I0112987

ALEXANDRE LEBRETON

MK ULTRA

Ritual Abuse & Mind Control

Tools of domination for the nameless religion

OMNIA VERITAS

Alexandre Lebreton

MK ULTRA
Ritual Abuse & Mind Control
Tools of domination for the nameless religion

*MK ULTRA, Abus rituel et contrôle mental,
outils de domination de la religion sans nom*, 2016.

Translated from French by Omnia Veritas Limited.

Published by
Omnia Veritas Ltd

⊘MNIA VERITAS®

www.omnia-veritas.com

© Omnia Veritas Limited – Alexandre Lebreton - 2021

All rights reserved. No part of this publication may be reproduced by any means without the prior permission of the publisher. The Intellectual Property Code prohibits copying or reproduction for collective use. Any representation or reproduction in whole or in part by any means whatsoever without the consent of the publisher is illegal and constitutes an infringement punishable by the articles of the Intellectual Property Code.

WARNING

This book deals with a particularly painful subject and contains shocking information that can be very disturbing for everyone. Its sometimes very brutal content, especially in the testimonies, is intended to reveal a harsh reality masked by a massive societal denial syndrome. Some of the content can also potentially trigger negative reactions in survivors of ritual abuse and mind control, but also in anyone who has been a victim of incest or childhood abuse and neglect. Caution should therefore be exercised and reading should be stopped if it triggers inappropriate emotions or reactions. This book is intended for adult readers only.

This book is strictly informative, in no way can it be a substitute for therapeutic treatment.

It is intended for believers and non-believers alike, although some passages with biblical or eschatological content may be disturbing to the atheist reader. A relative knowledge of theology and the spiritual warfare that takes place here on earth may help to fully grasp the content of this book. Believing readers are advised to prepare themselves in prayer before such a reading.

Everything that is hidden must be brought to light,
everything that is secret must come to light. Mark 4:22

FOREWORD

When we look at paedocriminal cases, at some point we come across accounts of gang rape, occult rituals, mental slavery and even human sacrifice where the terror and suffering of the victims is brought to a climax. One solution may be to look away, to reject these testimonies because they are too shocking and upset our paradigm too much; or else to take them into consideration and accept them as possibly being a reality of the world in which we live... An eventuality that will gradually become a certainty in view of the very many testimonies that relate the same practices. From there, it is possible to dig into the subject and to realise that it is a sort of *Pandora's box*. Is the innocence of childhood a fountain of youth for certain circles? Is the immaculate consciousness of childhood a blank page on which some people grant themselves the right to engrave whatever they want to serve their own interests? Does elitist Satanism, also called *pedo-satanism*, really exist?

Channeling consciousness is a key to domination here on earth. Mind control takes many forms, from the simple to the complex. Learning methods that shape the brain, school and university curricula that format beliefs and critical thinking, are a first form of shaping the future adult to be compatible and useful to the current social system. Journalistic' information and media entertainment are other factors that will influence your consciousness in a certain way. Social pressure to submit to the so-called 'one-track thinking' is also a form of mind control. The various food and environmental pollutions alter your brain and consequently your capacity of reasoning and analysis... At this stage, the population still has a semblance of free will. Each individual has the possibility to question everything he has been taught since childhood. He can re-inform himself by choosing other sources, get rid of his television, change his way of eating, lighten up on the material world to turn to the spiritual world, etc. We could also mention the subliminal or psychotronic as tools that can influence and control human consciousness.

The 'nameless religion' (to be defined in Chapter 2) loves and needs robots and automatons. It needs to create a planet of illusions where your thoughts, ideas and creativity are under its control. Her world is a permanent war to manipulate your subconscious in every way possible. From misinformation to hidden symbols to invisible technological weapons, the modus operandi of the "nameless religion" is MENTAL CONTROL.

What will be studied in this book is a tool of slavery where the free will of the victim no longer exists at all, or hardly at all. It is trauma-based mind control and manipulation of the psychic world, a process that begins in early childhood. Mind control or *Mind-Kontrol* (MK-programming) can be defined as a systematic torture blocking the victim's ability to become aware of the treatment inflicted. Suggestions and conditioning are used to implant thoughts and directives into the subconscious mind, usually in new identities (dissociated or "alter" personalities) created artificially through extreme and repetitive trauma, forcing the victim through a natural protective mechanism of the brain to act, feel, think or perceive things as the programmer wishes. The aim is to make the victim carry out instructions without being aware of them. The installation of these MK programs relies on the victim's ability to dissociate deeply. Very young children who already have serious dissociative disorders are therefore 'prime candidates' for programming.

The child is like a piece of clay that can be shaped. During the first six years, the brain is in full development, its neurons are organised according to its experience, it is in "recording" mode and it is not able to criticise the information it receives. He therefore stores the data and thus builds the foundations of his subconscious which will direct his adult life. This is why the internal structures of split personality programming are set up during early childhood, before the age of 6. We are talking about a real *psychic surgery*. The child will very quickly be encouraged to dissociate during traumatic sessions, to *pass through the mirror*, to *cross the rainbow*, to access an alternative reality, other dimensions. In a child, the profoundly altered states of consciousness during a traumatic experience create a kind of psychic and energetic "unlocking".

The *culture of* dissociative states is as old as the world and is an integral part of the practices of the "nameless religion" which systematically uses it on its descendants. This psycho-spiritual process is therefore a kind of doorway to other dimensions and gives *enlightenment to the person* who experiences dissociative states. The most direct way of accessing this modified state of consciousness is through pure trauma caused by terror and extreme pain, which can even go as far as near-death experiences, as we shall see. These techniques are systematically employed by Satanic/Luciferian fraternities as a process of reversal of sanctification: counter-initiation. They are used as tools to control society. As the famous hacker Kevin Mitnick says: *"The weak link in any security system is the human factor. "* In order to secure a system of global domination, it is therefore imperative to implement a *hacking of* the minds of the human pawns placed in strategic positions behind the democratic facades. The MK is the focal point of the various occult organisations on this planet. The main axis on which this tool of control is based is dissociative identity disorder, i.e. multiple personality syndrome, a consequence of traumatic ritual initiations practiced from early childhood.

This book is like a memory split into a thousand pieces that has been put together like a puzzle. Indeed, the subjects of ritual abuse and mind control are difficult to understand when one only has access to snippets of testimonies or rare articles on paedocriminal networks, Satanism and mind control. This is all the more true since the information available in the French-speaking world is still very limited.

To begin to understand this heavy subject, this puzzle required putting together pieces of anthropology, psychotraumatology, governmental MK-Ultra programs, transgenerational Satanism, the *"soul fragments"* of shamanic traditions, demonology, but also the societal aspect of the thing: that is, all the MK symbolism infused before our eyes in popular culture via the entertainment industry. Once all these pieces are connected to each other in a coherent way, a part of the arcane of this world becomes accessible to the layperson... the eye of the storm, an essential key to understanding the pedo-satanic system and more globally what we call today the *New World Order*.

This book tries to put the *MK puzzle* together as best as possible, and should help you to grasp one of the more obscure aspects of our world, and perhaps also enlighten you about our present situation, both material and spiritual.

The Canadian sociologist Herbert Marshall McLuhan said: "Only the smallest secrets need protection. The biggest are guarded by public disbelief."

Those who do not suffer from the common madness are called mad...

CHAPTER 1

MENTAL CONTROL: FROM SIMPLE TO COMPLEX

The inter-individual influence or social influence fascinates and frightens. (...) the terrible events attributed to it (collective suicides, ritual crimes...) as well as disturbing scientific studies (work on hypnosis, experimental studies on conformism or submission to authority...) affirm the existence of an almost irresistible force that could push us to do or think things we would not want to, a force that could even lead us to our ruin. There is, with influence, the idea of an intrusion, a real rape of the conscience, of the will... which seems to be able to pass under the control or the will of another. It is no longer oneself that wants or acts, it is the will of another that has entered oneself and it is another that acts through oneself (feeling of possession) - Stéphane Laurens, "Les dangers de la manipulation mentale".

There are different types of mind control. There is large-scale, mass control, and individual control, which focuses on a single subject. It can be direct and violent or indirect and non-violent (known as *silent* or *invisible war*). In mass mind control, individuals retain their overall free will, whereas the most complex individual mind control will totally suppress it. Through biology, neurology and applied psychology, the *wizard-controllers* have achieved an advanced knowledge of the human being, both biologically and psychologically. This system has come to know humans better than they know themselves, which means that it has great power to control individuals, for the most effective way to conquer a man is to capture his mind. Control a man's mind and you control his body, not all men have the same thoughts, but all think with the same mechanism: the brain. Mass or individual mind control can also be called hard or soft mind control, direct or indirect, active or passive. The military type of brainwashing is the active and direct method, while the television type of brainwashing is the passive and indirect method, certainly the most effective because the victims are unaware of what is happening to them and continue their brainwashing tirelessly and voluntarily.

1 - MIND CONTROL OF THE MASSES

It is not only the victims of MK-Ultra (US individual mind control programme, chapter 3) who are programmed, but the whole world, subjected to a form of mind control. We have, for example, been programmed to believe that our political leaders are men of honour and loyalty with great respectability because of the social status they hold... Whereas our current governing elites are nothing but corrupt, child-raping psychopaths and cocaine addicts, individuals steeped in the darkest occult. The death of a child or the use of a human slave reduced to the state of a robot does not make them hot or cold. Does this deliberately affirmative and provocative statement shock you? Does it erode your paradigm? ... Perhaps you will close this book here to protect your image of the world you live in. This would be a very natural defensive reaction: the instinctive preservation of your paradigm.

The now famous parable of the *"Matrix"* in which we are immersed could not be more accurate, people are permanently plugged into a *current* that keeps them in a secure and infantilising daydream. The functioning of our brain, our mind, our emotions and even our spiritual world is perfectly known by the "architects of control", who only have to press this or that button to trigger this or that reaction.

An important principle of mind control is distraction. Distraction allows consciousness to be focused on one or more of the five senses (sight, touch, hearing, smell, taste) in order to program the subconscious mind in parallel. This principle applies as much to magic tricks as to state propaganda, marketing and advertising. The second principle of mind control that accompanies the first is repetition. The combination of distraction and repetition is highly effective in programming the human subconscious. Television, radio, various circuses (entertainment and variety), are all directed at your subconscious, the art of propaganda is to address your subconscious directly. And this art has now become a real science applied on a large scale. Humans need entertainment, indeed, but we can see today that what is offered to us all the time on television, with reality TV for example, is more a sabotage of consciousness than an innocent game of belote...

People submit to mind control because they are born into it. The science of social engineering (the analysis and automation of a society) that works on mass control sets up manipulation, domination and oppression in a gradual way so that people can never be able to see it coming... It's the famous allegory of the frog in a pot of hot water. If you put a frog in very hot water, it will react very quickly to escape. But if you put it in cold water and gradually heat it up to boiling, the frog will get used to the temperature, it will become numb and will not have the strength to run away, it will end up being scalded. This is a good illustration of the phenomenon of habituation which leads to not reacting to a serious situation and our modern society is totally numb in this *"Matrix"* whose boiling point does not seem to be far away...

a/ Television

"Media stupidity is not an epiphenomenon. It is waging a war of annihilation against culture. There are many battles to be fought. But if the media industry wins its war against the mind, all will be lost."

Pierre Jourde

One of the sources that immerse the masses in this *"Matrix"* is directly in your living room, the television, which has replaced the fireplace as the "heart of the home"... This device is a tool of mental control of the first order, perhaps even the most important in terms of global control. Imagine for a few minutes a society without television, needless to say that consciences would have a completely different way of functioning, desires and needs would have nothing to do with those of today. Imagine a society without the infantilization, the dumbing down, the polemics, the division, the fear, the advertising conditioning, the deculturation, the standardization and the conformism that this device broadcasts all the time. Imagine the *"available brain time"* (a term used by Patrick Le Lay, CEO of TF1) that could be made available for other family, social, creative, truly educational and pedagogical activities, knowing that on average 75% of our free time (INSEE) is taken up by television programmes! No household appliance has ever managed to enter the home so quickly and so massively. The family organises its furniture around the television set, mealtimes and bedtimes are organised according to the programme schedule (and vice versa), it has in a way become the mistress of the house, programming the family schedule and the minds of the most assiduous members of the family to this schedule...

We are dealing here with a real technology of mental control, television has a powerful hypnotic effect. In *"Vie et Santé"* (1992) Liliane Lurçat writes: *"Children and adults are fascinated by images and words. Once the viewer is in front of the television set, he cannot detach himself from it. This behaviour is particularly impressive in children, since television is the only thing capable of immobilising a small child, who is usually very active in other circumstances."*

In 1997, the philosopher Jean-Jacques Wunenberg wrote in Télérama: "As the first agent of the globalisation of morals, television gives rise to a quasi-ritual set of uniform behaviours, whatever the environment and the visual messages: layout of the furniture, assembly of spectators oriented towards the light source, timetables constrained by a show that is generally programmed at a fixed time, etc.[1]

Several studies have been conducted on the effects of television on the brain. The overall finding is that it weakens attention span and critical thinking. Television creates a state of hypnosis under the guise of relaxation. The world's most popular pastime also leads to a form of addiction, the criteria of which are: *"spending a great deal of time using the substance, using it more often than one would like, thinking about reducing use or making repeated but unsuccessful efforts to reduce use, dropping important social, family or work activities to use it, and showing withdrawal symptoms when one stops using it."* All these criteria can be applied to heavy television users.

In 1986, Byron Reeves of Stanford University, Esther Thorson of the University of Missouri and their colleagues began to study whether the formal features of television content, i.e. cuts, edits, zooms, pans, sudden noises, etc.,

---

[1] *Télérama'*, 15/10/97

activated an orienting response in the individual and consequently kept his or her attention focused on the screen. The orientation response is the mobilisation of attention following a change in the subject's environment, accompanied by a complex set of sensory, somatic and autonomic changes that aim to prepare the subject to react to a possible contingency. By looking at how brain waves were affected by formal television features, the researchers concluded that video montages could indeed trigger involuntary responses in the individual... It is the form, not the content, that makes television unique. This orienting response may partly explain remarks such as: *'If a television is on, I can't stop watching it'* or *'I feel hypnotised when I watch television'*. Producers of educational programmes for children have found that these formal features can enhance learning, but that the increased number of cuts and shots eventually overloads the brain. Clips and commercials that use quick cuts with unrelated scenes are designed to capture the viewer's attention more than to deliver information. People may remember the name of the product or the brand name, but the details of the ad are in one ear and out the other; or should we say in one eye and out the other. This is the consequence of an overloaded orientation response.[2]

In 1964, the philosopher Marshall McLuhan published *"Understanding the Media"*, a book in which he explained that television is the preferred tool of advertisers because it is capable of bringing down the feeling of exteriority with the scenes watched, just as if it were an extension of the brain. This phenomenon is confirmed by an experiment conducted by Marshall and his son Eric McLuhan, reproduced twenty years later at the University of Toronto by his son in Peter Entell's documentary *"The Tube"*. The experiment consists of demonstrating that a film watched on television or in the cinema will not be perceived in the same way. In this experiment, two groups of individuals watch the same film on either side of a suspended screen, one receiving light reflected from the screen (similar to cinema), the other (on the other side of the screen) receiving light directly from the source (similar to television). Then each participant in both groups is asked to write a one-page commentary on their impressions and what they found significant about the projection. The experiment shows that "reflected light" and "direct light" do not have the same effects on the body and mind. In the "reflected light" group (cinema), people were aware of something outside themselves and were relatively objective about the content of the film. In contrast, in the "direct light" group (television), people talked more about themselves, their feelings and thoughts. Their comments were much more subjective than those of the other group. In direct light, such as television, the viewer is no more and no less than the screen on which the light is projected and experiences the content of the programmes with a much stronger emotional impregnation, with a loss of the feeling of exteriority of the scenes watched. There is no longer any distance: you are the screen and the projection of the image is imprinted on you like a tattoo. This direct light gives television images the power to invade the mind as in a dream, neutralising the critical mind.

---

[2] *"Addiction to Television"* - Kubey, Csikszentmihalyi - Scientific American, 2003.

As demonstrated in the previous experiment on the orientation response, it is more the medium (the tool) than the content that acts on the brain.

The American neurologist Thomas Mulholland has demonstrated by means of an electroencephalogram (EEG) that television creates a state of deep relaxation, even drowsiness in the subject. He found that the EEG showed Alpha brain waves when the subject watches television. These brain waves are the same as those seen when humans are inactive, the less the brain works, the more Alpha waves it produces. This hypnotic relaxation explains to a large extent the addiction caused by television, particularly after a day's work. Hypnotic relaxation is therefore an effective way of absorbing advertising content and other propaganda messages. Thanks to this hypnotic effect and its entertainment role, television keeps the citizen in an illusory distraction and detaches him from the real issues in order to better govern him. Frederick Emery, one of the most brilliant social scientists of his generation and a member of the Tavistock Institute said: *"Television can be conceptualised as the technological analogue of hypnosis."*

What Herbert Krugman said about television is also very interesting. Krugman is a former advertising agency executive, when he was a consultant for the Office of Intelligence Research at the US State Department, and his work was on the infiltration of communism into American society, as well as on brainwashing during the Korean War and resistance to propaganda. In the documentary *"The Tube"*, Herbert Krugman states that advertisers were fascinated by brainwashing techniques, and he says that he himself knew a few first-rate *"brainwashers"* whom he then recruited for his services... He does not hesitate to compare television with certain techniques used by the military, such as sensory deprivation chambers, which were also used in the MK-Ultra project. According to him, such techniques are based on a phase of desensitisation very similar to the mental state caused by television. The television image is indeed poor in sensory data, leading to the viewer losing the feeling of his or her body. In the case of individual brainwashing, the loss of the sensory cues by which the person recognises himself is the preparatory phase of the change imposed on his mental world. In the case of television, the images plunge the viewer into a waking sleep, his brain works in alpha waves, his identity dissolves and the 'image box' provides him with dreams programmed at fixed times for him.[3]

Television is the ideal tool for the application of the "tension and release" principle. It allows tension to be created in a controlled environment, thereby increasing the level of stress, and then provides a series of options for the release of tension and stress. As long as the victim believes that the choices offered are the only possible solutions, even if at first sight they seem unacceptable, he or she will end up making one of these unacceptable choices. In such a situation, humans are conditioned to respond to the tension like an animal looking for the pressure release valve. The key to the success of this process of mental control is the balanced management of the tension and the choices to relieve the tension. As long as these two things are controlled, the victim can be made to choose and

---

[3] "Studies attack television" - Louise Renard.

accept more and more unacceptable things. This is social engineering, *cultural psychiatry*, and television is the essential vehicle for infusing every home with the tension on the one hand and the valve to release that tension on the other. Television infuses images that create tension and then serves the solutions on a plate.[4]

Television with its world of semi-reality, illusion and escapism, broadcast 24/7, is a real mental programming box, its truly cultural and educational role remains very secondary.

Anton Szandor Lavey, the founder of *the Church of Satan* and author of the Satanic Bible, has a very clear idea of the role of television in our modern society... he writes in his book *"The Devil's Notebook"*: *The birth of television is a magical event with satanic significance (...) What began modestly in families with small boxes has gradually grown into large satellite dishes and antennas that dominate the horizon and replace the crosses atop churches. Television, or the satanic altar, has grown rapidly since the 1950s from a small, fuzzy screen to a huge piece of equipment that covers entire walls. What started as innocent entertainment in the daily lives of families has ended up replacing real life for millions of people, it has become a major religion for the masses.*

The clergy of the television religion are the artists, the presenters, especially those who propagate darkness through the rays of the cathode ray tube. The network presenters are the high priests and high priestesses of the consumer market. The local presenters are the parish priests, making hay out of the latest local tragedy. The celebrities, whether local, national or international, are all part of the hierarchy of the church, of the web.

Comedies, dramas and sitcoms are broadcast night and day, seven days a week, to activate and sustain the lifestyle of the parishioners, previously only the most fanatical practiced devotion daily. With the satanic stratification intensifying (aided by this diabolical machine), one of our tasks is to gradually develop a system for people to fit in perfectly with their TV lifestyle."[5]

It is also interesting to note about television that its centrepiece, the cathode ray tube, was invented by a British occultist named William Crookes. Crookes was a member of the *Golden Dawn* secret society and president of the Psychic Research Society, and it was he who inspired Oliver Lodge's research into the ether and the spirit world. This physicist invented several devices whose purpose was to interact with tiny elementary particles such as electrons. Crookes, who was a fan of spiritualism, believed that spirits were able to interact with particles such as electrons and protons to manipulate them. In his autobiography, Crookes said that it must be possible for spirits to influence these tiny particles; working on this question, he invented the *'Crookes Tube'*. A device for projecting electrons in a beam: this was the birth of cathode rays. Crookes' version of the cathode ray tube was to become the foundation for the development of television, invented forty years later by the Scotsman John Logie

---

[4] *Turn off your TV"*, Lonnie *Wolfe*, New Federalist, p.6, 1997.

[5] *The Devil Notebook* - Anton Lavey, 1992, p. 86.

Baird. Television, an invention that would ultimately subdue and hypnotise the entire world, was inspired in part by research into the spirit world...

b/ The subliminal

Subliminal means *"under the threshold"* of consciousness, it is an unconscious perception penetrating the so-called "subconscious" area of the brain. The subliminal message can be formal with one or more words, or visual with an image, a photo, a symbol. But it can also be sound waves.

Subliminal images are undetectable to the naked eye, but the brain perceives and processes them at a subconscious level. The brain processes a lot of information but seems to have different levels of perception and some information can then influence our actions and emotions without the cognitive brain having access to it. In 1997, an experiment by Ahmed Channouf demonstrated that electrodermal reactions (E.D.R.) occur when subjects are exposed to famous or unfamiliar faces in a subliminal way (the faces are presented for 50 milliseconds). The subjects' electrodermal reactions were longer when the face was known. They concluded that even when the subject is not aware of seeing these faces, there are physiological cues that demonstrate that there is nevertheless implicit perception and recognition.[6]

Subliminal images can therefore be used as a means of crowd manipulation. There are many cases of subliminal images being broadcast on television. In 1958, subliminal messages were banned in the USA, England and Australia. In 1992, France issued a decree (No. 92-280) banning *subliminal techniques,* which states: *"Advertising must not use subliminal techniques understood as aiming to reach the viewer's subconscious through the very brief exposure of images.* Despite this law and the supervision of the CSA, several cases of subliminal images being embedded in television programmes, films or advertisements have been observed. In France, the best-known case took place during an election campaign in 1988: the portrait of François Mitterrand was subliminally inserted into the Antenne 2 logo during the credits of the television news. This subliminal photo was broadcast from September 1987 to May 1988, 2949 times. François Mitterrand was elected on 8 May 1988. The TV news credits were finally replaced discreetly on 28 May 1988 at the request of the CNCL (Commission Nationale de la Communication et de la Liberté, predecessor of the CSA). This case was tried in court but the trial was lost because the image lasted more than 60 ms (milliseconds), which excludes the qualification of subliminal, the law considering that an image is subliminal when it lasts less than 50 ms.

In 2000, during an American election, a subliminal image embedded in a commercial for George W. Bush was discovered by chance. It was a formal subliminal message. The insult *"rats"* appeared at the same time as the advert referred to the competitor Al Gore.

---

[6] *Emotions and Cognitions"* - Ahmed Channouf and Georges Rouan, 2002.

In 2008, again in the United States, *FOX 5 News* introduced a very stealthy image of Republican candidate John McCain and his wife in its credits. The French TV channel M6 has also been nailed twice for broadcasting subliminal advertising images during the programmes *"Popstars"* and *"Caméra café"*.

In the February 1997 military journal *Orienteer*, Commander Shemishev of the Russian army listed a list of 'psy-weapons' in which he cites *the '25th frame effect'*. This is a technique where every 25th frame of a film reel or feature film contains a message captured by the unconscious. This technique, if successful, could be used to curb alcohol and tobacco abuse, but could also be applied to other more worrying areas if used on television viewers or computer system operators. Chemishev also claims that the Japanese have developed the ability to insert voice sequences at sub-low frequencies into music, voices that are only detected at the subconscious level. The Russians claim to use similar 'subliminal bombardment' in combination with computer programmes to treat alcoholism or smoking.[7]

Some Japanese retailers even play CDs with subliminal messages in their shops to combat shoplifting. These mind-control CDs play music or nature sounds but are encoded with a message in seven languages warning that anyone caught shoplifting will be reported to the police.[8]

In 1993 and 1994, several articles in the American press[9] reported that Igor Smirnov, a Russian expert in non-lethal weapons, had been experimenting for the US Secret Service and the FBI with technology capable of subliminally inserting thoughts into the minds of individuals in order to control their actions. The FBI considered using Smirnov's device against David Koresh of *David's cult* during the siege of Waco. Smirnov said: *'I suggested that the voices of children and families urging suicidal people to go home could be mixed with the sounds of police cars* (the building was surrounded by them)'. It was also a matter of sending messages to Koresh to make him believe that he was hearing the voice of God directly in his head. The FBI reportedly did not pursue this option for the (official) reason that Smirnov only guaranteed a 70% chance of success. The Russian press also published articles on Igor Smirnov. *Pravda* wrote on 6 March 1994: *"Village Voice published the 'scandalous news' that the Russians are able to control human behaviour"*.[10] Two weeks later the *Moscow News* published a long article, which explained how the scientist, for medical purposes, used 'psycho-correction'. Noises' containing questions, which are not audible but are perceived by the brain, are sent into the patient's

---

[7] *"The mind has no intrusion software"*, Timothy L. Thomas, in Parameters, pp. 84-92, 1998.

[8] *"Mind Control Music' Stops Shoplifters"* - McGill, Peter, The Sydney Morning Herald, 04/02/1995.

[9] Defense Electronics, July 1993, "DOD, intel Agencies Look at Russian Mind Control Technology, Claims FBI Concidered testing on Koresh"; Newsweek, 7 February 1994, "Soon Phasers on Stun"; Village Voice, 8 March 1994, "Mind Control in Waco".

[10] The Art to Control the Crowd", Pravda, 6 March 1994.

ears. The brain responds to these questions, and these responses are recorded on the electroencephalograph and analysed by computer, enabling Smirnov to perform a very rapid psychoanalysis. Afterwards, "noises" containing therapeutic messages are sent back to the patient's brain, which integrates them at a subconscious level. Smirnov denies using this technology for anything other than medical or unethical purposes.[11]

c/ *"Peer pressure"* or social pressure

"Habit, then, is an enormous engine of society, its most precious conservative factor. It alone is what holds us all within decreed limits, and what saves the children of the rich from the envious uprisings of the poor." - William James - *The Principles of Psychology*

Television is undoubtedly a tool of mental control of the first order. *Because of* the conformity and uniformity of the masses that it brings about, it is an important vector of what is called *"peer pressure"* or social group pressure, another tool of control, or one could say of self-control or self-regulation of the people.

Everyone has had the experience of arriving at work the morning after an 'important' football match has been televised. You will find that you are somewhat marginalised if you have not watched the match because you will not be able to participate in the lively exchanges between colleagues on the subject... And if you do not even have a television, then you will very quickly be labelled as an 'outsider', a marginal individual or even a 'sectarian'. Not following the football championship may still be socially acceptable, but as soon as you express an opinion contrary to the mainstream in matters of health, for example, such as vaccines or diet, you will very quickly come up against the "One Thinking" that shapes and directs the masses. In 2015, a blatant example was the massive *"Je Suis Charlie"* movement, stigmatising individuals who refused to adopt this slogan. This single-mindedness leads the individual to conform to the group for fear of rejection. Reactions can indeed be very violent when a person feels destabilised by the achievements that have shaped their *reality*. He or she can then play the role of guardian of the single thought by attacking the black sheep... *Peer pressure,* which varies in intensity depending on the country, culture, religion and political regime, is exerted on each of us by family, neighbours, colleagues and friends... It is a natural human function that makes *"the sheep guard the sheep"*, the individual unconsciously self-disciplines himself in order to follow the imposed social model, thus the people limit and censor themselves through social pressure. This pressure allows for the establishment of rules underpinning the entire community and thus compartmentalising thought within a well-defined framework. This is another important factor in the mental control of the masses.

---

[11] Extract from the dossier "Offensive Technologies for Political Control".

"I would say that within 50 years, if a lot of people don't consciously become resistant to the mind control that is being exerted on society, we're going to see more and more people who look like androids. People induce this themselves by looking at the world and saying: It's too dangerous for me to tell the truth, to actually say what I believe or express what I feel. It's much easier if I make up a false personality that will keep me passive. That's how it works..."
John Rappoport - State of Mind (*Infowar*)

It is fear that is at the root of this self-control of the people, fear of rejection, exclusion, failure and sometimes even fear of physical violence and imprisonment. Social pressure works very well to stop people from talking about certain things around them... especially when it comes to sensitive subjects such as network paedophilia, which is an unusual subject for most people because it is totally absent from the official media sphere. Their defence will often be to close themselves off to the subject because it will quickly scratch their paradigm. Some will use irony and derision as a diversion and as a kind of self-protection against the unimaginable, to very quickly change the subject of conversation... denial is massive. People who are interested in it are somehow marginalised, the social pressure exacerbated by media propaganda (or silence) has passed through...

You'll notice that we're talking about *television programmes* and *school programmes*... It's all mental programming on a grand scale, but at that level it doesn't take away your free will yet.

This social group pressure also plays an important role in the school and education system. For an average of 17 years,[12] the individual will function for most of his or her time in a class, a group, in which he or she will be given programmes that must be perfectly integrated if he or she is to reach the higher levels. If the individual does not conform to the group or is unable to integrate and adapt to the contents of the programmes or the learning methods, then he or she will be excluded from this machine that builds and formats future workers. The formatting and indoctrination of youth is obviously the basis for controlling a society, and the school and university system plays its role in the same way as television, cinema and music. The line between education and propaganda is very thin or non-existent, propaganda cannot work effectively without education programmes and control of information. The formatting of the minds of children, adolescents and young adults who will build tomorrow's society is the soil in which the single thought takes root and leads to this permanent social pressure. It is a cement that is difficult to break down in an adult who refuses to question his or her knowledge and paradigm.

d/ Food, water and vaccines

General de Gaulle said that the *French are calves, the whole of France is a country of calves.* Does the daily consumption of cow's milk have anything to

---

[12] OECD, Education at a Glance 2011.

do with our condition as human beings reduced to the state of "milk cows"? A simple reflection that may lead to a smile, but when we look at the effects of what we ingest on our brain, it suggests that the psychological and emotional state of a society depends largely on what it consumes morning, noon and night...

Food has a great influence on humans. His nervous system, his mind and his emotions are partly influenced by the type of food he eats. The control of the masses is achieved through a whole range of chemicals introduced into our bodies through food, water, vaccinations and the atmosphere. These chemicals weaken the nervous system and mental capacities, not to mention the endocrine disruption and damage to the genetic heritage. We will not enter here into the (controversial) question of alternative diets whose followers extol the benefits of their various schools. Instead, we will look at the chemicals that interact with our brains through what we ingest, but also through what we are injected with from birth or sprayed over our heads...

In the documentary *"Sweet Remedy"* (2006), neurologist Russell Blaylock stated that there is indeed a "chemical dumbing down of society": *"Because of these various toxins that affect brain function in a notorious way, we are seeing a society that is producing not only an increase in a lower and lower IQ population, but also a decrease in the high IQ population. In other words: a chemical dumbing down of society. So everyone becomes mediocre, which reduces the population to being dependent on the government because they can no longer perform intellectually. There are those people with the lowest IQs who are completely dependent, we have this massive population who will believe anything they are told because they can't really think clearly. Then there's a minority of people with high IQs, with good brain function, who can understand all this, and that's what they want! So you can understand why they insist on spending hundreds of billions of dollars on advertising: the aim is to dumb down the population."*

Let's start with fluoride, recommended by *experts* three times a day in toothbrushes, in lozenges for children and in massive dilution in drinking water for everyone! Fluoridation of drinking water supplies is commonplace, but what is much less well known is that fluoride has a certain impact on the brain of populations. Fluoride is a major repressor of intellectual functions. Independent studies show that fluoride causes various mental disorders, makes people stupid, docile and subservient, in addition to decreasing longevity and damaging bone structure. The first use of fluoride in drinking water dates back to the Nazi concentration camps. The pharmaceutical company I.G. Farben supplied the fluoride. The Nazis obviously did not use this product to improve the dental health of their prisoners, of course not, this massive medication of the water supply with fluoride was used to sterilise the prisoners and to stupefy them to ensure their docility. The chemist Charles Perkins was one of the first to denounce the harmful effects of fluoridation of drinking water in an essay he published in 1952. He states that repeated doses of fluoride, even in infinitesimal quantities, reduce an individual's ability to resist domination by slowly poisoning a specific part of his brain through narcotism. It thus subjects him to the will of those who want to govern him... Nothing less! He even declares that fluoride is a *"light and convenient lobotomy"* and that the real reason behind water fluoridation has nothing to do with the dental health of children.[13] The fluoride issue does indeed seem to be a big one, but it is not the only one.

Drinking water intended for the population receives several additives during its treatment process, in addition to fluoride, we can also mention aluminium, implicated in serious neurological disorders, such as Alzheimer's. On this subject, see Sophie Le Gall's excellent investigation entitled *"Du poison dans l'eau du robinet"* (France 3, 2013), which explicitly shows the immobility of elected representatives and organisations such as the AFSSA (Agence Française de Sécurité Sanitaire et Alimentaire) in the face of so-called "drinking" water which is in fact totally poisoned in certain regions of France. We also find this aluminium in vaccinations as well as mercury which is also a poison for the nervous system. Mercury causes autism in young children, although the pharmaceutical industry is at pains to prove that there is no link because of the colossal financial stakes. Some vaccines also contain an adjuvant called polysorbate 80, which is used in pharmacology to allow certain drugs to pass through the blood-brain barrier. What exactly is the role of such a chemical in the vaccination process? Do neurotoxic heavy metals such as aluminium and mercury contained in vaccines cross the blood-brain barrier?

All this accumulation of heavy metals in the body (introduced by water, vaccines, dental amalgams, food...) will lead to the blocking of enzymes destined to degrade food proteins such as gluten or casein, resulting in chronic poisoning of the body. Indeed, when cereal and milk proteins are not completely degraded, they pass through the intestinal wall and enter the bloodstream. These "opiate peptides" will behave in the body like certain morphine drugs and bind to the specific biochemical receptors for these substances. In her book entitled *"Gluten and dairy free diet"*, Marion Kaplan explains that by occupying and saturating the opiate receptors, the peptides from gluten (contained in cereals such as wheat, oats, rye and barley) and casein (contained in cow's milk) will lead to behavioural disturbances and promote the development of certain 'diseases'. These behavioural disorders caused by the partial breakdown of gluten and casein have been highlighted in several medical publications, including those by Professor Reichelt and the Institute for Paediatric Research at the University of Oslo. Reichelt is a pioneer in the search for opioid peptides, which he discovered in 1981 in the urine of hyperactive children, autistics and schizophrenics. Between 1986 and 1991, he saw marked improvements and even cures following the elimination of gluten and casein from his patients' diets. Gluten and casein intoxication is the cause of a wide range of behavioural disorders from hyperactivity to autism, personality disorders and epilepsy. Opioid substances that saturate the brain have the effect of inhibiting social bonds. Indifference, withdrawal and lack of language are major consequences. At the same time, these harmful peptides that clutter the body disrupt serotonin management. Sometimes there is too much serotonin, and sometimes too little. This leads to

---

[13] *Operation Fluoride* - vivresansogm.org.

excessive information being transmitted through the senses, insomnia, impulsive reactions, etc.[14]

Today, you only have to read the labels on industrial food packaging to see that gluten and casein are systematically added to ready meals, desserts, sauces, soups, etc. This is in addition to the constant increase in the presence of chemical additives of all kinds in industrial food, which is already denatured, polluted and even genetically modified. This is in addition to the ever-increasing presence of chemical additives of all kinds in industrial food that is already denatured, polluted and even genetically modified. We should therefore not be surprised to see more and more children developing behavioural disorders, known as hyperactivity, minimal brain function or psycho-organic syndrome. These disorders have repercussions on school performance and create a certain malaise that leads to various addictions. Other additives, such as citric acid, certain preservatives and synthetic dyes can trigger intolerances in susceptible individuals, with a significant impact on the neurological systems that regulate gestures, movements and concentration.[15]

In Australia, a study entitled *"The role of diet and children's behaviour"* was conducted by J. Breakey and published in 1997 in the *Journal of Pediatrics & Child Health*. The research showed that dieting can affect the behaviour of some children. It has been reported that symptoms such as attention deficit disorder, hyperactivity syndrome, sleep problems and especially mood changes can be corrected by diet. Another Australian study, conducted by the *Institute for Child Health Research*, observed the electrical activity of the brains of fifteen children suffering from hyperkinetic syndrome with attention deficit induced by certain foods. During the intake of the offending foods, a significant increase in beta brain activity in the frontotemporal region of the brain was observed. This 1997 investigation, which was the first of its kind, clearly demonstrated an association between brain electrical activity and the ingestion of certain foods in children with ADHD (Attention Deficit Hyperactivity Disorder). This scientific data validates the hypothesis that in some children, foods may not only influence clinical symptoms but also alter the electrical activity of the brain.[16]

In an article entitled *"Phosphates in food: Children pushed to the brink of madness"*, the paediatrician Frédérique Caudal reports what he has observed. After two years of experiments in his practice, he has found that a diet without phosphate additives makes up for the condition of hyperactive children in four days and thus avoids the infamous 'drug' *Ritalin*. Phosphates are present in virtually all foods containing additives. Their use is such that, over the last 10 years, their presence has increased by 300%! Our industrialists are not going to mince their words when it comes to neuro-toxic additives!

The issue of phosphates was raised in Germany as early as 1976 by Mrs Hafer, a pharmacist specialising in the acid-base balance of the human body.

[14] Gluten and dairy free diet" - Marion Kaplan, 2010.

[15] "Children's nutrition and behaviour - phosphates", Aldo Massarotti, bromatologist chemist.

[16] Uhlig T., Merken schlager A, Brandmaier R, Egger J. - Eur. J. Pediatr. July 1997.

This woman had observed and studied the behavioural abnormalities of her adopted son and had come to the conclusion that the trigger was foods rich in natural phosphates (milk, eggs, etc.) or added phosphates (phosphoric acid in colas, diphosphates in processed cheeses, cooked hams and baking powders in lecithin cakes). Hafer's work has had a great impact in German-speaking countries.[17]

Let's move on to sodium glutamate or E621. This is a particularly vicious flavour enhancer that is widespread in industrial food. It is present in all sorts of additives such as sodium caseinate, yeast extract or the famous *"natural flavouring"*... Glutamate is an excitotoxin, i.e. a product that is toxic to the consumer's nervous system. This food additive causes mood disorders, mental confusion, anxiety attacks and behavioural problems, especially in children.

In 1991, the American television programme *60 Minutes* broadcast a report on the dangers of MSG. In this documentary, Dr. John Olney, a professor of neuropathology and psychiatry, states that he is convinced that people are at risk from this nerve-damaging additive, especially babies and children. It was Dr Olney's research pointing out the likely danger to infants that led to the removal of glutamate from baby food in the 1970s. But today Olney is still concerned about the millions of children who are exposed to it in their favourite foods - fast food and snacks - which are completely unmonitored. The report shows us the case of a ten year old child, Jeremy Larrows, who was diagnosed as hyperactive, which led to his failure at school. Everything was tried to help him, from chemical treatments to special educational programmes, but nothing helped the child. Everyone thought he had attention deficit disorder. For five years, Jeremy was angry and aggressive with his peers and family, to the point where he was unhappy. He could no longer manage his own behaviour. His family took him to see Dr. Schwartz who immediately ordered the total removal of glutamate from his diet. Very quickly there were dramatic changes, his hyperactivity disappeared, his grades improved dramatically, as did his relationships with friends and family. His mother told reporters: *'We lost him for five years, now we have him back, and he is a beautiful, bright child. It's been a long, hard search...'*

In the same family of excitotoxins, just as vicious and widespread as sodium glutamate, is aspartame (E951), a neurotoxic sweetener found in over 6,000 foods! This neurotoxicant has the unfortunate ability to destroy neurons. In 1971, Dr. John Olney, who had already demonstrated the danger of sodium glutamate, managed to prove that aspartic acid (40% of which makes up aspartame) literally causes holes in the brains of young mice. Despite this, aspartame is still permitted as a food additive and is even used in some pharmaceutical products. Aspartic acid accumulates in our bodies, affects our brains, and also crosses the placenta to reach the brain of the foetus.[18]

---

[17] "Alimentation et comportement des enfants - Phosphates", Aldo Massarotti, bromatologist chemist.

[18] Food additives danger" - Corinne Gouget, 2006.

Despite the evidence of its toxicity, it is still present in your supermarkets... especially at the checkout, in pretty little boxes of all colours attracting your children. Regularly, *"expert opinions"* (such as *the European Food Safety Authority*) confirm in headlines in our media that aspartame is safe for us, even highlighting its usefulness! Why does such a war of information with great blows of "expertise" try to systematically confirm the harmlessness of these neurotoxic additives? It's up to you to answer...

e/ Social engineering: *"Shock strategy"*, Tavistock Institute

"If terror can be induced on a widely disseminated basis in a society, then the society returns to a 'tabula rasa', a blank slate, a situation where control can easily be established. Kurt Lewin, German psychiatrist, director of the Tavistock Institute in the 1930s.

Lewin argued that through the creation of controlled chaos, the population could be brought to a point where they would voluntarily submit to greater control.

The *'shock strategy'*, a term popularised by Naomi Klein in her book *'The Strategy of Shock: The Rise of Disaster Capitalism'* (2007), is based on brainwashing techniques that aim to destroy the subject's memory, to break down his or her capacity to resist, in order to obtain a blank page on which a new personality can be printed. These techniques can be applied to an entire population by creating a *'tabula rasa'* (clean slate), i.e. wiping out a country's heritage as well as its social and economic structures in order to build a new society, a new order after the planned and controlled chaos. Once the people are deprived of their reference points, put in a state of shock and infantilised, they are defenceless and easily manipulated and despoiled. This process can be applied following a serious economic or political crisis, an environmental disaster or even an attack or war. But it can also be applied in a progressive way, over the long term.

The Tavistock Institute is a key point in the founding projects of global mind control, social engineering or more precisely here "organised social chaos". This complex organisation has succeeded in completely changing the paradigm of our modern society... According to its official website, the *Tavistock Institute* is a non-profit organisation formed in England in 1947. The Institute describes itself as focused on the application of social science in a variety of professional fields, including government, industry, business, health and education. The organisation writes and publishes the monthly journal *'Human Relations'*. Its clients range from large multinational companies to small community groups, both nationally and internationally. The Tavistock Institute is one of the most mysterious and influential groups of the last fifty years, but it is little known. Several elements make it unusual and unique: it is independent, being entirely self-funded and receiving no government funding; its field of activity straddles the academic and consultancy worlds; and its areas of research include anthropology, economics, behaviourism (behaviourism), political science, psychoanalysis, psychology and sociology.

This institute started its activities with the creation of the *"Tavistock Clinic"* which was founded in London in 1920. At that time it was a psychiatric institute. It was Herbrand Arthur Russell, Duke of Bedford and Marquess of Tavistock, who decided to assign a building in central London to a group of doctors, mostly psychologists, so that they could develop their research. The institute started with the study of traumatic psychosis and the *'breaking point'* in survivors of the First World War. The *'breaking point'* is the moment when the soldier's psyche breaks down under the effect of trauma, a sort of psychological tipping point in the face of intolerable stress. The aim of this research was to apply the results of these studies on war survivors directly to civilian populations. The project was supervised by the British Army's *Psychological Warfare Bureau under the* direction of psychiatrist John Rawling Rees, who later became co-founder of the *World Federation for Mental Health*. In 1940, Rees defined the objectives of this psychological warfare as follows: *"Since the last World War we have done a great deal of work to infiltrate the various social organisations throughout the country (...) We have launched a particularly effective offensive in many professions. The two easiest were teaching and the church, while the two most difficult were law and medicine. Anyone whose memory goes back only a dozen years will realise how important change is in the minds of professionals (...) If we want to infiltrate other social and professional activities, I think we must imitate the totalitarian regimes and set up a fifth-column type of activity (...) Parliament, the press and other publications are the surest means of disseminating our propaganda (...) We must aim to infiltrate every educational activity of national life."*[19]

In 1932, the leadership of the Institute was handed over to the German psychiatrist Kurt Lewin, founder of the *National Training Laboratories* (NTL, Harvard's clinical psychology research centre, established in 1947), which specialised in the study of human behaviour and behavioural psychology. Lewin is known for his work on the manipulation of mass behaviour, i.e. large-scale brainwashing... Much of his research for the Tavistock involved the development of mass brainwashing by applying the traumatic processes of repeated torture for individual mind control over society as a whole. It was Lewin who originated the *'tabula rasa'* theory that terror induced on a large scale in a society will lead to a kind of daze in that same society, a situation where *'control can easily be obtained from an external point."*[20]

For Lewin, society must be 'infantilised', according to him an immature state of mind must be developed in the population in order to control it as well as possible. He called this controlled social chaos 'fluidity'. In 1963, the head of the Tavistock Institute Trustees, Eric Trist, said exactly the same thing about controlling society: 'The administration of a series of successive traumatic shocks to a society has the effect of destabilising it and creating permanent conditions of social turbulence...' which will serve to generate a new society, a

---

[19] *Strategic Planning for Mental Health"*, Colonel John Rawlings Rees, Mental Health Vol.1, No.4, October 1940, pp. 103-104.

[20] *Fifty Years of the Tavistock Clinic"* - Henri Victor Dicks, London, Routledge and Paul, 1970.

new paradigm of society, an opportunity to shape a new face of the planet. For this, "social psychiatry" [21] had to be developed and applied on a large scale.[22]

Dr. William Sargant, another Tavistock researcher, wrote in 1957 in his book Battle for the Mind: A Physiology of Conversion and Brain-Washing: "Various types of belief can be implanted after the brain's functioning has been sufficiently disturbed by the deliberate induction of fear, anger, or excitement."

Traumatising to reprogram is the standard *modus operandi of* Tavistock. Here we find the protocol of individual mental programming based on trauma. It is a matter of erasing the subject's original personality through a succession of traumas, in order to install a new programmed personality, a new Order... *Ordo Ab Chao,* order is born from chaos, the motto of Freemasonry. Or *"Dissolve"* the elements and then *"Coagulate"* them, the great mystery of the alchemists... formulas that seem to apply well in the field of mental control, both individually and collectively.

The Tavistock Institute became the centre of psychiatric research par excellence and changed its name in 1947 to the *Tavistock Institute for Human Relations.* He then continued his work on strategy and psychological warfare for the OSS and its successor, the CIA. This organisation has a powerful network of influence helping it to infiltrate and permeate the various sectors of the materialistic society in which we live. This network includes generous patrons who enable the Institute to endure and operate effectively. Patrons such as the British Home Office, the Rockefeller Foundation, the Ford Foundation, the Carnegie Institute, etc. Tavistock is also closely linked to many *think tanks* and other globalist organisations such as the WHO (World Health Organisation), the World Federation for Mental Health, UNESCO and the Rand Corporation.[23]

The Rockefeller family has always had an important role in the advancement of Tavistock. In his book *"Mind Control, World Control",* Jim Keith reports the following statement by an official Tavistock columnist: *"The Rockefeller Foundation, before funding us, needed reassurance, not only about our policies... but also about the people who work there."*

In a funding document for the group, some of the objectives of the Tavistock are stated:[24]

a/ The invention of the 'psychiatric order' as a medico-social role leading to the observation and recognition of problems in the field of human relations and their management. "

b/ The invention of 'social psychiatry' as a political science to intervene for the prevention of large-scale problems.

c/ The establishment of a whole series of military institutions that will concretely implement the recommended policies.

---

[21] Mind control World control" - Jim Keith 1997, Chap 5.

[22] "The psychiatrisation of society, do conspiracy and psychiatry go together? " - Alain Gossens, Karmapolis.com.

[23] Conspirator's Hierarchy" - Dr John Coleman.

[24] Mind Control World Control" - Jim Keith 1997, p.45.

d/ The invention of new types of therapeutic communities.

e/ The invention of 'cultural psychiatry'.

The Tavistock Institute was the first of its kind and has seen hundreds of other similar centres such as the *ISR, Cornell ILR, Hudson Institute, National Training Laboratories, Walden Research, Stanford Research Institute* and many others established around the world along the Tavistock model. Ten major institutions are directly under its control, with four hundred subsidiaries and no less than three thousand diverse groups and *think tanks* specialising in behavioural organisation, political science, psychoanalysis, psychology and sociology. According to John Coleman, author of *"Conspirator's Hierarchy: the Story of The Committee of 300"*, Tavistock has a veritable *"invisible army"* of actors in the courts, the police, universities, the media, etc. Tavistock chooses the artists it wants to work with. Tavistock chooses the artists we watch, trains and introduces into society the experts we listen to and the politicians we elect...

Tavistock is said to have trained world leaders for use from strategic positions around the globe. This was the case for Henry Kissinger, a German refugee and former student of John R. Reese, who is one of the most important leaders to have passed through the Tavistock. As a result of his training, Kissinger was quickly promoted to high positions of political and strategic power and is still a man of great influence today. Another example is Jimmy Carter. In the 1970s, the future president of the United States was suspected of being a *'Clockwork Orange brainwashed zombie'*. In July 1976, Lyndon Larouche's newspaper *New Solidarity International Press Service* (No. 27) published an article entitled *'Has Jimmy Carter been brainwashed? There is much evidence to suggest that Carter's "Tavistockian" smile and pseudo-religion are the direct result of a behavioural modification programme carried out by his "close friend", psychiatrist Peter Bourne, and his sister Ruth Carter Stapleton... Carter has a history of psychological instability that makes him highly susceptible to being programmed into complete submission during a presidential election. In 1966, shortly after losing an election in Georgia, Carter fell into a depression and said: 'Life has no purpose... the smallest failure is an insurmountable disaster for me'.* This is not evidence of mental programming, but Carter was under the control of Dr. Peter Bourne, a psychiatrist from Tavistock. Bourne accompanied him throughout his political rise to the point of becoming his campaign manager during the presidential elections. Bourne saw in Carter the opportunity to create a *Manchurian Candidate* (the term used in MK-Ultra for an assassin who is not aware of his programming). According to Bourne's own father, a British Army Special Forces Major who regularly conducted gorilla and baboon studies at the Yerkes Research Centre, his son *"was always interested in how to get a President elected from a sociological and behavioural point of view. In Carter's team, he is the one who runs a real scientific presidential campaign."*

Tavistock is also behind some large-scale social movements. Take the example of the 'counterculture' of the 1960s, where the Tavistock network clearly steered the spread and use of drugs, especially LSD. Youth discontent and protests were an open door to infuse certain ideologies with drugs. This social destabilisation was to be a loophole for testing new methods of control, such as giant parties where LSD would be supplied on a large scale. Thus young guinea pigs would end up becoming agents of the new culture also known as the *New Age* (the spiritual project of Luciferian occultists such as Alice Bailey and Helena Blavatsky). One of the first of these giant festivals was held in 1967, the *Monterey Pop International* in California, with over 100,000 participants. A three-day concert that would become the model for mass festivals like Woodstock, organised two years later with the full complicity of the FBI. The Woodstock festival was a gigantic open-air mind control operation based on LSD. *Time* magazine called the Woodstock gathering the *'Aquarian Festival'* in reference to the end of the Age of Pisces and the beginning of the Age of Aquarius: the *New Age,* or New Order (more on this later), which was to be established following the social destabilisation of the 1960s.

The enormous media promotion of the Beatles in the United States (a group to which we will return in Chapter 9) was also organised as part of this large-scale social experiment. It was not a spontaneous revolt of the youth against the social system, but the big 'rock music' bands of the time served, among other things, to introduce a new vocabulary and expressions to form a new culture. Drugs, sex, rock'n'roll, nationwide protests... the new and the old world collided head-on and all these hippies had no idea that this was part of a social plan decided and organised behind prestigious philanthropic foundations, corporations and research centres dependent on the Rockefeller Foundation among others. These master puppeteers of finance and politics used pop culture to manipulate social development.

In the same way, we can also mention rap music, which was used to establish a liberal ideology in the United States and subsequently in Europe. The 'Tavistockian' technique was the same as for the hippie movements, i.e. *Cointelpro (Counter Intelligence Program)* operations consisting of a direct infiltration of the original movement to destabilise it, distort it in order to discredit it or divert it to specific ends, as was the case for example with the *'Black Panther'* (American revolutionary political movement) Rappers and hippies are two movements that seem to be totally opposed to each other... yet it is interesting to note that the *Zulu Nation* (the flagship organisation of rap) adopted as its motto in 1974 *"Peace, Unity, Love and Having Fun".* This is the same formula that the hippie movement had used ten years earlier, *"Peace and Love!* This is a libertarian philosophy that says *"make love not war".* A doctrine that consists in making the revolution through the sublimation of pleasures, through the apology of drugs and sex, nothing more and nothing less. Today, we can see that industrial rap, which raises millions of dollars, continues to propagate an exacerbated and decadent materialism in an ever more virulent manner, with productions propagated all the time on the major media networks. Indeed, this process of social engineering, which began in the 1950s, has not stopped and we are now seeing the consequences. John Coleman (author and former MI6 spy) wrote: *"The moral, spiritual, racial, economic, cultural and intellectual bankruptcy in which we find ourselves today is not a social phenomenon that happened by chance. Rather, it is the result of a carefully organised Tavistock programme.* "[25]

These social engineering programmes aimed particularly at young people are continued today by the propulsion to the forefront of the stage of hypersexualised and globally idolised 'starlets' such as Lady Gaga, Beyoncé, Miley Cirus, etc., the list is long. Stars whose song lyrics and on-stage behaviour are becoming more and more deviant, not to say completely deranged. We will come back to this in Chapter 9 on the entertainment industry.

In terms of social engineering, cinema is also an essential tool, in the same way as television and music broadcast in a loop on radio waves and specialised TV channels. Cinema, television and music have an 'alienating' effect by depersonalising us. Our external and internal image tends to be a reflection or copy of the models made by stars, actors, idols and other *sex symbols...* These 'life' scenarios that are exposed to us all the time, from Hollywood films to daily 'reality TV', addictive TV series and music videos, have a considerable influence on our look, our style, our thoughts, our attitudes, our behaviour, even our emotions and feelings. The omnipotence of the image aims to keep us in a state of infantilisation and therefore more docile and manipulable.

There is also a lot to be said about certain video games that are ultra-violent or steeped in occultism. Some productions are real alternative worlds which, unlike a film which lasts an hour or two, here the scenarios can last for dozens and dozens of hours during which the player is an actor in his own programming, the effect on the subconscious is therefore tenfold.

It is much easier to run a society by mental control than by physical coercion, and there is no shortage of methods for programming the masses. The basis for controlling the population is to keep them ignorant of the fundamentals of the system in which they live and to keep them confused, disorganised and permanently distracted.

Professor Noam Chomsky, an American linguist and philosopher, has described some strategies for manipulating the masses:

- The strategy of diversion

It consists of diverting the public's attention from important issues through a continuous barrage of distractions and trivial information. This strategy prevents the mass from being interested in knowledge in the fields of science, economics, psychology, neurobiology, etc., essential information. The hijacking of mental activities is also achieved through low quality curricula and learning methods that sabotage critical thinking and creativity. Schools thus keep young people ignorant about real mathematics, real laws, real history, etc. The media, on the other hand, carefully keep the public away from real social problems.

---

[25] The Tavistock Institute Of Human Relations: Shaping the Moral, Spiritual, Cultural, Political and Economic Decline of the United States of America - Johan Coleman, 2006, p.14.

- The arsonist's strategy or "problem-reaction-solution".

It is about creating problems in order to offer solutions. First, a situation is created that is intended to provoke a certain reaction from the public, so that the public itself will demand the measures that you want it to accept. For example, allowing violence to develop, organising bloody attacks, assaults, in order to get the public to demand liberticide and security laws. In the same vein, organising an economic crisis to make people accept as a necessary evil the rollback of social rights and the dismantling of public services.

- The gradient and deferral strategy

It consists in making people accept a measure, a law or unacceptable socio-economic conditions. To do this, it is sufficient to apply it progressively, in a 'degraded' manner, over a period of ten years or so. The strategy of deferral consists in getting the public to accept an unpopular *"painful but necessary"* decision by obtaining their agreement to apply it in the future. The masses always tend to naively hope that *'everything will be better tomorrow'* and that the required sacrifice can be avoided. This gives the public time to get used to the idea of change and to accept it with resignation when the time comes.

- The strategy of infantilisation

It consists of addressing the audience as if they were small children. Most advertisements aimed at the general public, particularly radio advertisements, use a particularly infantilizing, even debilitating, discourse, arguments, characters and tone, as if the viewer were a toddler or a mentally handicapped person. The more one tries to deceive the public, the more one uses an infantilizing tone. The propaganda of 'subculture' or 'crass ignorance' that encourages the public to wallow in mediocrity, to find it 'cool' to be vulgar, stupid and uneducated, is particularly present in reality TV programmes, which are aimed at a highly impressionable youth. These television productions act as programming on individuals who have already been uprooted and have no real spiritual reference points that would allow them to question what they watch and integrate every day.

Control of most of the media is obviously required for this to work. Mental programming of individuals in key/strategic positions is necessary for the proper functioning and security of the system, small amounts are not an option. Invisible warfare with its silent weapons does not fire missiles, it does not make noise, but it undoubtedly causes physical and mental damage. The public as a whole will find it hard to believe that they could be subjected to such a weapon, they will instinctively feel that something is wrong, but they will not be able to express this feeling in a coherent and rational way. Therefore, the call for help and the collective organisation of a defence against such an invisible weapon becomes very difficult.

- Electro-magnetic waves / psychotronics

All our actions, thoughts and physical sensations are powered by the bioelectricity produced by our neurons and transmitted through complex neural circuits inside our skull. An external electromagnetic wave can therefore interfere with this brain bioelectricity.

Psychotronic mind control can be applied to large populations as well as to a single individual. The development of electromagnetic antipersonnel weapons began in the mid-1940s, perhaps even earlier. The earliest known reference is in the American Strategic Bombing Survey (Pacific Survey, Military Analysis Division, Volume 63) which mentioned Japanese research into developing a *'death ray'*. The development of these technologies is linked to the mind control and behaviour modification research carried out by the US and Soviet military and intelligence services at the beginning of the Cold War. The aim was to develop technical means capable of manipulating, modifying or controlling the consciousness and behaviour of individuals or groups of individuals. As these experimental programmes had a military interest, they were very quickly covered by the secret of defence, both in the United States and the USSR.

Behavioural research' studies the fields of bioelectricity, electrical or radio stimulation of the brain, electronic destruction of memory, but also psychosurgery, hypnosis, parapsychology, telepathy, telekinesis, subliminal, *remote viewing,* irradiation, microwaves, ultrasound, etc.

In 1940, the scientist Walter Hess was awarded a Nobel Prize for being able to influence the behaviour of cats (making them suddenly ferocious) by means of electrodes implanted in their hypothalamus. Already in the early 1950s, Dr. Lilly had mapped out the body functions related to various areas of the brain. Using electrodes, he was able to activate nerve centres related to fear, anxiety, anger or sexual functions. His research was done on monkeys. During the 1950s and 1960s, Dr. Jose Delgado proved that human behaviour and the nervous system could be completely controlled by electrical signals transmitted to the brain by tiny electrodes.[26]

Influencing the human brain remotely with electromagnetic energy was obviously the next step in this field of research. At that time, a CIA document stated: *"The feasibility of remotely controlling the activities of several species of animals has been demonstrated (...) Specific research and evaluation will be conducted for the application of some of these techniques on humans."*[27]

As early as 1959, a CIA document (obtained by Harlan Girard, Chairman of the *International Commission on Offensive Electromagnetic Weapons,* through a Freedom of Information Act request), sub-project 119 of the MK-Ultra programme, proposed to "establish a critical review of the literature and scientific developments related to the recording, analysis and interpretation of bio-signals.), MK-Ultra subproject 119, already set out to *"establish a critical review of the literature and scientific developments related to the recording, analysis, and interpretation of bioelectrical signals from the human body and the activation of human behaviour at a distance (...) Techniques for activating the human body by remote electronic means. Progress has been made and the*

---

[26] Physical Control of the Mind, Toward a Psychocivilized Society" - Jose M.R. Delgado, 1969.

[27] The Search for The Manchurian Candidate" - John Marks, 1979.

list of laboratories, researchers and resources in the Bioelectronic study is in preparation. "

In 1985, journalist Kathleen McAuliffe met José Delgado in his laboratory in Spain, where he was experimenting with electromagnetic brain stimulation. In an article for *OMNI* magazine, she wrote that José Delgado had shown her how he could put a monkey to sleep or make it hyperactive, or how he could calm nervous fish using appropriately modulated microwave radiation.[28]

Delgado's work was fundamental in the field of psychotronics, his experiments on humans and animals proved that electronic stimulation of certain areas of the brain could trigger intense emotions, including rage, desire or fatigue. In his paper entitled *"Intracerebral Stimulation and Observation of Tracings in Patients"*, Delgado observed that *"radio stimulation of different points of the amygdala and hippocampus in his four patients caused various effects, including pleasant sensations, elation, deep concentration, intense relaxation (an essential precursor of deep hypnosis), coloured visions (hallucinations), etc. "*[29]

As early as 1966, Delgado stated: "My research confirms the unpleasant conclusion that movement, emotion and behaviour can be directed by electrical forces and that human beings can be controlled like robots by pressing buttons. In 1974, Delgado spoke in the US Congress and declared that "we need a psychosurgery programme for the control of our society. The goal is physical control of the mind.[30] The vast majority of Delgado's work on influencing perceptions and behaviour at a distance by means of electromagnetic waves has remained classified and inaccessible to the public.

Offensive Behaviour Control - USSR" is a US Army report (1972) presenting 500 studies on Soviet experimentation with electronic mind control, more precisely on the use of *Super High Frequency Electromagnetic Oscillations.* The Russian directed energy weapons programme focused on individuals, not groups. Some Soviet dissidents were targeted with anti-personnel microwave weapons, but also with mind-altering techniques that aimed at *the total submission of the individual will to an external force.*

In March 1967 *a co-ordinating group for psychotronic research* was formed in Prague under the chairmanship of Professor Jaroslav Stuchlik. In 1970, this group became the Psychotronic Research Section of the Czechoslovak Scientific and Technical Society under the leadership of Dr Zdenek Rejdak. It was Dr Rejdak who organised the first Russian symposium on psychotronic research in Prague in June 1973, after which an *International Association for*

---

[28] *The Mind Fields" -* Kathleen McAuliffe, OMNI magazine, February 1985.

[29] *"Thought Control and the US Government" -* Martin Cannon, LOBSTER 23 - From an analysis by journalist G. Guyatt presented at the International Committee of the Red Cross Symposium on *"The Medical Profession and the Effects of Weapons".*

[30] José Delgado, 24 February 1974, transcript in the edition of the *"Proceedings of the Sessions of the American Congress",* number 26, vol. 118.

Psychotronic Research was formed and its second congress was held in Monte Carlo in July 1975.

The programme of the Prague symposium included the following five topics:

- Erasing the subconscious
- Development of ESP (extra-sensory perception)
- Induction of paranormal effects in dreams
- The mechanical equivalent of neuro-psychic energy
- Psychic hygiene".

In 2001, US Congressman Dennis J. Kucinich proposed a space preservation bill in the House of Representatives (*Space Preservation Act - 107th Congress 1st Session H.R. 2977 - A Bill*). In Section 7 of the bill, technologies that access the human brain, alter health, or kill were defined as *"land-, sea-, or space-based systems that use radiation, electromagnetic, psychotronic, sonic, laser, or other energies directed against targeted individuals or populations for the purpose of information warfare, mood control, or mind control of those individuals or populations."*

The *psychotronics* mentioned in the list of Kucinich's bill is described in a book by Russian scientists Vladimir Tsygankov and Vladimir Lopatin (*"Psychotronic Weapons and the Security of Russia"*), as a weapon using "torsion field" radiation (scalar waves).

There are international human rights agreements that prohibit the non-consensual manipulation of human beings. On the initiative of US Senator John Glenn, discussions were opened in Congress in January 1997 (*Human Reasearch Protection Act*) concerning the risks of irradiating civilian populations. Today, pulsed microwaves are present in our environment on a massive scale. Few people question how this technology works and they do not necessarily realise the impact and, above all, the potential for control and manipulation generated by the systematic setting up of a global "communication" network.

Nerve impulses in the brain are carried out through electrical signals that trigger brain chemical changes. The human brain operates within a relatively narrow band of dominant frequencies, these frequencies indicate the type of activity that takes place in the brain. There are four main groups of brainwave frequencies, which are associated with most mental activities. The first group includes the Beta waves (13-35 Hertz), which correspond to a normal awake state, anything above this frequency will be associated with stress, states of agitation that can impair our thinking and weaken our reasoning abilities. The second group of frequencies includes the Alpha waves (from 7 to 13 Hertz), they correspond to a state of relaxation which allows us to concentrate mentally, these waves facilitate learning. The third group, the Theta waves (from 4 to 7 Hertz) correspond to mental imagery (imagination and daydreaming), access to memory and internal mental concentration. The last group includes the Delta waves (0.5 to 3 Hertz), which are ultra-slow waves that correspond to deep sleep. Generally speaking, the frequency of the brain waves will be at its lowest when the individual is in a state of deep relaxation and at its highest when the person is very active or agitated.[31]

Any signal external to the brain, with identical electromagnetic signals, can therefore interfere with the brain waves by influencing its frequency band. In other words, an external signal can impose its own rhythm on a person's brain: the normal frequencies are then artificially altered and the brain waves adapt to the new frequency band, triggering a change in brain chemistry and thus modifying thoughts, emotions and physical condition. Knowing that most human brain activity takes place in frequencies between 1 and 100 Hertz and that electromagnetic waves of this type of frequency have wavelengths of hundreds or even thousands of kilometres preventing them from targeting the human brain, scientists began experimenting with pulsed microwaves. This is the type of microwave that is used in mobile phones. There are pulsed microwave frequencies that penetrate deep enough into the brain tissue to trigger neural activity.

Dr. Ross Adey, one of the pioneers in the study of mind control by electromagnetic waves, has demonstrated that behaviour and emotional states can be influenced at a distance by placing the subject in an electromagnetic field. Adey and his colleagues have shown that microwaves modulated in different ways can impose a type of brain activity on different areas of the brain. Working with cats, they found that the frequency of certain brain waves that appeared during conditioned behaviour could be selectively increased. This is achieved by modifying the shape of the microwaves with rhythmic variations in amplitude, equivalent to EEG (electroencephalogram) frequencies. For example, a 3 Hertz modulation decreased the number of Alpha waves by 10 Hertz in one area of the animal's brain and increased Beta waves by 14 Hertz in another.[32] By directing a frequency to stimulate the brain and using amplitude modulation to make the waveform mimic a desired EEG frequency, Adey was able to impose a Theta wave rate of 4.5 cps (cycles per second) on his subjects.[33]

From 1965 to 1970, the *Defense Advanced Projects Research Agency (DARPA)*, with over 70-80% military funding, launched Operation *Pandora* to study the health and psychological effects of low-intensity microwaves. This project has conducted studies that have shown how to cause heart attacks, leaks in the blood-brain barrier and auditory hallucinations. Despite attempts to conceal Project *Pandora*, FOIA records revealed a memo from Richard Cesaro, then director of *DARPA*, confirming that the initial goal of the programme was to "*discover whether a precisely controlled microwave signal could control the mind.* Cesaro encouraged such studies "*to develop potential weapons applications.* Although many of the projects revolved around the use of narcotics

---

[31] Mega Brain, New Tools and Techniques for Brain Growth and Mind Expansion" - Michael Hutchinson, 1986.

[32] "Effects of Modulated Very High Frequency Fields on Specific Brain Rhythms in Cats", Brain Research, Vol 58, 1973.

[33] Extract from an analysis by journalist David G. Guyatt presented at the International Committee of the Red Cross Symposium on *'The Medical Profession and the Effects of Weapons'*.

and hallucinogens, the *Artichoke, Pandora* and *Chatter* projects clearly demonstrated that "psycho-electronic" devices were of the highest priority. From 1963 onwards, research into behavioural control therefore focused on electronics.

In September 1977, the director of the *MK-Ultra* project, Dr. Sydney Gottlieb, testified before the US Senate. When Senator Richard Schweicker asked him about MK-Ultra subprojects that might be related to hypnosis, or more precisely to radio-hypnotic intracerebral control (a combination of wave transmission and hypnosis), Gottlieb answered the Senator: "There *was a great deal of interest in the effects observed on subjects who are in a wave field and it is likely that among the innumerable subprojects, someone tried to verify that it was possible to hypnotise a person while in a wave beam.*"[34]

In 1974, J. F. Schapitz conducted a study to demonstrate that "words spoken by a hypnotist can be transmitted by modulated electromagnetic energy directly into the subconscious parts of the human brain, i.e., without using any technical device to receive them, without having to transcode the messages, and without the person exposed to such an influence being able to consciously control the input of the information. This study was disclosed under the Freedom of Information Act,[35] but Schapitz's results, funded by the Pentagon, were never made public.

In 1986, the US Air Force published *"Low Intensity Conflict and Modern Technology"*. The document has a chapter entitled *"The Electromagnetic Spectrum in Low Intensity Conflict"* which was written by Captain Paul Tyler. Tyler was the director of the US Navy's *Electromagnetic Radiation Project* from 1970 to 1977. At the beginning of this chapter, Tyler quotes from a 1982 Air Force report entitled: *"Final Report on Biotechnology Research Requirements for Aeronautical Structures for the Year 2000"* which states: *100 milliamperes through the myocardium can cause cardiac arrest and death... A radiation system could cause dizziness or death over a wide area. The effectiveness of this device will depend on the shape of the wave, the field strength, the amplitude of the pulse, the repetition of the radio frequency and the frequency of the carrier device."*

In a less intensive way, the use of microwaves could be adapted to simply influence human emotions and behaviour. Tyler also writes: *"Because of the many parameters involved and the specificity of each parameter, each can be tailored for a specific effect. Having this kind of flexibility provides a wide range of options for the user. This opens the door to appropriate responses for warfare, whether conventional or unconventional."*

To the objection that the range of frequencies in which a human nervous system operates is too narrow to provide such a wide choice of response, Tyler writes: *"There are unconfirmed reports that a change of 0.01 Hertz can make a*

---

[34] Mind Control, World Control" - Jim Keith, 1997.

[35] "Body Electric: Electromagnetism and the Foundation of Life" - Robert Becker, William Morrow and comp. New York, 1985.

difference.[36] However, the frequencies used in public scientific experiments do not have this degree of precision. Tyler mentions military research here which, if not unconfirmed, is covered by defence secrecy.

In 1960, Dr Joseph Sharp and Dr Allen Frey sought to transmit spoken words directly into the auditory cortex using pulsed microwaves similar to the sound vibrations a speaker can send out. This research gave rise to the *'Frey effect'*, more commonly known as the *'microwave auditory system'*. As early as 1962, Frey's device made it possible, with appropriate modulation, to induce sounds in both deaf people and people with no hearing problems, whether they were a few centimetres or several thousand kilometres away from the transmitter. In the early 1970s, Sharp, who was working on the military *Pandora* project, expanded on his colleague Frey's studies of sound transmission directly into the brain. In his experiments at the Walter Reed Military Institute, he found a way to reproduce and transmit not only sounds in the brain, but also fully comprehensible words. This experimentation, covered by the secret of defence, was finally made public in 1975 in an article by Don R. Justesen entitled *"Microwaves and Behavior".*[37]

In July 1968, the United States Patent Office registered Patent No. 3,393,279 for an invention by Patrick Flanagan described as a *"nervous system stimulating device"*, which was nothing less than the *"Neurophone"*: a device for transmitting sounds directly to the brain from a distance, with natural sound quality and without the need for any brain implant. The invention seemed so incredible that the Patent Office did not patent it until six years later, thinking it was not serious. No sooner had the patent been filed than the *Defense Intelligence Agency* classified the invention as "National Security". Flanagan was banned from further research.

According to the Department of Psychic Correction of the Moscow Medical Academy, acoustic psycho-correction involves the transmission of specific commands via white noise bands into the human subconscious without disrupting other intellectual functions. This Department of the Moscow Medical Academy has clearly recognised the potential danger of this technology. Russian experts, including George Kotov, a former KGB general who served in a high ministerial position, presented a report containing a list of software and hardware associated with the psychic correction programme, which could be supplied for the modest sum of $80,000. According to General Kotov: *"Once it has become possible to probe and correct the psychological content of humans, against their will and by material means, the results can escape our control and be used in a malicious and inhumane way to manipulate the collective psyche."*

Some Russian authors note that world opinion is not ready to deal adequately with the problems caused by the possibility of direct access to the human psyche. Therefore, these Russian authors have proposed a bi-lateral

---

[36] Low Intensity Conflict and Modern Technology", ed. Lt.Col. J. Dean, USAF, Air University Press, Center for Aerospace Doctrine, Research and Education, Maxwell Air Force Base, Alabama, June 1986 - Chapt: The Electromagnetic Spectrum in Low-Intensity Conflict, Capt Paul E. Tyler.

[37] *"Microwaves and Behavior"* - Don R. Justesen, American Psychologist, March 1975, p. 391.

centre for these psycho-electronic technologies through which the US and Russia could monitor and restrict these emerging technologies. Dr. Igor Smirnov, a Russian expert on non-lethal weapons, was invited to the United States in 1993 for a series of meetings devoted to the subject of psycho-electronics. The meetings included representatives from the CIA, DIA, FBI and DARPA, as well as civilians including representatives from the National Institute of Mental Health and bio-medical research. As mentioned above, Igor Smirnov is the creator of a technology capable of subliminally inserting thoughts into the minds of individuals. A firm called *Psychotechnologies Incorporated (Psi-Tech)*, based in Richmond, Virginia, has secured an agreement with the Russians to share and develop this technology for use in America. Dr Smirnov died of a heart attack in 2005 and his patent is now held exclusively by *Psi-Tech.* Note that *Psi-Tech* is controlled by Colonel John B. Alexander, NASA General Michael Aquino (member of the Church of Satan and founder of the Temple of Set) and Lieutenant Colonel Albert Stubblebine, among others...

Perhaps the declassified document that best describes the capabilities of psycho-electronic weaponry is the article by US Colonel Timothy L. Thomas entitled *"The Mind Has No Anti-Intrusion Software"* (1998), from which the following are excerpts:

An entirely new arsenal of weapons, based on devices designed to project subliminal messages or to change psychological and data processing abilities, could be used to incapacitate individuals. These weapons aim to control or alter the psyche, or to attack the various sensory and data analysis systems of the human body. In both cases, the aim is to distort or destroy the signals that normally keep the body in balance (...) The body can not only be deceived, manipulated, or misinformed, but it can also be paralysed or even destroyed - just like any other data processing system. The 'data' that the body receives from external sources - such as electromagnetic, vortex, or acoustic energy waves - or that it creates through its own chemical or electrical stimuli can be manipulated or changed in exactly the same way that the data (information) in any electronic system can be changed (...) In fact, the rules of the game (of information warfare) include protecting and gaining access to the signals, waves, and impulses that are capable of influencing the data-processing elements of systems, computers, and people (...). Dr. Janet Morris, co-author of "The Warrior's Edge", made several visits to the Moscow Institute of Psycho-Correction in 1991. She was introduced to a technology that allows researchers to electronically analyse the human mind so that they can influence it. They input subliminal commands using key words transmitted over "white noise" or music. By using infrasound, a very low frequency transmission, the psycho-corrective acoustic message is transmitted by bone conduction."[38]

In 1996, the US Air Force Scientific Advisory Board announced in a public document: "In the first half of the 21st century, there will be an explosion of knowledge in the field of neuroscience. We will come to a clear understanding

---

[38] *"The mind has no anti-intrusion software"* - Lieutenant Colonel Timothy L. Thomas, analyst at the Office of Foreign Military Affairs, Fort Leavenworth, Kansas, 1998.

of how the human brain works, how it actually controls the various functions of the body, and how it can be manipulated (both positively and negatively). One can envisage the development of a source of electromagnetic energy that could be pulsed and concentrated to act on the human body in such a way that it would inhibit voluntary muscle movements, control emotions (and thus actions), induce sleep, transmit suggestions, interfere with both short-term and long-term memory, and so on. This will open the door to the development of new capabilities that can be used in armed conflicts, in situations of terrorism or hostage taking, and in training situations."[39]

Luc Maempey of the Groupe de Recherche et d'Information sur la Paix et la Sécurité (GRIP) said about psycho-electronics: "The abundance of available publications, articles in the specialised press, websites maintained by the various institutions of the Department of Defence, could give us the illusion that transparency is perfect, that the information is complete and objective. However, this is not the case. Unclassified information remains very superficial and concerns only certain political aspects, doctrines, or basic technical information, while the bulk of programmes relating to non-lethal weapons is still covered by the secrecy of 'black programmes' which benefit from large budgetary envelopes that escape all control (...) The deceptions and cover-ups used by the Department of Defence and its contractors to conceal the true nature of certain programmes have taken on such a magnitude that they sometimes escape the control of the military authorities themselves."[40]

What is presented in this sub-chapter are archives available on the internet, notably in a French-speaking dossier entitled "Les Technologies Offensives de Contrôle Politique". Given the exponential evolution of technology, needless to say that research in the field of psycho-electronics dating back to the 70s, 80s or even 90s is very much outdated at the present time... Moreover, any declassified technology or information that comes out of the military is at least fifty years old, and academic research, especially in Europe, is at least one or two generations behind the military advances. As early as 1952, the CIA's Moonstruck project had the objective of implanting electronic devices in people in order to be able to track them remotely... A programme that is now declassified. What are the technologies and objectives of the programmes underway today in 2016? The lack of information and the absence of public debate on this serious subject is, on the one hand, very dangerous, because a number of states have developed and are still developing weapons of this type. On the other hand, it leaves an impressive margin of manoeuvre for the use of this technology, which can be used by private individuals, and one of its assets is precisely its discretion...

In December 2012, Jesse Ventura made a documentary on the issue of electromagnetic weapons and artificially induced 'voices in the head'. The

---

[39] USAF Scientific Advisory Board, New World Vistas Air and Space Power for the 21st Century", Ancillary Volume, 1996, p.89.

[40] Non-lethal weapons, the new arms race. Groupe de Recherche et d'Information sur la Paix et la Sécurité - Luc Maempey, 1999.

documentary, entitled *"Brain Invaders"*, gives voice to many victims, but also to people closely connected to mind control research. At the end of his investigation, Jesse Ventura meets Dr. Robert Duncan, a scientist who worked for the CIA. Duncan admits that he helped develop systems that allowed the government to *"get inside people's heads"*. It's a combination of several technologies to create a tool that can insert ideas and voices into the heads of Americans, which he calls *'Voice of God'*. Here is a transcript of their conversation:

- Jesse Ventura: What is the negative side of what you did?
- Robert Duncan: I have empowered the dark side with some of my work.
- JV: What do you mean by that?
- RD: Technology is neutral, it can be used for good as well as for evil. I have worked on projects for the CIA, the Department of Defense and the Department of Justice.
- JV: When you worked in these programmes for the CIA and the government, what exactly did you do? And where did you work?
- RD: This is confidential information, I can't tell you about it.
- JV: Was it about "voices in the head", that kind of stuff?
- RD: Yes
- JV: We've met people who say they hear voices in their heads and have to sleep in Faraday cages. They do crazy things, but when they talk to us they sound perfectly normal, they sound as sane as you and me. Are they really crazy? Or is it the government that does things to them?
- RD: The government does this to them. It's called "Voice of God".
- JV: So you know that the weapons you worked on are now being used on civilians?
- RD: Absolutely. You have to remember that the CIA has a long history of experimenting on our civilians, LSD, etc.
- JV: Of course. We hear about the MK-Ultra programme in the 60s and 70s and we are told that it has stopped, is that true?
- RD: That's not true! The programme continued under a new name and with a new budget. This is the ultimate weapon.
- JV: Do you recognise today that there are people, citizens of this country who are being harassed by this technology?
- RD: It's worse than being harassed, that's a mild word... They are truly tortured.
- JV: How do they get inside your head? I've heard about these GWEN towers, they would have been active in the past and they claim that now they are useless.
- RD: With this tool, they have the ability to easily transmit messages through the country into people's heads or cause them intense pain. This is part of the strategy for world domination, controlling the population from the conscious to the subconscious.
- JV: Who are the controllers? Is it the President? The Federal Reserve?
- RD: No.

- JV: So these people are indeed at some level in our government, they take decisions without being officially elected.

- RD: That's exactly it.

- JV: It makes it more difficult because they can't be removed from their position.

- RD: They cannot be removed and they are also difficult to find. They hide in the dark recesses of government.

- JV: You worked for these people, you helped them develop this technology.

- RD: I was naive, I didn't know how these technologies were going to be assembled to create the ultimate weapon.

- JV: You don't work for them anymore?

- RD: No...

- JV: You look me straight in the eye and tell me that you have no more connection with this research, and that you are here to denounce it...

- RD: Exactly...

- JV: Are you afraid for your life?

- RD: No.

- JV: Why?

- RD: I am not afraid to die (...)

In his book *Project: Soul Catcher - Secrets of Cyber and Cybernetic Warfare Revealed*, Dr. Robert Duncan makes it clear that there is a 60-year gap between military technology and civilian hardware in this area. He writes: *"The mind has no firewalls and no anti-virus software, which makes the public very vulnerable to these kinds of psychotronic attacks. In a direct intrusion into the mind, the manipulation is done with synthetic telepathy, which is a bio-communication technology. Sounds and voices can be pulsed to a target. Due to religious beliefs, "the voice of God" (which is the name given to this technology) becomes a reality for those who have never heard of this technology before. Others will believe that it is aliens because again, it is a technology that seems too advanced to come from this earth..."*

In 1994, the first tests of the world's most powerful radar equipment, the HAARP system, began in Alaska. This equipment has the characteristic of being able to heat up the ionosphere and thus make it change altitude. By manipulating this layer of our atmosphere, it is possible to use it to send electromagnetic waves to a targeted area of the planet. The applications of this technology range from climate change to earthquakes to influencing wireless communications. Officially, the HAARP system is designed for scientific research, but it is highly likely that it was developed for military purposes. What does ionospheric manipulation have to do with the mental and behavioural manipulation of humans? Nick Begich and Jeane Manning, the authors of the book *"Angels Don't Play This HAARP"* who have been investigating this device for over seven years, report that John Heckscher, the director of the HAARP programme, said in an interview that the frequencies and energies used in this system are adjustable and in some applications would be pulsed in the 1 to 20 Hertz band. The frequency bands are narrow and the energy levels are low, but they are distinct from the pulses of the Earth.[41] Heckscher goes into further detail when he says: *"The ELF and ULF waves that will be produced with HAARP interacting with the polar electroproject will have such low power levels compared to the surrounding noise, that very sensitive integrating receivers will be needed to record them.*[42] The most important point is that of controlled coherent signals which, as mentioned above, are 1/50th the energy level of the Earth's natural fields but which, however, can have profound effects on brain activity. The HAARP system creates a huge, coherent and adjustable electromagnetic field, which could be compared to José Delgado's EMF (electromagnetic field), except that HAARP's does not extend to a single room. It has the potential to cover an area the size of a large western state, or even a hemisphere. Patrick Flanagan, the inventor of the Neurophone, said of the technology: *"The HAARP project could be not only the world's largest 'ionospheric radiator', but also the most colossal brain control instrument ever conceived."*[43]

Finally, let's take a look at mobile telephony and its societal tidal wave similar to that of television... In France, the number of text messages sent has risen from 1.5 billion in 2000 to more than 100 billion in 2010 (figures from the Fédération Française des Télécoms). Never before has a technology imposed itself so rapidly; telecommunications satellites and relay antennas have covered the territories in an invasive and systematic way. Urban areas are overloaded with relay antennas, which sometimes multiply in an anarchic manner without local residents having any say in the matter. This means of telecommunication combines radar, radio and telephone technologies, and operates using low-frequency pulsed microwaves. By buying telephones and subscriptions, we are financing the installation of a gigantic network of pulsed microwave transmitters and receivers covering every square centimetre of the country. Because of the nature of the waves it uses, this telecommunications network has a huge potential to influence people's brain waves.

A mobile phone emits microwaves all the time even when it is switched off (to locate the nearest base station). Most people never leave their phone and even sleep a few centimetres away from it (addiction problem). Dr. Richard Gautier, the author of *"Votre GSM, votre santé: On vous ment - 100 pages pour rétablir la vérité"* has listed no less than thirty-two experiments published between 1995 and 2003 showing a notable change in the EEG (electroencephalogram) of human subjects exposed for a short period of time (from a few minutes to one night) to low frequency pulsed microwaves. This confirms once again all the research that has been done in this field for over fifty

---

[41] John Heckscher, HAARP programme manager, interviewed by Jeane Manning on 21/02/1995.

[42] Letter from John Heckscher to Mr Arthur Grey, Cabinet Secretary, US Department of Commerce, Administration for National Telecommunications and Information and responsible for radio frequency allocation - 08/11/1994.

[43] "Angels don't play this HAARP" - Jeane Manning and Dr Nick Begich.

years. According to Dr. Richard Gautier: *"A long-term experiment is currently underway on a planetary scale, of which we are all guinea pigs."*[44]

Mobile telephony or the art of introducing a silent weapon into the pocket of every citizen? One thing is certain: we have very little experience of this technology and yet it requires very special attention, both in terms of its impact on our cells and on our brain waves. Yet we note a deafening silence from the French health authorities on the subject. The situation is different in Russia, where the *National Commission for Protection against Non-Ionising Radiation* has drawn up a list of recommendations concerning mobile telephony:

- Children under the age of 16 should not use mobile phones.

- Pregnant women should not use mobile phones.

- Neurological disorders such as neurasthenia, psychopathy, psychosteny, as well as all neuroses with asthenic, obsessive or hysterical disorders reducing mental and physical activity, memory loss(s), sleep disorders, epilepsy and epileptic syndrome, predisposition to epilepsy

- Calls should be limited to a maximum of three minutes, and after each call the user should wait fifteen minutes before making another call. The use of headsets and hands-free kits is strongly encouraged.

- Manufacturers and retailers of mobile phones should include in the technical specifications the following information: all the above recommendations for use, all relevant health and epidemiological data on mobile phones, as well as the radiation levels associated with the phone and the name of the measurement laboratory.[45]

2 - INDIVIDUAL MIND CONTROL

Brainwashing is "indoctrination so intense and thorough as to create a radical transformation of psychological characters and beliefs. " - Webster's New World Dictionary

Individual mind control is a common practice in political, military, criminal, mafia and cult circles. But mind control can also be present within companies or the family structure when a narcissistic pervert harasses and manipulates an employee, a spouse or a child.

Some groups have always relied on coercive, so-called 'strong-arm' interrogation techniques, as well as various brainwashing methods to force the victim into submission, to extract information, or to indoctrinate them. These intrusive and violent techniques are used today by some political and military organisations, by intelligence services and by the criminal world (pornography, prostitution networks, human, arms and drug trafficking). Brainwashing is a process of indoctrination that was used on some American prisoners during the Korean War (1950-1953). In 1951, the journalist Edward Hunter reported on

---

[44] Annie Lobé - NEXUS n°30 of January-February 2005.

[45] "Mobile phones: how to protect yourself" - Annie Lobé, 2006.

these methods under the term *'thought reform'*. A technique developed and applied by the communists after their takeover of China in 1949. The Chinese communists also tried to manipulate some of their own citizens, in the same way as prisoners of war, to change their beliefs and convictions. The aim was to make them accept and integrate a 'truth' that was previously rejected and considered false. These methods use food deprivation, sleep deprivation, isolation and confinement of the victims in a small space over a long period of time. The victim, totally weakened physically and psychologically, comes to believe that he or she will actually die or go insane. The end result is that her political, religious and social beliefs conform to those of the torturers who hold her life in their hands. Any group that needs to subdue and dominate individuals uses these methods of *'thought reform'*. Intimidation, threats, social isolation, spiritual indoctrination, torture, deprivation of basic needs such as sleep or food, etc., are the techniques used to subjugate people. Intimidation, threats, social isolation, spiritual indoctrination, torture, deprivation of basic needs such as sleep or food, etc., are the techniques used for the submission and indoctrination of a human.

Subject conditioning is an important step in individual mind control. Ivan Pavlov and Frederic Skinner (father of radical behaviourism) are the forerunners in this field. Pavlov is known for his work with dogs; his experiments included first giving a signal with a bell to arouse the dog's attention (the conditioning stimulus), and then five seconds later he gave it food (the unconditioned stimulus). After a while, the mere sound of the bell produced a conditioned reflex in the dog, which began to salivate without any food in front of it. This type of conditioned reaction is called *Pavlov's reflex*. Pavlov describes two types of reflexes: innate reflexes, which are present from birth, and conditioned reflexes, which are acquired through learning.

One thing that is less well known is that Ivan Pavlov studied the effect of extreme stress on the conditioning of dogs. For this he used electric shocks.[46] This form of extreme conditioning is the basis of mind control, using the victim's fear and pain to program codes and signals that trigger automatic reactions.

During the 1924 flood in Leningrad, water flooded Pavlov's laboratory and the dogs were almost submerged, swimming with just their heads sticking out of the water at the top of the cages, they were totally terrified. Many of them then lost their previous conditioning. Pavlov reported that the dogs had undergone a kind of cerebral dissociation and were in a hypnotic state similar to some human "mental disorders". Pavlov then deduced that in the event of severe trauma, *"the brain may undergo an erasure, at least temporarily, of all conditioned behaviour previously implanted in it."*[47]

After several months, Pavlov, who had re-conditioned most of the dogs, purposely ran water into the laboratory to see how they reacted. The dogs then all panicked and were re-traumatised, losing again all the conditioning that had just been 'reprogrammed'. Pavlov's work and observations on dogs can be

---

[46] Conditioned Reflexes and Psychiatry, Vol.2 of Lectures on Conditioned Reflexes - Ivan Pavlov, 1941.

[47] *Battle for the Mind: A physiology of Conversion and Brain-washing* - William Sargant, 1957.

paralleled by the testimonies of survivors of *tabula-rasa* mind control methods, where all previous learning is lost, like a wiped slate, and where a conditioning trigger/stimulus can reactivate the traumatized state.[48]

One method of effectively subduing and manipulating an individual is to apply *the three Ds* or *DDDs*, which stand for *"Debility, Dependency,* Dread*".* Psychiatrists Farber, Harlow and Jolyon West described this protocol in their book *"Brainwashing, conditioning and DDD".* According to these psychiatrists, the victim should be debilitated, dependent and frightened in order to break him or her so that he or she can be dominated...

You will notice that this protocol of individual mind control *"DDD"* is today applied on a large scale in social engineering programmes that aim to condition society. Who could deny today that our modern world does not infantilise us, debilitate us all the time, make us dependent on everything and anything by taking away a maximum of autonomy, and induce constant fear?

There is also the *"PDH"* method, which stands for *Pain, Drug and Hypnosis,* i.e. the use of pain, drugs and hypnosis to subdue and program an individual. A *PDH* combination that we find in the Monarch type of mind control (developed in chapter 7).

In the book (report) for the CIA entitled "Communist Control Technics" (1956), psychiatrists Laurence Hinkle and Harold Wolff wrote: "The man with whom the interrogator deals may be regarded as a patient who has been intentionally created. The interrogator has at his disposal all the advantages and opportunities that a therapist might enjoy in dealing with a patient in desperate need of help."

It is about creating chaos in order to bring order. To intentionally create a *'patient'* is thus to take a healthy subject and weaken and terrorise him, in order to *'help'* him as a *'therapist'.* This disturbing correspondence between coercive interrogation and psychotherapy shows the interchangeable role that psychiatrists can have with torturers and vice versa. Psychiatric science is the nerve of mind control.

The list below contains different forms of mind control that can be applied to an individual. It combines brainwashing methods reported by prisoners of war with methods used in destructive cults and government programmes such as MK-Ultra. It ranges from 'simple' mental manipulation of the victim who is fully aware of and remembers it, to the most complex forms where the victim has no memory of the trauma and no awareness of their mental programming. The 'formula' of brainwashing is always the same: destructuring and erasing the identity and replacing it with a new 'programme'. Each of these techniques can be used in isolation, but they will usually be combined in some sort of "death" and "rebirth" process. By analysing these specific techniques of individual mind control, it is possible to detect power strategies applied in a more global and diffuse way, on a larger scale.

---

[48] "Ritual Abuse and Mind-Control: The manipulation of attachment needs" - Ellen P. Lacter, 2011.

- The individual finds himself alone among a group or community that will continue to profess particular beliefs and doctrines, while at the same time the individual is gradually isolated from his family and outside activities.

- The shrinking of the world. The victim is stripped of all personal belongings, as they symbolise their past life and can be a source of moral strength. The aim is to cut the victim off from what connects him or her to the world and to others in order to sabotage his or her ability to resist and persevere. The sense of this separation is to be intensified by all means, so that the victim becomes convinced that he or she is cut off from any relationship that can help. A fake, miniature world is also created around the victim, as a formwork for working on their psyche. It is a question of substituting the world of the interrogation for the outside world, the world outside is then erased to bring it into line with the standards of a micro-world, a closed-door, one-on-one meeting between four walls. In this small-scale world constructed by the torturers, the victim quickly becomes convinced of their omnipotence.

- Destructuring of identity. The victim is told that she is what she is not and that she is not what she really is. This is done in order to make them lose their bearings and start questioning their own identity. The victim is forced to question beliefs that she had never questioned before. Her certainties are shaken.

- Disorientation and confusion. The aim is to disrupt the person's natural expectations and conditioned reactions. The individual is used to a logical world, a world that makes sense and is naturally predictable, and he or she will cling to it in order to preserve his or her identity and capacity for resistance. The destabilisation begins with the systematic disruption of temporal reference points: fiddled clocks, which move forward and then backward, irregular schedules and variable geometry nights. The torturers become masters of space and time, they disrupt the natural rhythms in order to plunge the subject into a state of total disorientation. In addition to the strategy of temporal disorientation, the victim will be attacked on his logical and semantic reference points by an avalanche of absurd and incoherent questions, contradictory and far-fetched assertions, tones of voice totally inadequate with what is being said, etc. This disorientation is also achieved through the use of the "I" and "I" signs. This disorientation also involves the saturation of his interpretative capacity. Faced with the avalanche of nonsense with which he is inundated, the individual will lose his way in a sort of spiral of interpretative hypotheses that are as vain as they are infinite... to the point of madness. Letting the victim try to understand something where there is nothing to understand is part of these sadistic methods.

- Guilt-tripping. Repeatedly making accusations against the victim to imbue them with guilt. The individual will come to feel that he or she has done something wrong and will be convinced that he or she is guilty and that the punishment is therefore deserved. Perpetrators may also force the victim to commit wrongdoing so that they themselves are in a position of guilt and thus guilt. The victim's behaviour is shaped by the use of rewards and punishments, together with other conditioning processes.

- Self-predation. Turning the individual against himself until he finally becomes the agent of his own defeat. It is a question of turning the subject in on himself by depriving him of the outside world and of others, by radicalising his subjectivity in order to make him responsible for his own torments. The question may then be asked: "But why are you doing this to yourself?". Guilt and self-prediction go hand in hand.

- Betrayal and self-betrayal. Forcing the victim to denounce his friends, colleagues, entourage and family. This reinforces the feeling of guilt and shame but also the feeling of betraying one's own life. The victim is led to believe that no one in her family or community cares about what she has become.

- Voluntary submission. The victim voluntarily submits to the torturer in exchange for compensation, which may be material goods, drugs, sex, but also 'affection' and 'freedom'. The victim may be able to choose his or her master.

- Submission through terror. The torturer gains a form of respect by terrorising the victim, this can be done even if the victim still retains their own beliefs and personality.

- The breaking point. The combined effects of strong guilt and shame lead the victim to feel alienated from herself. She begins to fear madness and total annihilation. The victim is also subjected to violence, degradation and public humiliation aimed at destroying her self-esteem. Moreover, the deliberate unpredictability of the perpetrators' behaviour makes it impossible to detect their expectations and thoughts, which reinforces the victim's feeling that she really has no control.

- Brainwashing through deprivation of basic needs such as sleep, food, water, etc., combined with social isolation. combined with social isolation.

- Associate orders with pain. Directives and commands are given at the same time as the torture. This is to convince the individual that the violence will happen again if the orders and directives are not followed. The injunctions: *"You will forget"*, *"Don't talk about it"*, etc., are verbalised and imprinted in the mind of the individual. The injunctions: "You will forget", "Don't talk about it", etc., are verbalised and imprinted on the psyche at the same time as the pain is injected into the nervous system. It is a matter of maintaining a repetitive physical and psychological torture in order to install these commands deeply into the victim through the (usually subconscious) belief that there will be extremely painful consequences if he/she ever violates the directives. The re-experiencing of these initial tortures often involves somatic manifestations, such as slight bruising or swelling of the initial injuries.

- Clemency. The inevitable annihilation is suddenly reversed by the unexpected clemency of the executioners. A brief pause in the interrogations, a brief moment of appeasement where the victim is treated as a respectable human being. Suddenly, annihilation is no longer the only possible outcome. For an individual in such a situation, this sudden psychological decompression will serve to soften him or her up and bring him or her into the camp of the perpetrators. The individual then becomes almost grateful for the ongoing 'reform' process, and will have to participate in his or her own indoctrination, for example by writing instructions or organising activities.

- Stockholm syndrome. Situations of intense stress gradually lead to dependency and a certain loyalty of the victim to the aggressor. The term

"Stockholm syndrome" dates back to August 1973 when a hostage was taken in a bank in Stockholm, Sweden. A 32-year-old prison escapee named Jan-Erik Olsson took four bank employees hostage for five and a half days. A few days after their release, although the captives were unable to explain this reaction, they testified that they had shown a strange closeness to their captor, they sought to identify with him and even came to fear the police. In some cases, victims have even testified on behalf of the hostage taker or raised funds for his legal defence.

- Confession. The victim eventually agrees to make 'confessions' in order to relieve himself of the crushing guilt he is made to bear. Confessing, 'confessing' even if there is nothing to confess, becomes an irresistible act for the individual to end the horrors of mental confusion, guilt and loss of identity.

- Harmony'. When the victim's reformation is well under way, when her emotional needs have been met because of her good behaviour, the victim can then regain some relational life in a group, she is allowed to participate in common activities. This brings relief, the pressure is relieved and the alienation can disappear to make room for a better relationship with the environment. The need for human relationships leads the victim to become closer to her abusers.

- Rebirth and re-education. In this new 'harmonious' state of mind, the victim is ready to condemn and reject everything she has been in the past. Through confession, she must condemn all aspects of her past life, seeing them as a long series of shameful acts in order to rebuild something on a new basis. It is a form of rebirth.

- Spiritual indoctrination. The psychologically weak or addicted victim is subjected to a charismatic leader who claims to be connected to some kind of god. He claims to have been chosen for a spiritual mission and becomes a compass for the disoriented victim.

- Spiritual pollution. These are witchcraft rituals aimed at 'attaching' evil entities to traumatised and disassociated victims (see Chapter 5). These entities will harass and participate in mind control. Pacts, spells, curses, covenants, etc., are used to pollute and render the victim's mind unfit for purpose. Pacts, spells, curses, alliances, etc., are used to pollute and make the victim evil and unhealthy, physically or psychologically ill, socially isolated, devalued and enslaved.

- *Psychic driving'*. A method involving recorded messages that loop for hours while the victim is in an altered state of consciousness as a result of electroshock, sensory deprivation, deprivation of food, water, sleep, oxygen, confinement and other acts of torture.

- Hypnosis and trance: A trance state is a hypnotic dissociative state where memory and perceptions are altered. Dissociation being a separation, a split between psychic/mental elements, which usually are united and communicate with each other (this topic will be developed in chapter 5). The effects of a trance state can be caused by certain conditions such as: mental or physical exhaustion, terror, repetitive chanting, rituals or drugs. Susceptibility to trance or dissociation varies from person to person. Research has shown that people with high hypnotic suggestibility apparently have genetic predispositions, but trauma, especially childhood sexual abuse, also predisposes to high hypnotic suggestibility. Some trance states appear to be self-induced and function as a defence mechanism against massive pain and a violent environment. In some cases, self-induced trance and dissociation from severe abuse may result in the creation of a multiple personality. The trance may also be induced by another person, a hypnotist. The hypnotist may make post-hypnotic suggestions to the person to perform certain actions or experience certain emotions or physical sensations as a result of the hypnotic trance. These actions or emotions are usually triggered by certain discrete 'codes' that have been dictated to the subject while he (or she) was in trance. The mind control that many victims of ritual abuse suffer is partly due to having been repeatedly put into trance states and having received a complex series of post-hypnotic suggestions. However, hypnosis and trance also have an important role to play in the treatment of ritual abuse victims. The use of trance in a therapeutic context often allows the victim to recover memories dissociated from consciousness. This process is a very important aspect of recovery for victims of ritual abuse.

- Perverse manipulation of the victim's (in this case usually a child) psychic world. This involves, among other things, removing any notion of desire from the child and any inner desire. The child must systematically turn to the adult for permission in all areas of his or her life, including the inner world. This destroys all the safe places the child has created internally to escape the horrors he or she has experienced. It creates a sense that there is no real place (internal or external) where he can be safe and that his tormentors are omnipresent and know everything he thinks. At this stage an internal system with alter (split personality) starts to be set up by which the cult will manipulate and control him throughout his life.

- Trauma-informed mind control. This is a protocol based on the phenomenon of dissociation, or 'fragmentation' of the personality in response to extreme and repetitive trauma. An individual's personality can be fragmented into several different identities that can take over the body in turn. An 'amnesia wall' isolates each alter personality, preventing the victim from becoming aware of the activities of their alter. This method of mind control, called *Monarch* programming, is symbolised by the Monarch butterfly, which represents, among other things, the (sad) rebirth of the caterpillar-victim into a slave-butterfly, the chrysalis representing the process of "reformation" or "programming".[49] [50] [51] [52]

In an article entitled *'Behind the Democratic* Facades: *Mind-Control and the Satanic Cult of National Security'*, Dr. Hans Ulrish Gresch divided this trauma-based mind control process into three phases:

Phase 1: Preparing the victim's mind and nervous system for programming. The victim is placed in a condition of extreme vulnerability,

---

[49] Report of the Ritual Abuse Task Force Los Angeles County Commission for Women, 1989.

[50] The Manipulated Mind: Brainwashing, Conditioning, and Indoctrination", Denise Winn, 2002.

[51] The Relationship Between Mind Control Programming and Ritual Abuse" - Ellen P. Lacter.

[52] Kubark, the CIA's secret manual of mind control and psychological torture - www.editions-zones.fr.

disorientation and terror, and is then subjected to extreme physical and psychological stress. The victim's sense of self-preservation is threatened, his or her identity is weakened or destroyed and he or she regresses to the emotional and cognitive state of a child, his or her mind is dissociated.

Phase 2: Programming the victim as a robot or computer, with new attitudes, behaviour patterns and frames of reference in which these attitudes and behaviours will make sense. At least two personalities are created:

- A robotic personality that is consciously in contact with the controllers and receives programming.

- A new artificial personality that is totally unaware of being programmed and is also unaware of the existence of the robot personality.

The robotic personality is a kind of automaton, while the artificial personality defines itself as a human. The robot will be programmed with repetitive indoctrination and various means of conditioning (punishments and rewards). The robot is called a 'slave'. The slave is the interface between the controller and the artificial personality(ies).

Phase 3: Selective erasure of the victim's memory. This is not really memory erasure in the sense of destruction, but rather the suppression of the victim's ability to recall certain experiences. This amnesia concerns all experiences directly or indirectly linked to the mind control process, as well as all biographical elements that do not fit into the logic of the artificial personality, which is in fact the front personality.

The overall aim of this process is to program the victim to become totally powerless, it is the controllers who then become all-powerful, they are like 'gods'.[53]

It is this type of complex mind control that will be explored in the next few chapters.

---

[53] Behind the Democratic Facades: Mind-Control and the Satanic Cult of National Security" - Hans Ulrich Gresch, Phoenix Journal 155, 1995.

CHAPTER 2

THE ROOTS OF TRAUMATIC RITUAL ABUSE AND MIND CONTROL

"The methods of religious initiation are often so similar to modern political techniques of brainwashing and thought control that one sheds light on the mechanisms of the other." - William Sargant

"When we look at the historical and anthropological literature, we find content related to religions, cults, fraternal organisations apparently referring to traumatic rituals for the purpose of creating altered states of consciousness. These states of consciousness have sometimes been seen as something sacred, such as a magical catalyst for profound visions or possessions by gods. In other cases, these methods have been used to establish a kind of powerful psychological control, in an underground and secret way, unknown to mental health professionals. Cult and Ritual Abuse" - James Randall Noblitt & Pamela Perskin Noblitt

"The mind control techniques of these groups (according to police officials and survivors deemed credible) have been recognised as bridging applied science and shamanism. The occult as an expression of the religious has existed for thousands of years. It is only in the last 150 years that science has aggressively sought truths about the psychological manipulations involved in these occult belief systems. The Random House Dictionary describes occultism as "the use of pseudo-science claiming knowledge of supernatural intermediaries beyond the reach of ordinary knowledge. This is to remind us once again that 'secret information' equals 'power'." - TRANCE Formation of America: True life story of a mind control slave - Cathy O'Brien & Mark Phillips

1- INTRODUCTION

We will elaborate on satanic ritual abuse in Chapter 4, but the following definition will provide a better understanding of the content of this chapter: *"Severe and systematic abuse of one or more children, adolescents, or adults, usually by multiple perpetrators of both sexes, over a period of several years. Ritual abuse is associated with a belief system involving the worship of Satan and involving sexual, physical, psychological, emotional and spiritual abuse, usually of young children, often in ceremonies involving rituals, symbols and other 'magical' practices. The main aim is indoctrination and mind control, which is achieved through dissociation,*

*use of drugs, hypnosis, torture, humiliation, etc. In the case of transgenerational
Satanism, most of these things take place "at home", with family members."[54]*

Ritual abuse and mind control techniques based on trauma and
personality splitting are used by many organisations around the world, dating
back to Babylon, ancient Egypt and the Mystery religions. Cults with revelations
and rituals, the knowledge and practice of which is restricted to a small number
of initiates, are called 'mystery religions'. The *Egyptian Book of the Dead is* one
of the earliest writings to refer to the use of the occult for mental manipulation.
Torture, drugs, magic, hypnosis and demonology were used to put the individual
in a deep state of dissociation and mental control. Demonology being a branch
of theology that studies demons just as angelology studies angels. These
initiatory rites of passage are the ancient Mysteries of 'death' and 'rebirth' or
'resurrection', a secret and sacred procedure that involved powerful alterations
of consciousness. These cults were particularly present in the Mediterranean
basin, for example the Babylonian ceremonies of *Inanna* and *Tammuz*, the
Egyptian Mysteries of *Isis* and *Osiris*, the *Orphic* cult, the cult of *Bacchus*, the
Mysteries of *Eleusis, Mithras*, the *Corybantic* rituals or the Mysteries of *Attis*
and *Adonis*. The rituals of the Mysteries took place without interruption for a
very long period of time, the unveiling of the initiatory secrets of these cults was
punished by death.

Éliphas Lévi (French ecclesiastic and occultist born Alphonse-Louis
Constant) describes certain initiatory rituals allowing access *to* the Mysteries as
follows: *"The great trials of Memphis and Eleusis were intended to train kings
and priests, by entrusting science to courageous and strong men. To be admitted
to these tests, one had to give oneself body and soul to the priesthood and give
up one's life. One then descended into dark underground passages where one
had to cross, in turn, lighted bonfires, deep and rapid streams of water, and
movable bridges thrown over abysses, without letting a lamp held in one's hand
be extinguished and escape. He who faltered or was afraid was never to see the
light again; he who intrepidly overcame all obstacles was received among the
mystics, that is to say, he was initiated into the minor mysteries. But his fidelity
and his silence remained to be tested, and it was only after several years that he
became an epicist, a title which corresponds to that of adept (...) It is not in the
books of the philosophers, it is in the religious symbolism of the ancients that
one must seek the traces of science and find its mysteries (...) All the true initiates
have recognised the immense usefulness of work and pain. Pain," said a German
poet, "is the dog of that unknown shepherd who leads the flock of men. Learning
to suffer, learning to die, is the gymnastics of Eternity, it is the immortal
novitiate."[55]*

Initiatory rituals of the traumatic type are intended to transcend
consciousness. In her book *"A Course of Severe and Arduous Trials"* Lynn
Brunet explains that *the trials of the ancient Mystery Cults were designed to*

---

[54] "Ritual Abuse: An European Cross-Country Perspective" - Thorsten Becker & Joan Coleman,
ISSD Conference "The Spectrum of Dissociation", Manchester, 09/05/1999.

[55] *The History of Magic"* - Eliphas Levi, 1999, p.122.

produce altered states of consciousness, a mystical experience with a state of ecstasy and union with the divine. The methods involved the exploitation of pain, fear, humiliation and exhaustion. These techniques seem to have emerged in warrior cultures, where upon exposure to extreme violence and fear of imminent death, a warrior could experience this state of bliss with a sense of immortality (...) This relationship between the feeling of terror and the sensation of a 'sublime' experience became one of the key themes of philosophical enlightenment (...) Immanuel Kant and Edmund Burke were two Freemasons who studied this subject. Kant stated that the experience of the Sublime, induced through the sensation of being overwhelmed by terror, is a situation in which the individual can no longer grasp what is happening. In a similar way, Burke stated that terror has the capacity to induce reactions that put the individual in a particular state, "that state of mind in which everything is suspended", thus producing "the effect of the Sublime at its highest level" (...) "to make things terrifying".*In Druidic initiation, candidates are locked in caves, have to crawl through long tunnels, or are locked in chests or coffins for several days, only to emerge 'born again'. These initiatory practices were known as the 'mystic fire', and the outcome of these tortures was sometimes expressed as a 'blaze of light' (...) As Ross Nichols notes, the Druid magicians 'dipped or cooked the child in the mystic fire', a euphemism meaning that in pre-Christian times the child was sometimes subjected to these initiatory trials."[56]*

In 1756, Edmund Burke spoke of the "Sublime" as follows: "Whatever may provoke the feeling of pain or danger in the mind, it produces the strongest emotion that the human mind is capable of feeling. When danger and pain become too intense, it becomes utterly terrifying and therefore a priori incapable of bringing pleasure, yet, in retrospect, we observe that such things are delightful."[57]

Immanuel Kant described the *'Sublime'* as the encounter between the 'I' and that which has the potential to annihilate it completely, i.e. the trauma that can annihilate the will and disarticulate the personality. For example, Glenn Gray describes the altered states of consciousness of soldiers on the battlefield: *"In danger of death, many soldiers enter a dazed state in which clarity of mind has completely disappeared. In this state they may be caught up in the heat of collective ecstasy to the point of forgetting death because of their loss of individuality, or they may function as the cells of a military organism to do whatever is expected of them as they become automatons."*[58]

This altered state of consciousness in the face of extreme terror and/or pain, which some called the *"Sublime"* in the 18th century, this *"blaze of light"* or *"illumination"*, is what is known today as *dissociation*, an essential point to

---

[56] "A Course of Severe and Arduous Trials: Bacon, Beckett and Spurious" - Lynn Brunet, 2009, p.6, 7, 11.

[57] "A Philosophical Enquiry into the Origin of Ideas of the Sublime and Beautiful" - Edmund Burke, 1998, p.37-38.

[58] *The Warriors: Reflections on Men in Battle* - Jesse Glenn Gray, 1998, p.102.

which we will return throughout the book. Dissociation is the foundation on which MK-Monarch slave programming is built.

In his book *'Religion: An Anthropological View'*, Anthony Wallace describes a *'ritual learning process'* that essentially works with what he calls the *'law of dissociation'*. He writes that these practices of inducing an ecstatic spiritual state by directly and crudely manipulating human physiological functioning are found in all religious systems (ancient and primitive). Wallace classifies these manipulations into four broad categories:

- 1) Drugs
- 2) Sensory deprivation and mortification of the flesh through pain
- 3) Sleep deprivation leading to fatigue
- 4) Deprivation of food, water or oxygen

In his 1966 book, Wallace indirectly describes, on an anthropological basis, the origins of Satanic ritual abuse and mind control. He describes how the neophyte is put into a state where he is radically dissociated from all his past knowledge in order to receive new information. Indeed, cognitive and emotional restructuring (programming) is facilitated in these dissociative states where the subject's suggestibility is increased. Wallace writes: *"The effectiveness of these procedures in inducing physiological changes has even been demonstrated in non-religious settings, including clinical experiments on the effects of sensory deprivation and various 'brainwashing' or 'thought reform' techniques...* These include the MK-Ultra programme which will be discussed in the next chapter.

Anthony Wallace speaks of an *'ecstatic spiritual state'* brought about by certain rituals, an ecstasy caused by a deep dissociative state. The word 'ecstasy', which comes from the Greek word *'ekstasis'* meaning 'leaving the body', this dissociative 'illumination' during trauma is indeed considered by some to be ecstatic, that is to say a state of consciousness where past, present and future are transcended and unified. Some extreme traumatic rituals go so far as to provoke what is known as an NDE (*Near Death Experience*), a near-death experience in which our space-time is transcended... Victims of rape often report this phenomenon of extreme dissociation, where they feel they are leaving their physical body during the tragedy.

In the book "Le monde grec antique", the historian and archaeologist Marie-Claire Amouretti writes: "The Mysteries of Eleusis bring to the initiate a communication with the great goddesses of the earth Demeter and Korah, and with their parèdre Pluto. Most probably, one also receives a viaticum for the afterlife. The initiation is done in three stages: the small mysteries of Agrai, in the spring, the great mysteries in September-October, where the ultimate stage is reached only in the second year; from the 13th to the 20th Boedromion the preparations take place, from the 20th to the 23rd, the initiation. The preliminary ceremonies are somewhat known to us: procession, sacrifices, consumption of products of the earth, manipulation of possibly sexual objects, mystical drama evoking hierogamy (editor's note: sexual alliance between the divine and the human). But the obligation of secrecy was so well respected that we do not know the ultimate phase or "epicopia": it seems to have provoked a kind of contemplative ecstasy. The initiate entered into a personal relationship with the divinity; he received the promise of bliss. In Phaedrus, Plato speaks of the 'supreme bliss' attained by the myste (the initiate). We get the impression that these ceremonies have induced the participant to overcome the anguish of death through the conviction of being integrated into a chain of life, just as wheat dies and is reborn through the seed."[59]

In the A.M.O.R.C. publication 'Rosicrucian Digest' we read (Rosicrucian Digest), we read: "The path to knowledge is an esoteric path, as opposed to the exoteric one, the religion of devotion. This knowledge, which is the goal of true philosophy, has a twofold purpose. Firstly there is the teaching of techniques and practices for overcoming human limitations, such as the trauma of death. Secondly there is the study of the cosmic order and working within it. When these two aspects meet, we get a form of hermeticism."[60]

The ancient Greeks were well aware of the effects of profound physiological stress in altering an individual's perceptions of the world. Ancient Greek priests used traumatic rituals to 'cure' certain patients. The person was prepared for this rite by fasting, lustration (a water purification ceremony) and sleep deprivation. The person was then taken down into the underground and left alone in complete darkness. The intoxicating gases that were exhaled in this cave, or possibly the lack of oxygen, soon had an effect on the person, causing terrible dreams and visions. It was then that she would be rescued just in time and taken out of the cave and back into the light and air. This kind of ordeal caused a real trauma that was supposed to heal the patient. The psychiatrist William Sargant does not hesitate to use the term *'brainwashing'* to describe the rituals of the *Trophonios* oracle, during which the subject experienced sensory deprivation, visual and auditory confusion techniques as well as the taking of psychotropic drugs. Just as we go to a psychiatrist today when we need advice or treatment, the ancient Greeks consulted oracles for the same purpose. Before going to the oracle, the person had to first experience sleep deprivation, repetitive chanting, taking drugs and finally venturing alone into deep, dark caves. This long and exhausting struggle, which could last several days, put her in a state of extreme physiological stress. Then, when the oracle revealed certain things, the person was able to understand the meaning thanks to this altered state of consciousness which gave him another vision of the world. We find the same kind of initiation among the Amerindians, with sleep and food deprivation, isolation and extreme conditions aimed at accessing an altered state of consciousness causing visions and revelations linked to the spirit world. The *Eleusinian* Mystery Cult used a sacred potion called *Kykeon* in its rituals, which contained rye ergot and was very similar to today's LSD (a powerful hallucinogen). In *Orations XII*, Dion Chrysostom writes about initiation rites using psychotropic drugs: *'It is as if there were a hand above the man, Greek or barbarian, initiated in a sanctuary of exceptional beauty and grandeur. He will have many mystical visions and he will hear many mystical voices. Darkness and*

---

[59] *"Le monde grec antique"* - Marie-Claire Amouretti & Françoise Ruzé, 1978, p.108.

[60] *Rosicrucian Digest* - Volume 89, N°1, 2011, p. 5.

light will appear to him alternately and thousands of other things will happen to him. [61]

Hypnosis is also involved in these initiatory processes. The *Ebers* papyrus, more than three thousand years old, is one of the oldest medical treatises that clearly describes the use of hypnotic processes by Egyptian diviners. In the Temple of Isis, Egyptologists have found numerous engravings depicting figures with obvious characteristics of hypnotic trance. The hierophants (priests) of the ancient Egyptian Mystery Schools practised a very advanced form of hypnosis in which the initiate would enter a deep trance that could trigger what we today call an *NDE* (*Near Death Experience*). (As we will see later in this book, some modern Luciferian groups practice traumatic rituals called "Resurrection", which plunge the victim into a near-death experience) Today, some hypnotists acknowledge that they owe much to the ancient Greek *Asklepiades* priests who practised hypnosis as a form of behaviour modification medicine. They called these hypnosis techniques 'dream healing'. A Greek engraving from 928 BC shows Chiron putting his pupil Aesculapius into a hypnotic trance. The oracles of *Delphi,* among others, used hypnosis, drugs and inhalation of vapours to achieve deep alterations of consciousness.

Magic, psychotropic drugs and demonology have always been combined in religious rites. Drugs, but also deep traumas can remove the natural barrier that usually protects humans from demonic spirits, they are considered powerful tools to interact with other dimensions.

The MK-Ultra project did not invent anything in the field of brainwashing, except to have created a scientific framework using human guinea pigs for political and military purposes. The initiation ceremonies of the Mystery religions involved rites of passage that could be described as elaborate mind control programmes. These mind control protocols are still with us in modern times, a process to induce a deep altered state of consciousness in order to implant a new paradigm. All of these things have been experimented with and perfected over and over again in order to achieve mind control of an individual who then becomes an automaton, a golem. Order through chaos... rebirth through symbolic death. These states of trance and dissociation of the mind generated during traumatic rituals go back as far as humanity. They can be found all over the world, notably in Haitian voodoo, African juju, but also in the shamanism of North and South America, Asia, Polynesia and in Europe with the Druidic culture. When extreme trauma alters brain chemistry, perceptions of reality change and ancient occultists believed that the victim's reaction was mystical or magical. Today we call this dissociation and its biochemical mechanism is beginning to be well understood by trauma specialists, but the energetic and spiritual mechanism is much less understood... at least in secular circles. Paganism and Satanism have always used this psycho-spiritual process called "dissociation of the personality" to access other dimensions of being, but it is also used as a tool for mental control and enslavement. For Dr. James Randall Noblitt, trauma-based mind programming began when men found that accidental

---

[61] Source for the Study of Greek Religion - David Rice, John Stambaugh, 1979, p.144.

traumas and certain traumatic rituals could produce altered states of consciousness and even create personalities totally dissociated from the individual's original personality. In his book *"Blood Secret"*, the Nigerian shaman Isaiah Oke calls these dissociated alter personalities *Iko-Awo*, personalities that serve as slaves to witch doctors.

This knowledge about the functions of the brain, which consist in causing the dissociation of the personality, the occultation of memories and an opening towards other worlds during traumatic experiences, may have been encoded in certain mythological stories, certain rituals or symbols, totally hermetic to the layman. This is how this initiatory knowledge was able to cross the ages. These Mysteries of the human mind have been and still are today very much studied by certain secret societies. This occult knowledge gives access to psychic powers and the world of spirits. The dissociation of the psyche can therefore be considered as a kind of *enlightenment*, but above all it allows one to master the techniques of mental control over others and thus to obtain a certain power. Black magic combined with trauma-based mental programming is an initiatory knowledge that has now become a powerful tool for political and social control.

2 - RELIGION WITHOUT A NAME

The legacy of the ancient Babylonian Sumerian-Akkadian Mystery religion with its blood sacrifices and enslavement of human beings has been passed down through the generations. Jay Parker, a survivor of Satanic ritual abuse, revealed that his grandparents, descendants of Luciferian bloodlines, once told him about the Statue of Liberty that it was actually Semiramis, the Queen of Babylon, the wife of Nimrod. Nimrod was the builder of the Tower of Babel, the first man to establish a World Government with a Universal Religion in opposition to God. Nimrod seems to be an obvious role model for the elites of international Freemasonry. In *the History of Freemasonry*, published by the *Masonic History Company, it is* stated that Nimrod was honoured as a *"Grand Mason"* and that his attempt to build a *"New World Order"* earned him the distinction of *"First Grand Master"*. Freemason Albert Mackey has written that *"Legend attributes to Nimrod the creation of the Masons as an organised body and he was the first to give them a constitution or laws for a government. Masonry, according to the legend, was founded in Babylon, whence it was transmitted throughout the world."*[62]

The tradition of ritual abuse to create slaves is said to come from an ancient doctrine, the ancient Babylonian tradition of demon worship, devotion to fallen angels, which we will call "the nameless religion". In these ancient religions, the evil gods were feared and had to be appeased constantly. The polytheism of the Mesopotamians, Sumerians, Assyrians, Persians and Babylonians was completely linked to demonic entities. Demonism is the dynamic behind the magic and spiritual powers of these primitive and ancient

---

[62] *The History of Freemasonry: Its Legendary Origins* - Albert Gallatin Mackey, 2008, chap.19.

religions. The many Canaanite, Egyptian, Greek and Roman gods are of the same ilk as the Babylonian gods. All the practices of magic, quests for immortality, animal and human sacrifices, etc., derive from these ancient demon cults. In *Mackey's Revised Encyclopedia of Freemasonry*, Albert Mackey informs us that: *"According to Warburton, every pagan god receives, apart from what appears publicly and openly, a secret cult into which no one is admitted except those who have been selected by preparatory ceremonies which constitute initiation. This secret cult has been called the Mysteries."*[63]

Today, these cults no longer have their altars in the public square, and for the uninitiated they exist only in history books, and even then... But have they disappeared completely? Are demon worship, blood sacrifice rituals and traumatic initiation practices that create deep dissociative states ancient history?

There is still today a cult that perpetuates this tradition, like a 'nameless religion' passing on the *Mysteries* from generation to generation. Why a "religion without a name"? Because it does not officially exist. This cult, or rather this doctrine, is not supposed to exist for the common people of our time. It could just as well be called the "religion of a thousand faces", its multiple forms being nothing more than manifestations of a basic strain that adapts to human times and civilisations. It is a strain that is externalised in such and such a way according to the circumstances that are offered to it and that adapts to the material hazards, but that remains one in what it aims at on the spiritual level. It is a clandestine doctrine, a *Transhistorical Gnosis* which has no precise name but which has nevertheless shaped our modern society by infiltration for centuries. It leaves its mark by a symbolism that the initiates like to display in the profane world, but also by an influence leading to an increasingly marked decadence of morals. It is a subculture that emerges little by little and tries to impregnate the profane to become a worldwide hegemonic culture. This "nameless religion" is divided into a multitude of sects and groups that do not at first glance have the same interests, but all have in common that they are working more or less ardently to set up a world government, a *New World Order,* the cradle of the Antichrist. The "nameless religion" is the worship of Lucifer, and is divided into several branches, Kabbalists, Martinists, Rosicrucians, Theosophists, Luciferians, Gnostics and Neo-gnostics, etc. (all these schools overlapping each other). (Its true followers (i.e. those who are aware of the real issues they are defending and the war being waged here on earth) are descended from trans-generational Luciferian families or are initiated and corrupted in the high lodges of pyramidally structured secret societies. All are working to establish the reign of their Prince, the fallen angel Lucifer, the "civilising" god, while the God of the Bible is for them a "destructive" God who must be overthrown. One of their methods is the infiltration and subversion of religions, governments and important organisations to patiently and methodically infuse their Luciferian doctrine. This is accompanied by a formidable discretion thanks to the principle of the *"Massa Duma"*, the law of silence, guaranteed by the

---

[63] Mackey's Revised *Encyclopedia of Freemasonry* - Albert Mackey, The Masonic History Company, 1946, Vol.2, p.689.

dissociative states in which many followers are "engulfed". The aim is to destroy the social order (nation, family, religion...) and to reverse morality and traditional values in order to impose a new order through destruction: *Ordo ab Chao*, order through chaos. In our modern societies, we can see the results of this destructive doctrine of "redemption through sin" or "holiness through evil". It is a particularly unhealthy philosophy aimed at a systematic inversion of moral values, where evil becomes good and good becomes evil. In his book entitled *"The Militant Messiah"*, Arthur Mandel defines this notion of "redemption through sin" as follows: *"It is nothing other than the old Pauline-Gnostic idea of felix culpa, the holy sin of the road to God through sin, the perverse desire to fight evil with evil, to get rid of sin by sinning."*[64]

This scourge seems to have its roots in ancient Babylonian practices and Mystery Cults. A doctrine revived by Frankism and Sabbataoism, a satanic degeneration of Judaism and Kabbalah, founded by the false messiahs Sabbataï Tsevi (17th century) and Jacob Frank (18th century). *Sabbatao-Frankism* can be considered a close ancestor of the Bavarian *Illuminati*, Zionism, Communism, and Fascism. Strictly speaking, there is no Frankist or Sabbataist cult, since it is a doctrine and a philosophy propagated by the infiltration of religions, but also of Freemasonry and other secret societies working behind the scenes of governments and behind democratic facades.

In his book Jacob Frank, the False Messiah, Charles Novak writes: "Thus, while Judaism preaches virginity, fidelity, and love, Sabbatai and his successors such as Jacob Frank preach sex from an early age for girls, sexual orgies for young boys, and wife-swapping on Shabbat. So much so that some Frankist children do not know their real biological father. Jacob and his followers were caught in the middle of an orgiastic Shabbat in January 1756 in the town of Landskron and were, at the request of the rabbis, expelled from the town for orgies. A woman stood in the middle, naked, while the male followers sang the Jewish Shabbat prayer: Lekhu doidi likrass kalo (Prayer sung every Friday night to celebrate the coming of the Shabbat. Instituted by Rabbi Alkabets in the 16th century). Then they would rush to her, turning the ritual into a collective orgy. Frankish sexual rites later consisted of songs, ecstatic dances, mixing men and women. Frank would kneel down and fix two lighted candles to a wooden bench, drive a nail between them and wave the cross in all directions, exclaiming: Forsa damus para vert, seibuml grandi asserverti (Judeo-Spanish), Give us the strength to see you, the great happiness to serve you. The lights were then turned off, the men and women undressed and the collective orgy began, the nudity reminiscent of Adam and Eve before the fall. Frank, however, did not participate. He remained in the middle, in mystical contemplation (...) The Frankists were known for their sometimes violent collective sexual orgies. Through these nihilistic behaviours, where the 9th became a feast of joy, they exchanged

---

[64] *The Militant Messiah or Flight from the Ghetto: A History of Jacob Frank and the Frankist Movement* - Arthur Mandel, 1989, p.57.

women, where they wanted to destroy all dogma: "So that the real Good God may appear," in their own words."[65]

Here we find the sacred orgies practised in the ancient religions known as the "Mysteries", such as the cult of Dionysus (Bacchus in the Romans), a phallic cult linked to fertility, just like the Shivaic cult in India or the cult of Osiris in ancient Egypt with its obelisks symbolising the phallus.

This "nameless religion", Luciferian and elitist, has its roots in the ancient Mystery religions of Babylon and Egypt, but also in Celtic Druidism. It has incorporated into its doctrine what it considers to be the 'best' of each of these traditions, their fundamental practices. Deities such as "El", "Isis", "Osiris" or "Baal" continue to receive a secret cult today.

This 'religion' has an almost undetectable tool of domination, namely trauma-based mind control. The world's ruling elite is militarily applying this mind science of trauma and dissociation. This phenomenon of personality splitting was discovered by ancient and pre-industrial cultures, but today it is an occult knowledge that is used by a Luciferian elite to control not only their own members, their own offspring, but above all to dominate all of humanity and establish absolute rule. In a testimony posted on the internet in April 1999, Kim Campbell (Philippe-Eugène de Rothschild), one of the many adulterous children of Édouard Philippe de Rothschild, said: *"When I watch CNN, I can't believe how many familiar faces are in the limelight in politics, the arts, finance, fashion and business. I grew up with these people. I met them at rituals and in the corridors of power. Financiers, artists, crowned heads, and even heads of state, all of them are people with disassociated personalities, who are working today to bring humanity into a New World Order, where the human being occupies the highest place and God is only a secondary abstraction. All these people, like me, had undergone satanic ritual abuse that had dissociated their personalities."*

What are these initiations? What are these ancient Mysteries? Do their symbolism contain initiatory keys that cross the centuries? Through which modern organisations do these Mysteries continue to be transmitted from generation to generation?

3 - FROM THE ANCIENT MYSTERY CULTS
TO MODERN SECRET SOCIETIES

The question of the involvement of Masonic-type fraternal organisations in ritual abuse, mind control and unhealthy occult practices has long been a matter of debate. Some Freemason writers suggest that the Masonic Order is based on an ancestry containing not only the rituals of the cathedral builders, but also initiation rites that come from various ancient cults such as the Mystery religions involving traumatic rituals. Other Freemasons claim that there is a Black Masonry that dishonours so-called *"pure and authentic"* Masonry.

---

[65] "Jacob Franck, the false messiah: Kabbalah deviance or conspiracy theory" - Charles Novak, 2012, p.50-62.

Accusations are regularly made that Freemasons are involved in the sexual abuse of minors and the term *"Masonic ritual abuse"* is used. Here are a few books reporting testimonies which accuse members of Freemasonry: *"The brotherhood: The secret world of the freemasons"* by Stephen Knight - *"Larson's new book of cult"* by Bob Larson - *"The deadly deception"* by Shaw & McKenney - *"Inside the brotherhood: Further secrets of the freemasons"* by Martin Short - *"Ritual Abuse, what it is, why it happens, how to help"* by Margaret Smith - *"Terror, Trauma and The Eye In The Triangle"* by Lynn Brunet. Unfortunately, there are few or no sources in French.

In her book on ritual abuse, survivor Margaret Smith makes accusations against Freemasonry. She was a victim of a group of people who sometimes poked fun at the stupidity of those who label them as *'Satanists'*. According to her, from their point of view they are Luciferians and they see *Satan* as a Judeo-Christian myth or a mere metaphor. Some survivors also report that they were encouraged to attend Christian masses to develop a part of their personality on the "light side", while another part of themselves undergoes and participates in unhealthy and traumatic practices. This is Gnostic theology where this concept of *'light'* versus *'darkness'* is something essential.[66] Is this one of the reasons why our *Masonic* elites found powerful philanthropic foundations? This notion of *"light versus dark"* is commonly used by survivors of ritual abuse and mind control to describe their own inner world. Distorted Christian doctrine will often be used as a backdrop to manipulate the child. Margaret Smith and many other survivors have spoken of a certain Gnostic philosophy in the abuses they experienced and they have also reported the presence of Freemasons during these abuses, Masonic regalia or Masonic type ceremonies. This is not to accuse all of Freemasonry of perpetrating sadistic and violent rituals, it is likely that some Masons operate without the consent of the majority of lodge members. However, there are some things about Freemasonry that may be questionable: take the example of the symbol of the *Order of the Eastern Star* (a women's Masonic organisation) which is an inverted pentagram, a symbol generally used to represent Baphomet or Satanism more generally. [67]

In 2011, during a conference at the annual meetings of the group S.M.A.R.T. (*Stop Mind Control and Ritual Abuse Today*), Kristin Constance testified that she was a victim of ritual abuse and mind control by her grandparents, founders and members of a lodge of the *Order of the Eastern Star* in Australia. She reports that the Masonic emblem of the Eastern Star was used as a medium for her mental programming. (Her testimony is transcribed in full in the chapter on Monarch programming)

Neil Brick, ritual abuse survivor and founder of the S.M.A.R.T. group, said: "I believe Freemasonry is one of the largest organisations responsible for satanic ritual abuse in the world. Its connection goes all the way up to the

---

[66] *Manicheism an ancient Mesopotamian "Gnosticism"*, Journal of Ancient Near Eastern Religions, Vol. 5 - Mehmet-Ali Atac.

[67] *Cult and Ritual Abuse* - James Randall Noblitt & Pamela Perskin Noblitt, 2014.

government (federal and local), as well as some of the economic institutions in the country... I was born into Freemasonry." [68]

Sociologist Stephen Kent, who has investigated deviant religious cults, particularly Scientology, has met many people who have testified to having suffered Masonic-style ritual abuse, including children of Freemasons: *"From the very beginning of my research, people were coming forward with testimonies, some of which were linked to Masonic abuses. Some people claimed that their father had been a Freemason and that the abuse was linked to a lodge and its members. Sometimes the abuse seemed to have taken place within the Masonic lodges themselves, but I cannot say for sure. These appearances of Freemasonry in quite a large number of testimonies left me really puzzled."* [69]

Canadian Lynn Moss-Sharman, survivor and founder of *The Stone Angels* newspaper and spokesperson for ACHES-MC Canada (*Advocacy Committee for Human Experimentation Survivors & Mind-Control*), stated in an interview with Wayne Morris in 1998 that Freemasonry is a common denominator in accounts of ritual abuse and mind control. *"... There were conversations about this that took place at the meetings, the fear was about this Masonic connection. I put a few small ads in the Globe and Mail about this and about upcoming conferences. Those few words about the Masonic connection generated phone calls and letters from victims across Canada. People who described themselves as survivors of Masonic ritual abuse, still living in terror. They were always daughters of Scottish Rite Masons or daughters of Shriners (Masonic branch). From all over Canada, these people began to testify about memories of what could be described as mind control experimentation. This began to manifest itself in November 1994."* [70]

In a book published in 2007, *Terror, Trauma and The Eye In The Triangle: The Masonic Presence in Contemporary Art and Culture*, Lynn Brunet reveals that her father, a Freemason and Rosicrucian, sexually abused her as a child. He also confessed to the existence of certain Masonic factions that practice traumatic ritual abuse of children. Here are some excerpts from his testimony: *As the years passed, I remembered my father's sexual abuse as a child (...) I also discovered that sexual abuse and incest were woven through the family history over at least three generations (...).From the outside, my family looked normal, but the accumulated weight of this family history, fraught with trauma and tension, was a heavy burden for each generation to bear (...) In recent years, as the riddles of my own experience were resolved, I tried to talk to them about what I remembered. Fortunately for me, my mother was able to recall the night my father raped me at the age of four and thus validate her daughter's statements. However, the ritual abuse was beyond their comprehension, which is understandable in many ways. In mid-2004, my father began to develop Alzheimer's disease. During the initial period of the disorder, in an altered state*

---

[68] Surviving Masonic Ritual Abuse - Neil Brick, Beyond Survival magazine. 07/1996.

[69] *"Interview with Dr. Stephen Kent"*, Wayne Morris, CKLN-FM - Mind Control Series Part 13.

[70] *Interview with Lynn Moss Sharman*, Wayne Morris, CKLN-FM - Mind Control Series Part 16.

of consciousness, he began to tell me about the dark side of his Masonic involvement. He confessed to me that he was aware of the existence of certain groups that used Masonic rituals in violent contexts to initiate children. He told me: "There are a lot of these groups, there are a lot of people who know about them, but they don't talk about it because it's embarrassing. He had alternating coherent conversations with me in which he told me about his involvement with other men in these groups. Sometimes in the evening he would manage to get out of the nursing home and he would then start climbing trees like a military man on a mission to, he believed, observe the activities of the cult in order to 'get the children out of the cult'. This 'strategic mission' lasted for a fortnight until he thought he had retrieved each of the children. After that he seemed to be very satisfied with what he had accomplished and all signs of his inner turmoil subsided (...) The memories concerning irregular Masonic activities were clearly to be attributed to some part of his psyche which is not normally accessible to consciousness and may have become intertwined with his war experiences at that time. It is possible that by raising this issue I had plunged my father into an inner conflict, his memory loss having begun just after my confrontation with him. However, his brief period of honesty with me undoubtedly contributed to a mutual healing process. This confession, combined with the knowledge of the Masonic Order that I was able to acquire, redirected my focus away from anger towards the man himself. I am now led to understand the principles behind these age-old "magical" practices, which divide the psyche of these men into two: on the one hand, dedicated citizens and men, and on the other, the most childish, absurd and cruel of human creatures."[71]

In France, Maude Julien gave a disturbing testimony in her book entitled *"Derrière la grille"* published in 2014. Her father, who was a wealthy entrepreneur, initiated into Freemasonry, subjected her to extreme conditioning aimed at making her a *"goddess"*, but above all a robot who obeyed his every word. Maude Julien suffered total social isolation for fifteen years, she was locked in a mental straitjacket (just like her mother) with training of mind and body to make her a *"superior being"*, a *"Chosen One"*. The extreme and traumatic physical and mental exercises defied belief. Maude Julien said: *'This book is a manual of silent disobedience. I wanted to show how the hold is put in place. It's a perfect crime where the victim is so ashamed that she doesn't speak out. Today, I am well in my personal and professional life, my daughters are grown up. I wanted to write my story. For him, only his mental world counts. The others are instruments or obstacles. He has locked me and my mother in this mental straitjacket. The Ogre shows you that he is Love, with a capital A. Everything he does is for your own good. He sets up a timed life where he holds the remote control. Then he instills fear. The outside world is the danger. "*[72]

---

[71] "Terror, Trauma And The Eye In The Triangle" - Lynn Brunet, 2007, p.236-240.

[72] "Mon père m'a séquestrée pendant 15 ans: le récit terrifiant de Maude", Julien Balboni, www.dhnet.be, 2014.

In a television interview[73] with Thierry Ardisson, Maude Julien confided that she had traumatic amnesia about scars on her thighs and chest. She doesn't know what the origin is and the doctors say that they are not accidents. In this interview, Maude Julien says: *"My father's goal was indeed to make me an 'over-being', he had a very important mission for me. And for that I had to have physical and mental training so that the spirit would be stronger than matter (...)*

- Thierry Ardisson: And then there's the cellar, so there it's quite violent, that is to say that he wakes you up in the middle of the night and he puts you sitting on a chair in a cellar.

- Maude Julien: Always to stay put. But the purpose of this capital mission to which he dedicated me was that I should be able to move between universes, to learn to communicate with the dead (...)

- T.A: There's the electricity test too, it's amazing. It asks you to hold an electric wire and take shocks for ten minutes.

- M.J: When there are discharges, you must not react (...)

- T.A: (...) at eight o'clock you go to wake up your father, and there you have to hold his chamber pot while he urinates (...) the most disturbing thing is these scars on the thighs and on the chest, the origin of which you don't know. Are they initiation rites, do you think?

- M.J: What is certain for the doctors is that they were not done by health professionals, which rules out the accident theory (...) and I'm afraid I'll never know.

Is it the occult teachings of the Masonic lodges that inspire such projects to create *'higher beings'*, enslaved and traumatised to become mediums connected to other dimensions? As we will see later in this book, extreme trauma causes deep dissociative states that spiritually 'unlock' the child, allowing connection to other dimensions. Are there any *Masonic ritual abuses* whose purpose would be to initiate the child, i.e. to create an *"illumination"* in the child during the dissociation?

But let us now return to the Mystery Cults linked to Gnosticism, the Gnosis that some literature attributes a major role in the history of Satanism and ritual abuse. The Gnostics were sometimes referred to as *Borborites* or *libertines* because of the deviant practices they indulged in in their 'mysteries'. According to Kurt Rudoph, the author of *Gnosis: The Nature and History of Gnosticism*, the secret of some Gnostics includes a ritual handshake similar to the Masonic handshake, a specific handshake to which some survivors of ritual abuse often react with a change of consciousness without knowing why it is happening to them. These reactions may mean that there has been mental programming and that the particular handshake acts as a trigger that changes the individual's state of consciousness. We will come back to this in more detail in Chapter 7 on *Monarch-type* mind control.

In the Gnostic text entitled *'Gospel of Phillip'*, it is mentioned that *'God is a man-eater. It is for this reason that men are (sacrificed) to him.* Several sources reported that some Gnostic groups practised ceremonies involving

---

[73] "Tortured by her father to make her a superior being" - "Salut les terriens", 10/2014.

cannibalism and sexual orgies. From their description, some of these ceremonies clearly fall into the category of black mass and satanic ritual abuse. The most shocking of the reported Gnostic practices is certainly that of Epiphanius. A monk is said to have witnessed the orgiastic rituals practiced by a Gnostic group called the *Phibionites* (or Barbotians). Bishop Epiphanius of Salamis wrote in his *Panarion (Adversus Haereses: Against Heresies)* that the Ophite sect of the Phibionites practised abortion and that the dismembered foetus, coated with honey and spices, was devoured by the group as a kind of eucharist. These orgiastic ceremonies are linked to the Phibionites' view of the cosmos and how to free themselves from it. In addition to satisfying the demands of the archons (demons), these 'mores' respond to the need to gather the divine seed implanted in the world, which is currently dispersed in the male seed and the female menses. In his book *"The Gnostics"*, Jacques Lacarriere states that the violation of sexual morality and other blasphemous horrors demonstrate the clear "Luciferian" conviction of the practitioners. Some Gnostics associate Lucifer with Promotheus, the Titan of Greek mythology.[74]

The Satanist Aleister Crowley practised with his followers a 'Thelemic' version of the black mass which he called the *'Gnostic Mass'*. Freemasonry displays a 'G' in the middle of the compass and square, a letter that refers to its primary source: Gnosis. In his speech of initiation to the rank of Scottish knight, Adam Weishaupt (founder of the "Illuminated of Bavaria") declared: *"The illuminated alone are in possession of the secrets of the true Freemason. Even to the enlightened ones a great part of his secrets remains to be discovered. The new knight must devote his research to this. He is especially warned that it is by the study of the ancient Gnostics and Manichaeans that he will be able to make great discoveries about this true Masonry."*[75]

In his book entitled *"Son of the Widow"*, Professor Jean Claude Lozac'hmeur analyses the links between the contemporary Gnostic Masonic tradition and mythology. He concludes that the myth of the 'Widow's Son', so dear to the Freemasons, contains a real parable that transmits, in a veiled way, a secret tradition to which an initiatory cult was originally associated. According to him, once deciphered, this symbolic story reveals a dualistic religion opposing an 'evil god', author of the Flood, to a 'good god', of the Promethean (Luciferian) type. *In other words, the religion of the Widow's Son is based on the same traditional background as the Bible, with the fundamental difference that the values are reversed and that the Judeo-Christian God appears as a jealous and ruthless tyrant."*[76]

The 'good god' of the various Gnostics would therefore be Lucifer hidden in his most beautiful guise, *illuminating* the initiates with the light of knowledge... A 'civilising god' putting man at the centre of all things. His research into the occult origins of Freemasonry also leads Jean Claude

---

[74] *"Cult and Ritual Abuse"* - James Randall Noblitt & Pamela Perskin Noblitt, 2014. p.132.

[75] *"Memoirs"* - Barruel, vol. 111, p.107.

[76] Son of the Widow - Jean-Claude Lozac'hmeur, 2002, p.136.

Lozac'hmeur to conclude: *"In all civilisations there has existed a primitive religion diametrically opposed to the biblical tradition, and of which vestiges can be found in mythologies and folklore. In this mystery cult, which corresponds to the 'Primordial Tradition' of modern Gnostics, Satan was represented as the 'Civilising God of Light'.*[77]

In the book "Le monde grec antique", Marie-Claire Amouretti writes about the cult of Bacchus at the Mysteries: "Dionysus appears as the liberating god. The myth makes him an exile, linking him to the Near East to make him return triumphantly to Greek soil, accompanied by a procession of satyrs and maenads, musicians and dancers. The god of wine and unbridled desire, Dionysus offers himself to his followers in the form of a powerful animal that they skin and eat raw in order to appropriate his strength. Women in particular take part in this cult. The whole civic and family framework breaks down on the occasion of these celebrations, of which Euripides makes an extraordinary evocation in "The Bacchae": physical or spiritual drunkenness, joy, the dishevelled race in the wastelands, song and dance, sexual freedom and female domination, all this expresses a deep need to free oneself from a civic, moral and family system that is being organised with great rigidity. A necessary but dangerous outlet."[78]

All this is clearly linked to what we are experiencing today in our consumer society in which man is put at the centre of everything thanks to the liberating god of the *"brothers of the light"*. Unbridled "consumers" devoid of any spirituality and whose morality keeps falling year after year, this being the result of the global luciferian plan, based precisely on this trans-historical gnosis whose aim is to carry out the reign of the *"civilising and liberating god"*.

According to the Roman historian Titus Livy, the author of *"Rome and the Mediterranean"*, the Romans who investigated the Bacchus Mystery Cult discovered that its rituals included sexual transgressions and blood sacrifices. One of the cult's prophetesses had organised a vast swindle with her followers that led to several murders, the "Bacchanalian scandal", which is well documented in history. This cult only admitted young people under twenty to its initiation ceremonies, who were more docile during the orgies... *When her son was recovering, she had to initiate him into the Bacchic rites (...) Then his mistress Hispala told him that when she was a slave, she entered this sanctuary as a subordinate to her mistress, but that when she was free she had never been near it. She knew that it was a workshop for all sorts of corruptions, and it was well known that for two years no one over twenty had been initiated here. They took him to a place which resounded with shouts, chants, music with cymbals and drums, so that the voice of the initiate could not be heard while shameful practices were perpetrated on him with violence..."* [79]

---

[77] *Les Origines Occultistes de la Franc-Maçonnerie* - Jean Claude Lozac'hmeur, 2015, p.42.

[78] *Le monde grec antique* - Marie Claire Amouretti & Françoise Ruzé, 1978, p.107.

[79] "Livy, History of Rome", "Source for the Study of Greek Religion" - David Rice, John Stambaugh, 1979 p.149.

In his book *"Les Divinités Génatrices"*, Jacques-Antoine Dulaure (at the time a Freemason of the *Osiris* Lodge *in Sèvres*) tells us that the Mystery cult of Bacchus originated in Egypt and that it was linked to the phallic cult (the worship of the penis). Dulaure writes in his book: *"Herodotus and Diodorus of Sicily agree that the cult of Bacchus was introduced into Greece by a man named Melampus, who was instructed by the Egyptians in a large number of ceremonies. Melampus, son of Amythaon, had, says Herodotus, a great knowledge of the sacred ceremony of the Phallus. It was he, in fact, who instructed the Greeks in the name of Bacchus, in the ceremonies of his cult, and who introduced among them the procession of the Phallus. It is true that he did not discover to them the depths of these mysteries; but the wise men who came after him gave a fuller explanation. It was Melampus, he adds, who instituted the procession of the Phallus which is carried in honour of Bacchus, and it was he who instructed the Greeks in the ceremonies which they still practise today."*[80]

The Freemason Dulaure also writes about this cult of the Phallus to which he devoted a whole book: "A particular and little known sect, called the sect of the Baptes, celebrated in Athens, Corinth, in the island of Chio, in Thrace and elsewhere, the nocturnal mysteries of Cotitto, a species of popular Venus. The initiates, who indulged in all the excesses of debauchery, used Phalluses in a particular way; they were made of glass, and served as drinking vessels. Those who see in this symbol of reproduction only the character of libertinism, must be astonished that it was an integral part of the ceremonies dedicated to Ceres, a divinity so recommended by her purity, and nicknamed the Holy Virgin; that it appeared in the mysteries of this goddess at Eleusis, called mysteries par excellence, to which all the men of antiquity, distinguished by their talents and virtues, honoured themselves with initiation (...) It is Tertullian who tells us that the Phallus was, at Eleusis, part of the mysterious objects. No other writer of antiquity had made known this particularity, no initiate had revealed this secret before him: "All that is holiest in these mysteries," he says, "that which is hidden with such care, that which is not allowed to be known until very late, that which the ministers of the cult, called Epoptes, make us desire so ardently, is the simulacrum of the virile member."[81]

Here are some extracts from the book *"Shiva et Dionysos"* (Alain Daniélou - 1979) concerning the similarities between the initiations of ancient religions and those of modern secret societies aiming to divinise man: *Certain ritual techniques will allow us to act on the latent energies present in the human being and thus to transform him and make him the vehicle for the transmission of certain powers, to raise him to a higher plane in the hierarchy of beings, to make him a sort of demi-god or superman closer to the invisible world of spirits. This is the role of initiation. This process of transformation of the human being is long and difficult, which is why initiation can only be done by degrees. The*

---

[80] "Les Divinités génératrices ou du culte du phallus chez les anciens et les modernes" - Jacques-Antoine Dulaure, 1805, p.106-107.

[81] Ibid, p.117-118.

pashu (animal man) will first become a sâdhaka (apprentice), then a vîra (hero) or adept, i.e. a being who can dominate and go beyond the appearances of the material world. The next degree is that of siddaha (realised), also called, among the Tantrikas, the stage of kaula (member of the group), a word which corresponds to the title of "companion" in Masonic initiation, where the rank of apprentice is also found. The kaula has reached the 'state of truth'. Only then do the barriers between the human and the divine disappear and the adept can be considered divya (divinised). In the language of the Greco-Roman mysteries, the adept, the initiate, was called a "hero". The higher degrees were probably kept secret. This transformation concerns the entire human being. (...) Only an initiate can transmit powers to a new initiate. This is essential for the initiatory transmission to be valid. This is why an interrupted tradition cannot be re-established. Initiation is the actual transmission of a shakti, a power, which takes the form of enlightenment. The continuity of the transmission from one initiate to another is compared to the transmission of a flame that lights another. Initiates form groups of men who are different from others. These groups are called kula (families) in Tantrism, hence the name kaula (family members or "companions") given to their followers. The kula corresponds to the Dionysian thiasis. (...) The ritual bath preceded, for the Eleusian mysteries, the phase considered the most mysterious of the initiations. It was preceded, according to Plutarch, by a ten-day abstinence from sexual intercourse. The same rule is applied in India. (...) "The novice is then led into the initiation area, carefully marked on the ground. The western entrance is the best for disciples of all castes, but especially for those of the royal caste, the Kshatriyas... The novice must walk three times around the phallic image and, according to his means, offer to God a handful of flowers mixed with gold, or only gold if flowers are missing, while reciting the hymn to Rudra (Rudrâdhyaya). Then he will meditate on Shiva by repeating only the pranava, the syllable AUM. (Linga Purâna, II, chap. 21, 40-42). Similarly, in the Dionysian rite, "the initiate has his head veiled and is guided by the officiant... A basket filled with fruits and symbolic objects, among which one in the shape of a phallus, is placed on the head of the initiate. (H. Jeanmaire, Dionysus, p.459) (...) "The blindfold that blinded the disciple is then removed and the yantra is shown to him.... " (Linga Purana, II, chap.21, 45). "

We find the same protocol in Freemasonry when the apprentice must be blindfolded to receive initiation.

Some current testimonies seem to confirm that the cult of Dionysus/Bacchus and generally all these Luciferian cults are still practiced today in the West. The book *"Ritual Abuse and Mind Control: The Manipulation of Attachment Needs"* contains the testimony of a survivor of Satanic ritual abuse and mind control. The woman was born into a family that allegedly practises these rituals from generation to generation, here is an excerpt from her testimony: *"The first child murder that I can consciously remember was when I was four or five years old. My mother was knocked up by X (...) We were taken to a large stately home, it was during the summer on the occasion of an important date (...) On Friday evening there was a ritual followed by an orgy involving a lot of people dressed in costumes and doing 'antics' in this huge salon. Bacchus was one of the gods they worshipped. The next day we went outside to a big meadow, there were a hundred people, it was a big ritual. My mother was lying on the ground, she was in labour while X was singing (...) The child was born, it was a little girl. He then put a knife in my left hand and told me certain things about the child. Then he put his hand on mine and we pointed the knife at the baby's chest and killed it. He removed the heart, everyone cheered and went wild, then the child was dismembered and consumed.* "[82]

In his book The Occult Conspiracy: Secret Societies, Their Influence and Power in World History, Michael Howard writes about the Mystery Cults of antiquity: "The Mystery Cults perform initiation ceremonies that contain arcane symbolism and drama to reveal to the initiate the spiritual realities hidden behind the illusion of the material world. During initiation, the neophyte is put into a trance and experiences contact with the gods on a journey into the 'Other World'. Initiates pass through a symbolic death and are reborn with a perfect soul."

What Howard reports here is interesting because it shows the similarities between the ancient Mystery Cults, shamanism, possession cults and witchcraft... But what he describes also shows a similarity with contemporary Masonic-type secret societies, i.e. symbolic death for rebirth to a new life. A symbolism that we also find among Christians with the rebirth in Jesus Christ through the sacrament of baptism: *'So he who is joined to Christ is a new creature: the old has passed away; behold, the new is already here'* (2 Corinthians 5:17). Jesus Christ came to earth to reform all those pagan religions that practised blood sacrifice in honour of fallen angels. Blood baptism was replaced by the baptism of water and the Holy Spirit, and the blood sacrifice was permanently replaced by His own Sacrifice.

Benjamin Walker, the author of *The Woman's Encyclopedia of Myths and Secrets*, describes an initiation ceremony of the cult of Mithras, which was another of these Mystery religions, as follows: *"First there are a few days of abstinence from food and sex, then an ablution ceremony after which the candidate's hands are tied behind his back, and he is laid on the ground as if he were dead. After certain solemn rites, his right hand is seized by the hierophant and he is resurrected. Then comes the baptism of blood. The initiate finds himself naked in a pit covered with a grate, above this grate an animal is sacrificed so that the blood flows over the candidate. No matter which animal is involved, it always symbolises the bull of Mithras. The Christian poet Prudentius described this ritual in his personal memory: 'Through the grate flows into the pit the red liquid which the neophyte receives on his body, on his head, on his cheeks, on his lips and on his nostrils. He drips the liquid over his eyes and mouth to soak his tongue with blood and to swallow as much as he can. Symbolically, the initiate has been raised from the dead and cleansed by the revitalising blood of the bull. He is now considered "born again into eternity". He will be welcomed into the community of initiates as a brother and will now be allowed to*

---

[82] *Ritual Abuse and Mind Control: The Manipulation of Attachment Needs* - Orit Badouk Epstein, Joseph Schwartz, Rachel Wingfield Schwartz, 2011, p.149.

participate in the sacramental meal of bread and water, thus establishing his status as a chosen one. "

The survivor "Svali", an ex-illuminati, herself born into a Luciferian cult, reports in her testimony that the group to which she belonged has practices similar to the ancient Babylonian Mystery religions with blood baptism: *"They (the children) will participate in rituals during which the adults wear robes, and they will have to, among other things, prostrate themselves before the guardian deity of their cult. Moloch, Ashtaroth, Baal, Enokkim, are demons that are commonly worshiped. The child may witness a real or staged sacrifice serving as an offering for these deities. Animal sacrifices are common. The child will be forced to participate in the sacrifices and will have to go through blood baptism. He will have to take the heart or other organs of the sacrificed animal and eat them (...) They do initiation rituals with children or with older followers, the initiate is tied up and an animal is bled to death over him. "*[83]

A document[84] containing the hearings and minutes of the Dutroux case in Belgium reports some testimonies about blood sacrifices during rituals, sometimes with a kind of blood baptism. These are depositions and complaints, and no proper investigation has been carried out to determine whether these testimonies were true. All these cases are systematically hushed up... Why is that? Here are some excerpts:

X1 killed two rabbits and a dwarf goat on B's orders. The orgy took place in the garage. Participants with special costumes: leather, capes, masks... C. must eat the heart of the sacrificed rabbit. Children tied to rings in the garage. The blood of the goat is poured on C." (PV 118.452, 10/12/96, Hearing of witness X1 (Regina Louf), page 542)

Paragraph 29 (W.'s diary) mentions a family who performs human sacrifices, including their own daughter (...) She was taken to a house where there is a big pool outside. There are many men and women. They make her drink in the car. There is a big fire in the garden. There are three other girls (...) During a game in this house, hot blood was poured on her (PV 117.753, 754 and 118.904, W.'s Hearing, page 749)

He attended a black mass in the posh suburb of Gent in April 1987. Satanist mass. Animals were sacrificed, disemboweled and then killed. The blood of the animals was drunk by the participants (...) T4 could not attend the whole ceremony. Description of the villa. Luxurious vehicles (...) J. and E. reported that there were parliamentarians and other personalities. Incantations in an unknown language. Priests and priestesses naked under their cloaks. Everyone in cloak and mask. The suffering of sacrificed animals is the means to obtain power and might. (PV 118.220, 04/12/96, information T4, page 125)

He knows satanic churches in Hasselt, Brussels, Gent, Knokke, Liège, Charleroi and Mozet (...) The sacrifices range from animal to human. The sacrifices are followed by orgies (...) Sometimes the woman is sacrificed and her blood is used for the rites. (PV 100.693, 06/01/97, Hearing of L. P., page 126)

---

[83] How The Cult Programs People - Svali.

[84] "Belgium: Dutroux X-Dossier summary", 2005 - Wikileaks.org.

W. allegedly participated in "black masses" with other minors. She speaks of minors being branded with red-hot iron and of human sacrifices. She also speaks of prepared human meat that the girls had to eat. During these parties, the girls were raped by the participants. (PV 116.780 21/11/96, Hearing of W., page 746)

He participated in 1985 in several satanic sessions near Charleroi. On one occasion, the blood of a 12-year-old girl was offered to the audience. He did not attend the murder (...) On the spot, he was drugged before being taken to a room with people wearing masks and black robes. The participants were drinking blood. There was a naked girl lying on an altar, she was dead. (PV 250 and 466, 08/01/97 and 16/01/97, Hearing of T.J., page 260)

She first went to the castle when she was 14 years old in V's beige Jaguar. (...) during the full moons (...) She writes: In a circle around the fire - there are candles - everyone stands except the baby and the sheep - the baby cries (...) She describes the killing of the baby and the mixing of its blood with that of the sheep. Then the baby and the sheep are burned and everyone 'makes love together'. The baby's heart is torn out. (PV 150.035, 30/01/97, Hearing of N. W., page 756)

In 2000, France 3 broadcast a report entitled *"Child rape, the end of silence?"*. The documentary contains the testimony of a little girl who was a victim of satanic ritual abuse. She describes a cult scene in or near Paris: *"Then we went down into a labyrinth where it was cold, it was dark, and it looked like a basement. Here there was a changing room where we went to get dressed in the white and red clothes. Then we would go here* (ed. note: showing his drawing), *there was a room where they raped the children, it was a big room, like a big cave in the shape of a cathedral or a cot and there were many, many people here. There was also a very, very large statue of an African or black god, and when he growled, people put money in large baskets that were passed around. Around this statue there were ashes, with children's heads on spikes in the ashes."*

Doesn't the Old Testament repeatedly describe child sacrifices? Rituals consisting of sacrificing children to fire in honour of the demon Moloch (see the end of this chapter). These practices of sacrificial cults do not seem to have ended with the modern world... In different forms, the *Mysteries* are like dark funerals, celebrating a mystical death and resurrection in the form of a heroic or divine figure. In his book *"Antichrist Osiris"*, Chris Relitz explains that this ritual initiation of the Mysteries could take different forms consisting of a replay of a deity's life, death and resurrection. Secret knowledge was encoded in these initiation ceremonies and could thus be passed down through the centuries. Firstly, the candidate for initiation must die symbolically by re-enacting the story of a god. Then comes the search for and discovery of his body, and finally the *'resurrection'* where the initiate receives a secret that he must keep. A secret that at first seems insignificant, but the priest is perfectly aware that this information is of extreme importance. What the initiate has just been entrusted with is in fact *"the secret of all secrets"*, it is information encoded and veiled in symbolism that the initiate will not usually be able to understand directly. All they can do is to continue to blindly and eternally pass on this occult symbolism to other candidates for initiation.[85]

In 1928, the founder of the Revue Internationale des Sociétés Secrètes (R.I.S.S.), Mgr Jouin, declared in the first issue of the R.I.S.S.'s "Occultist Supplement": "Yes, the great secret of occultism is there: that is, not in the sensational discovery of an as yet unpublished confession or accusation, but in the obviousness of the truth. Yes, the great secret of occultism is there: that is, not in the sensational discovery of a confession or an as yet unpublished accusation, but in the obvious and serene conclusion of a sort of comparative grammar of the symbolism of all the sects. For the adepts, condemned to hide their 'truth' under impenetrable veils, have undoubtedly forbidden themselves at all times categorical formulae, since what they teach would be so repugnant to the minds and hearts of men...(...) But it is easy to see that a fixed interpretation of these symbols has always been in use among mankind, that a traditional cabala, long oral, then written, has developed from time immemorial side by side with the canon of the Scriptures and is finally found in a certain number of works, at first sight incomprehensible or contradictory, but whose true meaning can be reconstructed by the key to symbolism."

Christian Lagrave, the author of the book entitled "Les Dangers de la Gnose Contemporaine", declared during a conference: "How could these Gnostic errors have been transmitted and persisted since antiquity? Several modes of transmission are possible and can be combined with each other. First of all, there is the clandestine persistence of these doctrines in religious sects or secret societies, with an 'esoteric' transmission (reserved for a small number of initiates) carried out in an occult manner, i.e. these perverse doctrines are never fully and explicitly revealed, but are hidden under symbols and myths, gradually leading the initiate to discover them for himself. This tactic of progressive initiation was already in use in the ancient and medieval Manichean sects. It is still practised in modern occultist cults, particularly in Freemasonry. The aim of this tactic is to lead the new initiates gradually to doctrines which would scare them away if they were revealed to them completely at once."

All these sects, called schools of the Mysteries or religions of the Mysteries, were thus intended to transmit a certain esoteric and occult knowledge. Only aristocrats could join such groups to receive initiation into the 'famous' Mysteries. These initiates were trained with a methodical combination of teachings and indoctrinations. Sleep deprivation, ritualised torture, drugs and sometimes demonology were used to programme the minds of the 'students'. These aristocrats, initiated into the Mysteries and linked by rituals to certain demonic entities (which could provide them with material assistance), thus felt superior to the rest of the population. Thus, little by little, a sort of aristocratic caste was born, which developed a feeling of spiritual superiority that translated into 'enlightenment'. That is, access to a knowledge hidden from the majority of profane humans. A number of authors have clearly detected the strong resemblance between these ancient Mystery cults and the modern fraternal

---

[85] "Antichrist Osiris: The History of the Luciferian Conspiracy" - Chris Relitz, 2012.

organisations, secret societies that appeared later in Europe. Jean-Marie R. Lance, a member of A.M.O.R.C. (Rosicrucian), stated in a Canadian television documentary: *"The history of the Order, in its traditional aspect, goes back to ancient Egypt and we can even go back to 1500 years before Christ with, for example, Akhenaten who was associated with these schools of the Mysteries, with these "Houses of Life" which were places that allowed men and women to study the mysteries of life together.*"[86]

Some authors claim that Freemasonry was built on the one hand on the tradition of the cathedral builders and on the other hand on the model of those ancient schools of the Mysteries with the practice of unhealthy and traumatic initiation rituals. In these traumatic rituals, the terror that the candidate undergoes is the central point of the initiation process, his or her vulnerability in this experience marks the power of the group over the individual: *'We could have killed you, but we didn't'*. After going through this process, the initiate will be helped and protected by the group/cult on condition that he/she respects the strict requirements of secrecy. This principle of initiation through trauma is common to all Luciferian or Satanist fraternal structures, where initiation in early childhood is the best way to obtain a loyal, faithful adult who will perfectly respect the law of silence while perpetuating the obscure tradition. Rituals involving perverse and immoral acts, including vile paedocriminality, also provide a means of blackmailing those who have taken part. This allows for the creation of *'brotherly'* bonds, all the stronger when a human sacrifice, a ritual crime, was committed in a group and cameras were filming the scene to immortalise it. The adepts who plunge into this addictive violence feel connected to each other by a secret that is strictly impossible to reveal to the outside world; it is an unhealthy cement that binds the members together and gives them a feeling of superiority over the human mass.

A relatively well-known example of a secret society that practised satanic rituals is the *Brethren of St Francis of Wycombe*, better known as *'The Hell Fire Club'*. This group was founded in May 1746 by Francis Dashwood at the *George and Vulture public house* in London. Francis Dashwood was a close friend of King George III, who later became Britain's finance minister. This *'club'* was located in the underground of a church-like building, with a series of tunnels, halls and caverns that were used by the members (the 'brethren') for their occult activities, which consisted of fornicating with prostitutes, worshipping Bacchus and Venus and offering sacrifices to Satan. Although not a direct member, Benjamin Franklin occasionally attended *Hell Fire Club* meetings. Franklin was himself a Freemason, Grand Master of St John's Lodge in Philadelphia and Grand Master of the Nine Sisters Lodge in Paris. He was also a Rosicrucian Grand Master.

In February 1998, a worker on a building site discovered the bones of six children and four adults. The site was the restoration of a London house at 36 Craven Street, which was the home of Benjamin Franklin, the Father of the American Constitution. The bodies were dated to the period when Franklin

---

[86] "The secret sign: Order of the Rosicrucian" - Historia, 03/2012.

occupied the house, i.e. from 1757 to 1762 and from 1764 to 1775. The discovery of the bones was even announced in the British press, notably by *The Sunday Times*. Evangeline Hunter-Jones, MP and president of the *Friends of Benjamin Franklin House*, reported that *"the burnt bones were buried deep, probably to hide them, and there is every reason to believe that there are still some.* To exonerate Benjamin Franklin, it was quickly put forward that during his absences, his friend Dr. Hewson might have used the house to perform dissections of human cadavers for his students.[87]

Albert Mackey is a famous Freemason (the one who co-opted Albert Pike) who studied the philosophical roots of Freemasonry going back to biblical times. Mackey deduced that the *"pure"* form that was practiced by the Israelites (Noachites) involved a belief in one God and the immortality of the soul. He argues that its *'parasitic'* form was that set of initiatory rites practised by the pagans, and in particular the Dionysian practices of the Tyrians. Pagan practices which he says involved *'severe and difficult trials... a long and painful initiation... with a series of initiatory grades'*. According to Mackey, these two forms of Masonry merged during the construction of Solomon's Temple to produce a prototype of the modern (Masonic) institution. Mackey thus identifies a corrupted form of Freemasonry combined with a pure form dating back to its origins. He argues that this gives this secret institution both a light and a dark side. He defines this dark side, this 'parasitic' form of masonry, as a kind of black masonry with terrifying and traumatic initiation practices, which uses the symbolic representation of the mythical descent into Hades, the tomb or hell, and then returns to the light of day: the initiatory rebirth.[88]

Mackey reveals that there are two sides to Masonry, one of which is unaware of the other's existence, which can be translated as *"the good guys don't know the bad guys, but the bad guys know the good guys"*.

The Masonic author Manly P. Hall, honoured by the Journal of the Scottish Rite as *"the greatest philosopher of Freemasonry"*, clearly described the two distinct aspects of the Masonic organisation: *"Freemasonry is a fraternity hidden within another fraternity: a visible organisation concealing an invisible fraternity of the elect... It is necessary to establish the existence of these two separate and yet interdependent orders, one visible, the other invisible. The visible organisation is a splendid comradeship composed of "free and equal men," dedicated to ethical, educational, fraternal, patriotic and humanitarian projects. The invisible organisation is a secret, most august fraternity, majestic in dignity and grandeur, whose members are dedicated to the service of a mysterious "arcanum arcandrum," i.e., a hidden mystery.[89]

To complete this description of Hall, here is what Albert Pike says in "Morals and Dogma": "Like all Religions, all Mysteries, Hermeticism and

---

[87] "The Satanist and Freemason Benjamin Franklin" - Laurent Glauzy, 2014.

[88] "The Symbolism of Freemasonry: Illustrating and Explaining its Science and Philosophy, its Legends, Myths and Symbols" - Mackey, Albert G, 1955.

[89] "Lectures on Ancient Philosophy", Manly P. Hall, p.433.

Alchemy, Freemasonry reveals its secrets to no one but the Adepts, the Sages and the Elect. It resorts to false explanations to interpret its symbols, to mislead those who deserve to be misled, to hide from them the Truth, which it calls the Light, and thus to keep them away from it (...) Freemasonry jealously hides its secrets, and intentionally misleads its pretentious interpreters."[90]

In her book *"The Externalisation of the Hierarchy"*, the famous *New Age* occultist Alice Bailey, writes of this totally occult fringe of Freemasonry: *"The Masonic Movement is the guardian of the law. It is the House of Mysteries, and the seat of initiation. It holds in its symbolism the ritual of the Divinity, and preserves in its pictorial work the way of salvation. The methods of the Divinity are demonstrated in his Temples. The world can advance under the gaze of this Eye from which nothing escapes. Freemasonry is a far more occult organisation than one can imagine. It is destined to be the training school for the most advanced future occultists (...) These Mysteries, when restored, will unify all beliefs."[91]*

Alice Bailey tells us about Lucifer (*the Eye from which nothing escapes*) and the construction of a new world order (*the Mysteries that will unify all beliefs*).

There are a number of Masonic sources concerning the connection between the Mystery religions and contemporary Freemasonry. Some brethren have openly acknowledged this in several publications. The Masonic book entitled *"The Master Mason"* clearly describes the link between the Mystery Cults of antiquity and modern Masonry: *"The idea behind the Hiram legend is as old as religious thought among men. The same elements existed in the story of Osiris, celebrated by the Egyptians in their temples, just as the ancient Persians referred to it with their god Mithras. In Syria, the Dionysian Mysteries contain very similar elements with the story of Dionysius and Bacchus, a god who died and rose again. There is also the story of Tammuz, as old as all the others. All these refer to the ancient Mysteries. They are celebrated by secret societies, just like ours, with allegorical ceremonies in which the initiates progress through these ancient societies from one degree to another. Read these ancient stories and marvel at how many men have all received the same great truth in the same way."[92]*

The Master Mason book therefore invites Freemason readers to read the stories of the ancient Mystery religions to see how they teach the same *"great truth"* as Freemasonry. In the book *"A Bridge to Light"*, 32nd degree Freemason Rex R. Hutchens also talks about the *"great truths"* of the Mysteries. This is how he describes the 23rd degree in the Scottish Rite: *"Here we begin the*

---

[90] *Morals and Dogmas*, Volume 1, Albert Pike, p.104.

[91] The Externalization of the Hierarchy - Alice Bailey, 1974, pp.511-573.

[92] *The Master Mason"*, p.9-10 - Grand Lodge F. & A. M. of Indiana, Committee on Masonic Education.

symbolic initiation into the Mysteries practised by the ancients and through which Masonry has received the great truths. "[93]

In his book Symbolism of Freemasonry or Mystic Masonry, 32nd degree Mason J.D. Buck writes that "Freemasonry is modelled on the Ancient Mysteries, with their symbols and allegories, which is more than coincidental because of the strong similarities."[94]

Henry C. Clausen, a 33rd degree Freemason, wrote in his book "Your Amazing Mystic Powers": "Freemasonry is on the threshold of a new day. Because of the inadequacy of modern theology, the impossibility of materialism and the sterility of academic philosophy, men are turning to the eternal truths perpetuated in the arcane of the ancient Mysteries."[95]

The Freemason S.R. Parchment stated in his book Ancient Operative Masonry: "The hierophants of universal science and sublime philosophy teach the Great Mysteries of Egypt, India, Persia and other ancient nations. They reveal the secrets concerning the subtle forces of nature to worthy and qualified candidates. These devotees are also instructed in the doctrine of the Universal Brotherhood, and finally initiated into the consciousness of "I am that I am". These ideals are the landmarks, symbols and traditions of Ancient Operative Freemasonry, nothing more."[96]

In 1896, in the History of Freemasonry, Albert Mackey wrote of the Mystery religions: "It is known that in the Mysteries as in Freemasonry, there are solemn obligations of secrecy with penalties for violation of the oath (...) I have traced the analogies between the ancient Mysteries and modern Freemasonry: 1/ The Preparation, which is called the 'Lustration' in the Mysteries, is the first stage of the Mysteries and is also the work to be done in the degree of Apprentice Mason (who will have to 'polish' or roughen his stone). 2/ Initiation (...) 3/ Perfection (...) Freemasonry is the unbroken continuity of the ancient Mysteries, the succession of what was transmitted through the initiations of Mithras."

Indeed, the analogies between the Mystery cult of Mithras and contemporary Freemasonry are numerous and undeniable. In his book *"Son of the Widow"*, Jean-Claude Lozac'hmeur cites several of these similarities. First of all, the Mystery Room of Mithras was underground and had a crypt whose ceiling could be decorated with stars symbolising the universe, just like the ceiling of Masonic temples. The two cults have the same layout: on each side of the hall, lengthwise, were benches between which stood four small pillars for the Mithraic temple and three pillars in the Masonic temple. The two columns Jakin and Boaz of the modern lodges correspond to the two columns framing the bas-reliefs of Mithras. Last but not least, both cults involve an initiation that is preceded by trials and they also involve several degrees of initiation. The

---

[93] *A Bridge To Light"* - Rex R. Hutchens, 1988, p.194.

[94] "Symbolism of Freemasonry or Mystic Masonry" - J.D. Bruck, 1925.

[95] *Your Amazing Mystic Powers"* - Henry C. Clausen, 1985, p.xvii.

[96] "Ancient Operative Masonry and The Mysteries of Antiquity" - S.R. Parchment, 1996, p.11.

initiation ritual of the first Masonic degree is almost identical to the representations of the initiation into Mithraism. In both cases, the candidate's eyes are veiled by a blindfold held behind him by a figure and in both cases the master of the ceremony presents him with a sword. In the Mithras initiation the candidate is naked and sits with his hands tied behind his back, whereas in the Masonic initiation the candidate has one arm and one leg naked and stands with his hands free. It is more than likely that we are dealing here with the same cult that has survived the centuries. As we have seen above, the Mystery Cult of Mithras practised actual blood sacrifices to baptise the initiate in a form of resurrection and purification by the blood of the Bull.

Albert Pike himself admitted that Freemasonry was a vestige of the antediluvian religion, i.e. the religion of the Mysteries, the Babylonian religion: *"The legend of the granite, brass or bronze columns which survived the flood, is supposed to symbolise the Mysteries, of which Masonry is the legitimate succession."*[97]

Albert Mackey states in "The History of Freemasonry" that "the traditional history of Freemasonry begins before the flood. There was a system of religious instruction which, because of its resemblance to Freemasonry on the legendary and symbolic level, has been called by some authors "Antediluvian Masonry."[98]

In his book "La Symbolique Maçonnique", Jules Boucher, also a Freemason, states that "present-day Masonry is not a survivor of the mysteries of antiquity, but a continuation of the said Mysteries."[99]

Faced with all these quotations, it is therefore legitimate to ask this question: does modern masonry transmit initiations and knowledge similar to those taught before the flood, then at the time of Nimrod and Babylon? Has this secret Masonic knowledge retained a purely Luciferian doctrine, i.e. based on paganism and Satanism, including among other things depraved sexual practices and blood sacrifices (sexual magic and demonology)? Do they still sacrifice the *Bull* of Mithras? Do they still practice blood baptism? Is this the *"parasite masonry"*, the black masonry with traumatic initiation rituals that Albert Mackey talks about? Are traumas leading to altered states of consciousness, blood sacrifices and paedocriminal sexual magic initiatory keys that some modern secret societies use to establish connections with certain entities and thus acquire power and might?

This claim of descent from the most shameful mysteries of antiquity by many Freemason writers proves that Freemasonry tends by its doctrines and practices to the restoration of ancient paganism in its greatest perversion. Are modern secret societies of the Masonic type the direct descendants of the ancient Mystery religions and fertility cults? Cults that worshipped gods such as Baal,

---

[97] Morals and Dogma, Level 8 " - Albert Pike.

[98] "The History of Freemasonry: Its Legendary Origins, Pt.1 Prehistoric Masonry" - Albert Gallatin Mackey, 2008, p.61.

[99] *"La Symbolique Maçonnique"* - Jules Boucher, 1985, p.253.

Moloch or Dionysus (Bacchus) and whose rites included sacrifices. Group sexuality was also an essential element of these pagan cults, the solar phallic cult being represented today by the obelisks that stand in honour of the 'royal masonic secret' in our great public squares...

The author of *Who Was Hiram Abiff*, J.S.M. Ward reports that human sacrifice rituals were practiced in the Mystery Cults of *Astarte, Tammuz* and *Adonis*, he writes: *"We have abundant evidence that at one time human victims were regularly sacrificed to Astarte ... The most usual method seemed to be by fire, the victim was killed before being placed on a funeral pyre. It was this particular form of sacrifice that was associated with Melcarth or Moloch. Melcarth was Baal, the god of fertility* (see at the end of this chapter 'Sacrificial Rituals in the Old Testament') (...) *These archaic beginnings evolved into the great Mystery Rites and Freemasonry itself, in which men are taught the doctrine of the resurrection of the soul and life beyond the grave. All these primitive rituals are associated with the fertility cult. "*[100]

In his book *The Golden Bough*, Sir James Frazer writes that fertility cults represent a universal primitive religion in which human sacrifices were regularly practised. In 1921, Margaret Murray popularised knowledge of such secret religions with the publication of her book *The Witch Cult in Western Europe*. Murray states that the *'witch hunters'* of the 16th and 17th centuries had discovered and exposed a real goddess cult linked to the *'Old Religion'*: that is, cults organised hierarchically and meeting in assemblies according to a certain calendar. These ceremonies are known as *Sabbaths*. The orgiastic rituals of the *Sabbath, which* may include blood sacrifices, are cults related to fertility.[101]

For the Indian historian Narendra nath Bhattacharyya, there is a kind of archaic matriarchal substratum on which all the religions of India and the Middle East are rooted, most of which are linked to a form of sexual magic. Bhattacharyya also suggests that the ancient mother-goddess cults of Isis, Astarte, etc., are rooted in a *"primitive sexual rite based on the magical association between the fertility of nature and human fertility. "*[102]

Here are some extracts from the book *"The Ancient Greek World"* illustrating the ritual practices of ancient religions, in particular the cults linked to fertility: *"Immediately, in order around the vast altar, they arrange for the god the splendid hecatomb (a large number of animals intended to be sacrificed) (...) arms raised, pray aloud: you whose bow is of silver, listen to my words... This is how he prays, and Phoebus Apollo listens to his prayer. The prayer is stopped, the barley grains are thrown, the heads of the victims are raised to the sky, the throats are slit, the skin is removed, the thighs are detached, they are covered with fat in a double layer; pieces of raw flesh are placed on top of them (...) Sacrifice of consumable goods, collective meal with what remains.*

---

[100] *"Who Was Hiram Abiff?* - J.S.M.Ward, 1925, pp.50-34-195.

[101] The Oxford Handbook of New Religious Movements - James R. Lewis, 2008.

[102] Magia Sexualis: Sex, Magic and Liberation in Modern Western Esotericism " - Hugh B. Urban, 2006, p.22.

Everything takes place in the open air around a simple altar (...) The sacrifice of the animal remains the most characteristic rite. It can be of the Uranian type, as here, with the animal's blood directed towards the sky, and the offal eaten in joy despite the seriousness of the circumstances (the Greeks are threatened by the plague). The Chthonic cult is practised over a pit where the blood flows directly into the earth; the flesh is entirely burnt as a holocaust (...) We note that both rituals can be used for the same god, depending on the circumstances. Chthonic rites are addressed to the infernal deities, accompany certain expiatory sacrifices, often oaths, sacrifices to the sea and to rivers, to dead heroes (...) Simple offerings of popular cults, often of a magical nature, small clay statuettes, the first fruits of the harvest, hair (...)) The daughter of Demeter, Kore-Persephone, the maiden of grain, goes down in summer, after the threshing of the cereals, to join her infernal husband, Pluto - or Ploutos, that is to say the rich one, rich of the silos dug in the ground or of the half-buried jars filled with the new harvest. In October she returns to her mother to witness the sowing and the resumption of vegetation. This return is marked by the festival of the Thesmophoria (...) it is reserved for married women, who alone are bearers of fertility. It is then that putrefied pigs are removed from the pits where they had been thrown in sacrifice to Eubouleus, and their remains, mixed with cereal seed, will ensure the fertility of the land (...) This is only one example of the innumerable ceremonies intended to ensure the fertility of the soil (...) A certain number of sanctuaries also draw their reputation from their oracular function. It is admitted that there are many signs by which the gods address themselves to humans (...) the flight of birds, the entrails of sacrificed victims (...) The most famous is undoubtedly the oracle of Delphi, which Apollo inherited from the land that had preceded him there. The consultation of the Pythia is the favourite procedure. After having completed the preliminary formalities (purifications, consecration of the "pelanos", sacrifice of a victim to Apollo, another to Athena) and having made sure that the god consented to listen, the consultant is introduced into the back of the temple, "the adyton", where the Pythia is located, installed on the tripod that covers the oracular pit. "[103]

In the Dictionnary of Satanism, Wade Baskin writes about fertility cults: "In classical mythology, Dionysus is the god of wine and fertility. His cult spread to Thrace, and women were particularly involved in these orgiastic rites. The Maenads, in their ecstatic frenzy, abandoned their homes, roamed the fields and hillsides, dancing while twirling their flaming torches. In their passion, they would catch and tear up animals, sometimes even children, and devour their flesh, thus acquiring communion with the divinity (...) Some pagan religions gave initiations through secret rituals, not disclosed to the public. The secret knowledge that the initiate received gave him advantages in his present life and in his life after death... The Dionysian Mysteries were present in many places. The orgiastic ceremonies required drinking the sacred wine, eating the raw flesh of the sacrificed animal and drinking its blood. The ultimate goal of such a cult was to achieve immortality."

---

[103] *Le monde grec antique"* - Marie Claire Amourreti & Françoise Ruzé, 1978, chap.8.

Walter Leslie Wilmshurst stated in his book *"The Meaning of Masonry"* that Freemasonry is indeed descended from the ancient Mysteries where achieving immortality, i.e. "becoming a god", is the central point. This quest for immortality is a constant in all Luciferian cults, all pagan doctrines: *"This notion, which concerns the evolution of man into a 'super-man', has always been the goal of the Ancient Mysteries. The real aim of modern Masonry is not the social or charitable works that are put forward, but rather the acceleration of the spiritual evolution of those who aspire to perfect their human nature in order to transform themselves into a kind of god. This thing is a precise science, a royal art, which each of us can put into practice. To join this Art for any other purpose than to study and practice this science is to misunderstand its true meaning... which is the conscious realisation of our divine potentialities."* [104]

In his book "The Lost Keys of Freemasonry", the Luciferian Manly Palmer Hall says: "When a Mason learns that the meaning of the warrior on the board actually represents a dynamo giving off living power, he then discovers the mystery of his noble profession. The bubbling energies of Lucifer are in his hands. Before he can begin to advance and ascend, he must prove that he is capable of using these energies properly (...) Man is a god in the making, and just as in the mystical myths of Egypt with the potter's wheel, he must be shaped." [105]

Wilmshurst writes in "The Masonic Initiation": "Few Masons know what true initiation involves... True initiation consists of an expansion of consciousness from the human to the divine state... Man has this thing within him, enabling him to evolve from the mortal animal stage to the immortal, super-human, divine being stage... Can this process of human evolution be accelerated? To transform the animal human into an enlightened divine being? To these questions, the Ancient Mysteries answer that "Yes, human evolution can be accelerated in initiated individuals." [106]

What are these occult practices that accelerate the spiritual evolution of the human being, leading him to become a divine being and even a god? These Mysteries remain reserved for the initiates of the High Lodges and Back Lodges, or rather of the *Arcanum Arcandrum,* the Invisible Brotherhood described above by Manly P. Hall. However, some seem to have broken the oath of silence, such as Bill Schnoebelen who describes this Masonic *"Royal Art"* or *"Royal Secret"* as the key to immortality. It would be an opening towards other alternative universes where the individual evolves as a god... Wilmshurst speaks of a real acceleration of evolution but without revealing any details on the practices which allow access to it. According to Schnoebelen, this royal art would employ operative sexual magic, *Trans-Yuggothian* magic, to allow access to certain dimensions. Some authors claim that the use of sexual magic can be a means of accessing the subconscious much faster than any meditation technique.

---

[104] *The Meaning of Masonry"* - Walter Leslie Wilmshurst, 1922, p.47.

[105] The Lost Keys To Freemasonry " - Manly P. Hall, 1976, p.48.

[106] *Masonic Initiation"* - Walter Leslie Wilmshurst, 1992, p.27.

Dissociative trance states also allow one to reach other dimensions of being, bringing about *a* kind of *enlightenment*. Satanic ritual abuse, which is linked to both trauma and sexuality, thus combines dissociation (deep altered states of consciousness) and sexual magic. Two powerful catalysts for accessing other dimensions and gaining 'power'. Therapist Patricia Baird Clarke speaks of 'living sacrifices' that literally serve as 'batteries': *'A helpless baby or child will be chosen to be the living sacrifice to Satan. The child is then subjected to many painful and terrifying rituals in which demons are called upon to possess the child, making him or her a 'reservoir' or battery for storing satanic powers that can be used at will by the cult members (...) The most common way in which these powers are accessed is through sexual perversion on the child. "*[107] We will return to sexual magic later in this chapter...

In *"The Masonic Initiation"*, Wilmshurst describes well how altered states of consciousness, deep dissociative states, are an essential point in Masonic initiation: *"Certain dissociative states occur naturally in even the most balanced and healthy persons (...) a complete 'ecstasy', a state in which the consciousness then separates from the ego and the physical body. Apparitions and even actions at a distance are well recognized facts. Such phenomena are explicable by the existence of a vehicle more subtle than the gross physical body and consciousness can transfer temporarily from one to the other. These two bodies are capable of functioning together in complete independence (...) A Master is one who has overcome those incapacities to which the average underdeveloped man is subject. He has full knowledge and control of all his parts, whether his physical body is awake or asleep, he maintains a continuous state of consciousness. He is able to cut himself off and disconnect from temporal affairs and replace them with others of a supra-physical nature. He can function at a distance from his physical body, he can move beyond the mundane to higher planes of the cosmic scale... Initiation always occurs when the physical body is in a state of trance or sleep and when the consciousness, temporarily released, is transferred to a higher level. "*[108]

In this extract, Wilmshurst clearly describes a dissociative state with decorporation, an 'astral exit'. He also describes in his book the 'silver cord' connecting the physical body to the astral body during these exits (more on this in Chapter 6). To trigger these deep altered states of consciousness and astral exits, trauma is one of the most radical and sadly effective techniques. How far can an initiate go to receive the *light...* or to give it to someone else? To initiate a child for example? Is learning to suffer and learning to make others suffer one of the darker initiations? Can the dissociation caused by suffering be a tool for accessing *"enlightenment"*, so sought after in certain circles?

A 1929 Masonic magazine entitled *"Freemasonry Universal (Vol.5)"* describes part of the initiation rite for the rank of Apprentice in which electroshock is mentioned. This sounds rather benign, but it should be noted that

---

[107] "Sanctification in Reverse: the essence of satanic ritual abuse" - Patricia Baird Clarke, Five Stone Publishing, 2013.

[108] *"Masonic Initiation"* - Walter Leslie Wilmshurst, 1992, p.84-86.

electroshock is one of the most effective methods of creating mental dissociation and a state of timelessness. Survivors of ritual abuse and mind control often report the use of electric prods to torture slaves into dissociative states. Here is the description of the Masonic ritual: *"Certain forces are sent through the body of the candidate during the ceremony, particularly at the time when he has been named and received as an Apprentice Mason. Certain parts of the lodge were heavily charged with magnetic force so that the candidate could absorb as much of this force as possible. The first thing in this curious method of initiation is to expose to this influence the various parts of one's body which are used during the ceremony. In ancient Egypt, a weak electric current was sent through the candidate by means of a rod or sword with which he was touched in certain places. It is partly for this reason that during this first initiation the candidate is deprived of all metals, as these can easily interfere with the flow of the electric current."*

The *Most Worshipful Master* (*V.W.*M.) must be an outstanding occultist, for it is he who 'charges' the candidate at initiation. As it is written in *Freemasonry Universal*: *"The V.M.T. gives the light, the pure white light of truth and illumination.* Illumination", aka Kundalini, the Serpent Power, aka electromagnetic force, aka sexual energy, etc.[109]

Lynn Brunet's book *'Terror, Trauma and The Eye In The Triangle'*, mentioned above, is an investigation into the influence of Masonic initiation practices in contemporary art production. Brunet argues that the rites and concepts of the Masonic tradition symbolically contain the process and impact of trauma on the functioning of the human psyche. Here is an extract: *"This human capacity to escape terror and intense emotional or physical pain through denial and dissociation may have been exploited by Freemasonry in order to achieve mystical experiences. By interfering with the brain process through physical or psychic trauma (shock, terror, hypnosis), the mind can experience a disruption of the sense of time and a sense of timelessness. As William James points out in Exploring the World of the Celts, such experiences can produce a sense of absolute courage, invincibility and immortality. The sense of invincibility that this produces is clearly used in warrior cultures. Prudence Jones and Nigel Pennick in their book "A History of Pagan Europe" state that Freemasonry is connected with the ancient practices of Druidism, warrior culture, sacrifices and magic."*[110]

Here is an illustration of these notions of timelessness, invincibility and immortality caused by dissociative states. In the Scandinavian tradition, the *Berserk* is a warrior who fights in a trance state caused by his animal spirit (a bear, a wolf or a boar). This animal spirit makes him super-powerful, he enters a state of invincibility and becomes capable of unbelievable feats. In English the term *'to go berserk'* means in colloquial language 'to go berserk' or 'to lose control of oneself'. These warriors of Odin were gathered in brotherhoods where

---

[109] *Occult Theocrasy"* - Edith Queenborough, 1933.

[110] "Terror, Trauma and The Eye In The Triangle: the masonic presence in contemporary art and culture" - Lynn Brunet, 2007, p.75.

each aspirant had to pass an initiation such as ritually killing the bear and then drinking its blood so that the power of the beast could be infused into him. The warrior then became a *Berserker* and, in addition to his fury, obtained a gift of metamorphosis allowing him to modify the perception that others have of him by appearing in an animal form. During their fits of rage, the *Bersekers* would let their human mind fade away and let the animal mind take control. All young warriors had to go through an important ritual with the sorcerer of their brotherhood: the Ritual of Awakening. This ritual was the source of their *sacred anger...* either they survived or they died. The *Ynglinga Saga* describes these warriors as follows: *"His (Odin's) men went forth unarmoured, enraged as dogs or wolves, biting their shields, strong as bears or bulls, and killing people in one blow, but they were not stung by iron or fire. They were called berserkers."* (Wikipedia)

Here we have a good example of what a deep state of altered consciousness is, a dissociative trance state in which the warrior achieves that *absolute courage* which causes a sense of physical invincibility and immortality. To let the human mind fade away and let the animal mind take control may mean that this is a splitting of the warrior's personality, a deep dissociative disorder that leads to the creation of an animal alter, in this case a bear or wolf. This is what is known today as Dissociative Identity Disorder, where one of the alter personalities truly believes that it is an animal (see Chapter 5). The brotherhood aspect involving initiation rituals with a witch-priest reinforces the possibility of some trauma-based programming if the *Ritual of Awakening is to be* believed, from which the candidate might not emerge alive! ... if he came out alive, it was with a *sacred anger*, i.e. a personality split by the traumas. The warrior was left with an alter personality "enraged" by the traumas experienced during the ritual. The dissociative process is a key to initiation that can be found in various types of cultures. It is likely that dissociation and personality splitting is still a key point in the initiation protocols of modern secret societies.

In his work entitled *"Metamorphoses"*, the writer Apuleius seems to describe his own initiation into the Mysteries of Isis and Osiris, to which he is said to have been initiated during his stay in Greece: *"The high priest then dismisses the profane, has me clothed in a robe of unbleached linen, and, taking me by the hand, leads me into the deepest part of the sanctuary. No doubt, my friend the reader, your curiosity will be aroused as to what was said and what was done afterwards. I would say it, if I were allowed to say it; you would learn it if you were allowed to learn it. But it would be a crime in the same degree for the confident ears and for the revealing mouth. If, however, it is a religious feeling which animates you, I would have the scruple of tormenting you. Listen and believe, for what I say is true. I have touched the gates of death; my foot has rested on the threshold of Proserpine. On my return I crossed the elements. In the depth of the night I saw the sun shine. Gods of hell, gods of the Empyrean, all were seen by me face to face, and adored at close quarters. This is what I have to tell you, and you will be no more enlightened."* [111]

---

[111] *"La Symbolique Maçonnique"* - Jules Boucher, 1985, p.253-254.

We thus find here three essential components of secret societies of the Masonic type: death and resurrection, the trial by the elements and finally illumination. It is possible that this is a traumatic ritual that involves the candidate for initiation in an experience on the borders of death (*I touched the gates of death*) with a deep state of dissociation *that illuminates* his consciousness (*I saw the sun shine*), just as the Amerindians enter a dissociative trance during the "Sun Dance". A "dance" that is neither more nor less than a traumatic ritual aimed at making the initiate enter altered states of consciousness (we will come back to this Amerindian "Sun Dance" below).

Ancient Egypt seems to be the meeting point between the dark side of modern secret societies and Satanism, the roots of the phallic cult. The work of David L. Carrico's work entitled *"The Egyptian-Masonic-Satanic Connection"* gives us some insights into this question.

The American Satanist Michael Aquino, who has been repeatedly accused of ritual abuse and mind control of children (without any conviction), founded the *Temple of Set*, a famous occult Satanic order in the United States, in 1975. *Set* is the Egyptian name for Satan, Albert Churchward writes: *"This Sut or Set was originally a god of the Egyptians, but he was also the god of the South Pole, or of the Southern Hemisphere, this is amply proved and confirmed by the monuments as well as by the Ritual. Set or Sut, according to Plutarch, is the Egyptian name for Typhon, the Satan of the Christian cult."*[112]

In his book *"Antichrist Osiris"*, Chris Relitz writes that according to Plutarch, the Greek historian of ancient Rome, it was the widow of Osiris who founded the Mystery religion. While the Mystery religions spread throughout the world from ancient Babylon, they manifested themselves in various places by changing only the names of the gods and making some variations in the rituals. It is in Egypt that the Mysteries seem to have developed to the highest level. The 33rd degree Freemason Manly Palmer Hall wrote in his book *"Freemasonry of the Ancient Egyptians"*: *"It is now generally recognised that of all the ancient peoples, the Egyptians were the best trained in the occult sciences of Nature. The wisest philosophers of other nations visit Egypt in order to be initiated into the sacred Mysteries by the priests of Thebes, Memphis and Hermopolis."*[113]

It is undeniable that the Egyptian Mystery cult has a deep connection with modern Freemasonry. In his book *Freemasonry its Hidden Meaning*, George H. Steinmetz writes: *"Regardless of the origin of the modern lodge, or of the name 'Freemason', we can, after removing the symbolism of modern adaptations, discern in Freemasonry the outline of the teachings of the ancient Mysteries of Egypt."*[114]

Manly P. Hall wrote in "The Lost Keys of Freemasonry": "Early Masonic historians such as Albert Mackey, Robert Freke Gould and Albert Pike had a

---

[112] The Arcana of Freemasonry: A History of Masonic Symbolism " - Albert Churchward, 2008, p.55.

[113] Freemasonry of the Ancient Egyptians" - Manly P. Hall, 1965, p.7.

[114] *"Freemasonry its Hidden Meaning"* - Georges H. Steinmetz, 1976, p.46.

common goal which was to establish a definitive correspondence between the Hiram legend of Freemasonry and the Osiris myth expounded in the initiatory rituals of the Egyptians."[115]

In his book entitled *"Les Origines Égyptiennes des Usages et Symboles Maçonniques"*, the Masonic historian Jean Mallinger states without a doubt that the candidate for the rank of Master symbolically represents Horus: *"Our Brother Goblet d'Alviella has shown us in his study on the Origins of the Master Grade that the Initiate was in reality symbolised by the young Horus, son of the Widow, his divine mother Isis, whose husband Osiris had been murdered by Set (or Typhon)."[116]*

This is confirmed in the very official 'Interpretative Catechism of the Master's Degree': To the question 'Who is the widow whose sons the Masons say they are?' the postulant to the degree must answer: 'It is Isis, personification of Nature, the Universal Mother, Widow of Osiris, the invisible god who enlightens the intelligences."

This is therefore a cult of the 'Mother Goddess', in opposition to God the Father (who as we have seen above is considered by this Luciferian doctrine to be the 'evil god'). The Mother Goddess is linked to fertility, a belief that is systematically found in the Mystery religions, which practised ritual group sex accompanied by blood sacrifices as part of a fertility cult. According to Sir James George Frazer, Egyptian rites included human sacrifice. In his book *'The Golden Bough'*, Frazer writes: *'As far as the ancient Egyptians are concerned, we may say from Manetho (Egyptian historian and priest) that they used to sacrifice and burn red-headed men and then scatter their ashes (...) these barbarous sacrifices were offered by the kings at the tomb of Osiris. We can assume that the victims represented Osiris himself, who was killed, dismembered and cremated each year through these victims to accelerate the growth of seeds in the earth (...) The red colour of the poor victims is significant. In Egypt, the oxen that were sacrificed also had to be red-haired, a single black or white hair on the beast disqualified it for sacrifice."[117]*

Do the ancient Egyptian Mystery Cults of which modern Freemasonry seems to be so proud contain traumatic rituals with orgies and blood sacrifices in honour of the 'Goddess'? Are all these doctrines related to the fertility cult still relevant in our 'modern' societies? Do all these gods and goddesses still receive offerings today by certain sects? Isn't the time of the Pharaohs ancient history? The numerous obelisks (the phallic cult) that have sprung up in the large squares of our modern capitals perhaps indicate that it is not... Just like certain revolutionaries and thinkers of the 'Enlightenment' for whom Isis was the goddess of Paris (Parisis). Pharaohs and modern Templars do not seem to have totally disappeared...

---

[115] *"The Lost Keys of Freemasonry"* - Manly P. Hall, Macoy Publishing & Masonic Supply Co, p.101.

[116] Les Origines Égyptiennes des Usages et Symboles Maçonniques" - Jean Mallinger, 1978, p.47.

[117] *The Golden Bough"* - George Frazer, 1922, p.439.

Let us now turn to the *Egyptian Book of the Dead*. It is a series of writings (papyri) that were discovered in Egyptian tombs. The ancient Egyptians attributed the *Book of the Dead* to the god Thoth, who is said to be the mythical author of the magical formulas in this sacred book. The *Egyptian Book of the Dead*, which dates from 1500 BC, clearly describes the practice of magical and traumatic rituals. In his book *'The Soul in Egyptian Metaphysics and The Book of the Dead'*, Manly P. Hall compares this ancient Egyptian holy book with transcendental magic: *"The Book of the Dead has been given a modern title which unfortunately does not really correspond to its Egyptian literary meaning. The reason for this title is obvious, but the impression it gives is strangely inadequate. The text is indeed dominated by a spirit of transcendental magic."*[118]

In The Lost Keys of Freemasonry, Manly P. Hall also writes that "if the identification of the myth of Osiris with that of Hiram is accepted, then the 'Book of the Dead' is the key to Masonic symbolism, revealing a hidden beauty beneath the rituals, an unsuspected splendour in the symbols, and a divine purpose activating the whole Masonic process."[119]

As you will see, *the Egyptian Book of the Dead* contains bloody doctrines and (symbolic?) practices that can be compared with some evidence of modern Satanic ritual abuse. The sacred book describes in some passages the interaction between the soul of the dead and the gods (demons). A symbolism full of *'splendour'* according to the Luciferian occultist Manly P. Hall... The gods, who are none other than fallen angels, are described as *'blood devourers'*, *'gut eaters'* and *'bone crushers'*. The book refers a few times to a *'torture chamber'*, a term that will certainly speak volumes to survivors of trauma-based mind control. Here are some excerpts from a translation: *"So here is this great god of slaughter, mighty with terror, he washes in your blood, he bathes in your blood. "I have obtained power over the animals by the knife in their heads"* / *"He has taken the hearts of the gods, he has eaten the red, he has swallowed the green, their charms (magic) are in his belly, he has swallowed the knowledge of every god. "* / *"Unas (the king) devours men and lives above the gods, the one who cuts the scalps"* / *"Unas weighed his words with the hidden god who has no name, on the day of the newborn's tearing apart"* / *"who devours the bodies of the dead and swallows their hearts, but he keeps himself invisible."*[120]

The priests of the Egyptian Mystery Cults practised theurgy, a so-called higher magic aimed at communicating directly with the gods. Porphyry (Neoplatonist philosopher) reports that the Greco-Roman philosopher Plotinus once agreed to attend a theurgy session: *"An Egyptian priest who came to Rome and was introduced to Plotinus by some friend, had a desire to demonstrate his powers to him and offered to evoke a sensible manifestation of Plotinus' guiding*

---

[118] "The Soul in Egyptian Metaphysics and The Book of the Dead" - Manly P. Hall, 1965, p.15.

[119] *"The Lost Keys of Freemasonry"* - Manly P. Hall, Macoy Publishing & Masonic Supply Co, p.106.

[120] "The Egyptian Book of The Dead (The Papyrus of Ani) Egyptian Text Transliteration and Translation" - E.A. Wallis Budge, 1967.

spirit. Plotinus readily accepted, and the evocation was made in the Temple of Isis, the only pure place, it is said, that he could find in Rome. At the call, a deity appeared who was not of the class of daimons, and the Egyptian exclaimed: 'You are singularly favoured, for the directing daimon in you is not of the lower degree, but a god."[121]

The word "daimon" is a Greek word meaning "demon" or "supernatural being" which can sometimes be interpreted as a "personal genie", a "guardian spirit", a "familiar" demon or an intermediary between gods and mortals. In this MK book, the word "demon" or "demonic" will be used regularly to describe Luciferian entities, i.e. fallen angels working to bring man *down* by any means with the stated intention of *elevating* him to the status of a god. This is the inversion that is currently taking place in our world and it is the main concern of our elites: the spiritual fall provoking material adoration to lead to the worship of man, finally worshipping the prince of this world, Lucifer, the "civilising" god bringing light, knowledge and emancipation from a so-called "evil" god: this is the Transhistorical Gnosis described by Prof. Jean Claude Lozac'hmeur.

The use of magic and traumatic rituals to contact demons, i.e. Luciferian rebellion, in order to obtain guidance to make man a god, is one of the main prerogatives of the Masonic-type Luciferian sects. The Freemason Oswald Wirth calls these entities from another dimension the *constructive intelligences of the world* or the *Masters* transmitting their directives to the high initiates (the *Unknown Superiors*) connected to the *high spheres of the beyond...* [122] A whole programme, chapter 6 will deal with this crucial question of the connection to other dimensions.

According to Charles Webster Leadbeater, there is a *"Black Masonry"* which is dedicated to the study of evil between the 19th and 30th degrees of the Scottish Rite, the 30th degree being known as the *Knight Kadosh*. In his book *The Ancient Mystic Rites*, Leadbeater defines this Black Masonry as follows: *"Few of the Egyptian brethren seem to have gone beyond the degree of the Rosicrucian, they are those who need to know more than the splendid revelation of the love of God which they received in what we call the 18th degree. But for those who feel that there is still much to learn about the nature of God, and who long to understand the meaning of evil and suffering and its relationship to the divine plan, the prototype of a Black Masonry exists, the teaching being between the 19th and 30th degrees. This section of the Mysteries was particularly interested in working on Karma in its various aspects (...) Thus, the first stage of the higher instruction, that of the Rose Cross or Red Masonry, is devoted to the knowledge of good, while the second stage, that of the Kadosh or Black Masonry, is devoted to the knowledge of evil.* " [123]

---

[121] "The Greeks and the Irrational" - E.R. Dodds, 1977, p.286.

[122] "Freemasonry made intelligible to its followers" Volume III - Oswald Wirth, 1986, p.219-130

[123] *"The Ancient Mystic Rites"* - C.L. Leadbeater, The Theosophical Publishing House, Wheaton, III, pp. 41-42.

Admittedly, all of this remains hermetic for a layman, but it still leaves one wondering...

In his book *"La Conjuration Antichrétienne"*, Mgr Henri Delassus states that certain sections of the Kadosh Knights worship Eblis (Iblis), which in the East is the name of the devil, the Sheitan. In his *Encyclopedia of Freemasonry*, Albert Mackey explains that the Kadosh doctrine represents the persecution suffered by the Knights Templar. He writes that *"the modern Kadosh Knights are the ancient Knights Templar and that the Builder of the Temple of Solomon is now replaced by Jacques de Molay, the martyred Templar Grand Master."*[124]

It should be noted that the Order of the Templars, to which this Black Masonry refers with the Kadosh doctrine, practised satanic rituals. Eliphas Levi wrote in his book *"History of Magic"*: *"The Templars had two doctrines, one hidden and reserved for the masters, it was that of Johannism; the other public, it was the Roman Catholic doctrine. The Johannine doctrine of the followers was the Kabbalah of the Gnostics, soon degenerated into a mystical pantheism pushed to the point of idolatry of nature and hatred of all revealed dogma. In order to succeed and gain supporters, they cherished the regrets of the fallen cults and the hopes of the new cults, promising freedom of conscience and a new orthodoxy to all, which would be the synthesis of all persecuted beliefs. Thus they came to recognise the pantheistic symbolism of the great masters of black magic, and, in order to detach themselves from obedience to the religion which had condemned them in advance, they paid divine homage to the monstrous idol of Baphomet, as the dissident tribes had formerly worshipped the golden calves of Dan and Bethel. Recently discovered monuments, and valuable documents dating back to the thirteenth century, prove more than sufficiently all that we have just stated. Other proofs are hidden in the annals and under the symbols of occult masonry."*[125]

In his book 'The Occult Conspiracy', Michael Howard listed the charges brought against the Knights Templar when they were arrested in 1307: "The Knights Templar were accused of denying the tenets of the Christian faith, spitting and urinating on the crucifix during secret initiation rituals, worshipping a skull or head of Baphomet, anointing with the blood or fat of unbaptized babies, worshipping the devil in the form of a black cat, and committing acts of sodomy and zoophilia (...) Candidates entering the Order were also required to kiss their initiator on the mouth, navel, penis and at the base of the spine. These kisses were considered by the Order's critics to be evidence of their perverse sexual activities, but in the occult tradition, the navel, sexual organs and perineum are the physical locations of the psychic centres of the human body, known in the East as the Chakras."[126]

Accusations also reported by Helen Nicholson in her book "The Knights Templar: A New History". The British historian Nesta H. Webster writes that

---

[124] Mackey's Revised Encyclopedia of Freemasonry - Albert G. Mackey, 1946, p.514.

[125] *History of Magic"* - Éliphas Lévy, 1930, book IV, chapter VI.

[126] *The Occult Conspiracy"* - Michael Howard, 1989, p.36-37.

"Are the confessions of the Knights (Templars) the result of pure imagination which men under the duress of torture could have invented? It is difficult to believe that the accounts of the initiation ceremony could be pure invention, it was given in detail by men in different countries, all the accounts were similar, only the phraseology was different. If they had been led to invent a story, the testimonies would have contradicted each other (...) But no, each one seems to have described the same ceremony more or less completely."[127]

Author Donald Michael Kraig states that the Knights Templar developed their sexual rituals from the Sufi teachings of the Arab world, which in turn came from the Indian Tantric tradition, teachings that were later found among medieval alchemists and eventually among modern occultist magicians. We will come back to sexual magic later on.

Black Masonry thus nurses a vengeance against the persecutors of the Knights Templar: the Catholic Church. In *"The Ancient Mystic Rites"*, Leadbeater writes that *"The Tradition of revenge against the execrable King, the Pope and the Traitor has been handed down through the ages, and is intimately connected with the Egyptian tradition corresponding to our Black Masonry which culminates in what we call today the 30th degree."*[128]

Black Masonry with the Kadosh Knights, the modern Knights Templar, thus worked ardently for the destruction of the Kingdom of France and its Church. The occult struggle of Freemasonry against the King and the Catholic Church is explained in detail in the excellent book by Bishop Henri Delassus entitled *"The Anti-Christian Conjuration"*. The Freemason made Knight Kadosh is therefore firmly anti-Catholic and "revenge" is a central point in this Masonic initiation grade. *When the Kadosh knight has taken his oath, the dagger is placed in his hand, and a crucifix is laid at his feet, then the 'Greatest' says to him: 'Smash this image of superstition, break it. If he does not do so, so as not to make anyone guess, they applaud and the 'Greatest' addresses him on his piety. He is received without revealing the great secrets. But if he crushes the crucifix, then he is made to approach the altar, where there are three representations, three corpses if they can be obtained. Bladders full of blood are at the place where he is shouted at to strike. He carries out the order and the blood gushes back upon him, and taking the severed heads by the hair, he cries out: 'Nekam! vengeance is done!' Then the 'Most Great' speaks to him thus: By your constancy and fidelity you have earned the right to learn the secrets of true masons. These three men whom you have just struck are superstition, the king and the pope. These three idols of the people are only tyrants in the eyes of the wise. It is in the name of superstition that the king and the pope commit every imaginable crime."*[129]

---

[127] *"Secret Societies and Subversive Movements"* - Nesta H.Webster, Christian Book Club of America, p.57.

[128] *The Ancient Mystic Rites"* - C.W. Leadbeater, The Theosophical Publishing House, Wheaton, III, p.167.

[129] *Conservateur belge, t.* XIX. p. 358, 259 - Eckert, la *Franc-maçonnerie*, 1.1, p. 333.

Eliphas Levi wrote that Masonry has not only been profaned, but has even served as a veil and pretext for the plots of anarchy, through the occult influence of the avengers of Jacques de Molay, and of the continuators of the schismatic work of the temple (...) The anarchists have taken up the ruler, the square and the mallet, and have written on them liberty, equality, fraternity. That is to say, liberty for covetousness, equality in baseness, and fraternity for destruction."[130]

One important thing to make clear is that the international high Masonic lodges, whether they are *"black"* or so-called *"pure"* or *"authentic"*, all agree and speak the same language when it comes to the destruction of the Catholic Church. It is therefore an occult anti-Christian force.

It is interesting to note that Eliphas Levi in his book *"The History of Magic"* attributed the establishment of Egyptian Masonry on the Old Continent to Count Cagliostro. He is indeed the founder of the *Misraïm* or *Egyptian* Rite, which is primarily concerned with esoteric research. Cagliostro also played an essential role in the propagation of cabalistic Masonry. Eliphas Levi accused Cagliostro of dishonouring the Order and states in his book that Cagliostro used black magic for the cult of Isis by hypnotising young girls to make them into priestesses: *"Cagliostro was the agent of the Templars, and so he wrote in a circular to all the Freemasons in London that the time had come to set to work to rebuild the Temple of the Lord. Like the Templars, Cagliostro was devoted to the practices of black magic, and practised the disastrous science of evocations; he divined the past and present, predicted the future, made marvellous cures and also claimed to make gold. He had introduced into Masonry a new rite which he called the Egyptian rite, and he tried to resurrect the mysterious cult of Isis. He himself, with his head wrapped in bandages and coiffed like a Theban sphinx, presided over nightly solemnities in flats full of hieroglyphs and torches. He had as priestesses young girls whom he called doves, and whom he exalted to the point of ecstasy in order to make them render oracles by means of hydromancy (...) This adept is not, however, without importance in the history of magic; his seal is as important as that of Solomon, and attests to his initiation into the highest secrets of the science. This seal, explained by the Kabbalistic letters of the names of Acharat and Althotas, expresses the principal characters of the great arcane and the great work (...).The name of Althotas, Cagliostro's master, is composed of the name of Thoth and the syllables al and as, which, read kabbalistically, are Sala meaning messenger, sent; the whole name therefore means Thoth, the messiah of the Egyptians, and such was indeed the one whom Cagliostro recognised above all as his master."[131]*

According to Fritz Springmeier, an American writer and lecturer on Monarch mind control, one of the secrets of these Mystery religions, particularly the Egyptian Mystery cult of Isis, was the ability to use drugs, torture and hypnosis to create multiple personalities in a human being. According to him, mind-controlled sex slaves are used today in Masonic high degrees and other black back lodges. A disassociated alter personality can serve as a priestess in

---

[130] *History of Magic"* - Eliphas Levi, 1913, Book V, Chap.VII.

[131] Ibid, Book VI, Chapter II.

certain rituals. These MK slaves undergo trances, demonic possessions and all sorts of perverse rituals based on sexual magic. This initiatory knowledge did not dissolve with the fall of ancient Egypt: the occult world has never stopped splitting and programming slaves through a process of psychic dissociation based on trauma. This knowledge has been transmitted to the modern world through secret initiatory societies that preciously guard Pandora's box...

In her book *Terror, Trauma and The Eye In The Triangle*, Lynn Brunet writes that the myth of Osiris and Isis, which plays a very important role in the Scottish Masonic rite, may well be a metaphorical illustration of the process of trauma and personality splitting. Brunet draws parallels between myths, rituals, Masonic symbolism and the psychology of trauma, i.e. the functions of the brain that can be linked to initiation practices aimed at creating a mystical experience. The human body can be taken as an external symbolic representation of the cosmos with an internal mystical reality and physiology that provides a structure for its understanding. Lynn Brunet exposes something complex that may not be very comprehensible at this stage of the book, which is why the extract has been put in appendix 1 under the title: *Trauma and Dissociation in Masonic Mythology.*

4 - SEXUAL MAGIC AND SECRET SOCIETIES

The occultist Pierre Manoury, author of a *practical treatise on sexual magic*, defines this "discipline" as follows:

Magical sexuality can therefore be categorised according to three main criteria.

1) Abstinence, privation, macerations and chastity. This is done in a mystical context, a symbolic process or in communion with spiritual hierarchies of a high nature.

2) By an exacerbation of the desire potentiating energies applied to rites and ceremonies of so-called practical magic, the eroticization being in this case only cerebral. This is the most widespread principle in most ceremonial magics and the basic rituals of high sorcery.

3) Finally, in the magics and sorceries grouped under the generic term of sexual magics, where exacerbation and potentiation of desire and energies are followed by a release in the ritual context itself, according to very special modalities... The applications in these specific cases are of a formidable effectiveness on the material, physical and psychic levels (...)

Sexual magic can therefore be considered as a basis for ritual practices applicable at a very high level, by trained (and responsible) people, and constituting one of the great instruments of power, if not the most powerful (...) Sexual magic is therefore a practice essentially based on the use of vital energy, which will have to be domesticated, filtered, captured, accumulated, developed, potentiated and then channelled within the framework of the ritual.[132]

---

[132] "Traité pratique de Magie Sexuelle" - Pierre Manoury, 1989, chap.1.

Red magic (blood magic) and sex magic are the two most powerful magics because they use the human life force to empower the practitioner. This is why they are usually combined. Sex magic is inspired by Eastern Tantrism and aims to master the *"Kundalini"* and the immense sexual energy potential. In Tantrism, Kundalini is identified with *"Shakti"*, the serpent goddess present in the human body at the base of the sacrum, who is supposed to rise along the spine, during a *Kundalini rising*, to reach the brain by irrigating all the energy centres (*Chakras*) with her power. In *The Voudon Gnostic Workbook*, Michael Bertiaux writes about Tantrism: *"The secret of the Brahmins lies in the foundations of Physical Tantric magic. This secret is the root essence of organic Hinduism and is found in the deepest levels of the Hindu brain, manifesting itself in strange genetic mutations, due to the direct intervention of the Mother Goddess herself. This secret manifests its Power (Shakti) through a particular state of consciousness, a level of ultra-consciousness."* [133]

Since their first encounters with Indian religions in the eighteenth and nineteenth centuries, Westerners have been both fascinated and repelled by the Tantra tradition; a very particular form of religious practice due to the deliberate use of impure substances and transgressive rituals. The Tantras are esoteric works related to the worship of the goddess, dealing with yoga, cosmology, alchemy, magic and sacrifice. Tantrism condenses all these thousand-year-old disciplines for the purpose of erotic-magical and spiritual realisation. For a long time, it has been both repulsive and enticing to Western writers. Today, especially through the growing influence of the *'New Age'*, Tantrism is seen as a simple method of liberation of the body and mind, a form of 'spiritual sexuality' in which sexual pleasure becomes a religious experience. It is seen as a way of transgressing the so-called 'repressive' Western morality on sexuality. Tantrism has now become a very lucrative fad for some gurus, yet few Western followers of *New Age* philosophy know what some of the rituals of authentic Tantra entail.

Krsnananda Aagamavagisa is one of the greatest authors of Tantrism, who lived in 6th century Bengal. In his works, he describes esoteric ritual practices involving the use of organic substances such as blood, semen and menstrual fluids. Krsnananda also describes tantric rituals including animal sacrifice, which is still practiced in Bengal today. Blood sacrifices are related to the Vedas and Brahamic ritual practices, however, in Tantrism the sacrifices deliberately transgress and violate the guidelines given in the Vedic tradition. For example, the Vedas recommend sacrificing the animal with as little violence and suffering as possible, whereas in Tantric sacrifice the animal is decapitated in a very bloody manner, with the ritual focusing on the blood and decapitated head, which are the offerings to the goddess. It would seem that Tantric sacrifices involve a calculated inversion of the ancient Vedic texts: the impure animal replaces the pure animal, a bloody decapitation replaces a non-violent

---

[133] The Voudon Gnostic Workbook: Expanded Edition " - Michael Bertiaux, 2007, p.308.

strangulation, the Goddess takes the place of the male God (here again we find this notion of Goddess versus God).[134]

The sacred text of the *Kalachakra* Tantra, the "Wheel of Time", contains a treatise on alchemy and demonology. It says in Strophe 125: *'The consumption of faeces and urine, sperm and menstrual blood, mixed with human flesh, prolongs life. These are the five ingredients in the composition of the nectar pills (...) The consumption of the five flesh, with honey and ghee, puts an end to all ailments.* Note that in the same text, it is stated in stanza 154 that veneration of subtle entities "brings supreme happiness": *"Snakes, demons, planets that influence men, evil Nâga who delight in human blood, the goblin Kushma, the tutelary deities of places, vampires, spirits that cause epilepsy and Garuda can bring supreme happiness, if they are venerated in a mandala."*

The ancient Tantric practices were taken up by twentieth-century Western occultists such as Aleister Crowley, a leading figure in the importation of Tantra into the West with all the transgression and 'power through impurity' (or redemption through sin) that it implies. Crowley was introduced to Tantrism during his trip to India and Sri Lanka in 1902, but he combined this Tantric practice with various other techniques of sexual magic.

Tantrism with its phenomenal energy can be diverted and combined with powerful black magic, which was already practiced in Vedic times at the risk and peril of the initiated. Sexual magic is not something innocuous that is simply an elaborate *"Kamasutra"*. The arcana of these occult practices can lead the most ambitious initiates to commit abominations, so much so that the search for power and psychic powers can transform them into real perverted monsters... Lilian Silburn wrote in his book "Kundalini: *The Energy of the* Depths*"*: *"The mysterious energy unleashed by Kundalini Yoga manifests itself with violence and cannot be manipulated without running certain risks. Some deviations are called 'demonic' because they lead to depression and madness... The awakening of the Kundalini can have disastrous consequences."*[135]

In 1922, Krishnamurti had a Kundalini surge which he called a "spiritual awakening" and which changed his life. Here is an excerpt from Darrel Irving's book *Serpent of Fire, a Modern View of Kundalini*, which shows us that this Kundalini opens doors to other dimensions and allows contact with demonic entities: *"Krishnamurti began to have shivers and tremors and complained of an intense headache. He was in great pain, he seemed to be half unconscious and experiencing out-of-body experiences... At this point the entity Krishnamurti called 'the elemental' took over and did what it wanted... "I throw myself down, moan, complain and whisper strange things, just like a possessed person. I get up thinking someone is calling me but I immediately collapse on the floor. I see strange faces and lights... all the time. I have a violent pain in my head and neck... I will become a clairvoyant once this is over or maybe I am going crazy!!!*
"... The Krishnamurti personality went into the background and it was the entity

---

[134] "The Power of the Impure: Transgression, Violence and Secrecy in Bengali Sakta Tantra and Modern Western Magic" - Hugh B. Urban, 2003.

[135] Kundalini: The Energy of the Depths" - Lilian Silburn, 1988, intro.

that took over the functions of the body... There was the perception of this invisible presence working on his body, opening it up and preparing it for the great spiritual mission... The process continued year after year... "Krishnamurti would even say that he was wounded inside because "they" had burned him inside."[136]

In his book *'Theories of the Chakras, Bridge to Higher Consciousness'*, the Japanese Hiroshi Motoyama reports similar things during a Kundalini rising: *'I hear like a buzzing of bees... and I see a kind of fireball about to explode... my body levitates... my whole body is on fire and I have a severe headache. I remained in a feverish state for two or three days. I felt as if my head was going to explode... During this experience I met a horrible demonic entity. It was a terrifying and indescribable experience."*[137]

The Kundalini is symbolically represented by a snake that climbs up and around the spine through the various *Chakras*. In his book *"The Secret Teachings of All Ages"*, the Freemason Manly P. Hall writes that the tree in the Garden of Eden would represent this fire. Hall writes that the tree in the Garden of Eden is said to represent this Kundalini fire and the knowledge of how to use this sacred fire is said to be the gift of the great serpent, the temptation of the forbidden fruit: *"There is sufficient similarity between the Masonic CHiram and the Kundalini of Hindu mysticism to justify the hypothesis that CHiram can also be considered as a symbol of the Fire of the Spirit moving through the sixth ventricle of the spine. The exact science of human regeneration is the Lost Key of Masonry, for when the Fire of the Spirit is lifted through the thirty-three degrees, or segments of the spine, and enters the dome-chamber of the human skull, it finally passes into the pituitary body (Isis) where it invokes Ra (the pineal gland) and demands the Sacred Name. Operative Masonry, in the full meaning of the term, signifies the process by which the Eye of Horus is opened (...) In the human brain there is a tiny gland called the pineal body (...) The pineal gland is the sacred pine cone in man. The one eye which cannot be opened without CHiram (the Fire of the Spirit) and augmented by the sacred points which are called the Seven Churches in Asia (the Chakras)."*[138]

In Greek mythology, the worshippers of Dionysus were often depicted carrying a staff with a pine cone on top. This represents the energy of the Kundalini as it moves up the spine (the staff) towards the pineal gland at the sixth *chakra*, symbolised here by the pine cone. Indeed, we find the conceptions and practices of Tantrism in Dionysism, Marcel Détienne writes in his book *"Dionysus put to death"*: *"The overcoming of the sacrifice that the Orphics and the Pythagoreans operate from above, Dionysism accomplishes it from below... The followers of Dionysus... become enslaved and behave like ferocious animals. Dionysism provides an escape from the human condition by escaping into*

---

[136] *Serpent of Fire, a Modern View of Kundalini* - Darrel Irving, 1995, p.27-32.

[137] *Theories of the Chakras, Bridge to Higher Consciousness* - Hiroshi Motoyama, 2003, p.240-250.

[138] *The Secret Teachings of All Ages, An Encyclopedic Outline of Masonic, Hermetic, Qabbalistic and Rosicrucian Philosophy* - Manly P. Hall, 1988, p.273.

bestiality from below, from the side of the animals, while Orphism offers the same escape from the side of the gods. In the Dionysian world, practices corresponding to those of Tantrism are called *"Orgiasm"*. Orgiasm consists of group ceremonies in which blood sacrifices, ecstatic dances and erotic rites take place. Dionysus presents himself as a god of nature and a god of orgiastic practices, just like Shiva in India or Osiris in Egypt. Orgiasm aims at the deconditioning of the being, which returns for a moment to its deepest and most repressed nature. This return to the bestial instincts is an important aspect of the Tantric method.

Sex magic and the experience of Kundalini are part of the teachings of some Western secret societies. It is an initiation reserved for members who already have a good knowledge of the occult. Like ritual sacrifice, satanic sex magic provides powers, 'spiritual power' and material favours. On the other hand, total abstinence and transmutation of sexual energy will bring an intense happiness that is much more stable than that brought by tantric sexual practice.

An article entitled *'Sex and the Occult'* in the journal of the *Dark Lily* Society refers to the use of sex as *a means of accessing the subconscious.* The author of this article states that *through a sexual ritual, participants are able to access their own subconscious much faster than with other techniques such as prolonged meditation.* With such a method *"the work of several weeks can be done in a few days or hours.* Could sex magic be the "Royal Art" (Masonic) of which Wilmshurst, a Freemason, speaks? A practice that would accelerate spiritual evolution to reach the status of a God?

Tantric teachings tell us that a carnal and sexual relationship is a sharing of energy and karma. This means that the individual can be contaminated by the partner's psychic disorders or "bad karma", or on the contrary, be deeply inspired if the partner is a very pure spiritual being. In Tantric practices, it is the sexual organ of a very young woman that is venerated. According to the *Mahamudra Tilaka Tantra: 'Young girls over twenty years of age have no occult power.* Is the purity and innocence of childhood sought in satanic sex magic practices? Probably yes, just as in a blood sacrifice, it is a matter of draining this reserve of energy and purity. All the more so when the child is in a deep state of dissociative trance that connects him to other dimensions. It is used as a tool of power. The child is purity incarnate, the innocence of God's creation, its defilement and sacrifice the ultimate offering to Satan. This is why we systematically find sexual perversions and blood sacrifices in Satanic ritual abuse. The blood of the child is of great purity and it is at puberty that the purest principle of the child passes into the seed. This is the basis of sexual magic and its aberrations.

In his treatise on sexual magic, Pierre Manoury describes the course of a ritual during which the woman will have multiple sexual encounters with several men at the same time, with the aim of carrying out an "energetic charge" in the woman. Here is what he wrote: *"These somewhat scabrous descriptions are in no way an incitement to debauchery, they are very discreet practices, stemming from thousand-year-old traditions. It should be noted that they are ritual practices of energy manipulation in several traditions. From certain very closed Western societies, to the sabbats of high sorcery, from Greek bacchanals to priapées, via Shiva orgiastic rituals, etc. (...) certain branches of magic are quite elitist, and sex magic is one of them.*"[139]

In his book *"Memory of Blood: Counter-Initiation"*, Alexandre de Dànann tells us that in the Assyro-Babylonian tradition, the priestesses had the duty, during the *"coitus sacer"* (sacred copulation) with the initiates of the Mysteries, to impose, by means of specific techniques of sexual magic, the orders coming from the power of the Chaldean priestly caste. This was to prepare the events desired by the one whom this caste called *"Justice or First Virtue"*, being none other than Lucifer.

One of the 'fathers' of Western sex magic is Paschal Beverly Randolph. According to him, *"true sexual power is the power of God"*, which can be used both as a mystical experience and for magical practices to obtain money, the return of a loved one, or for any other purpose. Randolph's teachings on sexual magic were widely circulated in many secret societies and other esoteric fraternities in Europe, particularly in the *Ordo Templi Orientis* (O.T.O.). Randolph, in addition to being a medium, had founded a religious order dedicated to the *spiritual regeneration of humanity*, called the Brotherhood of Eulis, officially founded in 1874. Randolph claimed that his new sect was rooted in the Eleusinian Mysteries, one of the many ancient Greek religions. Randolph was also connected with the Rosicrucian tradition, but he claimed that the Brotherhood of Eulis was much more connected to the Mysteries than is the Order of Rosicrucians, which he said is only a gateway to the sanctuary of Eulis. The deepest secrets of Eulis are largely centred around the rituals of sexual magic, linked to the fertility cult of the ancient Mystery religions.[140]

These various ancient sects seem to have mixed the notion of fertility of the mother earth with that of human fertility, thus bathing in ritual orgies and blood sacrifices linked to a certain calendar to honour and make offerings to gods and goddesses. The ritual abuses, blood sacrifices and sexual magic that still take place today, stem from these ancient Babylonian practices: it is the 'religion without a name', the worship of demons.

Sarane Alexandrian, the author of *"La Magie Sexuelle: Bréviaire des sortilèges amoureux"*, reports in her book that it is the initiatory organisations, i.e. the secret societies, that have taken on the task of teaching sexual magic to the initiated. Karl Kellner and Theodor Reuss, two high degree Freemasons, are the two founders of the *Ordo Templi Orientis*, which according to Alexandrian, is a real school of sexual magic. In 1912, the O.T.O. published in the *Oriflamme*: *'Our Order has rediscovered the great secret of the Knights Templar, which is the key that opens all Masonic and Hermetic mysticism, namely the teaching of sexual magic. This teaching explains, without exception, all the secrets of Nature, all the symbolism of Freemasonry and all the workings of religion.*"[141]

---

[139] *Traité pratique de Magie Sexuelle* - Pierre Manoury, 1989, chap.6.

[140] *Magia Sexualis: Sex Magic and Liberation in Modern Western Esotericism* - Hugh B. Urban, 2006, p.65.

[141] *Modern Ritual Magic: The Rise Of Western Occultism* - Francis King, 1989.

Freemason Karl Kellner claims to have been initiated by an Arab fakir and two Indian yogis through whom he received *"the mysteries of yoga and the philosophy of the left-hand path, which he calls 'sexual magic'"*[142]. Kellner was the head of a small group called the *"Inner Triangle"* which practised tantric-type rituals with the aim of creating an elixir composed of male and female fluids...

Satanist Aleister Crowley created a Gnostic Mass (a sexual ritual), a ceremony in which semen and menses symbolise the sacred host. A ritual that became a central practice for the *Ordo Templi Orientis*. Alexandrian states that the O.T.O. comprises 12 initiatory degrees and that it is only from the eighth degree that one can begin to approach sexual magic... starting with initiatory masturbation. The seventh degree focuses on the adoration of the phallus under the symbol of Baphomet. The ninth degree teaches sexual magic itself, i.e. how to perform the sexual act in order to obtain powers. This degree is considered the Royal and Priestly Art, making the adepts capable of the Great Erotic Work. This is how the initiate becomes superior to the profane. In his book *"Stealing from Heaven: the rise of modern western magic"*, Nevill Drury also states that the O.T.O. practices sexual rituals with the use of blood, excrement and semen (red, black and white, the colours of the alchemical Great Work). The book *"Secrets of the German Sex Magicians"* gives the three initiatory degrees of sex magic taught by Aleister Crowley and practised by members of the O.T.O.:

VIII°= Teaching of magical self-sexual practices (masturbation).

IX°= Teaching of heterosexual magical practices, interaction between sperm and menstrual blood or female secretions.

XI°= Teaching of homosexual magical practices, isolation of the anus (*per vas nefandum*), sodomy, interaction with excrement.

We find that the teachings on sexual magic that come last are those related to the rectum. In his book *"Shiva and Dionysus: The Religion of Nature and Eros"*, Alain Daniélou writes: *"There is a whole ritual linked to anal penetration through the narrow door that opens onto the labyrinth (in humans, the intestine). In Tantric Yoga, the centre of Ganesha, the gatekeeper, is in the region of the rectum. The male organ, if it penetrates directly into the area of the coiled energy (Kundalini), can allow it to be brutally awakened and bring about states of enlightenment and sudden perception of realities of a transcendent order. This is why this act can play an important role in initiation. This explains a male initiation rite, widespread among primitive peoples, though rarely reported by Western observers, in which adult male initiates have sex in the anus with novices (...) This act is, moreover, part of the accusations made against Dionysian organisations by their detractors, and against certain initiatory groups in the Christian and Islamic world."*

Australian psychologist Reina Michaelson, who received an award in 1996 for her work on the prevention of sexual abuse of minors, claims that in some O.T.O. rituals, children are literally massacred. The O.T.O. sued Michaelson for these accusations and won the case. The psychologist had stated,

---

[142] *The Magic of Aleister Crowley* - John Symonds, 1958.

according to her sources, that this secret society was a *paedophile ring*, some of whose members practise trauma-based mind control as well as ritual abuse involving sex magic. She also stated that *this satanic cult has a lot of power because it is run by very powerful and influential families,* also implying that high-level politicians and other TV personalities are part of a high-level paedophile network covered by the authorities. In 2008, a couple were sentenced to prison for refusing to withdraw their allegations that the O.T.O. was a genuine paedophile ring. Vivienne Legg and Dyson Devine had to apologise publicly in order to be released after seven weeks in prison.[143] These multiple denials and systematic legal attacks by the O.T.O. serve to destabilise investigators and create disorientation about the nature and practices of the cult. Beneath this surface swell, the occult hierarchy remains intact and in perfect working order.

Frater U∴D∴ the author of *"Secrets of the German Sex Magicians"* claims that altered states of consciousness are sought by occultists through sexual rituals to obtain what they call *"magical powers"*. He cites, for example, an experience he calls the *"Gnostic trance"*. This author encourages his readers to practice rituals that lead to the overcoming of sexual taboos and insists that *"through the use of bizarre and unusual practices, we gain access to altered states of consciousness that provide the key to magical powers.* These are the kinds of statements that could explain the testimonies of ritual abuse whose perversity is beyond comprehension, even to the point of human sacrifice.

The violent and sometimes murderous rituals and extreme sexual debauchery of these cults are linked to notions of transgression, excess of all kinds and violation of social morality. They are seen as the ultimate means of surpassing the human condition and the social order in order to reach a kind of human transcendence, especially when accompanied by altered states of consciousness due to drugs and dissociative states: *"Dionysian ecstasy means above all the surpassing of the human condition, the discovery of a total deliverance, the attainment of a freedom and spontaneity usually inaccessible to human beings... In addition to these freedoms, there is also deliverance from prohibition, from the rules and conventions of ethics and the social order."[144]*

"Do what you will is the whole of the Law", "There is no other Law but Do what you will." (Aleister Crowley)

The Thule Society, or Thule Order, was a German secret society that largely inspired Nazi mysticism and ideology. In his book *"Spear of Destiny"*, Trevor Ravenscroft (former British military officer and journalist) explains that Thule members, who practised black magic, were behind Hitler's rise to power before World War II. According to Ravenscroft, the cult's members, as Satanists, were *'uniquely concerned with raising their consciousness through the practice of rituals that could connect them to the evil, non-human intelligences of the universe, but also enable them to attain a means of communication with those intelligences. One of the main followers of this circle was Dietrich Eckart.* Thule

---

[143] "Australia: How a paedophile and satanist ring case is being hushed up" - Donde Vamos, 19/10/2013.

[144] *A History of Religious Ideas*, vol.1 - Mircea Eliade, 1978, p.365.

members also practised a form of sexual magic derived from the teachings of the Satanist Aleister Crowley, which Dietrich Eckart used to initiate Adolf Hitler.

Hitler joined the Thule Order in 1919. Until 1923, Dietrich Eckart, who was his mentor, spared no effort to make Hitler a particularly devout follower of occultism and black magic. Eckart had received a message from his *'spirit guide'* that he would have the privilege of training the *'Anti-Christ'*. From the beginning of their relationship, Eckart believed that Hitler was this avatar and therefore he left no teaching, no ritual, no perversion untouched, all in order to spiritually train Hitler for his future role. It was from his studies of the powers generated by perverse occult practices that Eckart devised a ritual which he used when he opened Adolf Hitler's chakra centres to give him the vision and means of communication with the 'Powers'. Once his initiatory training was complete, Hitler felt that he was *'born again'* with a *'super-personal'* strength, a strength he would need to carry out the mandate he was given. Hitler used the Christian term 'born again' to describe his initiation. It is interesting to note here that during a 1988 presidential campaign television interview with George W. Bush, journalist Barbara Walters asked him a question that startled him. The future President paused for a moment, looking puzzled, and after a few seconds replied: *"If by Christian you mean born again, then yes, I am a Christian.* This is the answer one would expect from an occultist for whom the initiatory rituals he has participated in make him a *"Born Again"*. This is the symbolic process of 'death and rebirth' applied in ritual abuse and mind control. The *Skull and Bones* secret society through which Bush Sr. and Jr. (and many others) passed practices rituals identical to those of the Thule Order where Hitler was initiated, namely black magic practices. Ron Rosenbaum wrote about the *Skull & Bones* in an article for *Esquire* magazine: *"The (ritual) death of the initiate will have to be so terrifying that it requires the use of human skeletons and psychological rituals (...) sexual perversion is part of these psychological rituals (...) naked in a coffin, the initiate will also have to recount his darkest and deepest sexual secrets at the initiation.* We shall return to this question of *'initiatory resurrection'* in more detail in Chapter 4.[145]

This black magic initiation that transcended Adolf Hitler combined sexual perversion and *enlightenment* brought about by profound altered states of consciousness, i.e. a mixture of sexual magic and trauma-related dissociation. These rituals involved highly perverse and sadistic practices: sodomy, orgies, animal sacrifices, floggings, etc. Ravenscroft reports that Hitler was severely tortured during these traumatic rituals, including a *'magical, sadistic and monstrous ritual'* after which he became impotent. This impotence had nothing to do with physical castration, it had a deep psychological origin because of the extreme sadism and masochism of the rituals. Hitler's relationship with Eva Braun was of the same order. Trevor Ravenscroft also wrote about Hitler: *'Sexual perversion was central to his life. A monstrous sexual perversion that was really at the heart of his existence and was the source of his mediumistic and clairvoyant powers.* In his book *"Hitler - A study in Tyranny"*, Alan Bullock

---

[145] The Last Secrets of Skull and Bones - Ron Rosenbaum, Esquire Magazine, 1977.

writes: *"His power to bewitch a crowd is related to the occult art of African medicine men or Asian shamans; others have compared it to the mediumistic sensitivity or magnetism of a hypnotist."*

These black magic and sex magic rituals open doors to the spirit world, which provide the initiates with power and psychic abilities. In 1921, at the age of 33, Hitler was totally possessed by a hierarchy of demonic spirits and was finally ready to take over the leadership of the National Socialist Party. No one can understand the monstrosity of Hitler's plans without knowing the satanic perversion into which he had plunged long before he came to power. Hitler received real protection of a supernatural order to carry out his mission. In his book *"Hitler, Médium de Satan"*, Jean Prieur reports that on several occasions the future Fürher was saved by "dark forces" during the First World War: *"However, a voice speaks in him in a muffled voice and orders him to get as far away from the trench as possible; so he continues to walk like a sleepwalker. Suddenly a burst of iron and fire forced him to the ground. The explosion was close at hand (...) When it was quiet, he hurried back to the trench and recognised nothing more. Instead of the squad's shelter, it was a gigantic funnel strewn with human debris. All his comrades had been killed. It was from that day on that he was convinced of his divine mission. For the fifth time, Providence intervened on his behalf ... In the summer of 1915 he was saved again in extraordinary circumstances which he recounted years later to an English journalist, Ward Price: 'I was having dinner in the trench with several comrades, when I felt a voice saying to me: "Get up and go over there! The voice was so sharp, so insistent that I obeyed mechanically as if it were a military order. I got up at once and walked twenty metres away, carrying my dinner in my lunch box. Then I sat down to continue my meal; my mind had calmed down. No sooner had I done this than a flash and a deafening bang came from the trench I had just left. A stray shell had burst over the group, killing everyone."*[146]

During the First World War, Hitler already seemed to have a serious background of occult and pagan knowledge. Jean Prieur reports in his book: *"It was during the autumn of 1915 that he composed this curious and disturbing poem, in which one should see much more than a literary exercise:*

On bitter nights, I often go
In the silent clearing at Wotan's oak
To unite with the dark powers...
With its magic formula
The moon traces the runic letters,
And all those who are full of impudence by day
Are made small by the magic formula[147]

In this poem, Hitler refers to *"Wotan"*, also called *"Wodan"*, corresponding to Odin, the Norse god of the dead, the god of victory and knowledge. Scandinavia called him Odin and Germania called him Wotan. Adolf Hitler was a total follower of this old Nordic paganism. This is why the

---

[146] *Hitler médium de Satan* - Jean Prieur, 2002, p.41-38.

[147] Ibid p.38.

Nazis created (or perhaps absorbed) the *Ahnenerbe*, a society for research and teaching on the esoteric ancestral heritage.

Hitler also escaped several attacks in an extraordinary way, as in 1936 at the Olympic Games in Berlin, but also in 1937 and 1939. When some people around him were astonished at the lack of measures taken for his security, Hitler replied: *'You have to have faith in providence, you have to listen to the inner voice and believe in your destiny. I deeply believe that fate has chosen me for the greater good of the German nation.* He once said to Eva Braun: *'Providence protects me and we need no longer fear our enemies.* Ravenscroft reports that in a press interview, Hitler said: *"I walk like a sleepwalker dictated by providence.* What providence is he talking about? Certainly the 'Luciferian providence', in other words the demonic possession for which he had been prepared during years of initiations...

Aleister Crowley was a self-proclaimed "Beast 666". His biographer, John Symonds, said: 'Sex had become for Crowley the means of reaching God... He performed the sexual act not for emotional joy or procreative purposes, but to renew his psychic strength. He believed that he was thus worshipping the god Pan. " In his diary Rex de Arte Regia, Crowley describes his practices of the "Royal Art" (sexual magic), stating that he makes a wish during the rituals, usually for an influx of money, and that he always ends up getting his desires.

Ex-Occultist William 'Bill' Schnoebelen has made several public revelations about the rituals of Luciferian High Masonry. Schnoebelen was a member of the Church of Satan, a Freemason for 9 years, initiated into the 32nd degree of the Scottish Rite, the 90th degree of the Memphis-Misraim Rite, and the 9th degree of the O.T.O. He also attained the 9th degree with the Rosicrucians. In 1984 he came out of occultism completely and became a Christian. Here is an excerpt from a lecture in which he states that *the* Masonic *"Royal Art"* is linked to the practice of sexual magic on children: *"These rituals contain a deeply sinister aspect, but one that I must address. I apologise in advance because it is something vulgar. But we must talk about the 'Royal Secret' of Masonry and how it operates in this spiritual hierarchical pyramid (...) In 1904, Crowley had contact with an extraterrestrial being (demon) called Iwas. This entity dictated a book to him during his wife's mediumistic trances: the Book of the Law. This book states that God has fallen from his throne and that a new conquering child-god is coming to take his place. As a result, Crowley declared the end of Christianity and the advent of 'Crowlianism'. In fact, he was a genius, he could play chess with his eyes closed. He was an accomplished poet, painter and writer. He was so covered with Masonic titles that he could have filled five pages of a book. This man was one of the most honoured Masons in the world, but he was also the most dangerous man of the 20th century. Following the Book of the Law, he began to perform rituals to bring back this child-god. To do this he founded what he called the "Fascinating Child" sect, and in doing so he unveiled and revealed the Royal Secret of Freemasonry. Following the publication of his book, a man came to him. This man was Theodore Reuss, a German occultist and leader of the O.T.O. (Order of the Temple of the East) which is the order of the Eastern Knights Templar... This man then told Crowley that he had revealed the greatest mystery in the history of occultism. To which Crowley replied that he did not understand what he was talking about. Reuss therefore initiated him into the 9th degree of the O.T.O. and revealed the secret to him. The secret is that as a Freemason you are promised immortality. If you go to a Masonic funeral, you will hear a preaching about immortality. You will hear promises that after they die, they will go to the great higher heavenly lodges for eternity. How do they get this immortality? They do not believe in Jesus. The name of Jesus is not even allowed to be quoted in the blue lodges of Freemasonry (...) So where do they get this promise of immortality? The secret that Crowley indirectly discovered, probably through demonic intervention, is that this immortality is accessible through operative sexual magic. This type of sexual magic we are talking about here is the rape of a young child, unfortunately. Crowley taught that you can live forever through the sexual vampirisation of young children (...) I apologise for that, it's so horrible... But Masons do that. Not all of them! Please understand. But it is a big enough problem that I feel compelled to tell you about it. This is the reason why Masons think they can achieve immortality. Every time they defile a child, they steal a bit of that child's youth. (...) Then they think they can access alternative universes in which they will become gods (...) Crowley reveals the secret of the symbolism of the 'All Seeing Eye' in one of his books, the Book of Toth, which is a very advanced manual. This is the eye of Lucifer, but believe it or not, this symbol also corresponds to an organ we delicately call the rectum. Which is ironic when you know that it also represents Lucifer. This refers to the occult and archeometric doctrine of Masonry which claims that through sodomy, especially with young boys, you can access alternate dimensions of reality, through what they call 'typhoon tunnels' (vortexes). They have this belief that through sexual perversion they can access these tunnels, and the purpose of this type of magic is to find one's own universe and become the god of that universe. Satan betrays these people by enticing them to practice evil. However, what is important is not whether it works or not, but that these people actually believe in it (...) This form of magic is 'Trans-Yuggothic' magic. This means that it is a magic that operates beyond Plutonian space, a planet that they think is beyond the reach of the Sun, and therefore beyond the reach of the rays of the Judeo-Christian God. They think that there are entities beyond Pluto that are far more powerful, dangerous and deadly than God or the devil. This is the thing that these people are trying to achieve. Understand me well! I cannot say it enough: One or two Masons out of a hundred practice such things... But that is more than enough! And that's a serious problem!"*[148]

According to Bill Schnoebelen, sex magic practised on children is a key to accessing other dimensions and to obtaining power. A child who has been tortured and raped during satanic ritual abuse is in a state of dissociation, i.e. he or she becomes an open door to other dimensions (see Chapter 6 on the connection between trauma, dissociation and access to other dimensions). Could the practice of sexual magic on a child in a dissociative trance state be a *source of rejuvenation*? In such a state of dissociation, would the child be a kind of

---

[148] "Exposing the illuminati from within" - The Prophecy Club - Bill Schnoebelen.

bridge, a medium acting as an intermediary to connect the earthly world and the spirit world? Unfortunately, this question comes to be asked because everything suggests that this is a Pandora's box of which mind control is an essential component.

In his book *Do What You Will: A History of Anti-Morality*, Geoffrey Ashe writes that Crowley had *'hypnotic powers'* which he frequently used to seduce women but he also writes that he was *'like three or four different men'*.[149] Crowley himself described his altered states of consciousness in which he confronted other imaginary, dissociative or spiritual entities. Did Crowley himself have a multiple personality, a personality split by childhood trauma? Did he have a dissociative identity disorder? In his book *Magick in Theory and Practice*, Crowley advocates self-punishment by scarification with a razor blade. Therapists working with ritual abuse survivors report that self-harm by scarification is the most common feature of patients with severe dissociative disorders. Crowley joined the *Hermetic Order of the Golden Dawn* in 1898 and was finally expelled in 1900. In 1901, a scandal engulfed the Golden Dawn when Theo Horos (Frank Jackson) and his wife were accused of raping a sixteen year old girl. At the time, the judge concluded that the couple had used Golden Dawn rituals for the sexual exploitation of minors. According to Richard Kaczynski, the author of *Of Heresy And Secrecy: Evidence of Golden Dawn Teachings On Mystic Sexuality*, sexual magic practices are said to be commonplace in this secret society. It is likely that sexual magic is a common teaching in all these different Luciferian lodges.

The Golden Dawn is said to have been created following the discovery of mysterious Germanic documents. These were coded manuscripts that were deciphered and transcribed by one of the founding members of the Order, Dr. William Wyn Westcott, a Freemason. Subsequently, the documents were suspected of being forged and in order to clarify the matter, the author of *The Magicians of the Golden Dawn*, Ellic Howe, passed Westcott's translations to a graphology expert. The expert concluded that Westcott probably had a multiple personality disorder (dissociative identity disorder) because of his different and very distinctive handwriting styles. In his book *What You Should Know About The Golden Dawn*, Gerald Suster, a lawyer for the Golden Dawn, challenged the multiple personality disorder argument by noting that another prominent member of the Order, Israel Regardie, also had a writing style that varied and that he had never been diagnosed with multiple personality or any psychiatric disorder... One interpretation of these writing variations would be that these men both have dissociative disorders caused by traumatic ritual experiences. But this is an accurate diagnosis that is rarely made because few mental health professionals are trained to detect these kinds of personality disorders.[150]

Another secret society with a Masonic-like doctrine and structure is the F.S., *Fraternitas Saturni* or Brotherhood of Saturn. In his book *Fire & Ice: Magical Teaching of Germany's Greatest Secret Occult Order*, Eldred Flowers

---

[149] Do What You Will: A History of Anti-Morality - Geoffrey Ashe, 1974, p.235.

[150] *"Cult & Ritual Abuse"* - James Randal Noblitt & Pamela Perskin Noblitt, 2014, p.141.

refers to the F.S. as a *"friendly Luciferian organisation"*. Like the O.T.O. and many Masonic works, the F.S. gives considerable importance to Gnostic concepts and terms. In this book, Eldred Flower frequently refers to the *"Saturnian Gnosis"* and specific sexual rituals. It should be noted that Linda Blood, in her book *"The New Satanists"*, reports that Eldred Flowers, for whom the F.S. is a *"friendly Luciferian organisation"*, was assisting Michael Aquino as head of the Temple of Set. Linda Blood knows what she is talking about because she was Aquino's mistress and a member of this sect.[151]

5 - SACRIFICES, WITCHCRAFT, SHAMANISM AND MULTIPLE PERSONALITIES

Archaeological evidence shows that the Moches, Incas, Mayans and Aztecs all practiced violent and bloody rituals. On further investigation, it also appears that human sacrifice was also practiced in Europe. In an article entitled *'Vessels of Death: Sacred Cauldrons in Archaeology and Myth'*, [152]Miranda Green refers to human sacrifices practised by the Germanic Cimbrian people and reported by the Greek geographer Strabo. The article describes that the ceremony was performed by 'holy women', one of whom would slit the throat of a prisoner of war and collect his blood in a large bronze cauldron. Then his body was opened to inspect his entrails and organs for divinatory purposes. Human sacrifice is a common heritage in human history, a practice linked to the worship of demonic and Luciferian gods. Historically, early pagan rites included both animal and human sacrifices. Human sacrifice and cannibalism seem to have had some place in ancestral and even contemporary rituals. In *"Kingship and Sacrifice: Ritual and Society in Ancient Hawaii"*, Valerio Valeri reports on the existence of ritual human sacrifices practiced by priests until 1819, before they were banned. Valeri states that human sacrifices were also used in witchcraft rites. The ancient Haitian Voodoo cult practised the sacrifice of the *"hornless goat"*, a euphemism for human sacrifice.[153] Just as the term *'long pig' refers* to human flesh among the cannibals of Polynesia. Cannibalism has also been attributed to certain shamanic practices. A cannibalistic ritual is probably a traumatic experience both for the victim before death, and for those who participate in and survive the ritual. In *"Dictionary of Folklore, Mythology and Legend (Funk & Wagnalls)"* R.D. Jamison writes: *"The Cambridge Expedition to the Torres Strait reported that sorcerers ate the flesh of corpses or mixed it with their food after ritual practices. This results in them becoming violent and committing murder in anger. We know little about the processes that induce shamanic trance except that cannibalism causes the consumer to enter an inhuman or superhuman state."*

---

[151] Ibid p.142.

[152] The Antiquaries Journal 78, 1998.

[153] *Voodoo* - Jacques d'Argent, 1970.

In an article entitled *"Sacrifices of raw, cooked and burnt humans"*,[154] Terje Oestigaard notes that human sacrifice is a common practice serving as an offering to the gods. This offering can be buried raw, cooked as a meal for the deities, or cremated to ascend directly to heaven. Cremation is a transformation and a medium through which a certain transmutation of the offering takes place. Animal or human sacrifice can be seen as a communion between man and the gods through a meal, and was often the central rite of paganism because it allowed one to *"share the table of the gods"*, but it also served as a cathartic act.

The Roman emperor Julian was known for his penchant for sacrificial acts and they are universally decried by his contemporaries, both faithful and detractors. He was described as never leaving his 'amulets and talismans' and dividing his life between concern for the state and devotion to the altars. Libanios gives him the title of glory of having performed more animal sacrifices in ten years than all the Greeks combined. The emperor Julian made blood sacrifices in the temple of Zeus as well as in that of Tyche (fortune) or Demeter (fertility).[155]

In *'History of the Wars'*, the historian Procopius refers to human sacrifice as the most 'noble', preferably the first human captured in war. The god of war, Mars, was to be appeased with the most savage and bloody rituals by putting prisoners to death. For these ancient peoples, the shedding of blood was a means of appeasing the prince of war.

In an account of a journey among the Volga Bulgars (Vikings), Ibn Fadlan tells how various animals were sacrificed while the men of the clan raped a slave girl before she was killed and placed on a boat by her master. The boat was then set on fire to reduce the human offering to smoke.[156]

Ritual murder seems to be a common practice among the sorcerers of the *Cebuano* culture in the Philippines. In the book *"Cebuano Sorcery: Malign Magic in the Philippines"*, Richard Lieban writes: *"To become one of those who can practice 'Hilo', it is said that a man must first kill a member of his own family, and then he must claim one or more victims each year. One such sorcerer revealed that the obligation to kill grows every year. The longer the sorcerer practices his magic, the more frequently he must kill. All informants agree that when the sorcerer assumes such obligations, if he does not commit the murders according to the calendar, he will himself become a victim, struck by his own instruments of sorcery which will turn against him. As one sorcerer says: 'If he does not kill, he will become seriously ill, and he will not get better until he is dead. If he does not kill, he will die."*[157]

In one of his conferences on the theme of the *'New Age'*, Father Jean Luc Lafitte reports what he experienced in Gabon: *'I preached several retreats in the bush (...) Every night we heard the melodies of these sorcerers who worked on*

---

[154] Norwegian Archeological Review, Vol 33, No 1, 2000.

[155] "Sharing the table of the gods: The emperor Julian and the sacrifices" - Nicolas Belayche.

[156] The Risalah of Ibn Fadlan: An Annotated Translation with Introduction" - Mc Keithen, 1979.

[157] "Cebuano Sorcery: Malign Magic in the Philippines" - Richard Lieban, 1967, p.23.

the followers of their religion. I was told that they were made to dance, but that before making them dance, the guru, the sorcerer, took great care to make all his followers drink a beverage called iboga. This is a hallucinogen that he crushed into powder and made the followers drink it to make them dance all night to the sound of the drum. After a while, all these people would go into a trance (...) Once they were in a trance, the witchdoctor managed to empty their personality completely, so much so that in order to progress in this system of false religion, you had to do something that the guru asked you to do. The first initiation was to kill an animal, so in the beginning you had to cut the neck of a chicken for example. The second step was to kill an enemy and the third step was to kill a family member. The fourth step was to kill oneself...' Here we find three things common to accounts of modern ritual abuse: drugs, trance states and blood sacrifices. Western survivors report that they were first forced to kill an animal and then sometimes a human being, usually a baby. The fourth stage described by Abbé Lafitte, which consists of killing oneself, may correspond to the suicide programming of victims of mind control (MK), but the Abbé does not specify in what setting or in what way this fourth stage may be triggered in the tradition he describes.

Traumatic initiation rituals are a common factor in many traditions practising witchcraft and spirit worship. In his book *"La Conjuration antichrétienne"*, Mgr Henri Delassus writes: *"Satan had temples built and altars erected in all the places of the earth, and he had himself worshipped in them in an impious and superstitious manner. How many times did the chosen people themselves allow themselves to be carried away by him, to the point of sacrificing even their children to 'Moloch'! (...) The missionaries of the twelfth century were quite surprised when, leaving the slightly sceptical France of the time, they landed in the East Indies and found themselves in the midst of the strangest diabolic manifestations. Travellers as well as missionaries today witness the same prodigies. Mr. Paul Verdun has published a book: "The Devil in the Missions" (...) Apparitions and possessions are frequent among them, known and accepted by everyone. In all these countries there are sorcerers. To become one, one must undergo cruel trials that go far beyond the most painful practices of Christian mortification. In most of these initiations, a manifestation of the devil shows that he accepts the candidate as his own, he makes a possessed person of him or he takes him away."*[158]

In Papua New Guinea, traumatic rituals to terrorise the initiate are an integral part of local cults. In his book *"Ritual and Knowledge Among the Baktaman of New Guinea"*, Frederik Barth describes how a *Baktaman* novice who was so terrified of the initiation process literally defecated on it. In the book *Rituals of Manhood: Male Initiation in Papua New Guniea*, Gilbert Herdt reports that in the *Bimin-Kuskusmin* initiation, the novices are totally terrorised by the ceremony of having their septum pierced and their forearm burned. This creates serious trauma and the author reports that signs of deep psychological shock have been observed in several individuals who have gone through this initiation. In

---

[158] *"La Conjuration antichrétienne"* - Mgr Henri Delassus, 2008 (Saint-Remi), p.259.

his analysis of the Orokaiva initiation of the Papuans, in the book *Exchange in the Social Structure of the Orokaiva*, Erik Schwimmer writes that one of the functions of these rites is to provoke '*absolute and lasting terror in the candidate*'. All ethnographers who have studied the Orokaiva have emphasised the particularly terrifying nature of the *embahi* ceremony. Several authors have reported that a real panic is deliberately induced in the young candidates for initiation, but they also describe the anguish of the parents who witness the suffering of the children. In *"The Concept of the Person and the Ritual Sytem; An Orokaiva View"*, André Iteanu even writes that there is always a risk that the child will not survive the trials of initiation. In his book *"Prey into Hunter: The Politics of Religious Experience"*, Maurice Bloch analyses the *embahi* ceremony with its sacred and transcendental character. According to Bloch, the most important effect of this ceremony is that the initiate is symbolically killed, or more precisely that his vitality is neutralised, and he becomes a purely transcendental (dissociated?) being. Following this initiation, the child becomes sacred, so it is a question of conquering its vitality and putting it under a certain control. To do this, the child is symbolically killed in order to transform him, to transcend his person so that he himself becomes a killer and no longer a victim.[159]

Here we have a description that may fit the '*modern*' satanic ritual abuse with its attendant mind control. These are traumatic initiation rituals which aim to sacralise the child through deep dissociative states and rebirth as a 'Monarch' child; making him a *killer* rather than a *victim*, a full member of the Luciferian/Satanic cult.

Cult and Ritual Abuse: Narratives, Evidence and Healing Approaches by James Randall Noblitt and Pamela Perskin Noblitt addresses the anthropological aspect of ritual abuse and mind control using dissociative identity disorders (multiple personality disorder). The book reports numerous sources that concern traumatic rituals where the line between dissociation and demonic possession remains very blurred. Here are some of the sources they report in their book...

Isaiah Oke's book, '*Blood Secrets: The True Story of Demon Worship and Ceremonial Murder*', clearly addresses the issue of ritual abuse in West Africa. Isaiah Oke is the grandson and successor of an important *Babalorisha*, a Juju high priest. In his book, he recounts *the education and training* he received to succeed his grandfather. Oke describes the traumatic ceremonies he went through in his apprenticeship to become a high priest. He also describes the hardships he had to inflict on others, ceremonies that involved torture and even murder, such as the '*200 cuts*' ceremony in which he had to put a man to death. He reports what appear to be classic dissociation experiences when he refers to memory loss and possession by the spirits of village ancestors. Oke writes in his book: *"Our rituals serve to appease the most horrible of our gods. These gods*

---

[159] "Rites of Terror, Metaphor and Memory in Melanesian Initiation Cults" - Harvey Whitehouse, The Journal of the Royal Anthropological Institute, Vol. 2, No. 4, 1996.

are so fearsome that our rituals must be equally so. We believe that there is nothing better than blood to appease the fierce spirits of Juju. "[160]

Oke compares African Juju to American Satanism. He explains that this cult is practiced openly in West Africa and even exploited commercially for tourists, but that it has another facade where the secrecy is such that some say there is another religion, unknown to the outside world, within Juju itself: *"There is another place of sacrifice which we call the 'Tomb', usually in the forest, away from prying eyes and ears. It is usually a simple, well camouflaged hut in which we call the Igbo-Awo (the secret of the forest). What is practised in the "Tomb" are not harmless ceremonies, but rather the macabre blood rituals."* [161]

In his book *Ritual: Power, Healing and Community*, Malidoma Somé confirms Isaiah Oke's statements about the African religion of Juju. Originally from West Africa, Somé studied at the Sorbonne and Brandeis University in the USA. He describes rituals in which people speak with different voices and show different personalities. He states that the priest conducting the rituals is able to act on the minds of those present so that they are unable to remember the events that have taken place. He reports the example of a tribesman who wanted to reveal the secrets of the cult to strangers. Before he was able to do so, he reportedly had a psychotic break and committed suicide. These testimonies can be compared with those reported by survivors of satanic ritual abuse in the West. Some say that they feel their minds blocked or 'shut down' when they try to recall the details of their abuse. They also say that they become particularly self-destructive, even suicidal, when they are about to talk or have just talked to someone about things that should be kept secret. In the West, this setting up of the inner secret is done by what is called MK-Monarch programming. This is a form of extreme conditioning that creates and manipulates programmed reactions through deep trauma. (See Chapter 7)

The British psychiatrist William Sargant (who worked for the MK-Ultra project), stated in his book '*The Mind Possessed: A Physiology of Possession, Mysticism and Faith Healing*' that dissociation, amnesia, personality modification as well as mental programming, was an essential part of the *Orisha* cult.

Orisha is the *Yoruba* term for the gods or the representation of the spirit of God. It is an African-American tradition originating in Africa. The term is used in *Juju* but also in *Santeria* which is a derivative of *Yoruba* culture. In his book, William Sargant quotes the author Pierre 'Fatumbi' Verger, who is said to have been initiated into these *Orisha* rituals: '*Pierre Verger himself became a priest of the Orisha cult. He could not tell me much about the secret ceremonies that took place in the convent, but he was able to reveal that this was a severe brainwashing process in which the ordinary personality of the adept is replaced by a new personality. The initiate is never allowed to remember who he was, what he looked like and how he behaved with his old personality. When the*

---

[160] "Blood Secrets: The True Story of Demon Worship and Ceremonial Murder" - Isaiah Oke, 1989, p.19.

[161] Ibid, p.19.

initiate leaves the convent, he is given back his old personality by a special process, but he keeps very little memory of what happened in the convent. When the adepts return to the nunnery, by the same reverse hypnotic process, they regain their devotional personality, which will again disappear into their ordinary personality when they return to the secular world."[162]

Here we have an example of mind control based on personality splitting with memories partitioned by amnesiac walls (see Chapter 5). William Sargant also stated that *"Some people are able to induce on themselves or on someone else a state of trance and dissociation caused by strong and repetitive emotional stresses, to the point where it can become a conditioning system of brain activity (...) If the trance is accompanied by a state of mental dissociation, the person can be deeply influenced in his thinking and subsequent behaviour.* Sargant makes a clear reference here to the process of mind control using dissociative states.

The author Fritz Springmeier described Haitian voodoo ceremonies involving trance and dissociation phenomena. Springmeier draws parallels between these voodoo ritual practices and MK-Monarch programming: *"The first reports on Haitian voodoo were written in 1884 by Spencer St John. His writings describe the blood rituals and cannibalism practiced in this religion (...) Blood sacrifices are often associated with demons and the possessed person will drink the blood of the sacrificed animal. Gems, herbs, trances and dissociative states are used to attract spirits. While the MK-Monarch slave undergoes trauma-induced dissociative states, the dissociative states of Voodoo practitioners are ritually induced. Voodoo rituals involve chanting, drumming, sometimes clapping and frenzied dancing to induce dissociative states. Several factors that induce these altered states of consciousness have been identified in Afro-Caribbean or South American religions. First, there is dancing to a fast and jerky rhythm. Secondly, dissociated states often follow a period of food deprivation, hyperventilation is also used to achieve these particular states of consciousness. The onset of demonic possession is characterised by a brief period of muscular inhibition with a collapse (...) During the trance, the limbs of the body as well as the head are shaken, the person becomes so dissociated that he or she can pick up glowing embers by hand. The possessed person may be conscious, semi-conscious or unconscious of what is happening to him (...) Voodoo rituals that induce dissociative states are usually accompanied by amnesia. During this period of amnesia, the person has behaved as if he or she were a spirit (a god). What has been described here is more of a ritual-induced dissociative state than a trauma-induced dissociative state. MK-Monarch programming aims to combine both: ritual and trauma, in order to create and reinforce a deeply dissociated state. This is why it is difficult to separate the religious factor from MK-Monarch programming.*"[163]

---

[162] *The Mind Possessed: A Physiology of Possession, Mysticism and Faith Healing* - William Sargant, 1974, p.149.

[163] "The Illuminati Formula Used to Create an Undetectable Total Mind Controlled Slave" - Fritz Springmeier & Cisco Wheeler, 1996.

Let us now turn our attention to shamanism, a subject that cannot be ignored when studying altered states of consciousness and interactions with other dimensions. Shamans are what are known as 'medicine men' or 'witch doctors'. This is a primitive system of medicine dating back to the earliest times, a discipline that combines communication with the spirits and the practice of exercises to obtain certain 'spiritual powers'. It is sometimes referred to as a 'shamanic warrior', an individual who is able to reach deep trance states in rituals, usually with the help of a drum, songs and ceremonial dances. He sometimes uses sleep deprivation and/or drugs to facilitate these states of deep dissociation. Once in trance, the shaman enters the spirit world, a dimension parallel to our own but just as real to the shaman. These journeys bring him visions that allow him to diagnose health problems for example, but he may also have to deal with other problems concerning his community. In his spiritual work, the shaman is assisted by entities sometimes called 'guardian spirit' or 'guiding spirit'.

Some shamans do not limit themselves to 'benevolent' spiritual activities and may use sorcery related to the dark forces when they need it. Francis Huxley, in his book "The Way of the Sacred", makes a clear distinction between black and white shamanism. Harry B. Wright, in his book "Witness to Witchcraft", makes a similar observation among the Amerindian sorcerers of the Amazon, with the benevolent curanderos and the malevolent feiteceros. It is also interesting to note that in the book "The Shaman and the Magician: Journeys Between the Worlds", Nevil Drury reports similarities between traditional shamanic practices and some of the modern rituals of magic practiced in certain Masonic-type occult lodges. For example, he cites the Hermetic Order of the Golden Dawn. It is clear that the psycho-spiritual function, called psychic dissociation, is an essential point in Luciferian occultism.

It is necessary to clarify here what is meant by 'white magic' and 'black magic', or 'benevolent' and 'malevolent' sorcerers. Here is what Anton LaVey, the founder of the Church of Satan, says about magic:

LaVey makes no distinction between white and black magic, saying that white Wicca witchcraft and new-agers freely call upon the forces of darkness to solicit them in their hypocritical desires. LaVey said: "All magic comes from the Devil's realm, no matter how you dress it up. The belief that 'black' magic is only used for destruction and 'white' for healing is wrong. Satanic magic is used to invoke the power of justice, it can be used to help you or someone else, as well as it can be used to harm someone."[164]

There is no difference between white magic and black magic, except in the blissful hypocrisy and self-deception of the 'white magicians' (...) No one on this earth has ever studied occultism, metaphysics, yoga, or anything else of the

---

[164] "Dinner with the Devil: An evening with, the High Priest of the Church of Satan" - Bob Johnson, High Times Magazine, 1994.

so-called 'white light', without ego gratification and for the purpose of gaining personal power."[165]

Pierre Manoury also writes that there is no such thing as "white magic" or "black magic": "You can often tell a specialist by the slight smile he gets when he mentions the words 'white magic'. The reason is quite simple, white magic does not exist! (...) Whatever the case may be for these good people and the brainless herd that serves as their audience, white magic does not exist and has never existed. The term white magician is commonly used in literature to designate an adept who performs only beneficial operations, as opposed to the black magician who makes an alliance with the forces of darkness. But this is literature, not initiation! In fact, there is only one type of magic, which is subdivided into several specialities. The notion of white or black magic is purely Manichean, simplistic and primary."[166]

An important question about shamanism is whether these practices involve traumatic ritual abuse. How do shamans obtain these communications with 'spirits'? The hypothesis that these 'spirits' may in some cases be dissociated personalities of the shaman cannot be excluded, and it is possible that this personality splitting is created by rituals. Some rituals are non-traumatic, others are traumatic and involve traumas that function to produce fierce and intrusive alter identities that can easily be mistaken for demonic entities.

In his book *"The Way of the Shaman"*, Michael Harner describes the initiatory journey of a shaman, but he does not elaborate on the way in which the so-called *"guiding"* or *"guardian"* spiritual entities come to be part of the inner psychic world of the shamanic initiate. According to Harner, *the guardian spirit* must come to the shaman as a result of severe illness or one must deliberately go to meet it during a *'vision quest'*. In his book, Harner uses terms such as *'another identity'*, *'alter ego'* or *'another self'* in reference to *the shaman's guardian spirit*. In *Primitive Magic: The Psychic Powers of Shamans and Sorcerers*, Ernesto De Martino cites an ethnographic account by Martin Gusinde who uses the terms *'dual personality'*, *'second personality'*, *'medium personality'* to describe the shaman's interaction with the spirits. De Martino also cites a text by another shamanist, Shirokogoroff, for whom the drum is intended to *"produce the attenuation of waking consciousness"* and to *"favour the splitting (the coming of the 'spirit') (...).During ecstasy, the degree of splitting of the personality and the elimination of conscious elements is variable, but in any case there are limits in both directions, i.e. the shaman's state must not turn into a crisis of uncontrolled hysteria, and on the other hand, ecstasy must not cease: Indeed, neither the crisis of uncontrolled hysteria nor the suppression of ecstasy allow the regular activity of the second personality and the subsequent autonomy of the intuitive thought"*. De Martino then takes up the story of *Aua* who interpreted his illness *"as an invitation to become a shaman, as a vocation (...)*

---

[165] The Re-Enchantment of the West ", Vol 2: Alternative Spiritualities, Sacralization, Popular Culture and Occulture - Christopher Partridge, 2006, p.229.

[166] "Cours de haute magie de sorcellerie pratique et de voyance", Vol.2 - Pierre Manoury, 1989, chap.1.

After various disorders, he finally finds a psychic balance, and *"instead of the threat of a dissolution of the unitary presence, he now constitutes a double existence (...) but an existence which, although double, is under the control of a single unitary presence, which emerges victorious from this extraordinary psychic adventure".[167]*

All the terms used here may correspond to alter personalities due to a splitting of the shaman's personality. It may be a controlled and mastered dissociation of identity, in a way a shamanic management of the dissociative identity disorder (see chapter 5). The shaman would thus transform an undergone state into a dominated state, a passive dissociation into an active dissociation. The shaman is above all a sick person who has succeeded in healing, a healer who has healed himself. *"In the course of dramatic and painful battles with evil spirits, shamans are engaged in a fierce battle with the physical and psychological forces they have experienced during their illness."[168]*

In her book 'How about Demons? Possession and Exorcism in the Modern World', Felicitas Goodman writes: 'The Yanomamo shaman Hekura entered is not the same person as before. His facial expression is radically different, he moves in a way that is nothing like his usual way... Even his voice is unrecognizable. Rarely will a practitioner of this kind remember what happened afterwards."[169]

Are we dealing here with a real possession or with a deep dissociation with a split personality and dissociative amnesia? Perhaps it is also a mixture of both... We will develop this particularly interesting subject in Chapter 6 concerning the link between trauma, dissociation and connection to other dimensions.

One element that could link shamanic 'possessions' to dissociative identity disorder (multiple personality) is that sometimes this 'possession' of the shaman is only partial. The shaman goes into a trance but the entity does not necessarily take control of the body. This experience is often described as an 'inner journey' in which the shaman attempts to communicate with the spirits. This kind of mental functioning may be related to the DSM-5 category of dissociative disorders and dissociative trance.

Michael Harner adds that a person can sometimes obtain a 'guardian spirit' in an *'involuntary way'*, but he does not say in what way. Is it through accidental trauma? Later in the book, Harner explains that the *Jivaro* tribe commonly give their newborns a hallucinogenic drug, the purpose of which is to accompany the child in a process to obtain a guardian spirit... After briefly mentioning this practice of drugging the newborn, he indicates that there are other involuntary ways in which the child can acquire a 'guardian spirit', but without going into detail.

---

[167] "Anthropological approach to dissociation and its inducing devices" - Georges Lapassade, 2004.

[168] *"Animism and shamanism for all"* - Igor Chamanovitch, 2010, p.106.

[169] "How about Demons? Possession and Exorcism in the Modern World" - Felicitas D. Goodman, 1988, p.12.

In his book *The Occult: A History*, Colin Wilson argues that trauma is part of the shamanic training of some tribes, he writes: *"The shaman himself has completed his priesthood through the most terrifying rituals and initiations through pain."*[170]

Dushan Gersi, the author of *"Face in the* Smoke*: An* Eyewitness *Experience of Voodoo, Chamanism, Psychic Healing and Other Amazing Human Powers"* wrote: *"Becoming a shaman requires years of painful initiations. I have heard that many neophytes die because of the harshness of the initiation. The neophyte endures the worst physical and psychological torments leading even to madness."*[171]

In an article entitled 'The Role of Fear in Traditional and Contemporary Shamanism', Michael York writes: 'The use of shamanic techniques as a rapidly accessible tool for developing human potential is at odds with traditional tribal shamanism in which it is very rare that the individual chooses to become a shaman of his or her own free will. In an indigenous context, the individual undergoes a long and arduous training to become a shaman, usually as a result of experiencing a profound unwanted trauma."[172]

Mircéa Eliade describes an initiation ritual of an Australian 'medicine man' as follows: 'Finally, the third method involves a long ritual in a deserted place where the candidate must suffer, in silence, the operation is performed by two old medicine men: These rub his body with rock crystals so as to flay the skin, press crystals on his scalp, drill a hole under the nail of his right hand and make an incision on his tongue (...) After this initiation the candidate is subjected to a special regime with countless taboos."[173]

In his book entitled "L'Héritage Makhuwa au Mozambique", Pierre Macaire writes about shamanic initiations: "The initiations take place in isolated places, huts, where the neophyte is delivered to sufferings that are similar to those of a monster that engulfs and digests (dismembers, tears the flesh from the bones and the eyes from their sockets) (...) The death of the neophyte then signifies a regression to the embryonic state, a regression that is not of a purely psychological order, but fundamentally cosmological."[174]

Perhaps this monster that engulfs and digests is to be compared to the great god of slaughter found in the Egyptian Book of the Dead, a flesh-eater and bone-crusher, powerful with terror who washes in blood. A morbid symbolism possibly linked to the initiation rituals of death and resurrection.

Mircéa Eliade reports that shamanic initiations sometimes involve traumatic rituals after which the initiate returns to the village with such amnesia

---

[170] *The Occult: A History"* - Colin Wilson, 1971, p.147.

[171] Face in the Smoke: An Eyewitness Experience of Voodoo, Chamanism, Psychic Healing and Other Amazing Human Powers" - Dushan Gersi, 1991, p.45.

[172] "The Role of Fear in Traditional and Contemporary Shamanism" - Michael York, Bath Spa University College, 2012.

[173] Shamanism and the Archaic Techniques of Ecstasy" - Mircéa Eliade, 1951, p.54.

[174] *"Animism and shamanism for all"* - Igor Chamanovich, 2010, p.104.

that even the basic gestures of daily life have to be relearned... and he is then given a new name... We find here the principle of *tabula rasa* following a radical trauma, a blank slate on which a new identity can be rewritten. This is the basis of the MK-Monarch type of mental programming. Just as the traditional shaman will develop connections with the spirit world during his initiation, the satanic/traumatic ritual abuses the child goes through will create a spiritual rift and a split in his personality making him an *initiate*. He then becomes a medium bridging the gap between our world and the spirit world, an indispensable piece to embody and carry out projects established from other spheres...

Jean Eisenhower, a survivor of mind control, described a method used by a tribe to train a shaman by intentionally inducing trauma in a young child. The child is separated from the tribe for a few years by being locked in a cage a short distance from the village. The child is not spoken to or cared for except for basic care. The child can hear the tribe but cannot interact with the members and will therefore split psychologically and turn his or her consciousness towards the *greatness of the cosmos*, the other dimensions of being. These other dimensions are inhabited by entities that will interact with the child and with which he will establish strong relationships. Eventually the tribe reintegrates him with honour and kindness into the village, but the young shaman will never be like the others again. For the rest of his life, he will do spiritual work for his tribe.[175]

The film *A Man Called Horse* (1970) depicts traumatic shamanic practices inspired by real events. The film tells the story of a white man held captive by a Sioux tribe. Once the *paleface* has managed to show his hunting prowess and earn the respect of the tribe, he is allowed to participate in an initiation ritual of tribal torture. The ceremony consists of suspending him in the air by hooks stuck in his pectoral muscles. During the torture, the man goes into a trance that seems to be the result of physical suffering. His altered state of consciousness causes him to see spectacular visions. According to North American Indian experts, such rituals were practised in the past and are still practised today by some tribes. White men sometimes refer to this ritual as *the Sun Dance*, but the Indian term for this ceremony is better translated as *the Sun Gazing* Dance. The author of '*Lame Deer Seeker of Visions: The life of a Sioux Medicine Man*', John Lame Deer, describes the ceremony as follows: '*The dance is not as violent as it once was, but it still requires a great deal of effort from a man. Even today, a man can faint from lack of food or water. He may be so thirsty when he blows his eagle-bone whistle that his throat becomes as cracked as a dry riverbed. For a time he will lose his sight as he stares at the sun and his eyes will see only glowing spirals and bright lights. When the eagle's talons* (editor's note: hooks at the end of a rope) *penetrate his chest, the pain in his flesh may become so intense that there will come a time when he will not feel them at all* (editor's note: dissociated state). *It is at this point, when the sun is burning in his head, his strength is gone and his legs have bent, that he goes into a trance and the visions occur. Visions of his transformation into a medicine man, visions of the future (...) It is when we fast on the hill or tear our flesh at the Sun Dance,*

---

[175] "Shamanism, Mind-Control, Christ, "Aliens", and Me" - Jean Eisenhower, 2014.

that we experience the sudden illumination from the Great Spirit. This enlightenment, this discernment, does not come easily, and we do not want angels or saints to bring it to us second hand. [176]The American authorities banned the Sun Dance and other tribal rites in 1881. However, the practice continued underground until 1934, when the ban was lifted by *the Indian Reorganization Act.*

Again, we find that rituals involving extreme physical and psychological suffering lead to deep dissociative states that open the door to a form of spiritual *enlightenment...* In the book *"Kahuna Magic"*, Brad Steiger indicates that circumcision was practiced among the Hawaiians as a kind of blood ritual. Without anaesthesia, circumcision is an extremely painful ritual experience that certainly causes a profound alteration of consciousness - to escape the unbearable pain - the infant then enters a deep dissociative state... What are the future consequences?

M.D. Lemonick, the author of a *Time* article entitled *The Secret of Maya*, reports that in the Mayan culture (of Mexico and Guatemala) deep altered states of consciousness had religious significance for the community. Lemonick writes that *macabre bloodletting rituals accompanied any major political or religious event in ancient Mayan culture ... The intense pain of such rituals provoked visions that allowed initiates to communicate with ancestors and mythological entities.* "[177]

Dr. James Randall Noblitt hypothesises that repeated experiences of trauma are necessary for the creation of dissociated identities. However, some blood rituals involving sacrifice and cannibalism may probably result in the mental integration of the image of the victim, or the entity (god or goddess) that the victim symbolises, thus facilitating the creation of disassociated identities or alter personalities in the cultists.

With the discovery of the deep states of dissociation caused by traumatic rituals, some shamans gave birth to a new spiritual tradition: witchcraft and black magic. Such a traumatic and diabolical practice has obvious disadvantages (violence, pain and the total abandonment of all morality) but on the other hand, this witchcraft is capable of producing powerful and lasting experiences of possession and dissociation creating links with demonic entities, providers of various powers.

In many pre-industrial cultures, there was a desire to have the immediate presence of the gods in the community. Such a thing was possible when a god took possession of an individual. Of all the methods of invoking the gods, the use of traumatic techniques was the most effective in producing possession and thus obtaining the immediate presence of a god or deity. In most cultures, traumatic rituals had to be kept secret, where personality splitting and traumatic amnesia worked effectively, so the victim could not reveal the details of the

---

[176] "Lame Deer Seeker of Visions: The life of a Sioux Medicine Man" - John Lame Deer, 1972, p.189-197.

[177] *Archeology: Secrets of Maya"* - Michael D. Lemonick, 09/08/1993.

ceremony. It has been shown with dissociative patients that when dissociation gradually disappears, it facilitates the return of traumatic memories.

Through repeated observation, malevolent sorcerers have come to understand that they can create particular 'entities' that can serve them. Isiah Oke calls this entity the *Iko-Awo* or *slave spirit*. The slave spirit is probably a dissociated alter personality that is created in the victim during a traumatic ritual. The *Iko-Awo is* instructed to do whatever the sorcerer commands, including committing suicide. The victim will have amnesia about the traumatic ritual and be unaware of the evil programming that took place during the initiation ritual. The "slave mind" is therefore a dissociated mental state, comparable to an alter identity in an individual with a multiple personality. The spirit slave is created by the sorcerer during a traumatic ritual, usually during childhood. The victim will remain amnesiac of the abuse and the existence of this programming. This process can be found in the same way in some patients with dissociative identity disorder. They usually have amnesia about the abuse that caused their dissociation and their alter personalities.

Black magic related to mind control probably works like this. When a spell is cast, a curse or a trigger signal is given, the 'slave mind' is called upon to surface and take over the victim's body. This 'slave spirit' is programmed by the sorcerer to perform particular tasks. The commands may be a simple signal to which the victim has been preconditioned in a traumatic ritual to respond to the sorcerer's request. When the witch doctor has effectively programmed several individuals from the same tribe, then his or her community will have great fear and respect for him or her, especially after such 'magical powers' have been publicly demonstrated. Sorcerers who themselves have disassociated personalities (likened to gods or deities by the uninitiated) are likely to be considered even more 'powerful'. Such practices are secretly passed down from generation to generation in the families of sorcerers and occultists. It is important to note that in many cultures, witchcraft is considered hereditary. In the United States, the problem of ritual abuse is frequently multi-generational, and another disturbing feature of witchcraft in many cultures is incest.[178]

Let us now turn to the alchemists and Kabbalists. The alchemists are known for their research into the 'philosopher's stone', which is supposed to turn lead into gold. Some interpret this as a metaphor for the process the individual goes through to transform into a spiritually higher being. According to Robert Ziegler, in alchemy suffering is seen as a process of *"purification of man's basic nature in order to transform it. Indeed,* the trials and sufferings of life allow one to evolve, they can be more or less difficult hazards occurring throughout an individual's life, sometimes painful experiences that shape the person and therefore allow him to overcome them and evolve. However, this notion of transcendence through suffering and pain is applied and embodied in a much more basic way through traumatic initiation rituals causing direct physical suffering. Suffering that triggers a neurological process of transcendence: dissociation, a function that allows the *initiate* to overcome the physical and

---

[178] *"Cult and Ritual Abuse"* - James Randall Noblitt & Pamela Perskin Noblitt, 2014, p.116-117.

psychological pain intentionally provoked during the rituals. This dissociative process also allows access to another reality. All this is summarised in the Masonic formula *'Ordo ab Chao'* (order through chaos), a formula closely linked to alchemy.

The alchemists' search for the elixir of life and the fountain of youth may represent the desire to escape the limitations of mortality through magic. The infamous Gilles de Rais was tried and convicted in 1440 for the murder of one hundred and forty children. The man nicknamed 'Bluebeard' sought the Philosopher's Stone in the blood of children, with whom he worked in the manner of an alchemist... An isolated madman? Unfortunately, the Child is a source of youth for the worst occultists of yesterday and today...

Alchemists are also interested in the creation of the homunculus, a replica of an artificially created human being, just like the 'golem' of the Kabbalists. In his book *The Sorcerer Handbook*, Wade Baskin explains that a golem is a kind of homunculus. In the Kabbalistic tradition and Jewish mysticism, the golem is a humanoid automaton, a zombie without soul or consciousness created by a magician, a sorcerer. It is possible that the homunculus of the alchemists and the golem of the kabbalists are in fact references to dissociated personality states that can be created by traumatic rituals. In *"The Golem and Ecstatic Mysticism"*, Bettina Knapp wrote that golems are created in the phenomenal or experimental world of occultists when they are in an altered state of consciousness. In Jewish mysticism, golems are soulless bodies and it can be argued that at one time, when traumatic rituals and dissociative trance eventually created an alter identity, this fraction of a *magical* personality could be considered an empty shell without a soul, as it was created solely by magic. For the sorcerer, this alter personality did not exist as a real person, it was simply a golem. It could therefore be abused and used as a soulless robot to serve as a slave.

In 1932, Joseph Achron composed a suite for orchestra entitled *"The Golem"*. The first part of the work introduces the golem while the last part, which is the exact mirror image of the first part, represents the disintegration, the dissolution of the golem. Fritz Springmeier claims that mind control techniques use musical sequences to bring out the deepest alter personalities in a programmed individual. The reversal of this musical sequence will *dissolve* the alter, the golem, back into the depths of the victim's psyche. We find here what William Sargant described with the *Orisha* cult, in which the different personalities of the adepts come and go according to certain occult processes, the workings of which are known only to the high initiates.

In his book Kabbalah, Gershom Scholem describes Kabbalistic doctrine with some of its magical practices. Various ideas and practices related to the concept of the golem also take their place in the practice of Kabbalah through the combination of the characteristics of Sefer Yezirah and a number of magical traditions. The operative part of Kabbalah that concerns the creation of the golem uses trances, magic and visualisations. Scholem writes: "In this circle, Sefer Yezirah is almost always interpreted in the manner of Saadiah and Shabbatai Donnolo, with the added tendency to see this book as a guide for mystics and magic practitioners. The study and understanding of this book is considered successful when the mystic attains the vision of the golem, which is linked to a specific ritual with a remarkable ecstatic result (editor's note: altered state of consciousness)."

Jewish sorcerers used the secret Kabbalistic names of God, according to precise instructions to create the golem. Once created, the golem must in turn recite the combination of Hebrew letters but in reverse order. In addition, the 'Seal of the Holy Name' must be inscribed on the golem's forehead along with the word 'emet(h)' ('truth' in Hebrew and one of the names of God). At a certain stage, in order to stop and dissolve the golem, the first letter (Aleph) of the inscription on its forehead is erased, resulting in the word "met(h)" which means "death". Fritz Springemeier argues that this type of occult programming is used today to manipulate the deeper alter personalities of MK slaves.

It is possible that the alchemists themselves knew how to create alter personalities. Through the experimentation with disassociated personalities, they would be able to achieve another of their quests, which is the discovery of 'spiritual gold': that is, eternal youth, the feeling of youth even in old age. Such a thing can happen when an alter child personality takes control of the individual. Another thing that can also produce the illusion of immortality is the creation of an alter personality whose identity is passed on from generation to generation. Some survivors of ritual abuse have testified that their families practice a kind of 'ancestor worship'. They believe that they can achieve immortality by inserting their identity into another individual who will live on after them, and that this identity or personality will be passed on successively in future generations. Do the damned souls of the ancestors then take possession of their descendants whose personalities are split up and therefore wide open to act as mediums?

The 20th century scientists who worked on mind control projects such as the MK-Ultra did not invent anything, they simply took up psycho-spiritual processes that had been discovered long ago by witch doctors, shamans and occultists.

Psychiatrist William Sargant, who worked in the MK-Ultra programme, said that "the methods of religious initiations are often so similar to modern political techniques of brainwashing and thought control that one sheds light on the mechanisms of the other. He also wrote in his book Battle for the Mind: "It is one thing to break down a person's mind by inflicting extreme stress... it is quite another to get new ideas to take firm root in his mind. That's what MK programmers are all about...

This governmental and scientific interest in trance states, dissociation and psychic powers has been motivated by the desire for absolute control over the individual, and more globally over the whole of society and the whole world; in contrast to shamans and other tribal witchdoctors who have no plans for global conquest and whose practices only touch or affect their own community.

Witchdoctors have understood the advantage of using this mind science to manipulate programmed, amnesiac and loyal individuals. MK-Ultra mental programming is a perverse deviation from the ancient practice of training a shaman. Through sensory isolation, torture, drugs, hypnosis, electric shocks and sexual trauma, the subject becomes both amnesiac and totally enslaved. He or she may be programmed for one function or another; functions in which his or her physical and intellectual capacities will be far above average. During this traumatic process, he or she may also have developed paranormal psychic abilities such as mediumship and remote viewing (discussed in Chapter 6).

It is only recently that mind control has been modernised to become a science in its own right. Thousands of non-consenting human guinea pigs have been and still are subjected to such experiments. It is a real science, a psychic and spiritual surgery that does a lot of damage.

4 - SACRIFICIAL RITUALS IN THE OLD TESTAMENT

The Bible tells us that sacrificial rituals were a common practice in the pagan nations of the Old Testament. The Bible calls this type of ritual *'passing through the fire'* (Jeremiah 32:35, Leviticus 18:21, 2 Kings 23:10). This ritual of sacrificing children to fire is cited by Moses when he declared the list of laws against sexual crimes: *"Thou shalt not deliver up any of thy seed to be burned in the fire to Moloch"* (Leviticus 18:21).

Moloch is a demonic entity represented as a horned beast, an idol in the form of a bull or a giant goat. The Bible did not include these child sacrifice rituals in the list of sexual crimes for nothing. Modern satanic ritual abuse of child sacrifice also involves rape and sexual orgies. Here are some passages from the Bible relating to child sacrifices as offerings to demons:

> Whoever among the Israelites or among the immigrants who stay in Israel delivers to Moloch one of his descendants, shall be punished by death. (*Leviticus* 20:2).

> You shall not do so to the LORD your God, for they did all kinds of evil to their gods, which are hateful to the LORD, and they burned their sons and daughters in the fire to honour their gods. (*Deuteronomy* 12:31)

> Those of Avva made Nibhaz and Tartak; those of Sepharvaim burnt their sons with fire in honour of Adrammelech and Anammelech, gods of Sepharvaim. (2 *Kings* 17:31)

> They mingled with the nations and learned (to imitate their works),
> They worshiped their idols,
> Which were a trap for them,
> They sacrificed their sons and daughters to the demons,
> They shed innocent blood,
> The blood of their sons and daughters,
> That they sacrificed to the idols of Canaan,
> And the land was desecrated by murder,
> They prostituted themselves by their actions.
> (*Psalm* 106:35-39)

Who are you laughing at?
Against whom do you open your mouth wide and stick out your tongue?
Aren't you children in revolt?
A rabble full of falsehoods,
Burning near the terebinths,
Under any green tree,
Slashing children's throats in the ravines,
Under cracks in the rocks?
(*Isaiah* 57:4-5)

They built high places in Topheth,
In the Ben-Hinnom valley,
To burn their sons and daughters in the fire:
What I had not ordered,
This had not occurred to me.
(*Jeremiah* 7:31)

For they have abandoned me,
They have made this place unrecognisable,
There they offered incense to other gods,
Which neither they nor their fathers nor the kings of Judah knew,
And they filled this place with the blood of the innocent,
They built high places for Baal,
To burn their sons in the fire to Baal:
What I had not ordered,
What I had not mentioned,
This had not occurred to me.
(*Jeremiah* 19:4-5)

You have taken your sons and daughters, whom you bore to me, and sacrificed them to be devoured by them! Was it not enough of your whoredoms?
You slaughtered my sons and gave them away, making them pass through the fire in their honour.
(*Ezekiel* 16:20-21)

I defiled them with their gifts, when they made all their elders pass through the fire; so I wanted to plunge them into desolation and make them acknowledge that I am the LORD.
(*Ezekiel* 20:26)

The Lord said to me:
Son of a man,
Will you judge Oholah and Oholiba?
Describe their horrors to them,
For they have committed adultery,
And there is blood on their hands:
They have committed adultery with their idols;
Moreover, their sons whom they had borne to me,

They put them through the fire for them,
So that they are devoured.
Here is what they did to me:
They have defiled my sanctuary in the same day,
And have profaned my Sabbaths.
While immolating their sons to their idols,
They went to my shrine on the same day,
To desecrate it.
This is what they did in the middle of my house.
(*Ezekiel* 23:36-39)

You hate the good
And you love evil,
You take the skin and flesh off the bones.
They devour the flesh of my people,
Tear off his skin
And they break his bones.
And they put the pieces
Like (what is cooked) in a pot,
Like meat in a pot.
Then they will cry out to the Lord,
But he will not answer them;
He will hide his face from them at that time,
Because they have committed evil deeds.
(*Micah* 3:2-4)

You have the devil for a father, and you want to do your father's bidding. He was a murderer from the beginning, and he did not stand in the truth, because the truth is not in him. When he speaks a lie, his words come from himself, for he is a liar and the father of lies.
(*John* 8:44)

CHAPTER 3

THE MK-ULTRA PROGRAMME

"Mk-Ultra was designed with many sub-projects to develop the perfect soldier, the perfect spy. What I was told was that it was to serve our National Security more than any soldier or diplomat ever could... Nobody told me they were being used for drug trafficking and prostitution. No one told me they were being used as a breeding ground to supply children to sheikhs and world leaders. No one told me that we were using them for money laundering operations." Mark Philipps - *Mind-Control Out of Control* Conference, 31 October 1996.

1 - BRIEF HISTORY

During the "Cold War", the arms race included research on war materials but also on mind control and behaviour modification. The aim was to manipulate, alter and control the consciousness and behaviour of targeted individuals or groups. Following the war, both the US and the USSR considered this area of research to be of obvious military interest, and the development of these 'non-lethal weapons' (including psycho-electronic weapons) was quietly implemented in US and Soviet military and intelligence experimentation programmes, all under strict secrecy.

The forerunners of scientific experiments on mind control were the Nazis. In Nazism, there is the notion of "ideological warfare" to impose their ideology on the countries they occupied. The Americans took this doctrine and called it "psychological warfare". Psychological warfare is *"the use of propaganda or other mind control techniques to influence or confuse thought, or to subvert morality"* (*Webster's New World Dictionary*). This post-war psychological struggle was aimed at transforming the minds of populations, from the individual to the global scale. This is what we saw in Chapter 1 with social engineering/psychiatry.

The roots of the MK-Ultra programme go back to Nazi Germany. Adolf Hitler had indeed detected a certain satanic 'culture' in Northern European families steeped in transgenerational incest. Families that systematically practised ritual abuse of their offspring, practices that involved physical and psychological torture. The Nazis understood that the victims of such childhood abuse developed certain dissociative features that made them totally susceptible to "robotic" mind control. During the Second World War, the Nazis therefore experimented with drugs, hypnosis, trauma and various chemicals on concentration camp inmates as part of their research into mental and behavioural control. Following the war, in Operation *Paperclip* (made public in 1973), many Nazi scientists, including psychiatrists, were secretly brought back to the American continent and then infiltrated into the military, academic and private sectors for all kinds of scientific research, including psychiatry and government projects on mental programming. It was clear to the Americans that if they did not bring these scientists home, then their enemy, the Soviet Union, would use them. Major General Hugh Knerr, Deputy Commander of the US Air Force in Europe, wrote: *"The discovery and occupation of German scientific and industrial establishments has revealed that we are alarmingly behind in many areas of research. If we do not seize the opportunity to get the equipment and the brains that developed it back to work as soon as possible, we will be several years behind before we reach a level that is already being exploited."*[179]

In August 1945, President Truman approved Project *Paperclip* to transfer Hitler's best scientists to the United States. In November 1945, the first Nazi scientists arrived on American soil. From the beginning of the 1950s, the CIA and the American army conducted their own mind control programmes, codenamed *Chatter, Bluebird, Artichoke, MK-Often, MK-Ultra* and then *MK-Search, MK-Naomi, MK-Delta, Monarch...*

In 1977, the New York Times published a CIA directive on the objectives of Project Artichoke, launched in 1951: "To evolve and develop any method by which we can obtain information from a person against his will and without his knowledge (...) Can we gain control of an individual to the point where he will accomplish our objectives against his will and even against the basic laws of nature such as self-preservation?"[180]

Following on from Operation Paperclip, the MK-Ultra project, led by Sydney Gottlieb, was launched on 13 April 1953 by the then CIA Director, Allan Dulles. With an initial budget of $300,000, or 6% of the CIA's annual research budget, it was a major study programme. Over the next decade, US taxpayers gave more than $25 million to the classified MK-Ultra programme.[181] During this period many sub-projects focused on human mind control were initiated. Like Project Bluebird and Artichoke, the existence of MK-Ultra was known to very few people, and the US Congress itself was completely in the dark about this type of research. The MK-Ultra programme was conducted in 80 institutions including prestigious universities and hospitals, but also penal institutions. Examples include Princeton, Harvard, Yale, Columbia, Stanford, Baylor, Georgetown University Hospital, Boston Psychopathic Hospital, Mt Sinai Hospital...

Many scientists participated in this research, including James Hamilton, Louis Jolyon West, William Sargant, Ewen Cameron, Leonard Rubenstein, John Gittinger, Robert Heath, William Sweat, Harold Wolff, Lawrence Hinkle, Carl

---

[179] Project Paperclip: Dark side of the Moon " - Andrew Walker, BBC News.

[180] "Private Institutions Used in CIA Efforts to Control Behavior" - New York Times, 02/081977.

[181] "A Question of Torture: CIA interrogation, From the Cold War to the War on Terror - Alfred W. McCoy, 2006.

Pfeiffer, Harold Abramson, Martin Orme, Jose Delgado and many others... The four CIA directors who succeeded each other during the period of activity of the MK-Ultra and MK-Search programme were Allen W. Dulles, John A. McCone, William F. Raborn and Richard Helms.

This mind control research officially ended in the early 1970s. Most of the files were voluntarily destroyed in 1973 on the orders of Richard Helms, who explained his action in 1975: *"There were relationships in this programme with foreign scientists who were sensitive to this sort of thing, so when the project ended we thought that if we got rid of the files it would save all those who had helped us from embarrassing harassment..."* [182]

Richard Helms not only admitted that he had destroyed the files but also admitted that foreign scientists had been conducting mind control studies without having any idea that they were involved in the MK-Ultra programme by contract. Helms was determined to protect them and keep their identities secret, certainly because of the immoral nature of these psychiatric experiments.

Despite this, some documents have been preserved and testimony in the US Senate has subsequently made public the techniques that were used on hundreds, if not thousands, of non-consenting humans. Mind control' was induced by drugs, electroshock, overstimulation or sensory deprivation, hypnosis, ultrasound, radiation, psychosurgery including implants, and various extreme traumas designed to create dissociation and a veritable *tabula rasa* in the victims. This type of MK programme had three goals:

1/ Inducing hypnosis very quickly in an involuntary subject

2/ Creating lasting amnesia

3/ Implementing functional post-hypnotic suggestions in a sustainable way

One of the purposes of this research was to create *Manchurian Candidates*. This is an individual who has been brainwashed and programmed to kill with amnesia once the operation is complete. Dr. Colin Ross, a Canadian psychiatrist and former president of the *International Society for the Study of Dissociation* wrote in his book *"Bluebird"*[183]:

The main objective of the Cold War mind control programmes was to deliberately create dissociative disorders, including multiple personality disorder. The Manchurian Candidate was created, not fiction. It was created by the CIA in the 1950s as part of operations Bluebird and Artichoke (...) In order to understand these "super-spy" experiments, you have to put them into their social and historical context. This was a time when mind control experiments were ubiquitous and systematic. It was not a matter of a few isolated 'mad scientists', but of the leaders of psychiatric institutions and major medical schools (...) According to my definition, the Manchurian Candidate is an

---

[182] Advisory Committee on Human Radiation Experiments: Interim Report" - Church Committee, Book I.

[183] Bluebird: The Deliberate Creation of Multiple Personality by Psychiatrists " - Colin A. Ross, 2000, chap.4

individual with an experimentally created dissociative identity disorder who meets the following four criteria:

1/ It is deliberately created.
2/ A new identity is implanted in him.
3/ Amnesic barriers are created.
4/ It is used in real or simulated operations.

A declassified CIA document entitled *"Hypnotic Experimentation and Reasearch, 10 February 1954"* describes a simulation related to research on Manchu Candidates. The experiment proves that it is possible to program an individual into an undetectable assassin who is totally unaware of his actions:

"Miss X has been instructed (She has previously expressed her fear of firearms) to use all means at her disposal to wake Miss Y (kept in a deep hypnotic sleep). If she fails to do so, she may take the nearby gun and fire it at Miss Y. She has been programmed to be so angry that she would not hesitate to kill Y for failing to wake her up. Miss X followed the instructions to the letter, including firing (unloaded gun) at Y, only to fall into a deep sleep herself. After some appropriate suggestions, both were awakened. Miss X expressed total denial of what had just happened (i.e. she had amnesia). " (CIA Mori ID 190691, 2/10/54)

This work on human mental and behavioural control also led to the writing of a confidential document of mind control and psychological torture codenamed *"Kubark"*. Written in 1963, it was made public in 1997 when journalists from the *Baltimore Sun* obtained its declassification in the name of freedom of information. The 128-page document was presented as an interrogation manual for counter-intelligence.

People who suffer from mental illnesses make good subjects for these experiments because they are often disenfranchised and it is easy to discredit them afterwards by blaming their testimony on their illness. Karen Wetmore is one such victim of the MK-Ultra programme and author of the book *"Surviving Evil: CIA Mind-Control Experiments in Vermont"*.

As a teenager in the early 1970s, she was committed for "schizophrenia" to a psychiatric hospital in Vermont. A long stay from which she has only fragmented memories. It was not until adulthood that she was diagnosed with dissociative identity disorder, a personality disorder that was most likely reinforced by her mind control experiments.

In 1995, a psychologist advised her to consult her medical file to find out what exactly had happened in the psychiatric hospital. She discovered that she had been subjected to a very strange treatment, which she described as *"psychological rape"*. When she researched the doctors who were treating her, she discovered a Dr. Robert W. Hyde who was regularly mentioned in her file. On further investigation she discovered that this doctor was connected to Sydney Gottlieb, one of the leaders of the MK-Ultra programme. According to psychiatrist Colin Ross, who investigated Karen Wetmore's case, she could have been selected because she already suffered from a dissociative disorder due to repeated sexual abuse as a child. According to Ross, the MK-Ultra scientists were interested in reactions to programmed stimuli with, for example, keywords, codes to create a trigger. A person with dissociative identity disorder already has multiple personalities, so it's easier to make them a killer who responds to orders without discussion than it is with a non-fractional person. In studying Karen Wetmore's file, Ross discovered that doctors had given her pentylenetetrazole, a drug used by the Soviets for interrogation and brainwashing. In addition, her medical records show that she received dozens of consecutive electroshock treatments in a single session. Several psychiatrists have shown that electroshock can lead to amnesia. Dr. Ross believes that there was no justification for such treatment of Karen Wetmore, that CIA doctors gave her electroshock therapy to erase her memory and that it is very likely that she was subjected to a mind control programme. He came to this conclusion by looking at the treatment she had undergone, i.e. the type of drugs she had been given, the systematic and repetitive electroshock sessions, but also by the diagnoses that were made by the doctors who followed her at the time.

An internal CIA document[184] from 1955 lists methods used in MK programs:

- Substances that cause illogical thinking and impulsivity to the point that the subject will discredit himself publicly.
- Substances that increase mental capacity and perception.
- Materials that prevent or counteract the toxic effects of alcohol.
- Materials that increase the toxic effects of alcohol.
- Materials that produce the signs and symptoms of known diseases in a reversible manner, and can thus be used to simulate them.
- Materials that increase the effectiveness of hypnosis.
- Substances that enhance an individual's ability to withstand deprivation, torture and coercion during interrogation or brainwashing.
- Physical materials and methods that produce amnesia of events occurring before and during their use.
- Physical methods to produce shock and confusion over long periods of time that can be used stealthily.
- Substances causing physical disabilities such as paralysis of the legs, acute anaemia, priapism.
- Substances causing a 'pure' euphoria, without 're-descent'.
- Substances that alter the personality in such a way that the subject will tend to become dependent on another person.
- Materials that cause such mental confusion that the individual will have difficulty sustaining a fabricated story under questioning.
- Substances that lower the subject's ambition and overall effectiveness even when administered in undetectable amounts.
- Substances that cause visual or auditory weakness and distortion, preferably without permanent effects.
- A knockout pill that can be administered surreptitiously in food, drink, cigarettes, or as an aerosol that can be used safely, causing maximum

---

[184] Senate MK-Ultra Hearing: Appendix C - Documents Referring to subprojects, Senate Select Committee on Intelligence and Committee on Human Resources.

amnesia, and which may be suitable for certain types of agents on an *ad hoc* basis.

- Materials that can be administered surreptitiously through the upper respiratory tract, and which in very small quantities make physical activity impossible.

Thanks to these experiments, the American intelligence services were able to make a general survey of the various techniques and technologies intended to modify the human psyche and behaviour. Subsequently, research quickly turned to the study of the brain's electrical and radioelectric activity for the design of electromagnetic weapons, known as 'psychotronic'. The report of the Groupe de Recherche sur la Paix et la Sécurité (GRIP) entitled *"Les armes non-létales: une nouvelle course aux armements"* (Luc Mampaey, GRIP 1999), defined behavioural altering devices as follows: *"the objective of these weapon systems is to interfere with the biological and/or psychological processes of the human organism, by subjecting it to physical, chemical, electromagnetic stimuli or "morphing" techniques, without the intention of causing death, but with the aim of inducing a certain behaviour, altering mental faculties or influencing memory."*

The *New York Times* publicly revealed these MK programmes in August 1977. The article in question contained, among other things, the following excerpt from a 1950 memorandum about the recruitment of psychiatrists to conduct the experiments: *"A candidate's ethics might be such that he would not wish to participate in some of the more revolutionary phases of our project (...) In 1963, an Inspector General's report apparently resulted in the termination of a program, it stated that the concepts involved in the manipulation of human behavior are considered by many people, both inside and outside the agency, to be repugnant and unethical."*[185]

The following is an extract from the report on MK-Ultra by Inspector General John S. Earman: "Research into the manipulation of human behaviour is considered by many medical authorities and related fields to be professionally unethical, and for this reason the reputation of professionals participating in the MK-Ultra programme may be at risk. Some of these activities raise questions of legality and ethics. Examination of MK-Ultra programmes reveals that the rights and interests of US citizens are impacted. Public disclosure of certain aspects of the MK-Ultra programme could induce a strong negative reaction in American public opinion."[186]

Senator Ted Kennedy stated on August 3, 1977 before the Intelligence Committee, Subcommittee on Health, Research Branch of the Human Resources Committee: *"The Deputy Director of the CIA revealed that more than thirty universities and institutions had been involved in a large-scale experimentation project that included drug testing on non-voluntary subjects from all walks of life, high and low, American and foreign. Many of these tests involved administering LSD to non-consenting subjects in various social situations. At*

---

[185] "Private Institutions Used in CIA Efforts to Control Behavior" - New York Times, 02/08/1977.

[186] American Torture: From the Cold War to Abu Ghraib and Beyond " - Michael Otterman, 2007.

least one death was recorded, that of Dr. Frank Olson. A death that was caused by these activities. The Agency itself acknowledged that these experiments had no scientific value. The agents doing the monitoring were not competent scientists."

Dr. Frank Olson was a scientist who worked for the *US Army* in a top secret division at *Fort Detrick* in Frederick, Maryland. Olson died under suspicious circumstances in New York (see the documentary *Project Artichoke: Secret CIA Experiments*). His research for the military is not well known, but he worked on biological weapons and mind control through drug use.

All this mind control research went much further than Senator Kennedy stated above, as did the then CIA Director Stanfield Turner, who described MK-Ultra as a mere drug experimentation programme. He told the Senate on 21 September 1977: *"We are not in a position to tell you the full facts about these activities, we are just going to tell you what we know. The files we have studied tell only a small part of the whole story."*

The MK-Ultra programme and its sub-projects are therefore a real puzzle whose pieces have been destroyed or dispersed. Moreover, the CIA had established a network of "front" companies such as the *Society for the Investigation of Human Ecology*, the *Washington Geschikter Fund Medical Research* and the *Josiah Macy Jr. Foundation*. This division into a multitude of different projects made it possible to discreetly finance the MK-Ultra programme, thus compartmentalising the projects, but also the researchers. Indeed, these scientists were often unaware of the identity of their real employer as well as the numerous research projects in progress, which were apparently unrelated but formed a single framework. All of this forms the pieces of a gigantic jigsaw puzzle of which only the sponsors have the assembly plan. The methods of compartmentalisation of these *'black projects'* are still in use: each individual in the network receives only what is *'good to know'*, i.e. he will only have access to what he needs to know to do his *'job'*. They remain totally unaware of the globality of the project(s), receiving only what is strictly necessary in terms of information for the work they are doing at their level.

In 1977, freelance journalist John Marks requested access to all documents from the Office of Research and Development (ORD) of the CIA's Directorate of Science and Technology (a specialised Agency office) concerning *"any research or operational activity related to bioelectricity, electrical or radio stimulation of the brain, electronic destruction of memory, stereotactic surgery, psychosurgery, hypnosis, parapsychology, radiation, microwaves, and ultrasound."* He was informed six months later that ORD had identified 130 boxes, or about 39 cubic metres of material. John Marks had obtained under the Freedom of Information Act the declassification of a thousand secret CIA documents. It was he who publicly revealed the appalling scale of these MK programmes by publishing his research in 1979 in the book *"The Search of the Manchurian Candidate"*. His access to CIA documents was abruptly stopped after the publication of his book in 1979.

Victor Marchetti, a former CIA agent who worked for 14 years for the agency, has stated in interviews that contrary to its propaganda claims, the CIA continues its research into mind control. Marchetti published a book with John Marks entitled *"The CIA and the Cult of Intelligence"* (1973). Before the book was published, the CIA sued Marchetti to remove 340 items from his book, and the author objected, resulting in 110 items being censored. This is the first book that the US federal government has had legally censored. Nevertheless, the publication was instrumental in setting up the first *Church Committee* enquiry into the MK-Ultra project in the US Congress in 1975.

In 1999, following a *FOIA* request, Carol Rutz received three CD-ROMs from the CIA.

Carol Rutz is a survivor of these MK programs, at the age of 52 she finally got the concrete evidence of all these experiments. For her, this was finally confirmation and validation of her memoirs about the mind control experiments. These files had remained for 48 years in government *vaults*, 18,000 pages of declassified documents concerning the Bluebird, Artichoke and MK-Ultra programmes. One of these documents states: *"In working with individual subjects, particular attention will be paid to dissociative states that tend to accompany ESP (electronic brain stimulation) spontaneously. These states can be induced and controlled to some extent with hypnosis and drugs... Data for this study will be obtained from particular groups of individuals, such as psychotics, children and psychics... The researchers will be particularly interested in the dissociative states, the 'lowering of the mental level', the 'loss of the soul', the multiple personality of those called mediums; and an attempt will be made to induce a number of altered states of consciousness using hypnosis.* (CIA MORI ID 17396, p.18)[187]

Declassified CIA documents clearly show the objectives of these mind control experiments: the creation of MK subjects with multiple personalities and with amnesia walls allowing them to do anything and everything... Here is an extract from a document dated 7 January 1953 which describes how two disassociated girls get programmed: *"These subjects have clearly demonstrated that they can go from a fully awake state to a deep hypnotic (H) state triggered by a telephone, by a question, by the use of a code, a signal or words. This hypnotic control can be transmitted without great difficulty. It has also been shown through experimentation with these girls that they can act as unwitting messengers for intelligence purposes.* (CIA Mori ID 190684, 1/7/53)

The document entitled "SI and H Experimentation, September 25, 1951" (SI standing for Sleep Induction and H for Hypnosis) reports: "X has been instructed that when she awakens she is to go to such and such a room where she will wait in the office for a telephone call. When the phone rings, a person named "Jim" will engage in a basic conversation with her. During the conversation, this individual will mention a code name. When she hears this code name, she will go into an IS trance state, but she will not close her eyes and will remain perfectly normal to continue the telephone conversation. X is instructed that following this phone call she should follow the following protocol: X, who is at that moment

---

[187] A Nation Betrayed: The Chilling True Story of Secret Cold War Experiments Performed on Our Children and Other Innocent People" - Carol Rutz, 2001.

in a deep SI state, is brought into the presence of a device with a timer. She is informed that this device is an incendiary bomb (...) Following the telephone conversation, she is then programmed to take this bomb which is in a briefcase, then to go to the toilet where she will meet a woman who is unknown to her and who will identify herself by the code name "New-York". X then shows this person how the device works and tells her that it must be taken to such and such a room and placed in the left-hand drawer of the desk, all within the 82 seconds set on the device's timer. X is further instructed to tell this girl that as soon as the device is placed and activated, she is to retrieve the case, leave the room and go and lie on the couch in the operating room and fall into a deep sleep. X is also programmed to return to the operating room and also fall into a deep sleep after giving instructions to the other girl (...) The experiment was carried out perfectly without any difficulty or hesitation on the part of the girls. Each acted appropriately, the device was placed correctly and both girls returned to the operating room to fall into a deep sleep. Throughout the experiment, their attitude was natural, there was no difficulty in movement. (CIA Mori ID 190527 9/25/51)

Another internal document describes the excesses of this kind of experimentation: "On July 2, 1951 at about 1 p.m., instruction began with X concerning his studies on sexuality. X stated that he had constantly used hypnosis as a means of inducing young girls to have sex with him. Y, a musical artist, was forced to have sex with X under the influence of hypnosis. X stated that he first put her in a hypnotic trance and then suggested that he was her husband and that she wanted to have sex with him. (CIA Mori ID 140393 7/2/51)

On 3 October 1995, faced with the accumulation of disturbing revelations about all these mind control experiments, Bill Clinton, then President, had to make a public apology to his nation: *Thousands of government experiments took place in hospitals and universities and on military bases across the country... In too many cases, no formal consent was sought, Americans were concealed from what they were being subjected to, and far beyond the test subjects themselves, this deception fooled their families and the entire nation. These experiments were kept secret and concealed not for security reasons but for fear of scandal, and this is abnormal. So today, on behalf of a new generation of American leaders and citizens, the United States of America sincerely apologizes to the citizens who were victims of these experiments, and to their families and loved ones.*[188]

It is clear that Bill Clinton was forced to make a public apology because the MK-Ultra dossier had been publicly revealed, an apology of a monstrous hypocrisy because these mind control programmes have never really stopped, on the contrary they have never stopped progressing like an arms race.

In the United States, the subject of mind control is now untouchable and unassailable because it is buried under *the National Security Act* of 1947. This *National* Security Act allows for the removal of any truly disturbing case from the public record, so that it cannot be tried in a fair manner like any other case.

---

[188] "A village poisoned by the CIA? Pont Saint-Esprit 1951" - France 3, 08/07/2015.

The case of Cathy O'Brien (a victim of the MK-Monarch programme) fully demonstrates how the *National Security Act* systematically cuts off any attempt to bring a case to court for harm (the word is weak) related to mind control, despite all the evidence. (More on this in Chapter 10)

2 - CHILD VICTIMS OF MK-ULTRA: TESTIMONIES

In 1995, Christine DeNicola, Claudia Mullen and therapist Valerie Wolf testified before a US Presidential Advisory Commission. Christine DeNicola was a guinea pig in the MK-Ultra programme from the age of 4, from 1966 to 1976. Claudia Mullen was subjected to mind control at the age of 7, from 1957 to 1984. Valerie Wolf told this Commission that about 40 therapists had contacted her when they heard she was going to testify publicly, wanting to talk to her about some of their patients who had also been subjected to radiation and mind control techniques. All these testimonies point to the close correlation between mental programming and all sorts of traumatic techniques, from electroshock to sexual abuse, hypnosis and hallucinogenic drugs. There are almost no publications about mental programming on children, but four MK-Ultra subprojects were specifically targeted at them. Children who were officially treated for dissociative disorders but who ended up being victims of traumas aimed at making them even more dissociated and fragmented, and therefore more easily programmable.

Here are the transcripts of the testimonies before the Presidential Advisory Commission involving the deliberate irradiation of human beings. Testimony that was filmed in 1995:

- **Valerie Wolf** (therapist):
I have listened to all the previous testimonies and they sound very familiar. I'm here to talk about the possible link between the radiation these victims were subjected to and mental programming (...) The doctors who exposed them to radiation and administered chemicals were the same ones who were doing research on mental programming (...) It is important to understand that mind control techniques may have been used to intimidate the subjects, even as adults, to prevent them from speaking out and revealing that they were victims of these government-funded research programs. I have been a therapist for 22 years. I have specialised in treating the victims of these programmes, and even some of their perpetrators, and their families (...) We are now seeing former victims all over the country who have no contact with each other (...) many of these survivors are afraid to tell their stories to their doctors, because they fear they will be thought of as crazy. Many of them named the same people, like Dr. Green, who many accused of torturing and raping children during mental programming experiments. One of my patients even managed to find out that his name was Dr. L. Wilson Green. We discovered that one of the Scientific Directors of the Army Chemical and Radiological Laboratories had this name. Also included are the names of Dr. Sidney Gottlieb and Dr. Martin Orne who

were also involved in the radiological research (...) We often tried to obtain information under the Freedom of Information Act, in order to gain access to the data concerning mental programming. In general, our requests were rejected, but we were able to obtain some information that confirmed what our patients had told us (...) We need access to these archives to enable the rehabilitation and treatment of the many victims who have serious psychological and physical disorders (...) It is true that a Commission was appointed in the late 1970s to investigate mental programming, but it was not interested in experiments on children. At that time, these children were too young to talk about it, some were still being experimented on. The only way to put an end to the suffering of all these victims is to make public everything that happened during the mind control research. Please recommend that an investigation be launched and that all records of mind control experiments on children be made public. Thank you.

- **Christine DeNicola** (victim):
My parents divorced in 1966. My father, Donald Richard Ebner, was associated with Dr Green's work. I was subjected to these experiments between 1966 and 1976. As far as radiation is concerned, in 1970 Dr. Green concentrated his experiments on my neck, throat and chest, and then on my uterus in 1975. Each time I felt dizzy, nauseous, and vomited. All these experiences were always associated with mental programming. This was in Tucson, Arizona. Dr. Green used me primarily as a guinea pig for mental programming between 1966 and 1973. His goal was to mentally control me to train me as a spy and assassin.

My earliest significant memories are from 1966 when I was driven to Kansas City University. My father flew me there at a time when my mother was away. He took me to a place that looked like a laboratory. I think there were other children there. I was stripped naked and strapped to a table, lying on my back. Dr Green placed electrodes on my body and on my head. He was using a kind of projector. While a flash of red light was directed at my forehead, he kept telling me that he was implanting different images in my brain. Between each sequence, he would give me electric shocks and ask me to go deeper and deeper into my brain, into my mind. He would repeat each sentence several times, telling me that it was going deep into my brain and that I had to obey whatever he asked me to do. I remember that he gave me a shot at the beginning of the session and I felt drugged. When it was all over, he gave me another injection. Then I remember that I ended up at my grandparents' house in Tucson. I was four years old. This experience shows you that Dr. Green was using drugs, trauma, hypnotic suggestions, and all kinds of other trauma, to try to control my brain and my intelligence. He used radiation to study its effects on various parts of my body, and also to terrorise me. It was part of his trauma toolkit to program me mentally.

The other experiments were done in Tucson, Arizona, somewhere in the desert. I was taught how to open locks, how to camouflage myself, how to use my photographic memory and how to use certain digital techniques to develop my memory. Dr Green made me 'kill' dolls that looked like real children. Once, after being severely traumatised, I stabbed a doll. But the next time I refused. He knew many techniques to make me suffer, but as I grew older I became more and more rebellious (...) Because of my increasing lack of cooperation, they finally abandoned their plan to make me a spy and an assassin. Therefore, during the years 1974 to 1976, Dr. Green used various techniques to remove my assassin programming and to inject me with self-destruction, suicide and death programming. For what reason? He simply wanted me to die. Throughout my adult life, I have struggled to stay alive. If I am still alive, I believe I owe it to the grace of God. These terrible experiences have deeply affected my life. My personality fragmented into a dissociative identity disorder. Dr. Green's goal was to fragment my personality as much as possible so that he could control me completely. He failed! But I have been in constant physical, mental and emotional pain for years. I have been in regular therapy for 12 years. It was only 2.5 years ago, when I met my current therapist, who knew about mental programming experiments, that I finally started to make real progress and began to heal. In conclusion, I ask you to bear in mind that the memories I have mentioned are only a small part of all that I experienced between 1966 and 1976 (...) I know that other people can also be helped, provided they are given the help they need. Please help us in our efforts to ensure that these heinous acts never happen again. Thank you.

- **Claudia Mullen** (victim):

Between 1957 and 1984, I was a toy in the hands of the government. Its ultimate goal was to program me mentally to become a perfect spy. This was achieved through the use of chemicals, radiation, drugs, hypnosis, electroshock, sensory isolation, sleep deprivation, brainwashing, and verbal, physical, emotional and sexual abuse. I was exploited against my will for almost 30 years. The only explanations I was given were that 'the end justifies the means' and that 'I was serving my country in its relentless fight against communism'. To sum up my life, I would say that they took a 7 year old girl, already traumatised by sexual abuse, and continued to make her suffer in ways that are beyond imagination. The sad thing is that I knew I was not the only one being treated this way. There were countless other children in the same situation. So far no one has been able to help us.

I have already provided you with a written report in which I have included as much information as possible, including conversations that I was able to overhear in a number of official departments responsible for these atrocities. I was able to describe all this in such detail because of my photographic memory, but also because of the arrogance of the people involved. They were sure that they could always control my brain. Remembering these atrocities is not an easy thing to do, and it is not safe for my family and myself. But I think it is worth the risk. Dr Green once explained to Dr Charles Brown that he preferred to choose children as subjects for his experiments, because it was more fun to work with them, and also cheaper. He needed subjects who were easier to handle than military or government officials. So he chose to use only 'willing girls'. He added: "Besides, I like to terrorise them. At the CIA, they think I'm like a god who can create subjects through his experiments who will obey anything Sid (Dr Sidney Gottlieb) and James (Dr James Hamilton) can think of without question."

In 1958 they told me that I had to be 'tested' by a number of important doctors of the Human Ecology Society. I was asked to cooperate with them. I was not to try to look at their faces, nor was I to try to find out their names, as this was a very secret project. They told me this to help me forget everything. Naturally, as all children do in such cases, I did the opposite, and tried to remember everything. A man named John Gittinger tested me. Dr. Cameron gave me electric shocks, and Dr. Green gave me X-rays. Then Sidney Gottlieb told me I was "ready for the big A". He wanted to talk about the Artichoke programme. When I got home, I could only remember the reasons given by Dr. Robert G. Heath of Tulane Medical School for all the marks on my body: bruises, puncture marks, burns and pain in my genitals. I had no reason to believe that any of this had been caused by anything other than what Heath had explained to me. They had already started to control my brain.

The following year, I was sent to a camp in Maryland called Deep Creek Cabins. There I was taught how to satisfy men's sexual desires. I was also taught how to force them to talk about themselves. There was Richard Helms, the Deputy Director of the CIA, Dr. Gottlieb, Captain George White, and Morris Allan. They planned to recruit as many high ranking officials and university presidents as possible so that their projects could continue, even in the event that funding for mental programming and radiation experiments were ever cut. I was used to trap all sorts of unsuspecting men using a hidden camera. I was only nine years old when I was subjected to all this sexual humiliation. One day I overheard a conversation about the ORD (Office of Research and Development). This office was run by Dr. Green and Drs. Steven Aldrich, Martin Orne and Morris Allan. Dr. Gottlieb made a rather cynical remark about a leaked report of a rather large group of mentally retarded children who had been subjected to massive doses of radiation. He had asked Dr Green why he was so concerned about these retarded children: "After all, they're certainly not the ones who are going to spill the beans! On another occasion I heard Dr Martin Orne, who headed the Scientific Office and later the Institute of Experimental Research, say that "to continue to receive funding for their projects, their experiments had to use even more coercive means, even blackmail. He added: "We have to go faster, and then get rid of the subjects, so that they don't come back later to ask us about what happened. I could tell you a lot more about these government-funded research projects: the names of the projects and sub-projects, the names of the people involved in the experiments, the locations, the nature of the tests and the different ways in which the subjects were made to suffer (...) I would so much rather that everything we went through was just a dream to be quickly forgotten. But to forget would be a tragic mistake, it would also be a lie.

These were real atrocities that I and so many other children suffered under the pretext of defending our country. Due to the accumulation of harmful effects of radiation, drugs, various chemicals, suffering, mental and physical trauma, I was deprived of the ability to work normally and even to have children. It is obvious that these experiences were not justified in any way. They should never have been allowed in the first place. Our only way to reveal and bring to light the horrible truth is to make public any records that may still exist regarding these projects, through the appointment of a new Presidential Commission to investigate mental programming. I believe that all citizens of our nation have a right to know how much of this is fact and how much is fiction. Our greatest protection is that this never happens again. In conclusion, I can only offer you what I have offered you today: the truth. Thank you for taking the time to listen to me.

- **Dr. Duncan C. Thomas** (Professor at the University of Southern California, School of Medicine, Department of Preventive Medicine, Los Angeles):
Can I ask you what your parents were doing in all this? Do you have any idea how you were recruited for these experiments? Did you have parents? Did your parents know what was going on?

- **Christine DeNicola**:
I can answer you briefly. It was my father who worked with Dr Green. My mother didn't know about it, because my parents divorced when I was four (...) As far as I'm concerned, it was my father who "delivered" me for the experiments. He took care of me when I was very young. He started abusing me sexually very early on. He voluntarily put me in the hands of Dr. Green, but my mother didn't know about it.

- **Claudia Mullen**:
As for me, I was adopted at the age of two and a half by a woman who sexually abused me. At that time, she was a friend of the President of Tulane University. At a very young age, I began to show the symptoms of a sexually abused child, including dissociation of my personality. So she asked the President of Tulane University to recommend a child psychiatrist. He recommended Dr. Heath, who was involved in this research (MK). I remember very well all the personality tests he gave me. That's how I was recruited for these experiments. My father had no idea. He died when I was very young. I don't know if my mother really knew. To tell you the truth, I don't think she cared much. She died when I was a teenager. Afterwards, because I was an orphan, they could use me more easily.[189]

In her book *A Nation Betrayed: The Chilling True Story of Secret Cold War Experiments Performed On Our Children and other Innocent People* Carol Rutz testifies:
In my family, paedophilia was passed on from generation to generation. I was still in nappies when my father started abusing me. It was at the age of two that my mind split in order to deal with the trauma of my father's and other family members' continued abuse (...) I was 'sold' by my grandfather to the CIA in 1952. Over the next twelve years, I was subjected to various experiments and

---

[189] Translation by "Parole de Vie" - Series "Survivors of the Illuminati

training: Electroconvulsions, drugs, hypnosis, sensory deprivation and other types of trauma to condition and split my personality to make me perform specific tasks. Each alter personality was created to activate with a post-hypnotic trigger and perform something that would later be forgotten. This "Manchurian Candidate" programming was just one of the possible uses of the CIA's vast mind control program, funded by your hard earned tax dollars...

I was told I was working for 'The Agency'. It was actually elites from the CIA and other branches of government working in collusion with some extremely wealthy individuals who wanted to shape the world while remaining in the shadows (...)

I too was subjected to Dr. Joseph Mengele's torture in 1956, I was almost nine years old... I was driven by my father along a winding road to an airplane hangar in the middle of the countryside. Inside, hanging from the beams by pulleys, were cages with naked children inside, most of whom I thought were younger than me. I was placed in one of the cages, and like the others, I was deprived of food and water. I was very cold and kept curling up to hide my nakedness. Every time I tried to sleep, someone would poke me through the bars with an electric prod. The torturer seemed to enjoy torturing the children. He stood at the height of the cages, perched on whatever he could. When he wasn't torturing us, he was on the floor with Dr. Black. They were both smiling evilly, and our tears had absolutely no impact on them. The purpose of all this torture was to prepare us for programming. There was a hospital where each of us was taken after the torture that made us "cooperative". I received training that taught me about the meridians of the body and how to manage the energy flowing through these meridians. This was a preparation for later experiences in which I would have to use my mind to try to psychically kill from a distance. In another experiment, an alter personality was created for the purpose of memorising binary codes. If this alter "Robert" failed to repeat perfectly what he had learned, I was put back in the cage. Trauma-informed programming is the cruelest form of brainwashing. It leaves the child completely dissociated and open to mental programming. Joseph Mengele was a master at this.

3 - DR. EWEN CAMERON IN CANADA

As Richard Helms admitted, several foreign scientists worked for the CIA's MK-Ultra programme. Among them was Canadian psychiatrist Ewen Cameron, who conducted brainwashing experiments for seven years. Between 1957 and 1964, Cameron conducted his experiments at the Allan Memorial Institute in Montreal, Canada. He was also the head of the World *Psychiatric* Association (*WPA*). Thirty years later, a Canadian radio programme described his work as follows: *"During treatment, patients are subjected to extreme psychiatric shocks. Under the influence of barbiturates and LSD, the subjects are stunned by pre-recorded messages played on a loop. They are subjected to massive doses of electroshock, prolonged sleep for several days, ice showers, etc. Electroshock therapy, a treatment procedure that was not well mastered at the time, was 20 to 40 times more severe than what was normally prescribed.*

The sessions lasted five hours a day, five days a week, and their purpose was to "deprogram" the patient's brain and then "reprogram" it. In 1960, the CIA stopped funding the secret research at the Allan Memorial Institute. Dr Cameron then turned to the Canadian government, which funded him until 1963. In all, some fifty patients were used as guinea pigs in these experiments."[190]

When Canadians learned that the CIA had been conducting brainwashing experiments on their citizens, and that their government had not only known about it but had even helped fund it, the shock was enormous. It was the television programme *"The Fitfh Estate"* (CBS) that first revealed the affair in 1984 by revealing the work that had been supervised by Dr. Ewen Cameron in his Montreal clinic: the scandal broke. Legal action was taken by the victims against Dr. Cameron but also against the CIA. A film was even made about this affair: *"The Sleep Room"* by Bernard Zuckerman, 1998.

Here is the three-step electroshock protocol used by Dr. Cameron:

- First stage: This is the first stage of post-electroshock amnesia, the subject loses a large part of his short-term memory. The subject still retains the "space-time image": he knows where he is, why he is there and he recognises familiar faces but he has more difficulty remembering names.

- Second stage: In the second stage of *Electroconvulsive Amnesia*, the subject loses the "space-time image" but is aware of this loss. This awareness causes him extreme anxiety and panic because he wants to remember but cannot. At this stage, he will repeatedly ask: *"Where am I?"*, *"How did I get here?"*, *"Why am I here?*

- Third and final stage: At this stage, the subject becomes extremely calm, all previous anxiety has disappeared. He is taken back to his room where a tape recorder placed near his pillow will repeat the same instruction over and over for hours. This technique is called *psychic driving*. In this state, the victims had urinary and faecal incontinence.

Ewen Cameron was also working on 'radical isolation'. These were sensory isolation chambers in which the subject was locked up for a certain period of time. Deprived of sensory stimuli, *'the subject's very identity began to disintegrate*. Cameron himself boasted that he had experimentally reproduced on human subjects the equivalent of the *"extraordinary political conversions"* that occurred in the East,[191] i.e. brainwashing for political purposes. In 1957, his application for a grant to study the *"effects of repetition of verbal signals on human behaviour"* which, he said, could *"break the individual down as if after a long interrogation"*, was accepted by the *Society for the Investigation of*

---

[190] *"Lavages de cerveaux financés par la CIA"* - Radio-Canada, archives, 5 October 1988, interview by journalist Pauline Valasse with psychiatrist Pierre Lalonde.

[191] Ibid.

Human Ecology.[192] His research programme was then integrated into the MK-Ultra project.[193]

In an article published by *Nexus* magazine, Sid Taylor reports that following a 'treatment' on a woman, Cameron is quoted as saying: *"Although the patient went through both prolonged sensory isolation (35 days) and repeated restructuring, even receiving 101 days of 'positive driving'* (supposedly 'psychic driving' with positive content messages), *we did not get favourable results."*[194]

Cameron also supervised experiments with electromagnetic frequencies. Human guinea pigs were treated in a radio telemetry laboratory set up by Leonard Rubenstein in the basement of the Institute. In this laboratory, patients were exposed to a range of electromagnetic waves designed to control and modify their behaviour.[195]

One of Dr. Cameron's victims was Linda McDonald, a young mother of five. During a moment of weakness and depression, her doctor advised her to go and see the famous psychiatrist. After three weeks, Cameron concluded that Linda had acute schizophrenia and sent her to *the 'Sleep Room'*. There she was put into an artificial sleep for 86 days, a comatose state. Dr. Peter Roper, who was one of Dr. Cameron's colleagues at the time, said: *"The goal was really to erase the thought patterns and behaviours that were lacking in the patient because they were suffering from them and then to replace them with healthy habits, thoughts and behaviours."*

According to her hospital records, Linda McDonald underwent electroshock treatment over a hundred times. In fact, she was admitted to hospital for what we now call post-natal depression, but her records show a radical and completely inappropriate drug treatment. Here is an extract from her medical report: *"May 15 (1963): Subject to some confusion June 3: Knows her name, but that's about it June 11: Does not know her name."* Linda testifies that she very quickly became a vegetable, she had no identity, no memories, it was as if she had never existed in the world before (*tabula rasa*). She was just like a baby to be fed and washed.

Another victim of Dr. Cameron was Robert Loguey. When he was 18 years old, he had pain in one of his legs and his doctor, who had not found the cause of the problem, thought it was psychosomatic. He sent his patient to the Allan Memorial Institute. As with Linda McDonald, this too was a nightmare, shock therapy with drugs, including a powerful hallucinogen. He was injected with LSD every other day, sometimes mixed with other drugs and psychotropics. Most of these drugs were experimental, but they seemed to be suitable for

---

[192] American Torture: From the Cold War to Abu Ghraib and Beyond " - Michael Otterman, 2007.

[193] "Kubark", the CIA's secret manual of mind control and psychological torture - www.editions-zones.fr.

[194] A History of Secret CIA Mind-Control Research " - Sid Taylor, Nexus Magazine 1992.

[195] "Journey into Madness: The True Story of Secret CIA Mind Control and Medical Abuse" - Gordon Thomas, 1989.

brainwashing. During these deep altered states of consciousness created by the electroshock and drugs, human guinea pigs were forced to listen to audio messages that were supposed to imprint new thoughts on their minds, the content of which was sometimes very bizarre: Robert reports that a tape recorder placed under his pillow played the words *"You killed your mother"* (who was alive and well at the time) over and over. These were very short messages lasting a few seconds and played on a loop. For Robert, this process lasted for 23 days.

These patients never knew that their treatment was part of a CIA-led project. Indeed, Dr. Cameron was far from being an isolated "mad scientist" who decided to apply these techniques on his own. He was indeed following a programme of experiments on human guinea pigs. Velma Orlikow, the wife of David Orlikow, a Canadian Member of Parliament, was one of Cameron's victims. She had gone to the Allan Memorial Institute in the late 1950s to treat depression. She had a high regard for the famous psychiatrist before she realised that he had absolutely no concern for the mental health of his patients, but was simply using them as guinea pigs, nothing more. He was just doing what his employers, the CIA, told him to do. So she decided, with the help of eight other former victims, to sue this powerful institution, the CIA. The trial lasted several years and the case became almost an obsession for American civil liberties lawyer Joseph Rauh. Rauh and his young assistant James Turner knew that they were facing a formidable enemy, but they also had an ally who could balance the trial. They relied heavily on the support of the Canadian government, led at the time by Brian Mulroney. Unfortunately, instead of helping its own citizens, the Canadian government, fearing that it would be held accountable, stabbed them in the back throughout the trial; even going so far as to suppress a key piece of evidence that CIA officials from the US embassy had apologised to the Canadian government when the MK-Ultra experiments were publicly revealed. This apology was very important, it was a legally admissible admission in a court of law that one of the two parties in the case had done something wrong and reprehensible. It was evidence of negligence and wrongdoing at the time and the case could have been closed quickly to the benefit of the victims. Instead, the legal battle went on for ten years.

Thanks to a campaign of support and the strength of the case put together by the victims, the CIA relented on the eve of the trial. A settlement was reached for the sum of $750,000. At the time, this was the largest amount of compensation the CIA had ever had to pay. However, troubling questions remain to this day, particularly about the Canadian government. Why did it act in such an ambiguous manner when it was helping many Canadian citizens? The simple answer is that the Canadian government was in fact even more involved than the Americans in the experiments at the Allan Memorial Institute. Dr. Cameron's experiments were funded to the tune of $1/2 million by the federal Department of Health and Welfare during the 1950s, but the funding didn't stop there... They pumped more than $51,000 into these experiments after the CIA project ended in 1961.

When Linda McDonald discovered that her own government had funded brainwashing experiments on her, she made the difficult decision to sue. The former victim hounded the Canadian federal government for four long years until finally, in 1992, Ottawa reluctantly agreed to compensate her and several other victims to the tune of $100,000 per person. In exchange, they had to agree to stop any legal action against the Canadian government or the Allan Memorial Institute. However, Ottawa has steadfastly refused to acknowledge any wrongdoing at the psychiatric institute, the stronghold of Dr. Ewen Cameron. A finding was written stating firstly that the patients had not suffered irreparable harm, and secondly that they had consented to the treatment! According to the victims, Dr. Cameron had never told them anything about the treatment they were going to undergo. He never gave a single explanation or description of what would happen to them. This was clearly not medical treatment, it was brainwashing experiments with human guinea pigs. Despite this, the Allan Memorial Institute in Montreal has maintained its international reputation as a leader in the treatment of mental illness. [196]

The Native American community in Canada was also the target of all kinds of experiments, mainly during the 1950s and 1960s, especially in hospitals. A large number of children were taken away from their families as part of the *"sixties scoop"* programme, which officially concerned 20,000 Amerindian children. They were automatically placed in residential schools. These boarding schools were intended for the *'schooling'*, *'evangelisation'* and *'assimilation'* of the country's children, i.e. the little natives, the Amerindians. These thousands of children were separated from their families without anyone being able to say anything about it at the time. This is a very serious matter, involving the sterilisation of young women, medical experiments on the human psyche and the massive spread of infectious diseases to reduce this population. Pedocriminality and ritual abuse have inevitably been added to this pool of children separated from their families and placed in boarding schools. Some testimonies suggest that the MK-Ultra programme was carried out on many Amerindians, obviously non-consenting and literally serving as guinea pigs.

The daughter of a Canadian officer, Sara Hunter (pseudonym), was experimented on with 25 other children and as many adults. According to her, this took place at the Lincoln Park air force in Calgary, Alberta between 1956 and 1958. She says it was a Nazi doctor who carried out the experiments and she says she was the only one to survive the two years of torture, most of the children killed were Native American, others were runaways or orphans.[197]

In the documentary *"Unrepentant: Kevin Annett and Canada's Genocide"* (2006) about the genocide of Native Americans in Canada, Pastor Kevin Annett says when asked if he believes all these native testimonies: *"Well, when people who don't know each other keep telling the same story over and over again, even if you're skeptical, you have to admit to those facts. You know, it's a story that's widely told and when people started going further and reporting things that I later rediscovered and was able to validate with*

---

[196] The Fifth Estate - MK-Ultra in Canada, Dr Ewen Cameron - CBC, 1984.

[197] "Canada: the massacre of the Indian people involves the destruction and exploitation of their children" - DondeVamos, 27/10/2012.

documents, then I couldn't deny those things. You know, when you are a pastor, you learn to detect quite quickly if the person in front of you is telling you nonsense. You can read the pain in people's eyes. It's incredibly painful for them to talk about their experiences, they don't need to add to it (...) This happened in the summer of 1998 in Vancouver. I brought a lot of survivors to testify at this tribunal. Everything you can imagine about what happened in the Nazi death camps... They told it. There was a group of people from the island of Kuper who told of being victims of medical experiments where doctors who spoke German injected them with chemicals that killed them. "

These testimonies, which state that the 'scientists' who carried out the experiments spoke German, may suggest that they were Nazi scientists exfiltrated from Germany to America during 'Operation *Paperclip*', described at the beginning of this chapter.

In the same documentary "Unrepentant", Aboriginal police officer George Brown of the RCMP (Royal Canadian Mount Police) says of his childhood: "I'm 100% sure we were used as guinea pigs in hospitals for some reason. We were taken to the hospital, I remember it wasn't to see a dentist, and I wasn't sick."

Another testimonial is from Nung Klaath Gaa (Douglas Wilson), who says he is from the Haida Gwaii people. He says: "I read Kevin Annett's document and it helped me understand how my memory is so weak. In some parts of the paper they talk about shock treatments (...) In my last year there in the spring of 1961, I was taken from school to Charles Camsell Hospital, and from Charles Camsell Hospital to the Ponoka Psychiatric Institute. I don't know if I was there for one or two weeks, but I have this vague memory, a memory that came back to me like a flash. I was lying on this table with something on my head, with flashes and lights blinking continuously."

Survivor Lynn Moss Sharman, an indigenous Canadian, also testified about the ritual abuse and mind control she suffered as a child. She has done a great deal of work to bring together the Native American victims of these horrors and to make this known to the general public. We will return to her testimony in Chapter 7.

4 - DR. WILLIAM SARGANT IN ENGLAND

The British psychiatrist William Walters Sargant wrote: "Although men are not dogs, they must humbly remind themselves how much their brain functions resemble those of dogs." or again: "We need to excite the mind before we can change it. William Sargant was directly involved with the CIA's mind control programmes. He used the same brainwashing protocols as Cameron: electroshock, deep sleep therapy, psychic driving and of course the use of all kinds of drugs."

British actress Celia Imrie was one of Dr. Sargant's victims. At the age of 14, Celia was anorexic and had to be hospitalised but her condition did not improve despite treatment. In desperation, her parents sent her to St Thomas'

Hospital in London where she was placed in the care of the internationally renowned psychiatrist William Sargant.

To this day, she says that Sargant still comes back in her nightmares. More than 20 years after his death, it is now known that this psychiatrist worked for MI5 and the CIA, particularly in the MK-Ultra programme.

In a 2011 *Daily* Mail article entitled *"My electric shock* nightmare *at the hands of the CIA's evil doctor"*, Celia Imrie says she has little memory of her own electric shock sessions but that she remembers perfectly the electric shocks the woman in the bed next to her was receiving: *"I remember every little detail, whether by sight, sound or smell. The huge rubber stopper stuck between her teeth; the strange, almost silent scream, like a sigh of pain; the jerky contortions of the tortured body; the smell of hair and burnt flesh. I also remember the famous "Narcosis Chamber"* (the equivalent of Dr. Cameron's "Sleep Chamber"), *a room where patients were put into a drug-induced sleep for several days while machines broadcast instructions under the pillows. I can describe Sargant's "Narcosis Room" perfectly because I used to sneak out of my room to look through the portholes or a swinging door at these women lying on the floor on grey mattresses, as if dead, in an electro-induced twilight silence. When asked if I myself have been in this room, I answer "no", because I don't remember. But I have recently realised that before being placed in the Chamber, the subject was first drugged and I have never seen anyone come back from there awake. You went in asleep and came out asleep. I think anyone who has been treated with Sargant sleep therapy has been in that chamber at one time or another. You were totally unconscious in there, so maybe I was put in there myself. I couldn't know (...) I can't know the methods of mind control he exercised over me, I don't know what was on the recordings under my pillow, what they told me to do or think...*

A few years ago I tried to find my medical records at St Thomas' Hospital, I wanted to check what my treatment was and whether I had been in that Narcosis Chamber. I wanted to know the precise instructions that were recorded on the tape looped under my pillow. I wanted to know what Sargant had relentlessly induced in my young unconscious brain. Unfortunately, my search turned up nothing. When William Sargant left St Thomas's, he illegally took all his patients' records with him. By the time of his death in 1988, every piece of evidence and paperwork concerning his inhumane work on human guinea pigs had been destroyed. So I will never know the truth.

I remember being given massive doses of the anti-psychotic drug Largactil. The effect of this drug was impressive, my hands would shake uncontrollably, I would wake up to find tufts of hair on my pillow. But the worst effect was that I saw everything multiplied in four. When Sargant entered my room, I saw four men! It was horrible and terrifying. Even simple tasks like lifting a glass of water became impossible. As the doses were increased, I remember one day hearing a nurse tell her colleague that I was showing "dangerous resistance" to the drugs. Dangerous for whom? I wonder... In that horrible place, as far as I could see, the real lunatics are the ones working there, not the patients. Sargant used to say that every dog has its breaking point, it just takes longer for the eccentrics. "I guess my 'dangerous resistance' was what he was talking about, that I was one of those eccentric dogs he couldn't break."[198]

5 - PALLE HARDRUP'S PROGRAMMING

The 1958 book *"Antisocial or Criminal Acts and Hypnosis: A Case Study"* by Paul J. Reiter describes the case of a Danish man who was subjected to MK-Ultra mind control techniques. Palle Hardrup (or Hardwick) was 31 years old when he was found guilty on 17 July 1954 of robbing a bank and killing two employees a few months earlier. This case proves that an individual can be programmed to commit crimes and then have amnesia about their criminal acts. According to psychiatrist Colin Ross, Paul Reiter's book can be taken as a real manual describing how to create a *Manchurian Candidate*.

The Danish judges declared at the time that Palle Hardrup had a multiple personality (using their own words) and concluded that this personality disorder had been deliberately created by his programmer and master, a certain Bjorn Nielsen. A report from the Forensic Council dated 17 February 1954 stated that *'Although the symptoms of the mental disorder seem to have disappeared today, Hardrup cannot be considered cured. The deep split in his personality, which has been well established, will only heal very slowly.* The jury found Hardrup guilty on all charges but not responsible for his actions. Bjorn Nielsen, the man who turned Palle Hardrup into an amnesiac bank robber, was found guilty of robbery and manslaughter, even though he was not physically present at the scene. The jury found that Nielsen planned and organised the crimes by instructing Hardrup to commit them, manipulating him in various ways including hypnosis. Nielsen was sentenced to life imprisonment while Hardrup was committed to a mental institution. At the time, the case caused quite a stir in Denmark. For Nielsen, the 'perfect' crime was to ensure that no one could trace it back to him, a crime for which someone else would inevitably have to serve the prison sentence.

Hardrup and Nielsen were both members of the Nazi S.S., the former joined out of a naive need for brotherhood and the latter, Nielsen, joined in 1940 to get out of a reform school. Following the German debacle in 1945, they were both arrested and sentenced to several years in prison. It was there that they met for the first time in 1947. They soon became comrades and Nielsen became the leader and even the master, making Hardrup his disciple and slave, just as a young student would be recruited and indoctrinated by a sect. Alone, far from home, idealistic, naive, suggestible and unhappy, a condition that made him very vulnerable to mind control and manipulation. The two men finally get permission to share the same cell and they isolate themselves completely from the other prisoners. Gradually, they lock themselves into the practice of esoteric disciplines such as yoga, meditation, hypnosis, etc.

---

[198] "My electric shock nightmare at the hands of the CIA's evil doctor" - Celia Imrie, *Daily Mail*, 04/2011.

For 18 months, Hardrup was continuously alone in the cell with Nielsen, or working alongside him in the workshop. Nielsen immediately began his mind control experiments, working by instinct. There is no evidence, however, that he had any previous training in mental programming. Palle Hardrup was an excellent subject for hypnosis and Nielsen then started an intensive hypnotic conditioning programme involving several hours of trance exercises per day. This usually took place in the evening and Hardrup would often go to bed without coming out of the trance. Nielsen combined the hypnosis sessions with yoga, *Kundalini* awakening and self-hypnosis exercises. He taught Hardrup techniques for emptying his mind, for transcending and experiencing altered states of consciousness, which were supposed to bring inner peace. These practices were aimed at establishing direct contact with a 'deity'. For example, Nielsen told him that hypnosis would help him to become aware of his past lives. Through 'expansions of consciousness', Hardrup was to be able to become one with the 'divine cosmic principle' and thus have direct communion with God. Hardrup was also instructed to isolate himself from the other prisoners, his world was to focus only on Nielsen, his master, his guru. The total social isolation combined with these spiritual exercises resulted in Palle Hardrup being in a perpetual trance state in which he was constantly turned towards the 'divine'.

After some time, Nielsen introduced Hardrup to the guardian spirit 'X'. X was a guiding spirit who communicated through Nielsen, who was therefore psychic. X told Hardrup that all his previous unfortunate life was only a test to prepare him for his future role. It was X who also took control of the yoga training with Hardrup. After a while, the conditioning was such that hypnosis was no longer necessary, for Palle Hardrup, Nielsen was the incarnation of the entity X who spoke directly to him without the use of hypnosis. As soon as Nielsen spoke, it was X who spoke and gave the instructions. Hardrup was being taught about *Samadhi*, the state that yogis reach to transcend the needs of their bodies. The entity X was there to guide Hardrup towards *Samadhi* and enlightenment, even giving him various initiation tests. X also told him that he had a divine political mission to unite all Scandinavians under one flag. Hardrup was thus totally enslaved to a demonic entity whose intentions were very obscure.

In order to break all ties with the material world, Hardrup began a series of hypnotic exercises related to money. First, he had to mentally visualise moving a sum of cash into their cell to give to a 'poor beggar woman'; Hardrup saw this as a transcendent exercise in love and charity. But the exercises multiplied and got worse. Still under the orders of Entity X, Hardrup was to visualise himself robbing a bank and committing murder.

Any qualms or refusals about the robbery or murders were interpreted by X as a reaction of the physical body which Hardrup had to reject and transcend... The virtual bank robbery in which Hardrup was immersed during the hypnotic trance sessions was rehearsed and visualised in great detail, including the murder of the employees...

After a while, Hardrup began to hear X's voice talking to him even when medium Nielsen was not present: guardian spirit X was now connected to

Hardrup. Upon their release from prison, Nielsen ordered and arranged for Palle Hardrup to marry a woman named Bente. Nielsen beat her in black magic sessions and took advantage of her while Hardrup watched from the sidelines as a mind-controlled machine. The two men were looking for money to start a new political party; Hardrup was to become a robbery and killing machine... In August 1950, Nielsen first launched his robot, which was programmed for a bank robbery. The loot was 25,000 kroner, a sum of money that Hardrup immediately handed over to Nielsen after the robbery. There were no casualties that time, but two people were killed in the attack on 21 March 1951. A few days after his arrest, Hardrup told the police that a 'guardian spirit' (X) had ordered him to commit the robbery for political purposes. He said that this entity X had totally reoriented his life and influenced his actions since he had met it in prison. But he claimed that the guardian spirit X was not Nielsen and that Nielsen had nothing to do with the case. He even said that he had met the guardian spirit long before his first meeting with Nielsen. Hardrup finally confessed in December 1951 about the hypnotic conditioning of his guru Nielsen. In April 1952, Hardrup was subjected to a psychiatric examination by Dr. Reiter, who wrote a 370-page report on his case. Dr. Reiter reported that at the beginning of the examination it was impossible to hypnotise Hardrup until he could break a 'locking' mechanism. Hardrup had been programmed by Nielsen not to be hypnotised by anyone else. George Estabrooks in his book *Hypnotism* (1943) calls this process 'blocking'. Once this blocking system was deactivated, Hardrup became an easily hypnotised subject. Dr. Reiter stated in his report that Hardrup had been under intense hypnotic influence by Nielsen and that in committing the crimes he had acted involuntarily. He demonstrated that Hardrup had been subjected to somnambulistic amnesia induced by hypnosis and post-hypnotic suggestions. An altered state of consciousness in which critical thinking and free will are completely abolished.

In November 1952, Nielsen had a conversation with Hardrup at a court meeting. During the next two weeks Hardrup began to hear the voice of Entity X again, while showing great anxiety and agitation. In 1961 Hardrup was finally released from the asylum, but now he had to convince the public that he was no longer a programmed instrument and that if he met Nielsen again, the drama would not be repeated.[199] Nielsen was probably introduced to the occult and mind control techniques, perhaps during his time in the Nazi S.S., knowing that they were very interested in all these things.[200]

6 - OCCULTISM, THE PARANORMAL AND THE C.I.A.

Officially, the CIA's programmes on human behavioural control and mental programming ceased in 1963, with the exception of the MK-Search project, which was officially halted in 1972. However, similar clandestine

[199] The CIA Doctors: Human Rights Violations by American Psychiatrists ", Collin Ross, 2011.

[200] Les Dossiers extraordinaires Vol.1, "L'hypnotiseur", Pierre Bellemare.

programmes continued in other forms, refocusing on the use of electromagnetic radiation to affect human psyche and behaviour, but also through the use of parapsychological techniques. In 1976, parapsychology research received the direct support of the then Director of the CIA, George Bush. For the CIA, the word "parapsychology" is classified, i.e. any document mentioning the term "*psi*", which refers to all paranormal phenomena linked to the human psyche, is automatically classified as top-secret or higher.[201]

One of the CIA psychiatrists, John Gittinger, told a US Senate hearing: "The general idea we had arrived at was that brainwashing essentially involved a process of isolating human beings by depriving them of all outside contact and subjecting them to long periods of stress ... without the need for any esoteric means.[202]

This means that the field of research into esotericism, the occult, is not to be excluded if necessary. In their quest for absolute control over humans, the CIA and the army have taken a close interest in esotericism and parapsychology. This is not surprising, given that the source of their studies on mind control comes from the observation of alterations of consciousness during traumatic rituals, trances, demonic possessions and psychic powers developed in religious cults. The esoteric aspect of mind control is therefore as important, if not more so, than the purely scientific and psychiatric aspect. Occultism, ritual practices and black magic are essential points in the MK-Monarch programming protocols because they are linked to other dimensions of the being, as we will see later...

In the December 1980 *Military Review*, Lieutenant John B. Alexander of the U.S. Army wrote an article entitled *"The New Mental Battlefield: Beam me up, Spock! The* New Mental Battlefield*"*. In this article, Alexander highlights the growing importance of Soviet and American research on electromagnetic weapons but also research in the field of parapsychology. He cites disciplines such as out-of-body travel, *remote viewing*, precognition, extrasensory perception, telepathy, telekinesis, bio-energy circulation (fluid, aura), etc. In his article, John B. Alexander writes: *"The extent of parapsychological research in the United States is not well known and is not centrally organised. The US government has reportedly funded some research projects, but they have not been published (...) The use of telepathic hypnosis also has great potential. This capability could allow programming to be deeply implanted into agents without their awareness. Cinematically speaking, we would then have a Manchurian Candidate who would not even require a phone call* to trigger programming.*"*

Lieutenant Alexander concludes his article: "The impact that psychotronic weapons and other paranormal techniques will have in the future is difficult to determine at this time. We can assume that whoever makes the first major breakthrough in these areas will have a considerable advantage over his opponent, similar to the possession of nuclear weapons. Obviously, progress in

---

[201] Mind Wars: The True Story of Government Research into the Military Potential of Psychic Weapons", Ronald McRae, 1984.

[202] Amercian Torture: From the Cold War to Abu Ghraib and Beyond " - Michael Otterman, 1977, p. 52.

any of the above areas will add a new dimension to the battlefield. The Soviets have been working on these techniques for several years (...) The information presented here may be considered by some as ridiculous because it does not fit their paradigm, some people still believe that the world is flat (...) This is to underline the need for more coordinated research in the field of the paranormal. This is an article published in 1980, where is the research 35 years later? Knowing that it is exponential...

Lieutenant John B. Alexander worked with Colonel Michael Aquino (founder of the *Temple of Set*) on the Monarch slaves. According to Fritz Springemeier, he was one of the military men most involved in the training of elite units of *'Warrior-Monks'* who could fight using both martial arts and paranormal psychic powers. The recruits were obviously subjects who had undergone a mental programming protocol resulting in a multiple personality, a traumatic process that could develop special psychic abilities in the victims (see Chapter 6).[203]

In 1987, the *Seattle Times* published an article on Lieutenant Colonel Jim Channon entitled "The *New Army's* experiment with 'New *Age*' thinking". Here is an excerpt: *"The Army is therefore interested in New Age philosophy, the idea that the world can be changed by changing the way people think, and that the mind has invisible but tangible powers that are just waiting to be tapped. Centres were set up in Ford Ord, California and Washington DC to explore this intriguing idea that the power of the mind could be more effective than gun power in winning a war. From 1980 to 1982, these ideas were tested at Fort Lewis by Lieutenant Colonel Jim Channon. The army recruited young officers who were enthusiastic about this 'new thinking' to join forces with rather sceptical scientists (...) a think tank was set up at the Pentagon to assess the issue of paranormal psychic phenomena. These meetings covered the subjects of ESP, mediumship and even a helmet designed to synchronise the left side (logic) and the right side (intuition) of the brain."*[204]

This elite military *'new-age'* unit founded by Jim Channon was named *the First Earth Battalion*, with MK subjects (previously split and programmed) receiving martial arts training as well as an introduction to esotericism and the occult. The following is an excerpt from a letter from one of these New Age Battalion soldiers that was forwarded to Texe Marrs, an ex-US Air Force officer turned Protestant minister. This letter was published in his newsletter *"Flashpoint"* in September 1994:

We are a group of highly selected soldiers. We are to be 'Purified Psychic Soldiers'. We have all received our directives for "The Plan". We are preparing for the emergence of a "New Order. We are encouraged to read all types of books that deal with New Age and the occult, to study the various martial arts and to exercise the powers of the spirit. Communication with spirit guides (editor's note: demonic entities) is also encouraged. We are taught to become 'sages'. My

---

[203] "The Illuminati Formula Used to Create an Undetectable Total Mind Controlled Slave - Fritz Springmeier & Cisco Wheeler 1996"

[204] Ibid.

best friend and I study and practice our meditation and psychic warrior skills daily. I also study Ninjutsu, Tai Kwon Do and Tai Chi. We are not supposed to talk to people in this special unit (...) At the end of the Eleventh Delta Force Conference, the instructor said: "I have witnessed a process of unique and majestic value, an army of Excellence. (...) As our faculties grew, we were told that we were becoming 'like gods', that there were no limits to a soldier of the First Earth Battalion. We could travel to different places with our mind, walk through fire, move or bend objects with the power of our mind, see into the future, stop our heart (editor's note: extreme biofeedback as practised by Indian yogis), etc. (...) In the end, all martial arts serve only one real purpose: To bring the soldier-warrior to the truth (...) There are six levels of psychic soldier, from the beginner to the highest, who then becomes a Warrior-Minor or a Warrior-Master (...) The New Age military forces involve rituals, chants, meditations, prayers to the Earth and pledges of allegiance to the planet and the people. The first book we are recommended to read is The Aquarian Consipracy, the standard book of the New Age movement..."[205]

Gordon Thomas reports in his book *"Secrets and Lies: A History of CIA Mind-Control"*, that Dr. Stanley Gottlieb, Director of ORD (CIA Office of Research and Development), launched Operation *Often* in the late 1960s. This project aimed to expand research into the mysteries of human consciousness by exploring the world of black magic and according to Thomas *"harnessing the forces of darkness to demonstrate that the far reaches of the human mind are accessible. As part of* this operation on the paranormal, black magic and demonology, the CIA is said to have recruited clairvoyants, astrologers, mediums, demonology specialists, but also Wicca witchdoctors, Satanists and other experienced kabbalists and occultists... According to Thomas, the CIA even financed a chair of witchcraft at the University of South Carolina

Operation Often took a keen interest in demonology. In April 1972, the CIA attempted a discreet approach to the exorcist of the Catholic Archdiocese of New York. He categorically refused to cooperate. The agency also approached Sybil Leek, a Houston witch who cast spells with the help of her tame raven. With the bird perched on her shoulder, Sybil Leek gave black magic lessons to 'fine gentlemen' in Washington, D.C., and gave them an update on the state of the occult in the U.S. at that time: 400 witchcraft groups, led by 5,000 initiated witches or wizards... a thriving market with thousands of 'fortune tellers' and a growing array of anti-Christian products and items. Satan was not only alive, but flourishing throughout the country."[206]

In *TRANCE Formation of America: True life story of a mind control slave*, Mark Phillips writes: "In 1971, the New York Times published an article on the Central Intelligence Agency (CIA) and occult research, which was based on a collection of documents obtained from the U.S. Government Printing Office

---

[205] "New Age Menace: The Secret War Against the Followers of Christ" - David N. Balmforth, 1997, p.76.

[206] "The CIA's Secret Weapons: Torture, Manipulation and Chemical Weapons" - Gordon Thomas, 2006.

under the Freedom of Information Act. This was a report to Congress, which made it clear that the CIA was interested in clinical findings about causal relationships regarding the impact of religious practices on black magic users and/or the mind of an observer. Of particular interest to the CIA were the increased levels of suggestibility that certain occult rituals produced in the minds of practitioners. Cannibalism and blood rituals figured prominently in their research."[207]

7 - CONCLUSION

So here we are in the 1970s and the MK-Ultra programme is officially closed... to make room for new mind control projects that combine the previous achievements on mind programming with occultism, black magic, demonology but also with black psychotronic technology.

The Monarch project is the continuation of all this research that began at the end of the Second World War. Monarch, which seems to be the most important programme, is still classified as top-secret and under the guise of *'National Security'* (see Chapter 10). The Bluebird, Artichoke and MK-Ultra programmes eventually came out into the public domain after 30, 40 or 50 years... The mind control research projects are still operational, they have simply been moved even deeper into the recesses of government institutions. Mind-controlled slaves are a fact of life, you see them every day on your TV screen...

Bill Schnoebelen, describes MK-Monarch programming as follows: "We have good reason to believe that MK-Ultra still exists today in an even more atrocious form as Project Monarch. The difference between Project Monarch and Project MK-Ultra is that it merges child abuse with Satanism, again under the auspices of the government... Children are not only tortured, drugged, electrocuted, etc., but also hypnotised. but they are also hypnotised and undergo the scientific insertion of demons inside their multiple personalities resulting in Dissociative Identity Disorder (DID)... By doing this, they create different types of "super-slaves"...[208]

These "super-slaves" can be used as sex slaves, spies, drug runners, assassins... The alter satanist/luciferian personalities of priest or high priestess will be part of the deeper programming. MK slaves can be injected into many fields such as politics, the judiciary, science, etc. The aim is to have the best subjects in key positions of domination where the 'weak link' option is not an option. They are also found in the entertainment industry and in high-level sport. (This will be developed further in Chapter 7)

The *"Monarch network"* was formed by the meeting of two milieus that fit perfectly because of their hidden and compartmentalised nature, a common occult subculture, but also because of their mutual interests: on the one hand, the

---

[207] *TRANCE Formation of America: True life story of a mind control slave* - Cathy O'Brien & Mark Phillips - New Earth Publishing, 2013, p.22.

[208] "Exposing the illuminati from within" - The Prophecy Club, Bill Schnoebelen.

intelligence services, the military and organised crime, and on the other hand, networks composed of families practising systematic incest, child prostitution, paedo-pornography, satanic ritual abuse, etc. Families that are mired in these occult practices from generation to generation. Apart from sharing a taste for depravity, violence, occultism and power, the trauma-dissociated children in some families are ideal candidates for the mind control programmes of others... Whether it is mafia, religious, political or military groups, in general and internationally, they all know that dissociation, the fragmentation of the personality, is the linchpin and cornerstone of secrecy and power. Canadian therapist Alison Miller writes: *"What better source than an already dissociated child whose parents have abused them in a ritual abuse group?"*

For these MK-Ultra and now MK-Monarch mind control programmes, children with dissociative identity disorders are therefore sought after because they are more easily programmed than a child with an unfractionated psyche. This was the case with Cathy O'Brien, who was subjected to repeated rapes by her father and uncles during her early childhood and fatally developed severe dissociative disorders. Her father, who produced child pornography, was 'caught' by intelligence. He was forced to make his children available to the government's MK-Monarch project in exchange for impunity and protection for his trafficking. This is how Cathy O'Brien describes her family in her autobiography *TRANCE Formation of America: True life story of a mind control slave:*

> Stays at my father's house were devastating, but instructive. My mother had come to suffer deep psychological wounds from her own DID condition and had become an insomniac. My father was by this time travelling regularly to London, Germany and Mexico, as well as taking his family to Disney World in Florida and Washington D.C. My older brother Bill was still working for and with my father, travelling with him every year to the Cheney hunting lodge in Greybull, Wyoming to "hunt", and following my father's instructions to keep his wife and three children in mind control through trauma. My brother Mike ran a video business as a front for some of my father's and Uncle Bob Tanis' juicy porn video business. My sister Kelly Jo became a contortionist belly dancer excelling in "gymnastics" as she became "as limber as Gumby" in accordance with her prostitution programming. Her educational background enabled her to work in day care centres, where she actually scouted out abused children for my father as potential candidates for 'elected' office. In 1990, she graduated to open a formal daycare, "The Little Apprentices," in Grand Haven, Michigan, for my father. My brother Tom ("Beaver") is a Compu-Kid (CIA project), a programmed computer genius. My brother Tim broke his leg (where my mother had broken hers years earlier) for following my father's sports programming that was far beyond human capabilities. My younger sister Kimmy developed a hysterical obsession with a certain 'Mr. Rogers.' She expressed an inordinate fear of his enormous "electric" dollhouse, which lit

up at night to resemble the White House, and was under medical care for anorexia at age seven."[209]

Monarch-type mind control organisations and institutions infiltrate satanic cults and luciferian and incestuous families to gain access to these children who are already deeply disassociated. In exchange for access to these children to install programming that serves their interests, these organisations provide the network or parents with generous remuneration, favours that may include protection from the law, support for their occult or illegal activities, and information about MK programming techniques. Indeed, trauma-based MK programming is not "reserved" for governmental projects, it is a systematic practice on children of satanic/Luciferian cults that goes back much further than governmental experimentation. These various cults practicing traumatic ritual abuse of their offspring apply MK protocols according to the level of knowledge they have on the subject.

---

[209] *TRANCE Formation of America: True life story of a mind control slave* - Cathy O'Brien & Mark Phillips - New Earth Publishing, 2013, p.275.

CHAPTER 4

RITUAL ABUSE

... a vaulted room in the shape of a cellar where religious festivals were to be celebrated. The atmosphere is reminiscent of those rites of destruction of the individual personality, of that second state in which man becomes an empty vessel in which edifying feelings are drunkenly poured out. Description of the crypt of Wewelsburg Castle in Germany. Excerpt from the documentary *Schwarze Sonne* (The Black Sun of the Nazis - The occult roots of Nazism, 1998)

1 - INTRODUCTION

The mind control research carried out by the Nazis and later by the CIA was developed to make "religious" ritual abuse and the resulting personality disorders a true psychiatric science. Secret government MK programmes and transgenerational satanic ritual abuse are thus intimately linked. This doctrine of objectifying a human being is satanic, whether it is practised by a doctor in a white coat or a priest in a black robe. One of the purposes of the traumatic ritual abuse practised by these cults is to *initiate* the child through dissociation. This dissociative process causes a breach, a fragmentation of the soul opening the door to other dimensions, i.e. the deep traumas create an *unlocking of the* child's energy bodies, it is a real spiritual robbery... (This will be discussed further in chapter 6). During these traumatic rituals, the child becomes "initiated and sacred", and is thus linked to the spirit world in spite of himself, and this connection opens the way to demonic possessions and paranormal psychic faculties. As a result of these *"initiatory"* protocols, this inverted sanctification, the child finds himself split and parasitized by one or more entities, the crack letting the *light* through... One fact is that most survivors of satanic ritual abuse suffer from a dissociative identity disorder (formerly called multiple personality disorder). Is it a real demonic possession, a multiple personality or a mixture of both? We will come back to this...

Here is what Father Georges Morand, who was an exorcist priest for ten years, said on *France Culture in* 2011 in the programme *"Sur les docks"* about Satanic ritual abuse:

- Journalist: Father Morand, when you speak of a young girl being put naked on a cross, sprinkled with animal blood... When you speak of foetuses being torn from their mother's womb and sacrificed... What are you talking about?

- George Morand: I'm talking about people I've met, helped and accompanied for years, who only got out of their affairs through exorcism prayer. People whose names I could give you... who have fallen prey to extremely fearsome satanist groups practising what are called black masses linked to rites of witchcraft and magic, with ritual murders... under the double cover, and I weigh my words, on the one hand of the mafia, all the worldwide networks of low and high level prostitution, drug trafficking, and on the other hand of personalities who could be said to be beyond suspicion and who hold key positions in our civilisation, whether in the world of politics, all political tendencies combined... in the world of the judiciary, in the world of science, in the world of finance, in the intellectual world... and I would even say alas, three times alas, in the ecclesiastical world."[210]

In 2012, Father Gary Thomas, exorcist of the Diocese of San Jose in the United States, said in a lecture at Rutgers University: *"I sometimes perform the rite of exorcism for survivors of ritual abuse. Satanic ritual abuse is a reality. It is also something that is incredibly criminal, illegal and highly secretive. These satanic cults that are linked with the 'illuminati' are real and they are active, some for hundreds of years. They will kill people, they will sexually abuse all members of the cult in order to control them. They sometimes select outsiders to perform human sacrifices. This is all real. If you go to your local police, they won't be able to tell you about it openly, but law enforcement deals with this kind of thing regularly."*

In 1990, Mormon Bishop Elder Glenn Pace issued a memorandum denouncing ritual abuse practices within his Church, which reads: *"This ritualised abuse is the most vile of all child abuse. The fundamental and premeditated purpose is to torture and terrorise these children until they are forced to systematically and methodically disassociate themselves. This torture is not a consequence of 'anger', it is the execution of well thought out and planned rituals, often carried out by close relatives. The only way out for these children is to disassociate themselves."*

In 1989, the *ITV* television programme *'The Cook Report'* devoted an episode to the issue of Satanic ritual abuse. In this documentary, Reverend Kevin Logan said: *"In my listening and counselling capacity, I have seen some terrible things. I've heard really disgusting things that have happened to young people, children who have been raped on the altar, the initiation into Satanism. Children who had to eat excrement and drink blood, all these horrible things that Satanists are involved in, and most of all I saw the effect that all this has on these young people."*[211]

In a survey of 125 Chicago police officers in 1992, reported in the book *What Cops Know*, author Connie Fletcher concluded that *"Satanic ritual murders exist. This is not to say that it is widespread, but people do practice this kind of thing. In a satanic murder, the victim's right arm may be tied behind the body; the right testicle may be missing; the body may be drained of blood; the*

---

[210] "Spirits, are you there? Sorcery and exorcism in France" - Sur les docks, France Culture, 12/2011.

[211] The Cook Report: The Devil's Work " - Roger Cook, ITV, 17/07/1989.

heart may be removed; human or animal excrement may be found in the body cavities. There will be missing body parts: the heart, genitals, an index finger, the tongue... So much for confidences. "[212]

2 - RITUAL ABUSE IN THE MODERN WORLD

It's time to come to terms with this reality. Twenty years ago, if you talked about paedophilia, you were locked up. Fifteen years ago, it was the same with incest. Today, it is the case with ritual abuse. The children are still suffering. David Poulton, former Australian Federal Police Sergeant - Preston 1990[213]

We have just understood that paedophilia exists. We cannot yet understand that there are even worse things than paedophilia, and there are people who still resist with all their strength and all their inner strength. Martine Bouillon, former deputy public prosecutor in Bobigny.[214]

a/ Definition

One of the earliest references to Satanic ritual abuse was reported in a book in 1930 in Karl Menniger's *The Human Mind*, a reference book on psychiatry. The book mentioned the existence of black masses, Satanism and demon worship as real events taking place in major cities in Europe and the United States.[215]

The term *"Ritual Abuse"* was first used in 1980 by a Canadian psychiatrist named Lawrence Pazder, who defined the phenomenon as *"repetitive physical, emotional, mental and spiritual attacks combined with the systematic use of symbols, ceremonies and manipulations for malicious purposes."*

In a 1992 issue of the Journal of Child Sexual Abuse, David W. Lloyd defined ritual abuse as: "Intentional physical, sexual or psychological abuse of a child by a person normally responsible for the child's welfare. Such abuse is repeated and practiced during religious ceremonies, and typically involves cruelty to animals and threats to the child."[216]

For David Finkelhor, the author of "Child Sexual Abuse" and "Nursery Crime", it is abuse that occurs in the context of certain symbols or group activities that have a religious, magical or supernatural connotation. These

---

[212] *What Cops Know"* - Connie Fletcher, 1992, p.90.

[213] Preston Y. - Annie's Agony', Sydney Morning Herald, 1990 / "Ritual Abuse & Torture in Australia", ASCA, April 2006.

[214] "Child Rape, the End of Silence? " - France 3, 2000.

[215] *"Cult and Ritual Abuse"* - James Randall Noblitt & Pamela Perskin Noblitt, 2014.

[216] "Ritual Child Abuse: Definition and Assumptions" - David W. Lloyd, The Journal of Child Sexual Abuse, Vol.1(3), 1992.

activities, repeated over time, are used to frighten and intimidate children. Ritual abuse systematically involves mind control over the young victims.

In the UK there is a Department of Health document on child protection called *"Working Together under the Children Act"*. The document does not talk about ritual abuse but uses the term *organised abuse*, i.e. paedophile rings. A report that at least has the merit of recognising the existence of these networks, which are generally denied by political, legal and journalistic institutions, an omerta that seems to be international...

In 1991, this government document defined it as follows: "Organised abuse is an umbrella term for abuse involving a number of abusers, a number of children, and generally encompasses different forms of abuse (...) A wide range of activities are covered by this term, from small paedophile or pornography rings, often but not always organised for profit, where most participants know each other, to large networks of individuals or families which may be more widely distributed and where not all members may know each other. Some organised groups may exhibit strange and ritualistic behaviour, sometimes associated with particular 'beliefs'. This can be a powerful mechanism to terrify abused children from disclosing what they are experiencing."[217]

In 2004, the updated document no longer referred to "bizarre and ritualised behaviour" but added that "abusers act in concert to abuse children, sometimes in isolation or by using an institutional network or position of authority to recruit children for the purpose of abuse. Organised and multiple abuse occurs both as part of an abuse network involving families or a community, and within institutions such as schools or residential homes. Such abuse is deeply traumatic for the children involved. Investigations are time-consuming and require specialist skills from both the police and social workers. Some investigations become extremely complex because of the number of locations and people involved."[218]

Valerie Sinason, child psychotherapist and director of the Clinic *for Dissociative* Studies in London, defined ritual and spiritual abuse in a series of lectures entitled *'Safeguarding London's Children'* in 2007: *"Spiritual abuse is the establishment of a position of power and attachment that results in total blind obedience by thought, word and deed, over a child, young person or adult, through threats of physical and spiritual punishment from the victim themselves, their family or those who want to help them. In this type of abuse there is no room for a relationship with the divine, the victim is not allowed to have a spiritual relationship other than the one she has with her abusers. Many abuses involve a ritualised protocol, with specific dates, times and repetition of the same gestures and actions. Ritual abuse involves children being involved against their will in physical, psychological, emotional, sexual and spiritual violence. This is done under the guise of religious, magical or supernatural beliefs. Total*

---

[217] Working Together under the Children Act 1989 " - Department of Health 1991: 38 - "Beyond disbelief: The Politics and Experience of Ritual Abuse" - Sara Scott, 2001, p.2.

[218] Working Together under the Children Act 2004 " p.225.

submission and obedience are obtained through threats of violence against the victims, their families or those who would help them. "[219]

In 2006, ASCA (*Advocates for Survivors Child Abuse*), an Australian organisation of lawyers, published a report entitled *'Ritual Abuse & Torture in Australia'*, from which the following is extracted: *'Ritual abuse is a multi-layered crime in which dysfunctional families band together to organise these crimes, exploiting the children for profit. The exploiter and primary abuser of the ritually abused child is most often a parent. These groups of abusers usually consist of two or three families forming a network that offers their own children for abuse by other members of the network. In his book "Trauma Organised Systems: Physical and Sexual Abuse in Families", Arnon Bentovim describes these families as an "organised trauma system" in which severe trauma defines and shapes the family structure and the interaction between its members. Victims grow up from childhood in an environment where violence, sexual abuse and extreme trauma are the norm. In this context of organised sexual exploitation, the violence and incest committed by abusers against their own children can be seen not only as sadistic behaviour, but also as a kind of training for these sexual exploitation practices.* "[220]

In 1992, the Utah Attorney General's Office in the USA established a *Ritualistic Abuse Crime Unit*, linked to the *Child Abuse Prosecution Assistance* Unit. This specialist unit was headed by police officers Matt Jacobson and Michael King. It was responsible for investigating and providing assistance to Utah police officers regarding ritual crimes or other illegal activities of local cults. After a year of investigating this issue, Utah Attorney General Jan Graham requested to meet individually with each township manager, sheriff, senior police officer, and magistrate to discuss the creation of a jurisdiction over this issue. During two years, this unit investigated more than 125 cases related to ritual abuse, of which 40 cases involved homicides. At the same time, the investigators met with hundreds of citizens who claimed to have been victims of these satanic practices themselves. This government initiative produced a 60-page report entitled *"Ritual Crime in the State of Utah"*, written in 1995 by investigators Jacobson and King for the Attorney General's office. The report defines ritual crime as follows: *"Ritual abuse is a brutal form of child, adolescent, or adult abuse involving physical, sexual, and psychological violence with the use of rituals. Ritual abuse rarely occurs in isolation, but is repeated over a long period of time. Physical abuse is extreme, including torture, sometimes to the point of murder. Sexual abuse is painful, sadistic and humiliating. By definition, ritual abuse is not an impulsive crime, but rather a maliciously thought-out crime.* "[221]

---

[219] "Ritual Abuse and Mind-Control, The Manipulation of Attachment" - chap. "What has changed in twenty years? - Valerie Sinason, 2011, p.11.

[220] "Ritual Abuse & Torture in Australia" - Advocate for Survivors of Child Abuse, 04/2006, p.12-13.

[221] "Ritual Crime in the State of Utah, Investigation, Analysis & A Look Forward" - Utah Attorney General's Office, Michael R. King, Matt Jacobson, 1995, p.7.

This government report was obviously not intended to discredit the issue of satanic ritual abuse and its content is rather objective. It states for example: *"There is evidence that there are many cases of ritual abuse of children by individuals or small groups. Sometimes these people use Satanism or another religion, as well as 'magical' practices as part of the abuse. What has not been corroborated is the multitude of testimonies of 'survivors' who say they have been involved in human sacrifices, sexual abuse of young children, torture or other atrocities committed by highly organised groups, affecting all levels of government, all social strata and all states of the country. The lack of investigation and prosecution of such complaints does not mean that these accounts are false. This report aims to highlight in detail the problems associated with the investigation and evaluation of ritual crime cases. The help and assistance of senior police officers, magistrates, therapists, etc., is greatly appreciated (...) In conclusion, ritual crime cases should be treated like any other case. Investigators are encouraged to keep an open mind when dealing with cases involving the occult, religious beliefs or ritual criminal activities (...) Training and education regarding the many facets of ritual crime/abuse is necessary and should be of great value to all levels of the police force. Police officers should be instructed on the basic elements of ritual crimes. This training should include the types of organisations involved in occult activities, their aims and the symbols used by their members (...) This training should include information on the bizarre nature of ritual abuse as well as the problems associated with multiple personality disorder, amnesia and repressed memories, hypnosis, etc."*[222]

Despite the detailed evidence of ritual abuse from children, families, adult survivors, police officers, therapists and associations working with victims; despite the remarkable consistency of these reports both nationally and internationally; despite the similarities and overlaps between the various cases and testimonies; society as a whole still resists believing in the harsh reality of ritual abuse. There remains the mistaken belief that Satanism and other occult activities are isolated and rare (if not totally non-existent). This is not a new problem, but society is only beginning to recognise the seriousness and extent of this phenomenon. We all need to learn about it. Many professionals encounter victims of ritual abuse but do not necessarily understand the extent of the abuse behind their patients' mental health problems. The concept of ritual abuse, whereby groups of adults terrorise and torture children in order to control and exploit them, is terrifying and therefore very controversial (always this notion of a paradigm to preserve).

A destructive cult practising ritual abuse can be defined as a network, system or closed group, whose followers are manipulated and conditioned through the use of mind control techniques. It is a system that is imposed without the person's consent, and aims to change their personality and behaviour. The leader(s) are all-powerful, the ideology of the group is totalitarian and the will of the individual is totally subordinated to the group. The destructive cult creates

---

[222] Ibid, p.5, 44, 46.

its own values with little or no respect for ethics and morality. It is engaged in illegal activities such as the sexual exploitation of children and adults: prostitution and child pornography, the production of snuff films, drug and gun trafficking, but also all sorts of schemes that bring in money. In this kind of network, all the members hold each other's tongues, as they are all involved in highly criminal activities.

Most victims report being sexually abused and tortured by several people at the same time and in the company of other child victims. The testimonies report that women are just as active as men in these ritualised abuses. The word 'ritual' does not necessarily mean 'satanic' but rather protocol or methodical, as well as repetitive. For example, the juju cult in West Africa described by Isiah Oke practices ritual abuse with altered states of consciousness but without any particular belief in Satan. Some groups of Gnostic occultists could certainly be mistaken for Satanic cults, however in some cases it would be more appropriate to label them as Luciferian or Neo-Gnostic. There are many cults that incorporate rituals where Satan is invoked among other entities, but he is not consistently considered the central and only god of the cult. However, most survivors in our Western societies report that they have been ritually abused as part of a satanic cult, with the aim of indoctrinating them into satanic beliefs and practices. Ritual abuse is rarely isolated, but is usually repeated over a long period of time in a systematic way. Physical violence is extreme, with torture, rape and murder (simulated or real) used to traumatise and create deep dissociative states in victims. Sadistic sexual abuse is aimed at humiliating and causing pain. It is intended to dominate, dissociate and subdue the victim. According to psychotraumatologist Muriel Salmona, sexual violence is the worst form of psychological trauma. The WHO has also stated that sexual mutilation is the most traumatic abuse that can be inflicted on a human being. This type of barbarism is therefore used repeatedly in these hyper-violent cults. Harassment and psychological violence in addition to physical violence are devastating, indoctrination involves the use of drugs, hypnosis and mind control techniques. The intimidation and extreme violence of the cult members deeply terrorise the victim, following the traumas, he/she is in a state of dissociation and mental control (mental confusion and even traumatic amnesia), and communication with the outside world is therefore extremely difficult. If contact with the network has not been broken and therapy has not been undertaken, victims may live under this control for a very long time. It is important to understand that ritual abuse and mind control are inextricably linked; traumatic memories are a prison without walls.

This ritualised violence seems to have three purposes:

1- The rituals of some groups are part of a religious belief in which the victim is indoctrinated.

2- Rituals are used to intimidate and silence victims.

3- The elements of the ritual (devil worship, satanic symbols, animal or human sacrifices...) seem so incredible that they undermine the credibility of the testimonies and make the prosecution of these crimes very difficult.[223]

The Belgian survivor, Regina Louf (witness *X1* of the Dutroux case), reported in an interview given to Annemie Bulté and Douglas De Coninck (the authors of *"Les dossiers X: Ce que la Belgique ne devait pas savoir sur l'affaire Dutroux"*, 1999) that *"when they received a new victim in their network, it was extremely important that she could not talk to anyone about what happened to her. That is why they organised 'ceremonies'... The only objective of these rituals was to totally disorientate the victims."*[224]

In her book "Trauma and Recovery", Judith Lewis Herman writes: "Secrecy and silence are the first protection for abusers. If secrecy is broken, the abuser will attack the victim's credibility. If he cannot silence her completely, he will try to make sure that no one listens. Rituals contribute to this objective of discrediting, especially in a modern society that is increasingly materialistic and totally closed to the existence of "diabolic" religious practices described as "medieval". The devil's strength is to make people believe that he does not exist... However, there seems to be no doubt that these "diabolic" practices exist and are practised in our so-called "civilised" and "modern" societies, perhaps more than ever...

A 218-page thesis entitled *"Ritual abuse: the point of view of sexual assault workers"* was submitted in 2008 to the Université du Québec en Outaouais. Here is the text of the presentation of this thesis: *"Ritual abuse remains a little known subject in the various intervention environments. The lack of consensus on how to conceptualise ritual abuse and the controversy surrounding it hinder its recognition. This qualitative research has three objectives: to document and analyze information about ritual abuse, to advance knowledge and understanding of this type of abuse from the perspective of sexual assault workers who have supported women who have experienced it in early childhood, and to contribute to the advancement of knowledge on the subject in the francophone intervention community. Semi-structured interviews were conducted with eight workers who practice in various sexual assault services and who acknowledged having worked with at least two survivors of ritual abuse. The results obtained are presented in three distinct parts: those describing the overall characteristics of the concept of ritual abuse, those allowing us to learn about the after-effects of this type of abuse, and those resulting from the participants' experiences in their interventions with ritual abuse survivors. This research recognises some of the problems with the conceptualisation of ritual abuse, including the use of the word cult to address the subject. It is hoped that the definition of ritual abuse developed in this research will be used as a starting point for consultation among practitioners*

---

[223] Report of the Ritual Abuse Task Force Los Angeles County Commission for Women " - 15/09/1989.

[224] *Interview with Regina Louf, Witness XI at Neufchateau"* - Annemie Bulté and Douglas De Coninck, De Morgen, 1998.

who have experience working with ritual abuse survivors so that they can agree on how to define this type of abuse. It is also recommended that more research be done on ritual abuse, particularly with regard to programming, a method of thought control, and dissociation in ritual abuse survivors. Above all, there is a need to develop more practical intervention knowledge in this area. More research is also needed on the links between ritual abuse and sexual sadism, and ritual abuse and child sexual exploitation networks. "[225]

In 2011 the journal "Trauma & Dissociation" (International Society for the Study of Trauma and Dissociation) published a French-language dossier entitled "Lignes directrices pour le traitement du trouble dissociatif de l'identité chez l'adulte". This file contains a chapter entitled "Abus organisés" showing that this subject of ritual abuse is totally linked to the phenomenon of dissociative disorders:

A substantial minority of patients with Dissociative Identity Disorder (DID) report sadistic, exploitative, coercive abuse at the hands of organised groups. This type of organised abuse victimises individuals through extreme control of their environments in childhood and frequently involves multiple abusers. It may be organised around the activities of paedophile rings, child pornography or child prostitution rings, various 'religious' or cult groups, multi-generational family systems and human trafficking and prostitution rings. Organised abuse frequently incorporates activities that are sexually perverse, horrific and sadistic, and may involve coercion of the child as a witness or participant in the abuse of other children. Survivors of organised abuse - particularly ongoing abuse - are among the most traumatised of dissociative patients. They are most prone to self-destruction and serious suicide attempts. They very often appear to be caught up in very ambivalent attachments to their abusers and often present complex forms of IDD. Some of these highly traumatized patients show marked amnesia for much of their abuse and the history of organized abuse only emerges during treatment."[226]

Ritual abuse leading to deep trauma will develop a complex form of post-traumatic stress disorder which can lead to many symptoms in victims: panic attacks, uncontrollable crying, uncontrollable anger, eating disorders, suicidal tendencies, self-mutilation, hyper-vigilance, somatic symptoms, obsessions, terrors, sleep disturbances, nightmares, flashbacks, photographic memory, addictions: alcohol, drugs, sex, over-reaction to minor stress, violent or flight reactions, extreme mood swings, risk-taking behaviour, shame and guilt, dehumanisation, inordinate preoccupation with the abuser, attribution of total power to the abuser, idealisation of the abuser, gratitude to the abuser, belief in some form of special or supernatural relationship with the abuser, acceptance of

---

[225] *"Ritual abuse: the point of view of sexual assault workers"* - Jacques, Christine (2008). Dissertation. Gatineau, Université du Québec en Outaouais (UQO), Department of Social Work. Date of submission: 11 Oct. 2011 - http://dpndev.uqo.ca/id/eprint/339.

[226] Guidelines for Treating Dissociative Identity Disorder in Adults - Journal of Trauma & Dissociation - ISSTD: International Society for the Study of Trauma and Dissociation

the abuser's beliefs and assertions, repeated failures to protect oneself, helplessness and hopelessness.

Such ritual abuse is an integral part of the lives of some families where one or both parents are involved or collaborate in a network. This type of practice is also carried out by military or political groups with the knowledge to programme individuals, usually children. Children are thus sexually abused with rituals and intimidation to terrorise and silence them; but the aim is also to convert and format them into a belief system, a cult. In these Satanist or Luciferian groups, the basic programming instilled in the child is loyalty and fidelity to the group and the law of silence. The child will be indoctrinated to believe that the group's way of life is the only way and that its leaders and entities (deity and demons) must be obeyed and loyal. The cult, the network, must represent its only 'family'. The child is conditioned to believe that the abuses are for his or her own good, it is a military type of conditioning in which thinking for oneself is not tolerated, the children must obey without thinking. In these mind control protocols, the abusers separate and isolate the victim from the rest of humanity by forcing them to do things that are vile and unthinkable to a normal human. Very soon, children will have to participate in the rapes and tortures. This is a way of making them feel guilty and complicit so that they do not disclose the criminal activities outside the group. This means that the child will witness and participate in rape, animal sacrifice and real or simulated human sacrifice. These children are manipulated into believing that the abuse they may have committed against animals or other children was of their own choosing. This makes them feel guilty and ashamed, fearing revenge or even the police and prison. This cements the law of silence as well as the excruciating and overwhelming feeling of being a perpetrator and criminal themselves. All of this combined with dissociative disorders will lead the child to isolate the painful experiences psychologically and to carry on with life 'as if nothing had happened' and of course without any external disclosure.

These practices therefore involve, on the one hand, the children of these Luciferian families, destined to occupy key positions within our society, and on the other, small victims destined to be tortured and sacrificed by the former. They are literally fresh flesh used in rituals to programme the younger generation of the elitist cult. In the same way that there are two categories of MK-Monarch slaves: firstly, those who are "second class", used for prostitution, drug trafficking, etc., destined to be sacrificed; and secondly, those who are part of the Luciferian bloodlines who will be destined to serve the hierarchy throughout their lives by occupying strategic positions (we will come back to this in Chapter 7 on MK-Monarch programming). This forced participation of children in ritual abuse also serves to externalise the 'inner rage' that has built up as a result of their own abuse and torture. The child develops a considerable negative emotional charge (traumatic memory) during the abuse, which he or she can either turn against himself or herself or against other children or animals. The training of these "rabies children" is also done by forcing them to kill a pet to which they have previously become closely related. Everything is done to 'break' the child, to neutralise all natural empathy and innocence in the early years by creating deep dissociative disorders in the child. Ritual abuse is practised in families that systematically repeat the violence on their descendants. Families that are mired in a transgenerational pathological continuity and loaded with demonic ties due to the occult that they indulge in from generation to generation. The children of these bloodlines are programmed to perpetuate the unfortunate *tradition*, the victim child will in turn become a perpetrator reproducing the abuse he or she has suffered if not taken care of and removed from the destructive cult. In the German documentary *"Sexzwang"* (forced sex), Dr. Jim Phillips (former forensic scientist for the British police) states: *"All Satanists have been abused, all of them! I can't imagine that a normal human being would be capable of doing something so horrible, disgusting and repulsive..."*

Clinical psychologist Ellen P. Lacter wrote: "All the victims were forced to commit violence against others, often from early childhood. All abusers have been victims of severe abuse themselves. It is essential to bear this in mind when dealing with survivors. The 'Black-White' or 'Good-Evil' schema is to be avoided as it will feed the patient's fear that they may be irredeemably bad."[227]

Living in such a chaotic environment will cause sudden changes in the child's body chemistry. This type of traumatic life leads to high levels of adrenaline which can be very addictive for the child or adolescent. In adulthood (and even before) the victim will consciously or unconsciously provoke situations to raise their adrenaline level. Violence is a very effective way to do this. It is therefore important to take into account this phenomenon of addiction to violence and its systematic repetition from one generation to the next in violent families linked or not to ritual abuse. This violence against others triggers a sudden production of endorphins in the perpetrator during the act, which also allows him to dissociate himself and anaesthetise his own increasingly explosive traumatic memory, all in an unconscious manner. The aggressor (himself a former victim) thus relieves his own inner pain with a *"shot"* of endorphins. This is a vicious circle and a real addiction to endorphins and violence (more on this in Chapter 5). The book *"Ritual Abuse and Mind Control: The Manipulation of Attachment Needs"* contains the testimony of a survivor who illustrates this phenomenon of dissociative disorders that are repeated from generation to generation: *"My first memory of X was when he came into the room and grabbed me by the hair and twirled me around. When he stopped, everyone laughed because I was all confused. He could go from being incredibly cold and cruel to being extremely kind. Many times I tried to please him to get to his kind side (...) she* (editor's note: the mother) *also abused me from birth, not only in rituals, but also at home. There was a part of her that lost control, she would show her teeth, her eyes would light up in a certain way and she would go crazy..."*[228]

---

[227] *Advocating for Ritualistically Abused Children "* - Dr. Ellen P. Lacter, 2002, CALAPT Newsletter.

[228] *"Ritual Abuse and Mind Control: The Manipulation of Attachment Needs"* - Orit Badouk Epstein, Joseph Schwartz, Rachel Wingfield Schwartz, 2011, p.144.

This dissociative phenomenon with alternating totally immoral and violent behaviour with normal and loving behaviour will create a kind of cognitive dissonance in the child's mind. The child will unconsciously block out contradictory memories in which a parent who is supposed to love and care for him behaves in a totally abnormal and dangerous way. This reinforces amnesia and dissociative states in children. Repetitive traumas will split the child into different personalities and the child will respond differently to the "good" mother and the "bad" mother. For example, when the "bad" mother inflicts torture, the child switches to a personality that knows how to react to the "bad" mother. If it is the "good" mother who takes care of him, the child is in another state of consciousness and is not aware of the "bad" mother or of his other alter linked to the dark side of his mother. This phenomenon of dissociation and amnesia explains some victims' testimonies that there was *the "night child"* and *the "day child"*, two personalities that were not aware of each other and that allowed the child to lead a normal life, until the day when the traumatic memories eventually came back in adulthood (see Chapter 5).

In her book *Unshackled*, Kathleen Sullivan, a survivor of ritual abuse and mind control, also describes the dissociative states her parents were in when they abused their daughter: *"Each time she used a white sheet to hang me from a beam. When she did this, her voice became that of a little girl. She seemed to be replaying what someone had done to her as a child. Then, strangely, her voice would become that of an elderly person saying horrible things about me (...) On several occasions, she also locked me in a wooden box in the basement. Sometimes I would be locked in pain for hours inside this cramped box. When she would come downstairs to get me, she would "rescue" me from the box and ask me how I got there. She didn't seem to remember and I couldn't tell her that she was responsible."*[229]

The psychotraumatologist Muriel Salmona describes this process of dissociation of the personality as follows: "Moreover, women often say that they no longer recognise their aggressor, their partner, when he becomes violent. He starts to have a different look, a different expression, different ways of speaking, of shouting, a different voice... Because often they reproduce their father's voice identically, for example. It's impressive because it's no longer the same person, the aggressors are suddenly colonised by someone else they can't control."[230]

Many victims or perpetrators who have been under the influence of these highly traumatic practices during childhood and adolescence therefore develop severe dissociative disorders; including a multiple personality syndrome (Dissociative Identity Disorder, D.I.D.) which is the most extreme level of psychic dissociation. The perpetrator may therefore be a second personality (an alter) of the individual who will be unaware of his or her *Dr Jekyll & Mr Hide* functioning because of the amnesic walls that partition the different personalities. He may be perfectly integrated into society and his public personality will give no hint of his occult and violent activities. The public alter

---

[229] Unshackled: a Survivor's Story of Mind-Control - Kathleen Sullivan, 2003, p.34.

[230] Muriel Salmona - Pratis TV, 20/01/2014.

personality may be that of a good sincere Christian, while a much deeper alter personality will be the worst Satanist. Ritual abuse aimed at personality splitting is the cornerstone of mind control, the key element in subduing, exploiting and silencing victims. This control is achieved through the deliberate creation of a dissociative identity disorder through repetitive trauma, combined with indoctrination, conditioning, hypnosis and various psychotropic drugs, all accompanied by programming, the effectiveness of which will depend on the level of instruction the network has in this type of mind control.

Dr. Lawrence Pazder describes a certain ubiquity of executioners in our society who have "a normal appearance and lead an equally normal life at first sight. They are present in all strata of society, which they have carefully infiltrated. Any position of power or influence over society must be considered for them as a target for infiltration. The executioners have money available, many have impeccable positions: doctors, ministers, professions of all kinds."[231]

Dr. Catherine Gould, a founding member of the Los Angeles *Task Force* on Ritual Abuse, is internationally recognised for her therapeutic work with child victims of Satanism. In 1994, in Antony Thomas' documentary *"In Satan's Name"*, she described the same thing as Dr. Pazder about the infiltration and control of society by these cults: *"There are certainly bankers, psychologists, media people, we've also heard from child protective services, but also from police officers, because they have a vested interest in being present in all of these social and professional settings. When I started this work, I thought that the motivations behind paedophilia were limited to sex and money, but I started to realise in the course of my ten years of research that the motivations are much more sinister... Children are abused for indoctrination purposes. Ritual child abuse is a protocol for formatting humans to a cult. It's about formatting children who have been so abused, so mind-controlled that they become very useful to the cult, at all levels... I think the purpose of this is to get maximum control, whether it's in this country or in another."*

British psychiatrist Vera Diamond, who also works with survivors of ritual abuse, says in the same documentary: *"People are indoctrinated in a way that is very difficult to understand. I am currently working with people who have been through this kind of conditioning. It's called 'mind control', they completely format the victim. According to our sources, this involves high level organisations such as the CIA. I've even heard of the involvement of the Royal family, but also of other equally high families."*

American pastor Bob Larson also speaks of a systematic infiltration of institutions to establish their control: 'It is perfectly possible that these activities are even above the Mafia and other criminal organisations. It is possible that this is the largest criminal network and organisation in the world. They infiltrate the judicial system, the legislative and executive branches of government, the positions and professions of power and authority. So they can have some control.

---

[231] Dr. Lawrence Pazder: *The Emergence of Ritualistic Crime in Today's Society,* Paper presented at the North Colorado-South Wyoming Detectives Association. Fort Collins, CO: September 9-12,1986. *Occult crime: a law enforcement primer.*

They believe, as the Bible prophesies, that one day the Antichrist will rule the whole world."

The government report "Ritual Crime in the State of Utah" mentioned earlier in this chapter describes what it calls "Generational Satanism" as follows: "This type of group includes male and female members of all ages. They are usually born into the group and cannot seem to get out of it except by death. They are highly organised, very disciplined and extremely discreet. The local groups have strong links with national and international groups (editor's note: extensive network). The rituals they perform are elaborate and completely planned. They are Satan worshippers and they do everything to advance their cause (...) Their roots and practices go back hundreds of years. These people practice ritual abuse and child sacrifice (...) Women in these groups are used as 'breeders' to provide babies for the cult. These cults achieve perfect control over the members who leave no evidence of their activities (...) Sceptics cannot believe in the existence of such groups, arguing that no one can torture and sacrifice babies and children. However, in the past children were sacrificed to Satan but under other names such as Moloch. There are also documented historical cases of child sacrifices. In our time, many people report the existence of this kind of Satanism. They are discredited by the sceptics as are the many people who are undergoing therapy for dissociative disorders caused by severe psychological and physical trauma."[232]

In the book *Breaking the Circle of Satanic Ritual*, Daniel Ryder writes that for Sergeant Jon Hinchcliff (retired Mineapolis Police), one of the factors that allows these occult activities to continue is the social status of the members of the network. Hinchcliff reports that victim testimonies show that some of these members are doctors, lawyers, respected businessmen, clerics, judges, etc. The ex-police officer said: "*It seems that all their bases are covered and protected.*" Because of their facade of respectability and strategic placement, these people can make very calculated counter-attacks before any public disclosure of criminal activities can be made.

In her book *"The New Satanists"*, Linda Blood (former member of the *Temple of Set* and former mistress of Michael Aquino) reports the testimony of a certain *Bill Carmody*, who is the pseudonym of a senior intelligence instructor at the *FLETC* (*Federal Law Enforcement Training Center*): "*Carmody investigated for some time disappearances of children that appeared to be related to cult activities. As a member of a specialised team, he investigated a network that operated in several states in the southwest of the United States. Carmody was able to infiltrate a total of three criminal Satanist cults. Carmody said of these cults: "The most serious ones are the ones that are the most hidden and covered up, in fact these clans have very sophisticated organisations while having the best means of communication, it's an international network. Carmody states that these groups are involved in drug, arms and human trafficking, as well as child pornography (...) According to him, the best organised criminal*

---

[232] "Ritual Crime in the State of Utah: Investigation, Analysis & A Look Forward" - Utah Attorney General's Office, Michael R. King and Matt Jacobson, 1995, p.15.

cults are led by intelligent and highly educated people, people from the upper classes of society where they hold important positions in their community, so-called "respectable" positions. These sectarian groups constitute a very secret subculture which is part of the underworld in the broadest sense. They are generally composed of members of transgenerational families whose blood ties help to maintain silence and secrecy.[233]

During his appearance on the web TV *Meta-TV* in 2015, the ex-gendarme and French activist Christian 'Stan' Maillaud described in part this elitist network practising systematic ritual abuse to train the elite of tomorrow:

At the present time, when all the key posts are not yet held by "MK-Ultra", when the entire societal elite is not yet held by these mentally ill people, there are still human beings in the camp of the armed forces and we must put all our energy in their direction (...).Because there must be a split in their forces and they must come to the camp of the sovereign people who must free themselves from this hold (...) I am talking about the bite of the vampire, that is to say that for me the act of sodomising a martyred child corresponds to the vampire who bites a creature in order to turn it into a vampire. A child who is raped, tortured, martyred throughout his childhood, who finds neither justice nor protection and who arrives at adulthood like that, maintained in the networks that martyr him, becomes a predator himself. Especially when it is explained to him that if he in turn attacks other children who are tortured and raped, this will relieve him of his own suffering. This is the protocol they apply (...) It's a recurrent thing (...) the people who are placed in the societal elite are those who are selected by Freemasonry or the Rosicrucians (...) You have to know that in Freemasonry, in order to rise in rank you have to go through rituals, so this little pyramid is to be superimposed on the pyramid of your career. You want to rise in rank? Then you have to pass rituals in the lodge you belong to. The more you are greedy for power and success, the more you will ask to pass the ranks and you will then be caught up in satanic rituals. The first practices are the collective rape of children, then the killing, etc... What makes you have completely degenerated people who arrive at the head of institutions and that these people thereafter bring their own children from a young age in rituals of this kind to make them the future societal elite. And this is something that people still don't understand at the moment. When we investigated, we saw that there is a protocol where there are two types of victims: there are disadvantaged children, abducted children, children born under X, of rape, who are used as "raw material" for the initiation of other children. That is to say, on the one hand you have children who are taken by a freemason father to these parties, and on the other hand, these children who come out of cages and are put there so that the child of the elite ends up opening the womb of this unfortunate person who has been collectively raped and tortured by everyone... Why? Because this will create the fragmentation of the personality or the compartmentalisation of memories (...) You can imagine the monsters that are put on the market... So that's why at the moment in all the little

---

[233] *The New Satanists* - Linda Blood, 1994, p.29-30.

societal elite, all the places are being taken by these monsters following these formal protocols that really originated in Auschwitz."

Despite the total silence of the mainstream media on the subject, many people are working to expose these inhumane practices. In 1996, an article entitled *"An Analysis of* Ritualistic *and Religion-Related Child Abuse Allegations"*[234] was written by three university psychology professors: Bette Bottoms, Phillip Shaver and Gail Goodman. The article contains a list of criteria that can be used to define cases of ritual abuse, these criteria were compiled from the testimonies of victims and therapists:

- Abuse by one or more individuals of a group in which members appear to follow the orders of one or more leaders.

- Abuse related to any practice or behaviour that is repeated in a specific way (which may include prayers, chants, incantations, wearing of particular clothes...)

- Abuses related to symbols (e.g. 666, inverted pentagram, inverted or broken crosses), invocations, clothing with symbols, beliefs associated with Satan.

- Abuse linked to a belief in the supernatural, paranormal, occult or special powers (e.g. *'magic surgery'* - detailed in Chapter 7 - , spiritualism, etc)

- Rituals associated with activities involving tombs, crypts, bones...

- Rituals involving animal or human excrement or blood.

- Rituals involving specific daggers, candles, altars...

- Rituals involving real or simulated torture and sacrifice of animals.

- Rituals involving sacrifices with real or simulated killings of humans.

- Rituals involving real or simulated acts of cannibalism.

- Rituals involving the obligation to attend or participate in sexual practices.

- Rituals involving child pornography.

- Rituals involving drugs.

- Rituals to bind a child to Satan or a demonic entity.

- Abuse by a priest, rabbi or pastor.

- Abuse committed in a religious setting, religious school or religious centre.

- "Breeding" of newborns for sacrificial rituals.

- Abuse causing periods of amnesia or recurring disturbance on certain dates.

- Abuse disclosed by an individual with a dissociative disorder or multiple personality caused by ritual or religious abuse.

This list is not exhaustive. In 1989, the Ritual Abuse Task Force Report was published by the Los Angeles Commission for Women, chaired by Myra B. Riddell, with input from Dr. Catherine Gould and Dr. Lynn Laboriel. Riddell, with the participation of Dr. Catherine Gould and Dr. Lynn Laboriel. The study

---

[234] An Analysis of Ritualistic and Religion-Related Child Abuse Allegations" - "Law and Human Behaviour" Vol. 20, N°1, 1996.

commission was composed of professionals from the medical, mental health, education and justice sectors, as well as members of victim support organisations. This report mentions the types of physical and psychological abuse described by the survivors and their therapists:

- Locking the victim in a cage, wardrobe, cellar or other confined area, telling them that they will die there. Some victims report being locked in a coffin and buried alive to simulate death. One of the members of the group then comes to the 'rescue' of the traumatised child who will establish a privileged link with his or her saviour who will be perceived as an ally. The confinement can be done with insects or animals. This 'game' of isolation and deliverance will make the child even more vulnerable to the indoctrination and destructive practices of the group.

- Humiliation through verbal abuse, forced nudity in front of the group, forced ingestion of urine, faeces, blood, human flesh or semen. Forced to commit heinous acts such as mutilation, murder, rape of a child or infant.

- With guilt and threats of denunciation, the victim is deceived into believing that her participation in the atrocities was voluntary. This sense of guilt and shame helps to show loyalty and allegiance to the cult and its doctrines. Victims are indoctrinated to believe that the hyper-violent group is the only safe haven that can accept and protect them and that there is no point in seeking help from outside. The child is indoctrinated to believe that God has rejected and abandoned them, that they are bound to Satan, and that there is no way out of the group.

- Physical violence involving rape and sexual torture usually carried out in groups, zoophilia, electric shocks, hanging by the hands or feet, immersion in water to the point of near drowning, deprivation of food, water and sleep. A victim in a state of exhaustion is much more open to mental control because fatigue will impair his or her ability to judge. Painful torture causes the child to disassociate, and like a prisoner of war under torture he or she becomes willing to do whatever is required to make the pain stop. Physical pain is often associated with sexual arousal that a child is not prepared to deal with. Pain and pleasure are combined to help establish an unhealthy relationship between children and abusers. Stockholm syndrome is exploited to the full to create an attachment between victims and perpetrators.

- Make the victim feel that he/she is constantly being watched and controlled by the perpetrators and their spiritual allies (spirits, demons, deities). The child is manipulated into believing that the "walls have ears" and that an "all-seeing eye" is constantly watching his or her actions. The child is subjected to all sorts of lies whose aim is to reinforce the omnipotence and omnipresence of the perpetrators.

- Oath of secrecy on pain of death if the victim discloses anything. Mental programming for the victim to commit suicide in case of recollection or disclosure of sectarian and criminal activities. High vulnerability to self-sabotage and self-destructive impulses when the victim begins therapy and attempts to leave the cult group.

- Use of psychotropic drugs that alter and confuse the victim's consciousness, thus facilitating sexual assault. Psychotropic drugs may be injected, administered orally, in the form of suppositories or incorporated into food or drink. The hypnotic and paralytic effects cause the victim to become mentally confused, drowsy, and have their memory impaired. Perpetrators rely on these drug-induced changes in consciousness to reinforce the illusion that they have absolute power over the child. Victims also lose the notion of the boundary between the group and the self, and come to identify with the group and feel like an extension of it. The loss of self-esteem contributes to the development of malice and inner rage.

- Use of mind control, hypnosis, conditioning and programming with the use of 'triggers' to manipulate the victim's different personalities. Survivors of ritual abuse report intense light projections into the eyes during programming sessions. These lights appear to cause disorientation and induce a trance-like state, thereby decreasing the victim's resistance and increasing their suggestibility to programming.

- Coercing the victim to work for the cult on the outside, by engaging in prostitution, drug trafficking and other illegal activities. Infiltration of social institutions (schools, churches, law enforcement, courts, psychiatry, politics...) to expand the group's sphere of influence.

- Exploitation of recurrent pregnancies following the rape of certain young girls in the group used as 'reproducers'. The aim is to regularly provide the cult with undeclared babies. These babies are used to fuel ritual sacrifices or the black market, while these traumatic pregnancies and deliveries serve to 'break' and further control the victim. Young victims may be forced to undergo hormonal treatment to accelerate puberty.

- Use of rituals such as *"magic surgery"* (more on this in Chapter 7), various "rites of passage" such as the *"rebirth ritual"* and the *"ritual marriage"*, *in* order to reinforce the subjection to the cult. Spiritual indoctrination is a key issue in these groups. A ritual marriage can be between a child and his tormentor, between two children or between the child and Satan. These 'rebirth' and 'marriage' rituals have the consequence of binding the victim psychologically but also spiritually to the group and to the powers of evil. Non-biological twinning is also used as a means of mind control. For example, two young children will be initiated in a ceremony with a *magical union of* their souls, they then become *inseparable twins for eternity*. They will each share half of the same mental programming making them interdependent on each other. These ritual alliances chain together the alter personalities created by the extreme traumas, alter personalities that will remain loyal to the cult until they are removed from the cult with deprogramming work.

b/ Symbolism of death and rebirth

As we saw in Chapter 2, 'rebirth rituals' with a passage through a symbolic death and rebirth were a common feature of the Mystery religions. This practice of symbolic 'resurrection' is also present in shamanic traditions. Here,

Lloyd deMause takes up the description of a shamanic ritual by comparing it to the real childbirth: *"When the drum roll accelerates (heartbeat and contractions)... the whole structure cracks like a cosmic wave over my head (breaking of the amniotic waters)... and in a supreme effort, I have to keep going, my legs are blocked (passage through the birth canal)... my skull is a drum, my veins will burst and pierce my skin (anoxia)... I am sucked and pulled apart both downwards and upwards (birth)... Finally, it's as if I'm coming back from a very long way away, from an infinite depth where I've been nestled. Then suddenly the surface, suddenly the air, suddenly this dazzling white. "[235]*

This type of initiatory resurrection is frequently mentioned in the testimonies of survivors of modern ritual abuse. This death and rebirth may be symbolised by an actual burial in a coffin or vault in a cemetery. Some survivors even report being placed in the carcass of a dead animal and in some cases in a human corpse. Dr. Judianne Densen-Gerber, an American lawyer and psychiatrist who specialises in child abuse, speaks of a satanic ritual in which a child is placed in the gaping womb of a woman who has just had a caesarean section to remove her baby. This ritual was also described by Kathleen Sorenson and survivor Paul Bonacci (more on their testimonies later). Senator John De Camp reports Densen-Gerber's words in his book *"The Franklin Cover-up"*: *"I've been in this business long enough and I had to realize what these three patients were telling me. It was something so horrible for me to imagine. To take a two-year-old child and put it in the open womb of a dying woman. To have that child covered in blood. I use denial myself after all these years... According to Sorenson, this happened in Nebraska, today she is dead. But the same thing, the same ceremony, was described by Bonacci, also in Nebraska. "[236]*

The ex-satanist Stella Katz describes the rebirth ceremony in which the child's personality is split up as follows: *"It can be a carcass of a cow, a large goat or a sheep. The children are told that they can only enter the realm of darkness if they are born from the blood and the beast. This is similar, but in a reverse way to the Christian belief that only those born of water and the Holy Spirit will be able to enter the Kingdom of God. The child is drugged and placed naked in a carcass. He or she is sewn into the body (...) The hand of the 'deliverer' is inserted and the child is pulled through the incision that has been made in the animal. During this experience, the child, who is used to splitting up when terrorised, will create a new split* (editor's note: new alter/personality). *The child's alter is then usually identified with a demon name by the one who delivers it. "[237]*

Fritz Springmeier also describes the same type of rituals also serving as Satanic baptism: "This ceremony may vary in some details, but here is the ritual

---

[235] The Emotional Life of Nations" - Lloyd deMause, 2002.

[236] "The Franklin Cover-Up: Child Abuse, Satanism, and Murder in Nebraska" - John W. De Camp, 2011, p.212.

[237] "Healing The Unimaginable: Treating Ritual Abuse And Mind-Control" - Alison Miller, 2012, p.110.

performed for a child destined for Monarch mind control: the child is undressed and put into a purple robe. It is placed inside a pentagram with a naked woman as an altar before which the child is presented. A horse or jackal with the inscription 'Nebebka' on its neck or forehead is then sacrificed in the name of Satan (the name given to it may vary according to the group, it may be 'Set' or 'Saman' for example). The abdomen of the beast is completely opened and the liver is removed. The four guardian spirits of the four cardinal points, the 'watchtowers', are then invoked. The Monarch child is then smeared with the fat of the dead animal. A gatekeeper spirit is then summoned with a bell and the child is placed in the belly of the animal. Part of the raw liver is given to the child and the rest is eaten by the group. The child is eventually baptised with the blood of the sacrificed animal."[238]

The re-enactment of the birth trauma (or even intrauterine regression) is a common feature of Satanic ritual abuse (perhaps unconsciously linked to the initial trauma of twin pregnancies where the foetus experiences its twin(s) dying alongside it in the womb...). It would seem that the initiate's anxiety to remain permanently in union with the mother, and thus avoid the repetition of the birth trauma, is illustrated in the ancient Gnostic cults. These Mystery religions expressed their rejection of God the Father by a desire to return to the Mother Goddess. The rituals of birth, or rebirth, come from the ancient fertility cults linked to the Mother Goddess. The "Mother" and the incestuous orgy was elevated to the status of a divine ritual in opposition to "God the Father". In the ancient Mysteries, the initiate received the promise of divine omnipotence, a cosmic union with the "whole", through symbolic union with "The Mother". In the Eleusinian Mysteries, there was an initiation called the 'Dark Descent' into the Mother. The hierophant was accompanied in this dark initiation by a priestess who represented the Mother Goddess, the descent into her womb. In the Phrygian Mystery cult, the initiate descends into a pit and the blood of an animal is poured over him, after which he receives the *'nourishing milk'*. As we saw in Chapter 2, the Phibionite sect aimed to gather male semen and female menstruation in a kind of *'sperm cult'* where even human foetuses were consumed. All these rites revolve around fertility, mixing both the fertility of the *'mother earth'* and human fertility, often resulting in totally depraved and criminal practices.

For the psycho-historian Lloyd deMause, the only way to make sense of certain elements present in ritual abuse is to consider that they symbolically and even physically relive the trauma of birth. These include confinement in symbolic wombs (cages, boxes, coffins, but also real organic wombs), hanging upside down, which reproduces the sensation of the foetus in the womb. Submersion of the head in water during torture replicates the experience of amniotic fluid while suffocation replicates the anoxia that all babies experience during childbirth. The victim is forced to drink blood and urine, just as the foetus 'drinks' placental blood and 'bathes' in its urine. Rituals are often performed in tunnels or cellars, dark and damp underground places symbolising the

---

[238] "The Illuminati Formula Used to Create an Undetectable Total Mind Controlled Slave" - Fritz Springmeier & Cisco Wheeler, 1996.

confinement of the vaginal canal or womb. The sixteen characteristic elements of ritual abuse that researchers Jean Goodwin and David Finkelhor have identified are all related to the re-enactment of the trauma of birth. Without a symbolic 'birth', all these acts would be meaningless. Some researchers have asked a question about these systematic protocols in ritual abuse: *"Why rape in such a complicated way?* Because this process represents the *fetal drama* that must be reproduced and relived, certainly in an unconscious way.

In the book *"The Witches'* Way: *Principles, Rituals and Beliefs of Modern Witchcraft"*, Janet and Stewart Fenar report a victim's testimony that she was tied up naked and in a trance-like state and carried to a cave by a group of naked women. Once in the cave, the women passed her under their legs, gesticulating and screaming, as if giving birth. Then a symbolic umbilical cord was cut and the victim was doused with water. In his book *Symbolic Wounds*, Bruno Bettelheim also describes puberty-related rites in which young boys have to crawl under the legs of older men, in a symbolic rebirth. In the book *'Michelle Remembers'*, survivor Michelle Smith recalls her 'birth' ritual. A baby was first stabbed, then placed between Michelle's legs and its blood smeared on her, as if it possessed 'power'. Then red symbols were painted on her body and she had to put her head between a woman's legs and crawl as if the woman was giving birth to her. She also describes another ritual where she was placed inside a plaster statue of the devil and covered in blood. She says she felt like she was in a "toothpaste tube" when she was expelled: *"I am being born, I have something thick wrapped around my neck but a man cuts this rope so I don't choke."*[239]

The secret society *Skull and* Bones practices a symbolic death ritual in which the initiate is placed naked in a coffin and has to undergo various traumatic steps in order to be reborn and have his life transformed. In this coffin, he must also confess his darkest sexual activities. For the *Skull and Bones*, during the night of the ritual the initiate *"dies to the world to be reborn into the Order (...) While in the coffin for a symbolic journey through the underworld for his rebirth, which will take place in chamber number 322, the Order then dresses the "newborn" knight in special clothes, indicating that from now on he will have to adapt to the Order's mission.*[240] The oath taken by the initiate during this rebirth ritual swears an allegiance to the secret Order that surpasses all that concerns the profane world. It is a total allegiance to the group...

This type of ritual is common in Satanism. In his book *The Satanic Rituals: Companion to the Satanic Bible*, Anton Lavey, the founder of the Church of Satan, wrote: *"The rebirth ceremony takes place in a large coffin, similarly this symbolism of the coffin is found in most lodge rituals."*[241]

The ex-illuminati 'Svali', a survivor of ritual abuse and mind control who has somehow deserted the cult to give her testimony, claimed that one of their

---

[239] "Why Cults Terrorize and Kill Children" - Lloyd de Mause, The journal of Psychohistory 21, 1994.

[240] The Last Secrets of Skull and Bones " - Ron Rosenbaum, Esquire Magazine, 1977.

[241] The Satanic Rituals: Companion to the Satanic Bible " - Aton Lavey, 1976, p.57.

oldest rituals is the *'resurrection ceremony'*. The Phoenix is one of the symbols they value most, and death and rebirth to a new life is very much a part of the rituals of the Luciferian elite. We will see in Chapter 6 what this "resurrection" (and MK programming) ritual consists of, which goes so far as to cause a near-death experience (NDE) in the little victim.

c/ Blood sacrifice

> *"The hardcore Satanist groups believe that the best way to raise energy is either through the sexual act or through sacrifice, whether it's an animal or a human... A huge amount of energy is then released, even more so with a human being. If you want to raise this ultimate power, you sacrifice someone. The greatest amount of energy will be with a baby, then with a virgin."* - Bill Schnoebelen

A sacrifice can be an object that serves as an offering to a god, entity or deity in order to establish, restore or maintain a good relationship of man with the sacred. It is also about obtaining help, material favours or spiritual power such as psychic and magical powers. Cremation is a way of making the offering directly available to the gods. Blood rituals (sacrifices or bloodletting) are based on the belief that the life force of the human or animal is in its blood. Sacrifices follow a certain religious calendar which varies according to the cult, they can also be carried out on an ad hoc basis for a birthday for example. In the past, the offering of a human life to a god (demon) was generally used as a ritual for earthly fertility and harvests, nowadays sacrifices are more often used to obtain powers and personal favours. Cannibalism is often combined with human sacrifice because of the belief that the ingestion of human blood and flesh can absorb the victim's life energy. Adult and child survivors of ritual abuse report that the purpose of such practices is to obtain certain magical powers. Survivors explain that the consumption of blood and cannibalism is a way for the abuser(s) to take possession of the victim's spiritual power. Wallis Budge wrote of the cannibalistic acts recorded in *the Egyptian Book of the Dead: "The notion that by eating flesh, or more particularly by drinking the blood of another living being, man absorbs the life of the victim into his own life, is something that appears in primitive cultures in various forms."*[242]

These accounts of human sacrifice always raise a question of credibility with the public. Where do the sacrificed victims come from and where are the *remains*? Some testimonies report that the victims often come from within the cult, i.e. they are babies born of rape to be sacrificed. But they can also be homeless, missing adults or children. There is a deafening silence in the media and a lack of official figures on the annual number of disappearances... The explanation for the absence of remains may also be cannibalism, access to morgues and crematoria by the sect, freezing of flesh, conservation of bones for magical practices... etc. In 2000, on a France 3 television set *(Viols d'Enfants, la*

---

[242] "The Egyptian Book of The Dead (The Papyrus of Ani) Egyptian Text Transliteration and Translation" - E. A. Wallis Budge, 1967.

Fin du Silence?), the former deputy prosecutor of Bobigny, Martine Bouillon, declared that several mass graves of children had been discovered in the Paris region and that an investigation was underway at the time...

The victim, adult or child, who has been tortured and terrorised during the ritual before being killed, will have his or her blood charged with endorphins (endogenous morphine). These endorphins are secreted naturally by the body during intense stress or physical activity and are a natural opiate that acts as a painkiller. In sportsmen and women, the release of endorphins allows them to maintain high levels of effort and they often develop an addiction to the feeling provided by the hormones, the so-called *"runner's* high". A victim of rape and torture, whose pain has been pushed to the limit, will have an extremely high level of endorphins in his or her blood. This blood will be consumed like a drug by the participants in the ritual, who are themselves already in a dissociative state. A form of addiction can therefore develop through the consumption of human or animal blood charged with endorphins.

The ex-Luciferian Svali reports that "The Celtic branch (of the 'illuminati' sect) believes that power is passed on at the moment of passage from life to death. They perform initiation rituals with children or with older followers. The initiate is tied up and an animal is bled to death over him. The belief is that the person then receives the power of the spirit that comes out of the body, this power 'enters' the initiate (...) These people really believe that there are other spiritual dimensions, and that to access them, a great sacrifice has to be made to 'open a portal', usually by the sacrifice of several animals. I have also seen animal sacrifices made for protection, the blood is used to "close the circle" so that certain demonic entities cannot enter. We still find this notion of baptism by blood, the animal bled over the initiate to cover him with haemoglobin, just as in the Mystery cult of Mithras.

For the Satanist Aleister Crowley, the *'best blood'* is the menstrual blood of a woman, then the *'fresh blood of a child'* and finally that of *'enemies'.*[243] In his book *'Magick in Theory and Practice'*, Crowley wrote: *'Blood is life. This simple statement is explained by the Hindus for whom blood is the main vehicle of vital 'Prana'... This is the theory of the ancient Magicians, for whom every living being is a reserve of energy varying in quantity according to the size and health of the animal, and in quality according to its mental and moral character. When the animal dies, this energy is suddenly released. (For magical purposes) The animal must first be killed in a circle, or triangle as the case may be, so that the energy cannot escape. The nature of the animal selected must be in keeping with the nature of the ceremony. For the highest spiritual work, therefore, the purest and most powerful victim should be chosen. A male child of perfect innocence and intelligence is the most suitable and desirable victim. Some magicians who refuse the use of blood have endeavoured to replace it with*

---

[243] "Painted Black: From Drug Killings to Heavy Metal: The Alarming True Story of How Satanism Is Terrorizing Our Communities" - Carl A. Raschke, 1990.

incense... But blood sacrifice, though more dangerous, is the most effective, and in almost all cases human sacrifice is the best. [244]

Fritz Springmeier explains that sex and blood sacrifices are used to interact with demons. Black masses with blood sacrifices also involve orgies. Depravity and sexual magic are ways of interacting with demons, it also releases the tension present during the murderous ceremony. Some particularly powerful entities can only be summoned if there are sacrifices. Demons do not come for free and the price to pay is blood. Satan demands a sacrifice and the child is the greatest offering because it is the purest, add torture and sexual abuse and you have the ultimate offering. Just as with human sacrifice, where the purity of the child is sacrificed and vamped, Satanic sex magic also requires this innocence and purity to be most effective. The combination of the two is the ultimate defilement and therefore the ultimate offering. The executioner will terrorise the child to raise his fear and *energy* to a maximum... Then he rapes him, and kills him at the moment of orgasm in order to vampire the totality of the vital energy. In the black mass, it is the sacrifice of blood (red magic) and then the orgiastic element (sexual magic) that will constitute the *"Vibration"* sought by Satanists. When blood is spilled, it attracts certain more or less hierarchically elevated demonic powers, but also the swarming larvae that populate the lower astral.

Serial killer Ottis Tool has claimed to have been involved in extreme satanic ceremonies. Here is what he told Stephane Bourgoin who interviewed him in prison for his documentary *"Paroles de Serial-Killers"*:

- The initiate, who cut the person's throat, first 'fucks' the person, and the animals 'fuck' them too. Then they 'fuck' the animals and then kill them. They cooked the person and the animals and made a big feast.

- Was it when you were part of the satanic cult?

- Yes... They were doing that... There were many of them. You couldn't... you couldn't recognise them, they usually had a mask or a bonnet covering their face. In some cases you knew who was a member, but... you can't give up the main obligations, because that would be hell, worse than it already is... You can't reveal the passwords and that crap...

In both Luciferian and Satanist cults, the objective is to prove that Satan or Lucifer is more powerful than God the Creator. Some strictly Satanist groups use a system based on the inversion of the Christian tradition, both in ceremonies and in symbols. The cross will be turned upside down, marriage to God is replaced by marriage to Satan. The baptism of water and the Holy Spirit is replaced by the baptism of animal or human blood. The black mass reverses the Catholic mass in the sense that the participants actually eat sacrificial flesh (human or animal) and drink the blood of the victim, thus Satanists practice a kind of communion with their Master, a reversed sanctification. As we shall now see, there is also a *"living sacrifice"*, which is also a total diversion and inversion of the Christic teachings.

---

[244] "Magick: in Theory and Practice" - Aleister Crowley, 1973, p.219.

d/ The living sacrifice

Therapist Patricia Baird Clarke, in her book *'Sanctification in* Reverse*: The* Essence *of Satanic Ritual Abuse'*, described how the 'living sacrifice' of a child among Satanists works:

- People involved in occult activities have a certain degree of separation between soul and spirit that allows them to see, hear and feel entities living on another plane. These people are all, without exception, deluded and mentally confused. Many believe, among other things, that they can communicate with the dead, although the Bible clearly states that this is impossible. Demonic spirits can appear or take on any form, including human form, and thus deceive humans into believing that they can give fame, fortune, and even blessing and eternal life.

Spiritual power can only come from two sources: Jesus Christ or Satan. God gives the power to overcome all sin and temptation by giving His Holy Spirit to those who believe in the atoning sacrifice of His Son Jesus Christ. Those involved in the darkness of the occult are fed by demons. In the world of Satanic worship, demons are powers. If someone were to say that he has the power of ESP, he could also say that he has the demon of ESP. Human beings do not have supernatural powers, these powers come from spiritual entities. The more demons one has, the more powers one has available to fulfil one's own selfish interests. The great powers (demons) must go through the ignoble practice of satanic ritual abuse.

In satanic ritual abuse, an infant or child will be "chosen" and selected as a "special" individual through whom followers can receive energy. To receive energy there must always be a sacrifice; this is a Kingdom principle. Jesus Christ was the perfect sacrifice who gave Himself once for all, and by believing in Him, Christians receive the power to overcome evil and live a victorious Christian life. However, this power is only available to Christians if they are willing to live according to God's instructions, including Romans 12:1, where we are told: "Offer your bodies as a living sacrifice, holy, acceptable to God, which is reasonable worship on your part." Most people who know anything about Satanic worship have heard of babies being killed as a sacrifice to Satan. However, few have heard of the notion of a living sacrifice required by Satan.

God commands Christians to become a living sacrifice for Him. A Satan worshipper would not be willing to be a living sacrifice to anyone, because the very essence of Satanism is based on selfishness and greed but in order to gain access to powers and might, there must be a living sacrifice. Therefore, a helpless baby or child will be chosen to be the living sacrifice to Satan. The child is then subjected to many painful and terrifying rituals in which demons are called upon to possess the child, thus making him or her a "reservoir" or "battery" for storing satanic powers that can be used at will by the cult members. The most common way in which these powers are accessed is through sexual perversion on the child. The child will of course grow and mature into an adult, but because of the severity of the abuse and psychological programming, he will never realise that he possesses these powers. He will suffer throughout his life as much from the harassment of the demons as from his mental programming and the abusers themselves. This person has become a living sacrifice to Satan and his life is a living hell.

This is an abhorrent misappropriation and perversion of a glorious scriptural truth given by God to bring His people into a close and loving relationship with Him and thus fill their lives with blessings!

It is now becoming clear that these consequences of satanic ritual abuse require spiritual ministry. The best psychological techniques or expertise known to man will never be able to deliver a person in torment caused by demonic spirits. Only Christians empowered by the Holy Spirit have the discernment and power to deliver people tortured by demons. Our power over these entities is directly proportional to the extent to which we have been willing to die to ourselves to allow Christ to fill us with Himself. If we are willing to be a living sacrifice to God, we have the love and power to deliver those who, against their will, have been living sacrifices to Satan.[245]

When Patricia Baird Clarke writes 'The most common way in which these powers are accessed is through sexual perversion of the child', this is real sexual magic.

e/ The children of rabies

"... the sudden emergence, in a docile and amiable child, of a personality that is delirious, screaming, laughing out loud, uttering appalling blasphemies and seemingly invaded by an alien being." Witchcraft in England - Barbara Rosen

"We therapists identify much more with the pain and suffering of our patients than with the other side of the split, i.e. rage, revenge, perpetration... These feelings, like all the others, are difficult, but they need to be addressed in therapy." Multiple Personality and Dissociation: Understanding Incest, Abuse, and MPD - David Calof

Because of the extreme violence involved, ritual abuse creates enormous inner tension in the child. This internalised rage is exploited by the group to indoctrinate the child into a system where violence and fury are valued and even encouraged. The child who has been repeatedly raped and tortured in a group is not allowed to express his anger, this violence (or negative charge) that he has to evacuate can only be done by torturing other children and sometimes even by killing them. These hyper-violent behaviours are therefore encouraged and rewarded by adults who use this to make the child feel that he or she is already as violent as they are and that this is proof that he or she is truly becoming a member of the group, and therefore just as guilty as the others...

---

[245] "Sanctification in Reverse: the essence of satanic ritual abuse" - Patricia Baird Clarke, Five Stone Publishing, 2013.

Very violent behaviour has its origins in the first two years of life; the same applies to the feeling of guilt, which is precious because it is the only way of preventing violent acts from being repeated. When this feeling is not formed at this early period, it is difficult to acquire it later on; behind the violent acts of a "primitive", summary appearance, there are complex processes whose main characteristics are the non-differentiation between oneself and others, disorders of the body schema and muscle tone, the inability to pretend, and neurological dysfunctions due to very inadequate mothering care Maurice Berger, "Soigner les enfants violents" (2012)

For groups practising ritual abuse and mind control, the child's mind must be *broken at* an early age. To do this, extremely traumatic experiences will be multiplied, the aim being to corrupt innocence and create dissociative states. Children who normally have a natural empathy and joy of life, become 'soldiers' or 'priests' capable of hurting and even killing without feeling any empathy. The only way to achieve such behaviour is through the process of dissociation. The fracturing of the child into several dissociated personalities is a protective phenomenon against severe trauma. It is the deep dissociative disorders that make it possible to torture and kill in a robotic way without any real awareness of the seriousness of the acts. For these hyper-violent groups, compassion is not acceptable and must be neutralised from the very first years of the child's life, who very quickly, under the weight of trauma, will develop multiple dehumanised personalities.

Children who are victims of physical, psychological and sexual abuse develop an inner negative charge in proportion to the suffering and repetition of the trauma. This negative charge is a latent traumatic memory, but it is nonetheless present in the child who will have to survive the psychotraumatic consequences of the violence. In order to deal with the awakening of this traumatic memory, the child will resort to dissociative behaviours to create a disjunction that anaesthetises this intolerable tension, this negative emotional charge. This disjunction will occur during dissociative behaviours in two ways: either by extreme stress which will provoke a sudden production of hormones, or by using drugs. In a young child, these dissociative behaviours can take the form of self-destructive behaviours such as self-mutilation, scarification, hitting, biting or burning oneself; or even endangerment through risky games or violent behaviour against others, with the other being used as a fuse in a power struggle to make *oneself disconnected* and *anaesthetised*. Destructive cults encourage this chain of violence by pushing the (already traumatised) child to become an executioner and to understand very quickly that this dissociating behaviour, i.e. violence against others, relieves and anaesthetises the child's own traumatic memory: it's a vicious circle. (We will come back to these notions of dissociation and traumatic memory in more detail in the next chapter).

Jean Cartry, author and specialised educator, wrote about Maurice Berger's book "Do we want barbaric children? For about ten years, we took in four brothers, the two eldest of whom had lived for a year with their mother, alternating between erotic relationships and great violence. On the other hand, the two youngest benefited from early judicial protection, especially the last one whom we took in at the age of five months. The judge did not hesitate and removed him from the maternity ward. The first two boys, thirty and nineteen months old, were the most violent and dangerous little children we have ever known. In contrast, their younger brothers were never violent."

In 1990, a documentary entitled *"Child of rage" was* broadcast by *HBO* in its series *"America Undercover"*. This disturbing documentary reveals how a six-year-old girl, Beth Thomas, tortured animals and sexually abused her younger brother Jonathan. It is a compilation of video recordings that Dr. Ken Magid, a clinical psychologist specializing in the treatment of severely abused children, made during therapy sessions with little Beth. These children have been so traumatized in their early months or years that they do not develop a bond with other children or adults. They are children who cannot love or accept to receive love. They are not even aware that they can hurt or even kill (without remorse).

Beth's mother died when she was one year old and she and her younger brother Jonathan were left at the mercy of their father, a sadistic paedophile. The children were severely neglected and Beth was sexually abused until the age of 19 months, when social services took them away from the father and placed them for adoption. In 1984, the two children were given to a couple, Tim and Julie, who were given no information about the children's traumatic past. At the time of the adoption, Jonathan was seven months old, could not hold his head and could not roll onto his side. He had a severe lack of stimulation and feeding. After a few months, Tim and Julie began to observe the children's strange behaviours and learn some things about their past. They thought that Beth had probably been sexually abused and it wasn't long before she showed signs of it. She had a recurring nightmare that *"a man was lying on top of her and hurting her."*

The abuse by her biological father led Beth to engage in violent and sexualised behaviour, especially with her younger brother Jonathan. She also had a tendency to masturbate repeatedly, to the point where she developed an infection and had to be hospitalised. Julie caught her sexually abusing Jonathan one day, he was crying and his trousers were down. When Julie asked her what had happened, she said that she had *pinched his penis and put a finger in his buttocks*, that he had begged her to stop but she had continued. Sometimes Beth would stick needles into her brother and pets. When she was a little older, she even smashed Jonathan's head on the cement floor of the garage, requiring several stitches. At night, the foster parents had to lock her in her room. Beth's intention was not only to hurt her brother, but she wanted to kill him... On the video recordings, she expresses in a very calm and above all very cold way her desire to kill her brother, but also her parents. The most disturbing aspect of Beth's behaviour was her complete lack of remorse and embarrassment about her destructive behaviour. She was well aware that her actions were wrong and dangerous, but that did not matter to her.

Beth has been diagnosed with *an 'attachment disorder'*, characterised by emotional, behavioural and social disorders. This can take the form of an inability to establish appropriate social interactions. The child may show excessive detachment or excessive familiarity with strangers. Beth's case involved a complete inability to develop empathy and an inability to form normal emotional bonds with a human. Beth's behaviour was so extreme that in April 1989 she was removed from her adoptive parents' home and placed in intensive therapy with therapist Connell Watkins. Despite Beth's very dangerous behaviour, this therapist was convinced that she could help her as she had done with other children, sometimes murderers not yet ten years old... Gradually, in the course of therapy, Beth Thomas began to develop empathy, as well as remorse. She learned about right and wrong. Sometimes she would cry openly when she recalled her abusive behaviour towards her little brother. It took several years to bring Beth back into balance, but like all severely abused children, the scars will remain for life. As an adult, Beth obtained a degree in nursing. She wrote a book called *"More Than a* Thread *of Hope"*.

Another famous case of a hyper-violent, even murderous, child is that of the British Mary Flora Bell. At the age of eleven, she was found guilty of murdering two boys aged three and four. During her early childhood, Mary was severely sexually and physically abused. Her mother, who was a sado-masochistic prostitute, used her daughter during sessions with her clients, so the girl was subjected to atrocities. As she grew up, Mary developed a severe rage that manifested itself in the torture of animals and attempts to strangle other children. To her, these were simply *"massages"*, she was not aware of the deadly danger of such practices. It is likely that she had learned strangulation during S&M sessions with her mother. Like Beth Thomas, Mary developed no emotional bond with her parents, she did not know her father and her stepfather was an alcoholic criminal, so there was constant chaos in the house.

In May 1968, Mary strangled four-year-old Martin Brown. A few months later, together with her friend Norma, she strangled another boy, three-year-old Brian Howe. Mary signed her initial 'M' with a razor blade on the abdomen of the little victim, the girls also allegedly sexually mutilated the body with scissors. Mary was convicted of manslaughter on the grounds of diminished responsibility but was sentenced to life imprisonment even though she was still a child at the time of the crime: she will spend twelve years in prison. While in prison, Mary received behavioural therapy through which she developed a sense of right and wrong. She showed signs of remorse for the violence and murders she had committed.

Dr. Robert Orton, the first person to speak with Mary Bell during her incarceration, said of her that she showed the classic symptoms of a psychopathic personality in her total lack of feelings for others. *She showed not the slightest remorse, tear or anxiety. She was completely impassive and without resentment for her actions or her detention.* The psychiatrist also said he had seen many psychopathic children, but had never before encountered a case like Mary, so intelligent, so manipulative and so dangerous. Another psychiatrist, Dr. Westbury, said: *"Manipulation of people is her main goal."* A biography based on interviews with Mary Bell was written in 1998 by Gitta Sereny under the title *Cries Unheard: Why Children Kill, The Story of Mary Bell.*

In 1998, the book *"The Magic Castle"* was published. It is the story of a mother who adopted young Alex, a multiple and hyper-violent child. In 1984, at the age of 10, Alex came to live with Carole and Sam Smith. He had a file with a lot of information about his past. Alex had lived with his mother and stepfather until the age of 5 when he was taken into the custody of his biological father due to his mother's alcoholism. Then, due to severe abuse and neglect, Alex was placed in a home until the age of 7. He then spent 3 years in foster care before coming to Carole Smith. When Carole first went to collect him, she saw young Alex sitting on the lawn with two large bin bags containing his belongings lying next to him. She said afterwards: *'I kept him for a fortnight and it was the longest two weeks of my life!'*.

The trouble started for Carol and Sam as soon as Alex arrived at their house. He was constantly angry and withdrawn. In addition, he had the reactions of a 2-year-old. His behaviour was out of control and he broke things on several occasions. Carole was even afraid to take him out in public, *"The groceries became missiles and the supermarket trolley a destructive tank"* she says. It didn't take long for Carol to realise the serious psychological impact of the abuse he had suffered and that they would need a lot of help and support as a result. The social worker in charge of her case did not provide much help, so Carole and Sam eventually turned to psychiatrists and government social workers for help.

As Alex grew up, his problems increased, but Carole persevered in her care for the boy, who had now become a member of her family. As Alex's problems intensified, Carole sensed that there might be something even more profound about his behavioural problems. A therapist thought that he might have multiple personalities, Alex was 14 years old at the time. At that time he was seeing a therapist who used hypnosis as a form of treatment. To Carole's surprise, Alex was able to be hypnotised, and it was then that the other personalities began to reveal themselves. The next three years were a constant turmoil for Carole and Sam. They never knew which personality would emerge and they learned more and more about the horrors Alex had suffered in his early childhood. Through therapy, Alex learned to build a *"Magic Castle"* to help him deal with his split personality. In all, eight personalities were discovered, personalities that were created in childhood to help her cope with the immense stress of repetitive abuse. In the conclusion of the book, Carole quotes a statement by Alex: *'Being multiple is a means of survival, not a sign of insanity'*. At the time of writing, in 1998, Alex was still living with Carole and Sam, working alongside her adoptive father.[246]

Take a 7 year old child raised in ritual abuse who is given the high priest's dagger at initiation to sacrifice a baby... imagine what will become of this child at the age of thirty if he has not left the cult and has not been taken care of. Most likely he will have developed a deep dissociative disorder with a multiple

---

[246] The Magic Castle: A Mother's Harrowing True Story Of Her Adoptive Son's Multiple Personalities-- And The Triumph Of Healing - Carole Smith, 1998 / Book Review by Annette Petersmeyer Graduate Student University of Minnesota-Duluth, Duluth, MN.

personality containing one or more hyper-violent alter deeply buried in his internal system and emerging during certain ceremonies.

f/ Snuff films

Georges Glatz is a Swiss politician and the founder of the CIDE: *International Committee for the Dignity of the Child*. This Lausanne-based NGO produced an explosive report in 2012 showing the extent of the phenomenon of network paedocriminality. This report aims to explain why a leaden blanket covers all these cases. In 2000, on the France 3 television set, George Glatz told Élise Lucet that films showing the real death of children had been found in Belgium:

- Georges Glatz: Snuff film tapes sell for between ten and twenty thousand Swiss francs...
- Élise Lucet: What do you mean by "snuff-movies"? ...
- Georges Glatz: Tapes with real death of children...
- Élise Lucet: .... ?!?!!...
- Georges Glatz: Yes, these tapes exist, they were discovered a few years ago in Belgium, but they are not really talked about in the media.

"Child Rape: The end of silence", France 3 - 2000.

A rather shattering statement that left journalist Élise Lucet speechless...

In 2008, Father François Brune, in a video interview[247] about his book *"Dieu et Satan, le combat continue"*, said:

- It's the story of a young boy who was dragged unwillingly by a friend into satanic circles... but really satanic circles, that is to say that nobody knows about them, not even journalists or specialised investigators (...) but which can reach people with official positions in the very high level administration (...).) When I myself speak of Satanism as a priest, I am not very credible; but on the other hand, you have specialised investigators, notably on pornography and child pornography, who will reveal that there are indeed people who film children being tortured... and that this is sold at a premium...

- These are called snuff-movies....
- Here it is...
- So for you, behind this there is Satan?
- Of course! It exists... When it is said by psychologists, police or intelligence people, they are taken seriously, but it is the same thing, it is the same phenomenon...
- It is the destruction of God's creation...
- Of course... and in its purest and most fragile form... as soon as Satan can dirty it...

A *snuff-movie* or *snuff-film* (*To Snuff* means to murder in English slang), is an authentic video of torture and murder of children or adults, there is no

---

[247] *Dieu et Satan, le combat continue* - Yann-Erick interviews Father François Brune, *Élévation*, 2008.

faking, it is the direct capture on film of criminal acts. These productions are sold on the black market for several thousand euros and therefore reach a rather high social profile.

Many accounts of ritual abuse survivors report the presence of cameras during abuse and sacrifice, and this is a fairly common feature. The aim is to immortalise the sadistic and criminal acts, but also to have evidence so that all participants (when they do not have their faces masked) are bound by secrecy. But above all, these recordings are used to make a maximum amount of money, either through blackmail or through trade in specialised networks.

Officially, snuff films are only an 'urban legend', a kind of *'old fantasy'*. In 1978, Roman Polanski declared in the documentary *Confessions of a Blue Movie Star:*

"All the sexual taboos have been shown on screen and we can ask ourselves what will be the next step? It could be the murder of someone without tricks..."

The production of *snuff is a* terrible reality. A traffic of this kind was dismantled in Great Britain where Dimitri Vladimirovitch Kouznetsov, a 30-year-old Russian, had settled. This monster was arrested by the British police in 2000, he was producing videos for a list of Italian, English, American and German clients. In the course of the investigation, more than 600 homes were searched and 1,500 people came under police investigation, including businessmen and civil servants. Italian police seized about 3,000 videos produced by Kuznetsov. Investigators told journalists that the material included footage of children dying in torture and rape. The Naples prosecutor's office then considered charges against the clients for complicity in murder, some of whom specifically claimed recordings with the killing of children. A senior customs officer said: *"We have seen very, very violent things, sadistic abuse involving very young children, but the actual deaths take us to a whole new level..."*

The Naples newspaper *'Il Mattino'* published a transcript of an exchange between an Italian client and the Russian supplier, which is an *MI5* recording:

- Promise me you won't rip me off, tell me the truth," the Italian asks.
- Relax, I can assure you that this one really dies," the Russian replies.
- The last time I paid, I didn't get what I wanted.
- What do you want?
- To see them die...
- That's why I'm here...

The price of a single video ranged from 340 to 6,000 Euro, with the price set according to the type of content. Films with young naked children were called *'snipe video'*. The most gruesome category in which children are raped and tortured to death was codenamed *'necros pedo'*.[248]

In 1997, the "Draguignan trial" began. For the first time in France, the law against sex tourism could be applied and the investigations allowed the uncovering of a vast network of paedophiles organised both in France and abroad. During the trial, the snuff films that had been seized by the police were

---

[248] "British link to 'snuff' video" - theguardian.com / Jason Burke for "The Observer" 01/10/2000.

shown... The projection was stopped after 20 minutes and the prosecutor Etienne Ceccaldi declared before the cameras of Canal +: *"The vision of children being tortured to death, and all this for commercial purposes, is truly unbearable."*

Also in 1997, the English channel *ITV* broadcast a documentary entitled *'The Boy Business'* about the production of child pornography in Amsterdam. Film productions in which children are raped, tortured and killed. In this English documentary, three British people who lived in Amsterdam in the early 1990s testify independently of each other. They describe the *snuff* films they witnessed as children or teenagers.

In the documentary *""Dutsh Injustice: When Child traffickers rule a nation. In the documentary* "Dutch Injustice: When Child Traffickers Rule a Nation" about the Rolodex case, a victim of the Dutch network testifies: *"I also met people who were making snuff-movies. Snuff films are videos where several children, or one child, are sexually abused and then murdered at the end of the film. I was asked to take part in one of these films in exchange for a lot of money but I refused because I knew from what other boys had told me that it was very dangerous because you don't survive."*

The 2012 CIDE report mentioned above confirms the existence of snuff films through Michel Thirion, a private investigator who was in charge of investigating the disappearance of Julie Lejeune and Melissa Russo in the Dutroux case. His investigations led him to a *snuff* ring in the Netherlands (the same ring mentioned by the witnesses in the documentary *"The Boy Business"*). He told Jean Nicolas and Frédéric Lavachery about his meeting with an Englishman who owned a barge in Amsterdam: *"The Englishman offered me the best thing he had: the killing of children. The Englishman then suggested the best thing he had: the killing of children. The idea was for several people to get on his barge, set sail and satisfy themselves sexually with a child before the latter was thrown into the water, the Englishman explained to me."*[249]

In Belgium, too, the production of *snuff films* seems to have gone beyond mere 'fantasy'... In 1997, a case of paedophilia and paedo-pornography broke out in parallel with the Dutroux case. On 22 January 1997, the Nouvelle Gazette de Charleroi published an article mentioning the existence of this type of film: *"It was at Michel's home (and at his home alone, the investigators were keen to point out) that the gendarmes made the horrible discovery. They seized a dozen or so snuff films, video cassettes that show absolute horror. The children they show (European children, the youngest of whom appear to be 7 to 8 years old and the oldest 16 to 17 years old) are not only raped by unknown adults. They are also tortured by sadists: the investigators discreetly refer to hard sado-maso scenes. And, to top it all off, these infernal scenes end with the killing (real or simulated) of the little victims. We don't know if these children are really dead, the investigators admit. To be sure, their bodies would have to be found. But if they were staged, they are highly realistic. According to the investigators, we suspected that such horrors were circulating, even in our country. However,*

---

[249] "Dossier pédophilie, le scandale de l'affaire Dutroux" - Jean Nicolas and Frédéric Lavachery, 2001.

snuff films had never been seized in our country. I had seen a tape of this kind, seized in France," says an investigator. It showed a paedophile strangling a child. But what I saw here is beyond anything you can imagine. "[250]

In the document containing the minutes and hearings recorded during the Dutroux case, it is stated that in 1997, a letter relating to paedophilia was intercepted at the post office in Ixelles, which spoke of tapes with killings and/or rapes. It talks about a "Baroness and Dutroux". (PV 150.123/97)

In 2004, Belgian MP Albert Mahieu wrote a letter to the President of the Arlon Assize Court, Stéphane Goux, in which he mentioned the existence of a videotape of the murder of Julie Lejeune and Mélissa Russo. These are the two little victims found dead in Marc Dutroux's cellar. Officially, they died of hunger in Marc Dutroux's cellar while he was in prison. Deputy Mahieu starts his letter by saying that they did not die of hunger but of rape, abuse and torture. According to his sources, *"the recording, in colour and with sound, attests to the ordeal that Julie and Melissa endured before being put to death, in atrocious circumstances, by a masked executioner in the presence of a group of ten to twelve people.* According to the (now deceased) MP, there are several copies of this video recording.

Also in the Dutroux case, witness X1 (Regina Louf) described a world of sexual violence, torture and murder. Her testimony showed that she knew details of unsolved murders, which would not have been possible without access to police files. Régina Louf cited the Belgian company *ASCO* in her testimony. She called it the *"video recording factory"*, and gave the names of those involved in the torture and murder of children at the factory, all recorded on video tapes.[251]

In his book *"L'enfant sacrifié à Satan"*, which recounts the ordeal of Samir Aouchiche, Bruno Fouchereau notes that INTERPOL has repeatedly issued warnings at the European level concerning satanic crimes, as he writes in his book: *"Scotland Yard recently held a conference in Lyon in January 1996, aimed at alerting the European police to the increase in ritual crimes. Judge Sengelin, the senior investigating judge in Mulhouse, investigating the abduction of a little girl in 1990, was informed by the same Scotland Yard police officers that they had seized a batch of snuff films in which children were being murdered. These children, at least 15 of whom are of European origin, were killed on camera after being raped and tortured. "*

g/ Some figures

In 1984 the first meeting of the *International Society for Study of Trauma and Dissociation* (*ISSTD*) was held in Chicago. Following this meeting, Naomi Mattis (who later became co-chair of the *Utah Legislative Satanic Ritual Abuse Committee*), told the *Deseret News: "Of the 420 therapists in attendance, about*

---

[250] "Snuff-movies, an unthinkable reality", *Donde Vamos*, 13/08/2014.

[251] Scientology, the CIA & MIVILUDES: Cults of Abuse (video documentary).

75 percent raised their hands when asked if they had ever treated victims of ritual abuse."

Child sexual abuse psychiatrist Roland Summit has said of ritual abuse that it is the *most serious threat to the child and to society that we face.* Dr. Summit points out that he has dealt with *as many as 1,000 children who have demonstrated involvement in ritual abuse.*[252]

While getting real numbers on the prevalence of ritual trauma is a difficult task given the secrecy and criminality surrounding the phenomenon, there is nevertheless growing evidence that the problem of ritual trauma is considerably more prevalent than ever before. Dr. Kathleen Coulborn Faller of the University of Michigan has conducted analysis and empirical research on ritual abuse. She notes that there is a high degree of similarity in reports of abuse by individual children or adults, and that studies independently show confirmation of such allegations. Of the 2,709 members of the American Psychological Association *(APA)* who responded to a survey, 30% responded that they had dealt with ritual or religion-related abuse. Of this group, 93% responded that they believed ritual-related harm had occurred. In a 1995 article entitled *"Cultural and Economic Barriers to Protecting Children from Ritual Abuse and Mind Control"*, Dr. Catherine Gould reported that in 1992 alone, *Childhelp USA* logged 1,741 calls related to ritual abuse, *Monarch Resources* in Los Angeles logged approximately 5,000, *Real Active Survivors* logged almost 3,600, *Justus Unlimited* in Colorado received almost 7,000, and *Looking Up* in Maine handled approximately 6,000. This indicates a very alarming number of hotline requests.

One of the first studies concerning the existence of ritual abuse was conducted by Deborah Cole in 1992. The survey was entitled '*The Incidence of* Ritual *Abuse: A Preliminary Survey'*. Of 250 therapists, 46% indicated that they had had patients who reported ritual abuse or who met at least one of the criteria listed by Cole.[253]

In 1995, a study on ritual abuse was carried out by British psychologists (Andrews, Morton, Bekerian, Brewin, Davies, Mollon). These researchers collected data from 810 members of the *British* Psychological Society who had dealt with cases of sexual abuse. 50% of the therapists said they had worked with patients who reported satanic ritual abuse. 80% of the therapists who had one or more patients with a history of ritual abuse believed their statements. In a more recent British study in 2013, Ost, Wright, Easton, Hope and French collected data from an online survey of 183 clinical psychologists and 119 hypnotherapists. Among the psychologists, 38% had dealt with one or more cases of ritual abuse. The study showed that 25% of hypnotherapists had experienced one or more cases of ritual abuse. [254]

---

[252] Letter to California State Social Services Advisory Board. Summit, Roland - 26/10/1988, Occult crime: a law enforcement primer.

[253] *"Cult and Ritual Abuse"* James & Pamela Noblitt, 2014, p.53.

[254] Ibid p.55.

In Australia, Schmuttermaier and Veno published a study in 1999 in the *Journal of Child Sexual Abuse* entitled *"Counselor's belief about ritual abuse: An Australian study"*. The study targeted workers in 74 *Center Against Sexual Assault (CASA)* centres, 48 psychologists and 27 psychiatrists in Victoria were interviewed. 70% of the therapists validated the definition of ritual abuse and 26 of them reported 153 cases of ritual abuse identified between 1985 and 1995. Schmuttermaier and Veno conclude their study by saying that the identification and diagnosis of ritual abuse by professionals is always similar, whether in Australia, the USA or the UK. [255]

In South Africa, studies on child abuse including ritual abuse have been done on adolescents and young adults. The study by Madu S.N. and Peltze K. was published in 1998 in the *Southern African Journal of Child and* Adolescent *Mental Health*. 414 high school students were asked about their abuse experiences before the age of 17, 8% of whom reported ritual abuse experiences. In another study of 559 students from three high schools in Mpumalanga province, Madu noted that 10% had reported ritual abuse before the age of 17. Of 722 university students, 6% reported such abuse before the age of 17. [256]

In the article *"Ritual Abuse: A review of research"* (1994), Kathleen Faller cites a study by Susan Kelley on transgenerational ritual abuse. This study entitled *"Ritualistic Abuse: Recognition, Impact, and Current Controversy" was* presented by Kelley in 1992 at a San Diego conference on child abuse. Kelley investigated the testimony of 26 children from 14 families. The abusers were parents, grandparents, great-grandparents, uncles, aunts, cousins and siblings. Similar to other reports, a significant number of abusers were female (45%) and 61% of children were abused by the previous two generations. Reported abuses included threats and terrorising acts (89%), death threats (77%), production of child pornography (81%), threats with magic (89%), satanic references (92%), killing animals (54%), ingesting drugs (92%), singing and chanting (69%), and ingesting or touching faeces (85%) [257]

An international study on ritual abuse and mind control was conducted by German and American researchers: Carol Rutz, Thorsten Becker, Bettina Overcamp and Wanda Karriker. The study, launched in 2007, is available in English and German and is entitled the *"Extreme Abuse Survey"* (*EAS*). All questionnaires and results of the survey are available on the website *extreme-abuse-survey.net*. It includes a section for professionals, *the Professional Extreme Abuse Survey* (P-EAS), which is a questionnaire with 215 questions. 451 professionals from 20 different countries responded to the survey, which shows that 86% of professionals who have worked with at least one extreme trauma survivor report having had at least one case of satanic ritual abuse:

- 61% of them had patients reporting ritual abuse in the clergy.

---

[255] Ibid p.55.

[256] Ibid p. 68.

[257] Ibid p. 67-68.

- 85% reported that the majority of adult survivors of Ritual Abuse (RA)/Mental Control (MC) had a diagnosis of Dissociative Identity Disorder.
- 65% reported that their patients with AR/CM were based on continuous, non-dissociated memories.
- 89% reported that the RA/CM memories had a logical articulation with other aspects of the patient's life, forming a rather coherent whole.
- 86% reported that the dissociated personalities observed reported RA/CM
- 79% reported that the content of their patients' drawings, paintings and poems had RA/CM-related content.
- 75% report that some of their patients' medical and physical sequelae can be explained by RAs/CMs.
- 47% report that some of their patients' memories have been confirmed and validated by others.

The study also includes a section on survivors, here are some results from a sample of 1000 respondents:

- 79% report gang rape.
- 53% report being locked in a cage.
- 44% report cannibalism.
- 52% report zoophilia.
- 45% report being buried alive.
- 50% report having received electric shocks.
- 52% report having participated in child pornography.
- 46% report child prostitution.
- 65% report having been diagnosed with Dissociative Identity Disorder.
- 63% report that the perpetrator(s) deliberately created dissociative states (alter personality) to carry out programming on them.
- 41% report having been programmed as a sex slave.
- 18% report being programmed to be a murderer.
- 21% report having been programmed to develop psychic powers.
- 57% report being programmed to self-destruct when they begin to recall the abuse and programming.
- 34% report that one or more of their alter personalities have an access code.
- 28% report having an alter personality of a robot.
- 53% report that the torturers made them believe that entities, spirits or demons had taken control of their bodies.
- 15% report experiences of time travel.
- 26% report having been a victim of government mind control experiments.

Traumatic ritual abuse has been or is still practised in many cultures, with victims reporting altered states of consciousness such as dissociation, amnesia and altered personality. This list of symptoms of psychological trauma has been found to be almost consistently present in individuals who report accounts of ritual abuse. In the West, these accounts come from people who claim to be "survivors", many of them have the typical symptoms of severe dissociation, and many of their memories are brought up in therapy. However, it should be noted that these ritual abuse memories also come back as flashbacks outside of therapy, an important point to emphasise as therapists are sometimes accused of inducing "false memories" in their patients (see Chapter 10). Given that there are historical accounts of ritual abuse going back centuries, and that children as young as two and adults in their nineties continue to give accounts of traumatic ritual abuse all over the world, it is time to sound the alarm about how little has been done to raise awareness of the problem among professionals and institutions! Although it is totally impossible to stop or eradicate the problem, we must move beyond denial and begin to understand the dynamics of these abuses so that our investigative paradigms can change accordingly.

In a predominantly Christian society, satanic symbols can convey a powerful archetypal message to victims, especially if used in conjunction with torture and severe trauma. It is therefore not necessary for those responsible to have any spiritual belief system behind their practices or activities. This means that whatever the motivation, religious belief, sexual drive, power or mind control, these groups routinely use a ritualised framework to abuse, exploit and manipulate children or adults. Their structures operate to provide a constant supply of children and to protect Network members from possible prosecution.[258]

3 - SOME TESTIMONIALS

a/ Introduction

Testimonies of ritual abuse all describe the same thing: gang rapes, torture, occult rituals, drugs, hypnosis, trance and dissociation states, sacrifices (real or simulated), video recordings, etc., and these testimonies can be found on all continents.

Many of the testimonies are English-speaking: Cathy O'Brien, Mark Philips, "Svali", Jeannie Riseman, Kathleen Sullivan, Kim Campbell, Brice Taylor, Jay Parker, Fritz Springmeier, Cisco Wheeler, Ted Gunderson, Paul Bonacci, John DeCamp, David Shurter, Dejoly Labrier, Anne A. Johnson Davis, Vicki Polin, Linda Wiegand, Jenny Hill, Lynn Moss Sharman, Kristin Constance, Kim Noble, Lynn Schirmer, Bill Schnoebelen, Neil Brick, Carol Rutz, Caryn Stardancer, Kathleen Sorenson, Patricia Baird Clarke, Ruth Zandstra, Glenn Hobbs, etc. Most of these accounts of ritual abuse also involve trauma-based mind control, the two things being completely intertwined. But we will look at the MK programming aspect in more detail in Chapter 7.

The content of these testimonies is particularly atrocious and shocking. The rest of this chapter may contain some morbid repetitions, as some of the testimonies are so similar. Please forgive these repetitions, but the aim here is to

---

[258] Forensic Consideration in Ritual Trauma Cases " - Sylvia Gilotte.

present the words of child victims and adult survivors. A word that must be heard and taken into account despite its obviously very disturbing aspect. It is also a question of showing to what extent satanic ritual abuse practices are similar from one country to another and from one continent to another.

b/ United States

In 1989, Lieutenant Larry Jones of the Boise Police Department and director of the *Cult Crime Impact Network* (*CCIN*) said that those who discredited the evidence of ritual abuse were *"scum! We've found ritually sacrificed babies in Connecticut, Bend, Oregon and Los Angeles... When you add to that credible survivor testimony that can be circumstantially verified, there's no question."* [259]

In the documentary Devil Worship: The Rise of Satanism, Kurt Jackson of the Beaumont Police Department says: "Are human beings being sacrificed? Yes! They are! There are a lot of things I'm looking at to determine if this is a ritual crime. It could be something like a pentagram, it could be an inverted cross, the number 666, the body drained of blood, certain body parts removed in a certain way, etc."

In the same documentary, Sergeant Randy Emon says: "One problem we face is that senior officials in government agencies do not want to acknowledge that this is a reality. We have to lift this veil of misunderstanding and say to them: Hey, these are crimes we have to deal with!"

- Ted Gunderson

Ted Gunderson headed the Memphis FBI office (1973), then the Dallas office (1975), and in 1977 was appointed to head the Los Angeles FBI. He is one of the few (if not the only) senior American officials to have denounced the network of paedophile criminals who clandestinely control the judicial system. He has taken a close interest in the Martin School case and the Franklin case.

In 1988, Ted Gunderson appeared on a television programme hosted by Geraldo Rivera entitled *"Devil Worship: Exposing Satan's Underground"*. The debate was about the extent of Satanic crimes in the United States, here is an extract:

- Ted Gunderson, retired FBI agent, former head of the Los Angeles division. Is there really a network responsible for all these satanic murders in your opinion?

- What I can say, based on information provided to me by confidential sources, informants, I have also interviewed dozens of survivors of satanic cults in recent years: I affirm that there is a network of individuals who are very active in the country.

---

[259] *Occult Crime: a Law Enforcement Primer"*, Interview Lieutenant Larry Jones, Boise, Idaho Police Department and Director, Cult Crime Impact Network.

- Do you think these terrible accusations of sacrificial babies are true?

- I am sure of it, no doubt about it. This is based on the information I have gathered from all over the country, from several survivors and many informants.

In 1987, Ted Gunderson gave a lecture entitled *"Satanism and International Child Trafficking by the CIA"*. During this conference, he went into detail about the case of the Mc Martin nursery school, located in Manhattan Beach in the suburbs of Los Angeles, a case that caused a huge stir at the time. Some of the children claimed to have been forced to participate in animal sacrifices, but also in sacrifices of babies and other children. They said they were forced to drink blood and subjected to necrophiliac, zoophilic and scatological practices. Here are some excerpts from the conference:

Let's talk about the Martin case. In April 1985, the authorities looked into this case and searched for tunnels under the school. The children had said that they had been taken to tunnels under the school, including a room in the basement. There they were sexually assaulted, they described ceremonies with adults in robes, candles, religious songs (...) The adults were naked under their robes. They were led into a tunnel, through a trap door in the bathroom of a triplex. They were taken away in a car... we are talking about 2, 3 and 4 year old children who were prostituted in this network (...)

In the spring of 1993, I heard that the Martin School property had been sold by the Martin family to the defence lawyer, as agreed. He sold it to a contractor who was to build an office building in place of the school. So I contacted him immediately and said, 'Dear sir, I would like to have access to the property. He gave me two weeks. I signed a paper to take responsibility, and then I and some parents hired an archaeologist from UCLA, Dr. Gary Stickel, knowing full well that I was not qualified to validate the existence of these tunnels even though I had found them myself. So we started the excavation (...) Dr. Stickel told us: "I can say now without any doubt that there were tunnels under the school and that they have been filled in (...) I have a 186-page scientific report available on this. We found a large underground entrance 2.70 metres under the west wall (...) We found these tunnels during the second trial of Ray Buckey, so it could have been used to convict him. We informed the prosecutor who sent his investigator (...) This investigator, not qualified in archaeology, simply said: "There are no tunnels here. ' And of course the archaeologist kept his back to him. In any case, they did not use this evidence, solid evidence for this second trial, which they ignored (...)

In this tunnel we found a Disney plastic bag dating from 1982 about 1.40 metres below the concrete floor of the classroom, 1-2 metres from the entrance to the foundations (...) The tunnel faces south for 14 metres below classrooms 3 and 4 (...).A 2.70 metre wide chamber was found along the tunnel under Class 4, the ceiling of the chamber and the top of the tunnel sections had layers of plywood covered with tar paper and reinforced with breeze blocks. The characteristics of the tunnels confirmed that they had been dug by hand (...) The children described the entrance and exit of the tunnels well and this is exactly consistent with the tunnels discovered with the archaeologist (...) Another significant fact was the discovery by this archaeologist of a small plastic plate with three hand-drawn pentagrams (...) More than 2,000 artefacts were found underneath the floor of the school, including about 100 animal bones (...)

The team of archaeologist Gary E. Stickel found exactly what the children had described under the school. The tunnels had been backfilled with different types of soil. In the Martin case, *CII* director and member of the *Preschool-Age Molested Children's Professional Group*, Kee MacFarlane, was commissioned in 1983 by the prosecutor's office. She interviewed about 400 children who had all passed through the Martin School, including former students, and estimated that 80% of them had indeed been sexually abused. Of these hundreds of children, only 11 were heard at the trial. The private investigator Paul Bynum, hired at the time by the lawyers of the parents of the young victims, also came to the conclusion that children had been abused at the school. He committed suicide just before he could testify to the jury about the animal bones he had found in the tunnels. Those around him strongly denied that he was suicidal.

We find the same tunnel system in the case of the Haut de la Garenne orphanage in Jersey, where children were also tortured and raped during the night. This case was hushed up just like the Martin School case. In 2012, American investigative journalist Leah MacGrath Goodman was banned from English soil for trying to investigate this case in Jersey, which dates back to 2008. Children in the orphanage were allegedly tortured, raped and even murdered, and many of the little victims testified but were totally ignored. According to the journalist, all those who tried to investigate the case were expelled from the island or fired from their jobs. All indications are that this is a big cover-up. Just like the discovery of a mass grave of children in late 2011 on the grounds of the Mohawk Institute in Brantford, Ontario, Canada. These were Native American children from residential schools.

The case of Martin's Nursery School is therefore not isolated. In 1988, a study entitled *"Sexual Abuse in Day* Care: *a National Study"* looked at 270 cases of sexual abuse in day care centres and kindergartens, involving 1,639 victims. According to the experts who wrote the study, ritual abuse was reported in 13% of the cases, which could be true satanic rituals or pseudo-rituals designed to intimidate children.[260]

Later, Ted Gunderson also worked on the Franklin case, one of the biggest child sex ring scandals in US history, a case that was suppressed by all possible means, including murder. The Franklin case involved a ring that prostituted children mainly from *Boys Town* (a kind of orphanage village founded in 1917, with about 5000 children living there in the 1980s). The clients of this ring, the rapists designated by the children, were among the richest and most influential citizens of the state of Nebraska, including prominent businessmen, politicians, journalists and even police officers. In the Franklin case, there were also reports of ritual abuse involving child sacrifice.

---

[260] "Ritual sexual abuse: the case of Martin's kindergarten in the United States" - Donde Vamos 20/05/2012.

- John de Camp and Paul Bonacci

John de Camp was a Republican senator from Nebraska from 1971 to 1987 and a lawyer. In the Franklin case, he was put in charge of the case to prove that these extremely serious accusations were unfounded. But as a result of his investigations, he came into possession of incontrovertible evidence that paedophilia was being practised by certain American politicians, including those in the White House. He could no longer fulfil his mission of covering up the affair. In order to protect himself and his family, John De Camp wrote a book on the case entitled *"The* Franklin *Cover-up*: *Child* Abuse, *Satanism and Murder in Nebraska"*, a book that provides evidence of the existence and functioning of this paedocriminal and satanic network. This publication also makes the important connection between network paedocriminality and government mind control experiments on citizens, especially children.

There is also a journalistic report entitled *'Conspiracy of Silence'*, which describes the whole affair in detail. A documentary that was originally supposed to be broadcast by the *Discovery* channel, which retracted it a few days before due to pressure or threats. The rights were bought back in order to keep the material in boxes. However, a copy was sent anonymously to Senator John de Camp who then gave it to Ted Gunderson. Today, this important video archive is online on the internet.

In the documentary, Senator John de Camp states that this ring went all the way up to the highest authorities in the United States: "Obviously, the FBI was protecting something much more important than a bunch of old pedophiles having questionable relationships with little boys. They were protecting something much more important than a bunch of drug dealers. In my opinion, they were looking after the interests of some very prominent politicians. Very rich and powerful people were associated with these politicians and the political system in general, including the highest authorities in the country."

We also see in this documentary one of the survivors of the network, Paul Bonacci, who reports to Senator John de Camp the existence of parties organized in the house of Larry King (Lawrence E. King), rented for $5,000 a month, but also his escapades at the White House:

- I was about 14 years old in 1981. At first there were 3 or 4 parties in a year, then it was about one a month (...) Some of the children were kept in rooms on the floor below, in case they got agitated or panicked because of the drugs, because they were drugged. They would lock them in a room so they wouldn't escape.

- What kind of drugs?

- Everything you can imagine, cocaine, heroin, speed...

- You're telling me that this was all happening at these parties, at the same place where you saw Larry King and other prominent politicians?

- Yes.

(...)

- Have you been to the White House too?

- Yes.

- And how did you gain access to it?

- I went with Larry King, but Craig Spencer was one of the people who organised it for us. It was kind of a gift for the "services" we were doing for him.

- How many times have you done these kinds of parties there?

- I participated twice.

- And were you prostituted on these occasions?

- Yeah, after we left the White House late at night. It was really weird to be in the White House at that time, at night, and especially to go to places where the guy told us nobody ever went.

Paul Bonacci also testified that he had witnessed much bloodier scenes during satanic rituals in which babies or very young children could be murdered after being raped. The ritual would then continue with acts of cannibalism. According to Bonacci, Larry King had been involved in a satanic cult since at least December 1980. In his written testimony, he reports that he was taken by King in December 1980 to a *"Triangle"* located in a wooded area near *Sarpy County*, Nebraska. There he witnessed the sacrifice of a baby. The boy's blood was collected to be mixed with urine and consumed by the congregation. He himself was forced to drink from the chalice. According to Bonacci, the participants were all singing and making strange sounds, and he knew not to say a word about what he had seen, fearing that he himself would be the next victim sacrificed.

Bonacci was diagnosed with a dissociative identity disorder caused by the multiple traumas he experienced in early childhood. Senator John DeCamp reports on this in his book *"The Franklin Cover-up"*:

Dr. Judianne Densen-Gerber, a psychiatrist and lawyer mentioned above, is also a member of the *International Society of Multiple Personality and Dissociative States*. She has confirmed that Paul Bonacci suffers from Multiple Personality Disorder (now renamed Dissociative Identity Disorder, D.I.D.). It is not a psychosis, she says, but a neurosis resulting from the defence mechanism of a child's mind, a function to protect him from 'the unimaginable atrocity'. A total of three psychiatrists examined Paul Bonacci and all validated the diagnosis of multiple personality disorder.

On December 29, 1990, Dr. Densen-Gerber testified before the Franklin Legislative Committee in Omaha. She was questioned by Robert Creager about Paul Bonacci:

- Doctor, I believe the grand jury came to the conclusion that Mr. Bonacci was not capable of lying. Do you have any comment on that?

- I think it would be very difficult for Mr. Bonacci to lie... When you have a multiple personality, you don't have to lie, you change... There is nothing that Mr. Bonacci has told me that I haven't already heard from other patients or individuals. It's not nonsense and he often admits himself that he doesn't know. He hasn't fabricated anything and he doesn't try to give answers like most people who want to please do. He doesn't even want to give you the impression that he wants to please.[261]

Here is what Dr. Densen-Gerber wrote after visiting Bonacci in prison (Bonacci was indeed convicted of perjury):

1) He has an extraordinary memory for detail, making him a valuable witness.

2) He does not lie.

3) He accurately described satanic rituals practised internationally by cults, something he could not know without having participated in them himself.

He describes one of his personalities as a computer chip in his head that allows him to maintain obsessive attention to detail. He can give you dates and times with extreme accuracy. I've never seen a child who could do that. So he is a valuable witness. He doesn't make things up, he'll say "I don't know" if he really doesn't know.[262]

In October 1990, shortly before the opening of the Franklin Committee, a police psychiatrist, Dr. Beverly Mead, answered Senator Schmit's questions about the witness Bonacci:

- Senator De Camp: Doctor, do you now believe in these talks that we have heard here and those that we heard together earlier?

- Dr. Beverly Mead: I personally think that these details that he gave us came from experiences that he actually had...

- Senator Schmit: We have heard testimony from several of his personalities (alter) naming names like Larry King, Robert Wadman, etc. From your professional experience, do you think these descriptions are accurate?

- Mead: I would like to see them confirmed by other sources, for sure. But at the moment, my impression is that Paul or Alexandrew (editor's note: one of Bonacci's alter personalities) is reporting things honestly, as he remembers them.

- Schmit: Could he have imagined this or dreamt it and then told us here today? Could it be possible?

- Mead: It would be quite phenomenal to do something like that. I don't think it's possible. I think he's talking about things that he actually remembers (...) There may be some details that aren't very accurate, but I think the story overall happened as he says.[263]

Despite several psychiatric reports explaining the phenomenon of severe dissociative disorders, both Paul Bonacci and Alisha Owen, another Franklin survivor, were sentenced to prison for perjury. Bonacci's fractured psychological state, with its inconsistencies and contradictions, was deemed to undermine his testimony and necessitated his indictment for perjury! It is typical in such cases to put forward the psychological state of the dissociated victim in order to

---

[261] The Franklin Cover Up: Child Abuse, Satanism, and Murder in Nebraska" - John W. DeCamp, 1992, p.127.

[262] Ibid, p.212.

[263] Ibid, p.127.

discredit her testimony. The diagnosis of dissociative identity disorder should, on the contrary, be one more piece of evidence to be put in the file to support the fact that the victim has indeed experienced severe trauma, even mental control, and that the investigation should be pursued rather than dismissed. Victims should be listened to and cared for rather than condemned. But in such cases, the sad logic is rather to cover up the case to protect a network of *untouchables*.

John De Camp said that he had spoken with several of Paul Bonacci's alter personalities. He described how his writing style varies depending on which alter is in control and how memories can also vary from alter to alter. Bonacci even has a personality that speaks and writes German, even though he has hardly studied at all. Psychiatrists who have worked with him have reported that his different personalities are incapable of lying and have a very good photographic memory. It is believed that Bonacci was subjected to a trauma-based mind control program from an early age in order to make him a Monarch slave. Investigators reported that the network that turned him into a Satanist was centered at Offutt Air Force Base near Omaha, a major air force base. It was there that he was transported for sexual abuse when he was only three years old in the early 1970s. At Offutt, and later at other military facilities, the network 'trained' him through torture, drugs and sexual violence in order to train him militarily, including for assassinations. The idea was to split his personality through trauma and then program him.[264]

Paul Bonacci is one of the many victims who fell prey to the Network and were subjected to MK programmes. The outbreak of the Franklin case in the courts has allowed his testimony to be publicly revealed, but how many other victims remain trapped, whose word will never be heard?

In 2004, Senator John de Camp gave a radio interview to Alex Jones. Here are some excerpts concerning a testimony of Paul Bonacci who reports a snuff-film shooting in which he participated: *"I just took Paul Bonacci's diary and published a good part of it in my book, one passage is about a trip he made in 1984. He says he was taken to a place near Sacramento "with big trees. Then they went to a place where there was an owl, some kind of big carved owl or something (...) I didn't know then that there was a place called Bohemian Grove that fit the description, I didn't write Bohemian Grove in the book because I didn't know what it was at the time.* (editor's note: The *Bohemian Grove* or *Bohemian Club* is a group reserved for the world's elite (mainly Americans), it is one of the most closed in the world. Members meet once a year on a private property located in a Sequoia forest in Monte Rio, California. Ceremonies of pagan, Druidic and Babylonian inspiration take place there by a lake, at the foot of a giant owl statue representing Moloch, a Babylonian deity who is the symbol of this elitist club.) *Anyway, it's safe to say that he was brought there for a ceremony in which they did horrible things to another boy. There were three boys in all, and they filmed it. I just wrote down his words with the names he heard there (...) Remember I didn't know what the Bohemian Grove was at that time, the kid who wrote this didn't know either. All he knew was that he was*

---

[264] Ibid, p.327.

brought there. Let me read you the passage, Paul Bonacci wrote that. This is word for word what is written in his diary:

I went there in January 1984. I was paid by the men who were dating King for the prostitution stories. In the summer of 1984, I went to Dallas, Texas several times and had sex with different men that King knew, it was in a hotel. I traveled on YNR (private charter) and Cam (another private airline), which King routinely used. I never really dealt with King personally, except when he told me where I should go. On July 26, I went to Sacramento, California. King put me on a private plane from an airfield in Omaha to Denver, where we picked up Nicholas. A boy who was about 12 or 13 years old, and then we flew to Las Vegas where we were taken to ranches to get equipment. Then we headed back to Sacramento. We were picked up by a white limousine that took us to a hotel. We (Nicolas and I) were then driven to an area where there were tall trees, it took about an hour to get there. There was a cage with a naked boy inside. Nicolas and I had to dress up in a Tarzan outfit and stuff like that. They told me to *** the boy (I won't use the word). At first I refused and one of them held a gun to my genitals (I'll use that word) and said do it or you'll lose them. I started to *** the boy. Nicolas was subjected to anal sex and other stuff. We were told that he was a virgin and that we had to take it out on him. I did everything I could not to hurt him. We were told to put our *** in his mouth and other stuff... they filmed everything. We did these things to the boy for about 30 minutes or an hour when a man came and started hitting us on the genitals. He grabbed the boy and started to *** him and do other things to him (...) Then they put the boy next to me, one of them took a gun and blew the boy's head off. I had a lot of blood on me... I started screaming and crying, then the men grabbed Nicolas and me, they forced us to lie down. They put the dead boy on top of Nicolas who was crying and they put his hands on the boy's sex. They put the boy on me too and forced me to do the same. Then they forced me to *** with the dead child. They put a gun to our heads to force us, I had blood everywhere. They made us kiss the boy on the mouth. Then they made me do something else but I don't even want to write it down. After that, the men grabbed Nicolas and drugged him while he was screaming. They put me against a tree and held a gun to my head, but they shot in the air. I heard another shot, then I saw the man who had killed the boy dragging the boy to the ground like a toy. All these things, including when the men put the boy in a trunk, everything was filmed (...) Later we were taken to a house where men were gathered, they had the film and they watched it. While the men watched it, Nicolas and I passed through their hands as if we were toys."[265]

Paul Bonacci will describe this very same snuff-film scene, crying, in a prison interview filmed with Gary Caradori, the lead private investigator in the Franklin case. In 1990, Caradori died suddenly in the crash of his small private plane as he was about to disclose some damning evidence.

---

[265] *The Alex Jones Show* - Interview with John DeCamp, 21/07/2004.

- Kathleen Sorenson

Kathleen Sorenson was a social worker, and she and her husband Ron were foster parents for children with severe difficulties. In total, the couple collected about 30 testimonies from children they had cared for from a few months to several years. Kathleen Sorenson decided to talk about what she had learned from some of the children in her care. She and her eldest adopted daughter, a survivor of ritual abuse, testified publicly at forums and conferences throughout Nebraska. She has given radio and television interviews. In 1988, she appeared on Geraldo Rivera's program on Satanism. Kathleen Sorenson was very aware of the danger of talking publicly about these things. She died in a car accident in October 1989, shortly after testifying on a Christian television programme in Nebraska. Senator John De Camp published her testimony in his book *"The Franklin Cover-Up"*. Here is a transcript of some of what she said at the time:

We became aware of this topic because we were a foster family and worked with a number of children. A few years ago, several children started to talk after a period of trust building. They reported very strange things that had happened in their lives, which was frightening and at the same time very confusing. I really didn't know what to make of it. We went to the police first and then we went to social services but there was really nothing else we could do. These children we worked with have now been adopted into safe families. They probably would never have spoken out if they hadn't trusted the people they were living with.

There are some similarities in the children's stories regarding satanic cults. There are identical things that come up in each testimony, like candles for example. They all talk about rape. Sex is definitely a big part of it, all sorts of perverted sexual practices. That's the first thing you'll hear, sex, rape, incest, so it's hard to believe. But once this is accepted, we can continue to question gently to find out more. We then learn that it is child pornography, it is a systematic practice. They use this to threaten the children: "We have pictures, we'll show them to the police if you talk. The children then feel a great danger, a great fear of the police. They talk about strange make-up that people in the group wear, they talk about songs that they didn't understand. It was obviously singing, that's something that comes up in every story, but none of the children called it "singing". There were also dances. Most of the time it involves sexual practices. There is always a group leader that the children are very afraid of.

These children, from a very young age, I'm talking about young children, are born into families to worship the devil. That's all I can testify to and I don't pretend to be an expert on the subject. All I can tell you is what the children have told me. My husband and I are now aware of some things that we shouldn't know, it's true. That's why I thought a lot about it before I went on this show, we heard such ugly and scary things that we were reluctant to reveal publicly. It's a very heavy thing and I don't want to scare people away, turn their lives upside down or give them certain ideas. I don't want them to think that if a child starts talking about something like this, they've probably seen this TV show where I talk about it. But we are hearing more and more, and it is becoming very, very clear. I think it's time people knew that this is not a joke or a game, it's not something we can ignore or laugh at.

The children I spoke to all had to kill at a very young age. It was something that was beyond my understanding. Somehow, with the help of an adult's hand and by having them participate in the ceremony, they make the child commit a murder. And what is serious is that the children really believe that they wanted to do it of their own free will. They want to replicate what the adults do and they are encouraged to do so. It becomes their goal, to become like the adults. There is still a small part of them that retains that natural God-given sense of right and wrong, but with the excitement of the group, they want to do it. They also like sex, I didn't know that children could like sex. Why would they fight it? A child will eat a whole bag of sweets if you let them. They will take part in these things voluntarily. When they come out and start talking about it, it is very difficult for them to realise. At first, we ourselves did not realise that they were "volunteering" to do it.

They are told that they cannot get out, that no one will ever believe them, that there is no freedom. They are hopeless until they meet someone who is willing to listen to them. They are systematically threatened with death. Every time a child is killed in the group, they are told: "If you speak out, this is what will happen to you. And they have every reason to believe it... So even when they get to a foster home and start to feel a bit safe, they always expect one of the cult members to show up at the door one day and come after them. They believe that these people know everything they do and everything they say. One teenage girl told me that she was told that if she ever got married and her husband cheated on her, it would be with one of them. They are setting them up for failure in all areas. These practices seem to be prevalent in Iowa, Nebraska and Missouri. Some people have recently suggested that these states may be a kind of headquarters.

As you listen to me talk about these things, there will certainly be a part of you that will naturally reject much of what you hear here, and believe me, we too rejected it at first. I would like to share with you some of what the children have revealed to us, things that no child can know or invent. This is what finally convinced me with deep emotion. There is this pain and sorrow that comes out when these raw flayers start to talk.

The children I am talking about are those I have personally known at home. They are now between 5 and 17 years old. When they first spoke, they were between 5 and 15 years old and when these things happened they were still babies, we are talking about very young children... We are talking about children whose awareness and learning of right and wrong is then in full formation. These children do not know, they cannot know what is right. They are in total confusion. The monstrosities they have done before, and for which they have been rewarded, are of such horror that they will be systematically rejected by others when they talk about them. Usually they have been placed several times. When they come into a family, they will steal, they will hurt animals, etc. The kid may, for example, carve up the house and then take it away. For example, the kid might sharpen his pencils and try to stab people. Obviously, families don't want that kind of behaviour in their home, but they don't have a clue what's going on, they'll just think, 'We've got a very strange child. Many of these little ones are sent to psychiatric hospitals where they will be labelled "psychotic" or "schizophrenic", who would want them afterwards? I praise the Lord who has brought many of them into my life, into our family. There are other families like ours, it's just a way for the Holy Spirit... That's the only way I can explain it...

I will start with the first stories we heard. This one will sound horrible to you, but it's pretty soft to me, because we've been dealing with much more difficult stories. The first one is about two little boys who were 7 and 9 years old when they started talking about sexual violence, they had a lot of sadness in them. One afternoon when we were talking about various personal things, both negative and positive, the little one started to cry. When we couldn't get an explanation, his older brother confessed to us: 'He is probably crying because he was in the room when they killed his friend. That was the first case we heard. They started to describe the scene to us, they talked about this little victim whose hands were tied and whose mouth was gagged. There were crosses marked on her body, located at the vital organs. It was very unhealthy... A few weeks later we learned that it was not adults who had killed this child, but that it was that older boy, the one who had told us about it.

The next case we are going to talk about is a little boy who was very limited mentally. He had language problems, it was very difficult for him to express himself verbally. When he started talking about these things, everybody was surprised at the way he expressed himself. We were sure, we knew he couldn't have heard that from other children. But we started to wonder, there was indeed something strange with these children coming and pouring all these atrocities on us... The thing that made me believe in the truth of this child's story is that he talked about several babies that were killed, but one time he curled up in a fetal position while he was telling the story of the stabbed infant, he was 9 years old then. He was in the fetal position while his eyes became glassy and he said: "They cook the baby on the grill... it smells like rotten chicken or rotten deer. " He then told us how they cut up the heart and genitals to keep them in the fridge. A typical thing that keeps coming up in the testimonies is their interest in the genitals. I asked him where the remains of the bodies were put, I didn't get an answer from this child. But the two other boys I mentioned before told me afterwards that "babies were thrown into the fire. I asked them if they were dead when they were put in the fire, the smallest one said: "No, no, they were alive. At that time we were really panicked by all these things! What were we going to do? How could we help these children? Where could we find a therapist who could treat this problem? ... But God put in place a support system. Other families helped us and that really helped us a lot.

The next child is a little girl who was 9 years old when she spoke. It was very painful when she first started to talk about sexual abuse. Sexual abuse is so harmful for children... They are embarrassed to talk about it, it is so intimate. She started by drawing cats... All these cats had their tails drawn on the other side of the page, or their legs were separated from their bodies. As we started talking to her, she told us that she had to kill a cat that was expecting kittens. She confessed that she had to kill the cat: "With a knife, I put it in her backside and turned it. Now you're going to tell me, can a child make up such things? If I ask a child how he could kill a cat, do you think he would answer that way? These are the kind of horrible details that the children reported to us. Then the little girl told us that they ended up cutting the cat open and that's how she knew she was expecting babies. According to her, they ate parts of the animal, as well as the excrement. They also drank the blood. That was only the beginning, she also had to kill a baby, in the same way, "put the knife in the backside and turn". The baby was alive and screaming... This child to this day still has terrible nightmares and violent flashbacks. She told us that they cut up the baby and ate it. The remains were burnt and the bones crushed. The little girl spoke of petrol being poured over the remains to burn them in the backyard. I have often thought I was crazy, but I have heard this so many times that now I know it must be so... We know that there are morgues involved in the cremation of victims' bodies.

The most horrific cremation story I have to tell, something very disturbing, came from a victim who was a teenager when she told me. She described a gathering outside a barn where people were singing. Then when they went into the barn, they split into two groups. She was never with her whole family, they were always separated to go to different places. I asked her then where she had to go and she said, "I've always been at the cremation chamber. As she was describing the cremation chamber, I thought to myself, "How did she get away with all her sanity," I don't know. She was a very small child then.

This girl told us that these groups kidnap small children and tie them up. There may be 5 or even 10 of them tied up in a row. In the ritual she told me, they were fully clothed, which is unusual as they are usually naked. Candles were then given to other children, including this teenager, a child at the time. The candles were lit and then the adults poured liquid on the clothes of the tied children, which was obviously petrol. They would then give a signal to the children to come forward with the candles to set the little victims on fire. Once this was done, some of them were shot. The first child this girl had to kill was one of her little cousins. She says she couldn't object, because those who object are also killed (...) Two years ago, this girl collapsed at Christmas time. Everyone thinks that Christmas is a wonderful time. She told us that she hated Christmas, that she couldn't stand it because all she could hear were crying babies. For her, Christmas is the time when most babies die. She covered her ears and cried for hours, shouting: "Stop it! Stop it! Talk to God and tell Him to make it stop! All she could hear was screaming and crying babies... Christmas for the children I spoke to is one of the worst times. Three children told me about a very similar ceremony. They were taken to a church where all the children were together, it was apparently very festive. A young child is put forward, two of them talked about babies on an altar. The adults are all celebrating, singing and dancing. The children are drawn into this euphoria and a circle forms around the one who has been brought forward, of course he represents the baby Jesus. The adults then start laughing at him, spitting on him, insulting him and then encouraging the other children to do the same... You can imagine how quickly it gets out of hand.

At some point they give all the children a knife to go and stab and cut up the child or baby until it dies. Then they celebrate the death of the baby Jesus...[266]

- Sandi Gallant

In 1988, Sandi Gallant was a police officer in San Francisco when she wrote a report documenting numerous cases of ritual abuse throughout the United States, but also in Canada where the phenomenon is also present. Here is what she wrote for the parents of victims:

In recent years, police officers have been confronted with investigations that involve a change in vocabulary. This vocabulary has to be adapted to crimes now identified as cases of 'ritual sexual abuse' or 'ritual child abuse' (...) Until recently, the laws were applied in these cases in the same way as for habitual child abuse. This was not done to deny the existence of ritual abuse, but because these cases were never categorised before. In other words, these cases were treated the way all cases were treated because no one knew that they fit a particular crime scenario then developing in the country. However, this has caused problems in terms of successful investigations (...) The allegations involve unbearable and unbelievable types of abuse. Investigators believe the victims, but are unable to find evidence that would lead to prosecution. In the maze of problems that have arisen, investigators have found themselves, in many cases, faced with cases that they are unable to prove. The parents of victims, now totally frustrated by these failures of the system, need answers and, indeed, have a right to know why their children who have been abused do not have a right to justice. That is why this article was written. You, the parents, are worthy of having the laws enforced. At the same time, we need you to understand the situation.

Why are the laws like this? As a ritual crime investigator for the past several years, I can honestly tell you that we are making progress and this area of crime is being recognized as specific and real. I say this because not a day goes by that I am not in contact with other law enforcement agencies across the United States and Canada who are seeking information regarding the modus operandi and manner of ritual abuse. In this regard, we are making progress. Where previously officers were not aware of what they were seeing, they are now able to identify things more easily, whereas previously investigators had no training on how to identify these crimes when they encounter them. They are now being trained. This is all very good, but parents still don't see the results. In many cases, suspects do not even go to trial, let alone be found guilty. At the time of writing, there have only been a few successful prosecutions in the United States (...)

In her report Sandi Gallant will write to her superiors:

"The information contained in this document is unpleasant and strange, to such a degree that one might choose to discredit it. However, my research in

---

[266] "The Franklin Cover-Up: Child Abuse, Satanism, and Murder in Nebraska" - John W. DeCamp, 1992, p.204-210.

this area has revealed that many such cases are emerging in the country and in Canada. The similarities in the stories of each child victim used in these crimes tend to lend credibility to the information revealed by others. In addition, psychiatrists and therapists who have followed the victims say that the consistency of the stories and the explicit details revealed lead them to believe that the children are telling the truth. Every police officer who submitted information for this report believes that the victims are telling the truth and that, in fact, the children would be incapable of developing such stories.

In the course of my research, similarities began to emerge, indicating the strong likelihood that there is a network of people in this country involved in the sexual abuse and probable homicide of young children. These cases appear to differ from isolated cases of child abuse because the crimes mentioned here are committed with the deliberate intention of maiming and killing children for ritual or sacrificial purposes. Many of the reported cases also reveal child pornography that goes beyond the normal type of child pornography as children are photographed during rituals in which some people wear robes, costumes and candles, snakes, swords, altars are also present, but there are still other types of ritual material.

This report was never forwarded to the FBI, and the Department of Justice also refused to review it.[267]

- Elder Glenn Pace

On 19 July 1990, Glenn Pace, then a Mormon bishop, sent an internal memo to his church denouncing ritual abuse. Indeed, Glenn Pace had conducted an investigation into satanic ritual abuse within *the Church of Latter-day Saints* (Mormons) in order to denounce the systematic and widespread proliferation of mind control. He had collected some 60 testimonies concerning traumatic rituals and human sacrifices. At the time, this memorandum caused such a stir that a government investigation into ritual abuse in Utah was launched the following year (resulting in the report cited earlier in this chapter: *"Ritual Crime in the State of Utah"*). Note that in his book *The Darker* Side *of Evil, Corruption, Scandal and the Mormon Empire*, Anson Shupe reports on page 109 of his book that in the Hadfield case, children told *stories of sex orgies where participants wore costumes and adults took pictures.*

Here is the translation of the memorandum of this bishop who had the courage to denounce these horrors:

In accordance with the Committee's request, I am writing this note to pass on to you what I have learned about ritualised child abuse. I hope that this will be of some value to you in continuing to monitor this problem. You have already received the LDS Social Services report on Satanism dated May 24, 1989, a report from Brent Ward, and a memorandum from me dated October 20, 1989

---

[267] "Ritual sexual abuse: the case of Martin's kindergarten in the United States" - Donde Vamos 20/05/2012.

in response to Brother Ward's report. Therefore, I will limit this letter by passing on only the information that was not included in these documents.

I have met sixty victims. This number could be multiplied by two or three if I didn't limit myself to one session per week. At first I did not want to get involved in this issue, which could become a handicap for my position of responsibility. But later on, I felt that I had to pay the price in order to obtain an intellectual and spiritual conviction about the seriousness of this problem within the Church.

Of the sixty or so victims I met, fifty-three were women and seven were men, eight of whom were still children. These abuses took place in the following locations: Utah (37), Idaho (3), California (5), Mexico (2), and other locations (14). Fifty-three victims reported witnessing or participating in human sacrifices. The majority were abused by relatives, often by their own parents. All developed psychological problems and most were diagnosed with multiple personality disorder or other forms of dissociative disorder.

This ritualised child abuse is the most despicable of all child abuse. The fundamental and premeditated objective is to torture and terrorise these children until they are forced to systematically and methodically disassociate themselves. This torture is not the result of 'anger', it is the execution of well thought out and planned rituals, often carried out by close relatives. The only way out for these children is to dissociate. They will then develop a new personality to enable them to cope with the various forms of abuse. When the traumatic episode is over, the core personality takes control of the individual who is not aware of what has happened. Dissociation is also used to cover up all these things, as time goes by children don't remember these atrocities. They reach adolescence and adulthood with no active memory of what is happening (or what has happened). Usually they continue to be involved in rituals throughout their adolescence and early adulthood, without being fully aware of their participation in these occult activities. Many people I have spoken to have been used in certain missions and it was not until much later that they began to remember them. An individual may have memories of participating in rituals, while still serving the cult full time.

The victims lead a relatively normal life, the memories are locked up and compartmentalised in their minds. They don't know how to deal with some of their emotions because they can't find the source. When they become adults and find themselves in a different environment, certain things may trigger memories and flashbacks or nightmares may also occur. These people will live a normal life, and then overnight they will find themselves in a psychiatric hospital in a fetal position. The memories of their childhood come back in such detail that the victims feel again the pain that caused the initial dissociation.

There are two reasons why adults can remember such events in great detail about their past: first, the terror they experienced was so intense that it was indelibly marked in their minds. Secondly, the memory has been compartmentalised so that one part of the mind is not subjected to the trauma. When these memories resurface, they are as fresh as if they had happened yesterday.

Memories seem to come up in layers. For example, the first memory may be of incest, and then memories of dresses and candles come back. Then victims realise that their father or mother (or both) were present during the abuse. Another layer will contain memories of seeing others tortured and even killed, including babies, and finally the realisation that the person was involved in sacrifices. One of the most painful memories is sometimes that they themselves had to sacrifice their own baby. With each layer of memory comes new problems that the victims have to face.

Some people argue that witnesses reporting such treatment cannot be reliable because of the unstable state of the victim and because almost all of them suffer from dissociative disorders. In fact these stories are so bizarre that they do indeed raise the question of credibility. The irony is that one of the aims of these cults is to create multiple personalities in these children in order to keep the 'secrets'. They live in society without society having any idea that anything is wrong, because these children and teenagers do not even realise themselves that they have another life in the shadows and in secret. However, when sixty victims come forward to testify to the same kind of torture and sacrifice, it becomes personally impossible for me not to believe them (...)

The spiritual doctrine that is linked to this physical abuse is particularly difficult to overcome. In addition to pain and terror, the children are also taught Satanic doctrine. Everything is completely reversed: white is black, black becomes white, good becomes evil and evil becomes good, etc.

Children are put in situations where they really believe they will die, such as being buried alive or immersed in water. Before doing this, the executioner tells the child to pray to Jesus Christ to see if he will come and save him. Imagine a seven year old girl, who has been told that she is going to die and that she should pray to Jesus... and that for her, nothing comes to save her until the last moment when she is finally rescued by a person claiming to be a representative of Satan. She becomes a child of Satan and is in danger of becoming faithful to him.

Just before or shortly after their baptism into the Church, children are baptised by blood into the satanic order which is intended to cancel their Christian baptism (...) All these things are done with the personality that has been born in order to endure the physical, mental and spiritual pain. As a result, a kind of 'civil war' develops within these people. When the memories begin to resurface, there are personalities who feel that they themselves are devoted to Satan, with no hope of forgiveness, while the core personality is an active member of The Church. When the integration (merging of the alter) takes place, this is when the "civil war" breaks out. Sometimes, in an interview, the dark side personality emerges, perhaps petrified or filled with hatred for me and what I stand for. These personalities need to be dealt with both spiritually and psychologically.

Most of the victims are suicidal. They have been indoctrinated with drugs, hypnosis and other techniques to make them suicidal as soon as they start to reveal the secrets. The victim is threatened with death, their relatives are also threatened, etc. The victim has every reason to believe these threats because they have already seen people killed (...)

The purpose of this memorandum is to emphasise the complexity of psychological and spiritual therapy for these people. Our priests, when confronted with such cases, are naturally helpless, not knowing how to respond. As for the judiciary, it is totally ineffective. For example, some victims sometimes say that all these things are in the past and that they should put them aside and concentrate on their present life. This is simply impossible. Part of spiritual therapy is to convert the personalities that have been indoctrinated into Satanism. Victims need to integrate all their personalities so that they can function as a coherent whole, thus enabling them to cope with the problems and then to concentrate fully on their lives (...)

The perpetrators are living a double life, many of them are recognised members of the (Mormon) temple, which is why the Church needs to consider the seriousness of this problem (...) I refused to allow the victims to give me the names of the perpetrators. I told them that my responsibility was to help them in their spiritual healing and that the names of the perpetrators should be given to therapists and police officers (...) I don't pretend to say that this problem is widespread, all I know is that I have met sixty victims. When sixty victims testify to the same types of torture and killings, personally it becomes impossible for me not to believe them (...) Obviously, I only met those who were looking for help. Most of them were in their twenties or thirties. I can only guess, and I am horrified, at the number of children and teenagers currently involved in these occult practices (...)

- Jenny Hill

In October 2012, the US television channel *ABC4* broadcast a short report by Kimberley Nelson on the testimony of Jenny Hill, a female survivor of ritual abuse who was diagnosed with 22 different personalities. Jenny Hill's story is reported in *"22 Faces"*, a book written by her therapist, Judy Byington, who told the reporter:

"She was sexually assaulted in rituals when she was very young, she developed these multiple personalities whenever she was in a traumatic situation.

Her first alter personality was *"born"* when she was 4 years old. Just as her father, a devout Mormon, began to do the unthinkable...

He told me he loved me more than my mother and that this was our secret."

It was some years later, when the ritual abuse began, that her personality split again to cope with the rapes and torture. Jenny had no memory of the abuse, all she knew was that she had serious memory loss... Until one day she woke up confused in a psychiatric hospital. Dr. Weston Whatcott took care of her. He told the journalist that he met several of Jenny Hill's alter personalities:

If this was film, then she deserves to win several Oscars (...) She had a completely different voice! I mean a real change of voice, a change of accent, but also a change of demeanour, of facial expressions, all of that changed radically."

Dr. Whatcott also discovered that her different alter personalities come out in Jenny's writings. Both in the diary she wrote as a child and in the diary she kept as an adult. In this diary, the alter personalities reveal what happened in her past. Jenny herself was not convinced that she could have all these different personalities, until one day Dr. Whatcott made a video recording of one of the therapy sessions: *"She was fascinated by what she saw there, she was like a little child, she got down on her knees and got closer to the screen... She couldn't believe that it was her who was on that video.* Dr. Whatcott says the discovery of the recordings was a real turning point for Jenny. Memories began to surface, including memories of human sacrifice: *"I was tied up and they threatened to do the same thing to me as they did to the victim. At one point in the ceremony, the pain was so intense that the victim was crying hysterically... and I didn't cry, I didn't make a sound... as if I had been programmed to do that."*

Jenny says that on 21 June 1965 she saw this little girl being murdered. She says that she would probably have been the next victim but that she was saved by divine intervention...

Judy Byington: "Jenny said she saw a man's feet in a white light, she was lying on the altar and he was right on top of her, and it broke up the ceremony."

Jenny thought she was really alone with her memories, but her mother, before her death, admitted in a telephone conversation that she had been involved in Satanic rituals. She also confirmed and validated Jenny's memory of the saving white light. The telephone conversation between Mercy Hill (Jenny's mother), and Judy Byington, was recorded and broadcast in this *ABC4* report:

- Journalist: You mentioned this white light, can you tell us more about it?

- Mercy Hill: I don't know, I don't remember much about it, but I think there was a white light. It was a bit far away from us and it was coming down.

- Journalist: Did you see anything in the light?

- Mercy Hill: No, she was so bright you know... she was blinding...

- Vicki Polin

In 1989, Oprah Winfrey devoted one of her shows, *"The Oprah Winfrey Show"*, to Satanic ritual abuse. The programme was entitled *"Mexican Satanic Cult Murders"*. During the evening, a woman testified to the horrors she had experienced, claiming that her family had been involved in rituals for generations and generations. At the time of her testimony, she was undergoing intense therapy for her multiple personality disorder or dissociative identity disorder. Here is the transcript of her interview with Oprah Winfrey:

- Oprah Winfrey: Have you too experienced ritual abuse in your family?

- Vicki Polin: Yes, my family comes from a long line of abusers, going back to the 16th century.

- OW: And so they abused you?

- VP: I come from a family that believes in this...

- OW: And from the outside, everyone thought they were a respectable Jewish family?

- VP: That's exactly it.

- OW: While there was a cult to Satan inside the house itself...

- VP: Yes... There are many Jewish families all over the country, not only mine.

- OW: Really? And who knows about these things? A lot of people now. (laughs)

- VP: I've talked to a Chicago police investigator about it, and several of my friends know about it. I've also talked about it publicly before...

- OW: So you were brought up in the middle of all this horror. Did you think it was normal?

- VP: I buried a lot of my memories in myself because of my multiple personality disorder, but yeah... when you grow up with something, you think it's normal. I always thought that...

- OW: But what kind of things? You don't have to give us gory details, but what kind of things were going on in your family?

- VP: Well there were rituals where babies were sacrificed and you had to...

- OW: Whose babies?

- VP: There were people bringing babies to our family. Nobody noticed, many women were obese, you couldn't see if they were pregnant or not. And if there was any suspicion, they would go away for a while and then come back. Another thing I want to say is that not all Jews sacrifice babies, it's not a traditional thing.

- OW: So you witnessed a sacrifice?

- VP: Yes, when I was very young I was forced to participate in this and I had to sacrifice a child.

- OW: What is the purpose of these sacrifices, what do you get out of it?

- VP: It's about Power, Power...

- OW: Have you been used yourself?

- VP: I was sexually assaulted, raped several times...

- OW: What did your mother do? What was her role?

- VP: I'm not sure what role she might have had, I haven't got all my memories back yet, but my family were extremely involved in it... You know, they led me into it, both my parents led me into it.

- OW: And where is it now?

- VP: She lives in the metropolis of Chicago, she works at the Human Relations Commission of the city where she resides. She is a model citizen, no one would suspect her...

- OW: Were you brought up with the notion of right and wrong?

- VP: Yes... I had both notions. What I mean is that to the outside world, everything we did was good and respectable, and then there were certain nights when things were different...when what was bad became good, and what was good was something bad. All this was done in order to develop multiple personality disorders.

- OW: In your family, was it really called "devil worship" or was it just the things you did that were evil?

- VP: No, I don't know. I mean, I said it was bad, and they said it was good. There's a book I came across called "The Cave of Lilith", a book about Jewish mysticism and the supernatural. There's a lot in there that relates to what I experienced as a child. "

- Linda Weegan

Linda Weegan is a mother of two children who were victims of ritual abuse. She gave her testimony during a conference with Ted Gunderson. Here she describes the systematic protocol of injustice of attacking and judicially harassing the protective parent (usually the mother) to protect the alleged abusers and networks instead of conducting a proper investigation. Here is a transcript of her testimony:

I'm here to tell you an example of what happens when a satanic cult abuses your children. I go to church, I'm a Catholic... I go to church and yet the devil was something external that was not talked about and was even hidden. It was something that was very much in the realm of science fiction. My children started talking about sexual abuse in 1993. They would masturbate, they would try things with the dog like putting a pencil or a paintbrush up his rectum. These behaviours got worse and worse (...) I knew I had a very big problem but I had no idea what it was. So I went around the country looking for help. I gave my children's drawings to the police. So I had all these drawings with circles, people, black candles in the middle of tables, depictions of sodomy and so on. I went to the church and told them, 'I don't know what it is but these drawings look very significant. There are symbols I don't understand, devil heads, ghosts..." At that time I had no idea what satanic ritual abuse was. The only answer I got from the Church was that I had already had a psychiatric examination... Today I can say that I know what the symbols in these drawings mean.

Even though the father was charged with sodomy and oral sex on his children, no one would help me. Even though there are ongoing prosecutions, they say you made up these stories of satanic ritual abuse. Your credibility is zero, it just doesn't exist, "nothing like this happens in the US"... Just focus on the "simple" pedophilia your children suffered...

So I took my boys to an institute specialising in child sexual abuse. Mothers could also be admitted and I had legal custody of my two sons. My husband, his lawyers and the judge found out that my children were in a specialised institute... They then confiscated my house, everything I had, from my babies' photos to my clothes, I only had one suitcase with me. They took my car, my mail, my income, my assets... I lost everything for introducing my children to a sexual abuse specialist! They were trying to stop me because of what my children might disclose. They tried to break me financially so that my children would no longer have any therapeutic help at this institute. It was clearly acknowledged that my sons had been sexually abused and I can prove it with documents.

One day, the therapist who was taking care of them invited me into her office, and there she told me that it was a classic case of S.R.A. (Satanic Ritual Abuse). (Satanic Ritual Abuse)... I had no idea what she was talking about, S.R.A.... She then explained to me what Satanic Ritual Abuse was. She showed me the drawings that the children had made in her office. There was a picture of a blood sacrifice, where people cut their arms and collected the blood in a chalice. The chalice was shaped like a devil's head... etc... It included orgies, child sacrifices... It was a huge shock, I didn't know what to do, I didn't know where to go...

I called all the child protection associations and organisations in the country to ask for help, but no one admitted the existence of Satanic ritual abuse. Moreover, all the child protection associations only claim that they "love children"... but they don't actually help anyone. So my fight to save my children has brought me here, and I can tell you now that there are other mothers here today who have asked me for help because their children are also victims of ritual abuse. This is very hard for me, my life has been destroyed but I must say it has been rebuilt for the better. John and Ben, who are 11 and 8 years old, lived for 15 and 16 months in the home of a Satanist who is a member of a 25-person group located in Turney, Connecticut. They are actively involved in ritual sexual abuse. Neither the governor nor anyone else has protected my children. So I ask myself: How far will this go? (...)

- Glenn Hobbs

In 1988, *Jeremiah Films* produced a documentary entitled *"Halloween, Trick or Treat?* (in which Caryl Matrisciana interviews an ex-satanist, Glenn Hobbs, who was born into a cult of ritual abuse. Here is the transcript of the interview:

- Caryl Matrisciana: Glenn Hobbs was initiated by his grandfather into a Satanist cult as a child and continued to participate in these activities for years. I recently interviewed Glenn about his involvement and the importance of Halloween to these occultists.

- Glenn Hobbs: My involvement in Satanic worship began in childhood because I was a generational Satanist... That is, my family and its previous generations were involved in these occult practices. Today, my earliest memories of Halloween and everything related to it remind me that it was a very dark time in my childhood...

- CM: Glenn, can you tell us about the Halloween rituals you were involved in as a child?

- GH: There was another little girl involved in this with me. Her name was Becky. Becky was not like me, she was destined to be sacrificed. I was destined to be a high priest. She was born into this cult to be a human sacrifice. She and I were married together in a ritual. It was a marriage offered to "the Beast". When me and this little girl were married, there was a lot of sexual abuse, a lot of bloodshed, all to unite us.

- CM: When does the Halloween ritual begin? What is the real purpose of Halloween?

- GH: The rituals that I remember most clearly start at the end of September. Me and the little girl I just mentioned, Becky... The abuse was very repetitive during this time of year. We were taken to several rooms where we were stripped naked. We spent the next two weeks in some sort of huts where a lot of rituals took place, a lot of animals were sacrificed. Incantations to Lucifer and his demons were made so that they would come and take possession of me. I was destined to become a high priest when the time came. On Halloween night they took me and the little girl in the back of a van. The drive seemed long, again we were drugged... Finally we stopped, they got the little girl out and left me in the van. I could hear a lot of commotion outside, people shouting and screaming with this sort of murmur in the background... a sort of chant. So I was aware that a ritual was going on because I had heard this kind of thing many times before. It was something usual for me to see people lying on the ground and convulsing during these rituals, with always this demonic presence around... Finally a woman came and told me it was time for me to go... So she took me out of the van and there I could see that there were a lot of people present. Some people were dressed in some kind of dark robes with big hoods. They took me to a stone altar. I remember seeing the little girl, she was on the altar... I wondered at first what was going to happen, because you never know, they can use the altar for many things, it can be an animal sacrifice, sexual abuse by the high priest on a victim, it's hard to know in advance... They finally directed me in front of this altar, there I saw that they had tied her feet and she was tied to the altar. Her arms were also tied to the altar with some kind of hooks. She was very white... I remember she was incredibly white... They had made incisions in her feet and wrists. They had collected the blood that flowed from the wounds in a chalice, and then they passed this vessel to the people who were present. Then the high priest took the ritual dagger... He pointed it at the little victim, then he took my hand and put it on the dagger and forced me to stab the chest...

So as far as Halloween is concerned... You know, it was a climactic time of year, Halloween night when they killed that little innocent girl. This is something that happens every Halloween night, it's not just an isolated event. There are children all over the world who are sacrificed on Halloween night, and in our societies we celebrate it by going door to door asking for candy, it's a 'big holiday' for us. But I think it's very ironic, some people think it's something fun, while others are taking human lives... And yet nobody wants to face what's really going on (...)

- Anne A. Johnson Davis

Anne A. Johnson Davis is the author of *"Hell Minus One"*, an autobiographical book published in 2008 in which she recounts her childhood traumatized by ritual abuse from the age of 3 until she was 17 and finally ran away. Anne, whose real name is Rachel Hopkins, took a long time to go public and come out of anonymity, writing her autobiography took 7 1/2 years.

The book contains a foreword by Lieutenant Inspector Matt Jacobson of the Utah Attorney General's office (Jacobson is one of the authors of the report *"Ritual Crime in the State of Utah"* mentioned earlier in this chapter). In this foreword, Jacobson validates the testimony contained in the book, indicating that he himself personally met and questioned the abusers who confessed in his presence. Later, Anne even received written confessions from her abusers, who were none other than her mother and stepfather.

Here is an interview with Anne Johnson Davis that was conducted and posted online by the group S.M.A.R.T. (*Stop Mind-control And Ritual abuse Today*)[268]

- What is the book 'Hell Minus One' about?

- This book is all about hope and freedom, it is a biography, a segment of my life. As the subtitle of my book states, it is "my story of deliverance from satanic ritual abuse and my return to freedom".

This book reveals that there really are people who practice satanic ritual abuse. This is not a myth, as some claim. From the age of 3, my parents used me as an object in rituals until I left home at the age of 17. This book is about the abuse I suffered and the steps I took to regain my freedom, to heal myself and to finally forgive my abusers. The book talks about the choices I made, some miracles and some crucial help I received. Help that allowed me to overcome this tragic past. It is also about the commitment I made to live a new life in love, determination and positive resolutions.

- Why did you write this book?

- When I was in recovery, I began to understand that my life and mental health would not improve just because of me. I felt a calling to bring freedom and hope to others. My husband, Bruce, was also convinced of this calling and always encouraged me to write this book. He felt that my experience could make a contribution. At first I resisted because I wasn't ready to commit to something that required immense and painful effort. But as I healed, this desire to inspire courage in others grew within me. From my experience, I wanted victims of abuse to find some hope that they could get through this, that they could overcome the obstacles that seem totally insurmountable. What we face, we can overcome - and even do better. Then the doors will open and help will come when we give our all for the GOOD.

I have evidence of satanic ritual abuse. I also have memories that have come back to me and I have recorded all this clearly in letters. These letters were returned with written confessions from my abusers, who were my own mother and stepfather. My half-brothers also sent letters to the authorities to confirm my accusations. Two inspectors connected to the Prosecutor General's office subsequently obtained verbal and written confessions from the abusers.

- Who should read your book?

- The story in my book is meant to bring hope to the victims. Hope for those who are still captive. Hope that there are other options and that they have

---

[268] *"Interview With the Author of Hell Minus One"* - Anne A Johnson Davis, S.M.A.R.T. /ritualabuse.us.

a choice. It is also a call to those who are in a position to help them, such as lawyers, mental health professionals, the church and even people who open up to the testimonies they are sometimes given. This book is also for those who wish to read a biography where goodness and light have overcome evil and darkness.

- What are the most important message(s) of your book?

- That our adversity is not our identity. What we have done, or what has been done to us, is not who we are. No matter what has been done to us - or what mistakes we have made - we can overcome it and be true to our authentic, true self. Goodness and light always overcome evil and darkness. Our God-given ability to direct our own lives is never lost, never!

This book is for those who need encouragement, or who are in a professional or personal situation where they need to support and encourage someone. The subtitle of my book is: "My story of deliverance from satanic ritual abuse and my return to freedom". I say "deliverance" rather than "escape" because I could not have done this on my own. I received help from a higher power. I don't think anyone can get out of this bondage completely on their own. The message of this book goes beyond simply overcoming satanic ritual abuse, it is equally valid for everyone, individuals, associations, companies, as it deals with the issue of overcoming seemingly insurmountable obstacles. We all have Goliaths to face and overcome. This process of confronting and overcoming the obstacle is never easy and requires commitment and hard work. But the result of this work changes your life forever. The only way out is through it.

- How long did it take you to write this book?

- Let's see... How old am I? ... It took me a lifetime! First 47 years to live it, then I had to "relive" it and process it. Then it took 6 years of writing and finally 18 months to proofread and edit the final manuscript. The book was published in December 2008.

- What research have you done?

- Research? I didn't have to do any research. I lived it, then I remembered it. The memories came back with crystal clarity, one by one, day by day, week by week, month by month. It pieced together a shocking puzzle of which I was totally unaware. I wrote explicit letters about what had happened and eventually received written confessions from my parents: my mother and my stepfather. These written confessions were supplemented by verbal confessions to the Utah Attorney General.

- What was the most difficult thing, or challenge, in writing your book "Hell Minus One"?

- To find the determination and courage to stay on this project for over seven years, writing and re-reading a manuscript with horrific and painful details. But the dark side of my story was balanced by the light side which is ultimately the most important. These sources of positivity are my faith and spiritual experiences, as well as great circumstances and people who have passed through my life.

- In the first few chapters of the book, you describe a lot of detailed memories from when you were three years old. How did you remember it all? Was it always there, or did it come back to you as you wrote?

- Most of the memories came up in therapy. Additional details emerged over the years as I worked to put my story in writing. My editor and I worked together to finalise the manuscript. At one point, he asked me if I knew more. To preserve authenticity and accuracy, I took my time, quietly, to simply let the details emerge.

- Were your brothers and sisters victims like you? Or were they Satanists like your parents?

- My half-brothers have written letters to the church authorities supporting and confirming my testimony. I respect their privacy and I don't want to speak for them. They were not victims as I was, I was a "patch" in the family, considered a "bastard" and used as a sacrificial object.

- How did you manage to get these confession letters from your parents?

- At the beginning of my therapy, when I still had contact with them, I called them and asked them if they could write to the church authorities to confirm my accusations. And they did.

- Your parents' confession letters are published in detail in your book. You have used ellipses in several paragraphs. What did you leave out and why?

- These are paragraphs that were too insane and too violent to be published. This book conveys, above all, a message of hope and encouragement, of deliverance and healing. My intention in including these confessional letters was to give the reader enough information to know how unhealthy it was. But I did not want the content to be so offensive and shocking that the reader would close the book.

There were also references to my half-siblings, and out of respect for their privacy, I have removed these passages.

- Where are your parents' confession letters today?

- The originals are kept in a safe.

- Are they available to the public? If not, why not?

- They are not available to the public. They were made available to the Utah Attorney General during his investigation. They were also made available to the publishing house when the final manuscript was written. But due to the nature of the content of these letters, often with shocking graphic details, as well as a defamatory issue, as names are mentioned, they are not available to the public.

- Your parents started subjecting you to ritual abuse at the age of 3 and this continued until you left home at the age of 17. After that you started having rage attacks in your 30s... By the end of the 90s you had completed therapy and were on the road to recovery. That was over a decade ago and today you are in your 50s. You say it took seven years to write "Hell Minus One". Why didn't you write your book earlier? Was it an emotional issue, did you have to feel ready before revealing this memoir?

- Before 2001, I didn't feel the need to write a book that could possibly help others. Writing "Hell Minus One" took much longer than I had anticipated.

But I wanted the manuscript to be authentic in every detail and also to be of good writing quality. It took 18 months to rework and edit the manuscript, after 7 years of writing.

- Your parents did horrible and sadistic things to you. After these episodes, you didn't remember anything, you didn't even have hostile feelings towards them. What is the medical or psychological definition of this phenomenon? How and why does the brain work in this way? Can certain things experienced be erased?

- The definitions I have heard from professionals are not convincing. I tend to rely on my own experience rather than using labels that may be contradictory and misunderstood. In my case, my psyche prevented me from becoming aware of the abuse until I was mature enough to react. Before that, threats from my abusers that I would be destroyed if I spoke out about anything kept these memories of abuse in a compartmentalized, psychological silence.

- What exactly is satanic ritual abuse?

- For me, it is a criminal, inhumane and perverse form of devil worship. These crimes include physical, sexual, mental and spiritual torture of innocent victims.

- What is its origin? What is its history?

- First of all, I am not an expert on satanic ritual abuse and I do not wish to be. Sometimes, during the abuse, I heard my parents and their accomplices talking about going back to a distant time, so whatever was done on those nights did not refer to the present time. There are several sources on the internet describing in detail the origin of ritual abuse. Unfortunately, there are also many sources claiming that all this is false and that it is an urban legend born in the 1980s and discredited in the late 1990s. Mainly due to unproven and unsubstantiated claims.

What happened to me - the letters of confession from my parents - is one more argument to put in the balance. In fact, my parents' letters, their verbal confessions to the police and their excommunication from the Church, provide new evidence that researchers and sceptics of satanic ritual abuse did not have before. Without evidence, I can understand why this topic has not received more support in the past. One of my hopes is that "Hell Minus One" will receive good reviews, from the judiciary, mental health professionals and even the media. This is to reconsider the issue of ritual abuse.

- Why do these people engage in such behaviour? What do they get out of it?

- From my point of view, this is a means of fulfilling an addiction to sexual violence and perversion. I've seen them behave in a completely demented way - determined to appeal to the powers of darkness and evil - believing that this would give them superior power and might over other people, as well as an extraordinary way to get money.

- The ritual abuse you experienced took place in the 1950s and 1960s. If you do an internet search for "Satanic Ritual Abuse", hundreds of sites are listed. Some offer help, some describe disturbing details of today's practices. What comparison can you give us about what you have experienced and what is being done today?

- Over a year ago, after a few hours of research on this subject on the internet, I decided that I would never again subject myself to seeing or reading about such things. What I understand is that the purpose and intent of ritual abuse does not seem to have changed, even though the techniques have developed considerably. It is becoming more and more bizarre, more and more brutal and inhumane.

- For readers who are victims of ritual abuse, what do you recommend?

- Above all I would like them to know that they have a choice. I would like to urge them to be courageous and ask for help in any way they can, to get out and stay out of this evil, this bondage. If your family is toxic and completely sick, if they are involved in criminal activities, you should not turn to them anymore. You can't save them, but you can save yourself. I would like them to realise that they have a God-given right to their identity and their life. They have and will have inner signs and intuition that will guide them in the best way possible.

- For readers who worship Satan, or practice ritual abuse, what do you recommend?

- For those who practice satanism, they have the right to do what they want as long as it is not a question of criminal acts. Having experienced the satanic practices of these nauseating souls, I advise them to get out, whatever the cost, before it is too late.

- What do you hope to achieve with your book "Hell Minus One"?

- My hope and prayer is that this book will be a beacon, a light in the midst of darkness. A message of hope and encouragement. We can all overcome seemingly insurmountable obstacles. The epigraph to my book reminds us that we have all been endowed by the Creator with an inalienable right to our lives, a right to freedom and happiness.

- In your book, you explain why you and your husband chose not to press charges against your parents for their criminal acts. Now that several years have passed since that decision, do you regret it? Why did you make such a decision?

- No, I don't regret it. At the time, with the "false memory syndrome", the trial would not have gone in my favour. Whether I was telling the truth or not, it would have been my person who would have been put in the media spotlight rather than my parents; even though they made written and verbal confessions and were excommunicated from their church. A force within me warned me at the time that this would have resulted in a media explosion that would have torn my own little family apart and me with it.

v/ Canada

- Manon and Josée

In 1995, the Canadian newspaper *La Presse* published an article by journalist Marie-Claude Lortie entitled: *"The SQ has opened an investigation into a mysterious satanic sect in the Eastern Townships"* (SQ stands for Sûreté du Québec, the national police force of Quebec). A publication that is still available in the archives of the site www.lapresse.ca.

The article reports the testimonies of two young women, *'Manon'* and *'Josée'*, who were born into a satanic sect and got out despite everything. At the age of 28, Manon decided to talk to Luc Grégoire, an investigator with the Sûreté du Québec's major crime squad. The woman described black masses, gang rapes, physical abuse and sacrifices. Marie-Claude Lortie introduces her article with these words from Manon:

- I was born into a satanic cult. In a family where all members had to worship Satan, to love him unconditionally, to do everything to obey him. I was abused from the age of three and a half, tortured, martyred, raped. I saw animal sacrifices, but also human sacrifices...

- Humans?

- Yes, humans...

Manon recounts that she underwent initiation and traumatic rituals such as being buried alive in a coffin. She speaks of gang rapes and torture, of sacrifices in which she was forced to drink the blood and eat the flesh of the sacrificial offerings. As in many testimonies, she says that her family has been involved in these satanic activities for generations and generations: *"It is a cult that is transmitted by blood. And it is also with their blood that the followers must sign the obligatory pact before entering any black mass, a pact by which they commit themselves never to say anything about what they have seen or heard during the ceremonies. "*

The young woman explained to the investigator that every full moon, dozens of people crowd into basements to attend rituals led by Satanic priests. She speaks of ceremonies that usually gather around 100 people. The group to which she belonged often travelled long distances to attend black masses and she speaks of some ceremonies in Quebec with as many as 500 followers. She says she attended a ritual in the United States where there must have been 1500 people, according to her *"many people must have been there simply for voyeurism, for sensationalism, and to enjoy the sexual orgies that took place after the black masses"*.

The young women both claim that they were forced into prostitution and that this is the fate of all girls in the network. The rapes took place during the ceremonies, but they were also sexually abused in their families, *"Most of the atrocities were not spared to any of the young women in the sect"*, explains Josée. It was a priest from the Brothers of the Sacred Heart in Bromptonville, Guy Roux, who helped Manon through prayer in order to "free" her from what she had experienced. The priest said that the young woman was in the grip of the devil. Her psychotherapist also helped her a lot to overcome these traumatic experiences.

- Pierre Antoine Cotnareanu

Another testimony is that of psychoanalyst Pierre Antoine Cotnareanu. He described a disturbing case of one of his Canadian patients. His testimony was filmed and broadcast on the internet, here is the transcript:

- She was a person who came from a satanist cult, what she told us was quite atrocious, I didn't think that existed near my home. She said that she was part of a family that practised a Satanist cult from generation to generation. When she was little, she was educated, hypnotised, to be a kind of priestess, an altar for black magic ceremonies.

- Who did these things?

- She said that they were important people (...)

- As a therapist, were you destabilized by this discovery?

- Absolutely... it was very destabilising.

- What are the details that threw you off?

- The fact that it was used as an altar, that there was some sexual magic around it and that there were child sacrifices... I think that's enough to throw someone off.

- Sacrifices of children of what age?

- Young children, very young...

- Babies?

- She was the altar on which the sacrifices were made (...) She was a person in great distress when I met her and you could see that she had been hypnotised, so we worked to get her out of that kind of 'circle'...

- Did she give any figures on the number of people?

- There must have been 15 or 20 people at the ceremonies, sometimes less. They were families, and around these families, there were other more or less important people who gravitated.

- Was there a genetic aspect that was important to them?

- Yes, they've been like that for generations, so parents bring up their children that way and so on... There's not much tenderness there.

- Did they ever sacrifice one of their children?

- I don't know... But already, this patient, it's like a sacrifice, because to put her through this is rather demonic.

- How often were these rituals performed?

- It would happen quite regularly, it would start with a phone call and then I think the person's voice would put them into a trance and after that they would be available to do what they needed to do.

- Can you get out of a trauma like that?

- Yes, I think she got through it. It takes a lot of work, you need someone who knows the mechanics of hypnosis to be able to decode and defuse the process. I saw her some times when she was crying, she was crying... when she realised it... when there was this clash of different personalities that were meeting inside her: it was quite intense. Intense enough to destabilise me and make me think that there are people more qualified than I am for this. It's really a special qualification to work with these victims of cults who have undergone hypnosis (editor's note: mind control).

d/ France

- Véronique Liaigre

On 5 July 2001, the TF1 television news programme broadcast the testimony of Véronique Liaigre, who stated bluntly that she had been raped and prostituted by her parents from the age of 5. She clearly described a *Martinist* satanist sect in the Agen region that practised sacrificing children born of rape and not declared or foreign children. She said she was forced to participate in blood rituals under threat. Here is the transcript of this report broadcast at prime time:

- Patrick Poivre d'Arvor: Here is a terrible file on which Alain Ammar and his team have been working for several weeks. The accusations made in his investigation by a young woman who was a minor at the time of the events are extremely serious, some of them are even hard to believe, but it is her word. The names she mentions have been covered with a "beep" so as not to affect the presumption of innocence.

- Voice-over: Véronique is 20 years old and has lived through hell since the age of 5. Raped and prostituted by her parents, whom she denounced and who are waiting to appear before the court of appeal, she has managed to escape from those she calls her executioners. Her story is not an ordinary one and may even seem made up. However, if it is legitimate to have doubts, what this young woman told us and repeated spontaneously is shocking. In particular when she affirms, in spite of the threats she claims to have received, that she frequented a satanist sect, martinists, and that she herself was tortured and tortured.

- Véronique Liaigre: We are beaten, we have objects put in our orifices, there are sometimes sacrifices of children to give thanks to Satan, there are many things like that... An animal is killed, the blood is poured over our heads and the rest is put in a cupola which is placed on the altar.

- Journalist: So in fact, your parents, like all the parents of these children you are talking about, were selling their children?

- VL: Exactly, because it brings in a certain percentage of money. A child under 8 years old is worth 22,000 francs.

- J: Where do these children come from?

- VL: The children who are sacrificed are not declared, or are foreign children. In particular when I was in Agen, they were little Africans, they were black. In Jallais I also saw some, in Nanterre too, but they were white children, French, but they were children born of rape.

- J: Children born of rape?

- VL: Yes, which were not declared. These are deliveries that take place in the parents' home in abominable conditions.

- J: So, to the extent that they were not declared, they were sacrificed?

- VL: Here it is...

- J: Not only were you part of the cult, but you participated in these rituals...

- VL: Yes, in 1994, I had to sacrifice a child at gunpoint with two of my friends in Jallais. And the three of us had to murder him... At gunpoint, if we didn't do it, we would have been... They would have done it even more violently and they would have hurt us even more. So we had to do it...

- J: And who was pointing a gun at you?

- VL: "beep" the one who runs the "beep" gendarmerie.

- J: And these corpses, what do they do with them afterwards?

- VL: The one that marked me the most was the one I took part in. They took him to a cellar in Cholet, carried him in a black bag with an upside down white cross... And they had a big can, they put something in... I don't know if it was petrol or acid or something like that, but Cécile, Sophie and myself, we all saved ourselves.

- J: So they actually burn the corpses.

- VL: They have to burn them, yes.

- J: You think it's all a kind of network, people holding on a little bit so they don't fall...

- VL: That's it, and it's also to protect itself, because given that there are lawyers in it, it's true that it would make a strange fuss if we learned that there were judges and all that who were part of that network.

- J: Have you seen any personally?

- VL: I saw an e-mail from "bip", from Mr "bip" but I didn't know who it was...

- J: Who said what?

- VL: It was for a transfer of funds...

- J: And you think these people are part of the cults themselves? This elite you speak of?

- VL: They cover them... I wouldn't necessarily say that they are part of it, but they cover them, that's for sure.

- Voice-over: Jean-Claude Disses is Véronique's lawyer in Agen. She was transferred from Maine-et-Loire to a home frequented by paedophiles. Initially sceptical about his client's accusations, he is now convinced that she is telling the truth.

- Jean-Claude Disses (Véronique Liaigre's lawyer): I believe her when she tells me that she was raped in her family. I believe her when she says that she was prostituted by certain members of her family. I believe her when she explains that this prostitution necessarily and necessarily passed through many adults who came to abuse her for money. I believe her when she says at the same time that she was photographed during these scenes and I believe her all the more because we apparently find these photos on a CD-Rom in Amsterdan (editor's note: Affaire Zandvoort).

- Journalist: So it's her, she recognised herself and said "that's me".

- JCD: That's it, that's exactly it. She says "it's me", she says it in front of a police inspector and at the same time as she identifies herself, she also identifies five of her childhood friends. This means that if this is true, these children must have been subjected to pornographic scenes, these scenes must have been filmed, and these photos must have been sent to Amsterdam and ended up on a paedophile CD-Rom that was seized by the Dutch police in the context of proceedings in Holland. So there must be an organisation that takes photos, that distributes them, so there is an organisation and a network!

- Voice-over: Véronique led us to one of the many places where she said satanic ceremonies were held on the 21st of each month.

Véronique Liaigre (at the foot of a building in the city centre in front of a porte cochere): Here, I've been here several times. In particular, I remember well one time in 1994, when I found myself at a satanic ritual with a child murder. We went up to the second floor. There were rapes, there must have been 5 or 6 children, it wasn't a very big meeting. There were "beep", "beep", there were a lot of people, notably notables whose names I don't necessarily know.

- Journalist: And you yourself have suffered...

- VL: Yes, I was there and I suffered... My father was there, my mother was not there that time.

- Voice-over: Her incredible memory also allows Véronique to remember a phone call where she hears about little Marion Wagon, who disappeared on 14 November 1996.

- Véronique Liaigre: I was at the home of one of the paedophiles, "beep", and then the phone rang. She started screaming, she was upstairs, I was in her room downstairs. So I picked up the phone in her room and I heard a man I knew, Walter, demanding more money or he would report everything to the police. He said: "Anyway, I'm not going to jail, I didn't kill her, I only put her up under your orders, and only for six days. And now I want the money, I won't go to prison. And then I heard Jean-Marc say: "Anyway, where the dead bodies are buried, they won't find them any time soon. "

- Journalist: And do you know where they are buried?

- VL: I think they are buried in Granges sur Lot in the backyard.

- J: Marion's corpse would eventually be there...

- VL: Yes, I think so.

- Voice-over: Excavations have been carried out recently, but to no avail... Is Véronique making up stories? In any case, her statement leaves the father of the missing woman incredulous.

- Journalist: When we talk about a cult, have you never thought about it?

- Michel Wagon: Of course it is. We received a lot of letters, hundreds and hundreds of letters. But that's the side we don't want to think about, that we refuse to discuss. Now it's true that the events of the time, with the Dutroux affair, made us... We said to ourselves, well, it only happens in Belgium but in the end, it can happen in France. That's the side we don't think about...

- Voice-over: A former gendarmerie commander who was in charge of the Marion case at the time remembers the phone call Véronique mentioned:

- Michel Louvet: We weren't able to find out where the call came from, the call arrived at a private home. We weren't able to trace the call, so we don't know who made it. It's true that I heard that there was a young girl who made statements but I don't know them because I'm not currently in the gendarmerie. What I mean is that I trust my former colleagues to check all the leads.

- Jean-Claude Disses: How is it that these five children who were raped in Angers have their photos found in Amsterdam ten years later... That is the question! And you understand that this question is too serious for us not to ask ourselves!

- Véronique Liaigre: It's very hard, it comes back in your nightmares every night. Every second, when a child screams or cries... In the street, at any moment when you see a child, you say to yourself that maybe now he would be as big as that one.

- Voice-over: The police and the judiciary have taken Véronique's statements seriously and are trying to verify them one by one, however implausible they may seem. The eradication of certain paedophile and criminal networks may depend on these verifications...

- Patrick Poivre d'Arvor: Grave accusations, therefore, that the gendarmerie and the justice system are now working to verify...

This was a 10-minute report that explicitly dealt with satanic ritual abuse and the paedophile network that is rampant in France. A relatively long report which was broadcast at prime time on Patrick Poivre d'Arvor's news programme, something unthinkable today! Just like the broadcast on 27 March 2000 by France 3 of the report *"Viols d'enfants, la fin du silence?* which was followed by a debate where a certain unease was palpable on the set, and for good reason... Two children, "Pierre and Marie", denounced the unthinkable...

- Peter and Mary

In 2000, the report *"Rape of children, the end of silence?* showed the testimony of two children (aged 10 and 13) who said that their father had taken them to ceremonies with men and women in togas. These children described, face down, before the cameras of France 3: hypnosis sessions, drugs, torture, rape and ritual murder of children. Little Marie describes the basements of a large mansion, a sort of catacomb under a fancy building in Paris or its region, where the abominations took place. During the debate following the report, Martine Bouillon, former deputy public prosecutor in Bobigny, declared that she was aware of mass graves of children in the Paris region and that an investigation was underway! Georges Glatz, also present on the set, also confirmed the existence of mass graves, adding a layer on the reality of *snuff films*. Martine Bouillon was transferred within 24 hours of this shocking statement. She also stated during the programme: *"We have just realised that paedophilia exists... We still cannot understand that there are even worse things than paedophilia, I would say "simple"...".* Strangely, this documentary is not available in the archives of France 3, but it was recorded on VHS at the time, then digitised. It is now widely available on the internet. It is a reference documentary concerning testimonies of ritual abuse. Here are some extracts:

- Voice-over: Of the two children, it's the older one, Marie (pseudonym), who tells the story. Here she talks about her father and the places he took them to.

- Marie (drawing): There was a place in Paris where he was the leader. He said he was a great magician and that his name was "Bouknoubour". In this place, they wore big white robes with golden edges (here she draws a figure wearing a toga with a triangle in a circle on the bust). Then they made prayers, they raped the children, they frightened them... There were several other people who raped us, they put us to sleep with some kind of porridge. They also tied us to tables and then hit us or put needles near our eyes to make us believe that they wanted to gouge our eyes out.

- Journalist: Did they really hurt you? Did they hit you?

- M: Yes, they used to hit us...

- J: What did you draw for us Pierre (pseudonym)?

- Peter (drawing while crying): ...There were monsters... It was horrible... They raped me...

- J: They raped you? What's raping Pierre?

- P: It was touching the willy... playing with it... making... I was 6 years old, I didn't understand yet what they were doing...

(...)

Marie (also drawing in tears): *They were killing them...*

- J: They were killing the children?

- M: ...yes...

- J: How do you know that?

- M: Because I saw it... It was little children who were a bit Arab or something like that.... They used to cut their heads off...

- J: When you saw that they were cutting the head off a child, was it the truth, was it happening in front of you or could it have been a film?

- M: No, it was for real, because the children were shouting. And then they told us they were going to cut our heads off too, so they put us on this... And then we were very scared and we thought we were dead...

- J: But why were they doing that?

- M: I don't know, because they are bad, they are crazy! I don't know why they did that, they're mean! We didn't do anything, we were children (Marie is crying).

- Voice-over: In July 1996, as soon as the first revelations were made, the mother entrusted the children to a child psychiatrist who had already treated similar cases. For three years, Dr. Sabourin used drawings to gather their testimony. Dozens of drawings, dozens of hours of listening that forged his conviction: he believes the children.

- Dr. Sabourin: Of course, I think they have experienced incredible things, very difficult to synthesize for them and to put on stage. They both have a personal ability to draw them, which is not always the case...

- Voice-over: Mary drew a huge statue, which she said would stand in the middle of the ceremony room. Then she drew the pendulum and the wheel that would have been used for hypnosis sessions on the children, and always the disguises, big red or white capes, and crucifixes. We submitted to Dr. Sabourin the last drawing that Marie made for us.

- Dr. Sabourin: In her recent drawings, I find several themes... 4 themes that already existed, where we have a ceremony with people who are visibly disguised, with crosses on their shoulders, which we find here (showing other drawings), we have three of them here... and the crucifix here, it's a very special crucifix... She said it was a crucifix surrounded by grass. So where did she get it from?! I don't know... Is it her imagination, is she a delusional child? I don't think so... That is to say, when faced with this type of extremely precise and surprising thing, I tend to say that it's an element of memory that reappears. Always when it's a child and of course when it's an adolescent or an adult, these memories of early traumas are in a million pieces. And it is with a lot of difficulty, with a lot of emotions, a lot of inner tensions and fears - these are children who are afraid, they are under terror - that they manage to deliver a small passage, a small piece of memory, which leaves everyone dumbfounded. We say to ourselves, "Well, how come they didn't speak up earlier? How come they can't describe it like an adult would describe a scenario, that's the big job of the therapists and the police (...)

- Voice-over: The children describe a real organisation involving many adults, and although they are unable to indicate the location of the ceremonies, Marie has drawn us a very precise map of the building and its basement.

- Marie (describing her drawing): So we drive up here... We were turning at a roundabout. There was a bellman who came to open the door for us. Then we'd go into what looked like a fairly smart hotel. He'd go and get the keys and then we'd go down a corridor to a lift. Then we went down into a labyrinth where it was cold, it was dark, and it looked like a basement. Here there was a changing room where we went to get dressed in the white and red clothes, then we went here: a room where they raped the children. Here was the part where there were mostly girls raping the boys and my little brother, then here it was the men raping the girls. Then here, it was a big room, like a big cave in the shape of a cathedral or a cot and there were many, many people. There was also a very, very large statue of an African or black god here, and when he growled, people put money in large baskets that were passed around. Around this statue, there were ashes, with children's heads on spikes in the ashes...

- Voice-over: Children's heads on the end of spikes... Children's heads that Marie tells us have been decapitated before her eyes, and that we find in several of her drawings. To access these basements, Marie describes a building on the surface, a sort of grand hotel with a red carpet facing a roundabout in Paris or its region. A chic building with a rounded staircase (...)

- Marie (talking about her father): As he also raped us at home, someone would come to the house and undress. They would put their willy in our mouths and film us, or else, with my brother, they would tell us to do things...

- Journalist: And they were filming all this?

- M: Yes they would film... and then they would take the tapes to a place which I think was in Paris, where there were lots of books about sex and stuff... and they would drop the tapes off there. (...)

- Voice-over: So are the sectarian framework and the facts described by the children credible or unimaginable, as the investigating judge wrote? We put the question to Paul Ariès, a sociologist specialising in sects and child abuse, who has conducted studies for the Ministry of Health. We submitted all of Pierre and Marie's statements to him:

- Recording of Mary: They made prayers, they said they were "pure women", they said that one day all the people of this planet had been scattered over the earth and that now they had to gather them, the people... in fact there was a kind of god, a messenger of the gods... who came to tell them that they had to leave soon for their planet or something like that...

- Paul Ariès: I would tend to say that what we are told here is completely unimaginable, that is to say that a child cannot imagine it, a child cannot invent it. The first element is these elements of doctrine. That is to say that we are part of - if we look at it from the point of view of the followers of this group - we are part of an elite which comes from another planet and which is for the moment on earth and which will soon be called to leave. It's part of the general background of all kinds of networks today. The need to kill someone to save them or to save humanity. There are also all sorts of rites where we are told at some point that these men are "pure women". So this is something that we find relatively frequently in literature, the woman is the one who impregnates, and what we have to do here is to effectively impregnate what is called 'Homonculus', that is to say, the super-man. It seems to me that we are finally at a crossroads between two types of networks: on the one hand, saucerist networks - which believe in aliens - and on the other hand, sexual magic networks, and we know that these connections are being established more and more.

This 'saucerist' belief is also found in the case of Samir Aouchiche with the 'Alliance Kripten' sect, as we will see later. In chapter 2, we saw that Gnostics, in this case the Phibionite (or Barbotian) sect, practised orgiastic ceremonies related to the followers' vision of the cosmos and the way to free themselves from it. In addition to satisfying the demands of the archons (demons), these 'mores' respond to the need to gather the divine seed implanted in the world, which is currently dispersed in the male seed and female blood.

- Marie's recording: There were people with some kind of... not diving masks, but some kind of glasses with something over the mouth (gas masks?)... dressed in smocks. And there was a table with children's hands cut out on it, a child's head and then some sort of... I don't know if it was guts... things like that. And they put these things, the hands and all that, in jars.

- Paul Ariès: These hands cut off in jars, it's something that exists... So there again, there are several possible interpretations. One can simply have practices of the cannibalism type, the objective being to increase one's own power, also to learn to suffer, I was going to say to learn to make people suffer in order to become more powerful...

This France 3 investigation also makes the connection between the Pierre and Marie case and another incest case in eastern France with little Sylvie, who also describes gang rapes by her father and grandfather, and also speaks of a child murder. The most disturbing thing is that little Sylvie recognised in photos the father-rapist of Pierre and Marie, and they also recognised in photos the father-rapist of Sylvie. Just like Pierre and Marie's mother, Sylvie's mother filed a complaint, and she also gave the police the recording of a telephone message left on her ex-partner's personal answering machine by one of his friends, here is the transcript, the audio of which is broadcast in the report:

Hi, beep here, it's Saturday, 12.40, I'm calling back because you've called me several times and said it was urgent, we haven't spoken since. What I'd like to know most of all... we have to prepare the devilish weekends and the groups we want to do. I need you to tell me how many you're going to come to. Bye. "

The court dismissed the case, declaring that there was no link between the two cases, and even decided to withdraw custody of Sylvie and her sister from the mother and give it to the father, a classic procedure of French 'justice' in cases of paedocriminality. The mother then took refuge abroad with her children to avoid them being put in the hands of their executioner. This same 'justice' did not prosecute Pierre and Marie's father and therefore allowed him to retain custody, and no thorough investigation was carried out to determine whether the children were telling the truth, despite the extreme seriousness of the testimony! The mother also went to seek refuge abroad with her two children...

There are many similar cases in France where the mother has to literally flee the country to protect her children, who in such cases are systematically returned to the custody of the alleged paedocriminal by the *courts*. The protective parent is generally harassed, overwhelmed, even imprisoned or interned, while the abusive parent is totally protected by a well-oiled institutional system...

It *is* important to note here that in 2003, an investigation was carried out in France by the UN rapporteur Juan Miguel Petit on the subject of paedocriminality. This report was presented to the 59th session of the UN Commission on Human Rights. This official report called for *an urgent investigation by an independent body into the shortcomings of the justice system with regard to child victims of sexual abuse and those who try to protect them (...) Given the number of cases that indicate a serious denial of justice for child victims of sexual abuse and those who try to protect them, it would be appropriate for an independent body, preferably the National Consultative Commission on Human Rights, to urgently investigate the current situation.*

For example, on page 14 of the report, it is noted that: "The Special Rapporteur has referred to the enormous difficulties faced by individuals, particularly mothers, who file complaints against those they suspect of abusing their children in the knowledge that they may face action for false accusations, which in some cases may lead to the loss of custody of their child(ren). Some of these mothers use legal remedies until they can no longer afford the costs of legal assistance, at which point they are left with the choice of continuing to hand over the child to the person they believe is abusing them, or seeking refuge with the child abroad. It would even appear that some judges and lawyers, aware of the weaknesses of the judicial system, have informally advised some parents to do so. These parents expose themselves to criminal prosecution for such actions in France and, often, in the country to which they travel. "

- Deborah, Noémie and Pierre

In the early 2000s, the German channel *N24* aired a documentary showing the testimonies of several child victims of a paedo-satanist network in France. The report with French subtitles is entitled *"Snuff-Movies and Black Masses in France"*. As usual, these children come from families that practice these atrocities from generation to generation. In front of the cameras, they tell of satanic parties with ritual crimes, cannibalism and the shooting of snuff films. Pierre testifies that he participated in black masses from the age of 5 and that at the age of 7 he was initiated to become a high priest, during which time he had to sacrifice a baby in a ceremony. Some of these testimonies are linked to the Dutroux case, but they have never been taken into account. Here are some excerpts from the documentary:

- Mother of a child victim: I have always been ignorant of paedophilia issues, like most people. I think you have to experience it before you can understand what paedophilia is. What was disconcerting was that Robert would tell me about parties where he would go with his father and other adults dressed up in dresses and masks. What particularly struck me about his story was that he said, "Dad dressed up, but I still recognised his voice. And he also mentioned animal sacrifices and child sacrifices. He explained many things by imitating them with gestures. He didn't say literally "child sacrifices", he said that they made them bleed and then buried them.

- Voice-over: Like many other children, Robert mentions that there were also cameras. We found photos of Robert on the Zandvoort child pornography CD-ROMs. The mother clearly recognised her son in the photos. But even that is not sufficient evidence to prosecute the rapists. (...)

On the road from Scientrier to Lake Geneva, there is a house that Deborah calls "the green house". According to her, there was more than just child abuse here... Deborah, who is now 15, says there were satanic rituals.

- Deborah: There was a table with candles... There were candles on the table and all around and there were my attackers.

- Journalist: You say they put two of the other children who were there on the table? What happened? Without going into details.

- D:... They were cutting up the child... body parts.

- J: What did they do that with?

- D: With an electric knife.

- J: The child was alive?

- D: ... yes...

- J: Then they killed him?

- D: No, they let him suffer... He ended up dying.

- J: They were cutting off a finger for example?

- D: A foot... and they were raping it at the same time.

- J: They were raping him and the others had to watch?

- D: ... yes...

- Voice-over: Noémie is an 18-year-old woman trying to rebuild her life. A seemingly normal life, except for the fact that she will never be able to forget the horrors she has lived through.

- Noémie: If I testify today, it's obviously to cooperate with this report, but it's mainly because people need to hear about these things. So that people know that it is true, that children are raped and murdered every day. It is a reality! I have experienced it, I have seen it with my own eyes and that is why I want to convey this message. It is necessary to make sure that these things cannot happen to other children, so that children stop being raped. People need to wake up and be aware of what is going on, and stop saying that children are liars or fabricators. It's not true, children are telling the truth, but you have to be willing to hear it.

- Voice-over: Noémie was initiated by her father and other criminals, men from all sorts of backgrounds, into the barbaric practices that took place in front of a camera (...) Noémie was 5 years old when the first abuses took place, she lost her virginity at the age of 8.

- Noémie: It happened very quickly and brutally. They just did it for me and my cousin Camille. One day my father took me to my cousin's house, I liked going there because I liked her very much. My uncle André was there, as well as cousins Camille and Marie. And then it happened (...)

- Voice-over: Noémie's father showered her with tender words, reassuring her that touching was perfectly normal; she believed him. Then he revealed his big secret: a compound, an underground cellar where he kept children in cages. Noémie thus became her father's accomplice.

- Noémie: The children locked in these cages never stayed alive for long, between torture and rape, the children were eventually murdered. They were all alone there, they couldn't escape, because they were too beaten, too raped or too drugged... or dead (...)

My father and other men had already raped the girl. When I went in, I was a bit jealous because I knew that my father had also been involved in this. But then I was satisfied, probably because I could watch the ceremony and of all the children who belonged to this paedophile ring and were raped by these men, I was the only one who was allowed to watch the rapes. So instead of just being abused, I could participate in the abuse. They ordered me to boil water and pour it over the child. Meanwhile, they hit her, first with a belt, then with a piece of wood. They put cigarettes on her body and cut her hair. They ordered me to cut the girl's clitoris. I didn't know what it was, they showed me and said 'cut here!' My father told me I had to do it, then he showed me where to cut.

- Voice-over: Noémie talks about ten or so murders of children in one year. She shows the entrances to the underground passages on a map. The courts continue to deny that such underground complexes, catacombs, exist in Saint-Victor (Ardèche).

- Jacques Berthelot: I went to Saint-Victor, there are underground tunnels there. I was lucky enough to be able to take pictures of them. I gave these photos to the police in Privas, to Mr Marron. He promised that he would put my testimony in the police reports. I was heard by the police in April 1999. But today, the file seems to have been suddenly lost. My photos and statements to the police are nowhere to be found.

- Voice-over: Why are the alleged perpetrators not brought to justice? After several years of investigation, I have come to a conclusion. Many of the perpetrators are in high positions, they have the power to cover for each other and there is a lot of money involved. Noémie says about the children that they are abused, tortured, raped and sacrificed on camera. These snuff-films are said to sell for up to 20,000 euros each.

- Noémie: When I came in, the curtains were closed, it was dark. There were carpets on the floor, I was told to sit down, I sat at a table. The priests were standing with candles... They were wearing dark red robes, almost black. They were singing around the table. It went on for a long time... There was something that was covered with a cloth the same colour as their robes. There was a child, my grandfather took him in his arms, my brother Pierre was next to me. My grandfather then showed my brother how to kill the child. And then of course the child started to scream... then they said some prayers, and we went out. After 45 minutes or an hour, I don't remember exactly, they came out. The ceremonies always end the same way. The first black mass I saw, it was more or less the same, there was the sacrifice of the child and at the end on the terrace there were two big plates... with flesh... meat, now I know it was human flesh.

- Journalist: Are you sure it was human flesh?

- N: Yes, I'm sure it was part of the cult. You're part of the cult without realising it, all you have to do is attend a ceremony and perform certain rituals. But I was not aware of it when it happened. Now looking back, I think of all the things I was made to do to other children during the rituals, like cutting off parts of their genitals. (...)

- J: The outcome of these rituals once completed is nothing more than cannibalism?

- N: ... hmm ...

- J: Is it cannibalism?

- N: Yes.

- Voice-over: After talking to the psychologist, I realise that Noémie's father must have programmed her at an early age. Noémie couldn't bear the atrocities she endured and split into different personalities. One of these personalities is a robot who follows her father mechanically and then there is the girl who plays with her dolls at home.

- The psychologist: There are multiple factors in her story that make it absolutely credible to me. The first is the fact that today, at the age of 18, she has told the same story as when she was 11. The second point is that she describes all the details and she never contradicts herself. She never gives two different versions of everything that happened. Moreover, she gave me the same impression as other traumatised people I have met, i.e. the same detachment in the way she talks about her traumatic experiences. It seems paradoxical, but that's exactly what makes me think that what she's saying is the truth... She seems perfectly normal despite her past, she needs to keep that distance, otherwise she would fall apart. I don't doubt her story at all.

- Peter (Noémie's brother): The windows are closed, everything is shut, the curtains drawn and the blinds down. The children are tied to chairs with their hands behind their backs. They are gagged not to speak or scream. In this room were my father, Christian N. the owner of the place, André D. and André L. All of them were present at the two sessions I was forced to attend. What happened: first the children were raped, the child was almost dead, he was lying on the floor... My father took his belt and hit the child, all over his face and body. Everyone is beaten. They hit the child with a broomstick and then they tell me that now it's my turn. I don't want to... because it's as if I'm there, without being there (editor's note: dissociation). They take me and tell me to go ahead and do it! Do it! I couldn't do anything, there was no way out. I had to do it, they ordered me to do it. I hit him for like... 10 seconds and then I left.

- Voice-over: Pierre has not only been sexually abused by his father but worse. His paternal grandfather, a high priest of a cult, also rapes him. Since the age of 5, Pierre has been programmed by his grandfather.

- Peter: He tells me that I am the chosen one, that one day I will succeed him and that I will enter a circle of important people who will be my new family. He tells me that one day I too will be a high priest and that this is a great opportunity for me. Naturally I believed in it like a little 5 year old. Then the ceremonies came, they really existed and people took part in them. They explained me rituals, masses, prayers (...)

- Pierre describes the initiation ceremony he experienced at the age of 7: The ceremony started as always with songs and prayers. We prayed on red carpets, one red carpet for each participant. I was always next to my grandfather, the other priests together. We followed a certain chronology between the songs and the dances. We did this for about 20 minutes. Then my grandmother, who is not really part of the sect, who never participates in the big ceremonies, brought a baby that she was carrying in her arms. She gave the baby to my godmother Collette. Collette then walked over to us and gave the baby to my grandfather. He made a few signs that I didn't understand, then they passed the baby from hand to hand, until it came back into my grandfather's hands. My grandfather gave the baby back to my godmother, then he took out a rather long knife, with symbols and pictograms engraved on the handle. My grandfather took my hand, we approached the newborn baby and cut its throat. The baby didn't make a sound, he didn't even scream. He bled to death and the blood was collected with a cup, a kind of big cup.....

- Voice-over: The initiation of a new member always follows the same ritual. Each time the new members are ordered to kill. This should make them stronger and they have to swear to keep silent. We thought we had reached the abomination... But Pierre described another ritual practiced by this sect: cannibalism.

- Peter: My grandmother brought a big tray, there were the seven priests, there were ten of us around the table. Afterwards we were served with a piece of meat from the baby. We had to eat it to celebrate my arrival as the new priest of the sect. There was also a glass with blood in it. We had to eat and drink, we drank the blood. My grandfather said a prayer at the beginning and another at the end. He congratulated me saying that I had been very good, he flattered me saying that I was the best etc...

- The children of Judge Roche

In the Allègre affair in the Toulouse region, certain ritual abuse practices involving murder were revealed in private by Judge Pierre Roche himself. Shortly before his death, haunted by the idea that he knew too much (and remorse?), the high magistrate gave his two children, Diane and Charles-Louis, testimony of what he witnessed during surreal evenings between *people of power* (in the words of the Roche son). The Roche children testified on camera in September 2005 about what they call *"the secret part of the Allègre affair"*. In their testimony, one still finds this extreme depravity where there seems to be no limits and where torture and murder of children seem to be commonplace. According to the Roche children, these evenings of ritual abuse were filmed and these recordings were the object of a very lucrative traffic. Here are some extracts from Charles-Louis' testimony:

Our father came to Toulouse to reveal to us the existence of a secret group, of people of power from all types of milieu, politics, finance... He spoke to us of people from medical circles, even from universities. This secret group recruited a lot of people from judicial circles and even high-ranking police officers were very popular there. So it would be a secret group whose activities consisted of carrying out some sort of ceremony in the greatest secrecy, combining practices as strange and uniformly disgusting as group sex, scarification... He evoked images in front of us that would make your hair stand on end. He told us about charred flesh, cigarette burns, pierced flesh. He told us that the people who were tortured, sometimes killed during these sessions - well, the people killed were never consenting - and that among the tortured people, there were sick people who demanded this kind of treatment, and then there were non-consenting people, sometimes children, who were first tortured, then put to death, all filmed and the object of an illegal video traffic that would be traded under the table at crazy prices. He told us that the prey of this group of upper-class predators were recruited from the lowest strata of society in the categories of people who would never be wanted. He spoke to us of prostitutes, he spoke to us of "bums", I quote the term used by a magistrate, he even mentioned sometimes foreigners in an irregular situation depending on what they had at hand I imagine. That is to say, people who have either broken the ties with their environment or have no legal existence, people that nobody will go looking for or about whom any investigation will be more or less doomed from the start. And then, of course, the members of this group, because of the influential positions they hold, are in a position, in the event that certain cases threaten to come out, to nip it in the bud by manipulating the levers that are theirs, especially since they all hold each other by the short hairs...

- Samir Aouchiche

In France, we also have the testimony of Samir Aouchiche, revealed in Bruno Fouchereau's book entitled *"L'Enfant sacrifié à Satan"*, an investigation published in 1997. That same year, the France 2 television news devoted a short report on this case of satanic ritual abuse practised by a sectarian group called *"Alliance Kripten"*. Here is the transcript of the report:

- Daniel Bilalian: France is unfortunately not immune to the problems posed by paedophile networks. A young man of 26, Samir, has just told his terrible story in a book that has just been published. From the age of 12 in Paris, he was a victim of a satanic sect, tortured and then abused for nearly ten years...

- Voice-over: When he had to walk down that corridor, Samir knew that the horror was at hand. At the time he was only 12 years old, but for a year he had already been subjected to the fantasies of real torturers. Repeated rapes, torture sessions, here in the middle of Paris, he was spared nothing. And the life of this martyred child plunges a little further into delirium, to the rapes are added real sessions of torture and barbarism.

- Samir: Yes it was there... They brought me here, they tied me up, they put handcuffs on me and they put products on me...

- Journalist: What kind of products?

- S: According to the doctor, it was acid.

- Voice-over: Burnt with acid by the leaders of the sect, a small group of about twenty people called the "Kripten Alliance". Samir, like other children, has become their toy. A toy mutilated on 2500 square cm of skin...

- S: They couldn't live without torturing children. At the beginning it was done through rituals, through ceremonies and then it ended up in orgies... It ended up in sexual acts... And then you had to have sex with adults...

- J: Several adults?

- S: Yes.

- J: There were several children?

- S: Yes there were several children...

- Voice-over: Staring at him, Samir still bears the scars of his physical and moral suffering. Last Tuesday, accompanied by his friend Willy who pulled him out of his ordeal, Samir filed a complaint against two members of the Kripten Alliance. This ordeal could have been stopped. Between 1986 and 1988, i.e. two years after the first rapes, the Brigade for the Protection of Minors became aware of his case through cases involving other children. Samir's lawyer, Jean-Paul Baduel, now has documents to prove it.

- Jean Paul Baduel: There are elements that are inescapable, these are the after-effects that my client bears on his body. There are elements that are objective elements, these are photocopies of documents that were communicated to me by my client which show that during the years 1986, 1987, and even 1988, the police authorities who were in charge of the protection of minors, and even the magistrates, were fully informed of the existence of a group called "Kripten" and of the conduct of its members towards certain minors.

On 26 February 1997, the French-language newspaper '*La Nouvelle Gazette*' published an article on this case of Satanic ritual abuse. The paper was entitled "*La secte pédophile torturait les enfants*". In the article, Samir's lawyer, Maître Baduel, states that Samir had become *a passive subject subjected to the perversions of the Kripten leaders (...) They were all abused, some were even branded with a red-hot iron, they were in fact satanic role-playing games with torture and rape (...) The meetings he was going to attend had nothing to do with role-playing games, even for adults, but corresponded to a ritual of sexual magic.*

Samir remained under the influence of Kripten until 1994. An 'addiction' he says was maintained by hypnotics and other brainwashing. The article also contains an interview with Samir from which the following extracts are taken: "*I met someone from Kripten at the Foire du Trône. We were about fifteen children, boys, all underage (...) We were forced to prostitute ourselves with adults, sometimes during ceremonies. It was like being in a sect, the adults had black robes with a purple triangle. For years, the ceremonies took place in the basement of the Saint-Lazare station. In the beginning, it started with a little speech about aliens. There were usually as many adults as children. And then there was some pretty sordid stuff with blood, and it always ended with sexual orgies. They said it was to "purify the soul". Some of the adults were masked. (...) I was taken twice to Belgium, to the region of Charleroi and Forchies-la-Marche. I remember a big white house with a big garden. The interior walls were lined with mauve. There were several black masses which also ended in orgies. There were about twenty adults and ten children. I remember the presence of swastikas and the rape of a little girl. I also know that some children did not come back... we were told that they had left for Uranus.* "

In the book "*L'Enfant sacrifié à Satan*" we have a description of a ceremony of the sect "Alliance Kripten". The author adds in a note that this is one of the rituals of the *Golden Dawn*, a secret society that has already been mentioned in chapter 2:

A few minutes later, the three of them go down into the basement of the station to the tai-chi-chuan room (...) Here again, the decor has changed. The walls are now covered with black cloth, the neon lights are turned off and halogens light the room indirectly. A huge purple triangle is drawn on the floor, and a sort of checkerboard has been placed in its centre. On either side of the triangle, two kinds of columns about two metres high stand like obelisks. One is black and white, the other red and green. At the back of the room, facing the entrance, on a sort of platform framed by four candelabras, two large red and gold armchairs seem to be waiting for a royal operetta couple.

Five or six children are there, some visibly accompanied by their fathers or people close to them. A little boy of about six years old who refused to let go of his father's hand received a monumental slap that sent him rolling to the ground under the laughter of the adults, visibly delighted by the spectacle of this half-stunned boy (...)

Samir can't believe his eyes! The adults are unusually dressed. Most of them wear big white sarees, some are green and red. Others are dressed all in leather, which is the case of Ondathom, whom Samir has just seen walk past him. Others are bare-chested but wearing a mask. There are about twenty of them in all, wearing a variety of outfits. They are all clustered near the small room adjoining the hall. In this case, it seems to serve as a cloakroom, because the men and women all come out wearing more or less bizarre outfits, whereas they had entered in street clothes. Ajouilark is there too, draped in a red saie. On his chest is a huge purple triangle with a black border and a white cross on top. His face is masked, but Samir knows his eyes too well not to recognise him. Ajouilark grabs Steelarow and points to a large metal cup. With this chalice, the young man goes around the participants, so that each one puts in a big bundle of money. Samir has never seen so much money (...)

Mass music plays and the 'Emperor', followed by the Commander, makes her way to the podium. Meanwhile, Steerlarow is busy preparing on silver platters large lines of what Samir will later learn is cocaine. Ondathom grabs Samir's arm to lead him, the winning girls and the other children to the front of the stage, where everyone lines up. The adults spread out with a sort of saucy good humour on the sides of the triangle, facing the columns and the stage. Pröhne, who had been absent for a moment, returns with his dog and ties it to the handle of the exit door. As the trays are passed around the audience, Ondathom and the Chinese man unceremoniously undress the children. Some sob, others shield their faces as if expecting to be hit at any moment. Once everything seems to be in order, the Chinese man moves to the right of the platform and Ondathom to his left. Conversations are going well: a man wearing a red mask declares himself sensitive to Samir's buttocks, a woman dressed in a white saie only has disgust for Steerlarow's winners (...)

"Let us salute the triangle symbol of our order, let us salute the swastika, the eternal sun that regenerates our souls, let us salute the secret forces that, in the night, walk beside us. "

"Everyone shouted 'Ave! raising their arms. Ondathom and the Chinaman made the children kneel down (...) During the Emperor's speech, Ondathom, with a copper ciborium in his hand, made the children take a sip of a bitter red liquid. All of them quickly felt the same thing. Their heads were spinning. They do not fall into unconsciousness, but they are suddenly caught in a kind of fog. The adults notice the effects of the drug as the children slump on top of each other (...) Samir can hardly hear the Emperor's words, he feels as if he is falling, caught in a whirlpool. Everything is spinning, faces are blending together, and he can hardly hear the commander declaim:

The bodies of these children are the bread we share. They conceal our bonds and, through our sexuality finally freed from the yoke of the Judeo-Christian oppressors, we purify ourselves, we reintegrate the sacred plane of the celestial knights of the order of the Kripten Covenant. Sex and all the pleasures of our senses are the only law to be satisfied. Serve yourselves my brothers, in the name of the prince our lord, and honour Thule... "

The commander put his money where his mouth is and lifted his shirt, revealing an erect cock. He approaches a little girl of about twelve who has been sobbing since the beginning of the ceremony. The child barely resists Ajouilark when he forces her to take him into her mouth. Already, men and women have stepped aside to indulge in their pleasure, others are grabbing children... Samir feels palpated, turned inside out... then sinks into a kind of waking coma, a total insensitivity as if all this were not true, as if his body were not his body, as if he were only an observer of this odious meeting... (editor's note: a dissociative state)

When Samir opens his eyes again, he does not recognize anything. Neither the bed, nor the room, nor the strange paintings on the walls. He gets up to look out the window, but neither the garden nor the neighbouring houses he can see are any more familiar. The sound of washing up comes from the next room, and the smell of coffee soon tickles his nostrils. Samir is hungry and suddenly aware that he is naked. He looks for his clothes. They are lying in a heap on a chair. As he puts on his clothes, Samir feels the pain in his body awaken. His stomach hurts, his sex hurts, his head is spinning... With his trousers on his knees, he is forced to sit down again. The door opens on a pudgy man in his fifties who smiles at him:

- What's the matter, kid? "

Samir does not answer.

- Last night, the ceremony knocked you out and the Emperor thought you would be better off at my place to spend the night... I confess that I let myself go. "

A smile passes over the lips of the man, still wearing a red bathrobe, who remains silent for a moment in front of the child curled up in front of him.... [269]

e/ Germany

In October 1998, the Australian government granted refugee status with a protection visa to a German national, a survivor of ritual abuse, who had spent 15 years in a cult practising child pornography and trafficking. The Australian *Refugee Review Tribunal* said in the final hearing: *"It is accepted that ... thirdly, such groups exist in Germany, and the authorities have been largely ineffective in stopping their illegal activities.* The decision, taken by the Australian government, was to give this victim refugee status in need of protection, but there is no law to deal with such cases. This Australian court even stated that *"the German government is unwilling or unable to protect victims of ritual abuse."[270]*

- Antje, Nicki and Lucie

In 2003, a report by Liz Wieskerstrauch entitled 'Living Hell - The Victims' Fight: Ritual Abuse in Germany' (Höllenleben - Der Kampf der Opfer: Ritueller Missbrauch in Deutschland) was broadcast by the German channel

---

[269] *"L'Enfant sacrifié à Satan"* - Samir Aouchiche & Bruno Fouchereau, 1997, p. 66-71.

[270] "Ritual Abuse: An European Cross-Country Perspective" - Thorsten Becker & Joan Coleman, ISSD Conference "The Spectrum of Dissociation", Manchester, 09/05/1999.

NDR Fernsehen. The documentary gives voice to several survivors of ritual abuse. Once again, the testimonies overlap and describe the horrors which are also systematically filmed by cameras. Most of the women who testify in this documentary suffer from a dissociative identity disorder. Here are some excerpts in transcript:

- Voice-over: Black masses in churches, rituals in cemeteries. Torture and murder of newborn babies... These are the memories of Antje who spent her childhood in a Satanist environment. She has kept silent until now because of the atrocities... Now she wants to speak out and lodge a complaint against the culprits. In her case and in many others, strangers were hidden behind masks, but her own parents also participated in the rituals.

- Antje: My mother is still alive, she was the "powerful one", the Satanist (editor's note: priestess?). My father was the "messenger", the driver, the delivery man, the transporter... My father died in 1979 and the police didn't know if it was murder or suicide. No autopsy was performed and I suspect that he was murdered by my mother...

- Journalist: Did you confide in anyone?

- A: No.

- J: Why is that?

- A: I was afraid of dying... Under torture, I was "programmed" several times that if I talked about what was happening... I would die.

- Nicki: I was made to lie on a table and then pricked with needles, sometimes very deep under my fingernails. I felt this intense pain to the point where I thought I was going to die... At that point, a new personality is created to take over from this insurmountable pain and terror...

- Journalist: When did the abuse start?

- N: We don't remember exactly when it started, it started very early.

- Voice-over: Nicki uses the term "we" because she has multiple personalities, a diagnosis that is still controversial. As she explains, in order to cope with the excruciating pain, she has split herself into different personalities. Her memories are so fragmented that linking the atrocities to the place where it happened is very difficult. This poses a problem in providing evidence (...) Later, Nicki had the courage to file a complaint. Since then, other victims have also come forward, some openly, others anonymously for fear of the criminals (...) Antje also filed a complaint. Like Nicki, she has a multiple personality, which complicates the details of the places, dates and identity of the perpetrators... However, the prosecutor takes these testimonies seriously. To ensure that the investigation is not compromised by the authorities, her lawyer will testify anonymously in our documentary.

- Antje's lawyer: When you're dealing with a person with a psychological problem such as multiple personality disorder, then questions arise: what is fantasy, what belongs to this "identity" or that personality? Does it all fit together, is it coherent? The problem is that, from a legal point of view, these people are less credible than a person who has no personality disorder.

- Voice-over: In this report, there are also women who testify to satanic rituals but who do not have multiple personalities. They, too, are pressured by

Nicki to file a complaint, but many don't dare to break the law of silence, or else they remain anonymous. They also say that they have been indoctrinated by their families to perpetuate the rituals from generation to generation. In this way, each victim also becomes an accomplice... For Annegret, this is all the more reason not to go to the police.

- Annegret: The problem... it's not as simple as that... Firstly, we know how difficult it is to find figures, data or evidence. Secondly, we have a child, and if we start talking about these things, we are afraid that they will be taken away from us...

- Voice-over: The meaning of occult symbols and the practice of Satanism is uncharted territory for police and prosecutors.

- Ingolf Christiansen (German specialist on the subject of occultism and Satanism, giving a lecture): In the beginning, in the first degrees, I submit to the discipline "Arcanum", "Arcanum" is a Latin name meaning "the secret". This discipline of the Arcanum does not tolerate that the organisation of the group be revealed to an outside person who has not been initiated. The consequence of not respecting this discipline is martial punishment (editor's note: death). More commonly, they say: if you talk to anyone in any way, you will be made to pay... and people believe this.

- Voice-over: The satanic holidays, the teachings, the symbols... The victims will never forget them, often without really understanding them. For them, these are signs of excruciating pain, as for Lucie, who expresses herself here with the alter personality of a small child.

- Lucie (sitting cross-legged on the floor): They always had weird signs, sometimes drawn on our bodies... It was drawn like this I think... (gesturing on the floor with her finger)...

- Journalist: Three times the number six?

- L: I don't know but it was drawn in a circle...

- J: Three times the number six interlaced. Were there any other signs?

- L: Yes, stars... I don't like stars (drawing a pentagram with his finger). (...)

- J: What does the initiation ritual mean?

- L: Let them... let them... let them teach us, they teach us... what is important to live... For example to be happy when you hurt someone... because it's better this way, for everyone... For example, they would connect us to electric current... They would lock us in a cage... Then they would let dogs loose on the cage... It's done to make us obedient...

- Ingolf Christiansen: In the first instance, it is not about worshipping Satan, the devil or Lucifer, but it is a way to feel powerful. Man wants to become God, and from that point on, according to the vision of the Satanists or the occult ideology, it's about getting energy and power, and this is available in large quantities through the consumption of blood. Because blood is life and if this blood is consumed, it supplies this energy, this power. (...)

- Voice-over: Annette filed a complaint in Hamburg against her parents, but also against herself... because she was forced to kill. She has not been diagnosed with multiple personality disorder, but she explains that she led a double life. A quiet life in a pastor's house in Bielefeld and a violent and destructive life in a cult.

- Annette: My parents took me there when I was 4 years old. My first memories go back to when I was brought to kill a cat at the same age... Little by little I became more active in this group, I had to watch how other people raped children. Once I saw my parents and my brother... He was 11 or 12 years old, I was 2 years younger than him... I saw him while he was being raped, and then right after... he was like a lifeless body, moaning on the ground barely moving... It was just a body lying next to me... I swore to myself at the time that they wouldn't be able to do something like that to me.

- Journalist: What happened to your brother?

- A: My brother committed suicide three years ago. He shot himself...

- Voice-over: Antje is also looking for leads, witnesses, evidence... She's sure that her parents were behind the masked criminals. She has a witness, Sandra, her sister who is four years younger than her. They haven't seen each other for over 10 years. They have broken off contact as they did with their mother... the past being too painful. The two sisters were sold to paedophiles.

- Antje (showing a photo of herself as a child): This photo is typically meant to be circulated in paedophile networks. We are standing there on all fours, on my right hand you can clearly see a gold ring, which means that I am available for everything, helpful and obedient. That I will do whatever I am asked to do.

- Voice-over: We looked for Antje's sister and found her, but she will remain anonymous. Sandra does not have a multiple personality like her older sister. She offered to help in the search for clues and evidence, but also to give a statement to the police. The two women testified separately and without having spoken to each other before, they described in detail the same rituals... But they still do not want to meet again.

- Journalist: Did they believe in Satan?

- Sandra: For the mother yes... She believes in this power of darkness, she thinks it gives her the power to be someone she is not... to not be a victim anymore... To feel powerful, yes, she... yes!

- Antje's lawyer: Concrete facts are similar and partly complementary.

- Journalist: Does this authenticate the case?

- Lawyer: Yes, absolutely! It is well known that a story of this kind told by one person seems implausible. When they are told by one person, these stories are considered rather fanciful, whereas if someone else confirms and validates the testimony, if possible independently, then it is different.

- Voice-over: Antje remembers one night in particular when she was nine years old. It must have been a night with a very special ritual...

- Antje: That night it happened in a church, I'm quite sure. I saw my initiation again, if you can call it that... I had to receive and channel some satanic powers. We went to the cemetery, the church was nearby... a grave was opened... the coffin too... Inside was a man who had died recently. Everything had been cleaned up and I had to enter that grave to take out his heart... The high priest took this cup, and the other members of the lodge followed him into the church.

At the foot of the steps there was the symbol of the lodge, I don't know if it was drawn or just put there... I had to lie down on the altar... They drew things on my body... There was sexual abuse. At the end of the night... I had a new status in the lodge and suddenly I was an important person.

- Sandra: They prepared and conditioned her to become an evil person. They had really succeeded in instilling in her a sense of power and especially in making her like that power...

- Antje: I was taught the use of ritual practices... For example the sacrifice of a child, or the privilege of being next to the high priest when a person was lying on the altar.

- Sandra: Antje had really developed this sense of power, so she got closer and closer to the cult where she went up the ranks... It was a recognition for her, because otherwise she was nothing... That's how they do the initiations, systematically...

- Voice-over: Almost all the victims testify that during these rituals, films and photos "immortalise" the scenes: child pornography... So it's also about money and well-organised criminal networks. Without evidence, Lucie cannot file a complaint. She has a multiple personality... who would believe her? Today she is looking for pictorial evidence on the internet (...) Women from the GDR era have also reported this kind of ritual abuse, Lucie is one of them. She is looking for the places of her childhood, she is searching her memories, she is finding evidence.

- Lucie: At that time I didn't realise because I didn't know anything else. Now I realise that my family had a very high standard of living. We had video recorders, several cars (...)

There are 3 rooms, these rooms have no windows, they were cold, we think they were cellars. The floor was uneven, dusty and dirty. The walls were also in bad condition, there were lamps on the walls. There was a room where we waited and another room where it happened... We also remember another room, more like a big hall with some kind of steel beams... I don't know exactly, we just know that they are steel beams... and that this hall was not very clean...

- Journalist: What happened in this hall?

- L: It's part of our memories, there was a fire in the middle, there were men, black men, so to speak... And then we saw someone being led towards the fire, there was fear...

- J: Do you know how you got there?

- L: We arrived there by a transporter... There were no windows there either. Yes, we arrived there by a transporter. Sometimes there were other children, but we never spoke to each other... In these situations, it's not done...

- Voice-over: Underground rooms with a large hall... Looking for them is like looking for a needle in a haystack. The neighbours, teachers and villagers cannot be questioned, Lucie's parents would suspect something and the risk for her and her sisters is too great (...) Another possible place for child murders is Wewelsburg Castle: Wewelsburg Castle. But for the police and the public prosecutor in Paderborn, the facts go back too far (...) Karine, who also has a multiple personality, testified to ritual abuse in Wewelsburg Castle itself...

- Karine: I didn't know there was a castle with that name, but I recognised the ornaments in this room... with the columns... It's the castle that often came back in my childhood nightmares. I often reproduced these ornaments in drawings when I was little. In the crypt, first of all there is this swastika on the ceiling... I remember that in this crypt, there is a fireplace in the middle to make a fire. There is a kind of stone or altar, and it was on this altar that a child was sacrificed. This child was mine, he was sacrificed at the age of 6 months.

(...)

The documentary *Schwarze Sonne* (Black Sun of the Nazis), released in 1998, tells the story of this castle in Wewelsburg. The castle was completely restored by the Nazis and used as a place of worship and training for the SS during the Third Reich. Here is the description of the crypt quoted in Karin's testimony:

Just below the Obergruppenführer room is what was called the crypt. A vaulted room in the shape of a cellar where religious celebrations were planned. The atmosphere is reminiscent of those rites of destruction of the individual personality, of that second state in which man becomes an empty vessel in which edifying feelings are poured out in drunkenness... Clandestine groups of today's extreme right also feel attracted to this room. At night, they sometimes even break into it to hold mystical rituals..."

The director of the Wewelsburg Museum, Wulff E. Brebeck, states in this documentary: "On Christmas Eve 1992, we found the door broken. On the 12 podiums were white sheets decorated with runes. Of course, we never found out who had done this, but we know from our contacts with some visitors or groups of visitors that the tower is readily passed off as a place where black masses or similar ceremonies are held... And there are constant attempts to bribe our doorkeepers, to get the key or to enter this room at unusual times under all sorts of pretexts. We have to take very strict protective measures to prevent this kind of thing. Once we had a written confession from a group that they were able to have a baptism there, a black baptism, an admission into their order... and they were thanking us."

- Claudia Fliss

The German psychotherapist Claudia Fliss specialises in trauma caused by ritual abuse. She has helped many victims over the past twenty years and has examined many cases. In the documentary *"Sexzwang"* (forced sex), by the controversial Ivo Sasek, she states:

- The forms of violence are: physical violence, sexual violence, psychological violence, threats, extortion, the law of silence, animal and human sacrifices as part of rituals, the murder of infants, children and women. Sometimes it's one person who is killed, sometimes it's several people (...) The murders are always described in a similar way, there are different ways, but the testimonies always overlap. It always has something to do with blood, it has to do with a murderous frenzy, a lust for power, it has to do with cannibalism: drinking blood and eating human flesh (...) These are cults that have existed for generations, they recruit their members from their own ranks, children are born into them. From their earliest childhood they are used to these rituals, they will be trained daily to become fit for these things... It's brutal, but that's exactly how it happens.

- Have you heard of similar cases in Germany where people are killed by a satanic cult?

- Yes, this is what people almost always report. I have lived and worked in different parts of Germany and I had people in therapy who did not know each other but who reported exactly the same things. I know from colleagues working all over the country that there are victims who do not know each other but who report similar things. Then you realise that it's something structured.

- Gaby Breitenbach

Also in Germany, psychotherapist Gaby Breitenbach set up a safe place to receive and help victims of ritual abuse and mind control in early 2014. The centre is called *"Vielseits"* and is a first of its kind in Europe. All the women who come to the centre have been subjected to mind control. These women suffer from severe dissociative disorders and traumatic amnesia. Gaby Breitenbach was interviewed by journalist Antonia Oettingen:

From the outside, these are women who seem to have normal behaviour and normal lives. Their everyday personality is unaware of the abuse they are subjected to at night, at weekends or during holiday periods. These traumatic experiences are compartmentalised in the different parts of the personality, so that these memories are kept out of consciousness. The person is therefore unaware of the abuse and trauma (...) Victims are subjected at an early age to near-death situations, electric shocks, simulated drowning, all kinds of torture in which their torturers pose as 'saviours'. At a certain point, the victim's psyche will act in an automatic way: it will split up, in order to survive. As a result of this systematic torture, victims may develop different identities. The criminals who carry out these abuses hold the key to this internal system composed of a fragmented personality. They therefore have the ability to induce particular behaviours by using triggers. These can be hand signals, smells or sounds such as a particular ring tone (...) Young victims of ritual abuse are most often used for paedocriminal prostitution and trained to take part in sadistic child abuse themselves, which is filmed and photographed. These women will be prostitutes for much of their lives, they can also be used for sadistic violence and sometimes for espionage. Many of the alter personalities set up by the traumas do not feel the pain."[271]

---

[271] *"The Shelter for Women Having Their Minds Controlled By Criminal Gangs"* - Interview with Gaby Breitenbach by Antonia Oettingen - Vice.com, 12/02/2014.

f/ England

In the 1989 documentary Devil *Worship: The Rise of Satanism*, politician and Member of Parliament David Wilshire states:

Satanism is present in this country just as it is elsewhere. It is something terribly violent, it is child abuse, it is sexual abuse. This is no laughing matter, it has to be taken very seriously, it is a problem that has to be dealt with. The most tragic thing about this story is the children who talk about it and are told: 'Don't be stupid, this doesn't happen in our country', or: 'You are making up stories, you are lying'.

In 1989, psychiatrist Joan Coleman, with the help of other doctors, founded *RAINS* (*Ritual Abuse Information Network & Support*). She also ran the *Clinic for Dissociative Studies* in London. *RAINS* supports victims of ritual abuse and publishes studies on trauma and its consequences. In the book *"Forensic Aspects of Dissociative Identity Disorder"*, Joan Coleman recounts the cases of several victims of ritual abuse she has met, including the testimonies of 'Margaret', 'Theresa' and 'Monica' (pseudonyms).

- Margaret

In 1986, Joan Coleman had been working in a psychiatric hospital for 17 years. She worked with people who had mental health problems with physical repercussions. Margaret was one of her patients, a woman in her forties who had been a frequent visitor to the hospital for four years. Coleman was concerned about her health problems, she suffered from asthma as well as an ulcer and severe migraines. This was obviously related to her psychological problems but Coleman could not identify the cause of the problem. Margaret had a lot of visitors and according to her there were no family problems. She was prescribed medication, particularly when she was out at weekends. Fatally, one day there was an overdose accident and she was rushed to hospital. Shortly after this incident she began to confide in a nurse, Eileen, about a family friend whom she apparently did not like at all. It was from this point on that the floodgates opened for disclosure...

Initially, she spoke about what appeared to be a large paedophile ring: she described sadistic sexual abuse of children by men. She said that some of these people were family members or acquaintances, but also politicians and well-known media figures. During this first period of disclosure, her physical symptoms improved remarkably. She stopped vomiting and had almost no asthma or migraines. She then stopped the treatment and seemed ready to continue talking... Coleman and the nurse then decided to contact the police, whether or not the statements were true. However, as the names of the alleged assailants were not on police files, no investigation was carried out.

In the summer of 1987, Margaret was told that she had a terminal illness. She wanted to go home, but recanted any revelations she had made about ritual abuse. After only a few weeks, she was back in hospital after being found wandering on the road, totally drugged. It was then that she was moved to another part of the hospital where she must have felt safer as she began to speak again and to detail her earlier statements. She gave details of runaway children she had met at London Central Station who were being taken back to a hotel. There they were forcibly drugged so that they soon became addicted, the aim being to abuse them sexually. Margaret then described a house where some of these children were taken to be drugged and raped as well. She explained that although she refused, she was forced to watch the abuse and was photographed at the same time to keep her silent. After being raped or beaten by several men, some of these children were taken back to the "hotel", others were killed... She says that the murders were always done with a knife. The bodies were then dismembered and put in plastic bags to be taken to what she describes as a factory, a place where they are incinerated. The murders are filmed and the recordings sold for a high price.

Margaret described the same pattern each time, saying that *"it seemed to be some kind of ritual"*. She reported that the executioners wore robes and masks. She spoke of a Vietnamese girl who was bound to an altar and an inverted cross. It was as a result of these revelations that Joan Coleman began to research Satanism and ritual abuse. Margaret would later confess that her family had been Satanists for generations, and she never once recanted her testimony. Her mental state improved greatly after she confided.

Joan Coleman and her colleagues again contacted the police after witnessing child murders, this time providing them with names, addresses and details of the alleged perpetrators and the children, as well as the address of the "factory". But all this came to nothing... The police then appointed a psychiatrist to interview Margaret: the conclusion of this 'expert' was that it was the psychiatrist, Joan Coleman, who had made up the whole story. Margaret did disclose a lot about ritual activities, with descriptions of ceremonies, locations, but also about the hierarchy of the cult. She made a very clear distinction between the purely sadistic killings of children in London and the ritual sacrifices, i.e. the religious ceremonies in which both men and women participated. The sacrifices were always performed by the high priest on certain dates in the calendar. Margaret described the mind control methods used by the cult, she described how children are drugged and hypnotised into believing in *the magic of Satan*. On certain ceremonial dates, Maragret still barricaded herself in her room...

Joan Coleman and Nurse Eileen saw Margaret just before she died and she assured them that everything she had said about the ritual abuse was true and that she wanted everyone to know.

- Theresa

In 1989, in the course of her work, Joan Coleman met a 15-year-old girl who claimed to have been abused by family members from whom she had just escaped for a year. Theresa described cult activity with protocols almost identical to what Margaret had described. She gave many details of a kind of castle to which she and other children were taken regularly. They were drugged before they went there, so she had no idea where exactly this place was. According to her, this place was run by a doctor because one part of the house was used for experimental operations. In another part there were young children imprisoned in cages, they were taken out only for sexual abuse and torture, for experiments and finally for sacrifice.

In this case, the police mobilised and arrested five men for rape of minors and one woman for complicity and illegal abortion. Although Theresa testified before the police, there was no valid evidence to prove ritual activity, so this was not included in the charges. Shortly before the trial, the police went to Theresa's school to obtain records of her attendance, whereupon the headmaster gave them notes and drawings produced by Theresa a few months earlier: one of the drawings depicted the ritual sacrifice of a tramp. Theresa had put together a full dossier of her experiences, but despite this, the satanic ritual abuse was not pursued due to lack of evidence.

- Monica

In the late 1990s, Joan Coleman received a phone call from a nurse asking for advice on one of her patients. The patient was a 37-year-old woman named Monica, who was initially being treated for bulimia, but had started talking about ritual abuse from her early childhood. Joan Coleman began to meet regularly with this patient. At first Monica was terrified to talk about the cult, but after a few weeks she began to give details about her memories, which brought back the trauma when they surfaced. She described her traumatic memories with a child's voice, behaviour and facial expressions. This 'child' would say that *they* had different names and different ages, sometimes she would write in the handwriting of a 5 year old. At other times she seemed totally different and even became hostile towards Joan Coleman and the nurse. Gradually it was discovered that some of her personalities had remained loyal to the cult. While Monica thought she had stopped being involved in the rituals at the age of 15, some of her alter personalities had never stopped these activities and had no intention of stopping... These alter personalities regularly went to the ceremonies, without Monica's awareness.

Joan Coleman first encountered dissociative identity disorder (DID) with Monica's case. She learned a great deal from this patient, both about satanic ritual abuse and about the workings of a multiple personality system, especially how to work with alter personalities who are still cult loyal. As the amnesia barriers faded, Monica became more and more aware of her involvement in occult and cult activities, as well as her awareness of her other personalities. She gave names and locations of ceremonies. While Joan Coleman had never spoken to her about other ritual abuse survivors, some of the information she gave corresponded not only with that given by Margaret, but also with details of other cases. She spoke of a 'high priest', giving his cult name but also giving his real name. Coleman had heard of him before, he was a nationally important man.

One of her alter personalities was a 10 year old girl called *"Scumbag"*. The alter was created when her mother prostituted her in a back room of a pub.

The money collected was destined for the satanic cult. *Scumbag* was a heavy beer drinker, while Monica did not drink alcohol. Monica was a brave woman, she testified on a radio show in 1996, and for that she was punished... that is certainly what led to her death shortly after. [272]

Joan Coleman's association, RAINS, had set up a telephone line which received many calls from therapists seeking help and advice. Their patients were talking about exactly the same satanic-type ritual activities. In 2014, RAINS compiled a list of people involved in ritual abuse in England. The list, which gives both names and places of worship, was compiled from the testimony of a victim, but also thanks to a member of the network who decided to speak out. The list includes politicians, actors, journalists, policemen, doctors, entrepreneurs, churchmen... We will come back to the case of the *'star'* Jimmy Savile in the chapter on the entertainment industry.

g/ Belgium

- The X-File (Dutroux case)

In Belgium, during the Dutroux case, the X-file was full of testimonies related to ritual abuse. It was also the X-file that led to the Belgian elitist network... That is why it was quickly closed, Marc Dutroux remained the *"isolated predator"* and the media all shouted that paedophile networks: *"They don't exist! "*

Judge Jean-Marc Connerotte had however conducted the investigation well, so well that the case was taken away from him when it finally led to the trail of a very embarrassing network with testimonies of satanic ritual abuse linked to the Belgian top brass... It was then Judge Jacques Langlois who was appointed to take over the case, not seeming to be at all interested in these X-witnesses talking about ritual abuse nor in the 30 or so dead witnesses in this case... It was also he who did not consider it necessary to have the 6,000 hairs found in Marc Dutroux's cellar analyzed. Moreover, it should be pointed out that the Belgian authorities considered that the analysis of all these DNA traces would be too expensive... This is how the second file of the Dutroux case could be closed so easily. Former Belgian MP Laurent Louis said on his blog: *"How can we accept that the Dutroux BIS file was closed without any further action when there were thousands of DNA traces found in the Marcinelle cache to be analysed. Can we accept that the argument used was the cost of these analyses when every year we spend crazy amounts of money to ensure the lifestyle of our Ministers and the royal family? Isn't the search for the truth and the incrimination of paedophiles and child killers worth all the money in the world?"*

---

[272] "Forensic Aspects of Dissociative Identity Disorder" - Adah Sachs and Graeme Galton, 2008, p.11-20.

At the time, however, the X-witnesses clearly described satanic ritual abuse with the murder of children. In April 2009, the *Wikileaks* website put online a 1235-page PDF document containing the hearings and minutes of the Dutroux case, [273]the document contains testimonies describing extreme practices such as hunting with children as game! These are presumed facts because obviously no investigation worthy of the name was ever conducted to verify the statements. Here are some extracts from the document:

PV 151.044 - Hearing of witness X2 - 27/03/97 (page 1065)

Facts committed in Chimay: She went 5 or 6 times to a huge wood for hunting. She was obliged to go there (...) The most violent members of the Knokke gang, including the L brothers, took part. In Chimay she heard shouting and shooting, but she does not know what she was shooting at, she never saw any game (...) It was around Chimay castle - a description of the castle that she knew before. The wood is walled. It was the cries of children, maybe 10 years old. She thinks there were 4 or 5 children. The shouting stopped. She stayed with L. and at that moment the L. brothers left with 1 or 2 other people including the gamekeeper. The participants were all from Knokke and Eindhoven (...) The screams were horrible and indescribable (...) At the beginning the screams were not loud, rather cries of pain, then much louder screams for a few seconds and then they stopped. In Faulx, there were also screams but they did not stop. She never saw a girl come back from L.L.'s house in one piece. When the screaming stopped L. stopped 'making love' to her and went back to the car with her very quickly.

PV 151.150 - Hearing of witness X2 - 03/04/97 (page 1066):

A hunting trip in the south of the country with people on horseback - many were armed - During the hunt there is rape on X2 - She goes with C. in a Ranch or Land Rover or Cherokkee (...) The riders arrived on horseback, they shoot but she does not know what, she did not see any game or dog. One of the riders came towards her, got off his horse and raped her. The same rider also raped Eva. The hunt takes place at about 5pm. She was also raped by a smaller one. Violence but less than in Eindhoven (blows to the face and strangulation). X2 is strangled because she is screaming. Eva was only hit in the face and stomach. There was another minor under 15 (blonde) but she doesn't know if she was raped - she was with a woman.

PV 116. 022 - Hearing of witness X1 - 31/10/96 (page 411):

Murder of children in the Ardennes and in Luxenburg during hunting parties. Thatched villa. (...)

Says she was once taken away by someone who came to pick her up: man she did not know well - she associates him with serious things: ritual. (30 years old, glasses, short curly brown hair, moustache). He drove a black BMW (...) X1 describes the interior of the building (aerial photo, tiles, dark brown carpet in the office...). Present, the person who brought her, Tony, the old man from the 'decascoop', and 2 other men. X1 has to undress and is taken to a room. The man who brought her enters with a little girl of 2 or 3 years old (blonde with straight

---

[273] *Belgium: Dutroux X-Dossier summary*, 1235 pages, Wikileaks.org, 2005.

hair). In front of X1 the man with the BMW plays with the child and then takes out a knife and sticks it between the legs of the screaming child. The man with the BMW finishes off the child. X1 is then raped by him, Tony and the others.

X1 was 12 years old and this was the first time she had witnessed such an event. She had never seen the child before.

PV 100.403 - Information (14/01/97) (page 435)

Château d'Ameroix. Letter from a retired Gd (M.) In early April 1996 he was hosting a Mexican priest. A Dutch friend of the priest came to pick him up. The Dutchman mentioned the Ameroix castle as a place where satanic and paedophile parties with child sacrifice take place. The information was given to him by an American from NATO who had returned to the USA. This American participated in a party and was disgusted (...) Perhaps to be related to the hunting parties described by witness X1.

PV 150.364 - Hearing of witness X1 - 01/03/97 (page 478)

X1 says she went to Antwerp Castle 15 or 20 times between 1990-95. She witnessed 6 or 7 murders of children including Katrien De Cuyper. Description of the people who brought the children in a van (white - rusty - diesel). She can make sketches. The men drop the children off and leave (...) X1 confirms that this is the castle seen in Gravenwezel. X1 doesn't know what was done with the corpses - maybe Tony took care of them. He always brought it to the place and only brought it back when there was no death (...)

PV 118.452 - Hearing of witness X1 - 10/12/96 (page 542)

M. was killed in November 1984 in Knokke in the villa of X1's grandmother. First party: B. brought a little boy of 8 years old. Owner of the villa = man more or less 40 years old and his wife around 20 years old. Description of the villa. X1 killed two rabbits and a dwarf goat on B.'s orders. The orgy took place in the garage. Two Dobermans and a German Shepherd were involved in the orgy. Description of the garage: rings sealed in the wall, cupboard walled in with sado-masochistic material and paedophile tapes. Participants with special costumes: leather, capes, masks. C. was raped by T., N., B. and the owner. C. She has to eat the heart of the sacrificial rabbit. Children tied to rings in the garage. The blood of the goat is poured on C.

PV 151.829 - Hearing of witness X3 - 02/06/97 (page 1072)

(Royal family section)

Picked up in a pink American car with white roof driven by Charly. Always luxurious houses (...) On the spot the car stopped on a lawn in front of the house surrounded by a park. There were two supervisors: Ralf and Walter. The children were taken to a natural stone turret with a wooden door. There was probably a floor in the turret. An underground passage led from the turret to a cellar. A lightless underground - earthen and sloping. In the cellars there were cells where children were locked up waiting for their turn. There were also cells for dogs (Dobermans). The corridor led to an auditorium. In the turret: bodies of dead children in various stages of decomposition (sometimes dismembered and/or missing pieces) and dog carcasses. Spectators: always the same but difficult to identify - about 50. She recognised C., B. and .A. and two others whom she calls Charly and Polo. She thought she recognised W.C. and Dr. V.E..

The Dogs were drugged to be excited. Shows = orgies, killing of children and dogs. Show room with strong smell of dog excrement. Dogs running loose in the garden. Gilles (12 years old) was emasculated by POLO. The other children had to drink his blood. She thinks she saw him cut up again in the dead room. Girls slashed with razor blades (...) Hunt prepared by Charly and Polo.

At another location:

Large white house with upper floor and stables. Park with round pool and fountain coming out of a statue. The children were let loose naked and when caught they were raped. The hunt ended with torture in the theatre (...) (unbearable details)

PV 466 - Hearing of **** - 16/01/97 (page 260)

He is very scared. He was treasurer of the Young PSC. He frequented a lot M.D., P.S. and J.P.D. They tried to direct him towards the OPUS DEI which was the 'nec plus ultra' according to them. Under the pretext of tests of initiation to the OPUS DEI, he was brought to Black Masses with sexual acts. He mentions the presence of young girls from Eastern countries (13-14 years). In 1986, after a drunken political meeting, he went with S. and D. to a meeting they announced as being spicy. There he was drugged and then taken to a room with people wearing masks and black 'djellabas'. The participants drank blood. He was confronted with a naked girl lying on an altar - she was dead (12 years old). He woke up the next day in his car. He left the party and made a statement to the BSR in Charleroi (...)

PV 114.039 - Hearing of witness X1 - 13/01/96 (page 407)

French, English, German and Dutch were spoken in the house (...) An evening with an atmosphere comparable to the New Year's Eve party. After an hour or two, when everyone was present, we went down into the cellar where the children were waiting. Description of the room: (...) A cupboard with sado-maso objects (...) Generally 2 to 5 children for about 10 people, including couples (...) Violence towards the children: tied around the neck, cut with knives (...) Several children raped by V.. Photos taken (films?). A girl was cut in the vagina, a doctor who was participating in the orgy sewed her up. More violence during school holidays. Consumption of drugs and medicines during orgies. Killing animals (rabbit, cat, chicken...) in order to make children suffer.

Letter from **** - 13/12/96 (page 261)

Sect - Orgies - Pink ballets in Holland.

Letter to the Dutch Justice about sects in that country.

There is a group of 300 people in HOLLAND who form a sect. They organise orgies with minors (3 years and older). Members = lawyers - jurists - judges - policemen...

Meetings in country estates, hotels or at a member's home (...) Assembly on the first Saturday after the full moon and on Christian holidays and birthdays. Groups of 12 people with children. Rape and torture of children. Large assemblies = 50 adults and 50 children - drugs, drinks, orgies, rapes, video recording of child abuse. Children of group members attend parties. This leads to the creation of multiple personalities in the children. At Christmas, a 1-year-old child is simulated and abused but replaced by a doll when the real torture takes place. Simulated burial of a 15 year old child as a punishment. Multiple personalities are induced, for example, by making small children believe that a cat is introduced into them and grows into a panther that will watch them if they want to talk or leave the clan. These multiple personalities are maintained by psychotherapists. The multiple personalities induced allow for continuous control even of adults by creating a certain balance. This makes all perpetrators victims (...)

- The multiple personality of Regina Louf

In the Dutroux case document cited above, PV N°116.231 dated November 1996 reports that X1 (Regina Louf) speaks of her different personalities and the police note significant differences in her handwriting. PV N° 116.232 reports that Régina Louf speaks of another personality called *"Hoop"* ("hope" in Flemish) which can *"disappear very deeply and reappear at once.* In PV N°116.234, it is noted about Regina Louf: *"She finds herself whole and understands the reason for her multiple personalities. She understands that one person could not have endured. "*

In the X file of the Dutroux case, it is the testimony of Régina Louf (witness X1) that is the most complete and best known. Since her birth, her family conditioned her to serve as a sex slave. She herself states that this was a practice passed down from generation to generation, that her grandmother abused her mother and so on... The extreme abuse and violence she suffered from early childhood in this network eventually created in her a multiple personality, a dissociative identity disorder. This disorder was diagnosed by five therapists appointed by the Belgian justice system during the study of the Dutroux X file.

Here is an excerpt from the book *"Les dossiers X: Ce que la Belgique ne devait pas savoir sur l'affaire Dutroux"* which clearly addresses the issue of the multiple personality of witness X1, Régina Louf:

One of the few decisions taken during an Obelix meeting on 25 April was to engage a panel of five psychiatric experts to examine X1. The request for this was made a few months ago by Warrant Officer De Baets, but since magistrates from all over the country have been involved in the case, things have moved a little more slowly. Each of the five experts has his own specialisation. And each one has to assess X1 and his testimony from his own professional angle. The panel is headed by Professor Paul Igodt, a neuropsychiatrist from Leuven, and the rest is made up of his colleagues Peter Adriaenssens and Herman Vertommen, Johan Vanderlinden, a doctor from the psychiatric hospital in Kortenberg, and psychiatrist Rudy Verelst. Because of his specialisation, child psychiatrist Peter Adriaenssens was given the special task of examining the children of X1, but this never happened.

The panel of experts must check X1's memory skills and examine whether there was any question of suggestiveness on the part of the investigators during the hearings. What is literally written in the apostille of Judge Van Espen shows that he was already briefed at the end of April about the replay that started in secret under the leadership of Commander Duterme. So far, no one has ever commented on the conduct of the hearings, which are described as exemplary". Only Duterme and some of his followers disagree. I could feel it clearly', says Regina Louf, 'the psychiatrists knew very quickly that their work would not change anything. They started at about the same time as De Baets was put on the sidelines. In total I spent more than thirty hours talking and undergoing psychological tests. Sometimes they were really ridiculous tests, but these people were trying to do their job honestly. I think they got caught in the crossfire. They were in contact with the investigators who certainly told them that I was mad as hell. When they spoke to me, there was always an atmosphere of: we think you're fine, but they tell us that... At the last interview, Vertommen advised me not to accept an audition under hypnosis. He told me to think about my family and to resign myself to the fact that not much could be done with my testimony. "

When scientists are asked for their opinion, the answer is rarely black or white, and more often than not it is grey with many shifting shades. This is also the case with the eight-page report that Professor Igodt sent to Van Espen on 8 October 1997. This report indicates - just as X1 had done from day one - that we are dealing with a person with dissociative identity disorder. Igodt even speaks in his report of a 'borderline personality disorder'. But, he adds: 'Through many years of therapy, however, she has succeeded (...) in achieving an integrated mode of functioning; her different (alter) personalities, some of which she can name, work together quite well and she manages to control each of these partial personalities in such a way that losses of control occur only rarely and to a limited extent. This was also noted during the anamnestic psychiatric clinical examination: apart from some uncontrolled laughter, especially when it comes to the most horrific sexual abuse, the patient controls herself quite well and no dissociative changes could be found. As already mentioned, this is largely attributable to the fairly long period of psychotherapy she has already completed."

As regards the causes of these disorders, Igodt formally pleads in favour of X1: "The anamnestic psychiatric clinical examination, however, confirms the suspicion of massive sexual abuse in the past of the person concerned. To the question of whether this abuse occurred and was indeed significant in intensity, it seems that the answer is yes. This massive abuse seems to be the main etiological factor of the psychiatric syndromes observed, which is in line with the abundant results of examinations in this area. "

The Igodt report can probably be considered as one of the few objective pieces of evidence that are still on file after the summer of 1997. Igodt draws attention to the dangers of "contamination" with regard to X1's memory - "without there being any question of intentional lying" - because of her therapy, her attention to her own situation, as well as her obvious motivation to fight against child sexual abuse. Igodt explains that the credibility of a person's memories of their youth can be measured by the way they are told. If the account takes the form of a 'flowing story' from which doubt is absent, there is a good chance that the story is made up or 'reconstructed'. The more muddled the testimony appears, the more authentic it will be, he believes. For a testimony about things one experienced as a child must sound almost as if it were told by a child."[274]

In a France 3 documentary entitled *"Passé sous silence: Témoin X1 - Régina Louf"* broadcast in 2002, psychiatrist Paul Igodt, speaking about Régina Louf's dissociative disorders, said: *"When Régina Louf was examined, it was clear from many clues that this was a person who was severely disturbed by prolonged sexual abuse in early childhood. But at the same time, and we see this very often, she is a strong and intelligent person who has kept intact formidable defence and survival mechanisms. I think it is fair to say that the prolonged and very serious sexual abuse she suffered gave rise to the development of a multiple personality with alter-egos. Victims of rape or sexual abuse will tell you: "I wasn't there in that body, I was somewhere else... I was dissociating. But this is not madness, it is not schizophrenia, nor is it mythomania. It is obviously a search for one's own history, for one's truth, and it is a painful and groping process."*

At the age of 11, Régina Louf's mother introduced her to a certain Tony V., telling her: *"From now on you belong to him, he is your owner."* This individual then became her *"master"*. He had an ambiguous relationship with her, mixing pimping with an unhealthy attachment that passed for love between the child and her master. This is nothing more or less than trauma-based mind control. It was this Tony who was in charge of Regina, and it was he who 'guided' her into the paedophile ring. Even after she turned 18, Tony continued to pursue her, and although she had married, he managed to manipulate her into returning to ritual abuse at times: she had not been able to break away completely. Regina Louf's lawyer, Patricia van der Smissen, says in the documentary *"The X-Files"* that she thought *Tony* had somehow *"protected"* her and that this explained the fact that she remained alive.[275] Mind-controlled slaves are usually under the direction of one or more people who hold the codes, the triggers, to control and manipulate the victim. We find the same thing in the testimony of Cathy O'Brien who "belonged" to a certain Alex Houston, who was neither her husband, nor her friend, nor her guardian... he was her *"handler"*, her "owner", her "exploiter", her "master", her "trainer" holding the keys to her mind and directing her life from A to Z.

In her autobiography *'Zwijgen is voor daders - De getuigenis van X1'* (Silence is for the guilty, the testimony of X1) published in 1998, Regina Louf describes how her alter personalities are always the same age as when they were created during traumatic experiences. She also explains how her writing differs depending on which alter is active. In this book, she clearly describes the phenomenon of dissociation that occurs during traumas, dissociative disorders that can go as far as a split personality.

This book began to take shape in July 1988, when for the first time I wrote down my memories and nightmares in a notebook. I discovered that I had

---

[274] "Les dossiers X: Ce que la Belgique ne devait pas savoir sur l'affaire Dutroux" - Annemie Bulte and Douglas de Coninck, 1999, p.249-250.

[275] Zembla TV NED3 - 2004.

different styles of writing, and each type of writing was a very distinct part of 'me'. This was very frightening, especially as I often couldn't remember what I had written. When I re-read the pages, I would stumble over memories that had been buried in me for a long time. I had never really forgotten the facts, they had simply been dispersed in different personalities, each with their own traumas... Within six weeks I had already written much of the content of the book, a book that ended up with the BOB investigators (...)

More than ever, I discovered that I had black holes. I went to school, I got good grades, I even had several classmates, but somehow it all happened without me. It was as if someone else took over as soon as the school doors closed behind me. As if the abused 'Ginie' was put aside until Tony stood in my bed or at the school gate again. The abused 'Ginie' was hardly aware of school and family life, the other 'Ginie' didn't seem to be present during the abuse, so she could live 'normally' (...)

In Knokke, at my grandmother's house, the adults realised that I spoke with the voices in my head, that I changed my moods quickly, or even that I sometimes spoke with another voice or accent. Although I was only 5 or 6 years old, I understood that these things were weird and not allowed. So I learned to hide my inner voices, my other selves. After what happened to Clo, this strange feeling that I was sometimes directed by these inner voices became stronger. After the initiation, I could no longer resist the voices in my head. I was happy to disappear into nothingness, only to regain consciousness when Tony was there. The pain seemed more bearable (...)

Tony was the only adult who understood that something was wrong with my head. This did not bother him at all, on the contrary, he cultivated it... He gave me different names: Pietemuis, Meisje, Hoer, Bo. The names slowly became a part of me. The strange thing was that if he mentioned a name, the personality that matched the name was immediately called.

Pietemuis' (little mouse) became the name of the little girl he brought home from the abuse - a frightened, nervous little girl whom he could comfort by talking to her in a caring, fatherly way.

Meisje' (girl) was the name of the part of me that belonged exclusively to him. If he abused me in my bed early in the morning, for example, or if there was no one around.

Hoer' (whore) was the name of the part of me that worked for him.

Bo' was the young woman who looked after him if he was drunk and needed looking after.

"Now you leave that to me," he would say when I asked him curiously why he was giving me so many names, he would add: "Daddy Tony knows you better than you know yourself."... And that was sadly true.[276]

The question is who initiated this Tony on how to cultivate and exploit Regina Louf's dissociative identity disorder? Where did he receive instruction in these mind control techniques? Is he himself a member of an occult network, a secret society? Was he a victim of ritual abuse as a child and does he himself

---

[276] Zwijgen is voor daders - De getuigenis van X1 - Regina Louf, Houtekiet, 1998.

have a split and multiple personality? Is the splitting of the personality systematic in victims, and consequently in aggressors who have generally been victims themselves in these infernal networks?

One of the minutes of the Dutroux case contains a particularly interesting report of a hypnosis session performed by Dr. Mairlot on the witness Nathalie W., who was heard in the investigation of the X files: *"On December 12, while Nathalie is testifying, three gendarmes and a psychologist are needed to restrain and calm her down. She had just begun a series of hearings in which she spoke of extreme sexual sadism, ritual murders of babies and ceremonies that looked very much like black masses. This was the time when some investigators were seriously looking into secret satanic groups with which Dutroux and Weinstein had allegedly had contact. On 16, 23 and 30 January 1997, Nathalie was hypnotised in the interview room by Dr. Mairlot, a specialist in the field. This did not clarify the investigation. They mix the baby's blood with that of the slaughtered sheep (...). They burn the baby and the sheep, and everyone sleeps with everyone else (...) The monster is gone. They rip out the baby's heart. After this session, Nathalie says that she feels as if she has witnessed the show from several angles at once, as if she herself were present through several personalities. "If only part of what she tells us is true, it's perfectly normal that this should happen," Théo Vandyck tells his colleagues."*[277]

During the hypnotic trance, Nathalie W. reported in writing about satanic ritual abuse that took place in a castle during a full moon. She describes the sacrifice of a sheep and a baby around a fire, a ceremony followed by an orgy. The end of the report states cryptically:

When she woke up, she had the impression that there were several people watching what she described and that these people (these Nathalie) were fading away in front of each other. She thinks she disappeared about ten times."[278]

If one is not familiar with the phenomenon of split personality, dissociative identity disorder (DID), it is difficult to grasp the significance of this passage in the minutes. Indeed, here it is reported that upon awakening from the hypnotic trance, Nathalie described that several of her alter personalities emerged in succession during this hypnosis session. Each of them (*these Nathalie*) brought pieces of memory about this particular event. It is noted that *"these people faded away in front of each other, she thinks she disappeared about ten times"*. This means that ten or so alter personalities (or alternating personalities) followed each other during the hypnosis session, each having experienced part of the ceremony at one time or another. The memory of the event is therefore broken up into several pieces, like puzzle pieces held together by the different fragments of Nathalie's personality. It is therefore difficult for a victim to remember the whole event in a detailed, coherent and chronological way, unless you access the memories of each alter personality that was involved in it and you can put the puzzle together. Survivor Carole Rutz describes very

---

[277] "The X-Files: What Belgium should not have known about the Dutroux case" - Annemie Bulte and Douglas de Coninck, 1999, p.218.

[278] *Belgium: Dutroux X-Dossier summary"*, Wikileaks.org, 2005 - PV 150.035, 30/01/97, p.756.

well this phenomenon of memory splitting of a traumatic life moment in an already split child: the little victim goes from one alter personality to the other throughout the event, one personality will live the transport, the other the abuse, another will attend or participate in the sacrifices, etc...

In the France 3 report *"Passé sous silence: Témoin X1 - Régina Louf"*, Warrant Officer Patrick de Baets, who was in charge of the X file in the Dutroux case at the time, said of Régina Louf: *"She had a problem putting everything on a timeline, but she gave enough elements to make a good investigation. It was in fact a puzzle that was thrown on a table but which held together and was coherent."*

A large percentage of victims of ritual abuse and mind control therefore have Dissociative Identity Disorder, formerly known as Multiple Personality Disorder, with Dissociative Identity Disorder being the final stage in the scale of dissociative states. But it is important to remember that not everyone who has developed dissociative disorders has experienced trauma related to ritual abuse as described in this chapter.

CHAPTER 5

THE SPLIT PERSONALITY AND AMNESIA

Trauma of this nature, sexual aggression, triggers very specific psychological effects that produce a kind of psychological dissociation in the victim. This means, to put it simply, that her body is there but her head is elsewhere in order to survive the event.[279] Martine Nisse, co-founder of the Buttes-Chaumont centre

People have a range of abilities to cope with upsetting experiences. Some people, especially children, are able to disappear into a fantasy world, to disassociate, to pretend it never happened. They are able to go on with their lives as if nothing had happened. But sometimes it comes back to haunt them. Bessel van der Kolk - Trauma and Memory, 1993

As we learn more and more about dissociation, we come to the conclusion that in highly traumatised individuals, it is a fairly common defence process to keep themselves safe and to compartmentalise these things separately because they are far too difficult to integrate. Christine Courtois, author of "Healing the Incest Wound: Adult Survivors in Therapy"

1 - INTRODUCTION

The knowledge and understanding of dissociative disorders and more specifically of dissociative identity disorder (multiple personality) and traumatic amnesia is an essential point when trying to understand the process of trauma-based mind control. Knowledge of these psychotraumatic disorders allows us to understand that the human mind can split into several independent identities, separated, partitioned, by amnesic walls. We can thus understand that the mind of an individual is potentially programmable like a computer with files and access codes. This phenomenon of fracturing the personality is the cornerstone of ritual abuse because it "unlocks" the psyche, which then becomes accessible to integrate programming.

The horror and fear experienced by a ritually abused child causes the brain to react with varying degrees of dissociation in proportion to the severity and repetition of the traumatic experiences. This is a natural defence mechanism against intense psychic terror and extreme physical pain. Most children who have been abused in this way in early childhood will completely dissociate from the events and will often be unable to consciously remember what happened.

---

[279] "Child Rape, the End of Silence?" - France 3, 2000.

The dissociation can go as far as the splitting of the personality into multiple alterations, which is the most extreme stage, the one sought by the abusers who aim to establish mental control over the victim.

2 - DISSOCIATION

In humans, the phenomenon of dissociation manifests itself in various degrees. It can be a slight trance, a minor dissociation from everyday life, like when you read a page of a book and realise at the end that you have retained absolutely nothing of what you have just read. But this natural function can go as far as a serious psychopathology called Dissociative Identity Disorder (DID): the most extreme degree of dissociation resulting from severe trauma. The term *'dissociation'* was first used in 1812 in a medical text by Benjamin Rush, one of the fathers of American psychiatry.

In 1889, Dr. Pierre Janet (one of the French fathers of the concept of dissociation) wrote a thesis entitled *"L'automatisme mental"*, in which he presented 21 cases of hysteria and neurasthenia, more than half of which were traumatic. Janet demonstrates that these conditions can be treated and reduced through hypnosis. For him, it is a question of a *'dissociation of consciousness'*, hysteria being caused by the raw memory of the traumatic experience lying apart in a corner of the consciousness. Like a foreign body, this unconscious memory gives rise to archaic, maladaptive, automatic acts and reveries, without any connection with the rest of the consciousness, which continues to inspire detailed and adapted thoughts and acts.[280]

From the beginning of the 20th century, Pierre Janet and Charles Myers described this process of dissociation as a *"splitting of the personality"*. Janet, long before the neurochemical causes of this phenomenon were established, explained that it was, in a primary form, a dissociation between the individual's defence system and the systems that involve the management of daily life and the survival of the species. Myers describes this primary structural dissociation in terms of a division between *the 'apparently normal personality'* (PAN) and the *'emotional personality'* (EP). The EP is stuck in the traumatic experience and fails to become a recollection of the trauma, i.e. a narrative memory. Whereas PAN is associated with avoidance of traumatic memories, detachment, anaesthesia and partial or total amnesia. These are indeed two very different entities. There is some clinical evidence, for example, that they are associated with a different sense of self, and preliminary findings in experimental research on dissociative identity disorder (DID) suggest that they respond differently to memories of trauma and to threatening stimuli that are processed preconsciously.[281]

---

[280] "Psychotrauma: theoretical approaches. Tempête Xynthia, étude sur les sinistrés de La Faute-sur-Mer deux ans après" - Thesis by Anne-Sophie Baron, 2012.

[281] *"Dissociation structurelle de la personnalité et trauma"* - Nijenhuis, van der Hart, Steele, de Soir, Matthess, Revue francophone du stress et du trauma, 2006.

Psychotraumatic disorders were defined in the 1980s, starting with Post Traumatic Stress Disorder (PTSD), which manifests itself following a traumatic experience and which will persist over time with flashbacks, insomnia, nightmares, hypervigilance, etc. The definition of dissociative disorders came later in the DSM-IV (Diagnostic and Statistical Manual of Mental Disorders - USA) which characterises them as *"a sudden or progressive, transient or chronic disturbance of normally integrated functions (consciousness, memory, identity or perception of the environment)"*. They include the following five disorders:

- Dissociative amnesia: characterised by an inability to recall important personal memories, usually traumatic or stressful.

- Dissociative fugue: characterised by a sudden and unexpected departure from home or work, with an inability to remember one's past, either the adoption of a new identity or confusion about personal identity.

- Dissociative Identity Disorder (multiple personality): characterised by the presence of at least two distinct identities that alternately take control of the individual; the individual is unable to recall personal memories.

- Depersonalisation disorder: characterised by a prolonged or recurrent feeling of detachment from one's own mental functioning or body, with an unaffected appreciation of reality.

- Dissociative disorder not otherwise specified, whose main feature is a dissociative symptom that does not meet the previous criteria for specific dissociative disorders.

The American clinical psychologist James Randall Noblitt has classified the types of dissociation into five categories:

- Dissociation of consciousness: Occurs during trance states. Such states vary in intensity, ranging from a slightly foggy state to a deep state of stupefaction and physical numbness.

- Dissociative memory: When the person has large portions of their memory that disappear without explanation. Dissociative amnesia cannot be explained by a blow to the head or by neurochemical effects (drugs, alcohol).

- Dissociative Identity Disorder: When the individual suddenly experiences (consciously or unconsciously) that he or she is another person or an outside entity. This phenomenon is the main commonality between dissociative identity disorder and demonic possession.

- Dissociation of perception: Manifested by changes in auditory, visual and tactile perceptions that may be considered hallucinations. Perceptual dissociation may also include a distortion of the individual's sense of reality.

- Dissociation of will: Dissociation of will involves automatisms, automatic behaviours and cataplexy or dissociative conversion disorder (an inability to move and exercise muscle tone).

The book *"Thanks for the Memories"* by survivor Brice Taylor contains an interesting description of the phenomenon of physical and psychological dissociation. It is the testimony of a woman (Penny) who suffered repeated sexual abuse as a child: *"Dissociation is a way of escaping the intolerable. It happened from the first trauma, it was a way of coping with the unbearable physical pain but also the psychological pain. For me, it took the form of a numbness and a cooling of the body, and since that day, when I dissociate I become all numb. First it's my hands, then my feet, I can't feel them and if my eyes are closed I have no way of locating my limbs in space. Then the numbness in my face begins, I can't feel my lips or my cheeks. When I dissociate deeply, it takes over the whole body and I feel like a piece of wood... Even worse than the physical dissociation is what happens on the mental level when the whole body is numb. The only thing I can compare it with is the white noise of the static radio, it leaves me dizzy with my eyes lost in space. The thoughts that come in pass at the speed of light without any coherence, organisation or form. I am in total confusion. It can range from a slightly hazy, slightly hovering state to a real blank page where I can't see or hear anything (...) When I come back to myself, I don't immediately and consciously realise that I have lost hours."[282]*

Dissociation is a psychological and neurological defence mechanism that occurs at the time of trauma. During severe stress, the brain's amygdala will activate to produce stress hormones to provide the body with the means to cope with the danger. These hormones are produced immediately, like an alarm, and are adrenaline and cortisol. In a second phase, the frontal cortex will manage and modulate this hormone production, or even switch it off, depending on the degree of stress. In the case of an extreme situation where one is blocked and sequestered, such as a rape or torture, there is then a psychological sideration, i.e. the cortex is paralysed, it no longer responds. The consequence is that it will not be able to regulate the emotional response by controlling the flow of stress hormones coming from the alert amygdala. The amygdala will therefore produce adrenalin and cortisol in large quantities, too large quantities... These two hormones are useful in preparing the body for unusual efforts, but in too large quantities they can represent a vital risk at the cardiovascular and neurological level (cardiac arrest and epilepsy). Faced with this saturation in stress hormones, the body has an ultimate protection function, it will break down just like an electric circuit that is overloaded. To do this, it will isolate the cerebral amygdala, which will no longer be able to secrete adrenaline or cortisol.

When this process of disjunction occurs, the victim finds himself in a "second" state, in a kind of unreality... this is what is called dissociation. As adrenalin and cortisol are no longer injected into the body by the amygdala, the victim suddenly no longer feels this strong emotion and it is as if he or she becomes a stranger to the situation he or she is experiencing. The individual becomes a spectator of the traumatic scene in which he is involved, he is disconnected, and there may be a kind of decorporation. Some victims report that they were no longer in their physical body at the time of the dissociation, they could clearly see the scene from the outside (we will go into this in more detail in the next chapter).

According to psychotraumatologist Muriel Salmona, [283]this ultimate process of cerebral disjunction occurs when the brain secretes morphine and

---

[282] Thanks For The Memories: The Truth Has Set Me Free" - Brice Taylor, 1999, p.27.

[283] Muriel Salmona - Pratis TV, 16/01/2012.

ketamine-like substances. It is this chemical cocktail that seems to be at the origin of the natural phenomenon of dissociation during an extreme trauma. This cocktail creates an emotional anaesthesia but also a strong physical anaesthesia. The victim no longer feels anything and enters a sort of parallel world, sometimes leaving the physical body. It is said that the victim has passed through the *Mirror of Alice in Wonderland*, gone *Beyond the Rainbow* (in reference to the Wizard of Oz). These are the metaphorical images that are used by the MK programmer executioners to represent the process of dissociation. The programmers thus push the little victims to dissociate during the traumas by guiding them to an alternative reality in order to escape the terror and physical pain they inflict. Once the child is in this fully dissociated state, the deep programming work can begin as it is in this state that the child's subconscious and *spiritual doors are* wide open. Once the child is completely dissociated and disconnected from the body, a split occurs, another alter personality is created to "take over" the body of the little victim. It is this alter, this split personality, that records the unfolding traumatic memory, while the victim (the personality that slipped away during the traumatic experience) will be totally amnesiac of this memory. During this disjunction, all the usual memorization work by the hippocampus will be interrupted and the memory of the event will remain stored in standby, as in a "black box" that has recorded all the data. This is called traumatic memory, or traumatic amnesia. In a dissociative identity disorder, these 'black boxes' of memories are held by the different alter personalities.

Following these painful experiences, victims will generally continue to self-treat, to self-dissociate in order to be able to continue living relatively normally. This means that they will adopt strategies to anaesthetise this traumatic memory. The organism that has already experienced anaesthesia during the aggression will try to reproduce this process. This can be done by taking alcohol or drugs that have dissociative effects, so there can be strong addictions that are set up in a victim. But an important thing to add is that stress can also create these dissociative states, so it can also create a strong addiction. When a traumatic memory is awakened, the victim relives the event and his or her body reproduces the disjunction with the morphine/ketamine cocktail, which are hard drugs. A phenomenon of tolerance and addiction is therefore quickly established, hence the extreme behaviour of victims who scarify themselves, burn themselves, etc., in order to calm themselves down and get out of the situation. This is why victims behave in such an extreme way, scarifying themselves, burning themselves, etc., in order to calm themselves and anaesthetise themselves by increasing the level of stress in order to provoke disjunction and dissociation. They are not aware of the process that is taking place, but feel the "calming" effect of these acts of self-harm. It is nothing more or less than a question of chemicals in the brain, a kind of *'dissociative shot'*. Violence against others also creates this stress, which injects certain substances into the bloodstream.

Ritual abuse and mind control survivor Jay Parker, described how the Monarch mind control system is addictive to the endogenous brain chemistry that causes victims to perpetuate their dissociative states. In the global network of ritual abuse and mind control, the perpetrators are simply repeating on others what they have usually experienced themselves. It is a vicious circle, a vicious process. The child victims will develop a strong addiction to violence against others to create these anaesthetic and dissociative states, they will in turn become abusers. Just like a drug addict and the phenomenon of addiction that makes him or her constantly increase the doses, the abusers will have to constantly go further in the horror to continue to anaesthetise themselves.

The earlier the individual started practising ritual abuse, the more extreme practices he will need to dissociate himself... This is perhaps one of the reasons why the blood of victims who have been terrorised and then sacrificed is sometimes consumed: it contains a cocktail of hormones acting like drugs that will help the abuser to reach this state of disjunction, perched in an extreme dissociative anaesthesia. Practitioners of satanic ritual abuse seek to disjoin themselves, consciously or not, in order to self-treat their own traumatic memories. The more inhumane the acts of barbarism, the more sadly effective this will be. In transgenerational Satanist families, this is a real vicious circle where dissociation becomes a way of life. It is a process that is the automatic, natural and vital escape for these children during ritual abuse and mind control. But these dissociative disorders will continue to interfere throughout the individual's life. A child dissociates easily, in the face of traumatic situations he divides his own consciousness into several parts, often for long periods. The 'self' is put aside, buried in order to be protected. This is the safeguarding of what is most precious in the world, his divine essence, his true identity, the pearl that Satan cannot touch. The victim will always keep this divine root, his true "self", somewhere inside him. This precious seed is protected by the alter personalities that serve as armour against violence because they *encapsulate* the traumatic memories.

3 - TRAUMATIC (OR DISSOCIATIVE) AMNESIA

Traumatic amnesia is closely related to dissociation and dissociative identity disorder. It is characterised by an inability to recall important personal memories, usually traumatic or stressful, which cannot be explained by *poor memory*. The disorder involves a reversible impairment of memory, during which memories of personal experiences cannot be expressed verbally. Nor can it be explained by the direct physiological effect of a substance or a neurological or other medical disease factor. Traumatic amnesia is most often manifested as a memory lapse or a number of forgetfulnesses of aspects of the individual's personal history. These memory lapses are often associated with traumatic or extremely heavy events. In localised amnesia, the person does not remember events from a specific time period, usually the first few hours after an extremely heavy event.

Traumatic amnesia, which may be complete or fragmentary, is a frequent phenomenon among victims of sexual violence in childhood. This psychotraumatic consequence is unfortunately not taken into account in the legislation, which means that a victim who has had a long period of amnesia with the impossibility of denouncing sexual crimes in time will not be able to file a complaint because the statute of limitations will have expired. Numerous clinical studies have described this phenomenon, which has been known since the beginning of the 20th century and which was described in traumatised soldiers suffering from amnesia following combat. But it is among victims of sexual violence that we find the most traumatic amnesia. Studies have also shown that the recovered memories are reliable and in every way comparable with traumatic memories that have always been present in the individual's consciousness. These memories often reappear suddenly and uncontrollably, with very precise details and obviously with a great deal of emotion, distress and confusion, as the victim relives the memory as if it were happening in the present moment.

In 1996, at a psychiatry and neurology conference in Toulon, Jean-Michel Darves-Bornoz explained that traumatic memories are not like other memories. Indeed, the trauma will modify the normal mechanisms of encoding and recovering memories of the traumatic experience. On the one hand, trauma can cause hypermnesia (i.e. an exaltation of memory that allows access to extremely detailed autobiographical memories connected to the entire sensory system) as well as amnesia. In psychotraumatology, hypermnesia and amnesia are therefore paradoxically linked (this is a key point, to which we will return in Chapter 8). Indeed, when amnesic traumatic memories resurface in consciousness, it is with such force that it becomes hypermnesia, i.e. the memories that emerge become extremely clear, much clearer than a banal memory, assimilated by the explicit (narrative) and conscious memory. The traumatic experience *imprints itself* much more deeply on the victim than any other lived experience, which is why when these dissociative memories resurface, they are particularly invasive and very detailed as all the senses relive the scene. This issue of encoding and retrieval of traumatic memories is important because there is a controversy about true and false memories of sexual violence and ritual abuse. It is important to know that only memories that have been encoded in a language form (explicit memory) are likely to be accessible, while non-language memory (implicit memory) is not likely to be accessible to consciousness. This non-verbal encoding of memory, which is therefore difficult to put into a narrative, chronological and autobiographical context, will not be fully conscious of by the victim.[284]

These traumatic amnesias are the result of a dissociative mechanism triggered by the brain to protect itself from the terror and extreme stress generated by violence. There is a disjunction of the emotional circuit but also of the memory circuit in connection with the hippocampus: the area of the brain that manages memory and spatio-temporal location, without which no memory can be memorised, recalled or temporalised. As long as there is this disjunction in the memory circuit, the hippocampus cannot do its work and this emotional memory, like the *"black box of violence"*, is trapped outside time and consciousness... this is traumatic memory. Nowadays, it is possible to detect

---

[284] *Traumatic syndromes of rape and incest"* - Jean Michel Darves-Bornoz. Congress of psychiatry and neurology, Toulon, 1996.

signs of memory impairment through brain scans, as the amygdala complex and the hippocampus show a significantly smaller volume in people who have suffered severe trauma.

When the dissociation ceases, the traumatic memory can finally be reconnected to consciousness and re-emerge, for example, during an event that recalls the violence. It then invades the victim's psychic space, making her relive the violence like a time machine. These memories that come back to consciousness are unbearable for the victim, so she will set up avoidance behaviours to protect herself from anything that could trigger these memories again. As we have seen above, she will also set up dissociative behaviours to anaesthetise herself and make the emotional and memory circuit disconnect again. Alcohol, drugs, risky behaviour, endangerment, but also violence against others, allow this dissociation and disjunction by producing extreme stress again. The victim can therefore oscillate between periods of dissociation with major memory problems and periods of activation of the traumatic memory where he or she will relive the violence.

Traumatic memory can be treated, but unfortunately professionals do not seem to be trained in psycho-traumatology and the vast majority of victims of childhood sexual abuse are abandoned and not identified, protected and even less treated. Victims whose traumatic memories resurface are often not believed. They are told that the memories are fantasies, psychotic hallucinations or induced *"false memories"*.[285]

To complicate matters further, trauma can cause a closure of Broca's area, the area of the left hemisphere of the brain that allows us to verbally convey an experience, to put words to the trauma we have experienced. Since verbal communication is the way we usually tell others about our experiences, disruption of this function will further hinder the victim's recognition.[286]

In 1993, a study on traumatic amnesia was published in the *Journal of Traumatic Stress*. This study entitled *"Sef-reported* amnesia *for abuse in adults molested as children" was* conducted by Dr. John Briere. In this study, a sample of 450 adult patients (420 women and 30 men) who had reported sexual abuse were asked a questionnaire. The question relating to traumatic amnesia was: *"Between the time of the sexual abuse and your 18th birthday, was there a time when you did not remember the sexual abuse experience?* The results showed that out of a total of 450 subjects, 267 or 59.3% answered that they had no memory of their abuse before they were 18.[287]

The phenomenon of amnesia (traumatic memories) caused by dissociation during a trauma is still very controversial within psychiatric and judicial institutions. Why is this very serious field of psychotraumatology so

---

[285] "Raped at 5, she remembers it at 37: with terror, the brain can break down" - Muriel Salmona, nouvelobs.com 2013.

[286] The Myth of Sanity: Divided Consciousness and the Promise of Awareness " - Martha Stout, 2002.

[287] *"Sef-reported amnesia for abuse in adults molested as children"* - John Briere, Jon Conte, Journal of Traumatic Stress, Vol.6, N°1, 1993.

neglected and even discredited within the institutions responsible for justice, safety and the care of victims? Yet there is no shortage of concrete examples of dissociative amnesia, just as there is no shortage of research into this particular function of the human brain. The following testimonies show us that this is a recurring problem, but that it is covered by an institutional and media blanket that prevents the issue of traumatic amnesia, which is so crucial for understanding the paedocriminal system, from being brought to the forefront... Indeed, it is still a question of information control, which is dear to our "wizard-controllers" and to the prevailing social engineering...

During the French campaign *"Stop au Déni"* (2015) in support of young victims of sexual violence, a contributor testified about sexual abuse in schools. This is what she said about her traumatic amnesia: *"It took me more than 35 years to lift the fog that fell on my eyes that day, to know, to integrate in my memory, in which year and in which region I was in the first grade. and two more years to get out of this traumatic amnesia, to sort out, dismantle, and understand the punishment-rape strategy used. Today, I still get lost in the corridors when I enter a school, I can still feel that man's head, close by, I can still hear and feel his breath on my face, I can still feel myself pierced, scratched inside, I hurt. I wish I could finally let out the tears I swallowed in my throat that day, and I can't. Not yet. Not yet."*[288]

Here is also a testimony of traumatic amnesia reported by Isabelle Aubry, founder of the International Association of Victims of Incest (*AIVI*): *"It is now six months since I remembered things that the person who destroyed my life did to me. For seven, eight, nine years... I don't know... I had forgotten everything, or at least buried it in the depths of my memory... Now flashes have come back to me and I can't stop thinking about them. I remember a sentence that I can't hear today without thinking about it. When my parents weren't around and they weren't around much, I don't know how it started, I don't know how long it lasted, I don't know how far it went, I don't know when it happened, I just know it was when I was in primary school... he wanted me to massage him... I don't know, I know it wasn't just a back massage... I think he was naked but I don't know. I miss a lot of things from those moments and I find it very hard not to know how far it went. I think I would like to know what really happened. At that time I thought it was normal what I was doing, I was consenting. But now I suffer a lot. I mutilate myself, I make myself vomit, sometimes I eat a lot and sometimes not at all. In moments of despair I start drinking, taking medicine by the boxful. This past eats away at me and I can't get rid of it. I think that what I have become is hurting my friends and they have to be really understanding to be able to put up with me. I would like to see someone, a shrink, I have the numbers but I can't pick up the phone. I have more and more nightmares of rape, incest, suicide. My friends don't know what to do. I haven't told anyone in my family and it seems impossible!"*[289]

---

[288] *"Rape in school..."* - stopaudeni.com, 2015.

[289] How I overcame incest: from consequences to care" - Isabelle Aubry, 2010.

In 2013, in an article for the Nouvel Obs entitled "Raped at 5, she remembers it at 37: with terror, the brain can break down", the psychiatrist Muriel Salmona wrote: "When in 2009, during a first hypnotherapy session, after having relived very brutally and precisely - like a film - a scene of sexual violence committed by a close relative when she was 5, Cécile B. wanted to file a complaint, she learned that the facts were time-barred (...) She was 37 years old at the time. Cécile B. had lodged this appeal to contest the validity of the statute of limitations as far as she was concerned, since 32 years of traumatic amnesia had prevented her from being aware of the acts of rape she had suffered at the age of 5 and which had lasted for 10 years, and that consequently she had never been in a position to denounce them before they were remembered (...) As a specialist in psychotraumatology who takes care of victims of sexual violence, I can only fully understand and support her. Many of my patients are in the same situation as her, they have had long periods of traumatic amnesia and have been unable to denounce the sexual crimes they suffered as children in time because the statute of limitations has expired (sometimes by only a few days), others have been prevented from denouncing them for many years because of avoidance behaviours, or because of the influence and threats of their entourage, and when they are finally ready, they can no longer file a complaint."

In 2015, French journalist Mathilde Brasilier published an autobiographical book entitled *"Il y avait le jour, il y avait la nuit, il y avait l'inceste"* in which she recounts her traumatic amnesia. For 30 years, this woman had amnesia that totally obscured the memories of her father's rape that she had suffered as a child. Her brother was also a victim of the father's abuse and unfortunately committed suicide in 1985 a few days after telling his father *'After what you did to me, I have nothing more to say to you'*. It was after this tragedy that Mathilde Brasilier began to question herself and consult a therapist... For a long time she thought *she had lived a perfectly happy childhood in a privileged environment,* without having any memory of sexual abuse. In a radio interview she said about her father: *"The relationship was difficult because I couldn't stand to look him in the eye (...) This was one of the subjects I discussed with my mother: 'It's strange, I like Daddy, but looking him in the eye is unbearable for me. But I didn't know why (...)* Mathilde Brasilier said that her traumatic memories *came back all at once (...) one after the other (...) It's like a film that suddenly unfolds.*[290]

On 16 January 1998, the French actress and singer Marie Laforêt testified on the 8 o'clock news of France 2 about a traumatic amnesia. At the age of 3 she was raped several times by *a "neighbour"*, and this memory was repressed for years before reappearing in her forties. Here is the transcript of her testimony:

- Marie Laforêt: I relived exactly what had happened, the name of the man, his costume, his way of doing things, everything... Everything came back at once. It was impossible for me to talk about it for three days and three nights of crying spells... I received this in my face, you cannot in any way confuse it with anything else, neither with a premonition, nor with a story of mental

---

[290] "Incest: After amnesia, a painful reconstruction" - Mathilde Brasilier, VivreFm.com, 20/05/2015.

confusion... It is not a question of mental confusion, on the contrary, you are excessively precise.

- Journalist: How can you explain that your memory has buried this event for so many years?

- ML: I think it's in the same area as autism, fainting or coma. There is a painful episode, and one will decide to end it.

- Carole Damiani (Psychologist): The memory that remains in the unconscious has not been destroyed and sometimes it is due to associative links, i.e. from memory to memory we end up getting closer to the traumatic event. This may also mean that the person was ready to face the event at that time, when they had not been ready before.

Marilyn Van Derbur, the 1958 *Miss America* and daughter of millionaire Francis Van Derbur, has revealed in her autobiography the consequences of the paternal incest she suffered as a child. She says that until the age of 24, she had completely repressed the memory of her father's rapes. In her autobiography *Miss America By Day*, she publicly reveals: *"In order to survive, I divided myself into a happy, smiling 'child of the day' and a cowering 'child of the night' at the mercy of my father... Until I was 24 years old, the day child had no awareness of the existence of the night child (...) During the day, there was no anger or awkward looks between my father and me, because I was not aware of the night child's traumas and terrors. But the worse the night child got, the more necessary it was for the day child to excel; from the University of Colorado ski team, to Phi Beta Kappa, to being named Miss America, I thought I was the happiest person who ever lived."*

It was a young pastor in her church who sensed this dark secret. At the age of 24, he succeeded in breaking down the barricades she had built in her mind and the memories emerged. After that, she invested herself in her public career at an incredible rate in order to repress all these heavy traumatic memories a second time. At the age of 45, her life was turned upside down... From the age of 45 to 51, she went into a total tailspin, violent memories came up again, this time with physical pain and paralysis. Her body went completely off the rails, she could no longer move her arms or legs and she was hospitalised in a psychiatric institution. She wrote that she *could* never *have imagined that incest could have such repercussions! Who could believe that incest could have such effects on the body 30 years later?*

Marilyn Van Derbur had traumatic, dissociative amnesia for several years following the repeated rapes of her father. What she described later, from the age of 45 onwards, was a conversion disorder (or dissociative conversion disorder), i.e. a sudden loss of motor functions and sensitivity, without any medical explanation. For Marilyn Van Derbur, it was a paralysis most likely related to the sexual abuse she experienced as a child. She also writes in her book about her father: *He 'worked' on me night after night. Like a delicate piece of crystal shattered in concrete, my father stripped me of my own belief system and 'self', but also of my soul, which he broke into pieces."*

The autobiography of this Miss America contains both the glorious story of Marilyn Van Derbur's meteoric rise to fame, but also an essential source of information about child sexual abuse with its mechanism of dissociation and compartmentalisation of traumatic memories.[291]

The American actress and singer Laura Mackenzie also recounts that during her childhood she was regularly raped by her father, rock legend John Phillips... In 2009, she read a passage from her memoir 'High on Arrival' on the TV show 'The Oprah Winfrey Show': "I woke up that night coming out of a blackout, realising that I had been raped by my father... I don't remember when the abuse started or how it ended, was it the first time? Had it happened before? I don't know and I'm still in doubt. All I can say is that it was the first time I was aware of it. For a moment I was in my body, in this horrible reality, and then I went back into a blackout. Your father is supposed to protect you, he's supposed to protect you, not "fuck you."[292]

Mackenzie says she was 17 or 18 when she began to remember her father's rapes. At that time, she was known to millions as the child star of the sitcom One Day at a Time. No one realized what she was going through in private...

"Very early on I began to compartmentalise and repress difficult memories. And that is the root of all the difficult experiences that came afterwards."

She also said of her father: "I don't have any hatred for him. I understand that he's a really tortured man, somehow he gets that unhappiness through me (...) It's a kind of Stockholm syndrome where you start to love your abuser. I felt a great love for my father."

MK-Monarch victim Cathy O'Brien also describes how traumatic and dissociative memories work in a small child who experiences incest day after day: 'Even though I couldn't understand that what my father was doing to me was wrong, the pain and suffocation of his abuse was so unbearable that I developed a dissociative identity disorder. It was impossible to understand, there was no place in my mind to deal with such horror. So I compartmentalised my brain, small areas separated by amnesic barriers to block out memories of the abuse so that the rest of my mind could continue to function normally, as if nothing had happened... When I saw my father at the dinner table, I didn't remember the sexual abuse. But as soon as he unbuttoned his trousers, a part of me, the part of my brain that knew how to deal with this horrible abuse would wake up, it was as if a neural junction opened up so that this part of my mind could suffer my father over and over again, as needed... I certainly had a lot of experience in this "brain compartment" that was dealing with my father's abuse, but I didn't have the full range of perceptions, I had very limited perception, very limited vision."[293]

---

[291] Miss America By Day: Lessons Learned from Ultimate Betrayals and Unconditional Love" - Marilyn Van Derbur, 2003.

[292] "High on Arrivals: A Memoir" - Laura Mackenzie, 2011.

[293] "Mind-control out of control" - lecture by Cathy O'Brien and Mark Phillips, Granada Forum, 31/10/1996.

Régina Louf, Witness X1 in the Dutroux case, reported that a dissociated part of herself was never 'present' during the sexual abuse. This part of herself could therefore continue to live 'normally' without having to deal with the heavy memory of the abuse in her consciousness. Conversely, the part of her that was present and thus violated during the abuse, *Ginie*, was hardly aware of the life she led at school or in the family. It was as if *Ginie* was put aside until she resurfaced and took over when the abuser returned to Regina.[294]

In an article entitled *"Multiple Personality Disorder in Childhood"*, M.Vincent and M.R. Pickering give the example of a woman who described to them her experience at the age of 3 and 4 when she was repeatedly raped by her adoptive father. This is a description of the dissociative state with a passage into an alternative reality, where we find the splitting into two different selves: *"It became customary for her to remain passive and wait for the change of state of consciousness that would transport her from a heavy agony to a state of calm and even joy. She did this without even knowing that she was saving her own skin at every turn, feeding two 'selves' inside her, each unaware of the other's existence... Loving what is killing you is impossible. She couldn't do it. It's a hellish dilemma in the child's mind. So she left herself free to love, and left the other free to hate..."[295]*

In order to correctly diagnose a dissociative identity disorder, it is the alter personalities that are first looked for, not the traumatic amnesia itself. People with post-traumatic stress disorder, *borderline* personality disorder or other specified dissociative disorders may also experience occasional amnesia. Dissociative amnesia is caused by traumatic events that can be traced back through flashbacks, whereas the true amnesia in dissociative identity disorder is caused by alternating personalities that are quite distinct from each other.

4 - DISSOCIATIVE IDENTITY DISORDER (DID)

a/ Some historical cases

In 1793, Dr. Eberhardt Gmelin wrote the first detailed 87-page report on a case of 'dual personality', which he described as *'umgetaushte Persönlichkeit'* (personality exchange) in his publication *'Materialien für die Anthropologie'*. The case was taken up and described in detail in 1970 by Henri Hellenberger in *"Discovery of the Unconscious"*. It concerned a 21-year-old woman from Stuttgart who suddenly showed a new personality speaking French much better than German and adopting a complete change of behaviour. The two personalities, each speaking a different language, were completely unaware of each other. The "French woman" systematically remembered everything she had said or done, while the "German woman" forgot her actions. Gmelin had

---

[294] Zwijgen is voor daders - De getuigenis van X1" - Regina Louf, Houtekiet Publishing, 1998.

[295] *The Canadian Journal of Psychiatry"* / La Revue canadienne de psychiatrie, Vol 33(6), 08/1988.

discovered that he could easily trigger the personality change simply by a movement of the hands... This is reminiscent of the system of programmed trigger codes in MK slaves, as we shall see in Chapter 7.

In 1840, the psychotherapist Antoine Despine described the case of Estelle, an 11-year-old Swiss girl who had a paralysis with extreme sensitivity to touch. She had a second personality that could walk and play but could not tolerate her mother's presence, a reaction perhaps due to a traumatic memory related to her mother. Estelle showed a marked difference in behaviour from one personality to the other. In the late 19th and early 20th century, Dr. Pierre Janet reported a number of cases of multiple personalities in his patients: Léonie, Lucie, Rose, Marie and Marceline. Léonie had three, if not more, personalities including a child alter named "Nichette". In the case of Lucie, who was also described as having three personalities, there was an alter named "Adrienne" who regularly had flashbacks to a trauma from her early childhood. Rose had somnambulistic states and alternated between paralysis and the ability to walk.[296]

The first observation of a split personality popularised in the general public is known as the 'Lady of MacNish'. This famous case was published several times between 1816 and 1889. This young woman, whose real name was Mary Reynolds, alternated between two personalities between the ages of 19 and 35. Eventually one of the two personalities prevailed over the other. Her case is mentioned in the French philosopher and historian Hippolyte Taine's book *"De l'intelligence"*, and it was he who renamed Mary Reynolds the *"Lady of MacNish"*. The girl, who lived in the United States, was quiet, rather reserved and melancholic by nature and in good health. Her troubles began at the age of 18 with prolonged syncopations and she began to alternate between two very different personalities. One of them was very cheerful and sociable, a personality with a lively and cheerful character who was not afraid of anything and did not obey anyone. After about ten weeks she had a strange sort of syncope again and woke up with her original personality. She had no memory of the period that had just passed, but she had regained the same reserved and melancholic character. The alternation between these two personalities continued for years, often at night, while she was sleeping. When one of the personalities disappeared, Mary Reynolds found herself in exactly the same state as she had been the previous time, but without any memory of what had happened in the meantime. That is, with one personality or another, she had no idea what her second character was. If, for example, she was presented with someone in one of these states, she no longer recognised him in the other state. It was around the age of 35 that the sociable personality began to assert itself more often and for longer periods. This personality eventually took hold until 1853, when *Lady McNish* died at the age of 61.

Another known case from the 19th century is that of Felida, described by Dr. Azam who followed her from 1860 to 1890. Azam is the author of the book *"Hypnotism and Double Consciousness"* (1893) in which he describes the case of this young woman. In 1860, he made his patient known to the Surgical Society

---

[296] Diagnosis and Treatment of Multiple Personality Disorder " - Frank W. Putnam, 1989.

and the Academy of Medicine, and this case had a considerable influence on the question of the phenomenon of split personality. There is now a whole library on this case. Dr. Azam first met Félida in 1856 and followed her for 32 years. This is how he describes the personality changes: *"Almost every day, without any known cause or under the influence of an emotion, she is seized by what she calls her crisis, in fact, she enters her second state. Having witnessed this phenomenon hundreds of times, I can describe it accurately... I describe it now from what I have seen.*

Félida is sitting with a piece of sewing work on her lap; suddenly, without anything to predict it and after a more violent pain in the temples than usual, her head falls on her chest, her hands remain inactive and descend inertly along her body, she sleeps or seems to be sleeping, but a special sleep (...) After this time, Félida wakes up, but she is no longer in the intellectual state she was in when she fell asleep. Everything seems different. She raises her head and, opening her eyes, greets the newcomers with a smile, her face lights up and breathes cheerfulness, her speech is brief, and she continues, humming, the needlework that in the previous state she had begun. She stands up, her gait is agile and she hardly complains of the thousand pains which, a few minutes before, made her suffer (...) Her character is completely changed: from sadness she has become cheerful, for the slightest motive, she is moved into sadness or joy. In this life as in the other, her intellectual and moral faculties, though different, are unquestionably intact: no delusions, no false appraisals, no hallucinations. I would even say that in this second state, in this second condition, all his faculties appear more developed and more complete. This second life, in which physical pain is not felt, is far superior to the other; it is so above all by the considerable fact that Felida remembers not only what happened during the previous fits, but also her whole normal life, whereas during her normal life she has no memory of what happened during her fit."*[297]

Felida has the particularity of being amnesic in one direction only, her original personality having no memory of her second personality while the latter has access to all memories (we will come back to this in relation to MK-Monarch programming). Dr. Azam calls this phenomenon "periodic amnesia".

Gradually the second, more cheerful personality began to encroach on the first and eventually took over most of the time. When her old personality reappeared at times, she found herself confronted with large black holes where she had forgotten three quarters of her existence...

Félida episodically showed a third personality that Azam would only see emerge two or three times, Félida's husband had only observed her about thirty times in sixteen years. This third alter personality appeared in a state of unspeakable terror, her first words were: *"I'm afraid... I'm afraid...",* she didn't recognise anyone except her husband. Was it an alter traumatised by her memories? It should be noted that at that time, the link between dissociation of identity and trauma had not yet been established by the doctors who treated these patients.

---

[297] "Hypnotism and Double Consciousness" - Dr. Azam, 1893, p.43-44.

One of the most remarkable French cases is that of Louis Vivet. Between 1882 and 1889, he was studied by many scientific authors, notably Bourru and Burot who wrote in 1895: *"These facts of personality variation are less rare than we suppose"*. In 1882, Camuset noted in his report on Louis Vivet: *"We are tempted to believe that these cases are more numerous than one would suppose, in spite of the rather rare observations that we have"*. It was with Louis Vivet that the term *'multiple personality'* was first used to replace *'dual personality'*. Louis Vivet had six different personalities characterised by changes in memory, changes in character, and changes in sensitivity and behaviour. With each personality change, it was noted that his memories changed accordingly and that the personalities all ignored each other. This is how Bourru and Burot describe his personality change: *"All of a sudden, the subject's tastes have changed completely: character, language, physiognomy, everything is new. The subject is reserved in his dress. He no longer likes milk; it is, however, the only food he usually takes. The expression of his physiognomy has become softer, almost shy: the language is correct and polite. The patient who was once so arrogant is now remarkably polite, no longer on first-name terms and calls everyone 'Sir'. He smokes, but without passion. He has no opinion, neither in politics nor in religion, and these questions, he seems to say, are none of the business of an ignoramus like him. He is respectful and disciplined. His speech is much clearer than before the transfer, his reading aloud is remarkably clear, his pronunciation is quite distinct, he reads perfectly and writes fairly well. He is no longer the same character (...) In a few minutes the transformation is complete. It is no longer the same character: the constitution of the body has varied with the tendencies, and the feelings that translate it. It is a total transfer. The memory has been modified, the subject no longer recognizes either the places where he is, or the people around him with whom, a few moments ago, he was exchanging ideas. Such an unexpected and radical change was of a nature to astonish us and make us think (...) We repeated this application several times in the most diverse conditions and the result was constant. The same character reappeared, always identical to himself. It was a transformation, so to speak, mathematical, always the same for the same physical agent and the same point of application."*[298]

There is also the case of Clara Norton Fowler (under the pseudonym *Miss Christine Beauchamp*) whom Dr. Morton Prince, a Boston neurologist, met in 1898 when she was 23 years old. The use of hypnosis revealed the existence of four different personalities in her. In this particular case, it was reported that the girl had suffered many traumas during her childhood. *Miss Beauchamp* was a reserved and shy young woman, while her other personalities were outgoing, temperamental and angry. But the amnesic polarities between each personality were rather complicated: one was unaware of the existence of all the others, another was aware of the existence of only one other personality, and so on. One of her personalities showed total amnesia for the last six years before her appearance. A peculiarity in the case of *Miss Beauchamp* was the use of first

---

[298] *"Variations de la personnalité"* - H. Bourru and P. Burot, 1888, p.39-16.

names for the different alter, one of the personalities chose to call herself "Sally". Dr. Morton Prince considered Sally to be the most interesting personality and it was with her that he collaborated most readily. Prince looked for the one personality who was the authentic *Miss Beauchamp*, the true original personality. He came to the conclusion that this original personality had in fact disintegrated into several specific identities. Using hypnosis, he gradually dissolved the amnesiac barriers separating the alters and merged them together.[299]

Another case was reported in 1916 by Dr. James Hyslop and Dr. Walter Prince *in* the *Journal of the American Society for the Psychological Research*. This was Doris Fischer, born in Germany in 1889. This woman developed five distinct personalities, each with a particular name. The five alter personalities showed varied and very different characteristics from a psychological point of view. As is usually the case, they developed as a result of deep emotional shocks. Behind the personality of Doris, *"Real Doris"*, were:

- *Margaret:* The alter personality that was created by the first dissociative shock. An alter with the emotional and mental state of a five or six year old boy.

- *Sick Doris':* This is the alter personality that emerged after the second traumatic shock. *Sick Doris* had no memory of events or even any notion of verbal language, she did not recognise anyone and could no longer use everyday objects. She showed no affection.

- *Sleeping* Margaret": this alter personality seemed to sleep all the time, she hardly ever spoke except in a kind of foggy speech that was difficult to understand.

- *Sleeping Real* Doris: This was the name given by *Margaret* to the sleepwalking personality that was created at the age of eight. She had memories that *"Real Doris"* did not have.

Real Doris had no knowledge of the thoughts or actions of her secondary personalities. She could not remember anything that happened during the periods when another alter had emerged. The alter personalities merged one by one during the therapy sessions, leaving only the "Real Doris" in the end.

In 1928, another case of multiple personality was reported in the book *Multiple Personality* (W. Taylor and M. Martin, 1944). The patient was a man named Sorgel who lived in Bavaria and was epileptic. He showed two distinct organisations of consciousness: a criminal personality and an honest personality. The honest personality had almost no memory of his other life, while the criminal personality remembered both lives very well.[300]

Here again we find the notion of "one-way" amnesia, i.e. a deeper alter personality accesses all memories, while a surface personality remains totally unaware of its "other life"... A key point to which we will return in Chapter 7 on MK-Monarch programming.

---

[299] "La Femme Possédée", witches, hysterics and multiple personalities" - Jacques Antoine Malarewicz, 2005.

[300] "Multiple Personality and Channeling" - Rayna L. Rogers, Jefferson Journal of Psychiatry: Vol. 9: Iss. 1, Article 3, 1991.

The most publicised and therefore best-known cases *of* the 20th century are those of Christine Costner Sizemore (*The 3 Faces of Eve*), Shirley Ardell Mason (*Sybil*), Truddi Chase (*When Rabbit Howls*) and Billy Milligan (*The Man with 24 Personalities*).

The story of Christine Costner Sizemore was told in a book written by her psychiatrists, Corbett Thipgen and Hervey M. Cleckly. The sweet, shy young woman had come to them because she was suffering from terrible migraines that seemed incurable. During her therapy, a new rebellious and turbulent personality emerged. The first personality had no awareness of the existence of this other alter, the turbulent one, which was perfectly aware of the existence of the first. This case of multiple personality was brought to the screen by Nunaly Johnson in 1957, in a film entitled *"The Three Faces of Eve"*. The actress Joanne Woodward played the three personalities, *Eve White*, a docile and shy young woman, *Eve Black*, the turbulent seductress and finally *Jane*, a much more balanced personality, a sort of fusion of the two *Eves*. This film is one of the few that did not fall into the stereotypical portrayal of a T.D.I. with an alter criminal personality. The 1957 film version is introduced by journalist Alistair Cooke who states: *'This is a true story. You've often seen films that say such a thing. Sometimes this means that a certain Napoleon did exist, but that any resemblance between his real life and the film in question would be a miracle. Our story is true. It is the story of a kindly, self-effacing housewife who, in 1951, while living in her native Georgia, frightened her husband into behaving in a most unusual way. This is not uncommon: we all have our whims, we all repress an urge to ape someone we admire. One writer has said that in every fat man there sleeps a thin man. In this young housewife, frighteningly, two strong personalities were literally struggling to impose their will on her. It was a case of "multiple personality". You read about it in books, but few psychiatrists have seen it themselves. Until Dr. Thigpen and Dr. Cleckley of the Medical College of Georgia came across a woman with one more personality than Dr. Jekyll. In 1953 they presented this case to the American Psychiatric Association, a case that has become a classic in psychiatric literature. So this film was not about a screenwriter's imagination. The truth itself outweighed the fiction. Everything you will see actually happened to the woman known as "Eve White". Much of the dialogue comes from the clinical notes of Dr. Luther.*

However, the film, which shows only two personalities (which eventually merge), does not reflect the true reality, since Christine Costner in fact developed more than twenty different personalities, as she would later reveal in her memoirs, published only a year later under a pseudonym.

During the 1970s, *Sybil*'s case is certainly the one that most publicised dissociative identity disorder. Shirley Ardell Mason was a 25 year old woman who, because of visions, nightmares and terrible memories, went to see Dr. Cornelia Wilbur. It was then that six different personalities emerged during therapy. Shirley discovered that she had been severely humiliated and sexually abused by her mother as a child. This case could have remained in the shadows like many others, but Flora Rheta Schreiber published a novel based on Shirley's true story in 1973, a novel called *"Syblil"* which became a bestseller. Following this huge success, a few years later in 1976, Daniel Petries produced a film based on the novel. A film with the same name, *Sybil*, which was also a great success. For many therapists, this case marked the history of I.D.T. There was a before and an after to Sybil, leading to a whole controversy that still surrounds this mysterious multiple personality disorder today...

Truddi Chase, born in 1935, is the author of an autobiography entitled *"When Rabbit Howls"* (1987), and her case was also the subject of a television film: *"Voices Whithin The Lives of Truddi Chase"*, broadcast in 1990 by *ABC* (*American Broadcasting Company*). It was during therapy that it was discovered that Truddi had a multiple personality. She was abused from the age of two until she was a teenager. Her stepfather physically and sexually abused her while her mother neglected her. She always remembered the sexual abuse and mistreatment, but could never recall it in detail until she began therapy with Dr. Robert Phillips. Truddi Chase always refused to merge her many personalities, believing them to be a cooperating team. She died in March 2010 at the age of 75.

Another historical case of multiple personality is that of Billy Milligan, born in 1955 in the United States. In 1975, Milligan was arrested for several crimes including rape. This case was over-publicised at the time of the trial because of the particular psychological profile of the accused... His rape trial caused outrage when the defence pleaded not guilty on the grounds of *multiple personality*. Milligan claimed that it was not he who was present during the sexual assaults on female students, but an alter lesbian personality. The public obviously found it very difficult to believe the rapist's version of events. The Milligan case was studied for many years and reported in detail by Daniel Keyes, Milligan's biographer. Keyes spent sixteen years of his life gathering information, investigating and interviewing *"the Professor"* (Miligan's multiple alter personalities merged into one personality) as well as the people who were close to him. The result was two books: *"The Minds of Billy Milligan"* and *"The Milligan Wars"*, available in French under the titles: *"Billy Milligan, l'homme aux 24 personnalités"* and *"Les mille et une vies de Billy Milligan"*.

In Keyes' biography of Milligan, it is stated that his split personality occurred when he was constantly humiliated and beaten by his stepfather who also sexually abused him. Milligan was diagnosed with a total of 24 personalities. Some of these alter personalities had criminal and destructive tendencies, which got him into severe trouble. On the other hand, his other personalities showed extraordinary abilities and skills. *Arthur'* was one of his alter personalities who taught himself medicine and spoke several languages, and it was he who managed to connect all the alter personalities: *Arthur acted as a mediator in the internal system*. Other alter personalities had a real artistic talent for painting, each with a different style. There were also alter personalities who were the age of a child, a common occurrence in I.D.T. In his biography, Milligan explains the advantages of having multiple personalities, including child alter: *'It gives you a new perspective on the world. It gives you a whole new perspective on the world. A whole new perspective that allows you to see things that someone else wouldn't."*

In 1979, Billy Milligan was committed to the State Hospital for the Criminally Insane in Lima, Ohio. There, he suffered a real hell: racketeering, beatings, electroshock, chemical straitjacket... He remained in Lima until 1983, when he returned to the psychiatric hospital in Athens where he progressed in his therapy and finally managed to merge all his alter personalities. This is what he says about the fusion (integration, concepts that will be developed later) of his alter personalities: *"I was told that the union of all my parts would be even stronger than the sum of my individual personalities. But in my case this is not true, the union of my personalities is less strong."*

Despite the fusion of his alter, his mental state remained very precarious and unstable due to the many years during which he suffered prison, psychiatric internment, psychological and physical attacks, death threats, but also political instrumentalisation by senators, magistrates, hospital or prison directors... his recovery was therefore far from being favoured by a climate of security and stability. There were reports of sadistic behaviour by 'nursing staff' and everywhere there seemed to be brutality and instrumentalisation around him. Daniel Keyes denounces the American prison system for its opportunism, the corruption within its leadership and its inability to deal effectively with sensitive cases such as that of Billy Milligan.

A case that is less well known because it is not criminal and is much less publicised is that of Robert Oxnam. This man was the president for more than ten years of the *Asia Society,* a prestigious American cultural institution. Robert Oxnam is a specialist in Chinese culture and language and has accompanied people like Bill Gates, Warren Buffet and George Bush on their trips to Asia. He is the author of an autobiography entitled *"A Fractured Mind"* in which he reveals that he suffers from a dissociative identity disorder. In 2005, he was featured [301]on *CBS News' 60 Minutes* to expose this particular mental disorder.

Robert Oxnam had a very rigid upbringing and there was a lot of pressure on him to succeed socially and professionally. His father was a university president and his grandfather was a bishop and president of the World Council of Churches (WCC). Following a brilliant education, Oxnam was soon in the limelight in the mainstream media and soon gained a prestigious and elite position. By the age of thirty, he was appointed president of the *Asia Society.* Robert Oxnam was on *top of the world* but inside him there was a mixture of depression, anger and rage. On the one hand, there was this glittering social and professional success, and on the other a permanent malaise and depression that was getting worse. In the 1980s, Oxnam was treated for alcoholism and bulimia, and it was during this period that his first marriage collapsed. Visits to a psychiatrist for his addiction problems and recurring blackouts did not improve anything. He sometimes woke up with bruises and wounds on his body without any idea of what might have caused them or even in what context they might have happened. One day he was lost in a crowd in Central Station in New York, he was in a trance-like state and he heard voices nagging him, telling him that he was bad, that he was the worst person who ever lived. In 1990, during a therapy

---

[301] *Inside A Fractured Mind"* - Morley Safer, CBS News, 09/2005.

session with Dr. Jeffrey Smith, Robert Oxnam suddenly became someone else... His psychiatrist reports that there was a complete change in his voice, in his attitude and in his movements. During one session, Dr. Smith reported that Oxnam's hands were *like claws*, he was in a terrible rage. This anger came from a little boy named *"Tommy"*. When Smith told Oxnam what had happened during the session, Oxnam said that he did not know this *Tommy* and had no recollection of what had happened in the therapist's office. It was then that Dr. Smith realized that he might be dealing with a case of multiple personality. On hearing of this possible diagnosis, Robert Oxnam reacted strongly, saying: *"That's rubbish, I've seen Sybil, I'm not like Sybil!"*

In the course of the therapy, eleven distinct alter personalities emerged independently of each other. Among them were *"Tommy"*, an angry young boy, the *"Witch"*, a terrifying alter or *"Bobby" and "Robby"*. *Bob'* was the dominant personality, i.e. the 'host' personality: the public face, in this case an intellectual working at the *Asia Society*. In his public life, Robert Oxnam went about his business, meeting with high dignitaries like the Dalai Lama. But this public life gave no hint of his profound personality disorder... Childhood trauma is usually the cause of I.D.D., and Oxnam seems to be no exception. During his therapy, an alter named *"Baby"* reported memories of childhood abuse. These were severe sexual and physical abuses, always accompanied by the words: *"You are bad, this is punishment."*[302]

Did Robert Oxnam experience ritual abuse? Was he subjected to intentional personality splitting as a child? Was he a member of one of those elitist families who practised systematic mind control on his descendants? Where did the terrifying alter *'Witch'* come from? Did he undergo mental programming in preparation for the future elitist career into which he was quickly propelled? Still, his case demonstrates how an individual can have a dissociative identity disorder while conducting business in a high position and maintaining a completely normal public façade. Is this what Fritz Springmeier is referring to when he speaks of *totally undetectable mind-controlled slaves*, to describe these voluntarily split and programmed individuals?

b/ Definition of the I.D.T.

In the last thirty years, the assessment and treatment of dissociative disorders have been improved by better clinical identification, numerous research and academic publications and specialised instruments. International publications from clinicians and researchers have appeared in many countries, including clinical case studies, psychophysiology, neurobiology, neuroimaging, etc. All these publications confirm the existence of dissociative disorders. All these publications confirm the existence of I.D.T. and thus give it a validity comparable to other well-established psychiatric diagnoses. A 2001 study entitled *"An examination of the diagnostic validity of* dissociative *identity*

---

[302] A Fractured Mind: My Life with Multiple Personality Disorder " - Robert B. Oxnam, 2006.

disorder" by David H. Gleaves, Mary C. May and Etzel Cardena demonstrates that this psychiatric disorder is to be taken very seriously.[303]

Dissociative Identity Disorder has had many names throughout history: "dual existence", "dual personality", "dual consciousness", "personality state", "personality transference", "dual personality", "plural personality", "dissociated personality" (DSM-I, 1952), "multiple personality", "split personality", "alternating identity" and "multiple personality disorder" (DSM-IV, 1980).

It is a complex and chronic post-traumatic dissociative disorder that develops, in most cases, as a result of repeated severe sexual and/or physical abuse in early childhood. It is a disturbance in the functions of identity, memory or consciousness. The impairment may be sudden or progressive, transient or chronic. The person's usual identity or personality is then forgotten and a new personality (an alter) is imposed. This is often accompanied by memory impairment with important events not being able to be recalled (DSM III, 1987). Dr. Richard Kluft defines an alter as follows: *"It functions at the same time as a receiver, processor, storage centre for perceptions, experiences and their elaboration in connection with events and thoughts of the past and/or present and even the future. It has a sense of its own identity and ideation as well as an ability to initiate thought and action processes."*

Most patients with IDD will also suffer from various mental disorders such as chronic depression, post-traumatic stress, anxiety, severe addictions, eating disorders, narcissistic disorders and somatisation. They may be diagnosed with *borderline* personality disorder, schizophrenia, bipolar or psychotic disorder if the dissociation and presence of the alter personalities has not been detected or even investigated. These misdiagnoses occur especially if the assessment interview does not contain questions about dissociation and trauma or focuses only on the most apparent co-morbid problems (i.e. the associated disorders listed above).

The Diagnostic and Statistical Manual of Mental Disorders, DSM-IV (2000), defines the following criteria for Dissociative Identity Disorder:

A. Presence of two (or more) identities or personality states - each with its own relatively permanent way of perceiving, relating to, thinking about the environment and oneself.

B. At least two of these identities or personality states take control - repeatedly - of the person's behaviour.

C. Inability to remember very personal information: significant forgetfulness that must be distinguished from what is commonly forgotten.

D. The disturbance is not due to the direct physiological effects of a substance (e.g. drug or alcohol intoxication) or to a general medical problem (e.g. complex partial epilepsies). Note: in children, the symptoms are not due to imaginary companions or other fantasy games.

The individual is unable to recall important personal information and has memory gaps that are too large and deep for simple forgetfulness. Many patients

---

[303] Guidelines for the treatment of dissociative identity disorder in adults (2011), International Society for the Study of Trauma and Dissociation (ISSTD).

also complain of severe migraines. This disorder can lead to *dissociative fugue,* which is a sudden and unexpected departure from home or work, accompanied by an inability to remember the past. There is confusion about personal identity or the adoption of a new identity (partial or complete).

In his book *"Discovery of the Unconscious"*, Henri F. Ellenberger has established, on the basis of various historical cases, a classification of the different aspects that these split personalities could present:

1: Simultaneous multiple personalities.

2: Successive multiple personalities:

a/ mutually aware of each other.

b/ mutually amnesic.

c/ one-way amnesia.

Each personality lives with its own personal and individual history, its own memories, its own character and they may even have a different name. These personalities can also know and interact with each other within a complex inner world. It is an internal system where the alters can coexist peacefully but conflicts of varying severity can also divide them. In most cases, there is a dominant personality, called the "primary personality" or "host personality", which is surrounded by a series of secondary personalities, usually organised hierarchically.

The two largest case studies on this subject are Dr. Frank Putnam's *"The clinical phenomenology of multiple personality disorder: Review of 100 recent cases"* (*Journal of clinical Psychiatry* 47 - 1986) and Dr. Colin Ross' study of 236 cases.

When asked what they think they are, alter personalities say: a child (86%), a helper or assistant (84%), a demon (29%), a person of the opposite sex (63%) or they name another person (alive) (28%) or a dead family member (21%).[304]

German therapists Angelika Vogler and Imke Deister have listed the types of alter personalities frequently found in patients with IDD.:[305]

- *Host/Hostess:* The primary function of the host or hostess is to ensure the proper functioning of the multiple system in daily life. Their age usually corresponds to the physical age of the body and their sexual identity corresponds to the sex of the body. The host/hostess usually knows little or nothing about the existence of the other personalities in the system and has large memory gaps. The host/hostess usually comes across as a very reliable person, but their basic temperament is often depressive. As we will see in Chapter 7 on Monarch programming, it is these 'Host' personalities that serve as the front person, the public persona, in MK slaves.

- *The Observer:* In almost every system there is at least one observer who keeps an eye on everything that is going on and therefore has no memory gaps.

---

[304] Multiple Personality Disorder - Demons and Angels or Archetypal aspects of the inner self " - Dr. Haraldur Erlendsson, 2003.

[305] Imke Deistler und Angelika Vogler: Einführung in die Dissoziative Identitätsstörung - Multiple Persönlichkeit, Junfermann Verlag Paderborn, 2005 - Translation: www.multiples-pages.net.

This personality reacts rather rationally and does not show feelings, as it needs to keep a great distance from the inner and outer world in order to fulfil its role. For this reason the observer does not emerge in the foreground (does not take control of the body) but can make contact with different alterations in the system.

- *The Protector:* The protective personalities of a system emerge and take control of the body whenever an alter or the system feels threatened by a certain situation. These protective personalities can be very aggressive and it is important to understand and value their protective function.

- *Personalities who identify with the torturers:* These are the personalities who remain loyal to the cult. These personalities identify with their tormentors and their values. Their function is often to punish other alter personalities (e.g. by self-mutilation) who wish to break contact with the cult or who would, for example, like to reveal information about the cult in a therapy session. If the multiple person is still in contact with the cult, these alter personalities can pass on the contents of the therapy session to them without the other personalities in the system noticing.

- *Captive' children and adolescents:* In almost every multiple system there are children. They have remained captive for a certain period of time. There are children who retain a certain age for a long period of time while others mature. It is also possible that an alter-child who has kept the same age for a long time starts to grow old later on.

An amazing feature of I.D.T. is that within the same individual, alter personalities can show remarkable physiological differences in visual acuity, in reaction to medication and psychotropic drugs, in allergies, in heart rate, in blood pressure, in muscle tension, in immune function, but also in the electroencephalographic tracing. Irrational physiological differences since these alter personalities share the same physical body.

Already in 1887, Pierre Janet had demonstrated that some individuals could develop several psychic centres, each with its own particularities and activities. He had already named these dissociated centres "personalities". Janet worked with what were then called 'hysterics', women whose different personalities coexisted and operated at a subconscious level, only occasionally taking control of normal consciousness during hypnosis or automatic writing sessions. Janet had discovered that the subconscious personalities of these 'hysterics' were created in response to a traumatic event that had settled in the subconscious to become the seed of new personalities. With this understanding, Janet's therapeutic system finally became effective in understanding and treating this disorder in which a variety of personalities emerged spontaneously to interact with the outside world. From this point on, the *Dissociation/Trauma* model was established in psychotherapy and it began to appear in case descriptions of multiple personalities.[306]

In 1993, while researching multiple personality disorder, Dr. Adam Crabtree wrote: "The recognition of the phenomenon of dissociation as a means of treating a traumatic episode through the creation of multiple psychic centres,

---

[306] Multiple Personality Before "Eve" - Adam Crabtree, Journal "Dissociation", Vol.1 N°1, 03/1993.

leads to effective psychotherapy of multiple personality disorder. The etiological role of child abuse has not been recognised at all until modern times. But the statistical evidence of crimes against children from the late 19th century may offer a fruitful avenue for research. An examination of the historical cases raises questions about the equivocality of the multiple personality phenomenon; it also reveals data that have not yet been fully recognised by modern clinicians."[307]

I.D.D. develops during childhood. As we have seen, the process of dissociation is a natural protective mechanism in the face of a psychologically insurmountable situation. Just as a circuit breaker prevents a short circuit, this human function allows us to survive severe and repetitive traumas so that we can continue to live in a relatively normal way. This process has the effect of encapsulating memories, affects, sensations or even beliefs in order to mitigate their effects on the child's overall development. Depending on the severity of the trauma, the impact of dissociation can go as far as personality splitting. I.D.T. appears to be the most extreme level of dissociation. Pierre Janet himself recognised that *"extreme dissociation"* led to the creation of a multiple personality. The origin of this disorder, in at least 80% of the cases treated by psychiatry, lies in childhood trauma, particularly before the age of 5. Dr. Philip M. Coons compared twenty patients with I.D.D. with a control group of twenty people of the same sex and age, non-dissociated, non-schizophrenic, non-psychotic. While two people in the control group had suffered from childhood neglect or sexual abuse, 85% of the IDD patients had experienced physical and/or sexual abuse.[308]

Dr. Richard Kluft finds similar data linking I.D.T. to early childhood trauma: "In two large groups, 97% and 98% had experienced physical and sexual abuse in childhood, or psychological abuse and neglect."[309]

Dr. James P. Bloch has written that childhood trauma is now seen as a primary etiological factor in the formation of dissociative disorders.[310]

According to Dr. Colin Ross, *"the degree of dissociation is clearly related to the severity and chronicity of the abuse"*. Ross considers that, on statistical average, patients who have developed IDD would have suffered physical abuse for fifteen years and sexual abuse for almost thirteen years.[311]

We can therefore understand why many victims of satanic ritual abuse have developed a dissociative identity disorder. Indeed, DID is certainly a strong indicator of a history of ritual abuse. Dr. Frank Putnam stated in 1989: *"I am struck by the level of extreme sadism reported by most victims with I.D.D. Many*

---

[307] Ibid.

[308] "Psychophysiologic Aspects of Multiple Personality Disorder: A Review" - Philip M. Coons, Journal "Dissociation", 03/1988.

[309] Kluft, R.P. (1988). The dissociative disorders. In: J.A. Talbott, R.E. Hales & S.C. Yudofsky (Eds.). Textbook of Psychiatry, 557-585. Washington, DC: American Psychiatric Press.

[310] Assessment and Treatment of Multiple Personality and Dissociative Disorders" - James P. Bloch, 1991, p.3.

[311] Multiple Personality Disorder, Diagnosis, Clinical Features and Treatment " - Colin Ross, 1989.

of them have told me that they have a history of ritual abuse. Many of them told me that they had been sexually abused by groups of people, forced into prostitution by their families, or offered as sexual bait for their mothers' lovers. After working with a number of patients with IDD, it became clear that severe and repeated abuse in childhood is a major cause of multiple personality disorder."

Traumatic memories can therefore be "stored", or "encapsulated", in an alter personality and the host personality will have no awareness of this reality. It is when this alter personality emerges that it will be able to express and transmit this memory (usually by physically and emotionally reliving the trauma, a phenomenon known as abreaction). It will describe in great detail how the abuse happened, since it was he (or she) who experienced it directly, while the host personality was "deactivated"/dissociated to make room for the alter. Dr. Adam Crabtree reports that in 1926, the American psychologist Henry Herbert Goddard published a report describing the treatment of a young woman, Bernice R., diagnosed with multiple personality. Goddard used hypnosis to try to merge two personalities. He did this by putting one of the alter personalities into a trance state in an attempt to make it aware of the existence of the other in order to make them merge. Through this process, Goddard did a very good job of emotionally releasing the patient's traumatic memories. Among these memories, the young woman had clear and persistent memories of her father's rapes. Unfortunately Goddard classified these memories of sexual abuse as hallucinations, explaining that the incestuous acts that allegedly happened at the age of 14 were not mentioned by Bernice until she was 19. This tells us that Henry Goddard had no real knowledge of the functioning of dissociation and traumatic amnesia. He was therefore validating the frivolous theory *of "hysterical sexual hallucination"*... A theory that is still used today to discredit victims, as *"hysteria"* has given way to *"false memory syndrome"* (which we will develop in Chapter 10).[312]

It will take some time before the issue of childhood trauma is really taken into account and recognised as one of the major causes of personality splitting. Nowadays many clinicians have the idea that I.D.T. is a very rare disorder or simply do not recognise its existence. This is primarily due to the lack of information and training of clinicians about dissociation, dissociative disorders and the effects of psychological trauma; therefore, this diagnosis is rarely considered, let alone accepted. However, I.D.D. and dissociative disorders are not uncommon. Studies in North America, Europe and Turkey have shown that between 1 and 5% of patients in adult and adolescent psychiatric wards, as well as in substance abuse, eating disorder and obsessive-compulsive disorder (OCD) wards may meet the diagnostic criteria for BDD. But many of these patients will never be clinically diagnosed with a dissociative disorder.[313]

---

[312] Multiple Personality Before "Eve" - Adam Crabtree, Journal "Dissociation", Vol.1 N°1, 03/1993.

[313] Guidelines for the treatment of dissociative identity disorder in adults (2011), International Society for the Study of Trauma and Dissociation (ISSTD).

In his book *Cult and Ritual Abuse,* Dr. James Randall Noblitt gives some statistics on the recognition of I.D.T. in the professional psychiatric community:

A 1994 study surveyed 1120 psychologists and psychiatrists employed by the *Veterans* Administration, 80% of whom agreed with the diagnosis of I.D.D.[314]

Another study conducted in 1995 on 180 Canadian psychiatrists reported that 66.1% of them believed in the validity of the diagnosis of I.D.D. against 27.8% who did not validate this diagnosis, 3.3% were undecided.[315]

In 1999, a survey of 301 psychiatrists showed that 15% thought that I.D.D. should not be included in the DSM, 43% thought it should be included with reservations and 35% thought it should be included without reservations. On the question of evidence for the scientific validity of the diagnosis of I.D.D., 20% responded that there was little or no evidence of validity, 51% responded that there was partial evidence of validity and 21% felt that there was clear evidence that validated I.D.D.[316]

In 1999, the Washington State Supreme Court ruled that the diagnosis of I.D.D. met the criteria for the *Frye* standard (the *Frye test* is used to determine the admissibility of scientific evidence in a legal setting). This means that expert testimony on I.D.D. is admissible in federal court because it has been determined that this diagnosis is generally recognised in the mental health community.[317]

There are now a few tests that can be used to detect the presence of dissociative disorders in a patient. The *Dissociative Experiences* Scale (DES*) was* developed by psychiatrists Eve Bernstein Carlson and Frank W. Putnam in 1986 (Appendix 3). Putnam in 1986 (Appendix 3). Another test is *the Multidimensional Inventory of Dissociation (*MID) developed by Paul Dell. This test is of the same type as the previous one but with many more items. However, these tests do not allow a diagnosis to be made; it is only through more structured professional interviews that an I.D.D. can be established or excluded.

c/ I.D.T. and neurology

In recent decades, medical imaging tools to study brain function have improved considerably. Techniques such as magnetic resonance imaging (MRI) and positron emission tomography (PET) allow, among other things, to visualise the activation of different brain areas during certain tasks or behaviours.

---

[314] "Belief in the existence of multiple personality disorder among psychologists and psychiatrists" - Dunn, Paolo, Ryan, Van Fleet, Journal of clinical psychology, 1994.

[315] "Psychiatrists attitudes to multiple personality disorder: A questionnaire study" - F.M. Mai, The Canadian Journal of Psychiatry, 1995.

[316] "Attitudes toward DSM-IV dissociative disorders diagnoses among board-certified American psychiatrists" - Pope, Oliva, Hudson, Bodkin, Gruber, American Journal of Psychiatry, 1999.

[317] U.S. v. Greene, 1999 / "Dissociative identity disorder and criminal responsibility" Farmer, Middleton, Devereux, in "Forensic aspects of dissociative identity disorder", Sachs & Galton, 2008.

In November 2001, researchers in Melbourne, Australia, came together in what the *Herald Sun* described at the time as "the world's first study" of multiple personality disorder. The purpose of the meeting was to try to resolve the controversy within the psychiatric scientific community. The study concluded that *'individuals with multiple personality disorder (MPD) do not fake their identity changes'*. The brain waves of individuals diagnosed with MPD were compared with those of actors simulating personality changes. Although the actors convincingly reproduced identity changes, the researchers found that there were distinct changes in the brain waves of those who actually changed their personalities, while these changes did not appear in the brains of those who simulated a different personality.[318]

This same type of comparative study was conducted by Annedore Hopper and Dr. Joseph Ciorciari at Swiburne University in Victoria, Australia. Five patients with IDD and five professional actors participated in the experiment. The study clearly showed an electroencephalographic (EEG) difference between the host and alter personalities in the patients with I.D.D., while this EEG change was not seen in the actors who were simulating, for example, a child's personality. For Dr. Joseph Ciorciari, this study demonstrates that patients with I.D.D. do not simulate their different personalities, he said: *"Patients with I.D.D. were compared with professional actors who reproduced the age and personality corresponding to each of the patients' alter personalities and their host personalities. Significant EEG differences between the alter and host personalities were not found when the actors played the personalities, which is clear physiological evidence for the authenticity of I.D.D. "[319]*

In December 1999, the BBC's *Tomorrow's World* broadcast a report showing a neurological study of DID conducted by Dr. Guochuan Tsai (*Harvard Medical School*). For the first time, a patient with dissociative identity disorder was subjected to an MRI scan during the transition from one personality to another. Louise, the patient who volunteered for this study, had developed, with the help of Dr. Condie (her therapist), an ability to voluntarily trigger personality changes. This ability to change personalities on demand made it possible to observe first-hand how her brain functions in the MRI scanner as it transitions from one alter personality to another. Dr. Tsai says, *"Before we didn't have an MRI scanner, so we couldn't do this kind of study quickly and correctly. Also, we didn't have the right subject who could control the alter personality changes. Because we need to have that change during the MRI.*

The scan showed significant changes in the brain just as Louise was switching personalities. Curiously, the hippocampus, an area associated with long-term memory, shut down during the switch and reactivated once the transition was complete. A control test was also carried out: Louise was asked to simply imagine herself as an eight-year-old girl, without switching to another alter. The test did not show any of the changes seen previously. For Dr. Tsai, this

---

[318] "Programmed to Kill: The Politics of Serial Murder" - David McGowan, 2004, p.xiv.

[319] EEG Coherence and Dissociative Identity Disorder ", Journal "Trauma & Dissociation", Vol.3, 2002.

is a sufficient scientific basis for further research. For Louise, it is a proof to be given to all those people who deny the existence of I.D.T. Following the documentary, Dr Raj Persaud told the BBC: *"Like most psychiatrists, before this study came out, I was very sceptical about multiple personality disorder. This is because in England we make this diagnosis less frequently than in the US. In England, we generally think that these people can pretend to have this disorder to get some attention for themselves. But the important and very persuasive thing about this new study is that when this woman was in the scanner and she switched to another personality, there was a significant change in her brain activity, as opposed to when she just imagines having another personality. This is evidence that multiple personality disorder is not just faked but really exists."*

Neurological research has shown that repeated childhood abuse has a significant and measurable effect on the volume of certain brain areas such as the hippocampus and the amygdala complex. A 2006 study found that the volume of the hippocampus and amygdala is significantly smaller in people diagnosed with I.D.D. compared to a group of subjects without I.D.D.[320]

A study published in 2003 entitled *"One brain, two selves"* compared the activated areas of the brain of two different personalities of a subject with IDD. The brain areas of 11 women with I.D.D. were explored using a neuroimaging technique, PET (positron emission tomography). Following some therapeutic work, the women were able, like Louise, to control the personality changes required for the study. During the PET scan, the subjects listened to recordings with autobiographical and traumatic content in two different personality states. Only one of the two personalities studied confirmed that the content was autobiographical as it was the personality that had itself experienced the trauma, the other personality had no recollection of having experienced the trauma. The results of the study showed that this different perception of the same content is found in the different activated areas of the brain: the alter personality who recognises the content because it is recorded in his memory, shows a different brain activation profile than the alter personality who does not recognise the content. For the researchers, such a difference in the level of activity of certain brain areas cannot be explained simply by the imagination or by a change in the subject's mood.[321]

When we are inundated with danger stimuli in a traumatic situation, the collaboration of the amygdala complex with the hippocampus is strongly disrupted. The incomplete processing of information means that it is not integrated into a spatio-temporal order and therefore remains as isolated memories.

Research into brain physiological processes in traumatized people using computer tomography makes it possible to locate areas of the brain where changes in metabolism, in this case glucose, take place. With this imaging

---

[320] "Hippocampal and Amygdala Volumes in Dissociative Identity Disorder, American Journal of Psychiatry" - Vermetten, Schmahl, Lindner, Loewenstein, Bremner, 2006.

[321] *One Brain, Two Selves" NeuroImage 20* - Reinders, Nijenhuis, Paans, Korf, Willemsen, J.den Boer, 2003.

technique, it is possible to visualise the increase in glucose consumption in certain brain areas and deduce which areas are more or less activated. In a study conducted by Bessel Van der Kolk, traumatised people were asked to remember a personal trauma. Compared to non-traumatised people (control group) who were asked to recall a serious event in their lives, the traumatised people showed significantly higher activation of the amygdala complex, the insula, the medial aspect of the temporal lobe and the right visual cortex. During the evocation of traumatic memories, the right hemisphere of the brain was particularly active, while a decrease in activation of the left hemisphere was observed. The decrease was particularly pronounced in the lower frontal lobe and in Broca's area, which plays an important role in language. Professor Van der Kolk deduced from these results that the brain cannot fully process and understand a traumatic stimulus because Broca's area, which is responsible for verbalisation, is inhibited. These neurological studies show us how physiologically difficult, if not impossible, it is for victims of deep trauma to verbalise and explain clearly what they have experienced or are experiencing when a traumatic memory resurfaces. Van der Kolk explains that *"when these people relive their traumatic experiences, their frontal lobes are impacted, with the result that thinking and speaking are damaged. They are no longer able to communicate to others what is going on (...) The imprint of the trauma does not lie at the verbal level, at the level of the part of the brain related to understanding. It is much deeper in the amygdala, the hippocampus, the hypothalamus and the brainstem, areas that are only marginally connected to thinking and cognition."[322]*

Traumatic experiences are therefore not recorded via language, but mainly via the memory of bodily sensations, through smells and sounds. When a stimulus (such as physical contact, certain smells, motor noises, screams) activates the memory of a traumatic event, there is not necessarily a memory retrieval with narrative content. While narrative memory is capable of integration and adaptation, non-narrative traumatic memories seem to be inflexible, automatically activated and totally dissociated from the event. This dissociation of traumatic memories explains why they do not fade over time, but retain their initial strength and become what Van der Kolk calls *'soul parasites'* (we will see in the next chapter that these isolated traumatic memories are more likely to be related to *'soul fragments'*). The information about traumatic experiences is present in the memory at some level, but is therefore completely dissociated from the narrative memory. Without further processing to integrate them into the narrative and analytical memory, i.e. the autobiographical memory, these traumatic memories can potentially be reactivated negatively throughout life. They will manifest themselves, for example, in hypermnesia, flashbacks, hyperactivity, amnesia, emotional disturbances and avoidance behaviour. In trauma-informed MK programming, it is these unconscious traumatic memories that allow access to alter personalities through stimulus codes and trigger certain commands implanted during the trauma in the same way.

---

[322] Bessel van der Kolk wants to transform the treatment of trauma" - Mary Sykes Wylie, Psychotherapy Networker Magazine, 2004.

Physiological studies of the brain are now able to explain why traumatised people often cannot place their traumatic memories in time. When they do, they experience the traumatic memory as if it were happening in the present. Some research also explains why therapeutic methods that rely solely on verbal language are generally not effective in treating trauma. Effective psychotherapy must take into account narrative and explicit memory (located in the left hemisphere of the brain) but also implicit memory related to feelings and emotions (located in the right hemisphere of the brain). Events that are only recorded as implicit memory must be integrated to become explicit and autobiographical memory. In other words, the negative intrusions of these memories should be replaced by an integrated, coherent and chronological memory so that it no longer harms the person.[323]

d/ I.D.T. and schizophrenia

At the phenomenological level, there is a significant overlap between the symptoms of dissociative disorders (particularly I.D.D.) and schizophrenia. These similarities create confusion in hospital settings and therefore lead to misdiagnosis with significant repercussions for patients.

Dissociation caused by a split into several personalities involves the separation of normally well-integrated structures such as sensory perception, memory, attention, thought; whereas in schizophrenia these processes remain integrated, they are simply deteriorated. In I.D.D., the link with reality remains intact, whereas in schizophrenia there is an almost total break with reality. In I.D.D. the splitting of the personality is done by a division within the person, just like a cell division, as if each cell were a new and different personality. In schizophrenia, this division occurs between the 'inner self' and the outer world, the connection with reality is lost and the person lives in his or her own world.[324]

One study showed that a group of patients diagnosed with schizophrenia by a psychiatrist or psychologist, to whom you give a standardised interview related to dissociative symptoms, showed that 35-40% of these patients, supposedly schizophrenic, will emerge with a diagnosis of dissociative identity disorder. Conversely, in a group of patients diagnosed with DID who are interviewed for schizophrenic symptoms, two-thirds will emerge with a diagnosis of schizophrenia. A group of 236 patients with IDD showed that 40.8% of them had previously been diagnosed with schizophrenia.[325]

One of the commonalities between schizophrenia and I.D.D. may be auditory hallucinations, often involving 'voices in the head'. These voices can

---

[323] "Imke Deistler und Angelika Vogler: Einführung in die Dissoziative Identitätsstörung - Multiple Persönlichkeit, Junfermann Verlag Paderborn" 2005-www.multiples-pages.net.

[324] "I Was The Murderer! Or the Dissociative Identity Disorder In The Cinema" - Beatriz Vera Posek, 2006.

[325] "Multiple personality disorder patients with a prior diagnosis of schizophrenia" - Colin Ross, G. Ron Norton, Journal "Dissociation", Vol.1 N°2, 06/1988.

come from either inside or outside, they can be friendly or hostile. There is no reliable characteristic to automatically determine with certainty whether it is a "schizophrenic voice" or a "dissociative voice". Some therapists use the criterion of external voice or internal voice to discern whether it is schizophrenia or D.I.D. Auditory hallucinations that seem to come from the outside will show more of a schizophrenic tendency, whereas voices coming from the inside may be those of alter personalities, in which case there is probably a split personality. According to Dr. Colin Ross, another clue is that split personalities usually hear more children's voices than schizophrenics. In the 1994 edition of the DSM, symptoms of voices that talk to each other or systematically comment on the person's behaviour were considered schizophrenic. The doctor could therefore make a diagnosis of schizophrenia on this symptom alone, however many professionals have found that these voices are more common in multiple personalities than in schizophrenics.[326]

Many psychotherapists working with IDD patients have found that the phenomenon of voices in the head is a common occurrence in these people. More and more studies seem to link dissociation to these 'auditory hallucinations'. Some studies have focused exclusively on this issue, such as Charlotte Connor and Max Birchwood's *"Abuse and dysfunctional affiliations in childhood: An exploration of their impact on voice-hearer's appraisals of power and expressed emotion"*, or Vasiliki Fenekou and Eugenie Georgaca's *"Exploring the experience of hearing voices: A qualitative study"*.

The question of 'voices in the head' is a delicate one, knowing that psychotronic technologies such as 'The Voice of God' or 'Voice to Skull' can also produce this kind of phenomenon. (See Chapter 1: Psychotronics)

A study [327]conducted with the *Dissociative Experience Scale* (appendix 3) showed that 21% of psychiatric inpatients and 13% of psychiatric outpatients have a dissociative score above the pathological threshold. They conclude that dissociative disorders are still significantly under-diagnosed.[328] In a study entitled *"Dissociation and Schizophrenia"* published in 2004 in the journal *"Trauma and Dissociation"*, Dr. Colin Ross and Dr. Benjamin Keyes assessed dissociative symptoms in a group of 60 individuals treated for schizophrenia. They found that 36 subjects had significant dissociative features, representing 60% of their sample. These dissociative symptoms were accompanied by a high rate of childhood trauma as well as major disorders such as depression, *borderline* personality disorder or I.D.D. In both BDD and schizophrenia, dissociation is an underlying feature, as is the traumatic origin of these personality disorders.

---

[326] "C.I.A. doctors and the psychiatry scam" – Interview with Dr. Colin Ross, sott.net, 2013.

[327] *Dissociative disorder among psychiatric patients"* - T.Lipsanen, J.Korkeila, P.Pelolta, J.Järvinen, K.Langen, H.Lauerma, Eur Psychiatry 2004.

[328] "Dissociation and violent acting out: a literature review" - Jérémie Vandevoorde, Peggy Le Borgne, 2014.

Despite studies that have clearly shown the link between psychotic disorders and dissociative disorders, there has been a sharp decline in the use of the diagnosis of dissociative disorders. One reason for this decline is the introduction of the term 'schizophrenia' to describe patients with these symptoms. Between 1911 and 1927, the number of reported cases of multiple personality disorder, now called I.D.D., decreased by almost half after the Swiss psychiatrist Eugen Bleuler replaced the term *"dementia preacox"* with "schizophrenia". Dr. Rosenbaum explains this in detail in his article *'The role of the term schizophrenia in the decline of diagnoses of multiple personality'*.[329] In the *Oxford Textbook of Psychopathology*, Paul H. Blaney tells us that a search on PubMed (the main search engine for bibliographic data in all fields of biology and medicine) for schizophrenia generates a result of 25,421 articles, while a search for I.D.D. yields only 73 publications.

One of the negative consequences of these misdiagnoses is that the treatment given for "schizophrenia" will be based mainly on heavy, addictive and even dangerous medication. Whereas, as we shall see, in I.D.D. therapy, treatment with medication is something secondary. They can be used to treat comorbidity but they are not therapeutic as such. We have seen that firstly, I.D.D. has been replaced by a catch-all diagnosis called "schizophrenia", and secondly that the treatment protocol for the "schizophrenic" will be heavy chemical medication, usually inappropriate, which will never help the patient to understand and free himself from his disorders. Disorders that are mostly related to childhood traumas. Indeed, the psychiatric institution seems to have little will to really help victims and survivors of trauma by neglecting or totally ignoring the subject of psychotraumatology. Psycho-traumatologist Muriel Salmona says: *"We are very little informed about psychotraumatology, there is no training in medical studies, no training during specialisation in psychiatry. There are also many experts who are not trained in psychotraumatology, so they have no knowledge of traumatic memory and processes (...) Often the psychiatrists who take care of the aggressors have no training at all in psychotraumatology. They will treat them without taking into account the traumatic memory, and as a result, they will not treat what makes the people very dangerous."[330]*

Ritual abuse and mind control survivor Lynn Moss Sharman said in a radio interview with Wayne Morris (testimony in Chapter 7): *"I had come across some information - in a library - that the Scottish Rite (Freemasonry) in the United States had been funding schizophrenia research through its 'charitable' donations. I remember reading this and thinking that it was rather curious, even chilling, that the high ranks of this secret society would choose to use their 'charitable' funds to fund research into schizophrenia* (editor's note: *Scottish Rite Schizophrenia Research Program, SRSRP). A disorder which is very similar in some respects to the diagnosis of multiple personality disorder or dissociative identity disorder which is diagnosed in 99% of ritual abuse survivors, and*

---

[329] *Does discociative schizophrenia exist?* Marie-Christine Laferrière-Simard and Tania Lecomte, 2010.

[330] "Les conséquences psychotraumatiques" - Muriel Salmona, Pratis TV, 2011.

certainly in mind control survivors too. I very naively asked Mr. Tooey (Peter Tooey, Freemason, ex-police officer) if he was aware that funds were being used for these purposes, and he very proudly replied: "Well yes, here in Thunder Bay, all the money that the Scottish Rite contributed went to fund a research project on the study of schizophrenia at UBC. "I found it very disturbing, and again, very frightening that money from this community in Northwestern Ontario, received by this secret society, was going directly to a university on the West Coast of Canada. And then I came across another piece of information shortly after: There are research grants available at York University - something called the Rohr Institute, funded by the Masonic Foundation of Canada and based in Hamilton, Ontario. This institute offers grants for research and the $35,000 grant comes directly from the Scottish Rite Charitable Foundation of Canada, through the Rohr Institute. The purpose is to provide grants for studies/research in the field of "intellectual disability". I don't think it's something that's very well known and I wonder what kind of studies are actually being conducted at York University with these funds. "[331]

We have seen that IDD and schizophrenia are two interrelated psychiatric disorders, but schizophrenia seems to be a kind of *'catch-all drawer'* that serves rather to crowd out diagnoses that might be more precise, more detailed, and therefore more appropriate for treating patients.

e/ I.D.T. and psychophysiological variations

A number of studies and reports indicate that there are significant psychophysiological variations between the alter personalities of a patient with IDD. These may include differences in allergic or gastrointestinal reactions, the quality of vision may also vary between alters: there is evidence that blindness may vary according to the alter personality. Changes in voice and handwriting are recurrent. There are also differences in pain sensitivity, heart rate, blood pressure, blood circulation and immune function. Other differences have been noted in glucose levels in the alters of diabetic patients.[332] It has been shown that people who simulate alter personalities cannot cause such physiological differences. These sometimes extreme variations therefore validate the fact that patients with I.D.T. are not playing a role, but are undergoing a real personality change acting on biological functions that are not normally controllable.[333]

---

[331] "Wayne Morris, interview with Lynne Moss-Sharman" - CKLN-FM Mind-Control Series, Part 16.

[332] "Guidelines for Treating Dissociaitve Identity Disorder in Adults, Third Revision", Journal of Trauma & Dissociation, vol.12, 2011 - International Society for the Study of Trauma and Dissociation - ISSTD.

[333] *"Psychobiological characteristics of dissociative identity disorder: a symptom provocation study. "* - Reinders, Nijenhuis, Quak, Korf, Haaksma, Paans, Willemsen, den Boer, Biol Psychiatry, volume 60, 2006.

In a lecture given in 2009 on the phenomenon of multiple personalities, Father François Brune mentions several examples of these remarkable physiological changes: *"In fact they have already made some absolutely extraordinary discoveries, notably that we can deal with very strong differences according to the personalities that invade the main personality. We are therefore finally obliged to speak of 'primary persons' and 'secondary persons'. How do we distinguish between them? The main person is the one who controls the body most of the time, unlike the others (...) For example, we'll see that they don't need the same glasses (...) We'll also see that for certain medicines we'll have to change the doses, especially for diabetics. We will find that some people are left-handed at one time and right-handed at another time when their personality changes. We will also find that they are not all sensitive to the same anaesthetics (...) A mentally ill person (officially considered as such) suffering from split and even triple and quadruple personalities, who had to be operated, showed that his anaesthesia avoided suffering for some of the personalities that inhabited him, while the others complained of having suffered. They could describe the whole operation, so they were not asleep at all. When a few years later, this same person had to be operated on again, we had to wait patiently for all the personalities to emerge one by one in order to know which anaesthetic would suit each one (...) we are here in California with competent doctors... but in France, obviously it is difficult to imagine... Imagine a French hospital agreeing to go into this? Then their career would be over very quickly! There are also allergies which are not the same. There are cases of people who normally do not see colours, who when they are inhabited by others, report that they can distinguish them again. Another case studied in a very scientific way was that of a person who was asked to observe a flash lamp to study with an electroencephalogram the reactions in his brain. When the same personality was not in control, the brain reactions were not at all the same. This has been scientifically established in very serious and rigorous research.* (For Father François Brune, this phenomenon of multiple personalities is the result of possession by disembodied human souls. We will deal with this question of possessions in the next chapter)

A particularly strange aspect of these physiological changes concerns the effects of medications on alter personalities. According to some reports, it seems that their effects can be totally compartmentalised and even annihilated. Australian ritual abuse and mind control survivor Kristin Constance was hospitalised three times before finally being diagnosed with I.D.T. In 2011, at a conference, she described how she attempted suicide by swallowing a cocktail of anti-anxiety drugs, anti-depressants and anti-psychotics... She didn't even fall asleep... The chemical cocktail would have been locked into a certain alter personality and would have had no impact on the personality that was in control of the body (her testimony is transcribed in full in Chapter 7).

A phenomenon that is totally irrational, but as we will see in the next chapter, I.D.T. can also be paranormal.

Another ritual abuse survivor with I.D.T. also testified in 1997 on the *FOX13 News* programme *"Your Turn"*. Dejoly Labrier described how one of her alter personalities named *"Ginger"* needed *Prozac* because she was depressed. *They* (the alter system) took this drug for this alter *Ginger* for two years... but according to Labrier, only *Ginger* felt the effects... (his testimony is also transcribed in full in chapter 7).

Alter personalities seem to be able to block or enhance the effects of medication, as well as "fool" other alters by not taking the medication or by taking higher doses while the other alters would like to follow the treatment correctly, but they are not aware of these sabotaging behaviours from other alters due to amnesic walls.

An article in the journal *"Dissociation"*, published in September 1994, relates the case of a series of surgical operations with general anaesthesia performed on a patient with IDD. It was found that her anaesthetic requirements were rather atypical: She received a normal dose of muscle relaxant, however the dose of analgesics was totally different from the norm, she required only 16-33% of the dose that is usually used for an adult patient without IDD. The dose of anaesthetics was also lower than the norm, at 50-80% of the normal dose used in routine surgery. The patient explained that a child alter personality was in control of the body before each operation, the alter change would appear to have been anxiety induced. This could explain why the doses of painkillers and anaesthetics required were much lower than for an adult dosage. This phenomenon has been commonly observed by clinicians in several countries, who report that patients with IDD require smaller doses of sedatives when a child alter is in control of the body.[334]

Psychophysiological variations also relate to blindness. In November 2015, the Dailymail published an article entitled "Blind woman, 37, with multiple personalities lost her sight after an accident but can still see when in her teenage boy character". This article describes the case of a German woman who was diagnosed with cortical blindness at the age of 20 following an accident. Since then she had been walking with the help of a guide dog. Her medical records show that she received a series of tests which confirmed blindness. As there was no physical damage to her eyes, it was assumed that the problem was probably brain damage from the accident. 13 years later, in psychotherapy, she was diagnosed as suffering from I.D.D. with about ten alter personalities... It was during the treatment of her dissociative disorder that something remarkable happened: while her teenage boy alter was "in charge", her vision recovered. Her therapists reported that the woman's vision went from dark to light in seconds, depending on the alter personalities that emerged. German psychologists Hans Strasburger and Bruno Waldvogel, who conducted the study, used an EEG (electroencephalogram) to measure how the area of her cortex related to vision responded to visual stimuli. It was found that when the patient was in a 'blind' alter, her brain did not respond to the images, whereas with a 'sighted' alter personality, the measurements were normal. Her blindness came and went according to the alter personalities in control of the body. Doctors believe that

---

[334] *"The effect of multiple personality disorder on anesthesia: a case report"* - Moleman, Hulscher, van der Hart, Scheepstra, Journal "Dissociation" Vol.7 N°3, 09/1994.

his blindness was caused by a strong emotional reaction to the accident. Dr. Strasburger said: "It probably serves as a fallback function (...) In an emotionally intense situation, the patient can sometimes react by going blind, and thus not needing to see. There are other cases where blindness varies according to the alter that emerges, such as Diana's testimony in a documentary on I.D.T. in the series "The Extraordinary", broadcast on the Australian Seven Network in the 1990s.

It should be noted here that just as psychophysiology can vary from one alter to another, the style of handwriting can also change completely from one personality to another. An individual's handwriting is a mark by which they can be identified and their psychological profile analysed, it is unique and definitive, and therefore the police sometimes use graphology techniques in their investigations. Psychotherapists working with IDD patients have noted marked differences in handwriting style between alter personalities of the same person, and graphological analysis of this handwriting can reveal information about a particular alter. It is therefore possible to identify alter personalities by their handwriting style.[335]

f/ Transgenerational T.D.I.

It is common for adult women being treated for I.D.D. to clearly describe symptoms of I.D.D. in one or both of their parents. Testimonies may include clear descriptions of alternating personalities as well as the names of the parents' alter personalities. The Osiris Complex" - Dr. Colin Ross.

In his book "Childhood Antecedents of Multiple Personality", Dr. Richard Kluft reports cases of patients who had several family members suffering from dissociative states, from generation to generation. In particular, he describes the case of a 22-year-old man who was submitted to a psychiatric examination by a judge, at which time the possibility that he was suffering from I.D.D. was considered. The man was on trial for the murder of his father. He told the police that his father was a well-known pharmacist, one of the "pillars" of the local community. But he also reported that his father was involved in drug trafficking and had connections with organised crime. The defendant confessed that he himself was an accomplice in his father's drug trafficking as he sometimes made deliveries of goods. He also confessed that his father had large debts and that he had asked his father to kill him so that the life insurance money could be used to pay off these debts. The father also thought that a "suicide" could cancel the debt. All this information was validated by other people during the investigation. The young man could not kill his father himself, so he recruited another person to commit the murder. Both the son and the murderer were eventually arrested by the police.

---

[335] *Handwriting variations in individuals with MPD"* - Jane Redfield Yank, Journal "Dissociation", Vol.4 N°1, 03/1991.

Dr. Kluft spoke with this young man on a daily basis for some time and confirmed the diagnosis of multiple personality. Kluft himself observed changes in the individual's attitudes, voice, facial expression and body language. In addition, interviews with his two brothers, his sister, his wife, his cousins and his neighbours confirmed that the young man had behavioural changes characteristic of IDD. Based on the statements of the defendant, his family and his wife, it was also found that the father was most likely to have IDD. He was described as an unpredictable man who went into inappropriate rages with voice changes and unusual behaviour. Both the defendant and some of his family members reported that the father acted as if *"he was two different people"*, claiming that he was both a *"drug dealer"* and a *"pillar of the community"* (i.e. he had a hidden criminal activity on the one hand and a very respectable public front on the other). These statements may be consistent with an IDT.

Information gathered from the young defendant, his wife, brothers and sister, also suggested that the mother was also experiencing dissociative episodes. All sources testified that she was unstable and had a highly variable mood, and was described as *hysterical*. This woman, who was usually in a wheelchair, had periods of amazing physical improvement when she walked without any problems, something that was medically inexplicable (it is possible that this was a dissociative conversion disorder, which can manifest itself as occasional paralysis). The information given by the son and his family also suggests that the paternal grandmother suffered from I.D.D.: she was constantly described as *"unpredictable"*, *"changeable"*, and plagued by *"memory problems"*. All family members described her as a *"terror"* because of her inappropriate screaming and uncontrollable behaviour. In addition, her attitude with her children was totally random. There were reports of physical abuse of her children, but paradoxically she sometimes showed great affection. This illustrates the incompatible pattern of love and abuse frequently reported in families of IDD patients. In this case, the jury ignored the psychiatric report provided by the defence and the patient was sentenced to 25 years in prison.

Data collected by Dr. Richard Kluft from a number of patients support the hypothesis that dissociation and I.D.D. are likely transgenerational. Evidence of dissociative disorders was observed and reported in eighteen families of patients diagnosed with I.D.D. and followed by Dr. Kluft. This demonstrates a certain transgenerational connection, however, there are several factors that still need to be clarified about the mechanisms of this connection. Dr. Kluft legitimately states that this type of information is collected on an ad hoc basis, but it should be studied systematically and methodically in order to draw statistics and conclusions. More detailed studies would make it possible to identify the mechanisms underlying the transmission of I.D.T. from generation to generation.[336]

How are these dissociative disorders transmitted from one generation to the next? Perhaps we can answer this question in part through the practice of

---

[336] "Childhood Antecedents of Multiple Personality", Chap: "The transgenerational incidence of dissociation and multiple personality" - Richard P. Kluft, 1985, p.127-150.

transgenerational ritual abuse within occult networks? The case reported above by Richard Kluft shows us a young man suffering from an I.D.D., thus deeply traumatised since his early childhood. His father was a prominent pharmacist with a solid reputation who was obviously leading a double life by trafficking drugs in parallel with his professional activity. According to Kluft, there is every reason to believe that the father himself suffered from I.D.D., as did his wife and mother... So we have the classic context of a family practising ritual abuse from generation to generation, in which all the members are mired in dissociative states. I.D.D.s are caused by extreme and repetitive trauma, they do not appear overnight following a *bad flu*. Moreover, the illegal activities of the father, who leads a double life, reinforce the idea that this is a family that is part of an occult network, drug trafficking being a common occurrence in these circles.

The process of systematic repetition of traumas on the offspring is a vicious circle fed by traumatic memories that require dissociative anaesthesia. This process certainly has a great deal to do with the generational transmission of dissociative states and particularly of D.I.T. The victim will self-treat with physical and psychological violence against others, usually their children, who will in turn dissociate and repeat the violence, and so on from generation to generation. This phenomenon can happen without any satanic type rituals, "simple" recurrent family violence and incest can create this vicious circle if the disorders are not treated and cured. Sexual abuse also marks the victim's DNA, so the predisposition to dissociation and other negative consequences (depression, bipolarity...) are also passed on genetically. This genetic factor linked to dissociation is a mark sought and cultivated by certain Luciferian families (we will come back to the question of traumas that mark the DNA in chapter 7).

Let us recall here a case that took place in Paris in 2012. The case reported by *BFMTV* concerned the children of a Parisian couple whose man was (rightly) a pharmacist. *"It was the doctors at Necker Hospital who alerted the police. The two-and-a-half-year-old girl was taken to the emergency room for convulsions a month ago. Her blood and urine results showed that she had been regularly taking cocaine for almost a year. Her four-year-old brother underwent the same tests. Same conclusion. Except that the boy also consumes crack and in large quantities (!!)"* How can young children consume cocaine and crack? There is no doubt that these children were voluntarily drugged by adults... under what circumstances and for what purpose? A judicial investigation was opened by the Paris public prosecutor's office, where does this serious case stand today? Where are these children today?[337]

---

[337] "Paris: deux enfants de 2 et 4 ans drogués à la cocaïne et au crack" - Sarah-Lou Cohen and Cathelinne Bonnin, BFMTV, 02/03/2012.

g/ T.D.I. and animal alter

In an I.D.T., the presence of child or opposite sex alter personalities is very common. What is less common is the presence of a non-human alter. In some cases, the alter personality may be totally dehumanised to the point of believing that it is actually an animal. The presence of these 'animal alters' usually indicates that the person has experienced ritual abuse. The development of an animal alter occurs during extreme trauma in early childhood. The child may have been forced to behave and live like an animal. For example, the child may have witnessed the mutilation of an animal, been forced to participate in or witness acts of zoophilia or been forced to kill an animal. In Monarch mind control, the dehumanisation and the animal alter are deliberately created by the programmer in an extremely sadistic manner. However, these dehumanised alters may be present without any voluntary mental programming, but in any case it is the result of inhumane traumatic treatment, voluntarily dehumanising the little victim.

Here are some of the cases that the journal *Dissociation* reported in 1990 in an article entitled: *"Animal alters: case reports"*. It was written by psychiatrist Kate M. Hendrickson, Professor Jean M. Goodwin and Teresita McCarty. The content of this paper was presented at the Sixth Annual Conference on Dissociation and Multiple Personalities in Chicago in October 1989.

The first case report was of a 38-year-old woman who made frequent references to animals during her therapy. The patient described how her father would sometimes catch birds and lock them in the toilet with her when she was being punished, and they would come and bite her head with their beaks. This terrified her, she explained: *'When I am too terrified, I turn into a bird and fly into the toilet.* Sometimes her father would hang dead rabbits or birds over her bed. He would then tell his daughter that she could be strangled just like these animals if she didn't do what she was told or if she spoke out about the abuse. She was also forced to eat scraps from a dog bowl, etc. When the family cat gave birth, the father showed his daughter what he would do to her if she became pregnant. To do this, he would open the kittens' abdomens after strangling and dismembering them. These horrors done to the animals were a way to terrorise and traumatise the little girl.

When her father raped her at the age of eight, she became terrified of becoming pregnant and suffering the fate of kittens. When these horrors began to creep up in therapy, she said that she would hear *"strange baby cries inside her"*. These cries she heard were inconsolable and she was terrified to leave the therapist's office because she said *"everyone would know"*. She was terrified that other people would hear the screams and know that she herself had participated in the mutilation of the kittens. She said that she had tried to help the mother cat by taking her and her kittens inside her so that her father could not hurt them any more. She was terrorised by an alter of hers in which the suffering of the mother cat was internalised. This cat alter was itself terrified by the patient's father. After describing and understanding how the kittens had been internalized, it then became possible for her to talk about her incest pregnancies at the ages of fourteen and sixteen. The father had killed the babies as soon as they were born, hence the *strange cries* of *inconsolable babies* inside her. She says that one of her babies was dismembered like the kittens.

After the patient talked about the kittens inside her, she was able to recall the dissociated and repressed memories of incest, pregnancy and infanticide. At first she could only talk about these heavy traumatic memories through her cat alter. This cat alter could *'talk' about* these awful stories while the patient's main personality could not. It was found that when the patient was 'triggered' by the memory of not being able to save her children or the kittens, she would self-harm with a razor blade on her fingertips, fingers that came to resemble claws. She would also describe similar behaviour when she was ambivalently in bed with men: the alter cat would make numerous scratches on their face or chest.

Another reported case is that of a 35-year-old woman who, when terrified, turned into a dog. This may sound funny, but there is nothing comical about it. Her German parents punished her by making her eat from a dog bowl on all fours, forcing her to behave like a dog. In individual therapy, she was diagnosed with I.D.D. and revealed that she had been raped by her father, who also involved the family dog in zoophilic acts. Any reference to sex, being bad or evil made her "turn" into a dog. When this happened in therapy, the patient began to behave like a dog and speak in German (her usual language was English, it is possible that the parents spoke in German during the traumatic acts). The statements about dehumanising treatment by forcing her to behave like an animal preceded the statements about sexual abuse.

The *Dissociation* article also reports on a criminal case of a woman with dissociative disorder who was convicted of murder by disembowelment. There was evidence that she may have used her teeth and fingernails at some point in the crime. She also thought so because of the taste of blood in her mouth as she had total amnesia about the crime. During the investigation she was questioned under hypnosis. When she was in a hypnotic trance, it was suggested to her to imagine herself in a peaceful place, she then described that she was in a jungle and that she herself was a panther in the branches of a tree. After several hypnosis sessions to try to reconstruct and understand the crime, she stated in a trance that a warthog had attacked the panther and that it had been disembowelled. Evidence showed that her fingernails had been used in the crime but strangely no blood was found under her nails. One explanation is that she licked them just as a feline washes its paws. The woman's amnesia also covered a large part of her early childhood, but no history of violence could be found.

When a patient behaves like an animal, this may seem to be particularly severe psychotic behaviour. But these strange symptoms need to be observed and examined carefully, just as dreams and memory fragments should be systematically explored and dissected. Animal alterations may be partly related to dissociated memories and may serve to block access to a specific memory area. When the reasons for its development and the functions of the animal alter have been discovered and understood, this alter can then be connected with early childhood memories and the trauma that caused them. Contact with these animal alters is a doorway to the victim's most violent alters (which can be animal or human). These alter represent the victim's identification with the most violent acts of the perpetrators.[338]

In satanic ritual abuse, torture and killing of animals is commonly used to intimidate and silence victims. The child is told that he or she will suffer the same fate if he or she talks about anything. In addition, the child is forced to participate in the barbaric acts in order to make him/her feel guilty in order to make him/her 'guilty' in turn, as we saw in Chapter 4. The animal can thus internalise itself to become a fraction of the personality dissociated by the traumas, an alter that can show extreme rage. But through contact and reconciliation, an alliance can be created with the animal alter to make it a valuable tool that can help the victim in his or her healing.

h/ I.D.T. and therapies

This sub-chapter on therapy is not intended as a medical or therapeutic guide. It is intended to give some additional information to help understand a little more about how a split personality works and how to approach the problem for support and help.

The therapeutic strategy for I.D.D. is to "reunite", or "merge", the alter personalities with each other. It is a question of reducing their number until there is only one left, generally the one that was originally present, the so-called "host" personality. This mechanism is called *"integration"* and is based on the following principles listed by Dr. Colin Ross:
- Contacting all personalities using hypnosis.
- Gathering all the elements of the history of all the alter personalities.
- Consider each personality as part of the whole.
- To develop mutual understanding and cooperation between the different alter personalities.
- Controlling personality changes alter. (*switch*)
- Make agreements with each personality to oversee the whole system.
- First, establish mergers between personalities according to their affinities.
- To progress towards and consolidate final integration by supporting the patient's social relationships.
The following are the types of questions that can be asked when coming into contact with an alter personality, taking care to respect free will and to ask permission to ask certain questions:
- What is your name?
- How old are you?
- What is your function?
- Why are you here?
- How long have you been here?

---

[338] *"Animal alters: case reports"* - Kate M. Hendrickson, Jean M. Goodwin, Teresita McCarty, Journal "Dissociation", Vol.3 N°4, 12/1990.

- Following which event?
- What do you remember?
- Is there anyone else?
- How many are you?
- Are there any children?
- Who is in distress?
etc...

In an article entitled *"Dissociative phenomena in the everyday lives of trauma survivors"*, psychotherapist Janina Fisher gives four simple "laws" for understanding the internal system of a dissociated personality and for working with it/them:

- <u>An alter is only a fraction of a whole:</u> No matter what state the patient may be in at any given time, no matter how regressive, helpless and confused he or she may be, there will always be other adult alters who are confident and competent to move forward positively in therapy. No matter how self-destructive the patient may be at any given time, there are other alters who want to live and fight to survive. There are always alters who will fight to live and struggle to keep control over those overwhelming feelings of helplessness and demoralisation. The patient must keep in mind that no matter which alter or alters are dominant at any given time, they are only a fraction of a system designed to be in balance.

- <u>The system is designed for survival, not destruction:</u> This "law" will save the therapist unnecessary exhaustion during recurrent crises and prevent unnecessary hospitalisations. The therapeutic work consists of helping the patient to adapt to this system so that he/she can face its complexity and the challenges it poses in his/her present adult life. These dissociative functions, these personality changes, can be used constructively to be able to stay the course and to be able to live a meaningful life, to be able to find pleasure in living it and creating it. The fact that this system was designed to be adaptive also means that each crisis, each new 'glitch' that occurs, actually provides the opportunity to readjust the system in another way to make it even more relevant to the patient's life. These crises therefore allow us to understand the functioning of the internal system a little better.

- <u>For every action, there will be an equal and opposite reaction:</u> This means that each fraction, each part of the "I", will have its opposite polarity or its opposite. For example, suicidal and self-destructive alters will have opposing alters determined to live and fight and alters terrified of dying or having to feel pain. Alters who live in shame and want to hide and be invisible will be balanced by narcissistic and even exhibitionist alters. At any given moment, an outwardly expressed feeling, decision or viewpoint will be balanced internally by an equal opposite reaction. This systematic balancing of opposites can have both positive and negative consequences as there is also an opposite response to positive changes or events. For example, if some alters develop greater trust and closeness with the therapist, other alters will feel threatened and attempt to sabotage the therapy to distance themselves from the therapist. If some alters will relentlessly test the therapist's competence, consistency and reliability, other alters will feel sadness and desolation and will then want to redouble their efforts to please the therapist.

- <u>The therapist is the therapist of all the alter:</u> The therapist is the therapist of the whole system and therefore of all its parts. To work only with some of the alters while neglecting other parts would be to say that one is working only with one half of the patient. Whether it is the "nice half", the "young half", the "self-destructive half" or the "good half" of the patient, therapeutic work cannot be effective by taking into account only one part of a whole. If the therapist is the therapist of all parts, he will be neutral, he will not take sides and he will not keep secrets. He will discover the potential and usefulness that each alter brings to the therapy and to the system as a whole, including the violent, suicidal or self-destructive alters. He will see the interactions between the different alters, which will bring out the internal conflicts, just as a family therapist would. In the same way that the family system works, the patient will not be identified with any of his or her alters but rather with the overall alter system. Because in dissociative patients the system and the patient are one and the same person, the therapist must avoid a common trap in treating dissociation: that is, talking to the system as if it were a single person acting as a "revolving door" for the different "family members" to come and tell their stories in succession. It is usually more useful to work primarily with the "parent(s)", i.e. the adult alter or host personality, to teach them the skills necessary to foster communication and internal cooperation between all alters.

At the beginning of the therapy, due to the dissociative traumatic amnesia, the patient with I.D.D. will at first report a fragmented and incoherent experience. His complete and chronological personal history will come with time, through the progressive integration of dissociated memories and personalities. The process of integration can be compared to the construction of a jigsaw puzzle that could not take shape without the different pieces that make up the life experiences that have been broken up by dissociation. Integration therefore consists of putting these puzzle pieces together to recreate a coherent whole comprising all memories, whether valid or not. The pieces of memory belonging to the different senses (hearing, smell, touch, sight, taste: non-semantic memory) are managed by the hippocampus whose role is to transfer them to the cerebral cortex so that they can be consciously processed and integrated. In this way, they move from an unconscious to a conscious mode, from a dissociated to an associated or *resolidified* mode. They become an integrated memory that can now be coherently verbalised.[339]

The term fusion is also used to describe the process of integration. A trauma-free and dissociated mind works in a unified way. For a dissociated and split mind, fusion is the moment when two (or more) alternate personalities become aware of each other's existence. They then experience a kind of fusion, a dissolution of the amnesic walls which means that they will no longer have any separation and will therefore share the same memories. The "final fusion" is the

---

[339] "Healing The Unimaginable: Treating Ritual Abuse and Mind Control" - Alison Miller, 2012.

goal of the therapy. The patient moves from a state of multiple identities to a unified subjective self, *unification.*

It is recognised by therapists that there are three main stages in the integration process. First of all, however, it is essential to establish a feeling of physical and psychological security in the patient, as well as a stabilisation and reduction of symptoms (comorbidity). This stabilisation will allow the traumatic memories to be worked on, memories that must be consciously integrated. Integration, or merging of the alter personalities, and rehabilitation are the final phase. These three stages may overlap because one alter may be dragging on more than others, but usually the therapist treats one stage at a time.

- Phase 1: Safety, stabilisation and symptom reduction:

The first step is to create a kind of alliance between the patient and the therapist to establish trust and stability. In this stage, it is a question of minimising behaviours that may be dangerous for the patient as well as for those around him. It is also necessary to reduce negative thoughts that may make the patient vulnerable to further external attacks. Managing and controlling post-traumatic stress is also a priority in phase 1. Other behaviours that will need to be regulated are eating disorders, risk-taking, violence, aggression, etc. Alter personalities involved in violent behaviour and identifying with the aggressor(s) can be particularly difficult to manage. It is therefore important to identify them quickly in order to try to reach an agreement, a sort of contract with them to help the patient feel secure. These frightening, angry and violent alter often have a protective role, despite appearances, they are there to protect the patient.

The alter "observers" can be very useful in reconstructing chronologically the shattered memories in order to know what happened, the course of events (or the illusion and manipulation that the torturers wanted to create).

Generally, alter personalities see themselves as a truly separate person, outside the alter group and autonomous. It is when they become aware of the existence of other alters that they realise that they are multiple and that they belong to the same physical body. This awareness will, for example, prevent self-harm and a commitment can be made to each of them to avoid self-destructive behaviour. Many alters feel empty, depersonalised or unsure of their identity precisely because they are only part of a whole. Together they form a complete person. It is therefore a question of creating a form of cohesion where each alter knows the others and finds its place in the group, or internal system.

Making the alters assistants in the therapy is a major asset, but it is also necessary to develop strategies to improve their understanding and communication with each other, as the patient loses a lot of energy in dealing with the internal conflicts between them. The development of a trusting relationship and dialogue with the alter personalities will be the key to uncovering trauma (phase 2) and achieving stability and integration (phase 3).

Non-verbal and emotional communication is also important. Some alters will need to be hugged, while others will take this gesture as an attempt at sexual approach. Some alters are unable to look the person in front of them straight in the eye. Some will express themselves in an outgoing manner while others will be totally terrified and just need to hear reassuring words. Some cannot speak, they will need to communicate through writing, drawing or through another alter who will mediate. The therapist must not show favouritism and must treat each alter equally. The therapist should also not be frightened by those who appear hostile as they use anger to protect the more vulnerable alter, who are usually young children. During this phase there may also be the use of anchoring techniques in the present moment and self-hypnosis methods. Sometimes it will be necessary to use medication to address risky behaviours, but this should not be the focus of the treatment. It is also important in this first phase to develop acceptance and empathy for each part of the split personality, each alter should be seen for what it is and as having a role to play in the therapy and in the patient's life.

- Phase 2: Confrontation and integration of traumatic memories:

The second phase focuses on the patient's traumatic memories. Here there is still a lot of work to be done to help the patient accept the different parts of his or her personality and the alters must continue to get to know each other and live together. In this stage, the work also consists of overcoming the patient's blocking problems in his past. One of the most difficult tasks in this phase will be to overcome the fear of traumatic memories in order to be able to integrate them effectively. The patient and the therapist will have to discuss together to reach an agreement on which memories should be prioritised for processing. Once these traumatic memories are processed and integrated, they need to be shared with each alter personality who was not aware of them. This sharing of traumatic experiences with all the alters in the system is called "Synthesis". Once this Synthesis has been achieved, it must continue to lead to the full awareness that the traumas have been experienced and treated, and that they are now part of the past: this is called "Realisation". The patient will then be able to give a precise place to the trauma in the chronology of his life. As a result, the pieces of the memory puzzle will be reconstituted little by little to form a real chronological frieze. Synthesis is also followed by "Personification", i.e. the awareness that these traumatic memories belong to the patient, and to no one else. Finally, thanks to this work on the traumatic memories, the patient can transform his or her memories, previously dissociated and scattered, into a coherent and comprehensible narrative, this is the "Narration". This is the transition from a non-verbal memory to a narrative and analytical memory.

During this stage, strong emotions will erupt as the traumatic content of the memories emerges to consciousness. The patient may feel shame, horror, disgust, terror, anger, helplessness, confusion or grief. It is important to give adequate time for recovery between each session so as not to destabilise or re-traumatise the patient. But even with careful therapeutic planning, it may be necessary to return to phase 1 for further stabilisation when the resurfacing of a memory proves particularly violent. As the traumatic experiences are integrated, the alter personalities become less and less separate and distinct. Spontaneous fusion may also occur, but a premature attempt at global unification may cause stress that would be negative for the patient. As the patient's fragmentation subsides, he or she will gain a certain inner calm with a sense of peace, especially when the therapy is accompanied by spiritual renewal. With this new inner state, the patient will be better able to deal with his or her own traumatic history and with the problems of everyday life. The patient will begin to focus less on the traumas of the past and channel his or her energy into the present moment, which will greatly help him or her to develop new perspectives for the future.

- Phase 3: Integration and rehabilitation:

The third phase aims at the integration (final unification) of the personality. In the first two stages, the patient has learned to overcome the fear of other parts of his personality and the fear of his traumatic memories. He has also accepted and integrated the idea of having been abused as a child. Like a painful bereavement, the patient will have to let go of old beliefs to see new perspectives. He or she will now have to learn to deal with the emotions that may arise such as shame, fear, terror, anger and grief. The emotional manifestation of trauma can occur for more than two years, after which unification is considered safe. During this period, the patient may spontaneously return to phase 2 as new traumatic memories may still emerge. After the final integration, the unification of all alter personalities, the patient will usually retain the skills and attributes of the different alters that were dissociated from their personality.

These three phases of PTSD treatment are probably inspired by the work of Pierre Janet in the 19th century. His psychotherapeutic method for the treatment of post-traumatic stress included the following three stages:

1: The stabilisation of symptoms in preparation for the liquidation of traumatic memories.

2: The identification, exploration and modification of traumatic memories.

3: Relief of symptomatological residues. Reintegration and rehabilitation of the personality. Relapse prevention.

Regarding the use of medication, it is not a primary treatment for dissociative disorders, but it can be useful. Indeed, some patients require specialised treatment for substance abuse or eating disorders. Many therapists use hypnosis to calm, soothe, contain or strengthen the 'self'. Hypnosis also allows access to alter personalities that are not directly accessible without a modified state of consciousness. Since the beginning of the 19th century, hypnosis has been used for the treatment of I.D.D., resulting in numerous studies demonstrating that these patients are highly hypnotisable in comparison with other clinical groups. The higher the hypnotizability of the individual, the more effective the therapy. Hypnosis and self-hypnosis can also be highly effective in treating post-traumatic stress disorder (PTSD), which is usually present in patients with IDD.

Other specialised therapeutic methods may be useful for these patients, such as family or expressive therapy, remodulation and dialectical behaviour therapy (DBT), sensory-motor psychotherapy, 'primal' therapy, eye movement neuro-emotional integration (EMDR), etc.

EMDR (*Eye Movement Desensitization and Reprocessing*) is a rapid eye movement desensitization and reprocessing therapy, which was first used to clear post-traumatic shock and can be used to treat a wide range of psychological traumas. *Biofeedback* devices or *neurofeedback* can also be an additional help for the patient, as can acupuncture and even dietary changes.

Group therapy is not recommended for I.D.T., as many of these patients find it difficult to tolerate a process that encourages group discussion of the participants' traumatic experiences. However, after a certain stage of integration, group energy can be an effective support for the patient. Treatment of I.D.T. is usually done on an outpatient basis (not requiring hospitalisation), however, inpatient treatment will be necessary if the patient shows risks to themselves (self-harm, suicide attempts) or to others during the dissociative phases.

Expressive therapies will also play a positive role in the patient's recovery. Journaling, art therapy, music therapy, horticultural and animal therapy (especially with horses), movement therapy, psychodrama, occupational therapy and recreational therapy offer the patient the opportunity to use a wide range of techniques that can provide a means of expression and stabilisation. This will facilitate concentration, pragmatic thinking, organisation and cooperation of the internal world (the alter). Artistic practices such as painting, writing, collage, sculpture, etc., can serve as a visual and palpable record of the experience of the alter personalities, productions that can thus be examined at any time during the treatment.

To conclude this sub-chapter on therapies, here are some practical tips and exercises[340] aimed directly at patients with dissociative disorders:

It is about becoming aware of *the "here and now"*. To do this, it is helpful to observe and perceive yourself consciously, without judgement. When you notice that you are entering a dissociative state, in other words that you are starting to leave, that you are no longer quite there, that you perceive yourself less well, try to stop for a while. By practising, and perhaps even with therapeutic support, you can learn to answer the following questions:

- What was my situation when I started to dissociate?
- What did I feel on a physical level and on a psychological level?
- What is the last thing I remember?
- I knew I was entering a dissociative state because:

1/ I started, for example, to sway, to feel like I was in a fog, to have headaches....

2/ I stopped for example talking, thinking clearly, making eye contact...

3/ I started to tell myself that I could die, that no one can be trusted, that I never do anything right...

- What did I try to avoid?
- What could I have done instead?

If, over time, the patient is able to answer these questions better and better, they will be able to control their dissociative behaviours better and have more control.

What can you do when you enter a dissociative state?

---

[340] *EMDR Europe HAP Suisse romande* by Eva Zimmermann and Thomas Renz, based on Dr. Reddemann and Dr. Cornelia Dehner-Rau.

- Be aware that you are in a dissociative state, a state that will pass as everything passes.

- Also be aware that this behaviour is happening because it once protected you. Now you don't need it, you have other ways.

- Find a phrase like: *"Now I'm grown up and safe"*. Say this sentence out loud to yourself.

- Keep your eyes open and feel the ground beneath your feet.

- Do you have an object that you loved (e.g. a soft toy or other caring companion)? Drill into it consciously.

- Activate your senses with something cold (e.g. ice cubes or cold water on your hands, arms, face).

- Be aware of the difference between then and now. Say aloud to yourself today's date, where you are and how old you are.

- Breathe consciously. Feel the air flowing in and out of your lungs. Breathe with your eyes open, concentrating a little more on the exhalation.

- Do something that demands your attention and activates your senses: read or look at a picture, listen to music, touch a stone, smell a flower or an essential oil, consciously taste the aroma of a sultana, sunflower seeds or something spicy.

- Get moving: walk around, shake your limbs, stamp your feet, dance...

- Do something with your hands: writing, painting, gardening, a puzzle, crafts, etc.

- Take a shower and concentrate on the contact of the water.

- Be understanding of yourself. You deserve to be gentle with yourself.

- Make sure you surround yourself with people who make you feel good and with whom you do not feel threatened.

- When you are sure of this, you can say to yourself: I am now with so-and-so, I know that he wants me well. If I go into a dissociative state now, it has to do with old memories. In the present moment I am safe.

- Imagine that you put all the things from the past that weigh you down in a safe. Once locked away, they will no longer bother you.

5 - DEVELOPMENT OF I.D.T. IN CHILDREN

a/ Introduction

I.D.D. originates in early childhood, its development will be long term and it will usually be more obvious and recognisable in adulthood. Dr. Greaves writes that *"Personality fractions usually manifest themselves in early childhood, as early as 2 1/2 years of age and typically by the age of 6 or 8."*[341]

In an article entitled *"Incipient multiple personality in children: Four cases"*, Dr. Fagan and Dr. Mc Mahon reported on four children who developed

---

[341] Multiple personality: 165 years after Mary Reynolds" - G.B. Greaves, Journal of Nervous Mental Disease, 1980.

incipient split personality. The youngest was 4 years old and the oldest was 6 years old. Fagan and Mc Mahon state in this article that *"multiplicity is established by age 5 to 8 at the latest, but this will not usually be diagnosed until adulthood."*[342]

In an article entitled "Psychotherapy with a ritually abused 3-year-old: deceptive innocence", psychotherapist Leslie Ironside reports that "dissociated identities were diagnosed in a child as young as three years old, who was ritually abused and had endured extreme levels of trauma."[343]

The existence of I.D.T. in children was established by Dr. Antoine Despine in 1840. He reported the case of an 11-year-old Swiss girl, Estelle, which has been described earlier in this chapter. Dr. Richard Kluft has also published several papers on children and I.D.T., including the case of an 8-year-old child, Tom, which will be described later. Morris Weiss, Patricia Sutton and A.J. Utecht reported in 1985 in the *Journal of the American Academy of Child Psychiatry* on the case of a 10-year-old girl in an article entitled *"Multiple Personality in a 10-Year-Old Girl"*.

In her book Healing The Unimaginable, Canadian therapist Alison Miller writes: "I treated a 10-year-old girl who had just an alter personality in addition to her host personality, a 3-year-old alter (...).When she was bored at school, the 10-year-old would 'go inside her head', the 3-year-old alter would emerge and take over the body and behave like a 3-year-old, which was of course inappropriate in a classroom. The 10-year-old girl would then find herself in the headmaster's office with no idea of what had happened."[344]

Of course, the systematic response to such behaviour in a child will be to say that it is capriciousness, a voluntary regression of the child *'being a baby'*. But dissociative disorder and dissociative amnesia shed light on this kind of *'capricious'* behaviour from a completely different perspective. Of course, children do have tantrums and sometimes act in ways that are not age-appropriate, but there are criteria for determining whether it is a dissociative disorder, as in this case where the little girl does not seem to remember her baby behaviour.

Many patients have reported that their alter personalities originated in childhood. Unfortunately in children, dissociative disorders are usually undiagnosed for several reasons:

- Children with IDD usually have secondary signs and symptoms of the disorder. They will frequently have attention deficit, hyperactivity, behavioural problems, high anxiety, depression, somatisation, post-traumatic stress, dissociation and symptoms that may appear psychotic in nature. Vomiting and nausea, headaches and fainting are the most common somatisation in a child.

---

[342] "Incipient multiple personality in children: Four cases" - J. Flagan & P. Mc Mahon, Journal of Nervous Mental Disease, 1984.

[343] "Psychotherapy with a ritually abused 3-year-old: deceptive innocence" L. Ironside, 1994, in "Treating Survivors of Satanist Abuse" V. Sinason.

[344] "Healing The Unimaginable: Treating Ritual Abuse and Mind Control" - Alison Miller, 2012, p.28.

Trance states or conversion symptoms (dissociative paralysis), which are common in adult patients, are more rare in children. Inner voices that the child may hear may be misdiagnosed as 'schizophrenia'.

- Because dissociation and similar conditions are more common in healthy children than in healthy adults, these dissociative symptoms may be ignored and misinterpreted as normal child behaviour.

- Intra-familial abuse, a chaotic family environment and psychiatric disorders of family members will not only complicate the diagnosis but also prevent proper follow-up of the child.

- But above all, the most important cause of misdiagnosis is the inadequate training of clinicians and their lack of experience with I.D.D.. Their disbelief in the legitimacy of the diagnosis of Multiple Personality Disorder will result in them not looking for its presence at all.[345]

In children, amnesia, alternating totally different behaviours and hallucinations (usually auditory) are symptoms of a dissociative disorder. Amnesia may manifest itself as 'gaps' in the day, meaning that a dissociation has occurred at some point. In adolescence, symptoms will begin to be more pronounced than in children under 11 years of age, so adolescents will be more likely to be diagnosed with DID. Any child with a history of physical or sexual abuse should be assessed for dissociative disorder. When the abuse began in early childhood, was recurrent and sadistic, involved ritual practices and the parents themselves have severe psychic disorders, then a prolonged observation of the child should be done, as well as a history of any encounters the child may have had with adults. This work should be accompanied by careful interview sessions to establish an accurate diagnosis. Children whose parents themselves suffer from a dissociative disorder should be particularly monitored on a regular basis. Several authors have reported the link between dissociated patients and their dissociated family. The majority of these dissociated parents have a history of physical or sexual abuse from their early childhood.[346] This is a vicious circle that needs to be understood, especially in the case of transgenerational satanic families...

The following is a list of behavioural problems in children that may be related to IDD:

Intermittent depression - Trance or self-hypnotic state - Fluctuation in intellectual abilities and moods, rapid regressions - Amnesias - Auditory hallucinations (especially with inner voices) - Recurrent imaginary companions - Talks to himself - Sleepwalking - Night terrors - Sudden paralysis - Hysterical symptoms - Refers to himself in the third person - Answers to another name, or uses another name - Significant changes in personality and behaviour - Forgetfulness or confusion about elementary and basic things - Fluctuating schoolwork from one opposite to another - Hyper-destructive behaviour - Self-

---

[345] Dissociative identity disorder in childhood: five Turkish cases " - Journal "Dissociation", Vol.9 N°4, 12/1996.

[346] Recognition and differential diagnosis of dissociative disorders in children and adolescents" - Nancy L. Hornstein, Journal "Dissociation", Vol.6 N°2/3, June/September 1993.

harm - Violence against others - Suicidal speech or behaviour - Inappropriate sexual behaviour - Social isolation, anti-social behaviour.

b/ The case of a three-year-old child

In September 1988, the *International Society for the Trauma and Dissociation* (ISSTD) journal *"Dissociation"* published an article describing the case of a little girl showing personality dissociation caused by repetitive traumas. The authors of the article, entitled *"The development of symptoms of multiple personality disorder in a child of three"*, are Dr. Richard Riley, who worked for the U.S. Army in the *Exceptional Family Member* Program (EFMP) in Belgium, and Dr. John Mead, a private practitioner from Pasadena, California.

The child was followed from the age of 14 months, she suffered multiple repetitive traumas which developed a dissociative state in her. The progression of her dissociative disorder was videotaped during a legally ordered follow-up.

Cindy (pseudonym) was first seen by Dr. Riley at the age of 14 months. It was decided that she needed to be seen for an assessment following a dispute between the foster family, Joan and David (pseudonyms) and the biological mother Diane (pseudonym). Cindy had been released to the care of the foster family on the second day after her birth. She had had very limited contact with her biological mother between the ages of 3 months and 4.5 months, but had not had any contact since.

In the first evaluation session, Cindy showed a very positive attitude. She was curious and exploring the office, visibly happy and confident. She came across as a child receiving a lot of love and affection, there was clearly a strong attachment between her and her host family. She was also able to let the couple leave the room without showing any anxiety.

When Cindy was seen in the clinic at the age of 16 months, her biological mother came to visit her for a few hours twice a week at the foster home. It was reported that Cindy was sleeping poorly, that her appetite had deteriorated and that she was having tantrums. In contrast to the previous encounter, she was agitated, clung to her foster mother and became very anxious when she left the room to be alone with the doctor. All of these findings were reported to the judge, however, custody of the child was given to the birth mother with gradual access by the foster parents so that Cindy could adjust to the change. However, the birth mother was adhering to this visitation schedule very sporadically and it was learned too late that during this time she had given birth to another baby girl who died of SIDS at the age of 3 months.

At the age of 20 months, Cindy returned for a clinic visit, accompanied by Diane, the biological mother and Joan, the foster mother. Cindy had accepted everyone's company and seemed comfortable in this situation. At the age of 23 months, during another visit with her foster mother, Cindy was very frightened and clung to her foster mother. Over the next few months her emotional state deteriorated completely, she insisted on being held and would cry if she was not in physical contact with her foster mother. She had recurrent health problems and once arrived for a visit with a bruise on her earlobe. She then confessed that her biological mother had hit her. She also stated that she was called *"Lila"* by her biological family members. She repeatedly made it clear that her half-brother touched her genitals and inserted objects into her vagina. She regularly reported physical and sexual abuse.

As a result of these statements, a decision was made to limit custody with the biological family to daytime only, when Cindy was 2.5 years old. Her condition improved and her anxiety decreased, but she was still very angry and continued to cling to her foster mother. She even wanted to sleep with her and would wake up several times a night to check on her. Joan reported that the little one would talk in her sleep, repeating *"my name is Cindy R." (the name of the foster family).* (the name of the foster family). Cindy continued to talk about physical and sexual abuse during daytime visits with her biological family and began to replicate this abuse on her adopted sister, David and Joan's biological daughter...

Another medical *expert* was then appointed to examine the child in the environment of her biological family. He reported that Cindy was *"cheerful and outgoing and did not exhibit any abnormal or unusual behaviour.* During this period, the foster mother made an unexpected visit to Cindy's biological family and the child did not seem to recognise her or acted as if she did not know her...

The first filmed session took place when Cindy was 3 years old. Three sessions were scheduled to determine the status of the relationship between Cindy, her biological mother and her foster family, and to videotape all statements of abuse. She spontaneously reiterated her testimony about the sexual abuse by her brothers and the fact that her biological family consistently called her *"Lila"* instead of using her real name. At one point in a session, she reacted when the word Lila was mentioned by saying *"What?* She denied her visits to her biological family, but spoke of them in a direct manner. She also reported that her biological mother called her *"little bitch".* When she talked about the members of this biological family, the way she talked about them and her behaviour became totally different. Her language became immature, her body postures and mannerisms were like those of a doll. This series of video recordings was presented as evidence of abuse to the jury. As a result, the length of custody with the biological family was further reduced.

Three months later, the biological mother made a request through her lawyer for a session with her daughter to be filmed with her: the alter *Lila* personality presented itself directly in this session with the biological mother. There were then five sessions, four of which were recorded. During the first session, Cindy was ready to answer all questions about the foster family without hesitation. She gave emotional responses about the death of the foster family's paternal grandfather, while questions about the biological family were generally ignored or answered only with *"I don't know".* When she was told that she would be coming back the next day for another session, she agreed; but when it was added that she would be coming with her biological mother, she first remained silent, then replied negatively, and finally denied that she had just been told that she was to do a session the next day with her biological mother.

Following this, the child would alternately present herself with one of two distinct personalities, depending on the questions she was asked. These personalities were either Cindy or Lila. Lila would say that she wanted to be called that, and she would not answer questions about the foster family or would say that she did not know. Sometimes she would hide behind the dollhouse or chair, out of sight of her biological mother, and Cindy would emerge. At the end of one session, the child wanted to stay and clean up the mess she had made in the room, which was totally out of character for Cindy. During the next three sessions, Cindy and Lila appeared alternately: with the biological mother present, Lila was the active personality, but Cindy could sometimes emerge to play aggressively while criticising Lila for her behaviour. Lila could answer some questions about the foster family, but she had very limited knowledge about the family. She identified Joan R., the foster mother, as the "babysitter". In addition to this memory gap in her personal history, Lila seemed psychologically younger and her general knowledge was more limited than Cindy's. When Lila made a mistake, Cindy would say that she was not aware of it. When Lila made a mistake, Cindy could emerge to correct it. Lila also exhibited inappropriate sexual behaviour in some games. Her language was less developed than Cindy's and phonetically more immature. An important point to note is that Lila did not seem to know Cindy, whereas Cindy was aware of Lila, remembering every little thing she did. She didn't like her and she didn't like anyone in her biological family. Cindy was confident and dominant when not threatened. She also showed guilt and remorse when her behaviour offended someone.

Video recordings of the sessions were submitted as evidence but were never used. The court explained that because all the *experts did* not agree in their conclusions and recommendations, the court did not need the recordings. Instead, all custody and visits with the biological mother were stopped, and psychotherapy was set up for the girl. Twelve sessions were scheduled over a four-month period. Her foster mother was always present and her adopted sister, Cheri, was present for three sessions. In the first session, Cindy showed anger at her abusers and was encouraged to express it in her play. It was then that she let out the fear of her birth mother. The alter Lila emerged intermittently during this session and a few others afterwards. As the sessions progressed, Cindy began calling her adopted sister by the alter Lila's name. She would make requests or give orders in the same stern tone as her biological mother. Gradually Cindy began to like the alter and wanted Lila to live with her in the foster home. She then allowed the alter to participate more freely in the games. Both personalities also began to give information about the biological family without showing anxiety. At one point Cindy stated that she was older than Lila, she also strangely identified her foster mother as *"Lila's mum"*. During another session, Cindy responded positively to the idea that she and Lila could get together. As a result, she seemed to do much better and started to go to school. In one of the last sessions, she explained that she and her sister were both Lila, but one had grown up faster.

Little Cindy's case thus showed two criteria related to I.D.T.:

- The presence of two identities or personality states, each with its own way of perceiving, relating to others and thinking about the environment as well as about oneself.

- At least two of these identities or personality states take control of the person's behaviour on a recurrent basis.

Both Cindy and Lila are complex personalities, each with their own memories, their own behaviour and different social relationships. Cindy stated that she was older but also fatter than Lila. She referred to Lila as someone who was separate from her and living elsewhere. Lila was more immature than Cindy, both in her language and in her mannerisms. Her level of general knowledge was lower than Cindy's. Lila's alter also seemed more dependent and submissive, whereas Cindy's personality was aggressive, assertive and enterprising: she blamed Lila for things she had said or done. To Cindy, Joan was her mother, while to Lila she was simply her babysitter. Cindy knew Lila while Lila did not seem to know Cindy. Both personalities showed amnesia. The child could change personalities simply by moving or shifting her body position: the transitions (*switches*) were very quick.

Little Cindy's case fits five symptoms of I.D.D. listed by Dr. Fagan and Dr. McMahon in their article cited above:

1- She sometimes showed a dazed or trance-like behaviour.

2- She answered to more than one name.

3- She showed very marked changes in her behaviour.

4- She had memory loss about recent events.

5- She showed variation in her knowledge and skills.

The authors of the article conclude: "What would have happened to this child if she had not been removed from her biological family? Probably she would have continued to develop and strengthen her personality disorder with this alter Lila enabling her to cope with traumatic life circumstances."[347]

c/ The case of a seven-year-old child

Psychologist Wanda Karriker reported the case of a 7-year-old girl, whom she calls Katie (pseudonym). Her parents had brought her for a psychological assessment on the advice of her teacher because she was behaving oddly at school. She had extremely variable results and sometimes sucked her thumb while acting like a baby. Sometimes she seemed to be locked in her own world. In the interview with the parents, the mother said: *"It's like she has two extremes, sometimes she's totally passive and sometimes she gets violent, she's in a bad mood."*

Following an I.Q. assessment session, little Katie looked at the erasable board and asked if she could draw something on it, to which the psychologist obviously replied in the affirmative. The little girl then asked, *"Tell me what to*

---

[347] "The development of symptoms of multiple personality disorder in a child of three" - Richard Riley, John Mead, Journal "Dissociation", Vol.3 N°1, 09/1988.

draw? Why not a picture of your family? Karriker replied. Katie then began to draw three ghostly figures on the board, captioning them "Daddy", "Mommy" and "Lucy". She represented a child in her family named Lucy, but without representing herself as Katie... *"You know what?"* she said, looking down her shirt, *"I can press my belly button to get Lucy out.* The psychologist then asked if this Lucy looked like her and the little girl replied, *"She's cute, she has short blonde hair with blue eyes.* (Katie had long brown hair with dark eyes). The girl continued: *"You know what? She always gives me the answers in maths."* The psychologist then asked her if she could speak directly with Lucy and again Katie looked down her shirt, pressed her navel and said: *"Lucy, come here!"*. It was then that her facial expression changed to a much more mature child, with an obvious change in body language. She introduced herself by saying: *"Hi, I'm Lucy".* The psychologist then asked where Katie was now, to which the little girl replied *"Up there"*, while pointing to a corner of the ceiling... *"Can't you see her up there?"* she said. The child seemed to be experiencing depersonalisation, a phenomenon in which a person feels detached from his or her body (more on this in the next chapter).

When the girl saw the camera in the therapist's office, she immediately started dancing and singing, and then suddenly threw herself to the floor, kicking her feet in the air and moaning: *'No, no! Don't do this to me"*, while putting her hands over her mouth and rolling around in the fetal position. It was after this that Wanda Karriker began to seriously question whether little Katie had been abused to the point of developing these profound dissociative disorders. A disorder that her teacher described as a withdrawal into her *own world.*

When Karriker gave her findings to the parents, she pointed out the change in behaviour between Katie and Lucy, a dramatic change that had been caught on tape. The psychologist told the parents: *"I don't have to make a formal diagnosis, but I believe your daughter has created at least one imaginary friend, if not perhaps an alter personality, to help her cope with something she couldn't handle.* The psychologist explained to the doubtful parents that she herself had never observed multiple personality disorder in a child before. She explained that when a child is confronted with an unbearable trauma, he or she can unconsciously create different *"states of mind"* to help him or her mentally and emotionally cope with the pain. Following this interview with the parents and the explanation of the trauma issue, the psychologist never saw little Katie again so that she could say goodbye...

A few weeks later, Katie's mother called Karriker back to tell her that she had been diagnosed with an STD (Sexually Transmitted Disease) and that the pediatrician had recommended a psychiatrist for the girl. Shortly afterwards, Wanda Karriker was contacted by Katie's father's lawyer, informing her that she would soon receive a summons... Indeed, the child had just confided to the psychiatrist that her father had made her do *bad things...* sexual abuse which was therefore reported to social services.

During her deposition in the presence of defence lawyers, psychologist Wanda Karriker stated that the child had never verbalised the abuse to her, but that she had been removed from therapy when she suggested the possibility that trauma might have induced the little girl's dissociative behaviours... Wanda Karriker was only able to find out about the outcome of the case through the lawyers, but it would appear that the accusations of sexual abuse have been confirmed. Little Katie has been removed from her parents' care and has been placed in the custody of social services.

Subsequently, a therapist contacted Karriker for copies of the various psychological tests she had done with little Katie at the time, and wrote to her: 'Katie is an enigma. We are not making much progress with her. She always gets into conflicts, but then she denies doing anything wrong. Sometimes she acts like a baby, has lots of angry outbursts while at other times she can be totally passive, not responding to anything. For example the way she refuses to see her mother or father when they come for supervised visits. '

Wanda Karriker then couldn't help asking this therapist if the child had been treated for her deep dissociative disorders... To which the therapist replied: "But Dr. Karriker, this child shows no symptoms of multiple personality"...

Later, recalling how dissociated little Katie was, and how she behaved when a camera was rolling in the office, Karriker realised that if she had been able to work with her longer, the child would certainly have revealed more about the abuse. Her behaviour in front of a camera made the psychologist think that her parents were using her to produce child pornography and God knows what other horrors...[348]

The case of this little girl illustrates some of the practices denounced in Chapter 3, i.e. all those children dissociated and fractionated by intra-familial abuse, children removed from their families to be placed in care and who potentially become targets and prey for paedocriminal networks and mind control programmes. In the case reported here by Dr. Wanda Karriker, we have a little girl visibly fractured by trauma who is separated from her parents and it is interesting to note that the psychiatrist in charge of Katie's care once she was placed, states that she shows absolutely no symptoms of multiple personality... In other words, he is keeping Pandora's box closed by totally ignoring the little girl's dissociative disorders, or else he is not trained at all for that...

d/ the case of an eight-year-old child

The book "Childhood Antecedents of Multiple Personality" by Dr. Richard Kluft reports on some cases of children with split personalities. In particular, he describes in detail the case of an eight-year-old boy.

Tom was a boy who suffered from multiple personality disorder. It was later discovered that his grandmother also had a D.I.D. .... One of the grandmother's alter admitted to abusing the mother, who probably also suffered from severe dissociative disorder. So here again we are in a context of transgenerational I.D.D.

---

[348] Incest - The ultimate betrayal: Findings from a series of international extreme abuse surveys " - Wanda Karriker, 2008.

Tom was usually a good and exemplary child, but he could suddenly become extremely difficult while denying any bad behaviour he might have had, even if it had just happened a few moments earlier. He would blatantly lie while totally denying his involvement in acts that his whole family had witnessed. His voice, verbal and body language, and friendships varied with what seemed to be his "moods"... Sometimes he would even say he was a girl and then behave in an effeminate manner. Following these episodes he would admit in a very embarrassed way that he thought he was a girl, but that he had no memory of behaving in this way... He was accident prone but did not seem to learn anything from it. His school results were extremely erratic. Often it was found by his teachers that he did not understand certain subjects and when questioned he claimed that he had never been taught these things... His teachers therefore concluded that he was *slow-witted* and simply had learning difficulties.

Tom also frequently said that some of the clothes in his wardrobe were not his own and became confused when his mother tried to remind him when they had bought them together. The child was often depressed, particularly when he was called a liar, especially when confronted with acts that he had just denied participating in. The child was well aware of his efforts to cover up his recurring memory lapses as he knew that he was often *'in the dark'*.

Tom confessed that he was hearing voices in his head, both boys' and girls' voices.

During the interview with the therapist, several types of behaviour were noted, as well as changes in his voice. In addition, there was blatant amnesia about the content of the interview. His therapist used hypnosis to explore Tom's personality. The therapist reported that as soon as Tom was in a hypnotic trance, a personality with a deep voice spontaneously emerged. This alter said his name was *"Marvin"* and that he was an astronaut. Marvin told the therapist that Tom needed help because he *"wanted to be a girl"*, this alter also gave the therapist some advice in writing. Following this hypnosis session, Tom had total amnesia about the conversation between Marvin and the therapist. It was also found that Tom's and Marvin's handwriting was totally different. In all, five alter personalities were discovered in this child. Tom was depressed and rather weak, which is classic for the 'host' personality. The role of the alter Marvin was to help him with his inconceivable anger and fear. Tom had another alter named Teddy, as well as two female personalities named Wilma and Betty. Their characteristics were those of a mother, while Marvin and Teddy were more a representation of the father with a rational and brutal character.

It became clear during the therapy that the young patient had dissociated during an *NDE* (near-death experience) at the age of two and a half. He had fallen into a pond and almost drowned. He had been lifted out of the water lifelessly and finally "resurrected".[349]

---

[349] Childhood Antecedents of Multiple Personality " - Richard P. Kluft, 1985, p.179-180.

e/ Report on five cases

Here are five cases that have been described in a programme on dissociative disorders at the Psychiatric Department of Istanbul University in Turkey. The study was conducted by Dr. Salih Zoroglu. The cases were reported in 1996 by the journal *"Dissociation"* in an article entitled *"Dissociative disorder in childhood: five Turkish cases"*.

Hale:

Hale was a ten-year-old girl who had recurrent migraines and nausea. She was irritable and cried for no apparent reason, talked to herself, laughed inappropriately, had trance-like states and self-harmed. She even behaved like a delinquent and wore make-up and clothing inappropriately. In addition she had night terrors and visual hallucinations.

Her mother first took her to a *'Hoca'* (traditional healer) who said that she was possessed by *jinn* (demons in the Muslim tradition), but this consultation did not improve her mental state.

During the first clinical session, she told the therapist that she had been hearing voices in her head for a long time. One of these voices was that of *"Cisem"*, a very nice girl. The other voices were bad, they belonged to "people" of different ages and sexes. These were the voices that forced her to do bad things and systematically commented on her behaviour. As the therapy progressed, eleven alter personalities appeared. Among them was Cisem, an older girl who wanted Hale to be happy and well behaved. Cisem was afraid of the other alters who might punish her when she wanted to help Hale. The *"Big Boss"* was an older man who was the leader of the group of bad alters. Hale confided that this *"Big Boss"* alter and his cronies could connect directly to what she said and did through an (internal) computer. They could also use this computer in *observation* mode and know everything she was doing in great detail. So Hale sometimes felt like a robot when she was under the control of this computer. There were a total of six alter personalities that were under the control of *the Big Boss*. In addition, there were two other suicidal alters completely separate from the others.

Hale was severely beaten as a child. During therapy, she revealed that Cisem had been raped by a man named Erhan. He later became one of the alter persecutors, one of the assistants of the *'Big Boss'*. Memories of the rape came back in flashes, but Hale would not accept the fact that she was the one who had been raped and insisted that she was totally separated from Cisem. Eventually, after much therapeutic work, all the alter personalities were integrated and all the symptoms disappeared.

Mine:

The nine-year-old girl was taken to the child psychiatric ward of the clinic where her mother was already staying. Her father and brother had noticed that her behaviour changed abruptly when the father came home. She was very moody and aggressive. She often cried and acted as if she saw faces that she seemed to be afraid of and talked to continuously.

One day she went to the police and said that two men were following her. These two men were in fact her father and her brother whom she no longer recognised... She then spent the night in the police station (for her safety), and the next morning, after returning to her normal state, she could not remember anything that had happened the day before.

The girl told her mother that she had a friend inside her. A friend she could see and play with, and who also helped her keep her father and the boys at school at bay. Mine heard voices in her head, one of which was that of a girl a year younger than her. This alter emerged in a therapy session calling herself *"Ayse"*. This alter personality stated that she had been with Mine for three years and was on good terms with her. When asked where Mine was at that moment, she replied that she did not know while continuing to play with a puzzle. Later, when Mine "came back", she looked at the puzzle half reconstructed by Ayse but had no idea of the time that had passed or what Ayse had been doing during that time. Later, another alter personality of the opposite sex was identified. It was reported that her father was a chronic alcoholic who beat his wife and children. In Mine's case, the therapy was unfortunately very random as it depended on her mother's hospitalizations.

Mehmet:

Mehmet's family had regularly noticed that his behaviour was changing dramatically. The 11-year-old sometimes started to read and write in a way that was totally immature for his age. He could no longer pronounce the letter "R", he did not even know his name or age. The only thing he remembered was his parents. At such times he became like an introverted little child and played with toys inappropriate for his age. Moreover, he had no sense of time during his "fits".

Mehmet received therapy once a week for two months. At the fourth session he arrived with his premorbid personality, he did not recognise his therapist and did not seem to remember the previous sessions. This personality was that of a friendly boy with a very mature behaviour and speech for his age. He was particularly interested in science. He had complete amnesia of the times when he acted as a very young child.

His parents reported that the personality changes had started three months earlier. Each personality would emerge for three or four days, then he would not remember anything at all when another alter took over. Mehmet sometimes had paralysis in one arm that lasted ten to thirty minutes, after which he was hospitalised four times in different hospitals, including two university clinics. Comprehensive examinations (neurological, cranial, electroencephalogram) showed nothing abnormal, the arm paralysis was diagnosed as dissociative conversion disorder. Prescription of anti-psychotics, antidepressants, tranquilizers and anti-epileptics did not help him at all, on the contrary, these drugs provoked violent behaviour in him.

In the course of his therapy, two other alter personalities were observed. One in which he lost his ability to walk and talk: this was clearly an alter in the baby stage, as his voice and expressions attested. In the other alter personality he cried out "I'm crazy, I'm crazy! and he didn't recognise anyone at all.

In her case, no psychological or physical trauma was revealed. His older sister also stated that there was no abuse or neglect in the family. None of Mehmet's alter personalities had visual or auditory hallucinations, nor any such manifestations through which an alter could communicate. The boy could easily be hypnotized but the alter personalities did not emerge by this method. Instead, the changes occurred spontaneously and Mehmet had complete amnesia of these "seizures". The family eventually stopped the therapy and reported a year later that the dissociative disorders had ceased and that Mehmet had regained a good level of maturity.

Emre:

Emre was a five-year-old boy when he was admitted to a clinic at the request of his mother. The boy had sudden aggressive behaviours during which he broke objects, attacked friends, strangers and even his mother. He also had short periods when he was in a trance-like state, hearing voices, having horrible visions and many somatic symptoms such as migraines and nausea. Sometimes he seemed to be talking to himself, laughing and chatting for hours with who knows who... His behaviour was completely polarised and he had sexualised attitudes inappropriate for his age.

He confided that he could hear the voices of four girls and six boys in his head, all aged between four and twelve. He could see them, play with them and talk to them when he was alone. One of the girls, "Gamze the witch", had a gun with which she scared Emre and the other children. Sometimes she would hit Emre and break his toys, or she would have fun scaring him at night. At the third therapy session, Emre said that a twelve-year-old girl named "Cunyet" wanted to talk to the people present. This is how the alter Cunyet introduced herself: she was the eldest and it was she who protected Emre and the other children from the witch Gamze, the persecuting alter. When the therapist asked where Emre was, Cunyet pointed to an empty chair and said that he was sitting there listening to them. Although it was reported by his parents that the child often had amnesia, there was no evidence of amnesia between these two alter personalities during the therapy. No traumatic past was reported in this boy's case.

Nilgun:

This 10-year-old girl was once brought to therapy by her father. Her symptoms were recurrent boredom, sadness, crying for no apparent reason, loss of appetite, trance-like states, severe migraines, fainting spells, nausea, stomach pains and extreme tantrums.

Nilgun was diagnosed with depression by two psychiatrists. During the first interview, the girl said that there was an older girl inside her called *"Fatma"*. She confided that she had been hearing her voice almost every day for over two months. This voice comforted and encouraged her, and commented on her behaviour, feelings and thoughts. She also warned Nilgun never to talk about this to anyone including the therapist. At first the alter Fatma refused to talk to the therapist, then it started to communicate through Nilgun, and finally emerged completely: Fatma told the therapist that she had to "go" into Nilgun after a disastrous event that only she knows about, in order to help the girl. She said that she did not have the same parents as Nilgun and that she had taken control several times to help her but that Nilgun did not know what she was doing because she could not see her. She also said that she did not know everything that Nilgun did...

When the alter Fatma emerged, Nilgun's facial expressions, the way she spoke and the way she interacted with people changed completely. She seemed very serious and gave concise and precise answers. During the sessions, Nilgun liked to play with toys or puzzles, but Fatma was not interested at all. She said she was too old to play in this way. She also said that Nilgun was inside her. While Nilgun was a little blonde girl with blue eyes, Fatma described herself as having brown eyes and hair. Nilgun had amnesia about the periods of time when Fatma was in control. No past traumatic experiences were found in the case of this little girl.[350]

6 - I.D.T. IN THE MEDIA

a/ Documentaries

In the 1990s, the Australian television network *Seven Network* devoted a documentary to the phenomenon of multiple personalities in its series 'The Extraordinary'.

In 1993, the American channel *HBO* broadcast *"Multiple* Personalities: *The Search for Deadly Memories"*, a documentary entirely devoted to I.D.T.

In 1999 a French-language documentary was released in the series *"Phénomènes inexpliqués"* entitled *"Dédoublement de la personnalité"* (originally directed by *Gloria Sykes* and produced by *A&E Television Network*). This appears to be the only French-language documentary on the subject.

In 1999, a documentary entitled *"Mistaken Identity"* was broadcast on *BBC2* (in the series *"Horizon"*), in which several IDD patients and therapists spoke.

In 2004, a report entitled *"The Woman With Seven Personalities"* shows Dr. Ruth Selwyn accompanying Helen, a woman who developed multiple personalities as a result of ritual abuse including sexual violence.

---

[350] *Dissociative identity disorder in childhood: five Turkish cases"* - S. Zoroglu, L. Yargic, M. Ozturk, Journal "Dissociation", Vol.9 N°4, 12/1996.

The most recent documentary appears to be from 2010, entitled *"When The Devil Knocks"* and produced by *Bountiful Films* (Canada). It tells the story of Hilary Stanton, a woman diagnosed with I.D.D. and treated by therapist Cheryl Malmo.

b/ Cinema and TV series

It is interesting to note that despite the fact that this psychiatric disorder is more or less hidden from the general public, many film productions have used it as a basis for their screenplay:
- The Case of Becky (1921)
- Dr Jekyll & Mr Hyde (1941)
- *The Dark Mirror* (The Double Riddle, 1946)
- *The Three Face of* Eve (1957)
- *The Manchurian Candidate* (A Crime in the Head, 1962)
- The Nutty Professor (1963)
- *A Clockwork Orange* (1971)
- *Sybil* (1976)
- *Dressed to Kill* (Pulsions, 1980)
- *Zelig* (1983)
- Voices Within: The Lives Of Truddi Chase (Demons Within, 1990)
- *Raising Cain* (The Spirit of Cain, 1992)
- Plots (1997)
- Fight-Club (1999)
- Session 9 (2001)
- *The Bourne Identity* (Memory in the Skin, 2002)
- *Daedalus* (2002)
- Identity (2003)
- *Secret Window* (2004)
- *Hide & Seek* (Trouble jeu, 2005)
- Mr Brooks (2007)
- Shutter Island (2010)
- Frankie & Alice (2010)
- The Crowded Room (2015)

We can also mention the television series *Dollhouse*, featuring the exploitation of programmed and amnesiac human *'dolls'*, or *United State of Tara*, which tells the story of a mother suffering from IDD, but also the Canadian series *Shattered*, whose main character is a policeman with multiple personalities... The short film *"Inside"* by Trevor Sands features a patient with a rather motley multiple personality. The web series *Neuroblaste*, produced in 2011 by *Radio-Canada* in *motion comic* format, is inspired by the work on MK-Ultra brainwashing carried out in Montreal in the 1960s by psychiatrist Ewen Cameron.

Generally in film productions, IDD is portrayed in a stereotypical and biased way, showing only the attractive and sensational side of the multiple personality and overshadowing the other characteristics of the disease.

Furthermore, most films dealing with this subject feature extremely conflicted, violent and even murderous characters. This vision of I.D.T. is limiting. Furthermore, films tend to mix and confuse schizophrenia and I.D.D., which further aggravates the general confusion between these two diagnoses. As cinema is a visual art, the usual cinematic representation of I.D.D. does not allow for the distinction between true split personality and hallucination, which reinforces the confusion between schizophrenia and I.D.D.[351]

As for the media image of I.D.T.-based mind control, this is what therapist Alison Miller writes: "The popular media portrayal of mind control usually involves spies or assassins working for the CIA or other military, political, or even private business groups, without them being aware of it. This is because they have other 'personalities' involved in these activities. Take for example Jason Bourne, the hero of the film "Complots", or Echo in the series "Dollhouse", among other American productions. These dramas that feature special agents suggest to the audience that they were recruited as adults, even making a deliberate choice to participate in these things. Once they have been recruited, the story begins, their old memories are erased and a new personality with specific skills is then created. However, there is only one stage of life in which the programmers can create an individual who can do such activities without any awareness, without any resistance... There is only one way to do it and that is by abuse and torture of a young child. The ugly reality is that there are no adults who would willingly engage in such things, there are only little victims."[352]

c/ The Incredible Hulk...

Everyone knows the character "Hulk", the man who transforms into a sort of green giant with tenfold strength when something triggers an extreme rage in him. The Incredible Hulk was created by writer Stan Lee and cartoonist Jack Kirby. The fictional character was popularised by *Marvel Comics*, where he first appeared in the United States in 1962. What people don't know is that the story of the Incredible Hulk is based on a psychiatric disorder that is nothing more than I.D.T. with its dissociative amnesia. Without a split personality, the hero Bruce Banner would not turn into the Incredible Hulk...

On the website of the publishing[353] house we can read a very detailed description of the world of the Hulk and especially of his split personality. The publisher describes perfectly the traumatic and dissociative context behind the story of the 'green giant'. We learn that Bruce Banner is the son of an alcoholic who hated him deeply. His father abused and terrorised him, even killing his mother before being committed to a psychiatric hospital. Early on, Bruce showed

---

[351] I was the murderer! Or the Dissociative Identity Disorder in the cinema" - Beatriz Vera Posek, 2006.

[352] "Becoming Yourself: Overcoming Mind Control and Ritual Abuse" - Alison Miller, 2014, p.15.

[353] Marvel Universe Wiki: Hulk (Bruce Banner), www.marvel.com.

signs of great intelligence but also of being withdrawn. We can read on *Marvel.com* that he would have *"developed a split personality to help him deal with his pain and rage"*, the famous and incredible Hulk is therefore suffering from a dissociative identity disorder...

At school, Bruce Banner was so unsociable and violent that he ended up planting a bomb in the basement of his school... which drew the attention of the army to this little genius who would later become a physicist working for them. It was an accidental gamma ray irradiation that caused this radical physical transformation. At the beginning of the saga, Bruce transformed into a grey Hulk at sunset and returned to his human form at dawn. Later, his change into a 'green giant' will be triggered by a strong release of adrenaline when Bruce goes into an extreme rage at any time of day. The Green Hulk does not have the same intelligence as Bruce, nor does he have the same memory, he is a raving alter who can be a real threat to society. It is important to note that Bruce Banner suffers from amnesia, he never remembers what the Hulk has done and he has to reconstruct the events from the damage his green alter has caused in his path... This is clearly an uncontrollable rage where Bruce Banner enters a dissociative state. We are told that he is constantly struggling to control these *"switches"* and maintain a stability of his own personality...

The story continues... One day, psychiatrist Leonard *"Doc"* Samson captures the Hulk and manages to separate Bruce Banner's personality from the Hulk's. Without Bruce's personality to channel and hold him, the Hulk becomes even more dangerous. Bruce decides that the only way he can control the "green giant" is to merge with the monster. But the stress of reintegration creates another alter: *"Joe Fixit"*. This alter is a bad-tempered bully whose personality resembles that of Bruce's father. From this point on, there is a real battle in Bruce's subconscious as to which alter personality will take control and have supremacy. However, through hypnosis sessions, Banner, Hulk and Joe Fixit are all brought to the same level of consciousness so that together they can confront unresolved issues, finally facing their inner demons... Bruce Banner must then confront the memories of his father abusing him and murdering his mother. By integrating this, Bruce becomes able to merge the alter personalities to finally find inner peace: another personality will then emerge, a new Hulk who will have the mental abilities and intelligence of Bruce Banner while keeping the strength of the Incredible Hulk. This new personality will be called *"The Professor"*...

As you can see, we are right in the middle of the subject of the functioning of multiple personalities, or even the process of mental control.

The Hulk is one of those American superheroes (the Marvel universe of *comic books*) who are often implicitly linked to dissociative identity disorder. Superheroes with a classic civilian identity on the one hand and a secret identity with superpowers on the other, such as *Batman, Superman* and *Spiderman* (all three of whom retain the memory of their transformation). We can mention characters such as *Double* Face (one of the *super-villains* of the Batman universe) with a benevolent and a malevolent personality, or the character *Legion*, inhabited by multiple personalities each with psychic powers. There is also the superhero *Moon Knight*, who also has an I.D.T. with three alter personalities. Moreover, he has a relationship with an Egyptian god that allows him to become even stronger, especially on the nights of the full moon... All these characters illustrate the strong presence of the I.D.T. in the *comic book* and superhero culture. Dissociative amnesia is also present: The *X-Men* character, James Howlett, has an alter named *Wolverine* who is prone to amnesia, he never remembers the massacres he regularly engages in, just as the Hulk does not remember his destructive rages. This is a perfect illustration of the phenomenon of traumatic amnesia walls in dissociated states.

Note that in 1992, the *X-Men* series made a clear reference to the MK-Ultra programme in one of the episodes of season 4 entitled *"Weapon X, Lies and Videotape"*. In this episode the *X-Men* discover a laboratory where they were mind-controlled years before. They find a videotape that contains a description of the experiments that were done on them, and the cartoon says: *"Anonymous subjects have been tested and conditioned with trauma. We are able to reintegrate these men into society when the secret service needs them, without them having any memory of being programmed. They are conditioned and they don't remember anything... The key is to reach their subconscious. The key is to reach their subconscious. To do this the subject must be repeatedly exposed to simulations of extreme emotional trauma. Using drugs, we imprint false memories in the subject's mind in order to saturate him emotionally and split him up to make him controllable... This process seems to work best when the traumas are real...'* ... The MK-Ultra programme summarised in a few lines, but of course this is all science fiction for retarded teenagers...

7 - CONCLUSION

For Dr. Colin Ross, the serious study of I.D.T. should have caused a real paradigm shift in modern psychiatry, he writes: *"I.D.T. is the most important and interesting disorder in psychiatry, which is why I study it. I believe it is a key diagnosis in this impending paradigm shift in psychiatry, because I.D.T. best illustrates the characteristic response of the human organism to severe psychic trauma; but also because trauma is a major cause of mental illness from a public health perspective. I believe that trauma is a major underlying cause in many mental illnesses, such as depression, eating disorders, personality disorders, substance abuse, psychosomatic disorders and all forms of self-harm and violence. Biological psychiatry should achieve much better results if it focuses on the psychobiology of trauma."*[354]

It would seem that French-speaking psychiatry is poorly trained, if at all, in psychotraumatology and even less so in dissociative disorders.... The French-speaking resources (publications of scientific studies, publications of testimonies, specialised books, investigations and journalistic reports) concerning D.I.D., and more globally psychotraumatology, seem very limited if not non-existent. This is rather strange when this disorder is officially recognised

---

[354] "The Osiris Complex: Case Studies in Multiple Personality Disorder" - Colin Ross, 1994, p.xii.

in the DSM and when there is a large number of English-language works on the subject. Why is there such a gap in the French-speaking world? Why is psychotraumatology not more developed? This would allow us to better help the victims. Why is the existence of I.D.T. vigorously attacked and discredited by a certain medical elite or pseudo experts? Not only do they not recognise the phenomena of personality splitting, but they also relativise the consequences that childhood trauma can have on the child's future life.

It is a real lead cover for the Pandora's box of ritual abuse and trauma-based mind control: the neurological process of dissociation and traumatic amnesia. To teach in medical schools the scientific workings of dissociation, amnesic walls and personality splitting would be to reveal publicly and academically a certain occult knowledge. This knowledge is as old as the hills and is used systematically and maliciously by certain power groups today. The process of functioning of slaves under mental programming is not supposed to reach the public and lay sphere. Most students of psychology and psychiatry do not believe that such mind control is possible. This is because they have no knowledge of the basic concept behind MK, i.e. I.D.D., a personality disorder that is necessary for a human to work like a robot in clandestine operations... or not.

In an article entitled *"The Dissociative Disorders, Rarely Considered and Underdiagnosed"*, Dr. Philip M. Coons confirms that dissociative disorders are generally underdiagnosed because of a lack of training. Dr. Coons notes that psychiatric professionals are not familiar with this diagnosis or even with dissociative symptomatology because, according to him, *professionals seriously lack epidemiological data concerning dissociative disorders*. Why such an omission in the psychiatric community?

We have the beginnings of an answer in Cathy O'Brien's autobiography, *TRANCE Formation of America: True life story of a mind control slave*. Here is what Mark Phillips writes about psychiatric institutions: *"To date, neither the American Psychiatric Association nor the American Psychological Association has published a model for the development of an effective therapeutic protocol for dissociative disorders (considered to be the result of repeated trauma). A number of factors make the development of such a model difficult. The first of these is the secrecy that National Security applies to classified mind control research. In the current climate, referring mind control victims to psychiatric professionals for treatment would be like referring a patient in need of emergency surgery to a surgeon who has been blindfolded and handcuffed (...) What might allow us to lay the groundwork for an explanation would be to identify "who" in our government has an interest in blocking crucial medical research findings and other technological information from the psychiatric professions (...).) Taking the next step and getting a copy of the faculty professor's Oxford's Companion To The Mind (Oxford Press, 1987), you can find almost everything about mind research without any reference to mind control. Perhaps you will now have the opportunity to realise through the omissions of Random House, Webster and other Oxford Press, that you are a victim of information control.* "[355]

MK-Monarch survivor Cathy O'Brien writes in this book: "There are many such facilities in our country, within various CIA, military and NASA complexes, where hyper-advanced government knowledge is developed, tested and modified. The people I met, who had studied in depth the scientific mechanisms of the brain and the ins and outs of the mind, were using this accumulation of secret knowledge to manipulate and/or control others (...) (ed: Senator) Byrd explained to me that the 'New World Order' was 'empowered' by allowing its lobby, the American Psychiatric Association (APA), only partial information and/or deliberate misinformation of the psychiatric community regarding the treatment modalities for severe dissociative disorders resulting from mind control! Its authors believed that the withholding of knowledge and the proliferation of deliberate misinformation allowed them to control their secrets and, subsequently, humanity. This may well be the case if no one could or would respond to the information presented in this book."[356]

Here is a dialogue from the book *"For National Security"* which illustrates the lack of knowledge of the psychiatric world on this subject:

- I've made a lot of phone calls," Marsha begins, "it's really hard to approach psychiatric professionals about a 'classified' subject like mind control. They like to think they already know everything about it. Mark and I nod in agreement.

- Have you tried using the term 'brainwashing'?

- Yes," Marsha says, "I've even settled on the term 'behaviour modification', and I'm still having trouble describing the disorder, let alone finding a facility to deal with it. If you agree, I will start a search again, but this time to find someone who could diagnose her with BDD.

- Is there anyone in this state who knows how to treat this disorder? By today's psychiatric standards, it takes an average of eight and a half years to diagnose this syndrome, and during that time there must be treatment. Until the 'intelligence guys' get the data out into the psychiatric community for accurate diagnosis and treatment, our only solution is the old, obsolete, long-term therapies. How do you plan to find someone in this state to diagnose the consequences of the CIA's abuse of Cathy?[357]

Mental health professionals are clearly not trained to be able to correctly diagnose a person suffering from Dissociative Identity Disorder... This psychiatric disorder is not taught in the faculties, so you don't look for it and if you don't look for something, you don't find it... so it doesn't exist, the circle is closed. The lack of correct diagnosis, depriving the patient of proper treatment, is the most important and common problem for patients with I.D.D.. The latter

---

[355] *TRANCE Formation of America: True life story of a mind control slave* - Cathy O'Brien & Mark Phillips, 2013, pp.62-19.

[356] Ibid, pp.327-328.

[357] *"For the sake of National Security"* - Cathy O'Brien & Mark Phillips, 2015, p.101-102.

will usually be diagnosed as schizophrenic, bipolar or *borderline...* without forgetting of course the heavy prescription of psychotropic drugs that are part of the *therapeutic* protocol, fattening the pharmaceutical laboratories copiously, by the way...

In Canadian therapist Alison Miller's book, Healing the Unimaginable, a patient (LisaBri) testifies: 'In the early 90s I was diagnosed with everything from schizophrenia to PMS. I was told to find a hobby and not to drink at night. The psychiatrist would take a box of white pills out of his office every time I showed an emotional sign. Every therapist, doctor and psychiatrist I met wanted me to shut down my emotions or keep them away from me. But where could these emotions go? The more I suppressed them, the worse I got, until one day I found myself wandering around the secure ward of a psychiatric hospital... I managed to get off the drugs and alcohol and finally found a competent therapist to work with. I was determined to do everything I could to curb the intense emotional states I was experiencing. I was soon diagnosed with I.D.D."[358]

A closer look at I.D.T. shows that the dissociative and amnesic functions of the human mind can be exploited for the purpose of manipulation and exploitation of the individual. This is a true parallel psychiatric science, which in the wrong hands becomes a traumatic science and a weapon of undetectable mind control. If this split personality disorder with its amnesiac walls is not taught in medical schools and is systematically controversial and discredited by an elite of *experts,* it is for the simple reason that it is the main axis of the mental control practiced by certain dominant occult organisations. This is the cornerstone of the "nameless religion": the ritual abuses that enable MK programming, which is itself based on the structuring and organisation of an internal system resulting from an I.D.T.

Moreover, I.D.T. opens the way to the question of demonic possession and the possible existence of an occult science mastering the parameters of this possession by certain entities. For as we shall see in the next chapter, I.D.T. and demonic possession are intimately linked. Nowadays the ability to study both the spiritual and psychological aspects of mind control phenomena is often lacking, but there are exceptions, such as Dr. Loreda Fox's book *"The Spiritual Dimensions of MPD".* It is inevitable that the issue of demonic possession in the trauma-based mind control process will be addressed at some point. Traugott Konstantin Oesterreich, who was a professor of philosophy at the University of Tubingen in Germany, studied multiple personalities and demonic possession closely. He wrote a seminal book about it, which was translated into English in 1930 under the title *"Possession: Demoniacal and Other".* His anthology on the subject provides documented cases indirectly revealing that trauma-induced mind control was practised in Germany, France and Belgium long before the 20th century. Oesterreich's research in the early 1900s was the kind of research that Nazi MK programmers were very aware of. In 1921, Germans such as Oesterreich described abrupt personality changes by the term *"somnambuliform*

---

[358] "Healing the Unimaginable: Treating Ritual Abuse and Mind Control" - Alison Miller, 2012, p.136.

possession" (hypnotic states) or *"demonic somnambulism"* or what can be called *"Besessenheit von Hypnotismus und bösen Geistern"* (possession by hypnosis *and* evil spirits).[359]

---

[359] "The Illuminati Formula Used to Create an Undetectable Total Mind Controlled Slave" - Fritz Springmeier & Cisco Wheeler, 1996.

CHAPTER 6

TRAUMA, DISSOCIATION AND CONNECTION TO OTHER DIMENSIONS

If we walk in the flesh, we do not fight according to the flesh. For the weapons with which we fight are not carnal, but are powerful in the sight of God, to overthrow strongholds. 2 Corinthians 10:3-4

Father Hilarion Tissot believes that all nervous diseases accompanied by hallucinations and delusions are demonic possessions, and understanding things in the Kabbalist sense, he would be fully correct. The History of Magic - Eliphas Levi, 1913

In 1 Cor 15:44 we read: *'He is sown in the animal body, he is raised in the spiritual body, there is an animal body and there is a spiritual body'. So we know that we have a physical body and a spiritual body. It is through this biological body that we have physical contact with the material world around us. We are not aware that we have a spiritual body until our physical body dies. This is what God intended for us. Through rituals, Satanists use demons to separate the spiritual body from the physical body. When the soul and spirit have been separated and the spiritual body has been separated from the physical body, then the person enters in a fully conscious way into a whole other dimension. This is the dimension I call the inner world. This world is as vast and as real to the individual as the physical world is to us. We think of spirits as having a 'vaporous' state, but people who have been in this dimension have reported to me that demons do have weight and substance.* Restoring Survivors of Satanic Ritual Abuse - Patricia Baird Clark, 2000

1 - INTRODUCTION

We are now going to step into another dimension, into the paranormal... We are going to establish whether there is a link between dissociative identity disorder and demonic possessions; dissociation and psychic powers; with what seems to be a common factor: childhood traumas. We will see that severe trauma causes a kind of spiritual 'unlocking' that creates an opening to what we might call the *spirit world*, that is, dimensions beyond our physical and material reality. The dissociation that severe trauma brings about opens certain spiritual doors, but it also shapes the neurological construction in the child. As we shall see, these two things combined can lead to paranormal psychic faculties such as mediumship, clairvoyance, remote viewing, etc. But this traumatic process is also the door open to certain entities that will take advantage of these breaches, or fractures, to introduce themselves into the victim's spiritual world.

Initiatory rituals that deliberately provoke trauma are practised to open doors to other dimensions and spiritually link the *initiate* (the child victim) with the spirit world. The phenomenon of psychic dissociation linked to trauma would thus be a kind of bridge connecting *normal* cognitive functions to *paranormal* cognitive functions, linking the physical world to the metaphysical world. The corresponding metaphor is that of Alice *going through the mirror* to access another world. It is the access to this *'inner world' that* many survivors of ritual abuse and mind control talk about, a psychic and spiritual fracturing that creates an opening to another dimension of the human being... The process of dissociation is the basis of all spiritual practices aiming at accessing other dimensions (from mediumship to *'Astral Travel'*), and secret societies of the Masonic type study and teach these things.

Exploring the link between the phenomenon of dissociation and the phenomenon of demonic possession can pose a certain problem that must be overcome. Indeed, clinicians and other therapists working on psychotraumatology and dissociation already find it very difficult to have the reality of dissociative disorders credibly recognised, without having to be linked to the *"archaic, wild and primitive"* world of traditional indigenous healers and other *demon-hunting* exorcists. Yet these two worlds are inseparable if we are to understand the subject properly: dissociation and possession are integral parts of pre-industrial and even ancient religious traditions. The world of modern medicine could learn a lot from the world of traditional healers, especially in the psychiatric field. The spiritual side of personality disorders is usually neglected by therapists and mocked by Cartesian minds who will quickly criticise the subject of demonology, relegating it to *superstitious diablerie*, the relic of an *obscure medieval past*... Why not? But knowing that there are real adepts of occultism, rituals of all kinds and black magic, people who firmly believe that they are working hand in hand with Lucifer, the prince of this world, and his army of demons: rejecting the problem of the "devil" is not an option because it would be tantamount to falling into his trap, i.e. to denying his existence... We would then find ourselves totally subjected to his wiles and at the mercy of his spiritual attacks. Even if you don't believe in it, you should know that some people believe in it like hell and apply certain rituals to the letter...

The author Fritz Springmeier makes an interesting analogy between demonology and microbiology. Most people have never seen a demon just as they have never seen a virus. Yet they deny the existence of one and take antivirals to protect themselves against the other. There will always be differences of opinion on demonology, but just as it has been helpful to the health of many patients to treat viruses, victims of ritual abuse and mind control have found it helpful to treat demons, i.e. the spiritual side of their psychic disorders. Wasn't it Father Georges Morand who declared on France Culture in 2011 that the victims of satanic cults he had met had only escaped by praying an exorcism? Are the entities that the Siberian shamans meet or fight in their astral journeys nothing but frozen wind? Wasn't one of the main activities of Jesus Christ when he walked this earth to cast out demons, to deliver the sick through prayer? Did some of those healed by Christ have a split personality and even a split soul? In his book *Jesus: The Evidence,* Ian Wilson suggests that the many possessed people healed by Jesus Christ may have been suffering from I.D.D.

- As soon as Jesus came ashore, a man came to meet him from the tombs, possessed of an unclean spirit. He had his home in the tombs, and no one could bind him any more, not even with a chain. For many times he had been shackled and bound with chains, but he had broken the chains and broken the fetters, and no one had the strength to tame him. He was constantly night and day in the tombs and on the mountains, shouting and hurting himself with stones. He saw Jesus from afar, ran to him, bowed down to him, and cried out with a loud voice:

- What do you want from me, Jesus, Son of the Most High? I beseech you in the name of God, do not torment me. For Jesus said to him:

- Come out of the man, unclean spirit. And Jesus asked him:

- What is your name?"

- Legion is my name," he replied, "for there are many of us.

Mark 5:2-9

The possessed man answers Jesus Christ that he is *legion,* and that there are *many of them.* Is it an army of demons? A personality split into a thousand pieces? Or a mixture of both? Whatever the answer, the Lord has delivered and set this man free.

The Spirit of the Lord, the LORD, is upon me,

For the Lord has anointed me.

He has sent me to bring good news to the downtrodden;

To heal the brokenhearted,

To proclaim to the captives their release

And to the prisoners deliverance.

(Isaiah 61:1)

When the Bible speaks of *'broken heart',* it is natural to think at first that it is a figurative meaning, a metaphor sometimes used to describe a romantic relationship: *'he broke her heart'.* But just as Jesus Christ said *"eat, this is My Body, drink, this is My Blood",* there is nothing figurative or symbolic about the expression *"broken heart".*

John Eldredge, the author of *Wild at Heart: Discovering the Secret's of a Man's Soul,* has this to say about it:

When Isaiah speaks of the 'broken heart', God is not using a metaphor. In Hebrew it is called leb shabar ("leb" for "heart", and "shabar" for "broken"). Isaiah uses the word "shabar" to describe a bush whose dry twigs are broken (27:11), to describe the idols of Babylon lying broken on the ground (21:9) just as a statue breaks into a thousand pieces when you throw it on the ground; or to describe a broken bone (38:13). Here God is speaking literally, he says: "Your heart is in pieces, I want to heal it. "

The Hebrew word *'leb',* in addition to meaning *'heart',* can also be translated as *'spirit', 'soul'* or *'conscience'.* Theologians tell us that in the New and Old Testaments, references to spirit, soul and heart refer to one and the same thing. This means that in Isaiah the *'broken heart'* is equivalent to the broken conscience or the broken spirit, literally broken into a thousand pieces. Is this a reference to dissociation? To a splitting of the personality? Note that in the Old Testament, the Hebrew word for evil is *"ra"*, from the root *"Ra'a"*, a word that also means to break, to shatter, to tear apart.

Traumatic rituals leading to states of trance and possession, with the psycho-spiritual process of personality dissociation, were necessarily present in biblical times, but also in antediluvian and Babylonian times. The *Epic of Gilgamesh*, written in the third millennium B.C. in Mesopotamia, or the *Iliad of Omer around 800* B.C., report testimonies that correspond to what we would call today a dissociation during a trauma. Today the image of the crack and the break is a recurrent theme in the symbolism of Monarch mind control displayed in the entertainment industry. A doll or mannequin with a cracked or broken face, symbolising an alter, is a classic representation of an MK slave with a split personality (more on this in Chapter 9)

2 - MULTIPLE PERSONALITY AND DEMONIC POSSESSION

A curious phenomenon which has been observed for centuries but which has not yet received its full explanation is that in which the individual seems to be the vehicle of a personality which is not his own. Someone else's personality seems to "own" him and express itself through his words and actions, while the individual's true personality is temporarily absent. Dr. D. Laing - The Divided Self

Dr. James Randall Noblitt, referring to recent findings on dissociative disorders, said: "Perhaps we are approaching a new naturalistic theory of spirit possession. A theory not only applicable to mental health, but also to anthropology and historical interpretations of European witchcraft."

In dissociative identity disorder, the *"I"* is fragmented, whereas in possession, the body is divided. In D.I.D., it is the *"I"* entity (the main personality) that is split into several pieces, whereas in possession there is an invasion of an external entity. In other words, in I.D.T., the alters, although separate, are considered to be several aspects of a single individual. Whereas in possession, there are supposed to be several external entities independent and distinct from the individual. In I.D.T., the alters will have to be integrated and merged to reconstruct the personality in psychotherapy, whereas in possession, the outer entities are exorcised and cast out of the person in an exorcism. But as we shall see, these two phenomena, which are very close to each other, sometimes overlap and even seem to merge. It is therefore difficult to affirm that all cases of demonic possession are systematically related to a psychiatric disorder, just as it is difficult to affirm that the intervention of an external entity is only a superstition.

In his book "Occult Bondage and Deliverance", Dr. Kurt E. Koch writes Koch writes: The physician and famous preacher, Dr. Martyn Lloyd-Jones, invited me to speak to a group of psychiatrists on the subject of esotericism and the occult (...) As a result, I was attacked by two psychiatrists who claimed that the biblical accounts of demonic possessions to which I referred were actually cases of mental illness, such as epilepsy or hysteria (...).A man then rose to my defence, stating that from his own experience as a practitioner, he alone could name eleven different cases of demonic possession. Another psychiatrist then agreed with what his colleague had just said, adding that he himself had encountered three or four cases.[360] As we saw in the previous chapter with the work of Dr. Janet, what was called "hysteria" at one time generally referred to cases of multiple personality.

In *The Discovery of the Unconscious,* Henri Ellenberger traced the origins of dynamic psychiatry back to the magical worlds of shamans and medicine men, including historical reports of demonic possession in Europe. He writes in his book that *"Possession may have disappeared, but it has been replaced by the Multiple Personality".* With the modern age of scientism, the phenomenon of demonic possession has given way to a less than rational psychiatric symptom, the ins and outs of which academic medicine is still largely unaware...

Is it a question of sweeping away a 'diabolical', 'superstitious' phenomenon and replacing it with a purely 'neurological' phenomenon? Are the two not linked? Couldn't certain psychic disorders caused by traumatic fractures provoke an "opening" for outside entities? But are we really trying to find out the root cause of these personality disorders? It is true that today we are beginning to point the finger seriously at trauma and to understand its impact on the neurological level. But this phenomenon of multiple personality still hides many secrets, and we note that very few means are implemented to seriously study the question... which as we have seen, remains buried under a thick blanket of lead.

The first reported cases of *multiple personalities* mention individuals possessed by the devil or demons. This is the case of Jeanne Fery, a 25-year-old French Dominican nun who lived in the Mons area in the 16th century. Her case was described by Dr. Désiré Bourneville in 1886 in the book *'La Possession de Jeanne Fery'.* Bourneville himself said that Jeanne Fery represents *"the most perfect case of a split personality".*

Bourneville speaks of a case of "split personality" and his description of it contains all the criteria now referred to in the DSM psychiatric manual to describe IDD. Jeanne Fery's exorcist priest described a *"fragmentation of her identity"* and also mentions a history of trauma in her early childhood. Jeanne Fery was possessed by several 'demons' that had different functions. There was a demon who controlled her eating disorders and another called the *'Sanguinary'* who made her scarify herself because he *wanted pieces of flesh.* A third 'devil' was called *'Garga',* whose function was to protect her from feeling the pain of the beatings she received as a child. However, he made her relive the traumas by making her hit her head and body. Garga also made her attempt suicide several times by scarification or strangulation.

---

[360] Occult Bondage and Deliverance: Counseling the Occultly Oppressed " - Kurt E. Kock, 1972, p.11.

Jeanne Fery also showed dissociative symptoms such as amnesia during these *personality* changes, trance states, inner voices and second states where she showed extreme rage or extreme sadness. She was sometimes described as *"raging mad"*, unable to sit up, let alone lie down, for up to seven days and seven nights. Fery stated that she had visions of St Mary Magdalene who sometimes stood between her and the demons. Some authors claim that this was another of her personalities, the alter *Mary Magdalene*, the most rational and useful personality, who usually appeared at the most critical moments to calm the situation.

Cornau' was the first 'devil' to have possessed her, and he revealed from the nun that he had been her father since she was four years old. It was then learned that the little girl had been cursed by her biological father when she was 2 years old, which had opened the way to this *Cornau* who caused her very strange eating disorders. Jeanne could see these "devils", she could hear them inside her and they sometimes violently took control of her body with tantrums during which she had to be restrained and locked up. They also manifested themselves in childlike behaviour, or in sobbing and intense physical pain. The clinical picture was very similar to that of today's patients with severe dissociative disorders.

During the period when the exorcism rituals were performed, there were improvements and relapses where symptoms were exacerbated, but overall Jeanne's condition improved. Her treatment, which lasted 21 months, included the ongoing care of the sisters and Jeanne's consent to have her 'demons' who played the role of *father* and *grandfather* exorcised. Jeanne Fery kept a diary of her own exorcism in 1584, which was also described in detail by the priest who performed the ritual:

- 12 April 1584: The demon "Namon" reveals his name. Jeanne has lost all her religious knowledge.

- 28 June 1584: Mary Magdalene appears again and Joan tells her about contracts written inside her body, those written in blood link her to the demons.

- 25 August 1584: Mary Magdalene appears and speaks for the first time. Joan signs a written contract to break the link with her demons. Another episode of scarification, but the decision is made to continue the exorcism. The demons give back a piece of her flesh that Jeanne had given them. The exorcism is considered a success because the demons broke a tile as they left, a signal that had been concluded earlier.

- September 1584: Jeanne is very ill and suffers from her self-inflicted wounds. She now feels free of her demons, except for Garga and Cornau.

- 9 November 1584: When she was 4 years old, Cornau became her father. He seduced her with sweets and candy. Without him, she would be dumb and ignorant. Canon Jean Mainsent speaks to Cornau and promises to become Jeanne's father in his place. Mary Magdalene appears again and offers protection. Joan becomes like a child. She asks the archbishop to become her grandfather, which he accepts.

- November 12, 1584: During Mass, she plays with the holy image of Mary Magdalene like a child with a doll. She also shows her heart, indicating that there is pain there. Jeanne regresses to the pre-verbal stage. The Archbishop then begins to teach her as if she were really 4 years old. He blesses every part of her body and reads her previous written confession. After listening to her confession, Jeanne still behaves like a child, but she can walk and talk more assertively again. For nine days, the archbishop questions her about her early childhood. She receives absolution and goes to live for a year in the archdiocese with her nurse, Sister Barbe, to complete her liberation from the demons and for her rehabilitation. Mary Magdalene disappears. The sight impairment in her right eye, which had been present for 10 years, also disappeared.

- 6 January 1586: Joan falls into ecstasy during mass and sees Mary Magdalene. Jeanne tells the archbishop that Mary Magdalene has kept the promise she made a year earlier and is now free of demons. She has regained her spiritual strength and returns to the convent to resume her place in community life.

Here are some notes based on what Jeanne herself reported in her diary about the evolution of her troubles: "At the age of 2, she is given to the devil by her father who curses her. At the age of 4, she was seduced by the devil Cornau who appeared as a handsome young man offering her apples and white bread. She then accepts him as her father. From the age of 4 to 12, another devil appears (perhaps Garga). The devil Garga promises her that she will never feel the blows she receives again. As a teenager, for more freedom, she lives with her mother. She is apprenticed to a seamstress in the city of Mons. She has to do whatever her demons ask of her or she will be tortured. A multitude of new demons enter her. Previously she had only two or three (probably Namon, Cornau and Garga). She promises the demons to keep their presence a secret. At her first communion, she has to fight them. They undermine her resolutions in every way, take control of her tongue during confession, one gives her sweets during the Eucharistic fast, another hurts her throat to make her spit out the host, etc. Despite these obstacles, Jeanne entered the Dominican convent, but the inner conflict continued. New demons appear: "Traitor", "Magic Art", "Heresy", and many others. They demand control of her memory, intelligence and will. She starts to get involved in false ceremonies, she signs pacts written in foreign alphabets with her blood. The demons demand that she renounce all ties except those that bind her to them. They give her banquets, they give her pleasure, they also cause pain when she tries to eat on Christian feast days, they make her body reject the food. The demons True Freedom, Heresy and Namon will even involve her in sacrilege. The demons 'Bloody', 'Bow' and others make her cut off bits of flesh, she even agrees to be hanged by the demons and almost dies. She feels that she only loves demons and is afraid of people."

Jeanne Fery stated that she was no longer able to control her body and that she always said the opposite of what she meant, a symptom that is now considered a clinical sign of I.D.D. Another clinical sign is the amnesia she had when she had a child identity or lost objects "hidden" by demons. The alternation between good functioning and extreme dysfunction, the vision of the "demons", which she hears and which converse with each other, also suggest that it is a split personality. In addition to the amnesia and the manifestations of different personalities, Jeanne Fery had serious somatic disorders: she regularly suffered from loss of blood, vomiting, suffocation, spasmodic movements of her limbs, physical pains (head, heart and abdomen), insomnia, loss of appetite, loss of speech, blindness... but also sometimes extreme muscular strength... which is a criterion for demonic possessions according to exorcist priests. She said that certain "devils" inhabited and disturbed particular areas of her body, such as her blasphemous tongue, her blind eye, or her sore throat.

Jeanne Fery's case gives some indication of physical abuse in early childhood, perhaps even sexual abuse. One of her first dissociations appeared as a "devil" when she was beaten as a child. Later, the devil *Garga* helped her to stop feeling the beatings. Jeanne also mentions that her father cursed her and *"offered her to the power of the devil"* when she was two years old. She was then seduced by the devil *Cornau* at the age of four and took him as her father. This may possibly suggest sexual abuse by her father when she was 4 years old, as Jeanne seems to have created an alter to replace him. Indeed, a 4 year old child is unable to merge the image of the good father with that of the abuser. Today, very young children will attribute their abuse to monsters or vampires. The cultural context in which Jeanne lived could have given her this image of the devil.[361]

Another case, dating from 1623, is that of Sister Benedetta Carlini in Italy. This woman was described as being possessed by three *'angelic boys'* who sometimes took control of her body. Each of these "boys" spoke through her with a different dialect, a different voice and had different facial expressions. Benedetta had total amnesia about what was happening when the different "boys" emerged.

She also had eating disorders and self-mutilation. In her case, there were also references to childhood trauma, her parents were said to be possessed... The child had been put into a convent at the age of 9, the age at which her sexually abused alter *"Splenditello"* had remained fixed. Her symptoms became uncontrollable after the death of her father...

Did Jeanne Fery and Benedetta Carlini "simply" have a split personality without any intervention of external malevolent entities? It's hard to say... A normal psychiatrist would say that it's only a severe dissociative disorder, while a normal priest would say that it's a question of evil spirits outside the person. But researchers believe that the two phenomena are closely linked...

In a lecture given in 2008, Father François Brune cites a case of possession that took place in Italy. A case reported by the demonologist Mgr Corrado Balducci. This case lasted for seven years, from 1913, when the infestation began, to 1920, when she was delivered: *'After the blessing, she confided in the priest. She told him that at certain times of the day, a mysterious force, superior to her own, would take hold of her body and soul, and that then, despite her resistance, she would dance to the rhythm of a tango for hours and hours until she fell from exhaustion. She said that with a beautiful voice she sang*

---

[361] "Jeanne Fery: A Sixteen Century Case of Dissociative Identity Disorder" - Onno van der Hart, Ruth Lierens and Jean Goodwin, The Journal of Psychotherapy 24, 1996.

verses, romances, opera pieces that she had never heard before. She held endless lectures in foreign languages she did not know, before an imaginary crowd. She sang poems that foretold her own death and that of all her sisters. She often tore up everything she could with her teeth. She terrorised everyone in the house, roaring, meowing and screaming louder and louder, so much so that at certain times the whole house became a menagerie of ferocious beasts."

Father Brune tells us that the woman would have even shown a phenomenon of levitation 50 centimetres above the ground... Something that a psychotic alone cannot do, no one can usually do such a thing. This woman was perfectly aware of her strange actions directed by an evil force outside of herself. It was a situation that made her despair and even consider suicide. In this case, there was no amnesic wall between her possessed states and her normal state, and there was an 'outside force' influencing the person. Demon-possessed people have often shown behaviours that are supernatural and even beyond the realm of the unimaginable. The most *'spectacular'* demonic possessions cannot be explained by even the most extreme psychotic mental disorder. There is necessarily an intervention of external forces that transcend the laws of physics. In a 2008 conference entitled *"Demonic Possessions"*, Father François Brune described some rather impressive cases. In particular, he recounts an exorcism that was conducted in Germany in 1842 by a Protestant pastor to deliver a young woman named Gottliebin. The pastor's only weapons were prayer, faith and fasting... The doctors of the time who witnessed these phenomena did not understand a thing. The entities that possessed the young woman turned out to be a veritable legion. The demons first declared themselves to be 3, then 7, then 14, then 175, then 425... It is possible that the numbers given by these entities are obviously fanciful, but one thing is certain, it is that a host of demons *inhabited* this woman. In this case, there is apparently no mention of any personality change, amnesia or traumatic past concerning the woman, the pastor speaks only of acts of witchcraft. In his lecture, Father Brune quoted some passages from the report of this German pastor, Johan Christoph Blumhardt, translated into French by him:

It was terrifying for me to realise that what had previously been regarded as the most ridiculous folk superstition was emerging from the world of fairy tales into the real world. It began with vomiting sand and glass. Gradually it came to pieces of steel of all kinds, old wood nails all bent. I saw one day, after a long choking, twelve in a row fall into the basin we held in front of his mouth. Then there were shoelaces of different shapes and sizes, often so long that it was hard to understand how they could come out of the gullet. Once a piece of metal so large and wide that she lost her breath and remained as if dead for several minutes. There were also incredible quantities of pins, needles, and pieces of knitting needles, sometimes alone and sometimes mixed with paper and feathers (...) From the nose also I drew many pins (...) From the needles I drew quantities from the lower and upper jaws. At first she had a terrible toothache, although you couldn't see anything, and finally you could start to feel the spikes. They kept coming out more and more and there came a time when I could grab them but it still took a lot of effort to get them off. Two old pieces of wire, all bent to the length of a finger, once showed up in her tongue. On another occasion, she had two long wires twisted and tangled in several places under her skin. It took my wife and I an hour to remove them completely and Gottliebin lost consciousness more than once, as often happened. In addition, pieces of knitting needles or whole needles came out of his upper body so often at various times that I can estimate the number to be at least thirty. They were either lying down or stuck vertically, in the latter case often right in the heart area. If the needles were already halfway out, it took me half an hour of pulling with all my might. I can't really blame anyone for being sceptical about such stories, because it's too much to believe or imagine. But I was able to make all these observations and experiments for almost a whole year and always in the presence of many witnesses. I was very keen to avoid bad rumours, which is why I can tell these events in all serenity, because I am absolutely sure, if only because of Gottliebin's character, that there was never the slightest trickery. Every time I went to see her at that time, whether I was called or not, something would happen again and after a while a new trick of witchcraft would take place in some part of her body. The pain was always terrible and almost every time she would lose consciousness. She usually cried out, "I'm going to die! but the prayer alone would take care of everything. If she began to complain of pain anywhere, all I had to do was put my hand, usually on her head. Instructed by long experience in the Faith, I was sure to see at once the effectiveness of the short prayer I said. She immediately felt the thing move in her or turn around to find a way out. The most difficult part was the crossing of the skin, and it often felt for a long time that something was pushing from the inside out. It never bled, it was not like a wound. At most we could recognise for a moment where something had come from, at least as long as it had been done by the power of prayer alone."

In a *Planet* Channel programme on exorcists broadcast in April 2004, Msg Laroche, an Orthodox bishop, claimed to have personally seen a possessed woman spit out tiny toads and worms...

Conversely, certain supernatural phenomena, this time of a divine order, regularly manifested themselves in the lives of the saints, such as the gushing of fresh rose petals from the mouth. Father Brune notes that there is a parallelism between the phenomena of possessions and mystics. They are the same kind of manifestations but in a positive way, in something beautiful. This is the case of Mother Yvonne-Aimée de Jésus of the monastery of Malestroit who, in her bed, feeling oppressed, saw a red carnation coming out of her body at the level of her heart. *It seems to me that I can hear the flesh cracking, it tears, then when the carnation came out, the wound in her heart closed without a scar. (...) "The roses kept coming out of Aimée's heart. We now have five. The last one came while she was at the foot of the altar. (...) The rose was climbing towards her neck, I was pulling it with force, its long thorny stem was struggling to come out. It was this last rose that made Aimée suffer the most, the others were thornless."*

In his book entitled "What to do with all these devils? the Italian exorcist Raul Salvucci writes: "In the case of possession or diabolic obsession, the personality of the human being disappears; in its place, another entity takes over the body, the senses, the faculties, and speaks, acts, moves, and expresses itself through this human body. When liberation occurs, the person has two sensations:

- The first is that she doesn't remember anything she said or what happened, as if she had been anaesthetised for a surgical operation. Sometimes she also asks: "What time is it, where am I? After her release, looking at the bruises on her wrists, caused by those who had been trying to hold her down for several hours, a possessed person says: "Who did this to me?"

- The second is that she feels completely exhausted by the violence done to her to disable her 'evil' personality.

Why some people can be so cruelly stricken and how this dreadful form of diabolical possession is achieved is difficult to say."[362]

In 2010, a study was conducted in Uganda. Its aim was to explore the relationships between demonic possessions, dissociative symptoms and trauma. The study consisted of a group of 119 individuals diagnosed by traditional healers as possessed, compared to a control group of 71 unpossessed individuals. Assessments included demographic items, dissociation criteria and potentially traumatic elements of the individuals' lives. Compared to the control group, the possessed group showed more severe dissociative disorders but also more traumatic elements in their lives. The links between these traumatic events and dissociative disorders were significant. The study concluded that possession by entities was a dissociative disorder, or more accurately a *'dissociative trance state'* linked to traumatic events. Here is a short excerpt from the study showing the strong similarity between demonic possession and dissociative disorders:

"Entering another state of consciousness and speaking in a language that people have never learned before. Later, they do not remember speaking in these languages."[363]

The DSM-IV defines dissociative trance as follows:

Disruptions in consciousness, identity or memory that occur once or episodically, specific to certain places and cultures. Dissociative trance involves a narrowing of the field of perception of the immediate environment, as well as stereotyped behaviours or movements that the subjects feel are beyond their control. In the state of possession, instead of a sense of one's own identity, there is a new identity, attributed to the influence of a spirit, power, deity or other person. This may be accompanied by amnesia. It is perhaps the most common dissociative disorder in Asia. Amok (Indonesia), Behainan (Indonesia), Latab, (Malaysia), Pibloktoq (Arctic), Ataque de Nervios (Latin America) are known examples.

Another study concerning the link between possession, dissociative trance states and I.D.T. was conducted in Italy by Stefano Ferracuti in 1995. The subjects were recruited via the exorcist of the diocese of Rome, Don Gabriele Amorth. In this study, ten people who were undergoing exorcism sessions against demonic possessions were studied with the diagnostic criteria for

---

[362] What to do with all these devils? The testimony of an exorcist" - Raul Salvucci, 2001, p.41-42.

[363] "Dissociative Symptoms and Reported Trauma Among Patients with Spirit Possession and Matched Healthy Controls in Uganda" - van Duijl, Nijenhuis, Komproe, Gernaat, de Jong, 2010

dissociative disorders as well as with the Rorschach test. These people were overwhelmed by paranormal manifestations, claiming to be possessed by a demon. They obviously had great difficulty in maintaining a normal social life. These people had much in common with patients suffering from I.D.D. and the Rorschach tests showed that they too had a complex personality organisation. The dissociative trances of these 'possessed' people showed great similarities with I.D.D. The report of the study states that dissociative trance states, especially possession disorder, are probably more common than we think, but that precise clinical data on this subject are too few. In this study, subjects reported that psychiatric treatment did not improve their symptoms, while exorcism rituals brought some improvement. Almost all of them said that the exorcism helped to keep the demon under control, that it harassed them less after the prayers.[364]

For Father Angelo, exorcist of an Italian diocese, possession has nothing to do with I.D.T. In the book *"Confidences d'un Exorciste"*, here is what he confided to the two French journalists Nathalie Duplan and Valérie Raulin:

The demon, in the case of possession, invades the man's body and takes control of it, as if it were his own. Spiritual creatures lacking this, use the organs and limbs of the possessed person to move and speak, without the unfortunate person being able to stop them. Despite the torments inflicted by the devil, the soul remains free. This proves that the devil does not have unlimited power over man, as God does not allow him to possess the soul. I have also insisted that possession is not a 'multiple personality disorder' or a 'dissociative personality disorder', as psychiatrists argue, but a spiritual reality that is beyond our comprehension and is, in a mysterious way, part of God's plan. The demon cannot undertake what God forbids and his power to harm is not unlimited (...) It is very impressive to see Satan, or some other demon, inhabit a body, move it at will, manipulate it in an improbable way, and then be submissive, unable to resist when the priest lays hands on it. Again, submission is not immediate, especially when dealing with very powerful demons. I recall that, like angels, demons are spirits within which there is a hierarchy. Archangels are more powerful than angels. Among the demons, it is the same, some are superior to others. The powerful demons are quickly recognised because, at first, they do not react, they resist, while the demons of a lower rank are forced to leave first."[365]

In his book "Exorcisms and Powers of the Laity: Diabolical Influences", Father Ovila Melançon writes: "It is not known that there are neurosis-diseases and neurosis-demoniacs. One will sometimes attribute to a splitting of the personality what will be, in fact, only the intervention of a fallen spirit. It is also necessary to know that a true diabolic possession is almost always accompanied by mental and nervous disorders, which are produced and amplified by the

---

[364] Dissociative Trance Disorder: clinical and rorschach findings in ten persons reporting demon possession and treated by exorcism" - Stefano Ferracuti, Roberto Sacco and Renato Lazzari, Department of Psychiatry and Psychology, University of Rome. 1995.

[365] *Confidences d'un Exorciste"* - Nathalie Duplan and Valérie Raulin, 2012.

demon and whose manifestations and symptoms are medically identical to those produced by neuroses (...)Father Francesco Palau, beatified by Pope John Paul II on 25 April 1988, was right to welcome the mentally ill and to exorcise them all, so that "those who were possessed were healed; those who were ill remained ill", as Father Gabriele Amorth pointed out in his book entitled "An exorcist tells". The same author was quite right to write: "I have agreed with all the other exorcists I have consulted that recourse to an exorcism, in cases where it was not necessary, has never been harmful". This is the true pastoral care that should be found in the Church, pastoral care that corresponds to the authentic doctrine of the Church concerning exorcisms!"[366]

In a 2011 interview, the exorcist of the Diocese of San José in the United States, Father Gary Thomas, said: "Generally, people can be touched (by the demon) when they have experienced difficult things in their lives. That's my opinion based on my experience. With people who have a history of sexual abuse, it's even more telling. These are deep wounds of the soul and it affects the person's life on all levels (...) Demons want to attach themselves to people with a history of sexual abuse. I would say that eight out of ten people who come to me with demonic possession issues have been sexually abused, usually by a parent, brother or other family member. That doesn't mean that everyone who has been sexually abused will have demonic possession issues, but the risk is greater."[367]

In DSM-IV, both possession and DID were classified as 'dissociative disorders'. In its new definition of dissociative identity disorder, the 2013 DSM-V states: *"Disruption of identity by at least two distinct personalities, which may be described in some cultures as a possession experience."*

So we see that the ambiguity is real and that no serious study, at least publicly available, is being done to understand this phenomenon. The symptoms of demonic possession and multiple personality are indeed remarkably similar, the professor and clinical psychologist James Randall Noblitt has listed these commonalities:[368]

- Both possession and I.D.T. are more common in women than in men. A phenomenon seven times more common in women than in men, with women seeming to dissociate more easily than men.
- They are both reported as a result of traumatic experiences, rituals or initiation trials.
- They are both associated with primitive or pre-industrial cults, but also with modern ones.
- Secrecy is often a common factor in possession and I.D.T.
- Individuals report amnesia in both possession and I.D.T.
- Trance experiences are common.

---

[366] "Exorcisms and powers of the laity - diabolic influences" - Father Ovila Melançon, 1996, p.62.

[367] "Interview: Father Gary Thomas, inspiration for 'The Rite'" - Peg Aloi, 2011.

[368] *"Cult & Ritual Abuse"* - James Randall Noblitt & Pamela Perskin Noblitt, 2014, p.45.

- Individuals experience at some point a common consciousness shared with the alter personality or entity.
- Individuals act with behaviour that is not in their usual characteristics.
- The identity that is usually present is usually referred to as the *'host'*.
- Entities or alters that take control of the body may present themselves as an animal, spirit, demon or deity.
- Individuals may behave beyond the physical limits of the human body, particularly with regard to pain.
- A significant number of individuals affected by possession or I.D.D. believe that they have special psychic powers.

In psychic disorders or 'mental illnesses', the spiritual side, which affects the other dimensions of the being, is today totally ignored by modern medicine. Whereas in traditional pre-industrial cultures, this spiritual side was on the contrary the first thing to be treated in physical or mental disorders, notably through shamanism and exorcism. For example, in India, it was reported that 75% of psychiatric patients also consulted a religious healer. Similarly, in a rural community in South Korea, 15 to 25% of psychotic patients were treated with shamanic therapies.[369]

It is important to take into account all the dimensions of the human being when addressing the issue of I.D.D., which seems to go far beyond simple physical/neurological functioning.

Professor Emilio Servadio, an expert in psychoanalysis and honorary president of the Italian Psychoanalytical Society, also a specialist in paranormal manifestations, told the journalist Renzo Allegri about exorcisms: *"There are individuals everywhere with much more complicated problems and inexplicable and sometimes frightening pathological manifestations, which we are unable to classify and even less to cure. Faced with these cases, lay science stops, it ceases its research, because it no longer knows in which direction to investigate and refuses to formulate hypotheses. But the most open-minded psychiatrists and psychoanalysts sense that they are faced with phenomena that go beyond the limits of medical science into areas unexplored by human reason. They are aware that they cannot do anything and understand that it is their duty to leave the field open to theologians and, eventually, to the exorcists themselves. I consider that science must indeed recognise its own limitations. "[370]*

Professor Chris Cook of the Department of Theology and Religion at Durham University has written an article entitled *'Demon Possession and Mental Illness: Should We Be Making a Differential Diagnosis? from which the following excerpts are taken: "Demon Possession and Mental Illness: Should We Be Making a Differential Diagnosis? from which the following are excerpts: Demonic possession and mental illness are not simply two different diagnoses (...) However, if these two things are related, we need to know the nature of the connection between the two (...) We need to distinguish which of these two things*

---

[369] Historical, religious, and medical perspectives of possession phenomena" - SN Chiu, Hong-Kong Journal of Psychiatry, 2000.

[370] *Gente"* - Renzo Allegri, 30/12/1984, p.113.

we are dealing with, but we also need to identify which of the two problems causes the other as a secondary 'complication' (...).) Demonic possession is essentially a spiritual problem, but mental illness is a multifactorial affair, in which spiritual, social, psychological and physical factors must play an etiological role. The relationship between these two concepts is therefore complex. Different diagnoses may have a role to play in helping those whose problem may be demonic or medical/psychiatric in origin. However, spiritual discernment is of equal if not greater importance than scientific discernment.[371]

Pastor James Friesen is the author of the books *"Uncovering the Mystery of M.P.D."* and *"More Than Survivors.* (and *"More Than Survivors"*. He has worked with many patients and has described in detail how multiple personality disorder is linked to satanic ritual abuse. According to him, demonic possession is directly related to I.D.D. He states that individuals with dissociative identity disorder experience both split personality and possession by outside entities, but that these two kinds of *"takeovers"* are quite distinct from each other.

Dr. Haraldur Erlendsson also comes to the same conclusion regarding the simultaneity of possession and I.D.D. In a 2003 article entitled *"Multiple Personality Disorder - Demons and* Angels *or Archetypal Aspects of the Inner Self"*, he writes: *"If the different personalities claim to have a different history from the main personality, should we take this into account after asking a series of questions such as: 'Is there anyone? Who are you? How long have you been here? Where were you before? What effect do you have on the person? Why haven't you moved on? ". When the answers clearly give the conviction that the entity comes from outside the person, should we take these answers at face value? Should we use the answers given to differentiate between possession and multiple personality? Perhaps the diagnosis of I.D.D. should include possession trance. The problem here is that many clinicians are not comfortable with the notion of an afterlife or entities that may live in different worlds. Dr. Colin Ross, who wrote the most comprehensive book on I.D.D. (Dissociative Identity Disorder, Diagnosis, Clinical Features, and Treatment of Multiple Personality Disorder, 1997), has himself at times used techniques related to the spirit world, as have many others in this field. However, he prefers to treat alter claiming to come from outside in the same way as all other parts of the split personality. He helps them to cope with the traumatic content of the memories and seeks to achieve full integration with the rest of the person. My view is that possession and multiple personality do not happen separately but rather occur together. "*

We have seen that the causal link between severe trauma and dissociative disorders leading to multiple personality is now established. Do demonic possessions also originate in trauma? It would seem that this is indeed one of the many commonalities between I.D.D. and Possession. Father Jeffrey Steffon in his book *"Satanism: Is It Real?* (describes a number of causes that can lead to possession by one or more entities: *"First, a demonic spirit can attach itself to*

---

[371] ' 'Demon Possession and Mental Illness: Should We Be Making a Differential Diagnosis? - Chris Cook, Christian Medical Fellowship - Nucleus magazine, 09/1997.

someone through injury or trauma (...) A demonic spirit can also attach itself to a person through involvement in the occult."

Satanic ritual abuse is particularly attractive to demonic entities because of the black magic practices, but also because of the extreme trauma that occurs during the ceremonies. Demons are attracted to the suffering, pain and terror that cause the victim to be helpless and totally submissive to the abusers... but also to the spirits. This type of extreme emotion is a force of attraction and nourishment for fallen spirits, all the more so if blood is spilled. The deeply disassociated victims then become veritable receptacles for these entities attracted by the magic protocols and incantations that accompany the ritual. Moreover, these ceremonies are often performed in sites with particular telluric energies that facilitate interactions between different dimensions. Just as a cracked vase allows *light to* pass through, the splitting will allow certain entities to pass through and mingle with the fractures in the personality that are the *soul fragments*, a notion that will be developed later...

In 2010, Reverend Thomas J. Euteneuer identified 'seven levels of demonic persecution'. According to him, satanic ritual abuse is the most critical level: '*Children born into a family line of witches or satanic cults are initiated into them through rituals and consecrations. They are the most difficult to heal. The emotional and physical trauma of the rituals, inflicted from early childhood, even in the womb, is so extreme that it fractures the child's personality and makes him or her totally subject to possession, deliberately handed over to the demons of the cult. Such wounded and bruised individuals need compassionate help from the Church, but they cannot be healed by exorcism alone. In fact they need several elements combined together for true healing to take place. Firstly, they need to make a complete break with all occult activities and all the people involved in their abuse. Secondly, they need a qualified therapist with good knowledge to treat their dissociative identity disorder. Thirdly, they need a qualified exorcist and a good support team to offer regular prayers and mobilise all the spiritual resources of the parish for this particular case. Finally, they need a support group to rehabilitate them into a true Christian fellowship based on strong relationships of love and truth. They have a long healing journey ahead of them and therefore need maximum support and help. As with all demonic afflictions, healing is only possible with the grace of God and the active cooperation of the individual. Full healing may take years of hard work by all involved, but it is indeed possible.*"[372]

In the book "*Healing the Unimaginable*", ritual abuse survivor Stella Katz, who herself practised mind control on young children in a Satanist cult, testifies: "*According to some ancient writings, it is clear that the splitting of children is something that has been practised for many generations in some of these religions, with the aim of binding demons to children. When an alter emerges, it is its behaviour that will determine what type of demon it is, so the group will call this alter by a particular demon name. Afterwards, the group can*

---

[372] "Seven Degrees of Demonic Persecution" - Thomas J. Euteneuer, "Libera nos a malo", New Oxford Review, p.39, 05/2010.

use the demon's name to call it and make it emerge to take possession of the body. However, when a demon emerges without permission, which it usually does, the child will need to be exorcised. Children who cannot be exorcised may end up in a psychiatric hospital. As these occult groups have come to understand the process and consequences of splitting a child, their activities and the protocols they have created have become increasingly sophisticated.[373] Again, there is this ambiguity between internal alter personality and external demonic entity, but the notion of splitting (*spiritually unlocking*) the child is always present.

Author Fritz Springmeier makes a distinction between demonic possession and I.D.T., but acknowledges that there are many common characteristics and that the two are intrinsically linked in trauma-based mind control protocols: *"If we take MK programming from the programmer's point of view, the programmer believes in both personality splitting and demonic possession. For an MK programmer, you have to create alter personalities and at the same time 'demonise' them, i.e. link them to demons. Several former programmers told Springmeier that if someone wants to truly understand Monarch mind control, they have to realise that it is something fundamentally demonic (...) Programming and mind control cannot be separated from demonology and occult rituals."*[374]

Demonic entities could therefore bind to dissociated alters. This is also claimed by the Reverend Tom Ball, for whom demons are real entities that have been *"attached"* to alter personalities through *"curses"*, i.e. black magic protocols.[375]

As Dr. Haraldur Erlendsson has written: "My view is that possession and multiple personality do not happen separately but rather occur together."

According to the various data we have, it is more than likely that these two phenomena are indeed intimately linked. Unlike alter personalities, which have a basic protective role (even if some are very hostile and even violent), demonic entities coming from outside are not there to help the split person, their purpose is to steal, destroy, deceive and kill: they lead to madness and self-destruction. In a Monarch MK programming framework, the role of these demonic entities is to cooperate with the programmer to maintain control of the slave (to be discussed in the next chapter). The role of the alter personalities is to support and help the person survive the trauma as best they can. Their function is not destructive but rather protective. The alter personalities usually take great care of the original personality. The heavy traumatic memories and the pain they contain are 'encapsulated' in the various alters, which have the function of preserving the victim so that he or she can continue to live. It is for this reason

---

[373] "Healing the Unimaginable: Treating Ritual Abuse and Mind Control" - Alison Miller, 2012, p.94.

[374] "The Illuminati Formula Used to Create an Undetectable Total Mind Controlled Slave" - Fritz Springmeier & Cisco Wheeler, 1996.

[375] Ritual Abuse in the 21st Century ', Chap: 'The use of prayer for inner healing of memories and delivrance with ritual abuse survivors' - Tom Ball, 2008.

that alter personalities must be understood, accepted and loved; as opposed to destructive external entities that may also torment these alters as they torment the host personality. In the seminal book on the phenomenon of possessions, *Possession Demoniacal and Other*, Oesterreich speaks of evil spirits but he also speaks of "good" possessions. He cites a case reported by a certain van Müller in *the* book *Gründliche Nachncht*, where the possession alternated between an unhealthy evil spirit and a good spirit. It may be that [376]the "good spirit" did not come from outside but was in fact a fraction of the person's personality, an alter whose role was to help and protect him or her. If the other "conscience" is considered to be a part of the split personality, the treatment will be to integrate it (fusion or integration) with the main personality, but if the other "conscience" is considered to be an external spirit or demon, the treatment will be to expel it (expulsion by exorcism prayer).

The psychiatrist Ralph B. Allison was occasionally confronted in his work with patients suffering from I.D.D. with entities that behaved in an unusual way. Their "birth" could not be located in time, they were visibly useless, and they usually presented themselves as "spirits".[377] With an alter personality, it is usually possible to know when the splitting (dissociation) occurred, i.e. when it was "born". Furthermore, each alter normally has a well-defined function within the internal system: observer, protector, child, etc.

In his book *Uncovering the mystery of MPD*, Dr. James G. Friesen made a distinction in order to determine what is an alter personality and what is an external entity (demon). Friesen made a distinction in order to determine what is an alter personality and what is an external entity (demon):

---

[376] "Possession Demoniacal and Other Among Primitive Races, In Antiquity, The Middle Ages, And Modern Time" - Traugott Konstantin Oesterreich, 1930, p.27.

[377] "How About Demons ? Possession and Exorcism in the Modern World" - Felicitas D. Goodman, 1984.

Alter personalities	Demons
Most alters, and even "alter tormentors", can become powerful allies in therapy. It is possible to establish a positive relationship with them (even if it may be negative at first)	Demons are arrogant and there is no way to establish a relationship with them
In time, the alter becomes ego-synonymous, i.e. it can merge and harmonise with the original personality	Demons remain as 'ego-alien', external entities impossible to merge and 'integrate'
Confusion and fear are resolved when it is only a question of altering the situation.	Confusion, fear and lust persist despite therapy when demons are present
Alters tend to conform with their environment	Demons force undesirable behaviour and then blame a personality
Alters have their own personalities with specific voices	Demons have a negative voice without any corresponding personality
Irritation, discontent and rivalry between alter are very common	Hatred and bitterness are the most common feelings among demons
The imagery of the alter represents a human form and remains consistent	Demon imagery varies between human and non-human forms, with many variations

Dr. James Friesen warns well about the practice of exorcism: the fight against demons. It is necessary to have a solid spiritual foundation and never to engage in this kind of thing out of mere curiosity or financial interest. The risk is to "fight demons" that are not demons, or even worse, to fight demons without having the real capacity.

According to Father Gabriele Amorth, chief exorcist of the Vatican, in a possession there can be the presence of demons, but also the presence of *damned souls*, that is to say a soul of a deceased person who is slavishly attached to Satan. In his book *"Confessions"*, Father Amorth reports the case of a possessed woman. During the first exorcism prayers, she went into a trance and became very violent, speaking in several languages with different voices. After each session, the woman would come out of her trance state and ask what she had done and what she had said. Being totally amnesiac, she had no memory of what had happened, she was only tired and sore. After several exorcisms, obeying the priest's orders, a first demon revealed its name: *"Zago"*. He said he was the leader of a cult in a nearby village, near a ruined church, and that there was a legion of minor demons in this possession. The other demon introduced himself as *"Astarot"*, this one was concerned with destroying the love of the couple and the affection between parents and children. A third demon named *"Serpent"* had the mission of driving the woman to suicide. To the great surprise of the exorcist priest Gabriele Amorth, among these demonic entities there were three damned souls: *"Michelle"*, a woman who had worked at the Moulin Rouge and who had died of drugs at the age of 39. It was Michelle who often made the possessed Italian woman say the French phrases she repeated to solicit customers. During these moments, the woman's face became soft and persuasive. There was also *"Beelzebub"*, a Moroccan who had beheaded three missionaries in 1872 and then committed suicide, overwhelmed by remorse. The third damned soul was *"Jordan"*, a Scotsman who had murdered his mother. He often intervened by speaking in English during trances of possession. Later, during an exorcism, Amorth heard a new female voice, so he asked her forcefully: *'Who are you? To which* the voice replied: *'I am Vanessa, I am twenty-three years old. I was a student at the university. I met a young man who took me to black masses near the ruined church. That was the day I started to serve the devil. One night when I had drunk blood and was drunk from the ceremony, I crossed the street and died, hit by a car.* So there was the presence of a fourth damned soul. During the last exorcism prayers, a faded red cross appeared on the woman's forehead. When the husband touched the cross, he discovered that it was blood. The exorcist then questioned the entity to find out the cause, and the demon's answer was: *"It is the blood of a four-day-old child offered to me by its mother, one of my former followers."*[378]

Another case of what appears to be human soul possession was described in the Uganda study mentioned earlier in this chapter.[379] This was a 33 year old woman who had been suffering from spiritual attacks for years, according to her sister she had strange and aggressive behaviours during which she spoke with different voices. These attacks occurred when the family was about to go to church or say certain prayers. At the clinic, the patient would go into a trance, waving her hands as if she had claws while growling like a wild animal. Then she would start talking in a strange language with an equally strange voice. Her sister explained that it was the voice of an uncle who had been dead for many years. This uncle had retained the values and beliefs of traditional pagan culture, while their father had turned to Christianity. There was an unresolved conflict between their father and this uncle because the father refused to perform the rituals for the ancestors. Was this woman possessed by her uncle's soul?

A study conducted in 2000 in a Singaporean psychiatric hospital reported the case of a Malaysian man who, when possessed by the spirits of the ancestors,

---

[378] Confessions: Memoirs of the Official Exorcist of the Vatican" - Father Gabriele Amorth, 2010, p.145.

[379] "Dissociative Symptoms and Reported Trauma Among Patients with Spirit Possession and Matched Healthy Controls in Uganda" - van Duijl, Nijenhuis, Komproe, Gernaat, de Jong, 2010

began to speak *"Sundak"*, a Javanese dialect no longer used by his people and which he himself had never learned.[380]

For Father François Brune, there is a distinction between demonic possession and multiple personality, for him the phenomenon of multiple personality can only be explained by the incorporation of a disembodied and errant human soul. A soul that takes over the body of the individual to express itself through him.

This question of possession by the souls of the deceased is perhaps related to a form of "ancestor worship" practiced by Satanists and Luciferians. Certain families who practise ritual abuse and systematic personality splitting on their descendants would thus offer an open door to their ancestors so that they could 'live again' in the flesh through the punctual or permanent possession of their descendants (split and therefore open to mediumnity). If the ancestor was already split during his incarnation, fragments of his spirit can also remain linked to his incarnated descendants. They would thus obtain a kind of 'immortality', so much sought after by certain occultists.

The book *'Possession Demoniacal and Other'* is a study on the phenomenon of possession that has been recognised worldwide and remains a reference in the field today. In it, Oesterreich makes a clear differentiation between *voluntary* and *involuntary* possession and also a distinction between *lucid* and *somnambulistic* possession. In lucid possession, the individual is conscious and remembers it later. A contemporary example of voluntary possession is that of *'channels'*, the *New Age* mediums who voluntarily allow themselves to be possessed by an entity. Some of these mediums are lucid, others are not. Somnambulistic possession occurs when the individual is unable to remember his behaviour and what was going on around him during the trance state; whereas in lucid possession he is a passive spectator of what is going on inside him and of his actions being directed by another force. People with I.D.D. describe dissociative episodes in the same way that Oesterrich described possession states, they may be lucid, where the main personality and the alter are in common consciousness, or they may be separated by an amnesic wall.

It would seem, therefore, that a severe trauma leading to a profound dissociation can provoke both a fragmentation of the *"I"* into different alter personalities, or *soul fragments* as we shall see; and in parallel a phenomenon of possession by external entities which may be demonic or human in nature, or even fragments of disembodied human souls. The I.D.T. is therefore intimately linked to the phenomenon of mediumship and possession because of the 'spiritual breach' which has been caused by the traumas. Cases that could be mistaken for demonic possession can therefore turn out to be I.D.T. with alternating personalities that can lead one to believe that it is a question of external entities, just as external entities can effectively parasitise and infest a "fractured" person, with a split and multiple personality.

---

[380] "Phenomenology of Trance States Seen at a Psychiatric Hospital in Singapore: A Cross-Cultural Perspective" - Transcultural Psychiatry, 12/2000.

In her autobiography "Thanks For The Memories", Brice Taylor (MK Monarch survivor) writes: "I have met people with multiple personality disorder who thought they were psychic and channeling entities, when in fact they were contacting part of their own personality structure. One day, a female 'channel' named Shirley graciously offered me a private 'channeling' session (...) I told her I would be happy to ask any questions she had about herself when she was in a trance state, which she accepted. When asked if Shirley had been involved in any ritual abuse type activities, the answer was that "Shirley was not yet ready to face that reality". Channeling can be a clever way of covering up the reality of multiple personality disorder when personality fragments come to consciousness, explaining that it is an outside 'entity'."[381]

In an article entitled *"Multiple Personality and Channeling"* (*Jefferson Journal of Psychiatry*), Dr. Rayna L. Rogers draws parallels between *new-age* channels and people with I.D.D.. She concludes that the trances of these mediums (when they are genuine and not a fraud) are very similar in many respects to people suffering from split personality. As we shall see later, split people are also more open to the 'spirit world', to other dimensions, and therefore more likely to have access to mediumistic faculties (a *'channeling'* session is nothing more than a one-off possession, it may be unconscious or conscious, then evaporating just like the memory of a dream). From an external point of view, for example for an audience attending a séance, it is difficult to determine whether the *channel is* channelling an external entity, or whether it is an inner alter that is communicating to the outside world (we will come back to the channelling of spirits in Chapter 9).

3 - DISSOCIATION AND OUT OF BODY: THE DOOR TO POSSESSION?

In the book *"Diagnosis and Treatment of Multiple Personality Disorder"*, Dr. Frank Putnam says that there are two camps on the issue of out-of-body experience. Frank Putnam says that there are two camps on the out-of-body experience issue, one group he calls "separationists", those who believe that there is a "soul", an "astral body", which can actually leave the physical body and move to other places, and then there are psychologists for whom these out-of-body experiences are simply an altered state of consciousness and that it is a mere hallucination. The numerous testimonies tend to prove that there is indeed an astral body that can move outside the physical body.

People describe a feeling of floating weightlessness outside their body. Some people who have had a *NDE* (*Near Death Experience) have been* able to describe in detail the surgery that was being performed on them after an accident, while they were in a coma... They were also able to report the number of people in the operating theatre and what they were saying to each other. Their energy body was above the scene and could observe everything in great detail while

---

[381] Thanks For The Memories: The Truth Has Set Me Free" - Brice Taylor, 1999, p.114.

their physical body was unconscious on the operating table. These near-death experiences studied by Dr. Raymond Moody, but also the work of Robert Monroe or Dr. Jean Jacques Charbonier, show that an energetic body, known as the etheric body or astral body, with a consciousness, can leave the physical body and then return to it. Some people master this phenomenon and can provoke it at will, which is obviously not recommended. According to a Gallup poll in 1982, 25 to 30% of people have had this kind of experience following a hospitalization or a severe trauma.

Occultists are familiar with the technique of *'Astral Travel'*, or the astral projection of the *'body of light'* outside the physical body. It is a discipline studied by secret societies such as the Golden Dawn or Freemasonry, but it is a practice primarily mastered by the shamans of pre-industrial cultures, who travel through different dimensions using this technique.

The phenomenon of dissociation described in the previous chapter is sometimes accompanied by a feeling of separation of mind and body. Some victims of sexual abuse clearly describe a concrete exit from the physical body during their dissociation triggered by extreme violence, pain and terror. Psychotraumatologist Muriel Salmona, a specialist in dissociation, refers to these cases as 'decorporation'. Marie-Ange Le Boulaire, the author of the book *"Le viol"*, describes well how she found herself outside her body, observing her rape and analysing the situation in which she found herself in a very lucid way. She described this phenomenon during her appearance on the television programme *"Allô Docteur"* on France 5 in January 2014: *"I felt a metre away, like in a film. I was one metre behind and I was looking at the scene, which I was analysing very clearly, asking myself what I could do to get out of it... That was very clear."*

In the documentary *"A life after the cult"* (*Planète +*, 2014), Flora Jessop, born in a family of Mormon fundamentalists, testifies on her martyred childhood: *"It started with caresses, he told me that I should not talk about it, that it was our secret. At first I was proud, but at the same time I felt dirty and I didn't understand why. It was very strange, I was sharing a secret with my father and it made me want to throw up. I was terrified every time he wanted to talk to me. I became very good at detaching from myself. I would float above myself and watch him touch me and feel like it was happening to someone else. That way I could still love my father. Every child sees his father as his hero, he is a child's first hero. What I learned early on was that monsters don't hide under our bed, monsters walk through doors and have familiar faces. My hero was a monster..."*

The book *Wife Rape* reports a number of accounts of dissociation with an out-of-body exit during rape: *"One of the most common survival strategies is described by Debbie as an 'orbiting exit', she recalls: 'He was lying on top of me completely, and so I just went out with my mind, I just wasn't there anymore. I had transported myself somewhere else and I realised later that I had often done that, even growing up, when something hurt me, I would go out... I would become totally numb. (...) Karen also describes having had an out-of-body experience: "It's like I was watching the scene from the corner of the room and I couldn't feel anything. This happened only during the sexual abuse but not during the physical abuse. Annabel also described having an out-of-body experience during her rape, she said: "I was focusing on my arm while being somewhere above it, my arm was twisted under my body, like a rag doll. I didn't see the rape as if it was happening to me, but as if it was happening to someone else with a twisted arm."*[382]

In the book "Reach *for the Rainbow*", Lynn Finney reports on a survivor's account of her psychic disassociation and subsequent out-of-body experience:

I can't stand this another minute. I feel I am going to die. I want to die. Oh, please, let me die. What's the matter? I don't feel pain anymore. Why don't I feel any pain? I don't feel anything... I feel so peaceful. I'm floating, floating to the ceiling. What is happening? I can see my father's naked body on the bed below me. I can see his back and the back of his legs. He is on top of a little girl, a girl with long black hair like me. But that's me! I am so confused... I don't understand. How can I be there and here on the ceiling at the same time? I can see my father and the girl (me) moving on the bed, but my emotions and the pain are totally gone. I don't feel anything anymore but I can hear her crying. I'm glad I'm not down there anymore, I don't want to go back."[383]

Dr. David Gersten has reported a testimony about this extreme dissociation process. In his book *"Are You Getting Enlightened or Losing Your Mind?* he writes: *"Amanda was physically and psychologically abused and also sexually abused. Her alcoholic father began raping her when she was eight years old, and this continued for six years. An older brother also abused her (...) Amanda learned to cope with the agony by 'leaving her body'. In traditional psychiatry, we might say she was 'dissociating'. The question psychiatry does not answer is "where does consciousness go when it dissociates? ". I believe that what we call dissociation must often be an out-of-body experience. Amanda's consciousness was dissociating, or separating from her physical body. Her mind and consciousness were temporarily leaving the confines of her physical body. Thus, Amanda no longer personally experienced the emotional and physical devastation. In fact, she learned to "leave her body" at will and often found herself in ecstatic states of bliss while out of her body. I have since interviewed dozens of other people who have experienced extreme abuse, and more than half of them reported that they left their bodies during the abuse."*[384]

Extreme traumatic rituals are used to bring about this *'enlightenment'*: the transcendence of the physical body through the dissociative phenomenon. The core of Satanic perversion is to *"rip out the soul"* of the victim in order to vampire their energy and control their mind. It is not the rituals themselves that really matter, but rather their effects at levels beyond the material world...

---

[382] Wife Rape: Understanding the Response of Survivors and Service Providers' ' - Raquel Kennedy Bergen, 1996, p.30-31.

[383] Reach for the Rainbow: Advanced Healing for Survivors of Sexual Abuse " - Lynne D. Finney, 1992.

[384] "Are You Getting Enlightened or Losing Your Mind? " - David Gersten, 1997, p.147.

Some energeticists explain that a shock or trauma, especially in early life, will unlock the astral body so that it can detach from the physical body. Eileen Nauman describes this phenomenon as follows: *"People who have suffered shock and trauma, especially in early childhood, have their astral body come out above their head. The unlocked astral body looks like a coloured balloon floating around the head. A clairvoyant can see this and know that you are "uprooted" (disconnected) because of this event. The reason the astral body wants to "escape" is because it is our "motherboard" for all our emotions and feelings. During the attack, when a person is deeply hurt and traumatised, the astral body will come out through the upper part of our head (Crown Chakra), it simply does not want to experience that pain and suffering, it runs away from the anguish, grief or agony. If it unlocks and lets go, then you will feel less of these traumatic emotions. People who experience this also report a feeling of numbness and paralysis. This is another sign that the astral body is unlocked and out. Under extreme violence, the astral body unlocks and escapes. Is it as simple as that? What happens when this happens? We feel disconnected from the violence and trauma, there is no or much less emotion. Many people say that they "floated" above the scene of violence, with total detachment and without any emotion. They describe it as if they were watching a colour film, but without any emotional connection to the scene. Over time, the astral body learns how to escape instead of staying in the physical body and experiencing the powerful emotions of violence, trauma and post-traumatic stress. This allows it to remain unlocked following an event or series of events. Anyone who has had a traumatic or highly disturbed childhood may have had their astral body unlocked in order to escape the ongoing emotional pain."*[385]

It would seem that the neurochemical phenomenon that causes dissociation with physical as well as emotional anaesthesia is therefore linked to this detachment of the astral body where the victim sees the scene from the outside and no longer feels any emotion. Thus, "energetic" parts of our body can detach from it to evolve on other planes. As we will see later, these can be simple fragments of the soul that "tear" during trauma. In cases of I.D.D., we speak of personality splitting, but it is really the "energetic" splitting of a unified whole that the human being forms at birth.

It is interesting to note that the Quechua Indians of Peru use the word *"Susto"*, which means *"fear"*, to talk about this phenomenon of leaving the body, which they call the "loss of the soul" (or fragments of the soul). For them, this "loss of the soul" is called the disease of *Susto*: the disease of fear... In his book *"El mito del Jani o Susto de la medecina indigena del Peru"*, Dr. Frederico Sal y Rosas reports that *the Quechua Indians believe that the soul (or perhaps a part of it) can leave the body, either spontaneously or by being forced to do so. The disease of "Susto" can happen in two ways: either by a great fright, such as*

---

[385] "The Astral Body - And How to 'Ground' it to Your Physical Body" - Eileen Nauman, allthingshealing.com

thunder, the sight of a charging bull or a snake, etc., or in a malicious way not requiring fright.[386]

What about the examples given above such as fear of thunder, a bull or a snake that can trigger soul splitting, compared to Satanic ritual abuse? Rituals that include scenes that could not be more terrorising and painful, rape, torture and sacrifice (real or even simulated). In ritual abuse, the child's terror is deliberately pushed to the extreme, leading to extreme dissociation. In this deeply dissociated state, the mind becomes detached from the body. The child's energetic and spiritual doors are then left wide open, allowing the intrusion of demonic entities attracted by ritual, terror, blood, black magic and incantations. As nature abhors a vacuum, when a part of the soul splits and 'escapes', it creates a 'space' that can be invaded by an outside entity. This phenomenon of possession by a spirit when the soul splits is something we find in shamanic traditions. As a result of trauma, the child becomes disconnected from his or her "I", no longer *anchored*. Just as his personality is fragmented, his soul (his spiritual body) is also split. Furthermore, the child may find himself parasitized by one or more demonic entities that will attach themselves to him and interact with his inner world, that particular dimension to which he was connected during the traumatic rituals.

Now comes the disturbing testimony of a former member of the Luciferian *"illuminati"* order. The woman who has struggled out of this cult has converted to Jesus Christ and has decided to reveal what she has experienced since her early childhood, having been born into a family practising these horrors. Svali' (her pseudonym) was a victim of ritual abuse and mental programming, but she herself practised mind control on children in the San Diego group in the USA, to which she belonged. The following testimony was posted online in 2001, and concerns a ritual that went so far as to cause the victim's imminent death. This means that the victim is going to decorporate herself because of the extreme traumas that voluntarily push her physical body to the borders of death. This type of practice is one of the most extreme and complex of MK programming. We will therefore anticipate a little on the following chapter devoted to Monarch-type mind control.

Trauma is the basis of Luciferian mind control and the most extreme method is certainly what Svali calls the *'resurrection ceremony'*. According to her it is one of the oldest methods of the *Illuminati* Order. The ceremony, or ritual, is usually performed for a child of 2 or 3 years of age. The child will be strongly traumatised by various means: physical and sexual violence, electric shocks, asphyxiation, drugs, with the aim of making him/her dissociate as much as possible and bring him/her into a state close to death. It is a method of mental programming that voluntarily pushes a child to the edge of death. The little victim then feels presences around him/her, these are entities observing this little unconscious body between life and death... In these *"resurrection"* rituals, there will always be the presence of competent medical personnel with adequate

---

[386] "The Discovery of the Unconscious: The History and Evolution of Dynamic Psychiatry" - Henri F. Ellenberger, 1981, p.8.

equipment in order to monitor the child's condition and to be able to *"resuscitate"* it when the time comes... When he regains consciousness in extreme pain, he will be faced with a choice: face certain death or choose to live by integrating a demonic power into him. The child obviously chooses to live and a parasitic entity clings to him. Later, the child will wake up in clean clothes, in a soft bed, coated with healing ointments, but in a state of shock and extreme weakness. It is then that a person will come and tell him in a soft and reassuring voice that he was dead but that the demon *'brought him back to life'*, and that he must therefore be indebted to it as well as to the people who saved him by restarting his heartbeat. The child is also told that if he asks the demonic entity to leave, he will be returned to the near-death state he was in when it entered.

This type of near-death programming is used to terrify, split, demonise and ultimately totally control a very young child physically, psychically and spiritually. It forces the child to accept a totally Satanic/Luciferian spirituality in the worst possible traumatic and coercive circumstances. The ritual will profoundly affect the child's beliefs and this traumatic experience will most importantly alter the child's most basic reality. The purpose of this programming is to remove free will and willpower from the young subjects and make them slaves to higher, non-embodied forces.

Another mind control technique based on *NDE, or near death, was described by Svali as being practised in a government setting, such as MK-Ultra.* Another mind control technique based on NDE, or near death, was described by Svali as being practised in a governmental, MK-Ultra type setting. The subject is strapped in at the waist and neck and is wrapped in a sensory isolation chamber (suppressing all sensations in the limbs). In this state of sensory deprivation, he is fed intravenously and his brain is bombarded with extremely violent sound noises. The total darkness of the room will be interspersed with dazzling white lights and the subject will soon lose track of day and night. As the victim approaches the *breaking point* and is on the verge of *breaking*, he or she is given electric shocks and drugs. The level of pain and terror is at its peak and they are told repeatedly that they are dying, which they are... if necessary, they can be put on life support. It is then that the subject experiences this near-death state and finds herself floating out of her body, finally free of the physical and psychological torture. It is then that a programmer comes in as a "saviour" telling him that he deserves to live and that he will not let him die... In the end, the victim will owe him his life... Pre-recorded messages are also played in a loop (the *psychic driving* method of the MK-Ultra programme). Messages that contain the programming and future destiny of the subject in the *"Family"*. Hyper-traumatised, the victim is then very receptive to these messages which will be deeply integrated in his subconscious. Eventually, the victim is slowly brought back to a *correct* state of consciousness, always accompanied by the constant message that they are *"born again"* for the *"Family"*.

Again, one or more people will come to comfort the victim in a kind way and she will feel extremely grateful to be alive, to have been freed from all these horrors. She will even be like a young child clinging to the people around her...

This type of MK programming based on imminent death and out-of-body exit will implant itself in the victim at the deepest level, as it touches the very core of the being: His life. Subsequently, the person who has undergone this kind of protocol will have the certainty (programming) that he or she will die if he or she tries to break the mind control, and that he or she will again find himself or herself in a near-death state with the risk that his or her heart will stop permanently. Whatever lies and horrors are told and implanted in these states of near unconsciousness will be deeply embedded at the subconscious level. The child in such a situation has a desperate need to believe the adults who hold its life in their hands. The child, totally broken and programmed, will integrate all the data received as deep truth.[387]

In her autobiography, Cathy O'Brien writes: 'Whether I wanted to or not, I overheard a conversation between Aquino and a lab assistant about death and the brain as I lay deeply hypnotised on an icy metal table. Aquino said that I had often been close to death, which "enhanced my ability, being dead, to enter other dimensions (of the mind). I had listened to Aquino talk endlessly about these kinds of concepts, as if he were trying to convince himself of the existence of a theory of interdimensional time travel. "Whether it's a principle or a theory doesn't change the results," he claimed - the concept of time itself is abstract. Hypnotising me with past-present-future verbiage gave me an impetus which, combined with the Alice in Wonderland/NASA mirror world concepts, gave me the illusion of timeless dimensions (...) After moving me from the table into a complex-looking container (ed: After moving me from the table to a complex-looking container, Aquino then switched my mind to another area of my brain, claiming to have taken me to another dimension by means of the 'death gate'. He did this while I was being deprived of all my senses, combined with reprogramming using hypnosis and harmonics. The coffin-like structure in question was transformed in my mind into a crematorium, where I was subjected to a growing sensation of heat as I "burned slowly" as hypnotically suggested. Aquino, then, "took me across the threshold of death" into another dimension "void of time".[388]

4 - IN PURSUIT OF LOST SOUL FRAGMENTS

As we have just seen, the human soul can become detached from the physical body during extreme trauma. The victim remains alive, which indicates that the soul has not completely detached from the body but rather has fragmented. Although life may return to normal after this extreme experience, 'soul fragments' may remain separated from the 'I', lost fragments, loaded with traumatic memory and sailing in other dimensions... In her book '*Wife Rape*',

---

[387] Near Death Experiences / Near Death Programming " - Svali, 2001.

[388] *TRANCE Formation of America: True life story of a mind control slave* - Cathy O'Brien & Mark Phillips, 2013, p.328.

Raquel K. Bergen reports Sonya's words: *'I lost a part of me. I think a deep part of me has died.'*[389]

In the book *The Discovery of the Unconscious*, Henri F. Ellenberger explains that in ancient traditions, illnesses and mental disorders can occur when the soul leaves the body (spontaneously or by accident) or if it is stolen by a spirit or a sorcerer. The healer, or shaman, will then go in search of this lost soul in order to bring it back and thus restore the body and the psyche of the sick person. This is called 'soul retrieval'. This practice is widespread but not universal, and is found among the Negritos of the Malaysian peninsula, the indigenous people of the Philippines and Australia, among others. This belief is also present in other cultures such as Siberia, North West Africa, Indonesia and New Guinea. The nature of the soul, the causes of soul loss, the destination of the lost soul and the way to heal the sick person may vary according to each local culture.

These traditional cultures teach us that during sleep or fainting, the soul can separate from the physical body. This is the theory that a 'ghost-spirit' is present in the body during normal life, but is able to leave the physical body temporarily, particularly during sleep. The *travelling spirit* may then get lost, be attacked, captured and kept prisoner by an evil spirit or a witch. The spirit may also leave the body abruptly during an awakened state, particularly during a shock that causes great fear. It can also be forced out of the body by ghosts, demons or even witches. The treatment of the traditional healer is therefore to go on an *astral hunt* to find the soul fragment, bring it back and thus restore the patient. In Siberia, this healing can only be carried out by a shaman who has been put in contact with the spirit world during his initiation. He has the ability to mediate between this other dimension and that of the living. The Russian ethnologist Ksenofontov reports: *'When a human being "loses his soul", the shaman puts himself in a state of trance by means of a special technique during which his soul goes on a journey to the spirit world. Shamans are able to track down the lost soul in the other world in the same way that a hunter tracks down an animal in the physical world. They often have to make a deal with the spirits that have captured the soul, conciliate with them and give them gifts. Sometimes they also have to fight the spirits, preferably with the help of other spirits who are their allies. Even if they are victorious in their quest, they still have to anticipate the revenge of the evil spirits. Once they have retrieved the lost soul, they bring it back to reintegrate it into the body, resulting in the healing of the sick person.'*[390]

The ethnologist Guy Moréchand describes the role of the shaman as follows: "The exercise of shamanism is materially translated by the trance. When he enters a trance, the shaman is supposed to undertake a journey. He leaves his body, which will, on the spot, as the session progresses, mime and tell the story

---

[389] Wife Rape: Understanding the Response of Survivors and Service Providers' ' - Raquel Kennedy Bergen, 1996, p.60.

[390] *Schamanen-Geschichten aus Sibirien"* - J.G. Ksenofontov, Adolf Fiedrich and Georges Buddrus, 1955.

of the efforts and episodes of adventures that take place in worlds different from the earthly world. The representations of these shamanic journeys culminate in a cosmogony of three worlds, with a heaven and a hell, symmetrical to the earth, situated above and below it, the hell being sometimes subterranean, sometimes underwater. The three worlds (or series of worlds) are crossed by a vertical axis which is their access route. Heaven is reached by ascending with the help of a winged animal genie. The horse is, for many populations, the mount that leads to the underworld. In these worlds, which are practically unknown to ordinary humans and inaccessible to them, the shaman goes in search of a runaway soul whose absence has caused the illness. The end of the wanderings or the abduction of this soul by an evil spirit is sometimes the realm of a deity, celestial or infernal, from whom the shaman is obliged to go to claim and buy it."[391]

In his book entitled "Animism and Shamanism for All", Igor Chamanovich describes the trances of the "medicine men" as follows: "The 'medicine man' is an ecstatic par excellence. Now, in primitive religions, ecstasy means the flight of the soul into heaven, or its wandering through the earth, or finally its descent into the subterranean regions among the dead. The medicine man undertakes such ecstatic journeys to meet face to face with the god of heaven and present him with an offering on behalf of the community, to seek out the soul of a sick person who is supposed to have strayed from his body or been ravished by demons (...) The abandonment of the body by the soul during ecstasy is equivalent to a temporary death. The 'medicine man' is therefore the man who is able to 'die' and 'rise' a considerable number of times."[392]

The ecstasy (*ekstasis* = leaving the body) corresponds here to a deep, controlled dissociative state in which the shaman travels into other dimensions. As we saw in Chapter 2, the shaman himself probably went through traumatic rituals during his initiation, which created a split in him and led to the opening of a breach to the spirit world. He is a self-healing healer who controls his dissociative states.

In other traditions, the shaman does not work in a trance state and does not venture so far into the spirit world. His technique is simply to perform conjurations, a kind of exorcism, as among the Quechua Indians who, as we have seen, call this fracturing of the soul *the disease of fear* (*Susto*).

In the Kahuna tradition we also find this notion of the splitting of the soul. For this Hawaiian people, a man's spirit can split into different parts during an accident or illness. In his book *"The Secret Science Behind Miracles"*, Max Freedom Long reports on the four types of human *"ghosts"* or *"spirits"* that the Kahuna tradition has listed. These descriptions can be compared with the different alter personalities and traumatic amnesias that characterise an I.D.T.:

    - 1/ The spirit in a normal state of a deceased man: This entity is composed of a subconscious mind and a conscious mind, just as in

---

[391] *"Principaux traits du chamanisme mèo blanc en Indochine"* - Guy Moréchand, Bulletin de l'Ecole française d'Extrême- Orient. Tome 47 N°2, 1955. p. 511.

[392] "Animism and shamanism for all" - Igor Chamanovich, 2010, p.108.

physical life. It thinks and remembers like any ordinary incarnate man
(...)

- 2/ The subconscious mind of man separated from his consciousness by
accident or illness, before or after death. This mind remembers very well,
but it is illogical, it has the reasoning capacity of an animal. It responds
to hypnotic suggestions. It is like a child and often causes "poltergeists"
for fun.

- 3/ The conscious mind of man separated from his subconscious before
or after death. This mind remembers nothing, it is an almost totally
helpless spectre, wandering aimlessly (...) it will behave like a true 'lost
soul' until it is rescued and reconnected to its subconscious mind, which
will then provide it with the memories to restore its power (...)

- 4/ The spirit of super-consciousness, including what are called "nature
spirits" or "group souls" in theosophical terminology. Information about
this category of spirits is vague, although we can conclude that they often
take over the two lower categories of spirits mentioned above, unihipili
(subconscious) and uhane (consciousness), sometimes helping them to do
things of a spectacular nature.[393]

The *'loss of the soul'*, *or* rather the loss of *'soul fragments'*, is therefore
a widespread belief in traditional shamanic cultures. It is characterised by a loss
of life energy, personal power and part of the identity. These soul fragments can
be lost in another world, another dimension, especially when there has been
abuse, suffering and trauma in childhood. Just as some South American shamans
associate the loss of the soul with fear, for some South East Asian shamans the
'fall of the *fold'* is usually the result of a material accident, for example a blow,
a fall, or fear, anxiety or overwork.

A body with a fragmented soul is like a tree without roots, it is weakened.
This is similar to what some clairvoyants report about the 'unlocking' of the
astral body which splits from the physical body in extreme traumas, leaving the
victim in a kind of 'disconnected' state. They are no longer physically anchored
in matter and this weakens them considerably.

Shamans systematically do grounding work before embarking on a
journey into another dimension, it is important and even necessary for them to
keep their *"feet on the ground"* during an astral exit. In his book *The Way of the
Shaman*, Michael Harner notes that in all pre-industrial traditions, when a person
was physically ill or behaving abnormally, it was usually because they had lost
a part of themselves that had been uprooted. This problem could sometimes be
aggravated by outside entities because the trauma, the trigger for the loss of a
part of the soul, could allow the intrusion of demonic spirits into the person's
psychic space and cause significant damage.

In all these traditions, it is clearly recognised that the loss of the soul
occurs as a result of psychic, physical or spiritual trauma. As we have already
seen, the shaman's task is to find the lost pieces of the soul and return them to
the broken person, but sometimes he will perform an exorcism to drive out the

---

[393] The Secret Science Behind Miracles " - Max Freedom Long, 1948, Chap.5.

entities that may be parasitizing the patient. Some anthropologists who have studied the healing techniques of traditional shamans have described ceremonies aimed at first restoring the split soul and then exorcising it from parasitic entities.

So here we have the pattern: Trauma - Soul/personality splitting - Possession.

A pattern that seems to be common to survivors of satanic ritual abuse who have developed I.D.D. Just as the degree of severity of trauma will influence the level of dissociation, so too will the degree of severity of trauma influence the possibility of possession by entities. Personality splitting is linked to this *"loss of soul"*.

The phenomenon that psychology calls dissociation thus has both a neurochemical and a metaphysical aspect, yet psychiatry is unable to explain to us *where* the different pieces of the personality go with their dissociative amnesia... and even less to explain to us where the *fragments of souls go* that shamans look for in their astral journeys to heal the sick...

Some psychotraumatologists explain schematically that a forgotten traumatic memory is *lost and stored in a 'black box' in the hippocampus at the back of the brain...* But do we know what exactly a memory is? Memory is not a thing but a process. It is neither solid nor static, nor is it literally 'stored' in a tangible form. It does not lie somewhere in a cupboard and it has no manifest physical form in the sense that it cannot be touched, seen or heard.[394]

Our memories are not made up of neurons but rather of a "subatomic" energy that goes beyond our physical dimension, neurons being only a biological interface for the expression of information. From there, several questions can be asked:

- Is a child alter personality in a dissociated adult a fragment of the soul (more than "personality") that has become stuck in the past, in an alternate dimension, retaining the age and memory it had when it separated from the physical body in the trauma? Can these alter children be explained by this theory of lost soul fragments in another dimension outside our space-time?

- Is the I.D.T. linked to another space-time in which the "alter personalities" can be contacted, processed, delivered and reintegrated into the present moment with all the memories that accompany them?

In his book The Lost Secret of Death, Peter Novak gives us the beginning of an answer: "When shamans travel to these other realities to find the lost soul fragments of others, they report that these fragments are not dormant at all. On the contrary, they appear to be autonomous, self-conscious entities, engaged in their parallel reality. However, as long as they are separated from the person's consciousness, these fragments do not seem to progress at all. They remain frozen in the same state of emotional and intellectual development that they had when they split from the person's mind. The soul fragment that split off when the child was 4 years old will continue to behave and think as if it were 4 years old. It will believe itself to be 4 years old, even though the rest of the person has

---

[394] The unbearable truth about water" - Jacques Collin, 1997.

grown to be even an old man. These alienated fragments do not seem to grow and mature until healing occurs and the missing piece is restored. These fragments will usually have their own personal qualities, abilities, feelings, and a consciousness of themselves leading their own lives in this fantasy world. The part of the soul that was lost in infancy will be left playing in the schoolyard, or perhaps shivering under the stairs, hiding from a punishment that already took place 40 years earlier.

It is the job of the shaman to try to make this soul fragment understand the reality of its predicament in order to convince it to return and join the rest of the spirit of the person living in the "present moment". Often the soul fragment will have no idea what the shaman is talking about, thinking that it is a truly autonomous person (...) a few days or weeks after the reintegration of the lost soul fragment, the memories associated with that fragment will begin to emerge into the person's consciousness. When the soul fragment returns, the memories associated with it return with it. These memories are lost and forgotten when the soul splits, so the person no longer has access to that memory fragment. Once back, these memories usually require a lot of attention as they contain traumatic emotions and sensations that need to be integrated. This is usually what has caused the split in the mind."[395]

Here we find exactly the same symptoms and characteristics of I.D.T. functioning, with traumatic amnesic walls that disappear as the alter personalities emerge and merge, while the related dissociated memories are gradually made conscious and integrated. The alter personalities of an I.D.T. would appear to be lost soul fragments with their memory content. Therapist Alison Miller has written: *"I.D.T. patients have told me that it is impossible to keep the alters separate from each other once the traumatic memories that split them up have been fully processed.* This means that the integration and fusion of the alter personalities takes place automatically when the dissociative amnesia disappears and the memories become conscious.

In 2006, ritual abuse and mind control survivor Lynn Schirmer described at a conference the process of merging with her alter personalities *"frozen"* in another space of time: *"They integrate into the present, in fact they... I don't know how to explain it: They go through some kind of process... There is some integration, but when I recover a memory, usually the process is to bring that alter out of its 'frozen', dissociated state... I have to bring the alter that holds that memory into the present, I familiarize it with the present moment and transfer that isolated memory into a coherent timeline. Then my alters only have to adapt to this new world, i.e. the present. So they have to evolve and get used to it."*[396]

When Lynn Schirmer recovers a memory, she must therefore lead the associated alter into the present moment where it must evolve to adapt... she speaks very clearly here of soul fragments blocked, "frozen" as she puts it, in

---

[395] The Lost Secret of Death: Our Divided Souls and the Afterlife" - Peter Novak, 2003, Chap.6.

[396] Lynn Schirmer - The Ninth Annual Ritual Abuse, Secretive Organizations and Mind Control Conference, S.M.A.R.T., 08/2006.

what seems to be another space-time. An obscure past in which the alters continue to live "in a loop" with this traumatic memory...

Survivor Jen Callow describes the reluctance of soul fragments to merge with their main personality: *"I have parts* (alter) *children who are eager to 'grow up' by merging with another part. However, there are many parts that remain afraid of integration. Some see the inner world shrinking, with the loss of playmates, friends... when these different parts merge, it can lead to a great sense of loss for others. This reduction in the number of alters can also be interpreted as real people 'disappearing' and some parts may be afraid of disappearing too (...) For many of my alters, integration is something terrifying, because it means giving up their own identity and becoming someone new and unknown."*[397]

The existence of these lost soul fragments in another space-time was validated by the astral travel experiences of Robert Monroe, the founder of the Monroe Institute established in 1974 in Virginia, USA. He was a wealthy businessman who owned numerous media outlets and had had many out-of-body experiences himself. Monroe became one of the world's leading specialists in astral travel. The initial purpose of the institute was to research *remote viewing*, and today it is one of the largest centres for research into out-of-body experiences, relaxation, meditation and *Hemi-sync* techniques (synchronisation of the cerebral hemispheres by sound frequencies). According to some authors, the Monroe Institute is also involved (probably through the CIA's takeover of the institute) in trauma-based mind control, as *Hemi-sync* techniques can be used to work on the cerebral hemispheres in *Delta* and *Theta* MK programmes (more on this in the next chapter).

According to researcher Tom Porter, Robert Monroe is the son of James Monroe, who worked for years for the CIA but was also the director of a front company called *the Human Ecology Society*. As mentioned in Chapter 3, this front company was used by the CIA to fund the MK-Ultra programme. James Monroe would have personally supervised people like Dr. Ewen Cameron. It is therefore possible that Robert Monroe, the world's leading exponent of astral travel, was himself subjected to the MK-Ultra mind control programmes. According to Andrijah Puharich, Robert Monroe himself stimulated his abilities for astral travel for which he seemed to have a certain predisposition, perhaps because of childhood traumas? A common feature of people experiencing spontaneous astral exits is trauma.

Monroe has written extensively about his out-of-body experiences which began in 1958. In 1994, he published the book *"Ultimate Journey"* in which he describes profound out-of-body journeys during which he sometimes encountered souls of deceased people. Monroe describes these entities as confused, disoriented, and seemingly trapped in a particular space of time, emotion and memory. He describes them as semi-conscious entities unable to realise that they are dead. As noted above, the Kahuna tradition describes these types of entities as the conscious mind separated from its subconscious mind,

---

[397] "Healing the Unimaginable: Treating Ritual Abuse and Mind Control" - Alison Miller, 2012, pp.269-270.

which then becomes an amnesiac wandering soul needing to reconnect to its missing part in order to access restorative memories. Monroe also tells how these entities, these lost souls, could sometimes even be his own. So they were not just souls of dead people, they were also fragments of souls of living people, including his own... He reports in his book that he sometimes encountered what seemed to be another part of his own mind, lost fragments that seemed to be trapped in the past and unable to evolve. When he encountered and delivered his lost soul fragments, they were reincorporated into his mind at a particular level, which he calls the *"I-there"*.[398]

Just as Lynn Schirmer describes with her alter, he brought his lost soul fragments back into the present moment, into our space-time. Monroe's experiences in other dimensions could validate the shamanic tradition of *"hunting for lost souls"* during astral travel to retrieve the broken soul fragments of a person to be healed. However, it would be rather the ancestral shamanic tradition that should validate Monroe's testimony because what he had just discovered was precisely what the shamans had been practising for centuries...

In his book *"The Ultimate Journey"*, Monroe tells us about his students who go on a hunt for lost soul fragments to bring them back into the present moment: *"What surprises many candidates is that when they embark on this mission, they discover that at the same time they are recovering lost parts of themselves... Others may appear as fragments of personality from everyday life, which had escaped or been torn away from the core personality. For example, children who had run away from trauma and the pain of physical and psychological abuse in their families and were now seeking to be reunited with the other fragments (...) Clusters of light, fires of human energy forming an endless multidimensional carpet... how could I not have seen them before? Now I understand the inflow and outflow... my flow is there and I have to stay on track... the outflow of those who come to help and find the lost parts of their cluster... the inflow that brings them back... thousands and thousands... insertions of clusters of personality units into human individuals of the earth life system."*[399]

If Robert Monroe went through an MK-Ultra type programme as a child, did he himself have an I.D.T. and special psychic faculties caused by a violent early spiritual 'unlocking'? Ron Russell's book *"Journey of Robert Monroe"* reports a quote from Lesley Frans showing that he obviously had a complex and multiple personality: *"Among the things we often talked about with Bob (Robert) were the different aspects of his personality that came out at times. Uncle Bob or Daddy, Business-man Bob, Manager Bob, Old Man Bob, Cosmic Bob, Paranoid Bob, etc. These were the main Bobs I knew, but they were far from the only ones. Once you could finally figure out which Bob was in front of you and try to communicate with him, whoosh! He would change in no time. There was a Juggler Bob who caused a lot of frustration. Bob Business-man had left his ethics behind, he was hard and unemotional (...) Some of the other Bobs were*

---

[398] The Lost Secret of Death: Our Divided Souls and the Afterlife" - Peter Novak, 2003, Chap.6.

[399] *The Ultimate Journey"* - Robert Monroe, 1996, Chap.15.

refuting the evil he had done, and Bob Parano was trying to regain and follow some ethics. "[400]

In the case of satanic ritual abuse and mind control, do witch doctors capture the soul fragments of victims? Can soul fragments be held captive by outside entities, which could influence and manipulate the thoughts, behaviour and create emotional and physical problems for the victim? This seems to be the view of some shamanic traditions that *the lost soul* may be held captive by evil spirits or sorcerers. This is also stated by some survivors of ritual abuse. Is this just a superstitious belief or are these really operative occult techniques?

In Satanism, sexual abuse is used to gain access to the victim's mind, child prostitution and the production of child pornography are used solely for financial gain. Sexual abuse is used to hurt and dominate the victim's mind, to *'take away the soul'*. Victims describe how Satanists can capture a part of their spirit to keep it with them permanently. Conversely, the torturers can also introduce a part of their soul, a fragment of their spirit, into the victim when they are in altered states of consciousness (spiritual openness). For this they use their bodily fluids (menstrual blood, semen, etc.) or other substances to *implant themselves* inside the victim during a rape for example. The soul fragments of the witch-boy will then remain attached to the victim to continually reinforce the commands for control and obedience. All this is pure witchcraft, which also combines orgasm and pain to *appease the fertility deities.*

The theory of trauma-created spirit fragments being able to attach themselves to a person is a familiar one in the field of the paranormal and possession. As we have seen, Satanists who practice ritual abuse are usually dissociated and split themselves, so it is conceivable that they could deliberately bind some of their fragments to victims. This type of manipulation combined with I.D.T. creates a spiritual, psychological and physical bondage. American pastor Tom Hawkins wrote: *"Most survivors of ritual abuse have been forced to participate in rituals involving vows, oaths, sacrifices or covenants made with the spiritual realm of evil. These 'legal transactions' give the evil spirits, or demons, the right to bind specific alters who have been involved in these practices and to exert influence and control over them to varying degrees. They may play a role, for example, in reinforcing programming, blocking memories, or re-traumatising alters who have failed in their duties, divulged secrets, or sought outside help. These demonised alters have usually been enslaved to Satan and his plan (...) These connections can also be made with entities of a higher order than demons (...) Dissociated personalities can be tortured into deep trance states that will connect them to what we call the 'second heaven', referring to the 'kingdom of air' of which Satan is the reigning prince (Eph. 2:2). There, alters can be held "captive" by evil entities and used for Satan's world plan, transmitted directly from the spiritual realm. In the internal system of these*

---

[400] The Journey of Robert Monroe: From Out-of-body Explorer to Consciousness Pioneer - Ronald Russell, 2007.

people, these alters usually appear to be outside the physical body and are considered absent or even dead by the other alters. "[401]

This other dimension in which the soul fragments evolve can be seen in the distortions of time and reality that are very frequent and sometimes intense in patients suffering from IDD. Aren't the traumatic memories, in which the person really relives the scene with the images, sounds, smells, physical pain and psychological terror, a journey through time? It is an access to another space-time in which a precise scene is well and truly recorded *"somewhere"* in the smallest details, with all the sensory and emotional system linked to this memory capsule. Psychotraumatologists will explain this phenomenon by the neurological and chemical process of dissociative memories not processed by the hippocampus, but they do not take into account this notion of *"lost soul fragments"*... How do they explain shamanic journeys to another dimension to search for and bring back these soul fragments... with their pieces of dissociated memories?

In his book *'Being and Time'*, Martin Heidegger refers to the past, present and future as the *ecstasies* of temporality, the word ecstasy meaning 'being outside'. In his analysis of temporality Heidegger writes that the past, present and future can be found transcended and indissolubly unified. He calls this the *ecstatic unity of temporality. Dissociative illumination'* is sometimes described as an exit from our space-time where present, past and future are all on the same timeline. The experience of trauma becomes somehow frozen and trapped in an eternal present.

Pierre Janet noted that when a traumatic memory was reactivated, the person usually lost track of time and the present moment, their 'present' was the traumatic experience that was occurring again. In an article entitled *"Functional disorders of memory"*, it is noted that *the immersion in the automatic memory is sometimes so intense that temporal orientation is lost and the trauma is relived as if it were occurring in the present moment, rather than as a mere memory.* "[402]

In the article *"Time Distortions in Dissociative Identity* Disorder", Dr. Onno van der Hart and psychotherapist Kathy Steele report the testimony of an alter personality who experiences time distortions during flashbacks of traumatic memories: *"It continues to be a storm in my head. There is a lot of noise with all kinds of flashes all the time, sometimes films. I'm scared, I can't look at them and they are hard to stop (...) It's scary because it happens so suddenly, but also because it makes me totally confused. Confusion about time mainly, it's hard to know if these things are part of the present moment or the past. It is also becoming increasingly difficult to keep a grip on the present time. I can't seem*

---

[401] "Dissociative Identity Disorder, Vol.1 Psychological Dynamics" - Tom R. Hawkins, 2010, p.62.

[402] "Functional disorders of memory" - Spiegel, D., Frischholz, EJ., & Spira,J., American Psychiatric Press Review of Psychiatry, 1993.

to trust the clock anymore. It is suddenly an hour later, and then five minutes appear to have lasted more than three days. "[403]

This testimony shows us that this disorder is a phenomenon that goes beyond our 'matrix' and that we must therefore take into account its multidimensional aspect if we want to start studying it seriously... Clinicians, with their 'classic' scientific training, are generally not intellectually equipped to deal with this side of the problem.

Child alter personalities are often unable to give themselves a sense of time, to mark hours or days. They are in an endless, boundless space, locked in a timelessness or 'frozen in the eternal present' of their traumatic experience. The notion of time seems to be something specific to our existence in this three-dimensional physical world, but this notion of time seems to disappear for these alters, which would prove that they are evolving (or stagnating, we should say) in another dimension. In a way, we can say that trauma can create 'holes' or 'gaps' in our space-time. Hence the connections with certain entities and the paranormal psychic powers that can develop in some victims as we shall see later.

This notion of soul fragments being trapped or even captive in another dimension is a key point in understanding the nature of I.D.T. and how MK-Monarch programming works. Monarch mind control deliberately creates these soul fragments in order to control and exploit them. The "inner world" of the Monarch slave would be nothing more than the dimension where these soul fragments live, trapped in structures set up by the programmer and linked to demonic entities that act as guardians. The programmers thus interact with this space-time to imprison and dominate these dissociated fragments. Therapist Patricia Baird Clarke describes this dimension as follows: *'Through rituals, Satanists use demons to separate the spiritual body from the physical body. When the soul and spirit have been separated and the spiritual body separated from the physical body, then the person enters in a fully conscious way into a whole other dimension. This is the dimension I call the "inner world". This world is as vast and as real to the individual as the physical world is to us. We think of spirits as if they were in a "vaporous" state, but people who have been in this dimension have reported to me that demons do have weight and substance.* "[404]

This is how therapist Alison Miller describes this inner world, this space-time where the alters live: "Not all patients' inner worlds are the same. Some, like the one described by Trish Fotheringham, have magical castles and forests; others have prisons, fortresses, torture chambers, and various military installations (i.e. structures deliberately introduced into the inner world by the programmers). Some describe places that seem to represent another world or other planets. People whose I.D.T. was created spontaneously (i.e., without a deliberate attempt by others to split them up for programming), usually have

---

[403] "Time Distortions in Dissociative Identity Disorder: Janetian Concepts and Treatment" - Onno van der Hart and Kathy Steele, Journal Dissociation, 1997.

[404] Restoring Survivors of Satanic Ritual Abuse " - Patricia Baird Clark, 2000.

inner houses in which the alter lives. These are often internal representations of the house where they lived at the time of abuse."[405]

Jen Callow has undergone ritual abuse and mental programming protocols, this is how she describes this inner world where her soul fragments are: *"When we (alters) finally start therapy with someone who understands what dissociation is, many of us are isolated and live in terror. We are locked in our inner world: in boxes, in cold basements, or in other places related to our memories. We are locked in our programs, often starving or in pain. Our inner system can inflict torture and abuse similar to what our abusers did to us."*[406]

This notion of an inner world where alter stagnates, a world without limits and totally abstract, fitted out with all sorts of things, could seem implausible, absurd and psychotic if we did not take into account this phenomenon of an alternative dimension to ours. We will detail the techniques for structuring this inner world in the next chapter on Monarch programming.

Traditional shamanic beliefs about soul splitting are probably not that far removed from our own psychiatric concept of a *lost soul*. Even if we ignore the cultural elements and the ancestral roots of these things, we have some commonalities with these ancestral concepts: don't we say that a patient is "alienated", "foreign" to himself, that his personality has deteriorated or has even been destroyed? Doesn't the therapist who works with a so-called *"schizophrenic"* patient try to establish contact with the remaining part of the personality that still has *"feet on the ground"*? Does he not seek to reconstruct the split personality in the same way as the modern successor of those shamans who track down lost souls in the spirit world and fight the demons that keep them prisoner, in order to bring them back to the world of the living?[407]

5 - TRAUMA AND PARANORMAL PSYCHIC ABILITIES

Here are some of the factors that I have identified regarding "haunted people". They are usually bipolar, they usually have suffered sexual abuse or trauma in their past (often in childhood). The majority of cases involve extreme dysfunction in the family. These are people who have experienced the paranormal since early childhood. " "Haunted People, Haunted Minds" - Bobbie Atristain, 2006

In 1784, the Marquis de Puységur (Armand Marie Jacques de Chastenet), who was working on animal magnetism and the laying on of hands, reported a particular case with one of his employees, a peasant by the name of Victor Race, who showed an obvious change in personality with a separation of consciousness

---

[405] "Healing the Unimaginable: Treating Ritual Abuse and Mind Control" - Alison Miller, 2012, p.69.

[406] Ibid, p.272.

[407] The Discovery of the Unconscious' ', Henri F. Ellenberger, 1970.

accompanied by amnesia. During a session of laying on of hands to relieve Victor of a pulmonary congestion, the Marquis was surprised to see that the young man had quietly fallen asleep... He discovered that this was not a normal sleep but a special state of consciousness in which he was in a trance. Once in this state, Victor Race showed special abilities: he became extremely sensitive to suggestion and his personality changed completely. While he was usually rather slow-witted, this other personality showed a remarkable intelligence with phenomenal mental agility. Furthermore, in these altered states of consciousness, he was able to read the Marquis' mind and make accurate medical diagnoses for himself and others. He could also predict the progress of a disease and prescribe treatment, often with great success. Victor also showed strange memory problems. Indeed, when he came out of this unusual state of consciousness, he had absolutely no recollection of what had happened, whereas in the trance state he was fully aware of his two personalities. The Marquis de Puységur decided to call this discovery the state of *"magnetic sleep"*, which he linked to the artificial sleepwalking states he also called *"magnetic sleepwalking"*.[408]

34 years later, the Marquis met Victor Race again and put him into a trance-like state. He was surprised to find that his former employee remembered in great detail all his previous *magnetic sleep* states. In his book *"The Discovery of Unconscious"* Ellenberger tells us that in August 1785, the Marquis de Puységur was ordered to command the artillery regiment of Strasbourg. It was then that the local Masonic lodge asked him to teach the principles of animal magnetism to its members, who were always very interested in acquiring paranormal powers that could lead them to the *"light"* and raise them above the profane. The story does not tell us if Victor Race had suffered trauma in his early childhood, but it does show us that a multiple personality can develop paranormal psychic powers.

Can trauma be the cause of certain paranormal phenomena? Can they open the way to certain psychic faculties? Do they create a breach, the opening of a door to other dimensions? As we have seen above, it would seem so. Emotions open doors to other worlds and those that emanate from trauma are particularly powerful. However, psychic powers do not necessarily come from childhood trauma. They can come from certain transgenerational 'gifts' that are more or less sharpened. They can be developed through certain energetic practices and exercises. But they can also be the result of pacts made with entities. Satanists and luciferians seek these paranormal powers to increase their power, but they only obtain subjection to demons in exchange for these "powers"... The Holy Spirit can also transmit graces of this type, such as clairvoyance for example.

Joseph Mahoney, a Catholic priest from Detroit (USA) who works with I.D.D. patients, has listed a series of strange phenomena that are observed in these split people.[409] Generally, a paranormal faculty will be specific to one alter personality and absent in others. Here is what the priest writes about these

---

[408] Multiple Personality Before "Eve" - Adam Crabtree, Journal "Dissociation", Vol.6 N°1, 03/1993.

[409] "Exorcism and multiple personality disorder from a catholic perspective" - Fr. Joseph Mahoney.

paranormal phenomena related to D.I.D. (note that some of the phenomena reported in this list are often also reported in cases of demonic possession):

- A great sensitivity to hypnosis and a rare ability to induce hypnotic and trance-like states in others.
- Memories of the body that manifest themselves physically. These are traumas from the past that arise on the body in the same way as the classic phenomenon of stigmata. They can appear and disappear without any external intervention. They can be skin rashes, marks, cuts, burns, blood loss, bruising, swelling or other significant physiological changes.
- Telepathy, clairvoyance and unexplained knowledge, photographic memory, hypersensitivity leading to highly developed reading of others' body language, unusual mental prowess.
- A physical strength beyond what is humanly possible.
- Accelerated healings, control of bleeding and the ability to self-regulate physiological states in ways that are usually impossible to do.
- An ability to make the observer feel cold, uneasy or threatened.
- Extreme self-harm, hatred of God and religious objects.
- An ability to go for long periods without food or sleep.
- An ability to anaesthetise a specific alter personality or to block nerve transmission of pain.

In her book *The Secrets of Psychic Success*, psychic Angela Donovan writes that in her own experience there are three ways in which psychic abilities can develop, one of which is directly related to traumatic experiences: *"There are those who have experienced severe emotional trauma. I have met many psychics who have come into this field through the death of a loved one, or who have suffered a physical shock, such as a blow to the head. This can literally open the 'doors' and create a receptive state. This is something that can be positive if the person is trying to understand what is happening to them, but if not, it can be very disconcerting."*[410]

The development of paranormal psychic powers has sometimes been reported following accidents causing physical trauma or near-death experiences. This is the case of the famous Italian medium Eusapia Paladino who suffered a cranial (parietal bone) trauma in an accident during her early childhood. This is also the case of the famous Dutch medium Peter Hurkos who acquired extrasensory powers following a trauma to the head and a three-day coma after falling from a ladder... Hurkos was considered to be one of the world's foremost clairvoyants, working to solve many cases of unsolved disappearances and murders. Hurkos said: *"I see images in my mind like on a television screen. When I touch something, I can then tell what I see in connection with that thing."*

In the book *'The Psychic World of Peter Hurkos'*, Norma Lee Browning reports what Hurkos told her about his trauma:

I remember when I fell and I didn't want to die, then it was pitch black. When I woke up I didn't have my own mind. That's when I got my gift. I was in

---

[410] The Secrets of Psychic Success: The Complete Guide to Unlocking Your Psychic Gifts " - Angela Donovan, 2007, Chap.1.

someone else's mind and I was scared because I didn't know what was going on. My father and mother said that I was not the same Peter as before. They said that I had died and that I had come back with two spirits. You can ask my father, I swear. He will tell you that his real son Peter died and I came back with two different spirits. There are two spirits here my dear, two spirits, you understand? (...) You know there are people with two personalities? Well I have two minds. My father was right when he said I was not the same Peter. This one died and he came back hearing voices and seeing images (...) Was he really a psychic or a psychotic? Was it possible that he was schizophrenic or a true multiple personality? Was he "born again" as a clairvoyant because of the head injury, just as Bridey Murphy was born again under hypnosis? Did he really have a sixth sense, or was he mentally ill? These questions intrigued me. If the story of Peter's accident could be verified, some light would be shed on so-called 'psychic powers'. I always had the idea that these paranormal psychic phenomena were something natural, rather than supernatural. A physical rather than a metaphysical phenomenon, physiological rather than psychological. I am convinced that one day it will be proven that everything called "psychic experiences" has a physical explanation with the various electrochemical components of the most wonderful computing machine there is: the human brain."[411]

Altered states of consciousness, or dissociative states, are the key to paranormal psychic abilities. As we have seen, extreme trauma causes dissociation, which is a profound altered state of consciousness. Dissociation creates a certain opening towards an alternative world, towards other dimensions, towards the immaterial and the invisible... This is surely the reason why more or less extraordinary phenomena can occur with certain individuals. People who have developed an I.D.T. (having undergone trauma and strong dissociation) have shown extraordinary physical abilities, exceeding the usual human potential, but they can also show certain paranormal psychic powers. Extreme and repetitive trauma seems to change or create particular synapses (neural connections, more on this in the next chapter) but also to activate parts of the brain that are usually dormant. This causes a kind of *"bug in the matrix"*, knowing that our entire "reality" is based on our perceptions, and that these perceptions (our five senses) depend solely on these neural connections and the electrical flows that circulate in them. If we add to this the fact that we only use on average 10% of our brain, then we can say that our perception of "reality" is in fact very limited and that it is therefore possible that it can be greatly modified by a few neural connections that are created or modified during trauma. As we will see in the next chapter, it is the child's experience that shapes the synapses and the functioning of the brain. Extreme trauma shapes the brain while splitting the energy bodies, creating an opening to other dimensions and the development of certain psychic faculties.

Dr. John Smythies explains this phenomenon of the 'Matrix' to which our brains are connected: "There is ample neurological evidence to show that our

---

[411] The Psychic World of Peter Hurkos" - Norma Lee Browning, 2000, Chap.1.

sensory data, including somatic data, cannot be identical to external objects but only to specific brain states. If we were to remove a child's brain and connect it to a giant computer that would send appropriate stimuli to the sensory nerves, the individual in question would lead a kind of perfect average life; in fact, he or she would live whatever life we programmed. The sensory fields of consciousness are constructs of the nervous system, not the direct apprehension of external material objects. In other words, the physiological mechanisms of perception work like television, not like a telescope."[412]

The psychic and extrasensory faculties that can be brought about by dissociation and connection with other dimensions is a reality fully integrated and used in most pre-industrial traditions, but also by the dominant 'nameless religion', for which the capacity for dissociation is a very important genetic criterion. Anthropologist Ruth Inge-Heinz, who has studied possessions in many cultures, writes: *"The concept that defines a 'healthy mind' differs considerably from culture to culture (...) It can be very destructive to put the label of 'mental illness' on an extraordinary state of consciousness. A state of mental dissociation does not necessarily mean that an individual is in a straitjacket. Many dissociative states that occur in Southeast Asia, for example, are quite controlled and integrated into traditional culture."[413]*

As we saw in Chapter 2, the shaman transforms a subdued state into a dominated one, a passive dissociation into an active one: he is a self-healed healer. In some cultures, people who behave with characteristics of mental illness are traditionally associated with the divine, especially if they receive specific visions or messages. Possession by an outside entity is often seen as an aid to becoming a healer or diviner. The *DSM-IV Casebook* (a supplement to the *DSM* with case histories and testimonies) reports the case of a woman who is recognised by her community as being able to communicate with the ancestors and to predict the future: *"Sometimes God comes into me, it's very hot when he gives me visions. (...) "This woman has symptoms that would be considered psychotic if they were seen by someone from a society that does not share her culture and beliefs (Guinea). She believes that she has special powers, while for some she is just hallucinating. In her local culture, these phenomena are very common. Her community attributes the role of healer to her and accepts her experiences and abnormal behaviour as something quite normal for someone in this role. Indeed, she is a very successful healer. Her community therefore attributes the role of healer to her and her behaviour is not seen as something to be treated and healed."*

In the book "Le Défi Magique: Satanisme et Sorcellerie", Jean Baptiste Martin writes:

Ernesto De Martino begins by pointing out that in the cultures that are usually the subject of ethnological studies, it has very often been observed that

---

[412] The Unknown Powers of Man: Prior Knowledge" - Chap: "Conclusion on the Mind and Brain" - Dr John R. Smythies, 1977, p.284.

[413] "Shamans or mediums: Toward a definition of different states of consciousness. Ruth Inge-Heinz, Journal of Transpersonal Anthropology, 1982.

certain particular psychic states are very common, as if the natives seemed to be naturally predisposed to them. These states arise as a result of traumas or emotions which precipitate the subject into a particular condition, characterised by the loss of the unity of the ego...[414]

In other words, the ethnologist De Martino describes here a dissociation that can cause a splitting (*loss of the unity of the 'I'*) and a separation of the physical body from the spiritual body creating an opening to another dimension and access to possession and paranormal powers. This is a common process in pre-industrial cultures, but also practiced by Satanic/Luciferian cults.

In October 2014, TF1's *Sept à huit* broadcast a report on Thailand's *"Mah Song"*, also known as the *"possessed horses"*. These men, revered as gods, enter deep states of dissociative trance claiming to be possessed by gods. In these altered states of consciousness, the Mah Songs accomplish quite extraordinary things. In particular, the report followed *Ae*, a 36-year-old man, who, when in a trance, speaks with the voice of a little boy in a Chinese dialect that he has never learned. Again, it is possible that this is an I.D.T., but the report does not mention previous trauma or amnesia as a result of *Ae*'s trance states.

According to *Ae*, the deity who takes possession of him is a "child-god", which is why he has this particular voice when he is possessed. The journalist tells us that there are even "baby gods" who take possession of the Mah Song...

Once in a trance, these men pierce their cheeks, ears and body skin with long metal rods. They show no signs of pain and no blood flows. Leading French surgeons who have observed the phenomenon do not explain it because the cheeks are normally a highly vascularised area and cutting them can even cause facial paralysis. During the ceremonies, the Mah Song, in a trance, will also prove their powers through insane challenges such as climbing an 18-metre ladder whose rungs are finely sharpened blades, without opening the soles of their feet, or walking on glowing embers without burning themselves. Performances that are impossible to do without serious physical consequences, so the state of dissociative trance (and the help of demons) is highly recommended in this kind of practice...

Mircéa Eliade writes that "among the Manchus, the public initiation ceremony once involved the candidate (shaman) passing over burning coals: if the apprentice indeed had the 'spirits' he claimed to have, he could walk over the fire with impunity."[415]

In 1992, in an article entitled *"Paranormal experiences in the general population"* (*Journal of Nervous and Mental Disease*), Dr. Colin Ross and Dr. Joshi claim that there is a link between paranormal and dissociative experiences. According to them, paranormal experiences are a natural aspect of dissociation. Like dissociation, these psychic abilities can be triggered by physical or psychological trauma, usually in childhood. Several studies show that such paranormal experiences are more common in individuals with a traumatic past.

---

[414] *"Le Défi Magique: Satanisme et Sorcellerie"*, Vol.2 - Jean Baptiste Martin, François Laplantine, Massimo Introvigne, 1994, p.154.

[415] Shamanism and the Archaic Techniques of Ecstasy" - Mircéa Eliade, 1951, p.104.

In his book *"The Osiris Complex"*, Dr. Collin Ross is very clear about the link between trauma, dissociation and psychic abilities: *"According to my data, analogously speaking, the genes for dissociation and the paranormal are closely related to each other on the same chromosome (...) Any extra-genetic factor activating one will tend to activate the other because they are related. Severe and repetitive early childhood trauma is one such factor (...) Highly psychic people tend to be dissociative (...) Another way of looking at this is to say that trauma opens a door to the paranormal. This door is usually closed in our rather hostile western cultures. The dissociative fragmentation of the psyche as a result of childhood trauma will act on this door which normally remains closed (...) These facets of the human psyche (trauma, dissociation and the paranormal) were suddenly banished at the end of the 19th century in conjunction with Freud's renunciation of his seduction theory. Freud had decided that the incest revealed to him by his patient with a dissociative disorder must be fantasies, which led to a problem for him: if the trauma had never existed, why did his patient have these symptoms and pseudo-memories? To solve this problem, he abandoned hypnosis as a substantive treatment, discarded dissociation in favour of repression, continued to ignore the paranormal, broke with Jung, and moved away completely from theories that put severe trauma and its psychological consequences at the heart of psychopathology. In order to remove an element he did not understand, he had to remove four essential components, which is what caused him to distance himself from Jung, who continued to be closely interested in dissociation and the paranormal."*[416]

In a study on the link between dissociation and paranormal phenomena, Douglas G. Richards notes that: "Psychic experiences closely related to dissociation reveal clairvoyance, precognitions, apparitions, psychokinesis and telepathy (...) Psychic experiences are an obvious component of dissociation. Richards makes it clear that these psychic experiences can also be a natural function in a healthy developmental process without a traumatic past.[417]

In a 2003 article entitled *"Multiple Personality Disorder - Demons and Angels or Archetypal aspects of the inner self"*, Dr. Haraldur Erlendsson writes: *"A particular aspect of MPD is the frequency of headaches (79%) and extra-sensory perceptions; such as telepathy, telekinesis, clairvoyance, vision of 'ghosts'.A particular aspect of I.D.D. is the frequency of headaches (79%) and extra-sensory perceptions; such as telepathy, telekinesis, clairvoyance, vision of 'ghosts', out-of-body experience... These are the main non-clinical features of I.D.D."*

In the book "Les pouvoirs inconnus de l'homme: les extra-sensoriels", Dr. Gustave Geley writes that the main problems in uncovering second personalities are two equally difficult ones:

1° The problem of the psychological difference with the normal personality: difference not only of direction, of will; but of general character, of

---

[416] "The Osiris Complex: Case studies in Mulitple Personality Disorder" - Colin A. Ross, 1994, p.69-70.

[417] "Hauntings and Poltergeists: Multidisciplinary Perspectives" - James Houran, Rense Lange, 2008.

tendencies, of faculties, of knowledge; differences so radical sometimes, that they imply, between the normal self and the second personality, complete opposition and hostility.

2° The problem of supra-normal abilities, which are frequently linked to manifestations of the second personality.

Now, if the works on multiple personalities are innumerable today and have brought to light the frequency, the importance and the polymorphic character of these manifestations, they have done nothing for the solution of the second problem, which remains unresolved (...) They have shown above all the total impotence of the explanations of classical psycho-physiology with regard to the supra-normal faculties.[418]

Dr. James Randall Noblitt reports in his book *Cult and Ritual Abuse* the case of one of his ritual abuse patients. She had developed an I.D.T. with an alter personality that saw auras (the energetic halo that surrounds a person). *For some reason, these patients sometimes report having psychic abilities, such as the belief that they have the ability to see auras. These people sometimes believe that they have been given a gift that allows them to see the light around other people's bodies; and that from the colour and other aspects of that light, they can interpret it and make some kind of diagnosis about the person (...) As I was finding out more about this alter personality, she explained to me that she had the ability to see auras because of the rituals she was forced to participate in. Her father warned her that these experiments were to be kept strictly secret.*"[419]

The psychiatrist Milton H. Erickson saw multiple personality disorder as something not necessarily pathological but rather as a phenomenal resource of potential to be tapped. He used hypnosis to access alter personalities and to transform involuntary behaviour into voluntary actions. This involves reversing an a priori negative, uncontrollable and sometimes destructive force into a controllable force for positive and constructive benefit. MK-Monarch mind control seeks to develop and exploit the full potential of an individual with I.D.D...

In 2014, a study was conducted in Turkey to determine the possible relationship between possession experiences, paranormal phenomena, traumatic stress and dissociation. The study was conducted on a representative sample of 628 women who were tested in clinical interviews structured around dissociative disorders, post-traumatic stress disorder, *borderline* personality disorder and childhood abuse and neglect.

In women with a dissociative disorder, paranormal phenomena and possessions were more frequent than in those without a dissociative disorder. Women with a history of childhood trauma, or adult trauma with post-traumatic stress disorder, reported possession more frequently than those without trauma. Paranormal phenomena were also associated with childhood trauma. The group of women with trauma-related dissociative disorders had the highest scores for

---

[418] The Unknown Powers of Man: Les Extra-sensoriels" - Chap: "Rôle du subconscient" - Dr. Gustave Geley, 1976, p.221.

[419] *"Cult and Ritual Abuse"* - James Randall Noblitt & Pamela Perskin Noblitt, 2014, p.33.

possession or contact with demonic entities, extrasensory communication, possession by a human entity and precognitions. This study shows that paranormal phenomena and possession are related to the issue of trauma and dissociation. However, the doctors who conducted this study consider it still preliminary due to the small sample size.[420]

In her doctoral thesis, psychologist Margo Chandley found that *"many 'channels' appear to have experienced neglect or abuse."*[421]

In a study entitled *"A Study of the correlations between subjective psychic experience and dissociative experiences" (Dissociation* Journal, 1991) Douglas Richards concludes that dissociation is very often related to clairvoyance, premonitions, psychokinesis and telepathy. He reports that out-of-body experiences, *channeling* and contact with *"spirit guides"* necessarily involve a dissociative process...

In her autobiography, *'Adventures in the Supernormal'*, renowned psychic Eileen Garrett describes the connection between early childhood trauma, paranormal phenomena and the development of special psychic abilities. Garrett lost both her parents to suicide a few days after her birth. In her early childhood, she was abused almost daily by an aunt who raised her...

At the age of four she felt the presence of what is usually called an "imaginary friend", she began to see auras and to have visions and premonitions. As an adult, Garrett sought to understand how she acquired her psychic abilities, writing: *"I think the trance state is part of the explanation of how I developed my psychic abilities. I began to understand how the pain and suffering of my early days made me withdraw from the material world. I withdrew from that world to such an extent that even though I could see my aunt's lips twitching when she abused me, not a word of what she might say entered my ears. I remember that when the pain and fear became unbearable, I could go inside myself and I would become numb and not feel the pain. I had unconsciously developed an escape technique to avoid the pain. I can now understand how this process paved the way for the development of my mediumistic trance states."*[422]

Kenneth Ring, the author of *The Omega Project*, observed that adults who testified to near-death experiences and contact with UFO phenomena also frequently reported early childhood abuse and trauma. For Ring, these childhood ordeals may have developed a particular sensitivity to other dimensions of being and parallel worlds: *"After all, a child who is exposed to physical abuse, sexual abuse, or other severe trauma will be strongly urged to disconnect from his*

---

[420] "Experiences of possession and paranormal phenomena among women in the general population: are they related to traumatic stress and dissociation? " - Sar, Alioğlu, Akyüz, Journal "Trauma & Dissociation", 2014.

[421] "Multiple Personality and Channeling" - Rayna L. Rogers, Jefferson Journal of Psychiatry: Vol. 9: Iss. 1, Article 3.

[422] "Adventures in the Supernormal" - Eilen Garrett, 2002, p.90-91.

physical and social world by dissociating. But in doing so, he is more likely to connect with other realities. "[423]

In the book Reframing Consciousness, artist Kristine Stiles discusses the relationship between dissociation, hyper-vigilance and parallel worlds: "I believe that the ability to dissociate can be linked to psychic faculties through hyper-vigilance, which is a common symptom in response to trauma. Hyper-vigilance involves excessive attention to an external stimulus beyond what the threat level requires. Hyper-vigilance plays a vital role in protecting the victim from a risky environment (...) Hyper-vigilance also allows for the development of a very high concentration power. Hypnotic and dissociative states have long been associated with unusual effects on the body. These are mental functions in which cognitive resources are entirely focused on a specific point, with little or no distractions and with increased control of somatic and neurophysiological functions. In the case of Joseph McMoneagle grappling with his newly acquired psychic faculties after his near-death experience, he recalls that a psychologist suggested to him that this near-death experience had made him more sensitive to other forms of detail. He describes this new ability as 'spontaneous knowledge', a 'new psychic functioning'. Dissociative hyper-vigilance literally blocks out the noise, or external pollution, that usually interferes with the point of focus, allowing the consciousness to access remote viewing or other psychic phenomena (...) My hypothesis is that hyper-vigilance may well be a primary feature in the connection between trauma and multidimensional abilities. This may also explain why both Eastern forms of meditation and Western concentration techniques are becoming increasingly important in processes such as remote viewing (...) In my view, traumatic dissociation and hyper-vigilance may result in a process that filters out 'mental noise' and thus allows consciousness to function in a multidimensional mode."[424]

In *the* book *The* Shattered *Self: A Psychoanalytic Study of* Trauma, psychoanalysts Richard Ulman and Doris Brothers report the testimony of a 36-year-old woman, Jean, who was a victim of incest that began at the age of 10 with her uncle and continued with her stepfather and brother-in-law. The traumas seem to have developed some particular psychic faculties in this woman: *"Jean's usual reaction to the rapes was to 'disconnect completely from her body', repeating to herself that 'this is not really real'. Jean was proud of her ability to maintain control during the rapes by showing no visible signs of anxiety. She also recalled a ritual before going to bed where she would slow her breathing to a crawl and remain as still as a dead woman to reassure herself that she was in "total control" of her body. Jean said that often during the day she would "listen to the silence", convinced that she had extrasensory powers to detect danger. She would walk between the bungalows with her eyes closed to test her paranormal ability to sense anything that might threaten her safety (...)*

---

[423] The Omega Project: Near-Death Experiences " - Kenneth Ring, 1992, p.142-144.

[424] Reframing Consciousness: Art, Mind and Technology " - Chap: "Transcendence" - Kristine Stiles, 1999, p.53-54.

Jean also reported having premonitions about her mother's suicide attempt. She described recurring "visions" of her mother cutting her throat a few months before it happened. She described a similar premonition at the age of 17, before her biological father suddenly appeared at her door (...)

Jean also described her relationship with a "psychic" and charismatic man who produced and sold sadomasochistic pornographic films (...) Jean said that she often participated in sadomasochistic scenes, sometimes lasting several days, and that she would then find herself in a state of detachment: "I would sort of leave my body and concentrate on not being hurt. After these sessions, Jean says that her memories of what had happened were extremely vague and that only the pain and marks on her body could remind her of her experience. Jean found it very satisfying to be able to separate her emotions from the physical pain in her body. The aches and pains make me feel special. The marks and bruises are how I measure my self-esteem. she says.

Several years later, Jean went back to school to get a degree in criminology so that she could pursue a career in the police. However, after passing the entrance exam, she decided not to join the civil service. She herself had opened a private investigation office in connection with the police force (...) She helped solve criminal cases with her 'psychic powers', she says. She would go into a trance-like state in which she would provide investigators with information such as number plates or the hiding places of criminals (...)

One morning Jean woke up with a high fever, severe pain and swelling in her joints. The symptoms were so severe that she had to walk with crutches and then in a wheelchair. The doctor she consulted was unable to find the cause of the symptoms. He tried several medical treatments, but without success. In desperation, Jean went into a trance state in which she relived the sexual abuse of her father-in-law and brother-in-law (...) According to her, after each trance episode, the unexplainable symptoms disappeared, only to reappear later, necessitating the repetition of the process (...)

For a few years, Jean worked in an alternative health shop. She discovered that she had remarkable success in healing various physical ailments through the use of herbs and gems (semi-precious and precious stones). She noted that without any training, she instinctively "knew" how to heal the people who came to her (...) She also reported that she had many symptoms of post-traumatic stress disorder such as hyper-vigilance, heightened reactivity and sleep disturbances."[425]

According to Gardner Murphy, former president of the *American Psychological Association*, serious illnesses, or more generally disturbing elements or alarming situations, can lead to the development of a heightened psychic sensitivity. We can take as an example the case of people with an I.D.D. whose sense of sight has been modified, which has resulted in the creation of an exceptional photographic memory. This photographic memory is also linked to hypervigilance and hypersensitivity developed in response to trauma. The brains

---

[425] The Shattered Self: A Psychoanalytic Study of Trauma " - Richard Ulman and Doris Brothers, 1993, pp.92-96.

of abuse survivors develop a constant hypervigilance and an ability to *read* other people very accurately. They will be able to automatically and unconsciously decipher and analyse behaviour, body language, facial expressions, tone of voice and other signals from abusers in an attempt to get a head start on avoiding violence or even death. This systematic hypervigilance will remain for a long time and in all kinds of situations. With post-traumatic stress, the brain also develops very strong sensory faculties, increasing hearing, smell, taste, sight and touch. In a split personality, one of the five senses may be hyperdeveloped in an alter, while another alter has other particularities.

Therapist and social worker Susan Pease Banitt, author of *"The Trauma Tool Kit"*, also explains how certain paranormal abilities can develop in an individual who has experienced severe trauma. Growing up in a violent environment forces the child to anticipate the moods of the aggressors and to become hyper-intuitive as a result of their hypervigilance. The child can thus develop telepathic abilities as well as increased sensitivity of his mirror neurons and sensitivity to the electromagnetic energies emanating from people. Physical violence or sexual abuse will also disrupt the functioning of the *chakras* (energy centres) in the victim. Energy therapist Barbara Brennan, who has worked on the flow of energy in the human body, has noted that certain types of violence, such as sexual abuse, can *'tear'* the *chakras*, unlocking them in a brutal and inappropriate way, causing an unbalanced energy opening. This abnormal breach will make the person's energy body more permeable and therefore more vulnerable. As we have seen, this can lead to a particular connection to other dimensions with uncontrollable paranormal phenomena. Dissociation is an altered state of consciousness, and all shamans who dissociate, who go into trance, need to learn to anchor themselves, to 'connect to the earth' when they access other dimensions. A child who undergoes a deep dissociation during a trauma does not have this knowledge and capacity to anchor himself, to "keep his feet on the ground" in order to preserve his balance. He or she is no longer grounded, no longer centred, and thus may become subject to attacks by demonic entities and uncontrollable paranormal experiences.

In an article published in the *Journal of Spirituality and Paranormal Studies* entitled *"Childhood Influences That Heighten Psychic Powers"*, Sylvia Hart Wright cites several studies and testimonies on the link between trauma and paranormal powers. Over the years, Wright has interviewed hundreds of people with near-death experiences, mediumistic and other extrasensory abilities. From these interviews, it is clear that early childhood stress is an important factor in the development of psychic powers in adults. She interviewed an internationally known *remote viewer* who had a very difficult childhood, and he told her: *"All these things that children shouldn't have to deal with, we dealt with very often. It's sort of the Jekyll and Hyde thing. You become ultra-sensitive so you can gauge the state of the situation with either parent. The more they drank, the more they became Mr Hyde."*

Several other people with special psychic abilities have reported that their alcoholic fathers had some extrasensory abilities themselves. This reinforces the fact that psychic powers may be genetically transmitted, as are dissociative abilities. Moreover, a parent who has been a victim himself, and who reproduces violence or abuse on his children, will trigger and reinforce this predisposition to dissociation and extrasensory faculties in the latter: always this transgenerational vicious circle...

A study of 1,400 Americans (*NORC-Luce Foundation Basic Belief Study, National Opinion Center,* University of Chicago) found that people with psychic abilities had experienced more family conflicts in early childhood than those without. The American sociologist Andrew Greeley concludes, among other things, that paranormal psychic experiences seem to be partly due to a childhood with serious family tensions.[426]

A Canadian study also showed a link between adult creativity and the quality of family relationships in early childhood. It was reported that creative adults often came from high conflict families and that these traumas had a significant impact on the future adult's level of creativity.[427]

Another study from 2011 shows that there may indeed be a connection between creativity and trauma, particularly with post-traumatic stress. At the start of their research, Robert Miller and David Johnson thought that post-traumatic stress would have diminished a person's creative faculties. But the study revealed that the group of individuals who had suffered trauma, compared to a group without trauma, had much better abilities to make symbolic representations.[428]

Psychological disorders, particularly personality disorders, also seem to be linked to what is commonly called 'genius'. Bipolar disorder has been described by some as a *"brilliant madness"* because of the psychic expansion it can sometimes lead to, both towards constructive creativity and towards destructive psychosis. Daniel Smith, a professor at the University of Glasgow, conducted a study showing that mental disorders, including bipolarity, are indeed more common in people with above-average IQ and creativity. He told the British newspaper *The Guardian*: *"It is possible that serious behavioural disorders, such as bipolarity, are the price we pay for having coping skills such as intelligence, creativity and verbal control.* However, as Daniel Smith explains, if a correlation exists, there is nothing automatic about the mechanism, and bipolar disorder does not produce geniuses on a regular basis...

In the past, mental *illness* was even considered a gift and is still considered a gift in some cultures. Aristotle said: *'No great genius has ever existed without a touch of madness'.* One of the most representative scientists is certainly Nikola Tesla, the Serbian-American genius who invented countless patents such as the electric motor, alternating electric current, radio, remote control, robotics, laser, fluorescent light bulbs, free energy, etc. Tesla mastered

---

[426] The Sociology of the Paranormal: A Reconnaissance " - Andrew Greeley, 1975.

[427] Childhood parenting experiences and adult creativity " - R. Koestner, M. Walker, Journal of Research in Personality, 1999.

[428] "The Capacity for Symbolization in Posttraumatic Stress Disorder" - R. Miller and D. Johnson; Psychological Trauma: Theory, Research, Practice, and Policy, 2011.

no less than twelve different technologies. Tesla was fluent in no less than twelve languages and his photographic memory combined with his ability to animate his mind was an exceptional asset to his work as an engineer. This extremely ingenious and hyper-productive man suffered from several mental illnesses: Attention Deficit Disorder (often linked to hyperactivity), Obsessive Compulsive Disorder (OCD) and bipolar disorder. Nikola Tesla also suffered from numerous phobias or, on the contrary, excessive passions. One explanation for his psychic disorders and his genius is that he had near-death experiences in his youth. As a child, he almost drowned, and he is said to have had an out-of-body experience. Later in his career, Tesla had an accident while working on an electrical coil, he came into contact with an electromagnetic charge of several million volts. He reported that during this near-death experience, he entered a state where he could see the past, future and present on the same plane, in what he called *"mystical vision"*. He stated that he had travelled through space and time, which is common to accounts of out-of-body experiences in near-death experiences. This notion of alternative space-time is also found with lost soul fragments.

Some scientists such as Dr. Yehuda Elkana and Dr. Gerald Holton have argued that discoveries and great scientific innovations are associated with creative intuition. Intuition" is defined as *"the ability to feel or know things immediately without any reasoning.* Carl Jung defines intuition as *"perception by the unconscious".* Trauma that causes hypervigilance and hyper-intuitiveness can therefore indirectly develop a certain creativity in the victim. According to a Swedish scientific study: *"Creative people (in the arts and sciences) have a higher risk of bipolar disorder and schizophrenia...* It is important to note that it is the brain configuration and psychic state that lead to higher than normal creative abilities, not the creativity that leads to the risk of mental disorders...

The scientific team at the *Karolinska Institute* has shown that artists and scientists are more numerous in families affected by bipolar disorder and schizophrenia, compared to the general population.[429]

If we refer to certain studies showing that personality disorders such as bipolar disorder, *borderline* disorder or schizophrenia most often have a traumatic origin in childhood, the link between trauma and creativity can therefore be established. Artistic or scientific genius could have its origin in a *defect* in the organisation of cerebral connections, or should we say a particular *wiring* of the brain. This wiring develops during the life experiences of the young child, because it is the experiences of the child that will shape the neuronal organisation of the brain. Here is what the painter Lynn Schirmer, a survivor of ritual abuse and mind control, said on this subject at a *S.M.A.R.T.* conference in 2006

- Do you think that abuse has made you more creative?

---

[429] "Mental illness, suicide and creativity: 40-year prospective to a population study" - Dr Simon Kyaga, Journal of Psychiatric Research, 2012.

- Yes, I do. I used to think that artists were born with their talent, but I don't believe that at all anymore. I think it happens because of the effects of early childhood trauma on different parts of the brain.

Actress Meg Ryan said in 2003 in the Los Angeles Times: "I don't think you would willingly cultivate traumatic or dramatic experiences in your life in order to become an artist. Then I think you would be wrong. But you can use it... There is a redemptive power in your life when you go through difficulties."

The creative process in art and science has sometimes been described in terms very close to dissociation, trance, or even possession. Indeed, the second state that accompanies the activity of certain creators sometimes leads to phenomena so disconcerting that they have sometimes been classified as occult and paranormal. The person fades away and gives way to the artistic or scientific genius, and becomes the medium of something that often exceeds him, something that expresses itself through him. This is a common trait of many of the great artists of our world, as we will see in Chapter 9 on the entertainment industry. There is a close relationship between hypnosis, dissociation, imagination and paranormal experiences such as mediumship, both in artists and in people with a traumatic past, who are often the same...

In the 1980s, some psychologists found that people who had experienced severe trauma in early childhood very often reported paranormal psychic experiences. They concluded that the childhood traumas had led them to dissociate and that instead of being in the present moment, they had turned their attention to their imaginary world... which explained their paranormal "delusions". But later, British psychologist Tony Lawrence worked on a series of statistical studies showing that the link between trauma and paranormal psychic experiences was stronger than the link between trauma and the imaginary world. *You have a direct link between early childhood trauma and paranormal experiences. You don't necessarily have to have a good imagination to have a paranormal experience. Even people who have a weak imagination can experience the paranormal, because of the fact that they had a childhood trauma.* "[430]

Dr. Richard Boylan, who has written extensively on the subject of aliens and UFOs, has met and interviewed many witnesses. He has found five commonalities among abductees and alien/UFO sightings:

- These individuals have a high level of psychic ability.
- Similar phenomena are observed with other family members (multi or transgenerational)
- Children who have suffered severe abuse or trauma.
- Individuals or entire families linked to government and/or intelligence agencies or ministries.
- They were very often Amerindians, indigenous people.

There is also a strong correlation between sites of occult activity, such as ritual abuse, secret military installations and UFO manifestations and ET abductions. We will not dwell here on the question of aliens, which is linked to

---

[430] Paranormal experience and the traumatized mind " - Tony Lawrence, 1999.

the existence of fallen angels, the "demons", the Luciferian army. Here is an extract from *the* book *Satanic Ritual Abuse, Principle of Treatment* in which Dr. Colin Ross explains the strong similarities between the two. There are *thousands of people in North America today who have flashbacks to alien abductions from spaceships, with experiments performed on them (...) These "abductees" come to therapy with missing time periods and unexplained post-traumatic symptoms, just like survivors of Satanic ritual abuse. Abductees report having had hypnotic amnesia barriers deliberately implanted by ETs, satanic cult survivors describe exactly the same programming by their tormentors. Survivors of satanic ritual abuse also describe forced pregnancies, medical laboratory experiments and pre-term abortions. The difference is that Satanists would use the fetuses for ceremonies while ETs would raise them.* "[431]

In his book *Mind-Control, World Control*, Jim Keith writes that the alien abduction business is being used to cover up mind control experiments by real humans.

Brad Steiger, author of books on the paranormal and ufology, has interviewed many psychics and other people with extrasensory abilities. He reports that most of them have gone through a series of traumas during their early childhood or youth.[432] According to him, these individuals with traumatic pasts seem to be prime candidates for certain military programmes, especially for paranormal psychic experiments such *as remote* viewing. Lyn Buchanan, a former *remote viewer*, defines these psychic techniques as follows: *"It is the structured and scientific exploitation of natural human potential for intelligence purposes. It is the structured, scientific exploitation of natural human potential for intelligence purposes, without the need for the usual five senses or equipment such as photography, electronics or other devices."[433]*

Joseph McMoneagle, another veteran of the U.S. government's *remote* viewing programs, has acknowledged that these techniques are used for identification, that is, to learn specific details about something that can only be accessed through extrasensory perception. People like McMoneagle and David Morehouse have been recruited into these programmes following paranormal events in their lives: a near-death experience, contact with a UFO and spontaneous out-of-body experiences. He explains that for the *remote viewing* programs, the U.S. government recruited Vietnam veterans who had experienced extremely traumatic situations during the war. In his book *Mind Trek*, McMoneagle states that trauma is a necessary part of developing remote viewing abilities. He states that the first consequence of his near-death experience was a state of depression. The second consequence was what he calls *'spontaneous knowledge'*, i.e. he knew what people were thinking when they spoke to him. He knew certain private things about people, things that they had never disclosed

---

[431] "Satanic Ritual Abuse, Principle of Treatment" - Colin A. Ross, 1995, p.26.

[432] The World Beyond Death " - Brad Steiger, 1982.

[433] "The Emergence of Project SCANATE The First Espionage-Worthy Remote Viewing Experiment Requested by the CIA, 1973" - Ingo Swann, 1995.

openly and of which he was not supposed to be aware. The third effect of this NDE was spontaneous exits from his physical body, he would sometimes find himself hovering over unknown ocean shores.[434] One of Lyn Buchanan's *remote viewing* students describes one of his experiences as being very similar to personality dissociation: *"I was floating with a different personality base, I felt a slight but noticeable personality change taking place."*[435]

As we have seen in the chapter on MK-Ultra, the CIA has taken a keen interest in paranormal psychic phenomena. When it worked on dissociation and personality splitting, it opened a door to other dimensions (which shamans have known for thousands of years). NASA has also done research into the paranormal. On Mike Siegel's *Coast to Coast* radio show, astronaut Gordon Cooper confirmed the existence of a mind control programme involving young children. A project conducted by NASA in the 1950s and 1960s. During the programme, Mike Siegel asked the astronaut about these '*Star Kids*'. Cooper said that these were children with exceptional mental abilities, who were exploited in a kind of MK programme. He described how this NASA programme cultivated and exploited the psychic powers of certain children. Abilities such as telepathy, *remote viewing* and out-of-body experiences. The 'study groups' also included learning protocols that allowed the subjects to assimilate large amounts of knowledge in a very rapid manner, as well as to develop a high performance memory. The programme also consisted of developing clairvoyance and guided imagination in these children, which are the basis for effective *remote viewing*.[436]

Here is what MK-Monarch survivor Cathy O'Brien reports about the link between NASA and government mind control programs: *Whether I was in military, NASA or government buildings, the procedure of keeping my mind under absolute control continued to be consistent with the requirements of the Monarch project. This included, prior to any physical and/or psychological trauma, sleep, food and water deprivation, high voltage electroshock and hypnotic and/or harmonic programming of specific memory compartments/personalities. What I endured from that time onwards via various high-tech equipment and other methods, gave the US government absolute control over my mind and my existence (...) Wayne Cox and I visited Florida on several occasions, his mother's parents living in Mims, which was only a few minutes away from the NASA Kennedy Space Center in Titusville. Like my father, he saw to it that I went there on orders for tests and other programming sessions related to mind control. Cox considered me a "Chosen One," and often used the CIA's "Monarch" project term for me to proudly "justify" leaving me at the NASA facility (...) Military mind control was fast, effective, and high-tech, but it was my programming by NASA that launched me as a "presidential dummy.*

---

[434] Mind Trek: Exploring Consciousness, Time, and Space Through Remote Viewing " - Joseph McMoneagle, 1993.

[435] Reframing Consciousness: Art, Mind and Technology " - Roy Ascott, 1999.

[436] Astronaut Reveals NASA Mind Control Program Involving Children " - Andrew D. Basiago, 2000.

Although Aquino did my programming at both military and NASA facilities, it was through NASA that he had access to the latest advances in technology and techniques. These included "mind tricks" such as sensory deprivation containers, virtual realities, flight simulators and other harmonics. At the age of two, Kelly (Cathy's daughter) had already been subjected to Aquino and his programming via these ultimate technological advances, which shattered her fragile childlike mind before her basic personality had a chance to form (...) in the deep basement of NASA's mind control lab at the Godard Space Flight Center near D.C., Bill Bennett began to prepare me for the program in question. NASA uses various "CIA designer drugs" to chemically generate neural transformations and induce the required state of mind at a specific time. "Train'-quility," the drug of choice for NASA in Huntsville, Alabama, created a feeling of quiet subservience and gave the impression of walking on a cloud."[437]

Kathleen Sullivan is also a survivor of ritual abuse and MK programming in government and military settings. She describes in her book *"Unshackled"* how her multiple personality disorder was exploited to develop special psychic abilities: *"My alter 'Theta' personalities were given special psychic training. Children like me were chosen for this type of programming because like all victims of traumatic abuse, we were very sensitive to the moods and thoughts of others, especially those of our abusers. I am convinced that some people working or connected with the CIA were aware of this link between trauma and the paranormal long before mental health professionals discovered it. I believe that the continued withholding of information about these human faculties, as well as the decredibilization and systematic disinformation, occurred because the CIA and other intelligence agencies that funded paranormal research had a vested interest in keeping this knowledge out of the public domain.*

I have recurring memories from my childhood of some of my Theta programming by James Jesus Angleton, head of CIA counterintelligence. Because he may have known that I attended a Christian church every week, he used the contents of the New Testament to teach me to expand my consciousness. He began my mental programming by quoting to me the words of Jesus Christ: 'You shall do greater works than I have done'... with our minds, he added. Angleton then taught me that the biggest wall preventing people from accessing and using their natural psychic faculties was their belief that they could not or should not. He taught me that if I got around this mental block, then I could do whatever I wanted with my psychic energy. He said that I could even move a mountain telepathically as long as I believed I could (...) He said that the human brain has a potential that we haven't even begun to tap into yet and he encouraged me to use it as much as possible. Other MK programmers also conditioned my alter Theta to believe that they could read the minds of others, communicate telepathically and perform remote viewing. Some of this programming has been successful (...) If these abilities are legitimate, then I don't think they are anything other than a natural human faculty. However, I

---

[437] *TRANCE Formation of America: True life story of a mind control slave* - Cathy O'Brien & Mark Phillips, 2012, p.164.

think they can be considered as part of the forbidden fruit mentioned in the book of Genesis, as a person using them could easily think of himself as a God. I have chosen to stop using my Theta programming, not because I fear demons, but because I simply want to respect the mental, emotional and physical integrity of others."[438]

Let us now return to the subject of near-death experiences. The obvious trauma of an exit from the physical body seems to trigger particular psychological and physiological experiences. It is as if something is unlocked in the person's energetic/electromagnetic bodies. Phyllis Marie Atwater, the author of *"Dying to Know You: Proof of God in the Near-Death Experience"*, who has herself experienced three NDEs, wrote: *"About eighty percent of people who have experienced a near-death state have reported that their lives have been changed forever. Closer examination, however, shows that surprising dimensions emerge. People who had experienced this did not just return with an increased enthusiasm for life and a more spiritual outlook. They manifested specific psychological and physiological differences of a magnitude never before experienced."*

Atwater interviewed more than 4,000 people who had experienced a NDE to find out what impact it had had on their lives. She found that there was generally a noticeable increase in intuitive and mediumistic abilities, communication with spirits, plants and animals for example. But her research also revealed that many people had experienced a change in the electromagnetic field of their bodies: *"From the beginning of my research into near-death states in 1978, I consistently noticed that a large majority of experiencers (those in my study as well as in outside conversation with them) reported that they became more sensitive to electric and magnetic fields - disturbances from equipment, appliances, wristwatches - after their NDE episode."*

These lasting physiological changes, which create a kind of electrosensitivity, lead to interference between the person and the electronic equipment around him or her: problems with breakdowns and malfunctions of appliances, batteries that discharge more quickly, light bulbs that systematically burn out, etc., but also extreme sensitivity to earthly events such as thunderstorms, earthquakes or tornados.[439]

6 - THE MEDICINE MAN
AND HIS TOTEM ANIMALS...

Now here is an interesting case of a Native American "medicine man" (healer). In 1989, the journal *Dissociation* published an article entitled *"Multiple personality disorder with human and non-human subpersonality components"*.

---

[438] Unshackled: A Survivor Story of Mind Control " - Kathleen Sullivan, 2003, p.66-67.

[439] "The bizarre electromagnetic after effects of near death experiences" - Buck Rogers, Waking Times, 2014 / BistroBarBlog translation: "The bizarre electromagnetic after effects of NDEs".

This article describes the case of a 70 year old Native American patient diagnosed with I.D.D.. This man had healing powers and was *a* well known and respected *medicine man in* his community, a Native American tribe that had retained its ancestral traditions. His personality was split into eleven alters, four human and seven non-human. It was discovered that early childhood abuse was the cause of her IDD. Furthermore, the development and manifestation of these alter personalities had been reinforced and maintained by the cultural context in which this Native American had grown up. The strong connection to nature spirits and totem animals in traditional Native American culture reinforced his alter personality system. The man had presented himself for therapeutic help. The inner battle between the human and animal alters was becoming too violent and interfered with his ability to perform healing rituals.

The first alter to form was that of an eleven year old boy, called *"The Little One"*. It was discovered that all other alter personalities had dissociated from this one. At the age of three, the patient had been raped by an uncle. In therapy, the alter described that he was playing with a turtle when the rape occurred. He tells how he then focused on the turtle as if he was crawling away, just like it, dissociating himself from the traumatic reality. The uncle raped the child more and more frequently and it was the alter *Le Petit* who systematically endured the abuse thanks to this dissociation linked to the tortoise. One day, at the age of five, *Le Petit* observed a healer using a turtle shell in his therapeutic rituals. Shortly after this, a male relative of his became ill with cancer and was confined to bed. The alter personality *Le Petit* said that when he was dissociated into the turtle alter, he often reached out to touch the sick man and after a while the man recovered, his cancer was in remission. It was then that *Le Petit was* given a place of honour in his family. His mother said that he had a rainbow over his head on his birthday, which was a sign that he had the power within him to become a great medicine man. From then on, his family and neighbours began to come to him for consultations.

His turtle alter (named *Power*) possessed faculties related to the spirit world, which could be used to control pain and treat serious diseases. This alter began to develop when the patient was three years old. The physical characteristics of this alter personality were a stooped posture, very slow movements, his head swaying from right to left and a very slow and limited speech.

Another alter was *"The Old Man"*, a 70 year old personality. This split occurred when the patient was in training with an old medicine man. He underwent an initiation during which he had to stay in the forest for several days undergoing purification rites with the prohibition of eating and drinking. In addition, he had to consume hallucinogenic herbs and run long distances. During this period of intense initiation, he was told repeatedly that in order to become a good medicine man, he had to become like his teacher. Under the traumatic effect of the fasting, the intense physical exercise, the hallucinogenic herbs and the constant demands of the alter *The Little One* to become similar to the teacher, the old medicine man who abused him during the initiation, he dissociated into this alter *Old One*, representing his teacher. It was this alter *The Old Man* who thus enabled the patient to become a true medicine man. It should be noted that violence and beatings are not normally part of the initiation rituals of learning among the Amerindians; this is a serious deviation. The behaviour of this alter was that of an old man, as much in his posture as in his manners and voice.

The man also had a male eagle alter named *Wind Spirit*, which also appeared during his initiation with the old medicine man. According to him, the eagle feather is a great source of power for the *"dissociative medicine"* of Native American healers. During the initiation, *Le Petit* was taught that the eagle is a medium between the earth and the *"thunderbirds"*, powerful spirits in the Native American tradition. Still under the influence of fasting, physical exhaustion, beatings and hallucinogenic herbs, *Le Petit* also dissociated into this eagle alter: the *Spirit of the Wind*. In this medicine man's I.D.T. system, this alter allows communication with the thunderbirds in order to obtain information to diagnose a sick person and obtain power for their healing. One of these powers is the ability to induce in the sufferer a feeling of lightness, similar to a bird, which would have an analgesic effect.

This Native American patient also had a wolf alter, a panther alter, a bear alter, an owl alter and a snake alter. His other human alter personalities were those of a 28-year-old woman (*Moon Walker*), created when the uncle began to sexually share *Le Petit* with his alcoholic friends. There was also a warrior alter named *"Killer Man"*.

During the therapy, the fusion/integration of the alter personalities was complicated for several reasons. First of all, the patient's wife and the people he was treating thought that with this fusion, the medicine man would lose his powers and his ability to contact the spirit world. In addition, the animal alter group and the human alter group were in conflict and their fusion was very complicated. It was necessary to merge the animals with each other and the humans with each other while preserving the patient's spiritual needs and his abilities as a medicine man so that he could continue to help his community. During this therapy, each alter personality proved to be highly hypnotisable. Visual acuity tests and neuro-sensory assessments showed considerable differences between each alter personality.[440]

This case indicates that I.D.T., this dissociative defence mechanism in the face of trauma, can be found in a variety of cultures and may sometimes explain why some shamans possess animal alter personalities. Alters that are revealed during trance states, as we saw in Chapter 2 with the *Berserk* warriors becoming super-powerful *wolves, bears* or *boars*, capable of incredible feats.

7 - CONCLUSION

So we see that trauma, dissociation, astral exits, paranormal experiences and psychic powers go hand in hand, one triggering the others, although not

---

[440] Multiple personality disorder with human and non-human subpersonality components " - Stanley G. Smith, Journal "Dissociation", Vol.2 N°1, 03/1989.

systematically. This link between trauma/dissociation and connection to other dimensions is a key point in MK-Monarch mental programming. In ritual abuse, the aim is to 'unlock' the child to initiate and thus make him/her sacred to the Luciferian cult. The spiritual and metaphysical aspect of programming is just as important, and certainly more important than the purely scientific (neurological and psychiatric) aspect. Indeed, the connection between the members of this cult/world network and the spirit world is indispensable for the success of the project of domination here on earth. In a systematic way, the offspring in charge of bringing the World Order to a successful conclusion must therefore be spiritually connected to the Luciferian militias on the one hand, while being psychologically and physically attached to the terrestrial network (families and power networks, secret societies) on the other. An earthly network well incarnated in the material world and thus accomplishing a plan established from other spheres: the Luciferian rebellion continuing its accomplishment on earth... Without this protocol of systematically splitting up the children in these bloodlines and more globally in all these Luciferian cults, the connection to the other dimensions and the "root of violence" could not be transmitted from one generation to the next and the *cult of horror* would certainly not be able to subsist for centuries. The deep dissociation caused by the traumas, which can be described as a violent "spiritual unlocking" (a real spiritual rape), systematically practised on *the ground crew* thus produces mediums receiving *enlightenment* and connection to the *light bearer:* Lucifer. These totally split and multiple individuals therefore possess certain alter personalities connected to the spiritual realm of Satan. This is what Pastor Tom Hawkins describes when he writes that *dissociated personalities can be trained during trauma to enter trance states that will connect them to the 'second heaven', the 'air realm' of which Satan is the prince. These personality fragments are bound and held captive in this realm and are used to implement Satan's world plan here on earth.*

It is interesting to note here that Freemasonry also refers to mysterious entities from another dimension that inspire (not to say dictate) its own actions in setting up the World Order. Freemason Charles Webster Leadbeater (an Anglican priest and theosophist, himself accused of paedomania) clearly wrote that Freemasonry made certain connections with *'shining beings'* from beyond: *'When one of these luminous spirits attaches himself to us by a Masonic ceremony, we must not think of him in terms of a ruler or attendant, but simply as a brother. Our egocentricity is so ingrained that when we hear of such a wonderful association, our first thought, even unconsciously, is to ask ourselves what we could gain from this relationship. What could we learn from this shining being? Will he guide us, advise us, protect us? Or is he a servant whom we can use for our own purposes?*[441]

The Freemason Oswald Wirth also refers to this explicitly when he writes that the Masters - for this is what the Initiates call them - envelop themselves in an impenetrable mystery; they remain invisible behind the thick curtain that separates us from the beyond... They work only on the drawing board, that is to

---

[441] The Hidden Life in Freemasonry " - Charles Webster Leadbeater, p.334.

say intellectually, by conceiving what is to be built. They are the constructive intelligences of the World, effective powers for the Initiates who relate to the Unknown Superiors of the tradition.[442]

Here is a Freemason who clearly declares that Masters from the beyond dictate to the Unknown Superiors of the Masonic back lodges how to build the world, because they are, in his words, the constructive intelligences of the World...

The belief that humans can come into contact with and be used and manipulated by so-called 'higher' entities for a specific purpose is not something new. Indeed, humans can serve as tools for forces from another dimension. The author Malidoma Somé writes in his book The Healing Wisdom of Africa: "The ancestors are at a disadvantage because they know how to make things better but they do not have the physical body to act with what they know. We ourselves are at a disadvantage because even though we have physical bodies, we often lack the knowledge to do things properly. This is why Spirit likes to work through us. A person with a physical body is an ideal vehicle for Spirit to manifest things in this world."

The physical human body is therefore potentially a tool of expression for entities beyond our earthly dimension. The human can be the tool of Luciferian entities just as it can also be the tool of the Holy Spirit. In this world of duality two forces confront each other, but one could also say that they complement each other to organise this great theatre, this great school in which we evolve. These two forces, commonly called "Good" and "Evil", have many similarities, one being obviously the negative copy of the other, one imitating the other in its own way because it is unable to create anything really. We find this duality at all levels, including the link that humans can establish with other dimensions. Ultra-violent ritual abuse will abruptly force open the spiritual doors of the child through torture, rape, blood baptism and trauma of all kinds; whereas in the divine tradition, the spiritual doors are gradually opened through the parents' loving care for the child, through the baptism of water and the Holy Spirit, through the kindness and help of angels and archangels faithful to God. On the one hand, spiritual powers are acquired through connection to the rebellious Luciferian entities, the fallen angels, and on the other hand, these powers are given by the Holy Spirit directly from God. On the one hand the black masses with the sacrifice and consumption of human blood and flesh, on the other hand the Holy Mass with the sacrifice of Jesus Christ who gives his body and blood in the Eucharist: the reformation of those ancient Babylonian cults linked to demons and based on blood sacrifices, practices which the "nameless religion" continues to perpetuate. The process of traumatic ritual abuse to "initiate", "sacralise" and "baptise" children is nothing less than an inversion of sanctification, a counter-initiation or counter-revelation, aimed at establishing a Luciferian reign of supernatural order. Lucifer being considered by these groups as the civilising god, bringing knowledge and light to humans...

---

[442] "Freemasonry made intelligible to its followers" Volume III - Oswald Wirth, 1986, p.219-130.

God forgives that," said (Senator) Leahy, referring as much to my role in NAFTA as to his pedophile practices on my daughter. "It's not that God you have to worry about, of course. It is a passive God, a God who has died out and lives only in a Bible. The God you have to worry about is the all-seeing, all-knowing God. That big, big Eye in the Sky. He sees all, records all and passes on information precisely where it is needed. Let me give you some good advice - don't open it, because there is no need to know any of this. Probably only your vice president (Bush) will know, and he's been keeping secrets all his life. I don't mean that George Bush is God. Oh no, he's much more than that. He's a demigod, which means he straddles the earthly and heavenly planes, so that he acts according to what he sees with his eternally vigilant Eye in Heaven." - *TRANCE Formation of America: True life story of a mind control slave* - Cathy O'Brien

Some of the things reported in this chapter go beyond the commonly accepted laws of physics, but the facts are there. But as stated in the introduction to the chapter, you don't see the germ, but you do prevent it with antibiotics, because science has taught you that. The human ability to interact with other dimensions and with certain entities is a vast area that modern rationalist science has long neglected. It does not seem to have explored these areas yet, so it cannot understand them, let alone teach them to you. Yet, little by little, by going deeper and deeper into matter, this science ends up paradoxically reaching the immaterial and spiritual realm. The strictly materialistic study that led to digging into the heart of matter with quantum physics is now able to transcend this matter to enter the spiritual world... which is none other than the heart of the material world, a kind of infinite fractal. One day, the loop will be closed, the physical and biological sciences will find their "invisible" missing link for a full understanding of the world in which we live, a sort of unified field. For the moment, just as with I.D.T., quantum physics is little discussed in universities... the filtration of information and teaching is obviously a key to mass control. It is likely that today in some laboratories, the most advanced physicists, especially in quantum physics, are beginning to realise that there is indeed a Creator with his Creation. Unless these gentlemen take themselves for gods creators of their own reality and forget the main Creator... and their condition of simple creature...

CHAPTER 7

MONARCH PROGRAMMING

Perhaps there is a reason why the news media is not publicly opening the Pandora's box of legend. Would it be plausible then to consider that closer scrutiny - by the media and the public - of the leaders of these destructive cults, might reveal very real links to government-funded mind control research? These are questions that, if truly addressed for what they are, would provide important answers to this social epidemic that includes physical and psychological abuse. The answers provided by a serious and thorough investigation could be the beginning of a solution to the myriad of problems that these destructive cults, serial killers and child rapists are causing society - Mark Phillips

For an MK programmer, one has to create alter personalities and at the same time demonise them, i.e. link them to demons (...) if one wants to truly understand Monarch mind control, one has to realise that it is something fundamentally demonic (...) Programming and mind control cannot be separated from demonology and occult rituals - Fritz Springmeier.

1 - INTRODUCTION

To begin this chapter on Monarch programming, here are three examples reported by Dr. James Randall Noblitt in his book *Cult and Ritual Abuse* showing cases of sexual abuse with rather mysterious mind control. The first case is from *the* book *Criminal History of Mindkind*, in which Colin Wilson tells the story of a woman travelling by train to Heidelberg in Germany. She wants to see a doctor there for persistent stomach pains. According to Wilson, during her journey she met a certain Franz Walter who introduced himself to her as a 'healer' claiming to be able to cure her... He managed to persuade her to leave the train at one station to go for a coffee...

She was reluctant, but she was persuaded. As they both walked along the quay, he grabbed her arm and "it seemed as if I had no will left," she said. He took her to a hotel room in Heidelberg, put her in a trance by touching her forehead, then raped her. She tried to push him away but she was totally unable to move (...) He caressed me and said: 'You are fast asleep, you can't call for help, and you can't do anything else. Then he locked my arms and hands behind my back and said, "You can't move at all. When you wake up, you won't remember anything about what just happened. Later, Walter prostituted the woman to several men, giving his clients the code word to immobilise her (...) The police began to suspect that she had been hypnotised, and a psychiatrist, Dr

Ludwig Mayer, was able to retrieve the buried memories of the hypnosis sessions. Walter was sentenced to ten years in prison... How could Franz Walter have put her under mental control so quickly and easily?"[443]

Colin Wilson therefore questions such a power of control, but does not provide any answers other than possible paranormal faculties that Walter could have developed to induce a deep trance in this woman. Wilson's case is similar to many accounts of ritual abuse survivors. Dr. James Randall Noblitt notes that he had several patients who described an identical scenario. They recalled being raped or sexually abused by someone who made them completely unable to react after he said a word, a phrase, or made some kind of sign with his hand or touched their face in a certain way. In therapy, these patients were initially unable to explain this phenomenon with these signals or trigger codes. After a few therapy sessions, frequently an alter personality would emerge with the ability to explain the process and even give an explanation of how the programming had been set up. These are the alter personalities that serve as sexual objects and are accessed by certain *triggers*. This programming is usually installed in early childhood and can remain in place for a very long time. Anyone who has the trigger codes to induce the trance state or bring out the alter personality can then sexually abuse the victim.

In the case reported by Wilson, there is no indication that the rapist Walter already knew the woman he met on the train. For this reason, how can we know that this is a case of pre-programming? According to Dr. Noblitt, it would be possible for an individual to identify and understand the underlying levers of programming in order to identify the trigger codes. This can be done simply by talking to the person and observing their eyelids and other bodily responses in reaction to potential triggers that have been quietly introduced during the conversation. There are indeed some basic keywords, or gestures, that are systematically used in MK programming. We might call these "standard" triggers.

Another case reported by Colin Wilson, this time in the book Beyond the Occult, describes a story from 1865: "After lunch, Castellan made a sign with his fingers, as if he were dropping something on the girl's plate, and she felt all her senses leave her. He then took her into the next room and raped her. She would later testify that she was conscious but totally unable to move."[444]

These two cases reported by Colin Wilson describe a victim who is totally paralysed and at the mercy of the aggressor. This may be a dissociative conversion disorder (which can manifest itself as a one-time paralysis).

In his book *Transe: A Natural History of Altered States of Mind*, Brian Inglis describes a case that went to trial in Wales in 1988, that of hypnotist Michael Gill. He used a flashing light device to hypnotise a woman and rape her while she was in an altered state of consciousness. Mind control techniques involving light flashes have been reported by survivors of mind control, including in the MK-Ultra programme. These three criminal cases illustrate how

---

[443] A Criminal History of Mankind " - Colin Wilson, 1984.

[444] *Beyond The Occult"* - Colin Wilson, 1988.

women can be sexually abused while in trance states induced in a rapid and powerful way by a triggering stimulus. Hypnosis alone is not capable of allowing such abuse of a person.[445]

At a *S.M.A.R.T.* conference in 2003, survivor Carole Rutz explained that her trauma-based programming could be accessed and triggered with hypnosis: *"All the programming that was done on me by the CIA and the 'illuminati' was trauma-based such as electroshock, sensory deprivation and drugs. Later, traumas were no longer necessary, hypnosis alone, combined with implanted triggers and sometimes updates could suffice."*[446]

In Monarch mind control, programming to sexually enslave a person is the most common. These *"Beta"* programming types are used to create sex slaves, sometimes referred to as *"presidential models"* in the case of MK slaves for the elite. But any Monarch subject can have one or more alter personalities programmed for this function, this type of alter is also called a *"Kitten"* or *"Sex Kitten"*.

In October 2001, a famous French model made shocking revelations during the recording of a television programme. She denounced her alleged sexual exploitation by her family, her entourage and certain high-profile figures. She said that she was raped by her father when she was two years old, and that she realised this a few months before, as her memories surfaced in flashbacks. She also revealed that she was regularly raped by her employers (a famous modelling agency), by people close to her and by members of the gotha (royal families). She will say that the forgetting of her abuse was due to hypnosis or what she thought was hypnosis...

Shortly after these revelations during the recording of a television programme with Thierry Ardisson, she gave an interview to *VSD* magazine, a dossier entitled *"Le cri de détresse d'un grand super model"* published in January 2002 in *VSD* N°1271. The magazine reveals that this woman was received by the head of the brigade for the repression of pimping and that she told him about dinners organised between young top models and *wealthy old men*. The interview gives several clues that she has been subjected to Monarch-like mind control. Here are some excerpts from the interview:

"A person in my family circle (she names a name) sexually abused me when I was two years old. He is a psychopath. He put me under hypnosis. Since then, anyone with authority who knows my secret can manipulate me. As long as I had not evacuated the terror of my childhood, anyone who frightened me could have a hold on me (...) They tried to make me a prostitute: it was so easy, I didn't remember anything, I forgot everything (...) I was a toy that everyone wanted to have. Everyone took advantage of me (...) I had no will of my own, so they organised my life for me: everything, everything, everything (...) They did hypnotic things to me (...) Yes, it's huge. There is a whole plot around me, for a long time, it concerns people in the government, in the police. Everything in my

---

[445] *"Cult and Ritual Abuse"* - James Randall Noblitt & Pamela Perskin Noblitt, 2014, p.86-87.

[446] "Healing From Ritual Abuse and Mind Control, a Presentation to the Sixth Annual Ritual Abuse, Secretive Organizations and Mind Control Conference", Rutz, C., 2003, S.M.A.R.T. Lectures.

life has been organised! Everything, everything, everything! I had no will of my own (...) During the 'Restos du Cœur', an artist told me: "Someone close to you abused you, they are organising for you to be raped again and for you to know nothing. A famous singer said to me: "One of your relatives (she mentions a name) told me that you were raped, can you forget it? Look at me, you will forget it! And she laughed. And it worked: I forgot (...) I really began to suffer, that's when I had the first flashes. First of all of someone close to me who was raping me. I said to myself: I've found out why I was so bad (...) In fact, all the people my family met were paedophiles. It's a vicious circle, and today I broke it! (...) I was an asset. My image, my kindness, my goodness, served those who wanted to hide things. And here, we are dealing with very, very, very bad people... Those who wanted to speak out are dead today (...) It's one of my relatives in New York who had me raped by the president of a big company. One day she calls me and says: "Do you remember what they did to you when you were a little girl? I said, "Oh yes, oh yes!" "Well, X is going to come to you, he's going to have sex with you and you're going to get the biggest contract there is. I didn't want to, but I was like a doll with no will (...) I want justice, that's all! Paedophilia is still such a taboo. It's girls like that who want to be models. So it's easy for the thugs to then have power over them."

Is this woman under Monarch-like mind control? Is she a *"presidential dummy"*? What she describes as memory lapses following the rapes, *"I couldn't remember anything,"* could be a severe dissociative disorder with amnesic walls. The fact that she told *VSD* magazine that she was raped under hypnosis *from the age of two*, that her family *only dated paedophiles*, that it is a *vicious circle that she wants to break*, and that her sexual exploitation seems to have continued throughout her life, strongly suggests that she may have been subjected to the sad journey of an MK-Monarch slave, trapped in a network that exploited her dissociative disorder. During the taping of the television show in November 2001, she also mentioned several names related to the entertainment industry, saying that these people were either aware of or were themselves rapists or victims. She named another well-known French star, saying that she too was subjected to such treatment.

Despite a complaint and the opening of a judicial investigation, her family quickly had her committed to a psychiatric hospital shortly after her revelations... She was only released three months later. Was an update of the MK programming necessary? Indeed, after a certain age, amnesic walls tend to dissolve, hence the reappearance of certain memories in the form of flashbacks. Her family tried to pass the *incident* off as a paranoid delusional attack, but no one could prove that it was really a case of madness and that what she had said was false. The complaint that the woman lodged was very quickly dismissed, so no investigation was carried out to confirm or deny these very serious accusations... Some time after her forced hospitalisation, the supermodel gave an interview to Benjamain Castaldi on the M6 programme *"C'est leur destin"* in September 2002. An interview in which there is still some doubt that she really tried to disclose her condition as an MK slave, without even knowing herself exactly what she was involved in. Here are some excerpts:

- Benjamin Castaldi: If you had to sum up your destiny in a few words, what would you say?

- Top-model: On the one hand it's a fairy tale, and on the other hand it's a horror film, a real nightmare. And when it all came up, there were people who tried to stop me from talking. I was put in a clinic to stop me talking. I got out with the help of a lawyer, it was a whole thing... Oh dear, it was quite complicated! (...) The lawyer phoned me directly in my room. She said: "Listen, you don't look like a crazy person at all! I'm coming to pick you up in the next two hours". I packed my bags and went out like that. (...) Once I reached my goal in modelling, everything was fine on the surface but deep inside I felt that something was wrong. So I had psychoanalysis for five years, and things came back to me that were so serious that I became sort of paranoid (...) I tried to talk, but they didn't believe me. There was a certain part that was paranoia, because it is true that when things are so enormous, afterwards it degenerates a little. There is a little bit of delirium. But the more time goes by, the more I realise that in fact, not at all (...) Have you seen the film True Romance? That's kind of my life. Everything was set up. Everything was manipulated. I was someone who didn't see anything. In fact, I think I was really crazy, but now I'm not.

Actress Marie Laforêt said of the affair: "I don't know what happened to X, it's the same story, she was talking about the same people, except that she was cut off... So she had a little record made to stamp her since. So she knows that if she ever says anything of what she wanted to say at the time, she will have an even more miserable fate than the one she has at the moment. So it's in her best interest to crash... That's all... But she made an attempt! She made an attempt and she paid for it. We amused her by making her make a record, a promo... But then everyone is in on it? You'll answer for yourself... Obviously!"

2 - DEFINITION

The term Monarch comes from the Monarch butterfly, an insect that starts life as a caterpillar (the undeveloped potential), which then evolves into a cocoon (the splitting and programming process) to become a butterfly (the Monarch slave). Is a caterpillar aware that it will become a butterfly? Is the butterfly aware that it was a caterpillar? No, and this image fits perfectly with the image of programming based on dissociation and traumatic amnesia. The fluttering butterflies represent the scattered soul fragments. The term Monarch also refers to the sensation of dissociation, which can be a floating sensation, like a butterfly, following an electric shock for example. Electric shocks are commonly used by programmers as it is a very effective method of torture, leaving little trace.

In Brice Taylor's (ex-presidential model) autobiography, Thanks For The Memories, Monarch programming is defined as follows: "A puppet is a doll that is tied to strings and controlled by a master. Monarch programming is also called "Puppet Syndrome", "Imperial Conditioning" is another term used. Some mental health therapists recognise this type of mind control as "stimulus-response conditioning". Project Monarch can be described as a combination of structured trauma, dissociation and occultism to compartmentalise the mind into multiple personalities in a systematic way. In the process, a satanic ritual, usually involving kabbalistic mysticism, is performed with the aim of binding a demon or group of demons to the corresponding alter. Of course, most people will see this as simply reinforcing the trauma within the person, denying the irrational belief that demonic possession can actually happen..."[447]

The Monarch butterfly seems to be the strong symbol that comes up regularly in the entertainment industry to represent this process of personality splitting. This well-known butterfly has the distinction of migrating from south to north over several generations, whereas the journey from north to south is done in one generation. These unique and fascinating creatures always return to the same trees as previous generations, even though they have never been there. How is this possible? It means that the Monarch butterfly genetically passes on information about where it was born to its offspring. This insect has been scientifically studied for this amazing genetic feature.

This would be one of the main reasons for the name of the Monarch project, as genetics is an important point in the selection of subjects. Certain information related to ancestors crosses time and centuries and is therefore transmitted from generation to generation. It is a kind of transcendent influence, in line with the studies on psychogenealogy, a *charge*, both positive and negative, that is transmitted to the descendants. In the book *"Satanism: Is it real?"*, Father Jeffrey Steffon explains: *"A third way (of demonic links) is generational inheritance. If parents have been involved in the occult, this generational link will be passed on to their children.* In shamanic cultures, the role of shaman is often hereditary and is usually passed from father to son. Just as Asian shamanic lineages pass on certain paranormal abilities or psychic powers, so do Luciferian lineages practising occultism and ritual abuse pass on an intangible heritage with a heavy baggage of demonic links. Disassociation, hypersensitivity, mediumship and other psychic powers are also part of the genetic make-up and will be activated and reinforced by rituals and early childhood traumas.

It is interesting to note here that a Swiss scientific study in 2012 showed that trauma (especially sexual abuse) in childhood leaves traces in the DNA up to the third generation. Is this what the Bible is talking about when it states that *"the iniquity of the father"* is passed on to his descendants to the third and fourth generation? (Exodus 20:5-6)

The team found that the DNA of a girl whose grandmother had been raped by her father carried the same epigenetic changes as her grandmother, and that these changes were much greater than in the mother and grandmother. The little girl who is the product of incest and who has never been raped carries the largest scar in the genome of all her cells. (UNIGE Research 2012)

It was found that these genetic marks will not mutate the DNA, but will influence the development of the brain and will be passed on to subsequent generations. The research group of Professor Alain Malafosse from the

---

[447] "Thanks for the memories: the truth has set me free" - Brice Taylor, 1999, p.16.

Department of Psychiatry at the Faculty of Medicine in Geneva conducted research on adult subjects who had been abused as children (physical, sexual and emotional abuse, emotional deprivation, neglect) and who suffered from *borderline* personality disorder. By examining their DNA, obtained from a simple blood test, the researchers observed epi-genetic modifications, i.e. in the gene regulation mechanisms: *"This is the first time that we have seen such a clear link between an environmental factor and an epi-genetic modification. The link is all the stronger because the more severe the abuse was during childhood, the greater the genetic modification,"* emphasises Ariane Giacobino of the Department of Genetics and Development. Moreover,[448] it has been found that trauma experienced in adulthood does not mark the genes as deeply and permanently as trauma experienced in childhood.[449]

It would seem that genetic encoding leading to totally deviant self-generated behaviours occurs after three generations of child abuse, which would explain why some families are totally mired in these things. Luciferian families who systematically practice ritual abuse and mind control on their offspring are therefore deeply marked in their genetics. These bloodlines are preserved by the almost systematic arrangement of unions and marriages.

In the distant past, humans (especially children) had good dissociative abilities. When exposed to trauma, they had a far greater survival advantage than those who did not. As we have seen, dissociation has an initial purpose of survival in the face of deep trauma, i.e. to preserve the individual so that he or she is able to continue to function properly. As nomadic tribal life has been gradually replaced by sedentary village life, thus reducing natural traumatic factors, this human genetics associated with dissociation has also regressed. Some lineages still perpetuate and maintain this genetic transmission of the *'precious'* dissociation, the gateway to the spirit world. Genetic baggage plays an important role in Luciferian hierarchies and dissociative abilities are one of those sought-after genetic marks.

Why is dissociation so important to these cults? In a young, developing brain, trauma and the dissociation it causes will shape neural pathways in a particular way and thus create certain intellectual, physical and psychic faculties. As we saw in the previous chapter, extreme trauma and deep dissociation will also open up gaps to other dimensions. It is these bridges to the spirit world that will allow certain communications to be established and 'power' to be received. In addition, the splitting of the individual's personality with amnesiac walls allows for the control and programming of the offspring to carry out the goals of these Luciferian bloodlines, which span centuries. All children of the 'nameless religion' are systematically *'put through the mill'*: the process of splitting them up and 'veiling' their synapses with extremely traumatic and disassociating techniques.

---

[448] "Childhood abuse leaves genetic traces" - 24 Heures, 2012.

[449] "Childhood maltreatment is associated with distinct genomic and epigenetic profiles in posttraumatic stress disorder" - Divya Metha, PNAS, 2012.

MK conditioning and programming will be systematic and the child's dissociative abilities will be tested and reinforced at an early stage. The more easily the child dissociates, the faster the programming work will be done. In her book *"Ascent From Evil"*, psychotherapist and survivor Wendy Hoffman explains: *"The cult teaches the art of dissociation. The victims' lives will depend on their ability to learn this quickly and from an early age. Dissociation is a subject that is taught, just like mathematics (...) It's easy for cult members to tell by just looking at someone if they are dissociating. They can check a member's dissociative skills as easily as they can check whether his addition is correct."*[450]

As we saw in Chapter 2, the ancient initiation rituals of the Mystery religions incorporated elements symbolising death and resurrection. Initiation sometimes also included amnesia (due to drugs, deprivation and trauma), erasure of memory for the formation of a new identity: this is when the initiate received a new name. Survivors of ritual abuse and mind control report exactly the same things. Monarch programming is a kind of trauma initiation, creating in the *initiate* (child victims) a connection to the spirit world and giving birth to one or more other alter personalities. Alters that are given different names and are programmed for different functions. The *"Monarch"* child of the Luciferian Hierarchical Order is a chosen one and is considered sacred. These are initiation rituals that aim to make the child sacred through deep dissociative states and rebirth as a Monarch child; a *killer* rather than a *victim*, a full member of the Luciferian cult connected to higher entities.

In 2009, Dr. Lowell Routley wrote an article in which he described Monarch programming, although he did not use the term. The paper, entitled *'Restoring The Lost* Self: *Finding* Answers *to Healing from* Traumatic *Socialization and Mind Control in Twenty-first Century Neurocognitive Research'*, was presented by Routley at a conference in Geneva at the International *Cultic Studies Association (ICSA)* annual international conference on 4 July 2009. Here is an excerpt from the introduction: *"These survivors learned to disassociate at a very young age through certain transgenerational practices passed down through the family. The use of traumatic socialisation is designed to compartmentalise the child's mind, to maintain secrecy and to maintain the status quo. Asphyxiation, deprivation, isolation and pain are known to dissociate the child, to ensure behavioural conformity, to suppress autonomy and identity, to create amnesia about abnormal activities, and to create unquestioning loyalty (...) terror maintains and reinforces the dissociative compartmentalisation. The degree of dissociation that results in the victim's mind is determined by the age at which this traumatic socialisation occurred, its frequency and intensity. Clinical work with survivors has led to a new discovery about programmed changes in the structure of the 'mind', the 'self', and consciousness that are said to have been made by technological or scientific means. As the phenomenology of programming was explored clinically, the patterns of compartmentalisation of the mind that emerged indicated sophisticated manipulation of the child's mind (...) Clinical observations further*

---

[450] Ascent From Evil: The Healing Journey Out Of Satanic Cult Abuse " - Wendy Hoffman, 1995.

indicated that the sophistication of 'programming' evolved in parallel with scientific discoveries. Therapeutic intervention requires firstly an appropriate diagnosis of the traumatic symptoms, and secondly a means of resolving the beliefs held by the dissociative and amnesic barriers. These factors have driven research to determine effective tools for healing. The clinical observations of survivors raised in these transgenerational families, as well as the results of 21st century neurocognitive research, have become the basis upon which a model of intervention has emerged.[451]

The term 'programming' is used in two ways for mind control methods. Most commonly, it refers to coercive persuasion practiced in destructive cults or military groups, mafia groups, etc. The second use of the term "programming" is much more specific, referring to *the manipulation or traumatisation of alter personalities, fragments, dissociated mental states or entities for the purpose of mind control.*[452]

It is the latter type of programming that is applied in the MK-Monarch protocol. In the book *"Healing From The Unimaginable"*, therapist Alison Miller gives this definition of programming: *"Programming is the act of internally setting up predefined reactions in response to external stimuli so that the person automatically reacts in a predetermined way to such things as auditory, visual, tactile cues, or will be able to perform a series of actions in relation to a specific date or time."*

In one of her books, the German psychotraumatologist Michaela Huber gives her definition of this type of mental programming: *"Programming in the context of trauma is a process that can be described as learning under torture. The metaphor 'programming' is certainly of computer origin and represents in this context what psychologists call conditioning. This means that the person who has been 'programmed' must react in a stereotyped way to certain stimuli. The reaction of the person to a stimulus is in this case automatic, so it is neither a natural reflex nor a conscious and voluntary reaction. In order to achieve this, "the programmer", whom I will call the torturer, has used the fact that his victim is a young child, preferably already dissociated (with a split personality) to carry out the learning process by torturing him. Torture can include physical, sexual, emotional abuse and often the victim is threatened that they will die if they do not comply. Once a victim has been programmed, it is possible to control them with the stimuli that have been 'implanted' (these are called triggers). An alter personality that has been programmed is usually not a complex identity and is therefore also called a 'programme'. Usually this person has been programmed to serve certain purposes: prostitute himself to enrich the master, steal, smuggle drugs, etc. With the help of programming the master can also ensure that the*

---

[451] "Restoring the Lost Self: Finding Answers to Healing from Traumatic Socialization and Mind Control in Twenty-first Century Neurocognitive Research" - Lowell Routley, 2009.

[452] *"Cult and Ritual Abuse"* - James Randall Noblitt & Pamela Perskin Noblitt, 2014, p.85.

victim has amnesia about the abuse and programming, he can also make the victim commit suicide when he is about to denounce his tormentors. "[453]

Jeannie Riseman, a member of the American activist group *Survivorship*, describes high-level MK programming, i.e. using sophisticated technology, as follows: *"What we refer to when we talk about mind control experiments is the deliberate and skillful manipulation of different parts of a person's mind, so that the person becomes controlled by others. The experimenters, programmers and controllers have a specific goal in mind and will select the techniques that best accomplish that goal. They are familiar with a number of techniques and when they are not satisfied with the results of one of them, they modify and adapt their methods. They know exactly what they are doing. The technology they have at their disposal is far more complex and sophisticated than what is usually available to groups that practice ritual abuse. They use equipment that is state of the art, equipment that can be very expensive. This technology includes electroshock, implants, equipment to inject information into certain parts of the brain, technology to divide the cerebral hemispheres, etc.* "[454]

This is what Dr. Lowell Routley refers to above when he writes that clinical observations have further indicated that the sophistication of 'programming' has evolved in parallel with scientific discoveries.

As we saw in Chapter 2, Monarch programming is a distant legacy of ancient Mystery Cults and traumatic rituals leading to deep dissociative states. MK-Monarch is the culmination of centuries of effort by various Luciferian cults to gain total control over a human being. Today, these mental programming techniques are very sophisticated and generally use electronic equipment, particularly related to the use of harmonics (vibrational frequencies). Indeed, everything on this planet vibrates at a certain frequency and this multitude of frequencies can be used to influence the human brain via neural pathways (see the topic of psychotronics developed in Chapter 1). In MK research, harmonics are used to activate a particular neural network in order to compartmentalise a given memory. In the laboratories that were already developing these electronic mind control techniques in the 1970s and 1980s, the application of harmonics was called *"brain training"*.[455] These harmonics aim to penetrate deep into the MK slave's subconscious in order to control, for example, his breathing, heart rate, etc. This technology could easily replace the cyanide pill to ensure that spies and other agents die with their secrets...

What is presented in this chapter is based on testimonies of survivors and therapists from many years ago. The evolution of any technology is exponential and so are MK practices, so we may know more when documents are declassified, just as some have been declassified regarding the MK-Ultra of the 1950s and 60s.

---

[453] Multiple Persönlichkeit, Überlebende extremer Gewalt, Ein Handbuch" - Michaela Huber, 1995.

[454] "Healing The Unimaginable: Treating Ritual Abuse and Mind Control" - Alison Miller, 2012, p.15.

[455] *"For the sake of National Security"* - Cathy O'Brien & Mark Phillips, 2015, p.404.

The MK-Monarch encompasses several disciplines, the main ones being (the first three being closely related)

- The science of torture and trauma.
- The science of drugs.
- The science of altered states of consciousness (hypnotic, dissociative, trance)
- The science of psychological and behavioural development of the child.
- Neurological and psycho-traumatological science.
- Psycho-electronic or psychotronic science.
- The science of lying and language manipulation (reverse psychology).

And probably the most important one:

- Paranormal science, or the way to use spiritual and occult means to control someone. Also in this category is demonology.

In the higher levels of the Luciferian hierarchy, the result is subjects who are able to work for the "Network" by being perfectly integrated into key positions in society. The "Network" being all organisations applying a Luciferian doctrine and working more or less ardently towards the establishment of a *New World Order* (the "nameless religion"). These MK methods are therefore reserved for a certain "elite", for initiates. The level of programming of children in these transgenerational families or military and political groups will vary according to several criteria:

- The knowledge and understanding that the group (or family) has about this type of mind control.
- The child's ability to dissociate, his or her IQ and level of creativity.
- The region or country in which he/she grows up.
- The financial resources and equipment available to programmers.

The essential component of Monarch mind control is the deliberate creation of an I.D.T. with a number of identities, personality/soul fragments, separated by amnesiac walls. Each alter personality is created to receive a particular training assigning it a specific role within the cult or outside in society. The more complex the ritual abuse and mind control that the child has undergone, the more complex his or her I.D.T. and inner world will be. Overall, it is a question of setting up a system comprising so-called *surface* or *facade* alter personalities which will be able to interact with the profane world, i.e. in civil society, while other much deeper alter personalities will have roles and occult activities linked solely with the cult and its network.

On June 25, 1992, the fourth annual Eastern Region Ritual Abuse and Multiple Personality Conference was held at the Radisson Plaza Hotel in Alexandria, Virginia. Dr. Corydon Hammond gave a talk initially entitled *"Hypnosis in Multiple Personality Disorder" which was later* renamed *"The Greenbaum Lecture"* because the content of the talk was totally different from what was originally announced in the programme.[456]

---

[456] The Greenbaum Speach - A conference sponsored by the Center for Abuse Recovery and Empowerment and the Psychiatric Institute in Washington, D.C.

To the astonishment of the public, Corydon Hammond then described what he had discovered in some of his patients. He publicly revealed the existence of people who were victims of mind control and programming. People who all suffered from dissociative identity disorder. Among other things, he revealed the different levels of programming: *Alpha, Beta, Theta, Delta, Omega* and *Gamma* that had emerged in some of his patients. He described the characteristics of these different types of programming:

- *Alpha* is the basic programming, the first personality splits that will lay the foundation for mind control over the slave, with a dissociation of the two cerebral hemispheres.
- *Beta* is sexual programming aimed at eliminating all morality and stimulating primitive sexual instincts.
- *Delta* and *Theta* are programmed killers, special agents, elite soldiers who can have certain psychic abilities.
- *Omega* is the self-destructive programming, including suicidal and/or self-harming tendencies that activate when the retrieval of memories begins to be too great.
- *Gamma* would be the protective programming of the internal system, i.e. a function designed to deceive and misinform.

Fritz Springemeier also cites the *Epsilon* (animal alter) and *Zeta* (snuff-film related alter) programmes.

In a 1997 interview with Wayne Morris on Ryerson Polytechnic University radio in Toronto, Ontario (CKLN FM 88.1), survivor Kathleen Sullivan described the different levels of programming she herself underwent: *"The Alpha program was the basic program. That's what my father said. It was the program that activated the Alpha waves in the brain. You had to start with that one and then move on to the others. The Beta program, for me, was called "Barbie". A politician who is very closely connected with these MK programmes once told me that it was Klaus Barbie who was behind this programming, which was later called "Beta". It was a programming that turned me into a real robot, especially in the sexual area. I was a sexual slave to a number of personalities from early childhood to adulthood. In this "Beta" state, I could no longer resist, I didn't even have an angry reaction. I was an absolutely docile sex slave and did whatever these men asked me to do. I would never have done these things if I had been in my normal conscious state. The Delta programme was mainly about the military. I was put into a 'Delta' state when I was under the orders of the military. Through this programming I was absolutely loyal to my superiors. There were several sub-codes to activate different parts of the Delta program, there were three: Delta 1, Delta 2 and Delta 3. They were activated by coded numbers. When I was in the Delta mental state, if they spoke these codes I could kill a person in the room. I did this without question because I obeyed the person controlling me in an absolute way. In this state, I no longer thought, I no longer reflected. This programme makes a lot of use of amnesia, in the interest of my survival. I knew this, and I was used to it. The Theta program was mostly about paranormal abilities. I don't really like that word because it has a lot of negative connotations. But they were using my mental energy to do a number of things that are considered paranormal... Some movies or novels have these scenarios... We were taught that you could use these techniques to hurt people. We were filled with extreme rage and we used this very violent energy to attack people with our thoughts.* "[457]

The internal system of people who have undergone ritual abuse and mind control is different from that of people with I.D.D. resulting from less severe and less systematic abuse, not having a direct MK programming purpose. Victims of these criminal organisations who deliberately create an I.D.D. to carry out complex programming will therefore show certain identifiable features in their dissociative disorders. Canadian therapist Alison Miller has noted[458] several of these characteristics common to mind control survivors:

- Presence of a complex inner world and interlocking internal structures in which the dissociated personalities (soul fragments) are imprisoned.
- Use of age-appropriate games and activities to facilitate programming.
- The alter personalities are programmed to have a specific function.
- Presence of a 'dump' for alter that have not been exploited, so they are not used by the programmers but they remain in the system.
- Presence of a hierarchy in the alter.
- Assigning alter to particular colours.
- Presence of alter observers and reporters who know everything that has happened to the person, everything they do, and who can report it to the teachers or programmers.
- Presence of a security system including punishments for disobedience.
- Presence of alter with a caretaker function.
- Presence of a filing system for briefs, especially for programming sessions.
- Presence of alter who believe they are animals, demons or aliens.
- Blocking alter at a certain age so that they cannot discern reality from fantasy.
- Creation of internal copies of the aggressors (alter executioners, identical to the aggressors)
- Presence of an internal calendar with roles to be held on certain dates.
- Presence of alter whose function is to send certain feelings or impulses.
- Presence of deliberately placed 'triggers' to cause certain behaviours or symptoms.
- Presence of 'traps' causing despair or triggering suicidal behaviour when memories are retrieved and abuse is exposed.
- Use of technological equipment for programming.

MK techniques aim to break the victim, to reach the *breaking point* from which deep dissociative states arise. The aim is then to manipulate these dissociative states of consciousness in order to program the fragments. The

---

[457] *"Survivors of the Illuminati"* (3) - A.204: Interview with Kathleen Sullivan, Word of Life translation.

[458] "Healing the Unimaginable: Treating Ritual Abuse and Mind Control" - Alison Miller, 2012, p.46.

following is a list of barbaric techniques for creating the dissociative states necessary for programming. These are methods that are consistently found in survivor testimonies and therapist reports. These are the most violent and traumatic practices because the worst traumas will be the most effective for dissociation and spiritual "unlocking":

- Sensory deprivation, food and sleep deprivation, but also sensory saturation (smells, sounds, light flashes).
- Confinement and imprisonment in boxes, cages, coffins, etc.
- Systematic behavioural modification and use of hypnosis.
- Restraint with ropes, chains, handcuffs.
- Hanging in painful positions or upside down.
- Suffocation, near drowning.
- Experiences on the edge of death.
- Extreme rotation on a pivot, "like a top".
- Blinding light or flashes of light.
- Electric shock.
- Rape and sexual torture.
- Drugs (ingestion or intravenous).
- Guilt, shame, humiliation and belittlement.
- Threats with firearms.
- Containment with insects, spiders, rats, snakes, etc.
- Forced ingestion of blood, feces, urine or flesh.
- Torture and/or forced rape of animals or humans (children, babies).
- Double constraint making a situation a priori insoluble.
- Desecration of Christian beliefs and engagement with Satan.
- Use of lullabies, fairy tales, books, films and music for programming.
- Theatricality, trickery, verbal manipulation, inversions, illusions and lies.
- Actors, props, costumes and make-up for rituals.

Fritz Springmeier explains that MK-Monarch subjects are created for different purposes, both hierarchical and non-hierarchical. Some subjects will be destined to work within powerful circles of power, under excellent cover. These are the ones who are part of the hierarchy, the bloodlines. They will usually receive complex, multi-functional programming and will be used to assist in the programming of other slaves. On them, the abuse will not be physically visible, unlike those who are not intended to be part of the elite such as expendable subjects like sex slaves, drug couriers, breeders, etc. Sacrificial MK-Monarch children are those who are not descended from the elite bloodlines, will be programmed for certain functions and then generally *"thrown off the freedom train"* (sacrificed, murdered, "killed") when they reach their 30s. This is why a *presidential dummy* will usually end up being sacrificed. A great distinction must therefore be made between the Monarch slaves of the high hierarchy, the Luciferian Order, and those who are not. As we have seen, bloodlines are extremely important in these groups, for whom blood is a means of acquiring power (through rituals). For these cults, power is stored in the blood, so the most effective way to transmit it is through the transgenerational lineage.

The child of a Luciferian lineage is conceived according to certain rituals. All the steps that this child will go through for programming are well thought out and follow a detailed protocol, unlike disassociated children from ordinary incestuous homes or families who will not undergo the same regime. The MK subjects of the hierarchy will in turn be used to program and train other elite children, while the second-class slaves will be abandoned after a certain age. The women and men of the Luciferian hierarchy will continue to work for the group throughout their lives with regular programming updates.

A person's readiness for programming is also about their potential for demonic possession, a point that is closely related to their potential for dissociation. Transgenerational Luciferian families are all sold and linked to Satan, and their children belong to him. Because of the genetically engraved transgenerational occult links and the connection to these demonic forces, these children are prime candidates for Monarch programming. While a non-Monarch child may be programmed to become, for example, a baseball player or a drug courier, the most complex programming leading the child to the highest positions will be assigned to subjects who already have exceptional generational demonic power. Indeed, the demonic entities linked to these Luciferian families are a major criterion that will certify the success of a programming.

Part of the MK-Monarch process involves participation in blood rituals to summon the most powerful demons. *Moon Child* rituals are designed to bind the fetus to demonic entities. The creation of these *Moon Children* within the Monarch Project therefore involves high black magic and powerful demons.[459]

Aleister Crowley is the author of the book *"Moonchild"* which was first published in 1917. The rituals that must be performed to capture a soul and create a *Moonchild* are more or less described in three of his books. The magical protocol begins long before the birth of the chosen child, who will obviously have biological parents of a certain lineage. Its conception will be ritualised in a well-defined way, nothing less than consecrating a child to the demons through sexual magic at the time of its conception. The traumas to split the child will begin in the uterus, a foetus can be violated in different ways: electric shocks, needle blows, various traumas of the mother which will have repercussions on the child. The aim is to turn it into a *magical child* that will serve as a host for a superior entity. The *Moon Child* would thus be a sort of avatar raised according to the Monarch programming to carry out its incarnation here on earth by serving a plan of higher order. In his book *"Blood on the Altar"*, Craig Heimbichner states that in a secret instruction of the ninth degree of the O.T.O. (Ordo Templi Orientis), the creation of a *"Moon Child"* is mentioned through the demonic possession of a foetus during a ritualised copulation... This is the heritage of the Assyrian-Babylonian tradition, maintained by Satanists like Aleister Crowley.

The film *Rosemary's Baby*, directed by Roman Polanski in 1968, depicts the birth of this demonic *Moon Child*, whose conception took place during a specific ritual. The film depicts an obscure Satanist network whose members are

---

[459] The Illuminati Formula Used to Create an Undetectable Total Mind Controlled Slave - Fritz Springmeier & Cisco Wheeler, 1996, chap.1.

socially unsuspecting. It should be noted here that the young singer *Kerli*, whose very popular video *"Walking On Air"* (which explicitly represents the Monarch programming process in its symbolism, has named her fans the *"Moonchilds"* (more on this young artist in Chapter 9 on the entertainment industry).

Childhood is central to all these practices. In Alison Miller's book, *Healing the Unimaginable*, former Satanist Stella Katz describes a type of hierarchical organisation consisting of three *Circles* which illustrate how Satanist/Luciferian networks can function:

- The 'First Circle' of the group in which I was raised includes those members of the group who were born into this First Circle or into the highest rung of the Second Circle. Children born in this Circle are trained from birth through programming.

- The 'Second Circle' includes people who were not born into the group but were brought into it at a very young age, usually before the age of one. For example, the child of a Third Circle member or a child recruited by a babysitter or neighbour. They also receive programming, but it will not start as early as in the First Circle.

- The 'Third Circle' includes people who joined the group in their teens or adult years. If these people have children under the age of two, or children of brilliant intelligence under the age of four, then these will join the Second Circle. Older children will remain in the Third Circle. They will be used to 'produce' babies, for prostitution, or to act as 'moles' (infiltration, espionage). They are never allowed to attend a ritual up close, they are cloistered in the back rows, their bodies will form the outer circle while their backs are turned to the ceremony, or they will be placed further back for surveillance. People who are brought into a group as teenagers or adults will not usually have dissociative identity disorder because after the age of nine you cannot split an individual.[460]

We find here the notion of an elitist hierarchy described above, which preserves the bloodlines in the *First Circle*, while the children of the lower levels of the network will be the second-rate MK slaves (*Third Circle*). This example of hierarchical organisation shows us how important children are to these cults, which can only perpetuate their hyper-violent and murderous practices from one generation to the next through the corruption and programming of offspring. Mind control based on disassociation is thus the foundation of this "nameless religion", a systematic programming without which it would probably collapse. Moreover, if the *"spiritual unlocking"* of children were to stop, the contact - power and "guidance" - with demons would be greatly diminished.

The subjects who pass through these systematic MK protocols are also subject to strict rules that form the protective glue of the network:

- The law of silence: not to disclose the activities of the cult outside the network.

- Be loyal to past and present abusers.

---

[460] "Healing the Unimaginable: Treating Ritual Abuse and Mind Control" - Alison Miller, 2012, p.94.

- Obey all past and present aggressors and the alter in charge of the I.D.T. system.
- Do not establish close relationships with people outside the network.
- Maintain a public facade of normality, or insanity if there has been banishment from the group.

Loyalty and faithfulness to the group and the law of silence are therefore the first things that are deeply engraved in the child. But all his programming will be based on three fundamental principles without which it could not be maintained over time:

- Terror.
- The rejection of God.
- The link (chaining) to demonic entities.

If the victim is psychologically and physically paralysed by terror, they will be unable to turn to God for help. Furthermore, if they are bound/chained to demons, then the programming will be effectively maintained over time. The cult wants to ensure that all the potential for empowerment and empathy that the child is naturally born with will be totally neutralised, the aim being even to destroy these positive potentials. The victim will also have to feel totally rejected and ignored by God, which is why the work of spiritual sabotage begins at a very early age. Spiritual programming is a very important part of mind control. A traumatised and split individual, who is necessarily very unstable and at the mercy of the programmer's Luciferian/Satanic doctrines, will undergo what can be likened to the alchemical work: *"Disolve - Coagula":* dissolve to recompose. In the case of the MK-Ultra or the MK-Monarch, this corresponds to the trauma leading to dissociation, a splitting (dissolution, *tabula rasa*), then comes the recomposition (programming with a new identity and new functions). The Masonic formula *'ordo ab chao'* (order through chaos) also applies to trauma-based mind control. Indeed, the programmer is the only one who will be able to put *order* (organisation and programming of the internal system) in the psychic *chaos* that he has voluntarily created in the victim (successive traumas leading to the breakdown of the personality and memories). The MK slave will therefore need the programmer or his master to be able to function again, so that order can return following the chaos... These alchemical formulas are basically neutral, but they can be used to enslave and control humans, and they are. These techniques are most effective with a very young child whose subconscious is still a blank page *in recording mode.*

In MK's elaborate protocols for creating a future elite, children are profiled from the age of 18 months. That is, the programmers make an assessment of the child's character and personality to determine his or her potential. John Gittinger (who joined the MK-Ultra project in 1950) is the designer of the P.A.S. (*Personality Assessment System*), a personality assessment system for evaluating the future behaviour of an individual. This system makes it possible to distinguish between different types of people and thus to identify the child's potential in order to adapt his or her programming for his or her future role in society. The P.A.S. has remained classified, although some of Gittinger's work has escaped the secrecy of intelligence agencies and entered the public domain.[461] EEGs (electroencephalograms) are also used in parallel with the P.A.S.. These neurological and psychological assessment techniques therefore provide MK programmers with the perfect tool to assess the young child even before they acquire language skills. This allows them to fine-tune the programming to the individual child. The child will then follow the script that has been set for him from his early years... Later on in adolescence and adulthood, he will receive all the necessary support and money from the Network to be strategically injected into the company where he will appear with a front personality.[462] The aim is to place 'safe' individuals in key positions, as 'weak links' are not an option in such a system. MK programming optimises the initial potential of individuals and makes them the best in various fields of activity, from politics to high-level sport, science and art.

The child will usually have the same programmer for several years. The child will alternate between living with the family and the programmer, with the parents receiving specific instructions to maintain and reinforce the work in progress. Cathy O'Brien's testimony shows how her father received information about mind control techniques in order to apply them to his children: *"Shortly after that, my father flew to Boston for a two-week course at Harvard on how to raise me in connection with this branch of the Monarch project related to MK-Ultra. When he returned from Boston, my father was smiling and delighted with his new knowledge of what he called "reverse psychology". This is akin to "satanic inversions", and involves puns and other phrases that burned into my mind, such as: "You earn enough to be housed, and I'll house what you earn. To me he gave a trinket, a commemorative bracelet made of little dogs, and to my mother the news that they would "have more children" to raise as part of the project (I now have two sisters and four brothers, ranging in age from 16 to 37, who are still under mind control). My mother followed my father's suggestions, gradually mastering the art of manipulating language. For example, when I couldn't close the snaps on my own pyjamas from top to bottom, in an infantile attempt to deny my father access, I would ask my mother: 'Please close them. She would comply by pressing her index fingers against my skin as if they were goads. The pain I felt was psychological, as it proved to me once again that she had no intention of protecting me from my father's sexual abuse. While complying with the instructions given to him by the government, my father also started to work me like Cinderella in the fairy tale. I would clear the fireplace of ashes, bring in logs for the fire and pile them up, rake dead leaves, crush ice and sweep - "because," my father said, "your little hands are really made for the rake handle, the broom, the ash shovel and the broom. At that time, his sexual exploitation of me included prostituting me to his friends, local mobsters and Freemasons, relatives, Satanists, strangers and police officers. When I wasn't*

---

[461] An Introduction to the Personality Assessment System - John Winne and John Gittinger, Journal of Community Psychology Monograph Supplement No.38. Rutland, Vermont: Clinical Psychology Publishing Co, Inc. 1973. "The CIA Won't Go Public" - Rolling Stone magazine, 18/07/74.

[462] The Illuminati Formula Used to Create an Undetectable Total Mind Controlled Slave - Fritz Springmeier & Cisco Wheeler, 1996.

being worked to exhaustion, filmed in a pornographic way, prostituted or involved in incestuous relationships, I was dissociating myself from myself in books. I had learned to read at the early age of four because of my photographic memory, a natural consequence of my I.D.T. "[463]

The child's already heavily disassociated state was the doorway to initiating a Monarch programming process. Earl O'Brien sold his daughter to a lawless elite who covered up his illegal child pornography activities in exchange.

Many of the doctors who practice MK programming are also active in cults, if not participating in rituals they are at least aware of these occult activities and use the alter created by trauma in various programming. This is one of the reasons why children born into incestuous, Luciferian/satanic environments are ideal prey for government MK projects. It is also important to understand that a programmer is himself in a dissociated state when he violates and splits the child for programming. It is usually one of his alter personalities, totally devoid of empathy, that is in control during these sessions. Most of today's programmers therefore suffer from split personalities themselves. According to Fritz Springmeier, we are currently in the second or third generation of MK-Monarch slaves, who have sometimes become programmers themselves. According to him, programmed humans are currently doing most of the work in trauma-based mind control.

3 - BREAKING THE HEART AND REWIRING THE BRAIN

a/ the heart

Preferably the child will be born prematurely. According to Fritz Springmeier, a premature birth is important because the care of such a baby is 'naturally' traumatic: catheter in the bladder, intravenous lines, oxygen mask, etc.

The Network will ensure that the first thing the child sees when it is born is one of the individuals who will program it. Over the next few months, the programmer will regularly talk to the baby in a very gentle, loving and hypnotic way so that the baby naturally bonds with its future *trainer*. An infant is in a state of total dependence on its parents or guardian and as it grows it must gradually acquire autonomy and independence. However, in terms of relationships, they will remain very dependent on the protection and benevolence of their parents or guardians for a long time. This obviously requires the parents or guardians to be available to offer the child an encouraging, loving and reassuring presence.

When parents or guardians are hostile or even sadistic and violent, the child is then faced with a dilemma for which he has no solution; because whatever happens he is obliged to trust and rely totally on his parents, even if he feels a strong negativity emanating from them. He has no choice and faced with

---

[463] *TRANCE Formation of America: True life story of a mind control slave* - Cathy O'Brien & Mark Phillips, 2013, p.129.

this impossible mission, the young child will lose a lot of psychic energy, he will split into a *"double thought"*, a premise of dissociation. The child cannot flee externally, so it will flee internally through detachment, passivity, "absence".[464]

In the Monarch programming protocol described by Fritz Springmeier, the child will be inundated with love (*love bombing*, a classic cult technique) during the first months of life in preparation for the abrupt withdrawal of care and tenderness from about 1.5 years of age. According to Stella Katz, other MK protocols do not wait until the child is 18 months old to split the personality and the Alpha programming (the first basic splits) is done between the ages of 6 and 10 months, the dissociative process can even start on a foetus.

This first stage, described by Springmeier, consists of brutally depriving the child of all that is tender and pleasant in this world. Through trauma and sensory saturation, he will become deeply disassociated from harsh reality: caging, electric shocks, nudity, food deprivation, contact and forced consumption of excrement... It is then that *help* arrives: the programmer who had been playing the role of *"daddy hen"* enters the scene to make the child suffer his most sadistic and violent side... The individual who has loved and nurtured him for 18 months not only rejects him but even makes him suffer voluntarily. This extreme and inextricable situation creates a split in the child that adds to the trauma of the premature birth.

During the first few months, a *loving* fusion between the child and the programmer must necessarily be established in order to create a clean break when the first major trauma is imposed on the child. A *'clean'* fracturing of the child occurs when the child is confronted with the extreme duality of a person who means a lot to the child. The child cannot reconcile the two totally opposite aspects of the same individual, one being a loving and protective being, and the other being the worst offender. The person the child trusted most becomes the person the child will fear most. Springmeier calls this initial violence, which is the first major split in a young child's life, *'Breaking the Heart'*.

Paradoxically, following this violent rupture, an unhealthy attachment between the victim and the perpetrator will develop. The ambiguity between love and hate as well as the mixture between pleasure and suffering will be cultivated and maintained permanently in the dissociated child. Stockholm syndrome is a reality and these networks that practice ritual abuse and mind control deliberately exploit it: victims become attached to their tormentors.

In his book 'Dialogues with Forgotten Voices: Relational Perspectives on Child Abuse Trauma and the Treatment of Severe Dissociative Disorders', Harvey Schwartz explains that the shocking absence of any anger against the abusers is ingrained and will remain intact. It is as if this prolonged immersion in sadistic abuse and extreme trauma has almost completely reversed the victim's self-protection system.

Judith Herman describes a process she calls *'traumatic bonding'* between the victim and the perpetrator. In her book *Trauma and Recovery*, she describes this process as follows: *"This is the traumatic bonding that occurs with hostages*

---

[464] Trauma and memory: When pain infiltrates body and soul" - Dr Ansgar Rougemont-Bücking.

or victims of abuse, who see their captors as saviours... The repetition of terror and threats, especially in a context of isolation, can lead to an intense sense of dependence, almost of worship of some all-powerful, almost divine authority. Some victims have reported entering a kind of exclusive, almost delusional world, totally embracing the torturer's grandiloquent belief system and voluntarily suppressing their own critical faculties as a sign of loyalty and submission. Such behaviour is regularly reported by people who have been subjected to totalitarian religious cults. "[465]

This phenomenon of Stockholm syndrome is common among hostages. Brian Keenan was held prisoner for a year in Beirut, Lebanon. In his autobiography *'An Evil Cradling'* he describes how he became attached to his imprisonment: *'My days were spent in a slow, gentle delirium, like that comfort and security a child must feel when its mother sings it a lullaby. In my cell I looked wildly at a dead insect hanging in its cocoon and felt a strange contentment. I felt no desire to leave this place. I even caught myself with the beginning of a panic rising in me at the idea of leaving here, I didn't want to leave. I then began to dread my freedom if it were to come.* "[466]

The process of attachment to a situation of imprisonment or subjugation is also found in Satanic/Luciferian cults practising MK. The victim grows up in an environment where it seems impossible to escape, where it seems impossible to break the ambiguous psychological attachment to the perpetrators, who deliberately reinforce this Stockholm syndrome. The chains of programming will meticulously weave a kind of cocoon... the cradle of the Monarch slave butterfly.

This attachment process is strengthened when the individual feels in danger and in dire need of help. This is why ritual abuse sometimes involves a situation where the victim (usually a child) actually believes that he or she is going to die, or as we have seen, even goes so far as to induce a *DND*. These techniques will create a strong psychological attachment between the *"saviour"* and the totally terrorised and dissociated victim. It is the application of the *"fireman-pyromaniac"* method, which consists of voluntarily creating a disorder to bring "order"... Always the same satanic manipulations, whether on an individual or global scale.

The programmer therefore works on the attachment between victim and perpetrator, on the addiction to trauma, what the German psychoanalyst Karl Abraham called *"traumatophilia"* (probably linked to neurochemistry), but also on the mixture of the notions of pleasure and pain, in order to manipulate the victims and their alter personalities. This phenomenon of "traumatic attachment" or Stockholm syndrome is an important point in MK programming because the programmer becomes the only one who can bring order to the inner chaos he has caused in the slave who fatally defaults to him.

---

[465] "Trauma and Recovering: The Aftermath of Violence, from Domestic Abuse to Political Terror" - Judith Lewis Herman, 1997, p.92.

[466] *An Evil Cradling"* - Brian Keenan, 1993, p.73.

This is the testimony of a mind control victim who was programmed by Dr. Joseph Mengele in Kansas City in the early 1960s. This testimony is reported by Carol Rutz in her book *"A Nation Betrayed"*: *"In basic (Alpha) programming, i.e. traumas aimed at multiplying the number of alters that will then be programmed and used for specific functions in the internal structure, I have a memory of Mengele creating a specific traumatic link. He broke the alter with one fraction remembering him with great affection (but including much sexual abuse), while the other fraction was totally terrorized by his cruelty. With the first alter split, he programmed the belief that he was inside it and that he was nurturing and teaching it so well that this personality fraction became attached to it and did not want to leave it. Then later he abruptly rejected it, making it feel worthless and abandoned it. "*[467]

Rutz also reports the testimony of a female survivor who was repeatedly programmed by Dr. Joseph Mengele in Florida in 1954 and in Tennessee in 1955 and 1956:

As he had grown old and grey, he (Mengele) called himself "grandfather". He used the film "Heidi" with me and took the role of Heidi's grandfather. I think the insidious part of his work on me was "love". He loved me and he tortured me. He must have trained my father as well because my father did exactly the same thing. One of Mengele's favourite phrases was "Pain is pleasure and pleasure is pain my dear. I am here to make you very happy. You will love me forever!"[468]

Most mind control survivors report that programmers induce this unhealthy attachment with their little victims from the first years of their lives. Carol Rutz recalls her programmer, Sydney Gottlieb, telling one of her new alter: *"I am your mommy and daddy, you love only me and I am the only one who loves you. I feed you and carry you, you belong only to me. Our 'baby part' (alter) grew to depend on and love 'Papa Sid' as his only source of love and nourishment. Since then, a deep bond had been established... No matter what experiments he did on me, I loved him and remained loyal to the man my baby alter considered his sole provider of the most basic things in life: love and food. "*[469]

b/ The brain

The American biologist Bruce Harold Lipton has discovered that children build the foundations of their subconscious between birth and the age of 6. During this period, we can say that the child's brain is in *recording mode*. The subconscious mind shaped during these early years will be the foundation of the future adult's psychology. Bruce Lipton states that all children up to the age of

---

[467] A Nation Betrayed: The Chilling True Story of Secret Cold War Experiments Performed on Our Children and Other Innocent People" - Carol Rutz, 2001.

[468] Ibid.

[469] Ibid.

2 have brain waves in *delta* frequency, an ultra-slow wave frequency. Then from the age of 2 to 6, children are mostly in a *theta* wave state. These low *delta* and *theta* brain frequencies will cause the child to be in a particularly programmable state, a state called "hypnagogic trance". This is the same brain state that hypnotherapists use to induce new behaviours in the subconscious of their patients. In other words, during the first six years of life, children spend their lives in a kind of permanent *hypnotic trance* state. This is why at this age they are able to store large amounts of information... and why they keep asking questions. On the other hand, the child is unable to critically differentiate the multitude of information he receives through his five senses, he will record everything like a blank hard disk, integrating everything as a truth. It is this construction of the subconscious mind, a kind of computer programming, that will drive the child's future life. Every child is therefore *programmed* by the way he or she is brought up and by his or her life experiences. It is a blank slate, a blank hard disk, a piece of clay on a potter's wheel, the question being what will be the nature of the 'sculptor'...

Even without dissociative states, it is very easy to program and indoctrinate a child before the age of 6. As we have seen, children from Luciferian cults are systematically programmed in the first place to remain loyal to the group. This is the first thing that is deeply inculcated in them, a basis for being able to carry out long-term projects with secure and loyal individuals.

During the 1990s, neurobiologists began to understand that the child's brain contains a huge number of undefined connections between neurons, waiting to be set up according to life experiences. These neurons link to each other through synapses (or neural connections) which will therefore develop in response to the child's experiences and needs. As the child develops and learns, these connections are refined and refined by incoming data. Early childhood experiences therefore have a crucial impact on how the brain will organise its foundations. Traumatic experiences during the first years of life will obviously have a major impact on the deepest basic structures of the brain.

Faced with a trauma, the brain must respond to this stress in a certain way, firstly by a chemical modification with the release of certain hormones, but also by the modification or creation of neuronal connections. The ordinary stimuli of life will enrich the neural networks in a certain way, but the strong overload represented by early traumas will also have a major impact on the synapses. Genes contain the information for the general organisation of the brain structure, but it is life experiences that determine which genes will be active, how and when. The expression of these genes is linked to the production of proteins that allow neuronal growth and the formation of new synapses. It is therefore the child's experiences, both positive and negative, that directly influence the activation of specific synaptic pathways and shape the overall neural substrate of the brain. Dr. Daniel Siegel calls this "communicative neurobiology", which is the way in which the human brain develops according to the child's life experiences. Recent studies in neuroscience have shown that the brain constantly changes and adapts synapses throughout life, depending on the environment and the adult's experiences, but it is clear that this process of neural adaptation is particularly active during the growth phase of the brain.[470]

In an article entitled "Retraining the Brain: Harnessing our Neuralplasticity", psychotherapist Janina Fisher writes: "Since the revolution in neuroscience in the early 1970s (with radical advances in scanner technology that allowed us to study brain function in real time) we now know that all areas of the brain are 'plastic'. They are capable of reorganising themselves, growing new cells and neural networks while rendering other areas obsolete, in response to life experiences. Psychiatrist and researcher Norman Doidge, author of 'The Brain That Changes Itself', calls this neuroplasticity the 'plastic paradox'.

A child undergoing repetitive and extreme trauma in early childhood (causing dissociation and chemical modification of the brain) will therefore develop a neural network with particular connections that it would not normally develop. He will therefore use parts of his brain that are not normally used in order to cope with extreme life experiences. The chemical disruption of the traumatised brain will also lead to a dissociative addiction that will contribute to the enslavement of the Monarch slave. As all this neural construction work takes place mainly during early childhood, early trauma will influence both the child's intelligence quotient and creativity: hyperactivity, hypersensitivity, hypervigilance, hypermnesia, all potentially leading to extrasensory perceptions and paranormal faculties. In a MK process, a training and stimulation programme will work to strengthen certain areas of the brain that are not usually active. The traumatised child will split into several alter personalities whose physical, intellectual and psychic faculties can therefore be cultivated and exploited in their programming. The severe dissociation resulting from extreme trauma in a young brain under construction thus leads to a profound modification of the synapses and will develop the three main criteria of Monarch-type mental control:

- A multiple personality with amnesiac walls.
- Outstanding physical, intellectual and psychological abilities.
- A "spiritual unlocking" that opens a rift to other dimensions and a connection with certain entities. This *tearing of the soul* gives access to the vast inner world of the victim, which we talked about in the previous chapter, a dimension where the dissociated soul fragments are located, a dimension that will be arranged and structured by the programmer as we will see later.

The child's genetics are of great importance as they contain the potential for intelligence and creativity, but also the potential for dissociation and extrasensory faculties. The programming will work to strengthen this or that ability according to the future role that will be determined and assigned to the child. A weak mind can hardly be programmed with these extreme trauma-based methods. Individuals who go through this kind of I.D.T. programming are formatted to exceed the usual 10% of our brain capacity.

---

[470] The developing mind: toward a neurobiology of interpersonal experience " - Daniel Siegel, UCLA School of Medicine, 1999.

Good intelligence and creativity of the subject is extremely important for a programmer. In MK programming, the stimulation of the right (analogical and intuitive) or left (logical and analytical) hemisphere of the brain is used to make the two sides of the brain work independently of each other. These techniques aim to develop and strengthen a particular ability, but also to block certain functions in order to favour others. The neuroscientist Roger Wolcott Sperry demonstrated that the separate cerebral hemispheres (by callosotomy, *"split-brain"*) could function independently and lead to distinct reasoning based on the information to which each hemisphere had access. Sperry has even put forward the much-debated hypothesis that there are separate personalities or forms of consciousness within each hemisphere. Just as there is a splitting of the personality in the Monarch process, there is also work being done on splitting the brain in the two hemispheres so that they can function independently of each other.

One alter personality may, for example, be programmed to function with the left hemisphere while another will function with the right hemisphere. The left and right sides of the body, linked to the opposite cerebral hemispheres - the phenomenon of controlaterality - may contain on one side (left) the alter linked to occult activities and on the other side (right) the alter of daily and public life. This work of separating the cerebral hemispheres will also make it possible to integrate programmes or memories that will only affect one half of the victim's body (see the testimony of the Australian Kristin Constance in the second part of this chapter, she clearly describes programming techniques aimed at uncoupling the left and right parts of the body and therefore of the brain). The process consists of disconnecting, or unplugging, one of the hemispheres in order to be able to work fully with the other and thus be able to feed them with different information. Techniques for stimulating one hemisphere may include sending clear and audible messages to the right ear while the left ear is saturated with confusing noise. Or showing certain images or films to one eye while the other eye receives completely different visuals. One part of the brain may be watching a bloody horror film while the other will be watching happy family scenes. This obviously creates a split in the brain and the two hemispheres will then work differently, one trying to disassociate itself from the horror scene, while the other will experience something totally different. A facade alter personality of everyday life will view happy scenes through the left hemisphere, through the right eye, thinking they live in a perfect world, while the satanic alter linked to the right hemisphere will view horror scenes through the left eye. These programming methods may seem preposterous and like something out of a bad science fiction movie, but reality surpasses fiction... Even more so with today's technology.

In order to create hyper-intuitive alters who are able to access other dimensions of being, it is necessary to block the logic hemisphere, i.e. the left side of the brain. When this hemisphere is 'switched off', or put on hold, then the right hemisphere (which controls the left side of the body) can function fully without '*competing*' with the other hemisphere. When this right hemisphere is fully functioning, the intuitive, subjective and spontaneous side is also fully functioning... The Monarch subject must therefore be able to develop his or her intuitive faculties to 100% in order to access certain dimensions. The deepest alter personalities (linked to the darkest occultism) will have this particular programming of the right brain in order to reinforce to the maximum this hyper-intuitiveness creating extrasensory faculties. This mastery of the two cerebral hemispheres as well as full access to the functions of the right brain are part of the objectives to be reached in occultism, the right brain allowing access to timelessness, to other space-time. The journalist Pierre Manoury writes about the right brain: *"This right hemisphere is too 'magical', its truths, even when they are obvious, are rejected as belonging to the domain of the irrational. The right brain is capable of building 'bridges', of envisaging totally new solutions, of receiving and integrating feelings and impressions from the collective unconscious, of perceiving influences that are not normally received by the five senses. It is a source of inspiration. It is the one that should be awakened to learn about it in order to acquire magical consciousness. "[471]*

In contrast, a left-brain alter will have great faculties for languages, calculation, mathematics, rational and analytical thinking. These are essential skills for training scientists or computer geniuses to work for the Network. Cathy O'Brien, whose entire sibling group was subjected to the Monarch mind control programme, reports that her brother Tom O'Brien was formatted to be a *"Compu-Kid"* (literally an *Ordi-Kid*). That is, a computer genius with MK programming. In the protocols for creating super-slaves, brainstem manipulation is used to create child prodigies who can work on, among other things, super-powerful computer programs. According to Fritz Sprinmeier, this consists of surgery on the brain stem so that the brain faces overcompensation at the level of the scar, resulting in certain faculties such as an exceptional photographic memory. Mental programming work with torture, drugs, hypnosis and I.D.T. improves the memory storage capacity of victims (conscious or unconscious memories).

Federal researchers involved in the Monarch Project related to MK-Ultra were, of course, aware of this photographic memory aspect of I.D.T., as well as the other "superhuman" characteristics that resulted from it. I.D.T. visual acuity is 44 times greater than that of the average person. My acquisition of an abnormally high pain threshold, coupled with the compartmentalisation of my memory, were "necessary" for military and other covert operations applications. My sexuality had also been distorted since childhood. The appeal and usefulness of such programming (i.e. presidential dummy) was to perverted politicians who thought they could hide their actions in the depths of my compartmentalised memory, which clinicians refer to as personalities. - Cathy O'Brien, *TRANCE Formation of America: True life story of a mind control slave*, p.130

Just like dissociation, the child's creativity is an important factor in the success of MK-Monarch programming. For this reason, the programmer will stimulate it to the maximum. The child is naturally creative and builds up an imaginary world very easily. The programmer will be able to tell the child

---

[471] *Cours de haute magie de sorcellerie pratique et de voyance*, Vol.2 - Pierre Manoury, 1989, chap.1.

stories, scripts or programming scenarios in a very vivid way, so that they become deeply imprinted in the child's mind: the aim is that the child can really "touch", "taste" and "feel" the scenario that is being enacted in his mind. Terror and drugs enhance the focus of the little victim so that he or she can best integrate a fantasy world deep inside. As we saw in the previous chapter, creativity is enhanced at the neurological level by early childhood trauma; if everything has been in order and harmony in a person's life, his or her truly creative energy will not work or will work only minimally.

For creativity to be optimised, it must be channelled. According to Fritz Springmeier, the programmer will therefore carefully guide the child's creativity and define its limits, the spark of creativity occurring when there is an alternation between intense concentration (focus) and relaxation (release). The programmer will therefore work on both the suffering side with torture (focus) and the goodness side with secure and caring attention (release). A light trance will allow creative ideas to surface, a process that artists know well. In Monarch programming, creativity as well as dissociation must be taught and encouraged because if the child does not develop these abilities, he or she may end up losing his or her mind and ultimately his or her life. The richness of his creativity will feed his imaginary world which acts as a lifeline just as dissociation is a backup circuit breaker. Dissociation and creativity work together to somehow preserve the child's life in the face of traumatic horrors.[472]

Monarch programming also works with what is called *Biofeedback*. Blood pressure, pulse rate, heart rate, body or body part temperature, etc., can be consciously and voluntarily controlled by the brain. These are psycho-physiological abilities that Indian yogis have mastered for centuries. The control of blood pressure, among other things, as well as the ability to reach deep trance states in a controlled manner, are faculties that are programmed into an MK subject. According to Fritz Springmeier, Monarch programming is about controlling the victim's physical body in order to reinforce the phenomenon of being a totally submissive "doll" controlled by an external master. If a programmer has the power, through a hypnotic trigger, to alter, for example, the heartbeat, blood pressure or body temperature of the subject, the subject will feel no more and no less than a doll or a toy whose biological functions are activated at will. The body, as much as the mind of the slave, is the property of the master and the slave is not allowed to control his or her own body; it is the alter personalities that are subject to these biological feedbacks caused by external triggers.[473]

---

[472] *The Illuminati Formula Used to Create an Undetectable Total Mind Controlled Slave* - Fritz Springmeier & Cisco Wheeler, 1996.

[473] Ibid.

4 - THE MULTIPLICATION OF ALTER PERSONALITIES

The methods and protocols for deliberately creating an I.D.T. in a victim in order to program them certainly vary from group to group but the basics remain the same.

Alpha programming consists of establishing the first personality fragments that will serve as the basis/root for creating all the other alter that will be partitioned into different groups and different levels of the internal system.

Survivor Stella Katz described the protocol of the satanic cult, to which she belonged, for the splitting of children's personalities: the first splitting of the child, the primitive alter, is called the "firstborn" and will have a guardian role for the child. (It is interesting to note here that in some shamanic cultures there are various techniques for the very young child to obtain a 'guardian spirit', including the use of hallucinogenic drugs. Are the "guardian spirits" of shamans alter dissociated personalities? Some authors think so, but one thing is certain: the occultism behind satanic/Luciferic mind control is directly connected to an ancestral knowledge present in the four corners of the planet. A knowledge whose central point is the dissociation of the human psyche). Stella Katz then describes the second personality split, which she calls the "*Gatekeeper*". An alter that will always be present when a new alter personality is created. The gatekeeper will no longer experience any trauma (splitting) as a result of its birth, its role is to observe everything that happens and to record all the new alters created. According to Stella Katz, these first two alter in the role of "guardians" will be the same age as the physical body, they will grow up at the same time because they do not receive any more traumas after their birth. Katz states that the alter who will be in charge of the system, the one to whom all the others must submit, is designated during a traumatic rebirth ceremony in an animal carcass. He will then control all the other alters related to occult practices: "*If an already existing alter emerges during the rebirth, he will become the new leader, because if this alter is strong enough to take over the rebirth ceremony without leaving the body, he will be strong enough to lead the whole system, so he deserves this position.*"[474]

She also explains that the process of splitting the personality must be done meticulously in order to obtain controllable and exploitable alters: "*We (by which I mean the group I was working with) would voluntarily split the child because when they split themselves, without guidance, the alters that are created are unable to become productive members of the group, they cannot be controlled. We are aware that a child who has to endure all the pain and torture we inflict on him would die if he did not have parts within him to absorb the trauma. It is also important that the child we train has a 'normal' personality that is acceptable to the outside world. A personality that can go to school and play with outside children without showing or disclosing anything.*"[475]

---

[474] *Healing the Unimaginable: Treating Ritual Abuse and Mind Control* - Alison Miller, 2012, p.110.

[475] Ibid, p.94.

The years following the first major splits forming the basic alter will see successive sessions of unimaginable trauma in order to create a multitude of fragments separated from each other by amnesic walls. The dissociative process is the keystone for the programming and everything will be done to provoke these modified states of consciousness: a violent psychic and spiritual opening. During the sessions, strong pressure is put on the child to escape from the pain by dissociating, by *going through the mirror*, he/she thus escapes from an unbearable situation by accessing other dimensions of the being. Dissociation in the face of extreme trauma and the obvious threat of death is paradoxically manifested by a sudden and surprising calmness with an absence of fear and pain, regardless of the severity of the violence. This is the neurochemical result of the dissociative process described in Chapter 5. In this state, the victim becomes intensely focused, develops sensory hyperacuity, mental quickness and a kind of expansion of the notion of time.[476]

In such a dissociated and hypnotic state, the child becomes hyper-receptive to learning and programming. For this reason, in trauma programming sessions, the child is verbally encouraged to dissociate, *go through the mirror* or *beyond the rainbow* to escape the pain = *the breaking point*.

Many survivors describe this state of deep dissociation as a basic, neutral state without any identity. Ellen P. Lacter reports a survivor who compares it to a *kind of USB stick for a computer: a simple object on which to write something*. This comparison is reminiscent of the *'tabula rasa'* principle, the blank slate described by the fathers of social engineering at the Tavistock Institute.

According to some MK survivors, an experienced programmer can easily recognise the *'breaking point'*, i.e. the moment when a new alter is created. This is the moment when the child no longer reacts to terror and pain. Each new fragment, or alter, will immediately be named with a code, a first name, etc.

Extreme dissociation will unlock the subconscious, it exposes the mind and allows information to be recorded without the mind being able to question or criticise anything because there is no longer any emotional or self-awareness barrier. This doorway to the subconscious would be accessible before the victim creates a new alter (which, let's remember, has a protective function), it is a deeply dissociated psychic window where no alter is yet in control of the physical body. It is in these states of deep dissociation, where the subconscious mind is totally unlocked, that the structures of the inner world are installed, deep dissociative states also leaving the door open to entities that will play a role in maintaining the programming. Entities that are not perceived by the victims as part of their personality split, they are "foreign bodies" in the internal system of the I.D.T.. They are "installed" (demonised) by the programmer when the child is fully dissociated and unlocked. The information, structures, and programming stored in the subconscious when this window is opened will never be consciously integrated by the different alters, it is data that is much deeper but will greatly influence and control the MK-Monarch slave.

---

[476] "Dissociation and the Dissociative Disorders: DSM-V and Beyond" - P. Dell & J. O'Neil, 2009.

During the MK *sessions*, the victim's brain can be monitored to detect when the brain waves will best integrate the programming.

German psychologist Hans Ulrich Gresch, himself an MK survivor, describes this programming process when the "breaking point" is reached: *"To obtain this 'blank slate', the torture must continue until the victim ceases to resist, until the point of total submission is reached, when he or she abandons all personal will. Then the programmers push the process even further, until this "blank slate" state is achieved... It is then that the victim becomes calm and receptive. This process is a physiological reaction to torture when it is applied 'correctly' (...) The victim reaches a state in which he or she becomes extremely suggestible, a deeply hypnotic state in which he or she is ready to accept anything. Thanks to this state of hyper-receptivity, the programmers can then implant a 'personality', a personality script (...) This new state (alter) will not consciously register the torture that was used to create it. But this unconscious terror and pain will continually feed its receptivity and hyper-vigilance. Although the dissociative state isolates the manner (memory) in which this experience occurred, it remains inscribed to some extent in his mind. The programmed information will be retained intact, with very little deterioration over time, largely due to a network of neurons that will connect this information with the pain and terror that preceded its implantation."*[477]

The programmers therefore focus primarily on creating dissociation in the victim. Through the use of torture and drugs, they manage to disconnect experiences from consciousness that will remain locked in the dissociated identities they have created. This is nothing more or less than exploiting the natural neurological defence functions that we described in Chapter 5. The book *"Ritual Abuse and Mind Control: The Manipulation of Attachment Needs"* contains the testimony of an MK survivor who describes this process of alter creation: *"What the programmer would do, for example, was starve you, spin you (rotating chair) for hours, put you through certain sound frequencies, tie you up to inflict electric shocks until he senses the moment when your mind has "broken"* (the breaking point) *and he sees that you have left your body* (dissociation). *This is when he will give you another name, he will name this new alter and he will say for example: "You are an Egyptian goddess and your life is dedicated to death and destruction". There will be a ritual where people are dressed in robes, singing and burning things. In the beginning, for my conditioning and programming, I was taught how to kill animals and how to torture other children, and then a lot of other things..."*[478]

Stella Katz describes the process according to the practices of the group to which she belonged: "The programmer observes the child carefully. It is thought that a split occurs when the child's cries become peculiar (...) when his eyes roll back, he suddenly relaxes and suddenly becomes silent. At this point,

---

[477] "Ritual Abuse and Mind-Control" - Chap: Torture-based mind control: psychological mechanisms and psychotherapeutic approaches to overcoming mind control - Ellen P. Lacter, 2011, p.78.

[478] *"Ritual Abuse and Mind Control: The Manipulation of Attachment Needs"* - Orit Badouk Epstein, Joseph Schwartz, Rachel Wingfield Schwartz, 2011, p.146-147.

the programmer has a window of fifteen seconds to one minute in which he will name the child's new alter and assign it a colour and a magic symbol. The programmer wears this colour with a black symbol on his shoulder or chest. Then he takes the child and wraps it in a blanket of the same colour. The child then receives a lot of attention and affection for approximately one hour. The child is fed, washed, changed and pampered. He is continuously spoken to in his own language, which may or may not be his mother's, using his new name that has just been given to him. Then finally he is rocked to sleep (...) This process may take a few hours or a few days depending on the child."[479]

Survivor Trish Fotheringham describes dissociation and programming as follows: "Their abuse was carefully planned. My trainers (programmers) used enough trauma to accomplish their goals. Smoke and mirrors' (deceptions and illusions, accompanied by drugs) meant that each specific aspect of the training (programming) was linked to a particular alter personality in a very carefully planned way. For maximum effectiveness and potential, the science of the child's mental development was taken into account in order to adapt the levels of programming. These trainings, which my alter understood as 'life lessons', became progressively more frequent and traumatic as I grew up (...) 'I', the person who managed daily life at home and outside, was not aware that alternative personalities held other pieces of my life. It seemed natural to me that my life was broken into pieces, so the 'gaps' in my schedule went unnoticed. Chronological continuity was unknown to me, so I was not aware that there was a discontinuity. I was not aware that a dissociated lifestyle had been established and that in order to cope with the difficulties, my brain was switching off to simply create another alter!"[480]

Alpha programming will form the basis of the system by creating a certain number of primary alters forming a sort of foundation. These alters will then be broken down into a multitude of potentially programmable fragments. These fragments of soul, or personality, are a sort of neutral and empty file awaiting programming. A basic, or primary, alter can thus be itself split into a multitude of other "sub-alters" by repetitive traumas, and so on... just like Russian dolls attached to the same large doll. It is a real programming chain that is set up. Survivor Kathleen Sullivan describes how her father chained his primary alters: *"Although non-traumatic hypnosis might have been effective in controlling my mind, Dad clearly preferred trauma-based programming to create a new alter system (group). He would first trigger (call) a primary alter he had previously created, and when this alter emerged he would torture it (with electricity, for example) until this fragment could no longer bear the pain. By dissociating, this alter would make room for another part of my mind (a new fragment) to take the next trauma. Dad called this the chain programming technique. He would traumatise one alter after another, verbally giving each one a code name, until I couldn't take it anymore and the process stopped on its own.*

---

[479] "Healing the Unimaginable: Treating Ritual Abuse and Mind Control" - Alison Miller, 2012, p.101.

[480] Ibid, p.74.

At this point he knew he had gone as far as he could. He would then do it again another day in another session, bringing out yet another primary alter to traumatise him and create a new set of personalities linked to that primary alter (...) He would often repeat that I was his prototype and explain that if a technique worked well with me, he would then use it on other children. "[481]

The internal system, which is nothing more than the deliberate creation and operation of an I.D.T., can thus become *a* kind of complex *family tree* composed of a multitude of dissociated and amnesiac alters. It is then essential for programmers and masters to have a kind of *mind map* or structural diagram with access codes to be able to manage the multiple Monarch slave. The 'masters' being the people who will be in charge of the MK (second zone) slave once the programming is complete. In altered states of consciousness and deep dissociation, the programmer will be able to integrate the 'software', or programs, into the different personality fragments to give them various functions. So there are several stages of alter development. Some may be "collateral damage", i.e. fragments created involuntarily during traumas and not exploited, some may have been left aside voluntarily because they cannot be exploited (this is why we sometimes find a "dumping ground" in the inner world, containing the unexploited alters), some may be fragments trained to obey simple and basic commands, in a robotic manner. But alters can also be trained and refined through a longer and more complex conditioning process to program much more elaborate and specific functions. Most alter of a Monarch subject will only take control of the body when called (with trigger codes) by the programmers or masters.

The alter will be organised, or "housed", in different levels, or layers, of the subject's internal system. Like files in a computer, the data must be easily accessible and above all not be mixed up, hence the importance of "amnesic walls" to partition the personality fragments and all the memories they contain. The numerous alter will be grouped into "blocks" or groups that bring them together according to the different categories of activities that will be assigned to them and programmed. The programmer organises and assembles these multiple fragments and groups as he wishes with structural diagrams, symbols, sub-systems, access codes, scripts, etc. It is really a matter of creating a hyper-structured internal world to house all the different alter personalities and of course to be able to find one's way around easily. All the data from a child's programming is recorded in a notebook or laptop which the programmer keeps regularly updated. This data includes what was done on the child, how long it took to create a split and what worked best to achieve that split. The names of the alter personalities are archived along with their birth order, the gender of the alter, the language they speak, as well as the colours, symbols and words or phrases associated with them (the triggers). The function of each alter and the type of "physical body" it has been programmed with are also specified: human, animal, robot, etc. All this information will be transmitted to the various successive masters who will be responsible for operating the Monarch slave.

---

[481] *Unshackled: A Survivor Story of Mind Control* - Kathleen Sullivan, 2003, p.59.

This multitude of alters will be organised in a very strict hierarchy where each fragment will have a very precise function. Satanic/Luciferian cults are themselves organised in a very hierarchical manner, so they reproduce this pyramid scheme within the victim to reinforce loyalty to the cult organisation. The highest alter in this inner hierarchy will be those who have received the worst abuse and have been forced to practice the worst atrocities themselves. These are the darkest and deepest alter in the system, those who are linked to the darkest occultism. The tormentors take pleasure in making the child believe that he is so bad that no one would want him except the group he lives in. The child is programmed to believe that he or she is an executioner, an abuser and a criminal rather than a victim, and if he or she ever begins to recall certain memories this programming will overwhelm the child. As we saw in the chapter on ritual abuse, this is about creating *children of rage.* These alter personalities will have the function of making the victim remember that he or she is just a killer or a rapist who will go to hell when he or she dies. The natural human function of choosing good over evil and empathising with others is a target for destruction in the child undergoing MK programming. Monarch programming takes away the victim's free will, forced abuse of animals and other children takes away the ability to make good choices. The taste for dissociation, adrenaline and endorphins that relieve one's own traumatic memories, eventually overrides natural empathy. This systematic programming to violence allows these groups to continue their existence across generations. It is necessary to recall once again that such a hyper-violent culture cannot endure without the systematic implementation of "Initial Violence" corrupting childhood innocence from the earliest years of life. Usually, one of the alters in the system will identify with the abuser. Most IDD patients have a fraction of their personality that represents the perpetrator, with the same type of sadistic and violent behaviour. In a study published in 1997, Dr. Colin Ross found that out of 236 patients with IDD, 84% said they had a persecutor/executioner alter: *"On first encounter, they were frightful, hateful, demon-like figures totally focused on the patient's malicious abuse and harassment."*

In the case of Monarch programming, the alter executioner is deliberately created and programmed with the characteristics of the programmer, often even bearing the name or pseudonym of the programmer. The victim will then have to carry out his orders even when he is not present, and he will even implant himself in the victim's mind. The role of this 'executioner' alter will be to maintain the presence of the programmer in the victim at all times in order to control the victim by supervising all alters. This goes far beyond simple obedience, it is the internal injection of the predator. The cult thus cultivates the predatory side of its offspring by voluntarily creating tormentors fuelled by an inner rage. It is these ultra-violent alters who will in turn become aggressors and sometimes programmers on other little victims. Survivor Svali explains that *many trainers* (programmers) *will put themselves inside the victim, in order to supervise the internal programs... The survivor may be horrified to discover a representation of his own tormentor in himself, but this is a survival mechanism... The survivor* (the alter tormentor) *will be able to reproduce the programmer's facial expressions, accent, mannerisms, and even relate the programmer's life as his own life*".

Kathleen Sullivan also writes: "Because I myself have had many conflicts and struggles to accept the 'evil' or 'demonic' side of my personality, I understand why some highly disassociated survivors do not want to believe that their 'evil' or 'dark' alter personalities are pieces of their own original personality. My personality has been polarized with the "too good" on one side and the "too bad" on the other. This has prevented me from merging the two and being able to integrate them into one balanced personality. Accepting our fully human 'dark side' requires great courage but also a strong will to forgive ourselves."[482]

Generally speaking, when a programmer implements something in the victim, it will at some level be a reflection of himself, just as writing and art reflect the person who produced them. Although the comparison between artistic creation and mental programming may seem misplaced, it is not so for programmers.

Military or political groups program their killers using indoctrination and training to make the split child into an elite soldier. These children will usually be tortured to produce alter personalities who can commit acts of extreme cruelty without having to face the psychological consequences. In Uganda, *the Lord's Resistance Army* (*LRA*) practises this kind of trauma and mind control training, the victims of which are "child soldiers". A Canadian documentary entitled *'Uganda Rising'* (2006) focused on these children who were forced into the ranks of the *LRA*. These children who were forcibly removed from their (often decimated) families tell of being tortured, mutilated, raped, sometimes forced to commit murder, and then herded into camps and used as soldiers. The documentary does not mention *ritual abuse* or *mind control* but the strategy seems to be the same.

In Monarch programming, many of the alter personalities will be dehumanised and conditioned to believe that they are something other than human. The dehumanisation of an alter will be done by making it experience, for example, the extreme conditions of a caged animal. Just as with the magic surgery we will describe later, all sorts of mental manipulations can be done to implant in the alter the belief that it is a cat, a goddess, a robot, a puppet, etc...

One or more alter will be programmed to act as reporters. That is, they will be conditioned to record everything and to report to the executioners any disobedience or disclosure of secrets by the slave. These alter "reporters" are also programmed to inform the cult of all the movements of the victim. The paradox is that this type of alter is conditioned by pain and terror to believe that the torturers "already know everything" and that he himself will be punished if he does not report what the victim does.

In order for the Monarch slave to function properly in society without being detected, it needs an alter personality, a sort of shell that masks the individual's multiple states. This is the 'host' or 'public' personality, the main

---

[482] Ibid, p.289.

personality that behaves 'normally' and is totally amnesiac of the abuse and the existence of the internal system with the multiple alters. Therapist Alison Miller calls this type of alter the *"apparently normal personality"*. Most alter personalities will be dehumanised, whereas this one will be allowed to be human, to have a sense of family, a social and emotional life, etc. The host personality is usually well oriented in space and time, i.e. it evolves according to our timetable, while many other alters will be stuck in the space-time where the trauma happened. To understand how the interface between this host personality and the other alters works, let us take the example of a known case of a hypnotic experiment by Pierre Janet: Janet hypnotizes Lucia to make her perform post-hypnotic suggestions. Lucia carries out the commands but forgets everything immediately afterwards. In contrast, another of Lucie's alters named Adrienne remembers everything that happened when Lucie was hypnotised, and she claims that it was she who performed the post-hypnotic suggestions without Lucie's knowledge. This is a one-way amnesia. The amnesic wall isolates the host personality, but some alter who do not experience this wall are fully aware of the existence of the host personality and retain the memory of all its actions. In Monarch programming, the host personality is totally unaware of the programming, but the deepest, most important alters in the I.D.T. system are fully aware of its existence and can therefore control it. According to therapist Elle P. Lacter, there is usually a basic structure in place that separates the alter personality system into two parts. The "host" side, which will not be aware of the existence of the I.D.T. system, and on the other side the deeper, occult-related alter group, which will be aware of the existence of these surface personalities and can even control them.

The internal system of an MK slave thus includes one or more host personalities that are compartmentalised and totally amnesiac, various alter personalities with different functions installed more or less deeply in the system, and finally there always remains the core, the essence of the *"I"*, the original personality that Satan (or the programmer) cannot touch or destroy. He can only isolate it as best he can, but this divine seed will always be present in the victim for his eventual restructuring and healing. The alter personality detected as the youngest is probably the original personality from which the others split off.

Some alter will also have denial programming. Their goal is to deny ritual abuse and all occult activities of the network. If leaks do occur, their goal is to put forward explanations such as "false memories", nightmares that are not real at all, a book or movie that may have influenced the person, etc. These alter personalities believe that they are preserving the victim and even saving him/her. These alter personalities believe that they are preserving the victim and even saving their life. These alter personalities have a vested interest in doing this: they believe that their very existence and survival depends on it and that if real awareness of the traumatic events were to occur, violence and even death would then occur as punishment for not doing their job. This denial programming begins in the early years of the child's life. For example, he or she will be terribly abused and traumatised, and then the next morning the adults around him or her act normally, as if nothing had happened. This is how they model a lifestyle of denial in the child. This is reinforced by phrases like: *"It was just a bad dream"*, *"How can you believe such a thing? It's just your imagination, it didn't really happen"*. Family members suffering from dissociative states will also be in some denial about occult nocturnal activities. Denial is also reinforced by telling the child that no one will believe him/her anyway if he/she talks about it. The ultimate goal is to format the child so that he or she no longer trusts his or her own reality, but instead looks to adults for *reality*. For example, the adult will show the child an orange and ask what it is, and the child will be systematically abused when he or she answers that it is an orange and will be hammered that it is an apple... The process will be repeated until the child, terrorised and fearing pain, answers that it is an apple and even ends up believing it... [483]

Another method of proving to the child that their memories are unreliable is to stage a simulated murder of a person in which the child is forced to participate. The next day, the child will see this person alive and well in front of him/her, although he/she is supposed to have been murdered in front of his/her eyes the day before, resulting in a form of cognitive dissonance. If the child asks questions, he or she will be told that this atrocious event was surely just a bad dream and a product of his or her imagination. Because victims often suffer from traumatic amnesia with a chronological breakdown of memories, it is very easy for people who have power over their lives to convince them that nothing happened to them. When parents tell the little victim that his nightmares or flashbacks are pure imagination and that this kind of thing never happens, this obviously reassures the child who will remain in these dissociated states between two worlds, two opposite realities...

Trauma-based Monarch mind control is practiced on children before the age of 6. After that age, it becomes more complicated to practice this kind of I.D.T. programming, but that does not mean that people are not programmed after the age of 6. Personality fragments induced by trauma and dissociation remain better isolated in the mind than personality fragments induced by simple hypnosis, but most people can be hypnotised into alter personalities. Some survivors of satanic ritual abuse have been programmed but they do not have an internal system with alter personalities, they only have some dissociative states, such as a *night self,* and *a day self.*[484]

5 - "MAGIC SURGERY" AND THE STRUCTURING OF THE INNER WORLD

To understand what we are talking about here, it is important to understand that the Monarch slave has gone through a traumatic process of psychic and spiritual splitting that opens the doors to other dimensions of being.

---

[483] Breaking The Chains: Breaking free of cult programming " - Svali, 2000.

[484] "The Illuminati Formula Used to Create an Undetectable Total Mind Controlled Slave" - Fritz Springmeier & Cisco Wheeler, 1996.

This gives him access to an *inner* world (far beyond his *head*) that is as vast and as real as the physical world is to us, a world composed of his various soul fragments (alters), demonic entities and the hardware set up as part of the programming. This inner world, or 'internal system', will be arranged by the programmer with different structures, architectures, objects, landscapes, etc., material or symbolic representations serving as a support to work in this particular dimension. It is sometimes possible to identify the type of sect that has perpetuated the programming by the type of structures and symbols that form the inner world. The hierarchical organisation of the alter personalities also often reflects the type of group that programmed the victim, it may be a military, satanic, druidic, kabbalist, neo-Nazi group, etc.

Magic surgery' is a tool to feed and organise this internal system. It consists of hypnotising and/or drugging the child by telling him/her that he/she is going to be operated on in order to insert an object or an animal into him/her. The surgical operation will be only a staging after which the child will believe that he really has this object inside him (this programming is supposed to remain implanted throughout his life). Extreme pain may be caused at the site of the surgery and blood may be smeared on the child to reinforce the belief that he or she has actually undergone surgery. The child knows what the object or animal is and what its function is. He is programmed to believe that this 'thing' inside him will attack, explode or denounce him if he speaks, that it is now scanning his thoughts and will influence him to become evil and behave badly. The child is programmed to believe that these foreign bodies will torment and harass him if he does not conform to the doctrines of the cult. Ritually abused children often report somatisation such as abdominal pain in connection with this 'magic surgery' phenomenon.

In the file of minutes and depositions in the Dutroux case, page 261 contains a letter from a certain *Van Aller* dated 13 December 1996 referring to what appears to be magic surgery. This is a testimony concerning ritual abuse allegedly practised in villas by Dutch notables: *"For example, these disorders (IDD) are provoked by making small children believe that a cat is being introduced into them, which will grow up to become a panther that will watch them if they want to speak or leave the clan, this allows continuous control, even in adults, and makes victims of all the perpetrators. IDD is maintained by psychotherapists."*[485]

A British psychiatrist reported an example of mind control based on the same principle: the child is forced to eat a spider and is told that it will multiply and that all these spiders will then watch him from the inside. By being forced to eat maggots, the child will believe that they can turn into flies that will report him to his abusers if he speaks. Fritz Springemier says that the *'Golden Penis of Osiris'* is placed inside Monarch slaves. It may also be the *'Eye of Lucifer'* or the *'Eye of Horus'* which is *placed* in the child's womb for constant observation and surveillance. This process of abstract surveillance of the inner world seems

---

[485] Letter from Van Aller of 13/12/1996 (Z200) - *Belgium: Dutroux X-Dossier summary*, 1235 pages, 2005 - Wikileaks.org.

to be something essential and systematic in MK programming. The child may also be told that his or her fleshy heart has been replaced by a cold black stone, thus reinforcing his or her dehumanisation in the face of horror. This 'magic surgery' is limited only by the imagination of the programmers. The possibilities are endless, because everything in this physical world can be transferred to the inner world. But as we will see later, this very malleable inner world can also be used to help the survivor in therapy.

In the human brain, the right and left hemispheres are connected by the corpus callosum, which mediates and makes rational analysis possible. However, this structure only reaches maturity around the age of 10. The experiences of a child's right brain (which perceives the world in raw data) are therefore not transmitted to the left brain for rational analysis. The left hemisphere translates perceptions into semantic and phonetic data, i.e. words, concepts and language. Before the tenth year, many things will remain unconscious for the child because the information network of the brain is not yet fully constructed. As long as the corpus callosum is not fully developed, the child can, for example, perfectly believe that Father Christmas will bring his presents to him on 25 December in his living room, while knowing that he is too fat to go down the chimney. [486]The process of 'magic surgery' therefore exploits this lack of brain maturity. The child under 10 may believe that a doll's house, a castle, a merry-go-round or an animal has been inserted into him because he does not yet have the ability to rationalise something so fanciful. This is not naïveté or "daydreaming" on his part, but a cerebral limitation which, in the context of MK programming, allows manipulation for formidable mental control. These "surgeries" will be implanted all the more deeply if the child receives them in states of trance, extreme dissociation and under the effect of drugs.

Before the age of 5 or 6, the young child has absolutely no cerebral capacity to defend itself against "invasive" mental control. The cerebral cortex, which enables reasoning, deduction, reflection, logical analysis of situations, decision making, emotional management, morality and organisation, is not mature until the age of 6, when it starts to mature very gradually. So we can understand why some sources say that MK programming should be implemented before the age of 6.

The supports, or structures, used to organise the inner world can be introduced or 'programmed' in ways other than 'magic surgery'. Here are some examples of supports that can be used to structure and organise the internal system of an I.D.T. These things have been reported by survivors and therapists:

The double helix (symbol of infinity), letters or symbols, 2D geometries such as the pentagram, triangle or circle, elaborate 3D geometric volumes, dolls, spider webs, mirrors or shards of glass, chess boards (duality of the black and white checkerboard with arrangement of pieces according to programming), masks, castles, labyrinths, temples, pyramids, walls to reinforce amnesia, demons / monsters / aliens, robots, shells, hourglasses, clocks, butterflies, snakes, suns representing the god Ra, ribbons, flowers, command diagrams,

---

[486] Neuropsychology of suffering, cause of repression" - Jean-Luc Lasserre.

computer circuits that can be used as a flowchart for complex programming A two-dimensional grid can contain a category of alter housed and operating on the same level. A third dimension can be created to form a cube with each side corresponding to a particular level of the internal system with a particular category of alter. A cube that can be rotated according to the group of alters that need to be accessed. This cube structure is placed in a spiral lift shaft such as DNA: through this system, the alters can "rise" (emerge) or "fall" (sink) as needed.

The complexity of the structures will vary according to the child's ability to memorise and represent them in his or her inner world. The Cabalistic *Tree of Life* (Tree of the *Sephiroth*) is a structure that has also been reported by MK survivors and seems to be an essential element for the inner organisation of the slave. The alter *"Key"* of the split painter Kim Noble has depicted the cabalistic tree in several of her works, notably in her painting entitled *"Seven Level"* which seems to describe the programming process step by step (a painting which is analysed later in this chapter and can be seen in appendix 4). The Sephiroth tree represents the structure of man and the universe. It contains and provides a coherent and ready-to-use "system" of correspondence: each *Sephiroth* (world, dimension, field of consciousness) is associated with a number, a planet, a note, a quality, a defect, a day of the week, etc. It is a perfect structure for organising the world and the universe. It is a perfect structure for organising and classifying the multiple alter personalities, the fragments of souls. This cabalistic tree basically represents the structure of man and the different worlds, the parallel dimensions we spoke of in the previous chapter.

According to Fritz Springmeier, certain geometric shapes incorporated into the inner world of the slave serve as focal points for demonic entities, doors through which demons can enter the human body. Indeed, geometries that give off a certain shape wave are used in magic rituals to interact with other dimensions.

Another structure is the merry-go-round, a classic carousel with wooden horses that go up and down while spinning in circles. The merry-go-round is also part of the systems for structuring the inner world and accessing its different levels. It will be used to make the alter personalities "go up" or "go down" during the states of trance and dissociation. In his autobiography *Thanks For The Memories*, former presidential model Brice Taylor describes this inner carousel as follows: *"That day the carousel was created in my mind, I was standing in the middle of the carousel while the programming was slowly done as it spun. Then it stopped at Henry's request in a place in my mind, just like the Wheel of Fortune. He then said to me: 'There is a whole other world in the files of your mind. The carousel allows the files in your mind to spin easily and effortlessly"* (...) *I was not able to retrieve all of this memory, because it was spinning like a merry-go-round, swirling and spinning like a top, so I could not grasp it to remember it. This programming is called "spin programming", it is meant to disorient and induce confusion."*[487]

---

[487] Thanks For The Memories: The Truth Has Set Me Free" - Brice Taylor, 1999, p.68.

When the victim undergoes extreme rotation on a swivel chair, it makes them feel sick and terrified, they go through all sorts of physical and emotional sensations. These sensations will transfer to the alter personalities who are in control of the body at that moment and are therefore undergoing this treatment. Later on, these programmed spinning sensations will be triggered by these alters whenever the individual remembers anything about the abuse, this memory will come up with the spinning sensation which will cause mental confusion and physical discomfort.

This is how survivor Svali describes the protocol her group used to insert a structure into the child's inner world to house one or more alter: *'The structures will be integrated into the victim's inner world while drugged, hypnotized, and undergoing electroshock. The person is totally traumatised and in a deep trance state. It is in this altered state of consciousness that they are forced to open their eyes and look at a projected image of the structure. This can be a 3D model of the structure, a holographic image or even a virtual reality headset. The image will be "injected and imprinted" by using successive shocks and bringing it closer and closer into the subject's field of vision. The subject may be ordered to enter the structure if it is a temple or a pyramid. Under the effect of deep hypnosis, they (the alter personalities concerned) will now live "inside" this structure. This will also be used to reinforce the amnesia and internal isolation programming, this structure will reinforce the walls of compartmentalisation between the personality fragment enclosed within it and the other alters in the system."*

The alter personalities may be trapped within these structures, or they may be linked or connected to them in various ways. Alters define themselves by the reality that the programmer has implanted in them. Objects, structures and symbols thus serve to organise and control the inner system, but it is also structured with scenarios or scripts that serve as pictorial and symbolic supports on which the programmers will build the alter. Generally speaking, anything that usually makes a child dream will be used to program it. A book, a film or a video game can in theory be used as a support for MK programming, all the more effectively with young children. It is a matter of encrypting their minds with fairy tale themes or other fantastic scenarios in order to confuse fantasy and reality, i.e. to make them straddle two worlds. *Alice in Wonderland'* is a classic programming script, as is *'The Wizard of Oz'* or some Disney productions such as *'Pinocchio'*, the carved wooden puppet, and *'Cinderella'*, the filthy little slave girl who turns into a beautiful princess. Monarch slaves, or rather their alter personalities, are conditioned to be placed in such scenarios to reinforce the effect of the programming. They therefore live in a completely imaginary world. Certain phrases in the script will serve as an implanted cryptic language to control the slaves. In *Alice in Wonderland*, the little girl has to follow the white rabbit who allows her to access mysterious and normally inaccessible places. In MK programming, the white rabbit is an important figure, representing the master or programmer who hypnotises the victim or induces them to disassociate from reality to access an alternative world during the torture. The famous passage through the mirror represents access to a dissociative state, a change of reality. The programmer encourages the child to *go through the mirror* like Alice, he encourages him to go through the door to another dimension of his being, the mirror being the door that will facilitate the programming... In the film *"Matrix"*, when Neo comes out of the matrix for the first time, he touches a mirror that becomes liquid and that ends up covering him completely, swallowing him up and taking him to another world... where he will be deprogrammed. To get there, Neo had *followed the white rabbit* tattooed on a woman's shoulder... These are very strong symbols, rooted in this occult culture. In The *Wizard of Oz*, the subject dissociates from reality by going *beyond the rainbow* ("Somewhere *over the* Rainbow", which is the theme song of the film), i.e. by going beyond terror and pain thanks to dissociation. The horror then becomes a dream, reality becomes fiction and the imaginary world becomes reality. The dissociated victim will register the trauma as an illusion, a reality that he or she has nevertheless experienced for a while, but which is nevertheless registered by the mind as a kind of dream. This is a crypto-amnesia that sabotages the usual process of remembering through trauma and hypnosis. The inner world of the slave becomes his 'reality' and the outer world becomes, for example, the land of Oz. It should be noted that in some shamanic cultures, celestial ascension is achieved by the overlapping of the rainbow. A considerable number of cultures see the rainbow as a bridge between earth and sky, a bridge between gods and men. It is often through the rainbow that mythical heroes reach the sky, its climbing serving to reach the spirit world. Medicine men' ascend to the celestial spheres using, among many other means, the rainbow. It would seem that the MK-Monarch programming techniques take up this rainbow symbolism, which represents nothing less than a dissociative process that opens the door to other dimensions. As we have already seen, trauma-based mind control techniques are intimately linked to certain ancestral cultures and psycho-spiritual practices, particularly the exploitation of dissociative states.

Another important symbolism in The Wizard of Oz is *the yellow brick road*. The slave must follow *the yellow brick road* through which the alter emerges from the inner world to take control of the body. *Following the yellow brick road*' are key words used to trigger a particular programming in a slave. Another example concerning the Wizard of Oz is the character *Tin Man* who is a kind of empty metal carcass. This character will be used to create *a well-oiled machine* that performs the commands perfectly, this is the programming of the Tin Man that some alter will receive.

The author of The Wizard of Oz, L. Frank Baum, an occultist and member of the Theosophical Society, is said to have been inspired by a spirit who gave him the *'magic key'* to write this children's story. In other words, Baum was a medium and wrote this story by channeling an entity. In the book *The Annotated Wizard of Oz*, Baum wrote: *"It was pure inspiration... It came to me in some inexplicable way. I think that sometimes the 'Great Author' has a message to get across and has to use the instrument at hand. I happen to have been that medium, and I believe that a magic key was given to me to open the doors to sympathy, understanding, joy and peace.*[488] The *Wizard of Oz* in 14 volumes was published in 1900, this tale which can be described as "theosophical" incorporates the "ancient wisdom" of the Mystery religions, which others would call satanic or luciferian... its initiatory content has been taken up and used as a medium for trauma-based mind control. The entities that inspired this story probably knew the potential it contained and the occult use that would be made of it.

The film *"Frankie and Alice"*, based on the true story of a woman who developed I.D.D., contains a scene showing a hypnosis session where a child alter personality emerges talking about the Wizard of Oz... just a wink. In a 2009 *New York Times* video *(Screen Test)*, actress and model Megan Fox told Lynn Hirschberg about her obsession with the Wizard of Oz as a child: *"I remember the Wizard of Oz very well because it was my favourite movie for a long time. I was obsessed with it and watched it over and over again. For years I wanted to be Dorothy! Until I was six I wore pigtails and I think my grandmother made me the Dorothy costume, I also had the little ruby slippers. My mother called me Dorothy, I didn't answer her or listen to her if she called me Megan, because that wasn't my name. "*

Survivor Svali described the methods used to implant a film script in a fractionated young child: *"The programmer shows the child the film and tells them that they will be asked about what they have seen, which automatically triggers the child to use their photographic memory. The programmer can show the child the whole film or just a few scenes, or even one scene. After watching the whole film or just a few passages, the child is drugged to relax and then asked what he remembers. The child will be abused if he or she does not remember what the programmer deems important and will be forced to watch these scenes over and over again. When the child has finally memorised all that is deemed important, the programmer will tell the child that he or she is one of the characters in the film. The child will be heavily traumatised to create a blank alter personality that will become the character in question. The first thing this new blank slate (the new alter) will see is the entire film or a scene from the film, so this will be its first memory. The programmer will then link the scene of the film to the "illuminati" (luciferian) ideology, teach the child the "hidden meaning" of the film and congratulate him/her for being one of the few "illuminati" who can understand its real meaning. Script programming will usually be linked to other programming already present in the child. For example, the military type programming may be linked to the film Star Wars, the internal maze programming may be linked to the film Labyrinth, etc. The possibilities are very varied. The music of the film, or a particular scene, can be used as a trigger to access the programming or to bring out the corresponding alter personality. "*

According to Fritz Springmeier, American popular culture in the second half of the 20th century was transformed into a large catalogue for MK programming. Series like *Star Trek* or *Star Wars* were exploited by

---

[488] *The Annotated Wizard of Oz"* - Michael Patrick Hearn edition, New York: Clarkson N. Potter, 1973.

programmers, as were *Walt Disney* productions, *Alice in Wonderland* or *The Wizard of Oz*. Nowadays, it is likely that programmers will use recent productions, although the *classics will* certainly remain effective and important media. For example, in the *Star Trek* culture, there has been a whole series of highly technical manuals describing in detail the whole universe of the series, i.e. equipment, ships, planets, etc. According to Springmeier, when you look at these ultra-detailed manuals, the best way to explain the time and money spent to develop such complex descriptions for a simple fiction is that they serve MK programming purposes. For example, these manuals contain maps of the *Star Trek* universe and such a map can be used as a support for organising a T.D.I. system. When you split up a victim's personality, you then need this kind of schema / support to restructure it, as if recreating or reorganising their shattered soul into a thousand pieces. A star cluster or planet can be used to isolate or group alter, only being able to leave that place by entering a dissociation and travelling through space-time when an electric shock, light flash or other trigger is induced. As with magic surgery, the number of scripts will depend on the imagination of the programmers, who have a whole catalogue of exploitable structures at their disposal to organise the inner world of the split subject.

Brice Taylor reports how his inner world could be a real cosmos: "Henry worked with me rather early on, to set up all my systems. He even marked a cross on my forehead to delineate what he called the 'star map' of my system. Then he put me in front of the mirror so I could see this little face, 5 or 6 years old, with short hair, with this black cross on me. He said that there were planets within my inner universe and that they were asleep waiting for the day when they would be occupied. Later he added other areas and said they were little worlds for the different planets. This system kept the information totally separate and isolated because the planets had no way of communicating with each other. All data and information was kept separate, autonomous and in orbit in the great blue vastness of the stars. All these stars were used as files for movie stars or politicians who used to use me. The larger stars contained larger files of alter personalities and were linked to people I used to see regularly, while the smaller stars were reserved for people I only saw occasionally. The larger stars were reserved for the elite. The all-powerful group of men who secretly orchestrated this horror had set up a sophisticated satellite system that could travel anywhere inside my mind, constantly monitoring my 'inner worlds'. Henry told me that the files in my mind are unlimited because the universe is limitless and absolutely vast, and he also told me that there will always be new areas to map."[489]

Objects can be transferred to the inner world with magic surgery, but they can also be used as an external medium for programming. Some objects can be used as tools to manipulate the dissociated child. In her autobiography, Brice Taylor explains that her father had created a special doll wardrobe for her. This cupboard was filled with a collection of various dolls. They were dolls from all over the world, toys that were always given to her with 'love'. Her father used

---

[489] "Thanks For The Memories: the truth has set me free" - Brice Taylor, 1999, p.66.

them as a medium to manipulate and program the alter personalities of his daughter, who was fractured by repetitive abuse, night after night: *Often when my father tortured me, he would give me a new doll to create another part of me with a new identity, I would then deal with it and my young (dissociated) mind would then identify with this doll I was holding. It would tell me that this doll in my hand was a part of me while both were separate, and then it would give it a name. There was the little doll with red hair and freckles, the Baby doll, Cindy the Bride, Rebecca, Sally, Barbie, Mrs. Alexander... to name a few. I was literally surrounded by dolls (...) my father said I couldn't play with them until he gave me permission, until he told me it was time for them to come out of the closet. At night, when he woke me up to abuse me, he would take out the doll related to the alter personality that was to emerge from my internal system. When he would take out a doll, he would say, "It's not in the closet anymore, now it can come out and play," and at that tender age, I would immediately fall into the personality that my father was calling. Then he'd say, "You, Susie, are going to retire when Doll is fully inside your body. Every time I snap my fingers three times, Doll will enter the body and Susie will withdraw to the side. And he snapped his fingers three times and I followed my father's command perfectly."* [490]

MK programming also uses colours to organise internal systems and easily manipulate alters. With a split personality into a multitude of alters, colours will be a way of organising a group and accessing it easily. Moreover, young children recognise colours before they can read, they are very sensitive to them. This programming can therefore be done very early, from the age of two. The child will be programmed in a room painted or lit in a certain colour. If it is the colour blue, the programmer will bring up one of the child's alter to tell him that he is going to learn to *become blue* and learn what this colour means. The room will be bathed in blue, the programmer will be dressed in blue, possibly with a blue mask. All objects will also be blue. An alter personality will be called to emerge and then drugged, hypnotised and traumatised on a table or stretcher. When they are in a trance state, they will be told that blue is something good and that they themselves are blue. She will be told that blue will protect her from danger, that blue people don't get hurt, that she will wear nice blue clothes, etc. If the child resists and does not want to *become blue*, she will be tortured until she submits. Following these programming sessions, the child will be bathed in blue for a period of time, given blue-tinted glasses or contact lenses, and will wear the same colour clothes. Then, in gradual steps, the child is taught the meaning of this colour and the function related to it, which he or she must integrate. The trauma sessions will be multiplied while this colour is imprinted more and more deeply in his subconscious. The colour thus becomes a trigger through which the programmer or master can access a particular alter group or alter of the victim. Colour coding is a basic method of organising internal systems. [491]

---

[490] Ibid, p.48.

[491] Breaking the Chain: Breaking free of cult programming " - Svali, 2000.

Here is an excerpt from a lecture by Australian survivor Kristin Constance, who describes a process of MK colour programming (the full transcript of her testimony can be found later in this chapter): *"The colour programming I underwent took place in underground rooms. Each room had a different colour, corresponding to different programming. The colours seemed to correspond to those of the Eastern Star: blue, yellow, white, green, red and black for the centre. The red room had a red light, a stretcher, a table full of torture instruments and equipment for electroshock. The right side of my body was covered while the left side was subjected to electrical torture. Electrodes were placed on my left joints, causing paralysing pain... which I still feel today. My left ear was whispered to and electric shocks were applied to my temples. This is how 'Red' was created, and reinforced... A woman would ask me questions about programming, and no matter what I answered, I was always wrong. I disassociated many times... "Red" and his alter seem to be programmed to have no reaction to pain in any circumstance during sexual abuse. Red has been through a lot of blood rituals and rapes, and she* (ed. note: a group of alters) *has taken most of my pain."*

In therapist Alison Miller's book *Healing the Unimaginable*, survivor Trish Fotheringham also describes how colours were used to organise and structure her alter personalities: *"My deliberately created alters were all associated with particular colours, each colour representing a 'path' or type of programming. An alter who has been trained to follow a red path will only wear clothes of that colour, will be spoken to in a certain way and will experience specific situations with a particular type of person. The chances are slim that even the toys the child is allowed to play with are not part of his programming (...) The programming will then consist of including more and more connections with colours, gradually linking each colour to sounds, words, shapes, symbols, etc (...) as a child, when I was placed on a man's lap, my first alter of the red (sexual) pathway had to behave in a systematically sexualised way, for example, he had to wriggle around and laugh explicitly. From the age of 6 months to 2 years, my programming focused on installing basic commands and triggers in the primary alter. Certain programs such as "Obey", "Don't Talk", "Be Loyal", as well as internal safeguards and alarms, were set up from the beginning and reinforced as I grew up. Later, my masters would call these alters using phrases containing trigger codes or by inducing the emotional state I was in at the time of the initial split (...) Lights, clothing and props, words, phrases, specific physical contacts, smells, drugs, as well as several specific colour codes were all methodically used. This allowed my masters and programmers to create and develop in each alter an individual and autonomous belief system formed with values systematically shaping his conception and understanding of how the world works, what the 'rules of life' are, and almost everything he thinks, feels, says or does."[492]*

---

[492] "Healing the Unimaginable: Treating Ritual Abuse and Mind Control" - Alison Miller, 2012, p.75-76.

Fortheringham also described the methods used to arrange his inner world during his dissociated states: 'I must have been two years old when my programmers first used a special chair with straps and a helmet. It could swivel, rotate, tilt and send electric shocks. My programmers always told me that this chair was a "magic door" that allowed me to "ride through the rainbow" to strange and distant realms. At first, the vibration and electrical stimulation of the chair, combined with the drug and wind of a fan pointed at me, made me feel as if I were floating and actually moving through space. They gave the chair different purposes and different 'destinations' depending on the alter that emerged. By using specific lighting, sounds or music, they created particular atmospheres, alternative realities. The chair that tilted and turned on itself, combined with electrical impulses, could create a real tornado with lightning in the inner world (...) When I 'rode the rainbow' on this chair, the lights and special effects made me travel. Afterwards I was violently 'fixed' and punished on that chair (...) The inner world was easily arranged, sometimes it was outside, sometimes it was staged. The 'weather phenomena' were injected into the inner world in the same way as everything else, simply by suggestion, by saying they were there, with some special effects. Like all children of that age, I naturally believed everything I was told. Dust tornadoes and whirlwinds were produced with fans pointed at me when I was in the 'magic chair'. At first I was told to 'control' these phenomena and then to become these phenomena myself. Rainbows were created around me in this chair, apparently by projectors and water spray. I was told that these rainbows were magical multi-coloured paths to other worlds and that it was the chair that set the final destination. These other worlds were first staged externally, then integrated and became part of my inner world. The rainbows contain all the colours, so they can be used to simultaneously call up all the colour-related alters (...) After tests have confirmed that the programming is satisfactorily integrated, the inner world is sealed off, trapping the alter personalities inside with their own pre-programmed reality. These alter personalities trapped in inner structures are stuck at a certain age and level of development where they still believe in fairy tales and magic. They are unable to discern reality from fiction. They are also totally unable to distinguish between the inner and the outer world (...) They are isolated with only their personal belief system, personality traits and skills, everything that has been programmed for them."[493]

In her book *"Restoring Survivors of Satanic Ritual Abuse: Equipping and Releasing God's People for Spirit-Empowered Ministry"*, therapist Patricia Baird Clarke has written a chapter on inner world structures and magical surgery. Based on Scripture, she also explains that satanic ritual abuse (through trauma and extreme dissociation) will split the physical and spiritual bodies, opening up a breach to other dimensions, as we saw in the previous chapter. Here is the full chapter which explains what this 'inner world' is from a therapist's point of view:

---

[493] Ibid, pp.77-78.

We are going to look at what we may encounter in a person who has suffered satanic ritual abuse, causing a very complex psychic state. These people are usually born into families that practice Satanism and ritual abuse from generation to generation. Not everyone who has suffered this kind of abuse will have the complex internal structures that we will now discuss and detail; however, it is to be expected that such structures and personality fragmentations will be found, as these people are not at all rare. Those called upon to work spiritually on the subject of ritual abuse will need the practical knowledge given in this chapter.

Satanic ritual abuse and the I.D.T. it provokes create an incredibly complex inner state. The following concepts may seem bizarre or surreal to those new to the subject. However, we must bear in mind that the things we are going to describe, which seem extraordinary, represent the victims' perception of life and reality. Everything they say must be treated with respect and great care, no matter how fantastic it may seem to you. Demons are summoned and "placed" in the person to keep the alter separate, inaccessible to the victim. Specific negative emotions and cult activities are assigned to each alter. These alters work to bring the victim completely under the control of the cult. The victim then becomes a kind of 'zombie', a real hell. The split individual is forced to form a dark inner world through constant violence and demonic programming. The Hebrew word for darkness is 'cho-shek', which means misery, destruction, death, ignorance, sadness and wickedness. The objective of the occultist torturers is to imprison their victim in a web of misery, destruction, zombification where there is no escape. The person's soul is shattered and each piece (fraction, alter) is entangled in a maze of dungeons, prisons, traps, etc... This is their inner world.

Victims are left extremely traumatised and broken, they are in a state of great confusion. Most of them do not understand what happened to them. All they know is that they are suffering and that they need help. The only understanding we have about these occult practices, what they do and why they do it, we learn from these precious people, victims in great pain and totally lost. It is difficult to reconstruct an accurate picture of their inner world, how it works and why it was created. By combining my experience with victims of ritual abuse with my knowledge of the Holy Scriptures, I have developed my own theory to explain what we are dealing with. We know from the scriptures that we have a spirit, a soul and a body.

1 Thess 5.23: "May the God of peace himself sanctify you completely, and may your whole being, spirit, soul and body, be preserved blameless at the coming of our Lord Jesus Christ! He who calls you is faithful, and he will do it."

In Genesis 2:7 we are shown how we were created in three parts. "The Lord God formed man of the dust of the ground, and breathed into his nostrils the breath of life, and man became a living being."

The breath of God became the spirit of man. When the breath of God came into contact with the body of man, the soul was formed and these three elements are joined together in us. In Hebrews 4:12 we read that Jesus (Himself the Word of God) at one point separated the soul from the spirit. For the Word of God is living and effective, sharper than any two-edged sword, piercing even to the division of soul and spirit, of joints and marrow, and is a judge of the thoughts and feelings of the heart.

I believe that as long as our mind is connected to our soul and body, we are not able to 'see' into the spiritual realm. This is what God has intended for us since Satan and demons can appear as 'angels of light' and deceive us. God wants us to be innocent of evil.

Romans 16:19b: 'I desire you to be wise in what is good and simple in what is evil'. This concept of the separation of spirit and soul is difficult to explain because there is a separation of soul and spirit by Jesus, who is good. When we have matured our Christian faith and put to death our selfish motives, we become aware of the separation of soul and spirit. This means that our good works that come from our soul are not linked to the carnal motives of our spirit. This separation is not total, as there is still a link that holds our soul in our body. We become more aware of the Holy Spirit and then have more spiritual discernment, but yet we still remain "plugged in" to the physical body. However, through satanic ritual abuse, there is a seemingly sudden and total separation of soul and spirit, which then allows the person to see and hear demons.

In Cor 15:44 we read: 'He is sown in the animal body, he is raised in the spiritual body, there is an animal body and there is a spiritual body'. So we know that we have a physical body and a spiritual body. It is through this biological body that we have physical contact with the material world around us. We are not aware that we have a spiritual body until our physical body dies. This is what God intended for us. Through rituals, Satanists use demons to separate the spiritual body from the physical body. When the soul and spirit have been separated and the spiritual body has been separated from the physical body, then the person enters in a fully conscious way into a whole other dimension. This is the dimension I call the inner world. This world is as vast and as real to the individual as the physical world is to us. We think of spirits as having a 'vaporous' state, but people who have been in this dimension have reported to me that demons do have weight and substance.

This inner world is a world of demonic spirits and alter personalities and is accessible through the mind, through thought, specifically through the imagination. People who practice transcendental meditation or who seek (non-embodied) spirit guides, for example, use their imagination to communicate with the realm of evil spirits. God has given us an imagination, which is not a bad thing in itself, because we can use it for fabulous inventions of great use to humanity. We can use our imagination like Jesus did when he taught his disciples and told them to cast their nets on the right side of the boat. Imagination can be used for good as well as for evil.

When spiritual work is done on alter personalities, when memories come up, there comes a time when the person is in great distress stating that their "right side seems to be separated from their left side". At this point, a demon must be expelled from the person. This will be helpful for the person, but it will not release them from the connection to that particular spiritual dimension they are experiencing. This sense of division can occur through the memory of the ritual that caused the splitting. One woman described a ceremony where Satanists use the scriptures of 'Hebrews 4:12', but in a completely twisted way. In this ritual, a real sword is held over the victim and demons are summoned to split and divide the victim.

Because of the spiritual dimension that person is in, he or she is able to see and experience these objects as if they were a real thing identical to our three-dimensional world. Satanists use this for control purposes. For example, the child could be taken on a trip to Germany and there be shown a castle in great detail, both inside and out. The child will experience a few very stressful days in this castle, going through different rituals in the various rooms. The child is forced to memorise the castle layout. A miniature replica of this castle in the style of a doll's house will be built, a three-dimensional model with which the child can deeply integrate its structure. Once the castle has been memorised, the child is subjected to "magic surgery", i.e. he is told that the miniature model of the castle will be placed inside him just as he himself is placed inside the castle (editor's note: here we find a scheme of mise en abyme, just like the graphic representations of the painter Escher based on duality and mirror effects. According to Fritz Springmeier, the inversions, mirror images, illusions and other trompe l'oeil contained in Escher's paintings are excellent supports for the mental programming of split subjects.) The castle is now "inside" the child and becomes a workable structure for the internal world. In this inner world, it is now possible to walk through the different rooms of the castle in a way that is as real as in the physical world. In the rituals that follow this "surgery", the child will disassociate many times and the alter personalities that are born will then be programmed to take up residence in different rooms of the castle. These rooms will be guarded by outside entities, demons, and traps will be strategically placed so that there is no escape for the partitioned alter. These castles are cold and dark, filled with rats and snakes and torture chambers, it is a powerful control structure. If an alter does not submit, does not do exactly as commanded, he will be handed over to the demons in a torture chamber of the castle. This is extremely painful for the victim as the spiritual senses are heightened. According to some accounts, the spiritual senses are stronger than the physical ones. The pain experienced in this inner world is even transmitted to the physical body. When a Christian is willing to devote his life to Christ, the Lord gives him exceptional authority in this matter. Jesus Christ knows how to protect the alter when it starts to speak. HE gives us the power to lock up all demons and HE puts the alters in a place where they cannot be found and retaliated against.

With this magical surgery, the occultists place traps all over the inner world of the person. Of course, these things are not really inside, but because the child believes they are there, the demons can use them to control him. Satanists are well aware that an alter will eventually have the opportunity to start speaking and testifying outside the cult. In order to keep them silent, or to punish them for speaking out, traps are strategically placed that will be triggered with certain triggers whenever the system is threatened. These traps can be as perverse as a demon can imagine. A very common trap is the bomb. One afternoon I noticed that a woman who had just accessed some memories of abuse had not had a drink all day. After consulting the Lord, he revealed to me that there was a bomb inside her ready to explode if she drank anything. She was absolutely terrified. I asked the Lord to take it out of her, which He did. She was then able to drink two large glasses of water. In this inner world, it is her beliefs that bind and hold the victim. A demon can simulate the internal explosion of a bomb and the person will have the sound and pain of that "explosion. Many of these tools are designed to destroy the life or sanity of the person who begins to speak. This is just one example of why this type of treatment can only be done successfully by a Christian who will rely on Jesus Christ to do the work. If an atheist had tried to remove this bomb, it would have exploded and the woman would have needed medication and possibly even hospitalization. A lady once described to me what had happened to her when well-meaning believers had tried to drive the demons out of her. A bomb exploded and she literally felt shrapnel pierce every part of her body. The shards were actually demonic entities being propelled into her arms, legs, head... every part of her body... the bomb burst was accompanied by an implanted command telling her to kill those who tried to help her, and then to run outside and throw herself under a car. She knew what was happening, but it was totally out of control. Two men were present to control her but two other people had to step in to help hold her down.

Through magical surgery, anything from the physical world can be placed in a person's inner world. These are some of the things commonly found in this other dimension of being. These objects, intended to control the victim, can only be removed by the Grace of the Lord. Most of them are related to painful memories of abuse and will be removed as the memory is processed and integrated, but this is not always the case. This is why it is important to leave the reins to the Lord.

- Computers: The computer can be used by demons and/or an alter to control an object or alter personality in the system.

- Telephones: The person can actually hear the voice of the abuser giving instructions, the voice is obviously that of a demon. If the abuser wants the person to go to a certain place at a certain time, he calls a demon who will activate the telephone to transmit the instructions to the victim. A demon has the ability to perfectly reproduce the voice of a human but also its physical appearance.

- Tape recorders: These can play humiliating things, nasty and hurtful remarks. They can play instructions over and over again to get certain behaviours. For example, if the person receives an external compliment, a "recorded" voice will counter by saying humiliating things. Again, this is demonic trickery.

- Video/DVD tapes: With these tools, horrific scenes of human or other torture can be projected into the person's mind.

- Alarm clocks: These can be set to ring at different times of the night or day so that the person can never get a good night's sleep. (Editor's note: Cathy O'Brien reports in her autobiography how automatic 'mental alarm clocks' were implanted in her and her daughter so that they never got more than two hours sleep in a row).

- Oven: An oven may be used to suck all the energy out of the person or energetically drain an alter for destruction. The oven can keep the person overheated to perpetuate the trauma.

- Labyrinths: Alters are often trapped in labyrinths. Jesus will be able to get them out and destroy the maze.

These are just a few examples of things that are commonly found in the inner world of victims of satanic ritual abuse. The possibilities are endless, because with this magical surgery, everything in this physical world can be transferred to the inner world.

For people born into transgenerational satanic families, the abuse may begin at gestation, in the womb. A foetus can be traumatised in various ways, by electric shocks, needles, shocks to the mother's womb, rape of the mother, etc.

It is likely that they are using a device to measure the baby's heart rate. When the heart rate increases and then suddenly drops significantly, it is a sign that the baby is entering a state of dissociation in the womb. Occultists try to obtain 6, 13 or even 18 fragmentations from gestation, these are satanic numbers of power. However, they do not always succeed in obtaining these desired numbers. Each fragmentation of the foetus in the womb becomes a "seed" which will then be split up again to feed the different levels of the internal structure of the person with alter personalities.

The organisation of the internal world is not random. It is a structure in which every personality alter and every object is meticulously and strategically placed.

This structure will have as many levels, as there were fragmentations in the womb. If the victim has been fragmented 13 times in the womb, the internal structure will have 13 levels. In some cases, the number of divisions in the womb will not be as many as desired, so the newborn will be immediately split to complete the number of levels. These different levels, which can also be called strata or layers, should have a geometric shape that will often be the same for each level. For example, if a square has been used, each level will be square. They can also be formed by combinations of geometric shapes, for example squares combined with triangles or circles.

Each level is divided into sections, or rooms, in which the alters are 'under house arrest'. Guardians (demons) are stationed at strategic points on each level. Underneath all of these layers, there is usually some sort of pit, which will sometimes have as many levels as the base structure itself. The different levels are connected by staircases (often circular, spiral) with a doorway dividing each level. This system is similar to an apartment building but the design may be more sophisticated. The levels are not necessarily the same size and may be at different angles to each other. Often the levels are designed to rotate or spiral (ed. note: carousel system). The whole complex structure is therefore "injected" into the child's inner world at a very young age. A model of the structure can be built so that the child can visualise and memorise it. The child will eventually memorise it perfectly, including the location of the guardian entities in each level and the location of the seed-alters in each level. Then, using magical surgery, the structure is placed inside him and he is told that he must grow with it. During the 'surgery', the child believes that he has been opened from the throat down to his lower abdomen and that this structure now fills the entire trunk of his body.

Each alter created in the womb by a dissociative split will be assigned to a particular level of the structure. This alter becomes the "founding seed" that will fill that level of the structure with multiple other alters, all splits of this alter-core. This means that this alter-core will undergo a whole series of splits during successive traumas.

The top level of the structure is called the 'public level'. This is where the alter performing the tasks of daily life (host personalities) are housed. These are the ones who will manage family life, etc., these are the ones who communicate with the outside world... These alters are generally unaware of the existence of other, deeper alters until they reveal themselves one day through outside help. These "public" alters know nothing about the lower level alters, or even that a complex multi-level structure can exist. The upper level alters have been programmed into the victim to cope with daily life, these groups of alters are sometimes called the "home system" or the "public level". This level usually has a small number of personalities: 7 or 8. The area of this top level will be the smallest of all the levels (the tip of the iceberg). As we progress through the structure to its depths, we will find larger and more densely populated levels. It is common to find hundreds of alter in the lower levels. The deeper the level, the darker the alters will be as they are engaged in the "dark side", i.e. the occult activities of the group. Alters residing in the deepest lower levels know absolutely everything about the higher levels and are able to take control of the entire higher system. The most powerful and darkest alter are at the lowest level, in the deepest programming layer. When these alter from the deepest layers want to take control of the body, they go up through the doors, give a password to the guardian demons and thus access the higher levels, the public levels. The host personalities of this public level are not empowered to resist the occultist alter of the deep. An alter from the depths can punish and torture an alter from the 'public level' if the latter has spoken or committed any other infraction of the rules. After some time in ministry, it may be helpful to pray and ask the Lord to seal the doors so that the lower level alters and demons can no longer ascend to the "public level" to cause disorder. However, this is not something to be done systematically... God has led me to do this for some people, but with others, He has instructed me differently. We must be open to the Lord's guidance.

An alter can be programmed to be anyone or anything, depending on the programmer's will or the victim's needs. Someone who has been tortured in such a complex way knows only one coping mechanism: dissociation. By this means, the cult deliberately creates alter personalities to serve its unhealthy purpose, and the victim creates alter personalities to cope with the life he or she must continue to lead. Therefore, some alter personalities will be designated to work for the cult, while others will have a role in helping and supporting the abused person. There are also neutral alters, who do not fit into either category. Cult alter are created by particular rituals, they have various functions such as teaching, storing information, performing specific rituals, making the victim follow a certain schedule when going to ceremonies, attracting demons to them, storing satanic energy, blocking any advice from Christians, managing programming etc. This complex system will ensure that there will be many alters in charge of killing the victim if she comes into contact with Christian counsellors who can begin to free her. The programmers give a complete identity to the cult alter, sometimes even with their own physical characteristics. For example, the victim may be overweight and old, but to the controlling alter, her body is that of a slender young teenager. These cult alters may go against the well-being of the individual to the point of even trying to kill them, when it is necessary to remember that they inhabit the same body... yet they often vehemently deny this reality by saying degrading things about the person's physical appearance or personality. At this point, it is helpful to have them look in a mirror to show how the cult has deceived them. It is also not uncommon for them to say that the mirrors are things that the cult has warned them about. I then tell them to keep quiet while they look in the mirror, this will often convince them that they have been totally deceived. Many of them will gladly give up their self-destructive murderer programming when they realise that they would have actually committed suicide. Satanists access alter through the use of triggers, such as names, flashing lights, tones, numbers, etc. Through abuse and programming, the victim effectively becomes like a human computer accessible to anyone with the program and access codes. These alter can also be activated by other means. Some are activated by demons that the cult summons during rituals. Other alters have been created and programmed to emerge and become active at a specific time. For example, if the cult has decided that a person should die at the age of 50, an alter with self-destruct programming will activate at the age of 50. The cult's astrologers have known for eons when certain celestial phenomena will occur. For example, a full moon falling on the same day as an eclipse on a Friday the 13th (which happened in March 1998). These things are anticipated years in advance by Satanists. Some alter may therefore have been programmed to emerge on that day to lead the person into a ritual where they will have a particular function. Each cult alter must be delivered from demons and converted to Jesus Christ. This is usually done in 15 to 30 minutes. Jesus gives them a new function so that they can work in a constructive way and participate in the person's welfare. These worship alters have a lot of information that will be very helpful in reaching other alters. For example, I encountered a case where an alter named Bobby had tried to kill the host personality in my presence. Jesus gave him the task of revealing to me where all the traps in the system were. Bobby had been programmed to memorise the traps on the first 7 levels out of a total of 13 levels making up the internal structure. Once he was "on our side", this alter became a valuable asset to the victim's recovery. Other cult alters are fully aware that they live in the body of the host personality, but they still work against it. Some of these alters, whom I call "kamikaze alters," are so attached to the dark side that they will gladly sacrifice their own lives to kill the victim. Some will be won over by Jesus Christ, others will not, even if they can see and hear him. In this case, Jesus simply removes them. A woman with a very complex I.D.T. will have many male alterations. They may appear early in the healing ministry, or they may not appear for several months, but they are there. It is also common to encounter an alter who believes he is a dog. He will not be able to speak but only bark. It is then necessary to ask another observant alter to speak for him, he will be a precious help. A question that can be asked is how can someone come to believe that he is a dog? Satanists like to dehumanise their victims. The less human they feel, the better they will come into contact with the demons by adopting their behaviour (demons are bestial). This type of programming is really quite brutal. For example, they will place the child naked in a pen with dogs for up to a week. The child is not allowed to behave like a human. He is not allowed to stand, talk, eat and drink with his hands and he will sleep on the floor. He has to get around on all fours to eat and drink from a bowl like a dog. He will be raped several times by male dogs. Some alter can be a kitten. I met one of these alters while listening to the victim talk about her techniques/attempts to cope with the violence. A little girl's alter then told me that she had noticed that the kittens on her family's farm were being neglected. She thought that perhaps if she became a kitten herself, her abusers would leave her alone. Some of these alter animals will not be able to speak other than a simple "meow", but others will require an alter mediator to speak on their behalf. Still others, due to various programming, may believe they are aliens or robots. One woman recalled being subjected to a week of dog programming, followed by a week of ET programming and a third of robot programming. At the end of the three weeks she had no idea who she was, all she knew was that she was not human. One of the most memorable alters I met was "Rubber Man". He was part of the "public level", he had been created by the victim to do incredible things that his horrible stepmother forced him to do. Being made of rubber, he could stretch his arms and legs to reach inaccessible places and perform seemingly impossible tasks. He was particularly good at washing windows or cleaning gutters. But the "rubber man" never spoke... he sang in a loud rhyming voice and liked to cheer up the host personality when it was feeling sad (editor's note: Cathy O'Brien reports that one of her sisters, Kelly Jo, has an alter with programming for prostitution with which she becomes as flexible as "Gumby").Many alters, especially baby or child alters, will have no particular function. They may be locked up in dark dungeons, pits, prisons, etc., they are terrified and miserable. These alters are often "residue", or "collateral damage", created when the person is subjected to increasing degrees of pain and terror during rituals and programming. In order to produce the desired cult alter, Satanists subject the person to unbearable pain that will result in several dissociations, with each successive alter created being stronger and more connected to the darkness than the last. For example, if the person dissociates five times before the desired alter is created, the first four alters are not taken into account by the cult, which will not take any interest in them. They are therefore considered useless and are locked up in a sort of prison or dungeon, they are "put in the wardrobe". Sometimes an alter with very little insight may show up but not answer questions. Chances are that this is a pre-verbal alter (infant or baby). It is necessary to ask if another alter can then come and speak on its behalf. I came across the case of a 53 year old woman recently. With her hair covering her face, she was staring at me while sucking her thumb and rubbing the top of her nose with her index finger. She was obviously very frightened but also curious. When she didn't answer any of the questions I asked her, I asked if someone could speak for her. It was then that I met 11-year-old Lisa, who told me about the abuse Rini had suffered. Rini then came back and I asked Jesus to deliver her, and as he often does, he sent a little lamb to her. I saw how she stroked the lamb, how she laughed when it snuggled into her neck. After a short time with the lamb, she looked up at Jesus in total awe and then raised her arms for Him to come and get her. She then seemed to relax and rested her head on His shoulder as He took her to a safe place.[494]

6 - THE TRANCE STATE AND THE 'TRIGGERS'

The trance state can be defined by three criteria:
- Altered consciousness.
- Partial or total amnesia as a result of the trance.
- Presence of at least one alternative personality during the trance.

The extreme physical and emotional conditions of ritual abuse have a heavy impact on the child, especially with the combination of these trance states. It is important to look at the role of these altered states of consciousness in the process of mind control of children. When they are in a trance state they are more open to indoctrination and techniques to control their minds and behaviour. For example, a child in a trance who hears an adult tell him that Satan is in charge will deeply integrate this belief, much more than if he were in a normal waking state. There are many ways to put the child into these altered states of consciousness during ritual abuse. The ritual itself contains several trance-inducing elements: chanting, isolation, sensory deprivation and pain through all forms of extreme torture. Trance states are also induced by hypnosis and drugs. These experiences have a profound and lasting impact on the beliefs, feelings and behaviours of victims, despite the fact that they cannot always remember them consciously. Only later in life, usually with the help of a trained therapist, will some ritually abused victims be able to laboriously reconstruct what happened when they were in a trance or dissociative state.[495]

The programming works with *triggers*, which are access codes such as names, phrases, flashes of light, a tone, a voice with a particular tone, which allow the programmers, masters or superiors of the cult to have access to the alter personalities of the victims. This also allows the programmer to have access to the internal structures in order to modify them or retrieve information if necessary. The internal system can indeed be used to store information that will be held by a hypermnesic alter, data that can only be accessed with certain access codes. The information can also be stored in the subconscious, which is then

---

[494] Restoring Survivors of Satanic Ritual Abuse: Equipping and Releasing God's People for Spirit-Empowered Ministry " - Patricia Baird Clark, 2000.

[495] Report of the Ritual Abuse Task Force Los Angeles County Commission for Women, 1989.

used as a real secure hard disk. All these manipulations are done without the victim being aware of them.

The previously programmed functions are performed unconsciously, or with some awareness of obligation to do or not to do something. Alters trapped in internal structures will obey implanted commands until they are released. These types of programming can control a person's thoughts and actions for decades, usually without any awareness. Survivors of ritual abuse and MKs begin to recover memories between the ages of 30 and 50. It takes many more years before the victim becomes aware of the programming and its ongoing effects on them. Uncovering these internal structures often requires outside help to enable the survivor to access this information safely due to self-destructive programming.[496]

The naming of alter personalities is a central point in mind control. The programmer will systematically name the created alter because it will automatically perceive itself as belonging to the person who identified it by giving it a name. The names of the alter, the access codes, the various triggering stimuli, will enable the mechanisms of mental control to be triggered and the programming to be accessed.

Trauma-based mind control relies on the ability to unconsciously induce in the victim the fear of reliving the abuse and torture, so that he or she complies with the directives and commands implanted during programming. The American psychologist Joseph LeDoux, who has studied emotional memory, has focused his research on the link between memory and emotion, particularly on the mechanisms of fear. His work gives us insight into how MK programming works. In his book *"The Emotional Brain: The Mysterious Underpinnings of Emotional Life"*, he shows that there are two long-term memory systems in humans: an explicit, conscious, cognitive and verbal memory system and an implicit, unconscious, emotional and non-verbal memory system (as we have already seen in chapter 5). His research reveals that the unconscious memory system of fear and pain can *"represent an indelible form of learning"*. In post-traumatic responses, he writes that *"a stimulus associated with the danger of the trauma can become a built-in trigger that can provoke emotional responses in us.* LeDoux calls this form of conditioning *"fear conditioning"*. It is this fear conditioning that appears to be a fundamental element in the functioning of MK programming. LeDoux's research shows that emotional information is relayed through the amygdala during automatic, unconscious coping mechanisms during trauma, and that this *fear conditioning* operates independently of consciousness, which he calls *the emotional unconscious*. This largely unconscious emotional system affects the conscious cognitive system more strongly than the other way around. Thus, he says, *"people usually do all sorts of things for reasons they are not aware of, because these behaviours are produced by mechanisms in the brain that operate unconsciously.* Survivors report that programmers intentionally use torture and drugs to try to block the victims' conscious cognitive processing ability. This fear-conditioning of the trauma will therefore control the alter

---

[496] The Relationship Between Mind Control Programming and Ritual Abuse ", Ellen P. Lacter.

personalities. Fear-conditioned responses will automatically be carried out without awareness, without cognitive awareness. Conditioned and programmed triggers, such as the voice of the perpetrator, a hand signal, a word or series of words, etc., can then induce uncontrolled fear and pain in the unconscious emotional memory. This will then cause the person to behave in a conditioned and programmed way to avoid actually feeling the pain and terror that they already unconsciously perceive in this traumatic emotional memory.[497]

The fact that some events are not consciously remembered does not mean that they have no significant impact on the individual's life. Until the memories return and can be worked on and integrated in a safe environment, the victim of such abuse will always be controlled to some extent by their past experiences. The survivor may therefore react strongly when something or some event reminds him/her of this heavy past (consciously or unconsciously). For example, if the survivor was ritually abused as a child during each full moon, as an adult he or she may feel compelled to join the cult to participate in the full moon ceremonies. Or he or she may be "driven" to perform an act of physical or sexual violence on a particular date or in response to a trigger in the environment. This may also manifest as self-destructive compulsions to cope with the anxiety associated with this dissociative memory of the traumatic event.

Therapist Ellen P. Lacter has observed several indicators of programming in her patients. For example, he will suddenly change his state in response to a detail that triggers a kind of robotic state with a rigid posture, blank eyes and an inability to hear or respond to anything. Then he'll start wanting to go somewhere or go to the phone... Four of his patients reported an identical trigger code related to the same kind of programming. The code was about ten characters long with the same prefixes or suffixes and with only a few spelling variations. Yet this code is not referenced in any books or on the internet and these people lived in remote areas.[498]

Dr. James Randall Noblitt reports that some of his patients have reported that phone calls or knocks on their door in a particular way bring out an alter personality programmed to submit to anyone using that trigger signal. Many therapists have reported similar information that overlaps from patient to patient. Dr. Cory Hammond, in his lecture entitled *"The Greenbaum Lecture,"* said, *"When you start collecting the same information, of a highly esoteric nature, in different states from Florida to California, and in different countries, you start to think that something is going on... That this is a large-scale, very well-coordinated, systematic, and highly organised phenomenon.... So we found the same phenomenon in many different places (...) It's time to share more information between therapists."*

In his book *Cult and Ritual Abuse*, Dr. James Randall Noblitt reports that some of his patients describe the same types of child abuse involving ritual and

---

[497] "Ritual Abuse and Mind-Control", Chap: The manipulation of attachment" - Torture-based mind control: psychological mechanisms and psychotherapeutic approaches to overcoming mind control, Ellen P. Lacter.

[498] Ibid.

sadistic acts. These patients had no interaction with each other, came from different geographical locations, religions and socio-economic backgrounds. Despite these notable differences, these individuals not only shared similar memories of traumatic rituals, but also exhibited similarly structured internal systems of I.D.D. Some alter patient personalities even seemed to recognise other patients, Dr. Noblitt writes: *"I was saying goodbye to a male patient diagnosed with I.D.D. and I invited another patient, 'Alice', into my office. Once in the room, Alice shifted into another alter, she was now behaving like a frightened child, "Why is Robert James coming to see you? Don't you know he is very dangerous? Because of medical confidentiality I could not say anything about this patient who had just left my office. I couldn't even say that he was a patient of mine. His real name was Robert Dale. Robert James was one of his secret cult names. How come Alice recognized him, and identified him with his cult name? To my knowledge he had not told anyone about this name, at least outside the cult, just as to my knowledge he had never met Alice before. He didn't even seem to recognise her when they met in the waiting room. Alice had also identified three other patients of mine, two of them by their cult names, which she said were linked to rituals she underwent in early childhood (...) Alice was also recognised by alter personalities of two other patients who, in consultation, revealed that they each knew each other from past cult activities."*[499]

Noblitt also writes that the power that exists within the Satanic/Luciferian cults is reflected in a very strict pyramidal hierarchical organisation. Some of the higher positions are held permanently by the same individuals, however in some Gnostic traditions, the relatively important positions (priestess, priest) may be rotational. These hierarchical levels vary in number from one organisation to another and will also have different names such as Knight, Prince, Priest, High Priest, King, etc.

As one member moves up the hierarchy, more information about the programming and trigger codes used in the ceremonies is revealed to them about the other members of the cult. Some of these triggers are generic, basic access codes that can be used to control relatively large numbers of people. This is why therapist Ellen Lacter reported that four of her patients had identical triggers linked to the same programming. According to Dr. Noblitt, the trigger *"Deep"* or *"Deeper"* seems to be a common keyword. When used repeatedly or discreetly placed in conversation, many survivors of these cults will typically enter a trance state where they will show noticeable signs of a change in consciousness, such as a change in gaze and posture.

Noblitt explains that cult members who move up the hierarchy will not only have access to a variety of trigger codes that they can use to control people at lower levels, but they will also undergo an 'upgrade' so that these generic triggers no longer have as much hold and control over themselves. Thus, survivors who have risen to the highest ranks of these cult groups have been conditioned and programmed with much more specific and complex triggers so that the majority of other members cannot control them by having access to their

---

[499] *"Cult and Ritual Abuse"* - James Randall Noblitt and Pamela Perskin Noblitt, 2014, p.90.

programming. Such control is reserved for the elite in the upper echelons of the hierarchy, they have more advanced knowledge of the triggers and more sophisticated access codes to their own programming. While low-level cult members are used by leaders for all sorts of things, they can in some cases move up the hierarchy and be taught the protocols for accessing the programming of other members, and so in turn hold incredible power to control.[500]

Mental control with its access codes to programming is therefore an essential point in Luciferian occultism, in the "nameless religion". It is the major tool of domination because it is undetectable. In the Greenbaum lecture, Dr. Cory Hammond reports that some survivors may also have identification codes. This code includes their date of birth, it may also include where they were programmed, as well as other information about their family or the cult. As noted above, the subconscious mind and alters can serve as a hard drive for storing all sorts of information. When Mark Phillips began deprogramming Cathy O'Brien, he discovered bank account numbers, for example. According to him deprogramming is just like hacking. Just as you can hack into a computer, you can hack into the 'hard drive' of an MK slave...

Very early on, once the alter personalities have been created, the children in these groups will be programmed with simple, basic triggers using the tactile and visual senses. These touch triggers are very important in controlling a child. To the outside world, most of these innocuous gestures just look like affectionate touches. These triggers will usually be learned through a combination of play and pain, punishment and reward. These programmings are done through repetition when the child is in altered states of consciousness.

The alter personalities of *Grand Master, High Priest* or *High Priestess*, are considered the most important and hierarchically highest. A child destined for such positions will possess alter personalities who will receive various training in secret esoteric languages, high forms of black magic and demonology. According to Fritz Springmeier, in the Luciferian hierarchies, these deepest alter personalities, i.e. those linked to the world of occultism, will have goddess or god-like names, king or queen names. These are the names that the programmer or cult will use to identify them, but they are not trigger codes per se. Access codes follow patterns, it may be a standard and unique code. Passages from the Bible are very often used to encode triggers, but also extracts from popular fiction books. Access codes for the deeper layers of programming will have esoteric content, for example in Enochian languages, often languages foreign to the country of origin will be used. The nature of the codes will also be related to the branch of the cult, e.g. a Druidic group will use Druidic symbols, a Kabbalist group will use Kabalistic codes. An internal system can easily have six different languages used as programming codes, but imaginary words can also be implemented as well as sign language codes. Gematria (cabalistic teachings on numbers) also plays an important role in creating access codes to the deepest and darkest alter personalities, related to occultism and witchcraft. That said, most alter personalities have all been more or less indoctrinated into the occult. There

---

[500] Ibid p.158.

are several reasons why Monarch slaves have many internal codes and structures related to esotericism and witchcraft. First of all, it is because the programmers are usually practising high occultism themselves and their worldview is based on these things, so they transcribe this into the MK programming. Secondly, the slaves are drawn back into their connection to Satan and his cult as soon as they are triggered by these codes of an occult nature. Thirdly, the use of 'magic' words as triggers will also reinforce the belief that programming is real magic.[501] Overall, anything related to the ritual abuse the victim has suffered can potentially be a trigger for the traumatic memory: colours, jewellery, clothes, books, films, food, drink, a birth or birthday...

Survivor Jay Parker states that the MK-Monarch system also uses nature and its symbology to reinforce and perpetuate the programming. The repetition of ritual abuse according to a certain occult calendar based on lunar and planetary cycles will permeate every cell of the little victims, even more so when they are spiritually "unlocked" during the rituals, as we saw in the previous chapter. Thereafter, it is the date-specific gravitational fields that act as triggers. For example, during full moons, when the traumatic memory is particularly charged because of the important rituals that systematically take place there, as well as at the summer solstices (20-21 June) or winter solstices (21-22 December). When the planets are in certain positions, whether the victim is 15 or 50 years old, the unconsciously perceived gravitational field at the cellular level will help to trigger the traumatic memory in the victim again, to bring him or her into "phase" with the ceremonies that are to take place. For programming to be effective, it must be activated, reinforced and updated regularly by visual or auditory stimuli. These 'reminders' or 'triggers' need to be ubiquitous in everyday life in order to reach MK subjects. Survivor Trish Fotheringham wrote: *"Lullabies, songs, stories, well-known TV productions and movies; every time I hear these things in my daily life, outside of formal programming, the beliefs of my alter personalities are subconsciously solidified."*[502]

According to some authors, this is one of the reasons why we see more and more occult symbolism flourishing in the mass media, especially in the entertainment industry (music and fashion); the most recurrent 'trigger' sign being *the single eye* usually represented by an individual who somehow has a masked eye (generic trigger). These different signs serve on the one hand to stimulate the commands implanted in the MK subjects, on the other hand they are implanted in the popular lay culture, in the collective unconscious. MK-type programming is also coordinated with the general media propaganda to which the general public is subjected. This creates a kind of continuum of mental programming that consists of controlling the mass but also the leaders of society. Many politicians in key positions are mind-controlled individuals who have been programmed with implanted commands. The coordination (matching) of an

---

[501] "The Illuminati Formula Used to Create an Undetectable Total Mind Controlled Slave" - Fritz Springmeier & Cisco Wheeler 1996.

[502] "Healing the Unimaginable: Treating Ritual Abuse and Mind Control" - Alison Miller, 2012, p.77.

implanted sentence in a victim with a propaganda sentence repeated over and over in the mass media prevents the mind of the programmed victim from becoming discordant. The brainwashed politician will believe that he is perfectly aligned with society because his programming is constantly reflected in it through the mass media: the matrix. Modern society is based on individual and global mind control and the massive propaganda that sustains all of this programming. As we will see in Chapter 9 on the entertainment industry, Luciferian occultism is being vulgarised to create a kind of hegemonic MK culture that is gradually imprinted on the collective unconscious. This means that these occult practices are applied on a large scale, with very large means, and that they directly affect the ruling classes.

7 - SOME TESTIMONIES:

a/ Jay Parker

Jay Parker was born into a family practicing satanic ritual abuse and MK-Monarch programming from generation to generation. In April 2011, Parker gave a talk in Philadelphia (*Free Your Mind: A Conference On Consciousness, Mind-Control & The Occult*), excerpts from which include:
Satanic ritual abuse is an occult system of mind control. This occult system is the opposite of Truth, of life, it is in total opposition to natural laws. It is essentially the antithesis of nature... a huge lie. It is a system that is compartmentalised and controlled by a minority, whereas nature and our reality is actually a system based on openness where we must share everything equally. The religious system of Satanic ritual abuse and occultism is found in a certain mysticism. Their mysticism is a religious practice in which an outside power will control your life and your destiny. You are then a mere cog in a machine. This mysticism is a complete lie because we are born with spiritual, mental and emotional faculties that give us the opportunity to live a creative and fully positive life. The Illuminati have a caste system and this system is based on bloodlines. It is a very strict hierarchy, so if you are born into the Rockefeller family, for example, you are already "in the thick of it", you will be one of the great controllers. In this system, if the cult detects that you have particular mental or mediumistic faculties, you will be able to access specific positions. Today, it is these Illuminati lineages from ancient Babylon that are in complete control of the system. There is strictly no sharing with this group, it's all between them, they work with each other... with this very particular old vibration...
Ritual abuse is a system of physical and emotional trauma, the purpose of which is to create a mind-controlled slave who will obey and serve the worst occultists throughout his or her life. At birth you are in alignment and harmony with the natural energies of this planet. Your synaptic connections, in the first six years, are in full development, you are in 'recording' mode, you cannot critically differentiate the information that comes to you. You store it and build your subconscious mind with it, which will later direct 99% of your adult life.

So imagine the result if during your first six years of life you were programmed with negativity, lies and mysticism, instead of Truth... When the synaptic, or neural, pathways are disrupted by, for example, electric shocks, your mental body and emotional body will be in such a state of terror that your physical body will produce and release certain hormones. These hormones will become a chemistry that your body will feed on daily. Just like Pavlov's dogs, who salivated at the sound of the bell, thinking they were starving... The Monarch mind control system has the same effect as Pavlov's conditioned dogs.

It takes years to program an individual. It is something that is systematic and has been going on for hundreds of years. 10% of the world's population practices this ancient religion that goes back to the old Satanist lineages. Anyone who goes through this system, whether you are a simple mechanic born into a Satanist family, or whether you are a banker named Rockefeller: they all go through this system to "veil" the neural connections! The energy they give out and the energy they receive is the very antithesis of nature, it is totally negative. This is why we are in such a situation on this earth. When the neural pathways are clouded, it ends up causing a particular chemistry in the body, so you are gradually programmed as a Monarch slave. You will, for example, suffer from depression at certain times of the lunar cycle when particular rituals are performed, and this goes on continuously throughout your first six years of life. So when the Moon is at certain points, whether you are 15, 20 or 40, the gravitational field will trigger the experience of trauma again, at a subconscious level. It's a very sophisticated system that uses everything in nature, whether it's gravitational fields or symbology, to continually trigger and perpetuate the programming. That's how you stay in a state of permanent obedience (...) Politically, it's both Republicans and Democrats who are involved in this mind control business. It's not just a few people, it's a global system of control (...)

Let me tell you a little bit about my family... My father came from an Illuminati lineage. His family came from Northern Ireland and joined the Order around 1720. When it is said that the Illuminati Order was founded in Bavaria in 1776, it was really just a reorganisation of the sect to announce their plans for a global revolution to establish a New World Order. As we have seen with the French Revolution and the American Revolution, they are acting internationally, in a globalized and coordinated way. So this date of 1776 in Bavaria, is not the founding date of the Illuminati Order, it was just a starting point to actively begin the takeover of the nations of the world.

In public life, my father was not an important person, he was a teacher. But in the occult world, because of his family lineage, his knowledge and his occult power, he obviously had a certain charisma. My mother claimed that she was descended from a 5,000 year old lineage, a legacy of witchcraft passed down from mother to daughter and coming directly from an ancient civilisation. My paternal grandfather was a modest businessman from a small town in New Jersey. But an interesting thing to note is that when he died, 300 people from five neighbouring states, who my family and local people had never seen before, came to his funeral... Now I'm 54, so I've been to a few funerals, it's usually people from the town you live in who are there... and my grandfather was a modest businessman in that town... And there were 300 people there to attend his funeral, some of whom came from Ohio! What triggered such a gathering? The answer is that this was a genuine Illuminati leader. He was not very important behind his desk... But in the field of occult manipulation of society, he was someone important...

When I was five years old, while visiting my maternal grandparents in Pennsylvania, they gave me a small statue of liberty. I said, 'Cool! They told me that it wasn't what I thought it was, but that it was Semiramis, the Queen of Babylon... I distinctly remember insisting for at least ten minutes that it was the Statue of Liberty and not some stupid Queen of Babylon! One thing I would like to say about my family is that even though they are all satanists, they practice mind control and work for the powers that be; there will be a time when true consciousness will emerge their true humanity... You can program a person to be a true psychopath, but you cannot destroy their consciousness. I've seen my parents go completely off the rails with their programming. They killed with glee because they were under control, influenced by some "power". There should come a day when they will want to know who they were, why they were born, so that they will realise that this has gone far too far, so that they can finally say "No" to this cult... But they don't.

b/ Svali

The anonymous author known by the pseudonym 'Svali' is a former occultist, born into a family of Luciferian lineage, who was a trainer (programmer) in the *Illuminati* group in San Diego. After struggling to get out of the cult and programming, she converted to Jesus Christ. While remaining anonymous, she decided to reveal all she knew about this network and the dangers of this worldwide Luciferian cult.

She has written two books, *"Breaking the chain"* and *"Svali speaks"*, which have not been published but are freely available as PDFs on the internet. In 2006, she also gave an exclusive radio interview to journalist Greg Szymanski (*The Investigative Journal*). Svali mysteriously disappeared from circulation shortly after this interview, her website was shut down and her phone line cut off.

In this interview she reveals what she knows at her level about the structure and hierarchical organisation of the *Illuminati* Order. She describes how they systematically program their children, with the programming of obedience, loyalty and faithfulness to the group being the first and most important to be installed. She explains that on the one hand you can have a child trained for prostitution and at the other end of the spectrum, a child trained to become a major government figure, which requires much more complex programming. Adults receive updates to their programming throughout their lives, it is an ongoing process.

Svali explains that this cult works on six main branches of learning: science, military, politics, leadership (high level leaders), education and spirituality. Children are to be trained in each branch. They will be tested and profiled from an early age to find out their skills, and then they will be directed to specialise in one or two particular branches depending on their potential and the cult's planned future activities. The training of the children also includes twelve life disciplines which are:

1/ No need.

2/ No desire.

3/ No wishes.

4/ No scruples.

5/ Be as fit as possible for survival.

6/ Law of silence.

7/ Values of betrayal.

8/ Journeys in space-time (the child will learn the principles of "travel", both internal in consciousness and external in spirit. The objective is also to reach *"enlightenment"*, an ecstatic state of dissociation.

9,10,11/ Sexual trauma, learning to dissociate, erasing feelings, these three stages varying according to the child's future role in the network.

12/ Be faithful to ceremonies/rituals. One of the objectives is also to create a complete separation between daytime and night-time activities for the child.

Svali testifies that she was programmed and at the same time trained at the age of five by a doctor at the University of Washington to become a programmer herself. She says that these people believe that their methods are beneficial and useful to children and their cult, and she herself sincerely believed that she was helping others to develop their potential. Svali divides programming into five main "specialties":

1/ training in silence:

This initial training begins at an early age, even before the child can speak. This programming will be done in different ways: the child is questioned after a ceremony about what he has seen and heard, and if he talks about "bad things", he will be punished, i.e. severely abused. This will be repeated until the child has learnt that he/she must hide the rituals. Generally, these extreme punishments will create an alter who will be a 'guardian' whose role will be to ensure that the child does not remember what he/she sees during the ritual abuse. This alter is conditioned to fear violence if the child remembers. The child may also undergo hypnotic trances to make the worst atrocities seem like a 'bad dream'.

2/ strength training:

This type of training also starts at a very young age, often even as a baby. The child is subjected to a series of conditioning exercises aimed at:

- Increase resistance to pain.
- Increase physical fitness.
- Increase the capacity for dissociation.
- Creating a photographic memory.
- Creating fear and submission through the desire to please.

3/ Loyalty training:

Programming for cult loyalty is the most important. Loyalty is a total commitment to the beliefs and doctrines of the group. Desertion or questioning of these doctrines is rare and the reprisals are obviously very severe. A person who questions the doctrine or refuses to do his work will go back to "re-training", i.e. his programming will be updated and reinforced. To do this they will be shocked and tortured until they submit. Generally adults are sufficiently conditioned to believe that the practices and goals of the group are really positive and constructive things. They are convinced that they are really helping the children. The children hear about hierarchical development within the network and it is put into their heads that they can become leaders in turn. Positions of power in the hierarchy are carrots at the end of a stick to make members work hard for their success. For a higher position in the hierarchy means less abuse and more control over others, which is important in a life that has so little control over itself.

4/ training for one or more functions within the group:

This training is geared towards the work done within worship. Each member has a specific role that will be assigned to him or her from early childhood. Here is a non-exhaustive list of functions:

- Priests and priestesses.
- Cleaners (after the rituals).
- Couriers/transporters.
- Executioners responsible for punishing recalcitrant or erring members.
- Teachers (history of worship, dead languages, etc).
- Prostitutes (Beta Kitten).
- Assassins (Theta, Delta).
- Trainers (MK programmers).
- Scientists (behavioural science).
- Doctors, nurses, medical staff, psychologists, psychiatrists.
- Military leaders (for military-type exercises).
- etc...

These roles are interchangeable and a member can have several functions at the same time. The length of training a child needs will depend on the complexity of the future role they have been assigned. These trainings are based on the reproduction of a 'model' of behaviour, called neuro-linguistic programming (NLP). The child is shown how the adult or adolescent performs his or her function, and once the behavioural model has been visualised and integrated, the child is told that he or she is to be taught it by giving clear guidelines on what is expected of him or her. The work is divided into several chronological stages. The child can be abused to induce a 'tabula rasa', a 'blank' personality that will do whatever it is asked to do. Programming makes extensive use of the gratification versus punishment scheme. If the child performs the commands correctly, he or she is praised and even cajoled, otherwise he or she is severely abused. Once the conditioning is in place, the programmer praises the child by telling them that they are good and that they are both doing a wonderful job for the "Family" (the *Illuminati* world sect). The child's alter personalities are desperate to carry out the commands in the most perfect way possible because they are constantly seeking approval from the tormentor(s): the programmer and the parents. This unhealthy bond based on trauma and emotional attachment will last throughout their adult life, as alter personalities are often seeking approval and remain at the stage of maturity where they were formatted but in an adult body.

5/ spiritual training:

Occultism and demonology play an important role in the group, so the children are subjected to intense spiritual programming. The child is dedicated to a "celestial mother" or to a deity, even before birth. Very quickly, he or she will be immersed in a religious framework where participation in ceremonies will oblige him or her to repeat these occult activities. The child will undergo a blood baptism, numerous consecrations and other rituals creating an attachment to the spirits of family members, such as the mother or grandfather. Any MK programming session requires the invocation of demons to guide the programmer or to infuse energy into the current programming. Spiritualism, mediumship/channelling of spirits, predictions, psychic wars for power, magic of all kinds, are all common and necessary in these Luciferian groups.

c/ Kristin Constance

Kristin Constance was born in Australia into a family that practised ritual abuse from generation to generation, so she suffered the horrors herself and underwent therapy for some 20 years. She is now a social worker and counsellor. She works with people with disabilities, some of whom have suffered severe abuse.

In August 2011, Kristin Constance gave a lecture at the annual *S.M.A.R.T.* meetings on ritual abuse, secret societies and mind control (Connecticut, USA). The lecture was entitled *"Alleged Ritual Abuse by Freemasons of the Order of the Eastern Star in Australia.* Here is the full transcript of his testimony:

My name is Kristin Constance, I am 43 years old. I was born in Australia. I was ritually abused and mentally programmed between the ages of 3 and 9 in eastern Australia. Ritual abuse is something that exists in Australia and is at the heart of a criminal network producing child pornography. Some of the people in these criminal groups have been arrested, but the groups themselves and the networks are never bothered. Survivors of ritual abuse in Australia face a number of barriers to their safety. A former New South Wales police officer, who investigated cases of ritual abuse, said: "As soon as you meet someone who is determined to give evidence, they can quickly find themselves at the bottom of the harbour. In Australia, there are few victim support organisations and it is an issue that is not well recognised by the law and the government. Although Australia has recognised ritual abuse as a legitimate reason for refugee status, it has only a handful of prosecutions proving the link between child rape and Satan worship. Ritual abuse includes sadistic acts, but it is not limited to that.

In 1998, the Australian Refugee Tribunal accepted a German victim of ritual abuse. The tribunal stated, and I quote: "The German government has been ineffective in stopping these illegal activities. In Melbourne, Australia, a survey identified 153 cases of ritual abuse between 1985 and 1995. 98 social workers, psychologists and counsellors contributed to the survey (ASCA - Advocates for Survivors of Child Abuse - 2006). 38 Australian citizens responded to the Extreme Abuse Survey (EAS - 2007), more than half of them (55%) reported ritual abuse and mind control. Michael Salter, who wrote a chapter on ritual abuse in the book Ritual Abuse in the Twenty-First Century, has just completed a PhD entitled Adult Evidence of Organised Child Sexual Abuse in Australia. In his study he interviewed 15 survivors of ritual abuse and I was one of them. In my interview with him, under a pseudonym, I described the details of mental programming by colours. I also interviewed a well-known Australian psychologist who has worked with ritual abuse survivors for over 20 years. She had about 20 patients who had been victims of ritual abuse and mind control and of those 20 patients, two had been abused by Freemasons. My grandfather was a 33rd degree Freemason, he was attached to several lodges. He and my grandmother had founded a lodge of the Order of the Eastern Star in the suburbs of Sydney.

I have been in therapy for 20 years... 16 years with my current therapist. The hardest part of my recovery was healing from a mental programming based on colours and the exploitation of the left or right side of my body. This programming regularly caused me to dissociate. At the age of 18, in my second year of nursing school, I started to have memory problems and this is what prevented me from passing my exams. I started to remember incest at the age of 24, and ritual abuse and mind control soon after. I was hospitalised three times. During my first stay in a large psychiatric hospital on the west coast of Australia, I was diagnosed with a 'brief reactionary psychosis', Hashimoto's Thyroiditis, plus an abnormal electroencephalogram indicated temporal lobe epilepsy. That day I forgot to eat and drink and I couldn't stop crying... So I went to the hospital myself. My first psychiatrist diagnosed me with a borderline personality disorder. But she quickly corrected the diagnosis to Dissociative Identity Disorder (D.I.D.) when alter personalities started to emerge. Shortly after that, I attempted suicide in a park in front of a Masonic building. I survived a rather strong cocktail of drugs, I had swallowed a vial of anxiolytics, a box of antidepressants plus anti-psychotics... I didn't even fall asleep...

I consider myself lucky because my family moved from the east coast to the west coast when I was 9 years old. From that point on, the ritual abuse by cult members stopped. Other types of abuse continued, but being taken away in the middle of the night for rituals was over. My sister, who is 7 years older than me, also remembers being subjected to ritual abuse. One day when I was 26 she asked me if I remembered the underground rooms, I told her I did... She then asked me if I remembered the screaming children, I said I didn't but I knew they were there in other rooms. My sister doesn't remember as much, but I'm sure she has a lot more after-effects than I do because she didn't leave the East Coast until she was 16. She thinks she went through a process that Scientologists call P.D.H. (Pain, Drug, Hypnosis). Some organisations employ this technique using pain combined with drugs and hypnotic suggestions. These suggestions or "commands" are also known as "implants". Scientologists described this protocol as early as the 1950s (Science of Survival, 1951). When my sister had a session with a Galvanic Skin Response Monitor or E-meter, which Scientologists use, the device indicated that she had indeed undergone hypnosis in the past. The E-meter is a biofeedback device that instantly gives the patient's nervous state and emotional reactions. Just before coming to this weekend of lectures, my sister told me that the E-meter had given a positive response to some memories about being raped on an altar, being given electric shocks, being forced to drink blood and eat human excrement.

I also consider myself lucky because 17 years ago, when I confronted my mother and father on the subject of ritual abuse, my mother told me that she was not involved in it but she gave me the suitcase with all my grandfather's Masonic paraphernalia. She apologised for not being a good mother to me. I think that will be the only answer I get from her about ritual abuse. That suitcase confirmed many things to me. There were papers with passwords, hand signs and information for Masonic rituals. There were also the aprons, jewellery and medals that my grandfather and grandmother used to wear at meetings. I then remembered the colours of the Star and my alter personalities trapped in the points of the Star. I felt as if I had finally found the key... On the emblem of the Order of the Eastern Star (editor's note: an inverted pentagram with the branches of different colours), the colour red is in the upper left branch and the colour blue in the upper right branch. In my mind, Red controls the left side of my body, and Blue controls the right side of my body. This Masonic emblem was on paraphernalia found all over my grandfather's house.

I have integrated a total of 26 personalities during my years in therapy. Today I have only 2 that remain stubborn and need more probing and questioning before I can integrate them permanently. I have had animal alter personalities, most of which were cats and tigers. My animal alters have helped me survive life-threatening situations, my tigers have supported me through hardship and confinement. My Red/Left split (editor's note: alter group related to the colour red and the left side of the body) has taken all the pain, while my Blue/Right split (editor's note: alter group related to the colour blue and the right side of the body) has been strong and continues to get stronger. I still have many unanswered questions about my abuse, so I need to travel to find more information. I have never been able to work in a stable way, but now I work full time with patients.

I remember being put in cages, I remember electroshock, scarification, rape, photography, drugs, hypnosis, food/light/oxygen/sleep deprivation. I was also locked in a coffin with spiders. I have participated in indoor and outdoor rituals. I have been tied to altars. I participated in death and birth simulacra. I remember underground trapdoors in the halls but also being woken up countless times in the middle of the night to be taken to rituals. I was slashed, pierced, pricked so that my blood would be used in the rituals. I have been subjected to genital mutilation, which is the most traumatic abuse that can be inflicted on a human being, according to the World Health Organisation.

The colour programming I underwent took place in underground rooms. Each room had a different colour, corresponding to different programming. The colours seemed to correspond to those of the Eastern Star: blue, yellow, white, green, red and black for the centre. The red room had a red light, a stretcher, a table full of torture instruments and equipment for electroshock. In this room, the right side of my body was covered while the left side underwent the electric torture. Electrodes were placed on my joints, which caused a paralysing pain that I still feel today. My left ear was whispered to and electric shocks were applied to my temples. This is how "Red" was created and strengthened... A woman would ask me questions about programming, and no matter what I told her, I was always wrong. I disassociated myself many times... "Red" and its various alterations seem to be designed so that during sexual abuse, there is a passive reaction to pain, under any circumstances. Red' has been through a lot of blood rituals and rapes, and he has taken most of my pain.

In the blue room there was a blue light, a stretcher, electroshock equipment, buckets and a sink. The left side of my body was covered, and it was the right side that received electric shocks. Here the shocks were applied to my muscles, and I often felt stronger after these sessions. Blue' seems to be a personality created to obey orders and feel no pain. It can be very angry and aggressive and will do anything to survive. I feel I am mainly programmed with these two colours. My sister would be more programmed with White. I still don't quite understand the purpose behind this Left/Red and Right/Blue split. But I hope to find more answers one day... I became aware of this Red/Blue division at the beginning of my therapy, 20 years ago. As I became more and more aware of it, I came to understand how they could control each side of my body independently of the other. I found five sources of evidence about colour programming and there are strong similarities. Blue is described as protective, painless, non-injurious, strong, sometimes military-like. Red is about sexual slavery and blood rituals. I don't know if every person programmed by Freemasons receives this type of colour-based protocol. I suspect that depending on personality type, certain colours will be emphasised and worked on more than others. Perhaps birth dates influence the colours chosen. I don't understand what they are trying to do or create... I really wonder what the guideline is behind this.

Red' experienced pain in my left ankle, left knee, left hip, left elbow, left ear and left temple... When I was 'triggered', I found myself curled up on my left side in front of a radiator in pain... I feel my Right/Blue side as unaffected by the abuse. I don't have as many nightmares as I used to, but I still have problems sleeping. I have never been able to maintain relationships but I am proud to have a growing circle of friends now. I never wanted to have children. I've always wondered why people want to bring children into the world... probably because I must subconsciously think that all children would automatically go through what I went through, so I chose not to have any...

The methods that have helped me most in my recovery are Gestalt therapy, massage and exercise. I am doing a lot of walking and cross training at the moment, which helps to synchronise my two brain hemispheres. It's a long process for the left and right sides of my brain to learn to communicate and synchronise again. The left side of my body has suffered a lot of injuries and it's like my brain almost sacrificed that whole part for my survival.

So the ritual abuse stopped when my family moved to the other side of Australia. But the incest and rape continued until I was 18, when I left for good. My father was an alcoholic and my mother continues to live in denial, even though she answers my questions when she can... My sister continues to struggle with her mental illness... I am now working with patients and my therapy is coming to an end. I realised that I could never be fully integrated/merged, but the awareness work has helped me to achieve many goals that I never thought possible... Like giving this talk... But my biggest achievement is staying alive... and anything that happens now is a bonus.

d/ Lynn Moss Sharman

Lynn Moss-Sharman is the founder of *The Stone Angels* newspaper and spokesperson for *ACHES-MC* Canada (*Advocacy Committee for Human Experimentation Survivors & Mind-Control*). She was a victim of ritual abuse and mind control as a child. When she founded *The Stone Angels* newspaper in 1993, she began to connect with other survivors. This led to her meeting with about 60 adults from the Thunder Bay area and northwestern Ontario in Canada. Together they decided to publish in this journal writings and drawings by survivors and therapists as well as information about modern mind control. The *ACHES-MC* Canada committee was formed in 1996 when Sharman attended a conference by Claudia Mullen and Chris Denicola in Texas (whose testimonies are transcribed in Chapter 3). At this event she also met other survivors, including Blanche Chavoustie. It was at this point that she decided to do whatever was necessary to form a committee to defend the rights of victims of mind control in Canada. Gradually, a database was built up and the committee was officially established in October 1996, with the aim of gathering enough information to produce a reliable report. The data collected included the geographical areas where the experiments took place in the USA and Canada, as well as a list of alleged perpetrators.

As contact was made with other victims, Sharman realised that many of them had been involved in ritual abuse linked to Freemasonry. Their fathers or grandfathers were Freemasons, including Shriners (*AAONMS: Ancient Arabic Order of the Nobles of the Mystic Shrine*), which was something that seemed to be a common denominator in all of these accounts. She also found strong similarities between the testimonies of US citizens who were victims of MK-Ultra mind control and those of Canadian victims who reported the same kind of experiences. In addition, the victims had often grown up near a military base. Another common denominator among the victims is that the father was often in the armed forces (Canadian or American). According to Sharman, 90% of the victims she met said they had been "offered" ritual abuse with the resulting personality splitting and mind control. These cases are not child abductions, but one or both parents are always consenting and even actively participating in the MK programming process on the child.

In 1994, Lynn Moss Sharman organised a series of conferences and meetings in Thunder Bay. The event was called *"Making Up for The Lost Time"*, a series of three conferences that took place between November 1994 and June 1995. The aim was to bring as much information and testimony from victims and therapists as possible to the public. The aim was to make the information publicly available and thus make it safe for people to start talking openly about it, while at the same time allowing victims to get in touch with each other. This kind of gathering is important because it gives victims confidence and reassurance about their experiences. They are no longer alone and this reassures them that they are not crazy. The keynote speaker at the first meeting in November 1994 was Shirley Turcotte, a consultant and licensed clinical therapist based in Vancouver, British Columbia. She became known for the documentary film *"To a Safer Place"*, which shows her journey as a victim, herself a survivor of a child pornography ring. Among the many other speakers was Dr. Louise Million, psychologist and author of *"Breaking The Silence"*, a study on the abuse and torture of *First Nations* people in homes and schools. Native American children in Canada have been particularly targeted by the Paedocriminal Network with mind control experiments.

Sharman reports that these meetings in Thunder Bay received extensive media coverage. She recounts that the then Canadian Premier, Robert Keith Rae, received complaints from Freemasons across the province about the *Stone Angels...* an organisation that was putting its foot down, pointing the finger at network paedophilia and mind control! Indeed, Freemasonry was regularly cited in lectures and testimonies as being linked to ritual abuse and MK. Sharman herself received messages from Freemasons on her answering machine. She even claims that the wife of a senior Freemason at the *Moose Factory* who was a newspaper editor in Dryden refused to print the announcement of the lectures because her husband was a Freemason. As editor of a regional newspaper, she deliberately chose not to let people know about such a gathering. These public meetings aimed at denouncing ritual abuse and mind control caused a general outcry among Freemasons because it was announced that they were not allowed to attend the lectures (although it was obviously impossible to make such a filtration at the entrance, the effect of the announcement had some impact...). Moreover, the recordings of the conferences were strictly reserved for victims, therapists and certain associations.

A majority of the survivors Sharman met were Native Americans, *Ojibway* from Thunder Bay or Northwestern Ontario reserves. Soon, similarities were found in the testimonies of former residents of shelters. For example, there were reports of an electric chair at the Fort Albany residential school near *Moose Factory*, where skeletons of children were also found. Former residents have told of being raped in the middle of the night by men in white robes, some have also spoken of forced abortions, etc. These are the same cult practices described by American ritual abuse survivors. Such cult activities are also reported to have taken place on Manitoulin Island, and some victims have even reported that wealthy white people fly in from New York or California to participate in ritual abuse on that island. All of this is well known to the Aboriginal community in Canada because they are doing their own investigations on this subject. They are well aware of the existence of such practices and know the places where these activities take place. According to them, this cult network involves, among others, child and family social workers, and many Amerindian children have been victims of these people (this connection of the Network with child social services is recurrent, whether in America or in Europe). The elders see what happened to many of their brothers and sisters in residential schools and homes, but also in the prison system, many of which were near American or Canadian military bases (*NORAD* and *DEW* Line). Lynn Moss-Sharman's father himself worked in the Canadian military.

Sharman's memories began to emerge with the sexual abuse of her father, her uncle and a group of men in the army who were also involved in the sexual exploitation of children. Her memories were of this group of men but she found it difficult to determine what connection they might have had with her father, or the exact role he played in this group. Sharman has memories of ritual abuse at a very early age (as young as three) when she lived with her parents on Maria Street in Toronto. She remembers a ritual she calls *"forgiving with blood"*, which took place near the slaughterhouse or in churches near Hamilton and Toronto. She also remembers being transported to various locations, including military-affiliated sites, such as the *Stone Mountain* Underground or Uplands Air Force Base in Ottawa. Sharman was subjected to sensory deprivation and electroshock therapy, she remembers being told: *"First we break you, then we build you back up..."* (*Ordo Ab Chao*). She was subjected to MK projects funded by the University of Rochester in the late 1940s and early 1950s. She cites a Dr. George Estabrooks of the Department of Psychology at Colgate University in Hamilton, USA, and affiliated with *Oswego State Teatcher's College*. Dr. Estabrooks was directly involved in the creation of the Manchurian Candidates, he was in contact with J. Edgar Hoover (FBI) as early as 1937, as well as with José Delgado, Martin Orme, Ewen Cameron and many others... We find here the whole clique of scientists who were working at the time on brainwashing and mind control based on trauma.

Sharman insists that it is essential for people to realise that these mind control experiments are mainly carried out on children and that the research is extensive and has led to the development of increasingly sophisticated techniques. Children are even born in these laboratories to be subjected to experiments without ever seeing the light of day. These little victims are locked up in cages, subjected to electroshock, drugs, sensory deprivation, etc., all techniques that will serve to profoundly dissociate them and split their personality. Sharman also reports genetic and irradiation experiments, or chemical treatments to accelerate puberty, in order to quickly obtain reproductive subjects. The victims are literally used as guinea pigs to test the drugs to determine which will be the most effective and fastest in the brainwashing process preceding the MK programming. Sharman questions the extent to which these mind control experiments were carried out in the Native American community in Canada. She remembers being taken to a place where there was an Inuit woman with a shaved head and a baby in her arms. She also wonders about the fate of a number of Aboriginal people who were sent to southern Ontario or to state borders for so-called tuberculosis treatment in the 1950s and 1960s.

Sharman's recovery process was very long and she still has a disabled status. Indeed, such fragmentation is devastating and in her view irreversible. She describes how her body has retained the memory of each level of programming due to the fact that the cellular memory records everything the victim has experienced. These traumatic memories usually emerge with a powerful abreaction (emotional discharge, the person relives the traumatic memory live). For Sharman, her memories began to emerge when she went through a personal crisis, yet another abusive and unhealthy relationship that eventually led to her total collapse. The first memories to emerge were of the rapes, and then over time, fragments of more enigmatic memories such as being locked in a cage or being given electric shocks, also came back violently. When these flashbacks emerged, she could see someone's face, for example, but intense physical pain gripped her whole body and she became totally unable to speak. She could not explain to her therapist what she was remembering or what was going on in her head. She went through a long period where she was unable to talk about her traumatic memories. Sometimes she had to write them down or draw them. During these violent memories, she found herself in situations where she hid under the coffee table, for example, by wrapping herself in the therapist's carpet. Her body and mind were literally reliving the traumatic experience she had undergone years before, with equally intense pain. She says that she found herself in physical postures that she was completely unable to assume in a normal state. Her body would contort in unbelievable ways and she would spasm as the cellular memory of the electric shocks came back.

Her therapist told her that hypnosis would not be a good thing for her because of the intensity of her physical reactions when the memories came back. Indeed, hypnosis could flood her with too many memories that would have such an effect on her body that she could not bear it. The therapist preferred to take things gently, step by step, so that Sharman would be able to handle it, both emotionally and physically. His body, mind, spirit and "I" had to be able to process the traumatic information and understand how these different memories could be linked together. Another puzzle that had to be put together...

An important point to note is that Lynn Moss Sharman never had to take medication during her therapy and she carefully avoided any psychiatric intervention. Yet on many occasions she wanted to end her life and go into hospital to receive treatment that might have helped her. She also managed to avoid systematic addictions and self-destruction.

e/ Dejoly Labrier

Dejoly Labrier grew up in a military environment, both her parents were in the military and practiced ritual abuse. Dejoly developed a multiple personality as a result of the severe trauma she experienced in these military groups. She is the author of *"All* Together *Now*: *A Multiple* Story *of Hope & Healing"*. In 1997, she was a guest on Kathy Fountain's show *"Your Turn"* on

FOX 13 News. Here is the transcript of the programme in which she gave her testimony:

- Kathy Foutain: The drawings that you're going to see now were drawn by different personalities with different names, but they all come from one person... A woman with dissociative identity disorder. A disorder believed to be caused by repetitive trauma inflicted in early childhood. This woman says she was abused by her mother and father in a strange, ultra-violent cult operating in a military setting (...) So we welcome Dejoly Labrier. It takes a lot of courage to talk about these things and I'm delighted to be able to talk about them with you. I'd like to help people understand what you've been through... Your parents were both military, "Marines".

- Dejoly Labrier: They were both "Marines".

- KF: An iron discipline?

- DL: Yes, very rigid. From early childhood, my mother used to boast that her three-year-olds were as disciplined as a "Marine" in making their beds or answering at attention by shouting: "Yes Sir! or "No Sir! We were continually restricted to doing our daily chores. Every Saturday we also had to clean the house from top to bottom.

- KF: What about the cult, the sect? Were they both part of it? Was it a satanic cult or something else? What were they doing?

- DL: There were satanic rituals that were practised... What I understood from the memories of my alter personalities was that they were both involved. My father was the leader and my mother was his accomplice, I call her his 'accomplice' because she never protected us from all this violence (...) There are children who are raped, but who are also cut up... This 'feeds the party' so that the members of the cult receive power and might. There is the consumption of blood, but there is also cannibalism with sacrificed babies.

- KF: Where do they take the babies?

- DL: Within the group itself, some women are having babies. There are also young girls of child-bearing age. As soon as they reach puberty, they get knocked up by the rapes during the rituals. They also find babies where no one really cares.

- KF: You say in your book in a detailed way that you were used sexually by this cult, so you were raped by your father and by other men.

- DL: I was raped by many people, including women, by many "Marines"... We moved around the country regularly. In the army my father was a recruiter and he was also on reserve duty at different bases around the country recruiting and training, especially amphibious training.

- KF: And in each place he was posted to, he found a new group of people to do this kind of thing?

- DL: Yes, that's it...

- KF: Does the army know about these things? You never hear them on this...

- DL: There is a lot of anger from some of my alter towards the military. But what I can say is that the higher hierarchy of the military was well aware of what was going on. There is a lot going on that they know about but they don't do anything to stop it. They never arrest the people responsible.

- KF: When your father came to a new site, from what you tell us he just had to put an advert in the local military newspaper to find people interested in it...

- DL: There is a military sexual exploitation network at national level. You get into it depending on who you are and what your connections are. One thing leading to another, through meetings and discussions, you end up meeting people connected to this kind of thing. So they can build up a network very quickly, sometimes it's just three people but sometimes it's a lot more people: 20 or 30 people.

- KF: What are the objectives of these rituals? What are their goals? You said it was satanic... Is it sacrifice? Why do they do this?

- DL: There is a belief that eating human blood and flesh in rituals will give you power. They think that this will make them very powerful. On the other hand, there is a kind of Satanism where they take Christian beliefs and reverse them, which is something essential for them. It gives them a feeling of superiority over others: "We are powerful, we can kill without anyone knowing, who will be next? So they feel very powerful and superior to others.

- KF: I had the chance to speak to your therapist on the phone a short while ago and she confirmed that it was indeed a dissociative identity disorder. She also told me that she had seen your different personalities emerge in her practice. It's part of the therapy to get these alters to a place where they are safe to tell their stories. Sometimes they may behave violently towards you or other people. It's about knowing why these alter personalities act the way they do in order to be able to help you, the alters need to be able to express themselves. You have drawn a map, a kind of diagram which represents about fifty different personalities. It was drawn several years ago, these are the alter that successively emerged and gave their names. Who is the big one in the middle, "Competent one"... Is it you or someone else?

- DL: It's an alter, it's not me. I am all of these... combined in one person.

- KF: You have very destructive personalities...

- DL: Yes... against me, internally, but they do nothing to others. What I would like to point out is that they each have their own behaviour, because they were created to protect another alter or myself. So they may look like they're behaving badly, but they're not really bad at heart, they're doing it to protect us.

- KF: In the drawing, this black woman is one of your alter?

- DL: Yes.

- KF: What role does it play?

- DL: She is the guardian of our system. She protects and loves each of the alter personalities unconditionally. When there are conflicts between some of them, she is the one who takes them aside to talk to them individually.

- KF: And who is "Silent one? "

- DL: "Silent one" is one of the alters who has been abused militarily and satanically. She does not speak, she is mute...

- KF: You say that today you have established a consensus with all the alter personalities. That means that they all agree to get along and to cooperate. Are they here, listening to our conversation?

- DL: Yes... A lot of alter do what they call "board meetings", meetings between themselves, that kind of thing...

- KF: So you had some kind of meeting before you came to speak on television?

- DL: (laughs) Absolutely.

- KF: They all said it was a good idea because ....

- DJ: ... Because it needs to be said, people need to know that this kind of abuse exists, and that this kind of psychic disorder (I.D.D.) also occurs. Many victims with split personality are misdiagnosed in psychiatry. They are sometimes treated with inappropriate medication that does not address the problem of multiple personalities.

- KF: Yes, your therapist mentioned that often victims are misdiagnosed and receive heavy chemical treatment which does not help them at all. It's better to let it come, to let the alter personalities emerge in therapy and recognise their different functions to try to have a good cooperation...

- DL: Yes, help them to have different functions. I have an alter called "Druggie", its function is to put the system to sleep, as a protective measure. If there's a trigger that happens that might be a problem for one of the alters, then Druggie emerges and puts us all to sleep. It literally puts us to sleep...

- KF: Now a question from Lydia who calls us from Ruskin.

- Lydia: Did she try to talk to anyone about what was going on at the time? Was there anyone to talk to?

- DL: Unfortunately, there was no one to talk to... My whole family was involved. When you are so violently abused as a child, you quickly learn to keep quiet and not to talk to anyone because you might be the next victim sacrificed... So the fear is there...

- KF: Were you afraid of being killed?

- DL: I was completely terrified of being killed.

- KF: You know, the skeptics of your testimony will say, "How do I know this cult is real? Is this all real? Are babies really being killed and mutilated? Some may also say that you may have been sexually abused by your family but that your mind created the rest of the story.

- DL: I can understand this reaction, because all this may indeed seem very strange. However today there are more and more people revealing the truth about what they have experienced. This is my life. I'm not saying that every person who is sexually assaulted is going to develop a multiple personality, or that they come from a satanic cult, or that the military are all rapists... What I have to say is that this is my truth but you don't have to believe me. There are a lot of people who know this is real and they are coming forward. In the beginning of my healing process I met people from all over the world who were drawing the same kind of things, telling the same stories, they had alter personalities with the same names, and they all had this same psychiatric disorder because of their traumatic childhood...

- KF: You have two sisters and a brother, are they safe today?

- DL: No, because it takes a lot of courage and work to get through it and to be able to recover. It's just like an onion that you peel back layer by layer to discover another level of pain and to become aware of it. My brother was severely abused as a child (...) My father wrote me a letter admitting to raping me and other children... including my brother. My mother is in total denial and accuses my father of being the one who betrayed us...

- KF: Does your father not want to leave the cult?

- DL: Today I have no idea...

- KF: Some people have called and asked this question: Is it possible that the therapist can implant these memories in your mind?

- DL: They (editor's note: the Network) have a lot of power, and all over the world they try to put into people's heads that this kind of thing is imaginary, that all these horrors can't really exist... All of this came about through my own work, if I went to see a therapist, it was for him to guide me, not to do the work for me, or to tell me what to think...

- KF: We have Tammi online, ask your question.

- Tammi: Hi Dejoly, I'd like to know how old you were when you finally got out of all this? And how did you get out of it? You said that the sexual abuse stopped in your late teens...

- DL: Yes, actually the sexual abuse stopped on my twentieth birthday. I came home for the party and my father was there, all alone... That day he raped me. That day he raped me. After that I never saw him again, because I ran away. I ran away after I realised that there would be help outside, people who could really help me (...) When you are dissociated, with a multiple personality, you are also disconnected from human relationships. I've been married four times... and now, in my fourth marriage, I can finally say that I love my husband and have been able to connect with him. Before this I was not able to establish a real relationship, now I can...

- KF: Therapy has helped you a lot...

- DL: Yes.

- KF: Now a question from Barbara...

- Barbara: Hi, what kind of therapy did you have? In particular with regard to hypnosis and the type of medication.

- DL: I had a therapist for 5 years, but she died suddenly... For 5 years we worked without medication, because it doesn't really work... But I have an alter, "Ginger", who needed Prozac when she was depressed. So we took Prozac for two and a half years.

- KF: Was it the alter or everyone who took it?

- DL: It's very difficult to explain... I was taking it for her, but she was having the effects... My therapist at the time also used hypnosis. My therapist at the time also used hypnosis. We also drew, I kept a diary in which I wrote questions with answers, and then we went back to it with the therapist. We also did experimental therapy with movement, music, etc.

- KF: But you never 'integrated' and merged to become one with all the alter?

- DL: No. I personally think that sometimes the therapist's plan or method is not necessarily in the interest of all the alters.

- KF: There is a kind of cooperation and consensus between the alter...

- DL: *Yes.* (...)

It seems that in Europe too, there are such practices in the military. In July 2011, the Italian magistrate Paolo Ferraro publicly denounced the existence of a *'satanic-military sect'* during a press conference in his country. An Italian TV channel broadcast the magistrate's statements. Here is the transcript of the short Italian report on the subject:

A satanic sect based on sex and drugs, forming a high-level network, is said to be practising obscure manoeuvres to ensure that investigations are never concluded. After the Superior Council of the Magistracy decided to suspend a magistrate for four months for an alleged health problem, it decided to make public this case which started in 2008.

Paolo Ferraro: I limited myself to a simple observation: in a house, several people, some of whom were "officials", were living there, with women and children, and participating in activities that were not at all normal... I discovered an underground world, unknown, obscure and ambiguous... There were also sexual activities practised in a context that was completely unknown to me until then.

The defenders of the Public Ministry denounce anomalies in the actions of the Superior Council of the Magistracy and have already planned an appeal to invalidate this suspension while magistrate Ferraro will appeal.

Paolo Ferraro: The choice they made is perhaps because they did not read correctly everything I denounced in my report. But also because they didn't really understand the essence of the problem."

f/ Cisco Wheeler

Cisco Wheeler is a survivor of the *Illuminati* Luciferian network. She is the co-author with Fritz Springmeier of the books: *"The Illuminati* Formula *to Create an Undetectable Total Mind Control Slave"* and *"Deeper Insights Into The Illuminati Formula"*.

Wheeler was programmed from early childhood by her father, who came from a transgenerational Luciferian family. According to her, her father was a programmer for the *Illuminati* Order and the US government. Her family was very politically connected. Her great-uncle (a direct descendant of General Ulysses Grant) was General Earl Grant Wheeler, a Chief of Staff who commanded US forces in Vietnam. His father was a 33rd degree Freemason and Grand Master in the *Illuminati,* and was a member of the *Grand Council of Druids*. Because of this status, he had strong ties to the American political establishment. According to her, her father was also a 'multiple programmer', i.e. he himself had suffered traumas in childhood which had split his personality. So it's a generational problem and he was himself a prisoner of dissociative states, just as his daughter Cisco was. He was a genius in every way, an outstanding musician. Outwardly this Satanist gave a very bright image of himself, loving his family and doing a good job in the army. On the face of it he was sociable, he liked people and people liked him. Wheeler believes that at some point in his life he became aware of who he was and what he was really doing in private and in secret, some of the amnesiac barriers broke down but it must have been completely beyond him... to change direction would have cost him his life because he had gone too far.

From birth Wheeler entered a highly structured world with systematic protocols. As a child, she was trained to serve as a sex slave to the so-called "elite" of the American political scene. Cisco Wheeler began having flashbacks following the death of her father. For a long time, his host, or front, personality did not have access to the memories of the deeper alter personalities associated with the occult, until the traumatic amnesic walls finally broke down at the age of forty. Not understanding these memory flashes and her suicidal tendencies, she sought help and was hospitalised for nine weeks. This was the beginning of her therapy and exploration of her dissociative identity disorder.

Her family had programmed her life from scratch. They had structured and conditioned her to become what they decided for her. This programming was designed to dehumanise and degrade her to the point where at times she truly believed she was a pussy. When she looked in the mirror, she saw a porcelain doll with a kitten's head. One of her alters had been programmed to be a sex slave, a docile kitten, the *"Beta Kitten"* programming we mentioned at the beginning of this chapter. To dehumanise her and create these animal alters, she describes how they had set up two cages, one filled with pretty, healthy kittens and the other for her... Locked in the cage, she had a bowl next to her connected to an electric wire that gave her shocks whenever she wanted to eat or drink. In this cage, she was humiliated and spat upon whenever she behaved like a little girl. In the next cage, the kittens were always well fed, they did not lack anything, they received a lot of love, they were stroked, etc. This ordeal and this torture was not only a shame, but it was also a real shame. This ordeal and torture, which was nothing more than MK programming, lasted for days and Wheeler tells how her little brain decided at one point that she should no longer be a little girl but that she was a little cat too. The cats were fed and they didn't have to lie in their own feces like the little girl, they weren't hit like she was. Her personality was dissociated by this deeply traumatic situation and so she identified with the kittens. When her memories came back, her body had retained the memory of all the blows she had received during this programming. The pain would come out as the memories emerged. She also talks about being locked in a cage with monkeys. When she recovered her memories to reconstruct her real identity, it was extremely difficult and painful for her to accept that she had been a real little girl. Every time she expressed something human, she was severely tortured until she finally pushed the reality that she was a human girl out of her head, because *it was too painful to be a girl!*

She also says that she underwent "magic surgery" in which her heart was "removed" in a mock operation accompanied by hypnosis and drugs. She soon followed in her father's footsteps by training to become a programmer herself. She cites some of the places where MK programming sessions took place: the

China Lake Naval Base in California, the Presidio Base north of San Francisco, Letterman Hospital near the Presidio Base, Alcatraz Prison, Scotty Castle in *Death Valley* National Park, Salem Psychiatric Hospital in Oregon, and the large Dorenbecker Masonic Hospital in Portland. All of this took place from the mid-1940s to the mid-1960s.

Wheeler recounts how, with a group of four or five MK survivors from the same social background, they encouraged each other and found the strength, thanks to God, to fight against the programming, harassment and constant intimidation of the network. Together they fought to regain their freedom and health. During her first five years of therapy, Wheeler says that the network was still in contact with her and that they regularly brought her back to torture her again: electric shocks, drugs, repeated rapes, etc. Despite the repeated abuse over five years, she says that the strength that kept her in therapy was that for the first time she was aware of being a real human being: '*I am not a kitten! I am a woman! I was a little girl! Those programmes were all lies!*' She was ready to die for the truth to come out.

Wheeler describes well the phenomenon of ambiguity that is created in the relationship between the victim and the perpetrator. As a young girl, she recounts how a child who did not belong to the Luciferian hierarchy was coldly killed in front of her. This is how the executioners display their power and a morbid emotional bond is created so that the child will become unconditionally attached to the murderer... because the murderer spared her, in order to kill the other child... Try to understand what can happen at that moment in the brain of a child who is only four or five years old. As already noted earlier in this chapter, trauma is an important factor in the emotional bond between the child and the perpetrator. The victim never knows when she will be 'loved' or when she will be 'hated'. Indeed, the perpetrators change their attitude *"like a shirt"* and can at any moment switch to horror because of their own dissociative states. Wheeler's father could be extremely kind during a programming session as well as abominable and devoid of any human feeling. He would become meaner than a wild animal and would stop at nothing to make his victim understand something. She says that some of her alter personalities still love her father very much and will probably love him forever. For her, incest was a proof of love, she considered that a father's or mother's love consisted in raping their children... This is a belief she held as long as she was in this Luciferian system where incest is a 'cultural' practice.

Wheeler had three *"mothers"* who formed the foundation of his internal system. These *"mothers"* were his three great basic alters who were placed on a pedestal in his inner world. These are alter's deeply connected to the occult whose sole purpose is to reign with the Antichrist as queens when he ascends his throne. Lucifer has a bride who is composed of all the *'Mothers of Darkness'*, i.e. all the alter High Priestesses.

According to Wheeler, this is the essential aspect of their system, the mental programming and actions of this network really come out of the very heart of Lucifer. He wants to crush God's people, and the world as a whole. The *Illuminati* consider themselves gods and their only master is Lucifer. They have sworn an oath to their prince, their *"father of light"*. They have signed up to implement his plans by any means necessary, to bring about what is planned for the end times and eventually install the Antichrist on his throne. They have been working towards this for centuries and the MK programming of the children of the Luciferian Order is a key part of this.

These people have no fear of hell. If they rule as gods, if they obey Lucifer's call and stay true to their blood oaths, they will rule with him in hell, that is their belief... They are convinced that if they abide by this, they will be gods in hell, with Satan. It's a huge lie but they believe it... They all want to be gods, that's really the basis of their doctrine and the only master they obey is Lucifer. Cisco Wheeler says: *"They are motivated by power, money and fame, but it's actually the demons that have been motivating them for generations... Lucifer and his demons. They are completely possessed."*

g/ Brice Taylor

Susan Ford's testimony first appeared in 1978 under the pseudonym *"Lois"* in Walter Bowart's book *"Operation Mind Control"*, *a seminal* work on the subject of mind control. In 1999 she published her testimony under the pseudonym Brice Taylor in a book entitled *"Thanks for the Memories"* in which she describes her journey as a Monarch slave from early childhood. Brice Taylor was one of those 'presidential models' who were completely dissociated and exploited by a certain American elite. She was used as an MK slave at the highest level of society and is one of the few who have publicly testified about these occult practices.

Susan Ford began working with her split memories in 1985 to find her way to healing. As a child, the abuse and programming began with her father. Her mother also suffered from dissociative disorders and some form of programming, and was also involved in the abuse of her daughter. Her whole family was involved, both her paternal and maternal grandparents, her aunts, uncles and even her brothers. So here again we are dealing with transgenerational Satanism. His father dragged him into Satanic ceremonies, particularly with his grandfather who was a wealthy politician, himself belonging to a family that had practised ritual abuse for generations. Brice Taylor believes that her father was himself a "multiple programmer" who suffered horrors as a child, and she says that she often saw him change his personality. This is the classic family pattern of a vicious circle of trauma passed on like a vampire bite from one generation to the next...

From the age of 5, she was regularly taken to military bases in California to undergo MK programming protocols. She also cites the *UCLA* Neuropsychiatric Institute and *NASA* centres where such things are said to be done. Her family's connection to the military was through her political grandfather. When she was 10 years old, he introduced her to a paedophile network of politicians and other high-profile people from all walks of life.

Taylor testifies that the ritual abuse she suffered included being pricked with pins and needles, burned, hung by her feet and sometimes tied in a cross.

The torturers also spun her around like a top, she was raped and deprived of food and sleep. She was also forced to participate in orgies during rituals. At military sites, she was subjected to electric shocks, flashes of light and sound, and torture with all sorts of sophisticated instruments, combined with the effect of the drugs administered to her. All these barbaric practices had the sole purpose of splitting her personality into a multitude of alters, created to be programmed. She describes that during these MK programming sessions she was strapped to a special chair, just like the ones used to train astronauts. According to her, they used the same equipment as the astronauts: centrifuges, weightlessness simulators, sensory isolation chambers, etc. Some of the equipment used light signals or other signals to make the astronauts feel comfortable. Some of the equipment used light or sound signals combined with electric shocks. Taylor explains, for example, that she received a sound in her right ear and a completely different sound in her left ear. She was programmed to associate a sound with a specific command, usually in a hypnotic state.

In addition to these programming sessions in military institutions, her father was involved on a daily basis in strengthening her mind control. She says that he had a completely unsuspecting front personality. Outwardly, he behaved like a charming man, no one would have suspected what he might do in private, the torture he inflicted on his children, in order to split them up and program them. According to Taylor, her mother was also involved in the torture, and when her daughter recovered her memories and confronted her with this harsh reality, she was in total denial, she had no recollection of treating her in this way. The mother did not dispute or deny what her daughter was telling her, but she seemed obviously very troubled by her memory problems. She later even helped her daughter to publish her autobiographical book.

Let's make a small parenthesis here with Svali who reports exactly the same thing with her mother who also had deep dissociative disorders. Dissociation has the effect of a kind of 'glue' that keeps the denial in place and helps to perpetuate the darkness of all these practices. In an article published in 2001, Svali wrote about her mother: *"You are making this up, you know very well that it is not true! I don't remember any of the things you are talking about! The person who told me this was my mother two years ago. She told me clearly that she did not believe me. Her amnesia is intact and she is protecting her. I wanted to explain to her that she and I had spent part of our lives in a cult, that I loved her and that I wanted her to get out of it too. In that phone call, the first in a year, I gave her the exact names of the people involved that we both knew. Mum, you're in a state of disassociation, that's why you don't remember, I said. No, that's not true, nothing like that happened, she maintained. She knew very well that I had never consciously learnt German during the day, yet it was in this language that she had spoken to me at night since I was very young. She herself did not understand the language consciously at all... 'Why do I speak German fluently today?' I asked her in German and continued: 'I never learned this language, you know that. I learned Spanish and Latin at school'... There was then a blank and she replied: 'Perhaps you are a medium and you learned it by telepathy'... My mother had to maintain her denial at all costs by explaining even the inexplicable... But how had she understood my question, which I had asked her in German? (...) I think that denial is a serious barrier to healing. When a survivor begins to recover his or her memory, he or she will usually confront family members with his or her memories in an attempt to validate them. The survivor also frequently faces lack of recognition, crude denial, and even verbal abuse from family members. People who need to remain in denial to protect themselves from painful truths. 'You are crazy', 'You are sick', 'You have a sick imagination', 'How can you make up such things? You need help', "You need help", even crueller phrases may be thrown in the face of those who want to keep their amnesia. "*[503]

In 1985 and 1987 Brice Taylor had two serious accidents. It was the shock of these accidents that began to bring up memories of her past... lots of memories. This first triggered programming that made her think she was going completely crazy. She had flashbacks with increasingly vivid visions, accompanied by physical pain in certain parts of her body. At that time, she was preparing a master's degree in clinical psychology and had to interrupt her studies, as her traumatic memories were emerging so violently. She came into contact with the therapist Catherine Gould, who helped her a lot. First the sexual abuse in childhood came up, then the memories of satanic ritual abuse and finally the memories concerning MK programming. We find here the same process of recovery of traumatic memories as for Lynn Moss Sharman or Kristin Constance: first incest, then ritual abuse and finally MK programming, the most violent memories coming back last, although it is difficult to establish a traumatic scale in this kind of thing.

Taylor states that during her therapy she worked with a Secret Service person who revealed to her what he knew about MK programming, including the keys, or codes, to trigger and manipulate the alter personalities. She describes how he would switch her from one personality to another in order to bring to the surface all the split memories held by the many alters. As the alters emerged in succession, she would take a pencil and write pages and pages about what had happened when this or that alter personality was active. As with most split people who have developed I.D.D., some of the alter personalities have photographic memory or hypermnesia that reveals memories in great detail. In addition, soul fragments that remain "frozen" in a space-time where the experience of the trauma is constantly present can relive a scene as if the person were living it in real time, in the present moment, which allows for a very detailed description. This phenomenon explains how some survivors are able to give very precise information about events that may be twenty years old, whether it be dialogue or descriptions of places.

Taylor underwent hypnosis combined with drugs, which was constantly used by her father to embed the commands deep into her subconscious and thus program her bit by bit. She also describes how electricity was used as a tool to fragment her personality. According to her, electroshock not only creates a deep dissociative state, but also affects the entire energy field of the human body and

---

[503] *Svali Speaks - Overcoming Denial* - Svali, 05/2001.

thus allows the individual to be affected at a very deep level. When she was very young, she was shocked with simple electric wires, later the torturers used electric prods originally designed for cattle. The electronic equipment on military bases was even more sophisticated. According to Brice Taylor and Fritz Springmeier, electric prods are used to erase short-term memory, but memory does not seem to be totally destroyed, as the many testimonies of survivors attest.

Taylor describes well how a single element in her environment could bring up memories all at once. As soon as one of these memories presented itself to her, she focused on it as much as possible to make it as clear as possible in her consciousness. The next step was to write it down and validate it as much as possible. She describes very well how her memories came back in extremely precise flashes, as if the event had just happened, even though it was 10 or 20 years ago. These were bits and pieces of information that over time put together a complete puzzle, the puzzle of her life as an MK slave.

Some programming was designed to disrupt her physical and mental functioning when she began to access the traumatic memories. She had to fight for many years to stay alive, fighting against these "time bombs" that had been placed inside her to drive her crazy or to kill her.

Her MK programming served governmental interests, her photographic memory was exploited as a communication tool in the Network. She was also used as a sex slave for the Network's elite, used for money laundering, pornography and prostitution, as was survivor Cathy O'Brien, who was also exploited as a "presidential model".

Brice Taylor revealed that an intelligence officer had told him about the case of elite sex slaves, the so-called 'presidential models'. This agent gave the figure of 3000 women programmed in this way in the United States. But this type of MK programming is not only about sex slavery, according to her, some Hollywood actors but also heads of state have a totally split and programmed personality, people who would also be in great need of healing their deep traumas...

h/ Kathleen Sullivan

Kathleen Sullivan is the author of the book *Unshackled: A Survivor's Story of Mind Control*.

When her memories emerged after her father's suicide in 1990, she became totally withdrawn and disconnected from her emotions, acting like a robot. The traumatic memories resurfaced, first the sexual abuse and then the increasingly traumatic rituals...

In 1991, she was hospitalised in Dallas and it was there that she began to face her painful memories and gradually understand that she had undergone MK programming. It was during this hospitalization that she realized that she had multiple personalities and that each of them had a first name, a number, and a code name.

Sullivan says that her traumatic memories came back through sounds, through her father's voice or other people's voices, voices that she heard very clearly. She knew in her heart that these were voices she had heard as a child. A memory could also come back through a smell or through food that suddenly seemed to become foul... when the traumatic (and cellular) memory came back, she physically felt the rapes she had suffered. Many of the visual memories came back through flashbacks or recurring dreams. It was then that she decided to write everything down. She spent hours and hours writing a diary while physically and emotionally reliving the traumas encapsulated in her memories. In particular, memories that concerned her programming as a murderer, something that drove her crazy, not knowing if it was her imagination or reality. Indeed, she stubbornly refused to accept these things that were coming back to her, but when her other alter personalities began to manifest themselves, she could no longer remain in denial.

When he was hospitalised in 1991, a psychiatrist at the University of Dallas asked him to write down his "personality map". Five levels of programming came back to her: Alpha, Beta, Delta, Theta and Omicron. Of course, no one bothered to reassure her and explain what this meant because no other patient described similar terms. She later realised that these were programmes that had been implanted in her mind through hypnosis and other techniques. This was MK programming at a government level.

Sullivan's father had been her main programmer since early childhood. She later learned that he himself had suffered extreme trauma as a child and was therefore totally unhinged. He was, however, a competent engineer at *AT&T* (formerly *Western Electric*), with a very scientific mind. He regularly told his daughter that he was a "god" to her, and of course little Kathleen believed him... But she was simply a guinea pig and a prototype; the better the father could split his daughter's personality, the better he would be seen by the CIA, for whom he worked. Like all the other torturers, the father used electricity and sleep and food deprivation to program her. He was an occultist who was fully immersed in satanic ritual abuse and ran a small group in Reading, Pennsylvania, in which many children were involved. As a child, from the age of four, Kathleen Sullivan had to participate in sacrifices, rituals to desensitise and condition her for her programming as a killer.

His paternal grandfather was Welsh and attached to a Druidic tradition. The people involved in these occult practices of a Luciferian nature do not want to give up their ancient religion and so these traditions continue today in a 'clandestine' way ('the religion without a name'). Father Sullivan practised *chain* personality splitting on his daughter, systematically giving a new name to each alter that was born. He then implanted in these fragments what he wanted: beliefs, feelings and thoughts. According to Sullivan, his father had been programmed as a child. He was of German origin and had been recruited as an interpreter by the air force during the war. Later he spent a lot of time with neo-Nazi groups, which is when he became interested in Satanic doctrines. He was very close to some Templar groups, according to his daughter he was never a Freemason himself but he regularly worked with high degree initiates.

Kathleen Sullivan estimates that she was exploited as an MK slave for about 20 years. She had versatile programming and was used for various functions: theft, child trafficking (supplying small victims to paedophile networks), security (bodyguards for political figures or others), settling of accounts (assassinations), interrogations, transmission of information, but also programming on children and participation in ritual sacrifices... She was used by *many people*, she says, mainly by the CIA, then by the Pentagon, the Rangers, Delta Forces, special military forces, but also the mafia, which according to her, is totally connected to the CIA.

When she was not on *special missions*, she was used as a bodyguard for politicians. She says that they like to have an MK slave on hand to do the dirty work, such as supplying them with drugs or children. A bodyguard usually gets into the privacy of the personalities he protects, so an MK subject who won't talk about what he sees and hears is preferable to an unprogrammed individual who would be a weak link in the vast network that is currently in control of this planet.

All these people engaged in immoral and illegal acts would obviously like to be able to act publicly with impunity and completely reverse the moral values of society. For Sullivan, these people are driven by a powerful motivation to establish and run a world government that will allow them to commit in peace anything that is currently considered immoral and illegal, such as paedophilia. Indeed, incest is a *cultural* practice unique to this Luciferian milieu, something they would like to inject into society by legalising paedomania. They only want one thing: to get rid of the Christian moral code, and for that they advance their pawns step by step to establish the reign of their doctrine: that of the *Luciferian New World Order*.

i/ Cathy O'Brien

Cathy O'Brien is yet another victim of the MK-Monarch process to reduce her to a sex slave, serve as a diplomatic courier or a mule to transport cocaine (the fuel of our elites)... Her split personality with amnesia walls was used by the highest levels of the US government. She and her daughter Kelly (who was also subjected to MK programming) were rescued in 1988 by Mark Phillips who took them to Alaska to be safe from the Network to which they were bound. There, Cathy's memories were able to begin to recover from the shackles of the traumatic amnesia walls, and she was finally able to exercise her free will. The result was an autobiographical book entitled *TRANCE Formation of America: True life story of a mind control slave*.

In 1996, whistleblowers Cathy O'Brien and Mark Phillips gave a lecture entitled *"Mind-control out of control"* in which they describe both their background and our situation with regard to this *New World Order*. The full transcript can be found in Appendix 2 of this book.

j/ The artist with multiple personalities: Kim Noble

Kim Noble is an English painter. From the age of 14 onwards, she was in and out of psychiatric hospitals for about 20 years, until she met Dr. Valerie Sinason and Dr. Rob Hale. In 1995 she was finally diagnosed with I.D.D., a diagnosis that was validated by Professor John Morton of *UCL* (*University College London*). In 2004, during art therapy sessions, Kim Noble and her thirteen personalities discovered a great interest in drawing... A dozen alters began to express themselves with brushes and paint, each with a completely different name and style. The themes are also completely different, some painting landscapes or seemingly innocuous characters, while other works are much darker and more explicit about the ritual abuse Noble may have suffered as a child. The alter named '*Ria Pratt*' clearly depicts scenes of rape and torture of children, scenes that Noble undoubtedly experienced and whose traumatic memories have been preserved by certain alters. In these paintings depicting ritual abuse, we find a great similarity with the various testimonies of other MK survivors.

Kim Noble has had numerous painting exhibitions and newspapers such as *The Telegraph*, *The Guardian* and *The Independent have* featured her work and interviewed her. She has also appeared on *The Oprah Winfrey* Show. These media describe her as an "original", an artist with multiple personalities, but rarely do they go into depth to explain the causes of such a psychological state. Even less do they discuss the subject of ritual abuse and mind control, which is symbolically present in some of her paintings. Most articles about her mention her great courage and talent, but none of them dare to touch the essential content of her artistic work and what it describes: traumatic rituals causing dissociative states. People are fascinated by the extremely varied painting styles, but it is clear that her works also describe her past as an MK-Monarch victim.

The following are excerpts from an article entitled *"Kim Noble: a woman divided"*, published in 2006 by *The Independent*:

Each of Kim's alter personalities is an artist in their own right: Patricia paints lonely desert landscapes, Bonny often draws robotic figures dancing, Suzy has repeatedly painted a kneeling mother, Judy's canvases are very large, while Ria's work reveals deeply traumatic events involving children. These disturbing representations are the root of Kim's psychological condition, she suffers from Dissociative Identity Disorder, a disorder that is a mental survival strategy where the personality splits at a young age due to severe and repeated trauma. The number of personalities often depends on the repetition of trauma. Kim herself has no memory of being abused as a child. She has been protected over the years by her alter: "I have been told I was abused, but for me it is still too early, it goes in one ear and out the other. It's not good to remember things I don't want to know."

Kim has good reason to fear the return of the memories of her past because it is possible that if she receives too much information, she will not be able to cope and she will "disappear". It's happened twice before (...) This is where it gets really weird - for Kim who is not quite Kim...

The alter personality I interview is Patricia, she runs her life and Aimée's (her daughter) life, but Patricia was not always the dominant personality. Before Patricia re-emerged, Bonny was the dominant alter and two years before that, it was the alter Hayley.

Kim looks at me very carefully as she explains: "You see, Kim is just the 'house', the body. There isn't really a "Kim", she's completely divided. We answer to the name Kim but I am Patricia. When people call us "Kim" we take it as a nickname. But once people know you well, they usually don't use that name anymore. (...) Of the twenty (or more) personalities who share "Kim", some were identified 15 years ago: Judy, who is anorexic or bulimic; the mother, Bonny; the nun, Salome; the depressed, Ken; the sensitive, Hayley, Dawn and Patricia; the mute, MJ.

There are also a handful of children 'frozen' in time (stuck at a certain age and place). Some of the alters know they are part of an I.D.T. system, but many are unaware or refuse to accept it. "Judy doesn't believe in this reality," explains Kim: "She's just a teenager who insults the therapist when he tries to explain the situation to her. She is so young, she doesn't even think about Aimee, who is her daughter. She knows me and she thinks I'm a bad mother because I'm always neglecting Aimee. For her, it's perfectly normal to come and go all the time (dissociation). She probably thinks that everyone works like that. There are certain triggers that cause dissociation, personality change, but gradually Kim has learned to avoid them. However there can be up to three or four alter changes a day."[504]

The paintings of the alter *Ria Pratt* are certainly the most shocking of all her work. We discover children put in cages, gang rapes, an abortion scene... The executioners are often represented here holding what can be interpreted as electric prods. What is common to all of *Ria Pratt*'s paintings is that, whether it is the children or the perpetrators, each character is painted with his or her "double" floating above or beside him or her. The doubles represent the same figure as the character, but in a transparent and ghostly way. This most likely symbolises the dissociation of body and mind during ritual abuse. *Ria Pratt* systematically depicts the children with their double, but the perpetrators are also depicted with this doubling, which confirms that they themselves would be in a state of dissociation or possession when they unleash their violence during ritual abuse. A morbid detail is that the executioners are systematically represented in these paintings with a smile on their lips...

The alter *Golden Dawn* produces paintings that mostly depict disarticulated and amputated mannequins. The alter *Judy* gives an important place to duality in her work, notably by painting black and white checkerboards. The paintings of the alter *Key* deserve special attention. As the name suggests, this alter's paintings expose key elements of encryption, i.e. protocols and methodology for MK programming. His "*Seven Level*" chart describes in detail seven steps for designing a Monarch slave (see chart in Appendix 4). The number seven is a magical number that is associated with musical notes, the colours of

---

[504] *"Kim Noble: a woman divided"* - independent.co.uk, 08/2006.

the rainbow, the days of the week, the wonders of the world, the seven levels of consciousness, etc. This production is constructed in horizontal layers representing different scenes. The process described is read chronologically from the bottom to the top:

- Phase 1: Birth in hell

This scene clearly represents hell, the setting where the child will be born: a family devoted to Satan/Lucifer. This is the beginning of the MK programming process. We can read several words written: *"Deep"*, *"Satan"*, "Dark", *"No Help"*, *"Blood"*, *"Death"*, *"All Around"* and *"No Life"*.

In this first scene, there are two representations of the devil personified, with horns and a pitchfork as well as inverted Christian crosses that confirm the satanic character of the place. Crawling bodies are depicted as well as a woman who appears to be in labour or abortion. A snake and a dragon are also depicted in this scene.

- Phase 2: Traumatic shock

This scene depicts the multiple tortures suffered by the small victims of MK-Monarch. This stage involves the infliction of extreme abuse on the subject to create the dissociative states necessary for programming. In this part of the painting, at least 28 children are depicted. On the floor, 13 children are reduced to slaves and walk on all fours in single file. In the centre of the scene is a table or bed on which a subject is lying with wires connected to his head and hands, a design that certainly represents torture by electricity. Two figures are pushing what appear to be stretchers on which children are lying. We can also see in this scene many cages in which children are locked up, and others are hung by their feet. Sexual violence is not depicted in this scene, but it is explicitly depicted in paintings by the alter *Ria Pratt*.

- Phase 3: Dissociation and splitting

This scene shows us the different alter personalities created by the traumatic shocks in the previous phase. The alters are represented as little people floating and getting lost in meanders drawn by sinuosities totally devoid of any organisation. However, the sinuosities in which the Alters evolve eventually merge to join the next phase, the central point of which is the Kabbalistic tree of life. These sinuosities containing the alter personalities form, as it were, the roots of the tree of life, which will serve as the basis, the foundation, of phase n°4. In this scene, the alter personalities are isolated from each other by these sinuous roots which partition the memories of each of them. This symbolises the traumatic amnesic walls created in the previous phase.

- Phase 4: Conditioning and structuring of the internal system

Once the alters have been created, a structure must be organised to compartmentalise them and make them easily exploitable. This is what scene 4 represents: the structuring of the inner world of the MK slave. The drawing seems to represent a kind of labyrinth or technical plan whose different zones correspond to symbols. We see signs of the zodiac as well as eyes that are there to monitor the dissociated fragments in the inner world. The focal point of this phase is the Kabbalah tree of life, also called the tree of the Sephiroth. Several survivors have reported being programmed with such a structure as a framework for organising and accessing the various alter groups. It is likely that the alter personality *Key* who painted this picture represented here the actual pattern of assembly and structuring of Kim Noble's split personality.

- Phase 5: Integration of access codes

This scene shows a pile of numbers and letters with a book in the centre. On the left side are the numbers and on the right side are the letters. The number 666 is written under the left page of the book. This is the phase of encoding the series of words and numbers that will be used to bring out this or that alter. Codes to access the inner world of the slave are also programmed. The book in the centre of the scene probably represents the archiving material that will contain all the data concerning the programming of the MK slave.

- Phase 6: The transition

Phase 6 represents a kind of highway, a bridge over a sea or a river. The initiation ritual is complete, the Monarch butterfly can emerge from the chrysalis... This highway, whose perspective gives the appearance of a triangle or pyramid, also symbolises the path to dissociation, the *"yellow brick road"* of the Wizard of Oz on which the victim is encouraged to dissociate and through which the different alters can emerge according to the needs of the controllers. A road that leads here to the next scene representing the dissociative state as such, where the victim floats *through the rainbow*.

- Phase 7: Liberation

This scene represents the sky of the previous scene, the dimension where the dissociated spirit of the victim evolves. This sky has two suns, a rainbow and a figure with wings and a halo, is it an angel, a butterfly or a dove? This scene symbolises both the final state of the slave, who has been broken up and recomposed by the Monarch process and can now be 'released' into the secular world to fulfil his function as a slave. But this final scene also represents the dissociative, timeless state that will now be the cornerstone of the slave's life. We also see in this scene an eye... the eye of Lucifer (*who sees everything*) which will permanently monitor the new MK-Monarch slave.

This painting of the alter *Key* represents the evolution of the slave from the hell of trauma in the basements of the first levels to the heavenly 'paradise' (*enlightenment*) represented by the deep states of dissociation caused by pain and terror. The final phase shows us that the slave has finally accessed the rainbow to transcend his reality... into other dimensions. However, this psychic escape is not true freedom, for the Eye is watching...

It is important to note the presence of the tree of the Sephiroth in the central position of the painting, as it is a primordial symbolic element of the Kabbalah, which is itself at the origin of many magical practices. Dr. Cory Hammond describes in the Greenbaum lecture the presence of the Kabbalistic tree as a structural element of the internal system of some of his patients.

Witchcraft and the occult appear to be at the heart of the Monarch mind control process. Although Kim Noble refuses to admit to ritual abuse, her alter personalities *Ria Pratt* and *Key* have memories that are clearly related to ritual abuse and trauma-based mind control. A therapist would probably learn a lot from talking to the *Key* alter personality... Kim Noble's true inner inspiration is the MK-Monarch programming buried in her traumatic memories, but of course this will never be mentioned in the media that is interested in her work...

We can also mention Lynn Schirmer who is another painter suffering from I.D.T. as a result of ritual abuse and mind control. A woman who testified publicly and produced an exhibition called *"DIDiva & The Mad Machines"*, in reference to the barbaric tools used by the programmers.

8 - SUMMARY

In 1997, Wayne Morris conducted an in-depth investigation into the problem of trauma-informed mind control. For eight months he interviewed 24 people (survivors and therapists) on *CKLN FM 88.1*, the radio station of Ryerson Polytechnic University in Toronto, Ontario, Canada. This series of interviews entitled *"Mind-Control Series" has been* fully transcribed. Part of it was translated into French by the Christian group *"Parole de Vie"* and put on the internet under the title *"Survivors of the illuminati"*. After examining all these documents and testimonies, *"Parole de Vie"* produced an interesting synthesis, which is presented below:

- 1 / The mental programming of human beings exists. This is an undeniable fact. It is a phenomenon of which the scientific community has only recently become aware, on a historical scale. A few decades ago, almost nobody talked about it, and there were almost no serious published documents on the subject.

- 2 / On the other hand, the technique of mental programming is extremely ancient, and seems to date back to the time of Babylon and ancient Egypt. Men seem to have understood very early on that it was possible to transform other human beings into mental slaves, through appropriate conditioning, based on repeated traumas.

- 3 / The Illuminati, or those who make up the "ruling elite" of the planet, also seem to have quickly realised the advantage they could gain from these techniques for world domination. In fact, Christians will have recognised that behind these abominable techniques and tortures lies the hand of Satan, who wants to enslave mankind, and make himself worshipped as God, in the form of the Antichrist announced by the Bible.

- 4 / Mental programming is based on the phenomenon called "dissociation", or "fragmentation" of the personality into multiple personalities. It is as if an individual's personality can be fragmented into several different personalities, which can take over the body in turn. Moreover, there are like 'walls of amnesia' between these different personality fragments, so that each fragment does not remember what happened to the other fragments. In fact, these are not multiple personalities in the absolute sense. The individual retains a single personality, but it is fragmented into different components apparently independent of each other.

- 5 / This splitting of the personality is generally caused by a violent and painful trauma. This trauma provokes physico-chemical reactions in the brain. The splitting of the personality would be a defence reaction of our organism against a too violent trauma. The brain creates a "special memory zone", which records the trauma at a subconscious or unconscious level, to spare the conscious memory from too much pain. A fragmentation of the personality is thus created, which will allow the memory of the trauma to be preserved, but at a level that is no longer conscious. This hidden memory will be surrounded by an "amnesic wall", so that the waking personality is not aware of it. It is therefore the victims of these traumas who "naturally" create this split in their personality, in order to be able to manage and absorb the traumas they have suffered. This splitting of the personality can therefore occur naturally in all those who experience violent trauma. But it can also be artificially induced, by inflicting controlled traumas on victims, combined with hypnosis or various drugs. It is then possible not only to fragment the personality, but also to condition, or program, each fragment of the personality. All these programmed fragments remain dormant at the subconscious level. But they can be activated, that is, they can go up to the conscious level and take control of the body. They are activated by means of secret codes defined in advance. The reception of this code by the victim plunges him into a hypnotic or second state, and the fragment of his personality that has been activated then takes control of his body, to carry out the programme coded in advance: spying, murdering, seducing, etc... One understands the advantage of this abominable technique for all the secret services. The CIA or the KGB have carried out or sponsored the most important research in this field, research financed by the American and Russian governments. They also "benefited" from the research carried out by Nazi doctors in the death camps, under the direction of the infamous Doctor Josef Mengele, who later took refuge in the United States.

- 6 / Over the past few decades, many doctors, psychiatrists, psychologists and other therapists have seen an increasing number of patients with similar symptoms coming into their practices. They had all experienced childhood sexual trauma, had severe personality disorders, and various characteristic symptoms: depression, alcoholism, drug addiction, eating disorders, sleep disorders, anxiety... All these patients also recounted all kinds of very disturbing personal memories, which spoke of satanic ceremonies, planned assassinations, money laundering, contacts with political, religious and economic circles, world conspiracy, New World Order... Many therapists were content to consider these patients as seriously mentally deranged. But others were astonished by the similarity of their testimonies and symptoms, and decided to make serious investigations into this phenomenon, in a scientific and systematic way.

They began to verify the memories of the victims, to learn about the satanic cults and their practices, and to have access to highly confidential information or documents proving that the government had financed extensive research on mental programming, and had carried out all sorts of experiments in military bases, hospitals and research centres, NASA centres, etc. They calculated that hundreds of thousands of innocent citizens had been used as involuntary guinea pigs in these very traumatic experiments. Favourite populations were the mentally ill, prisoners, military personnel, prostitutes, orphans and children in general. As the number of survivors grew, they organised themselves and, aided by a large number of therapists, demanded official investigations. Presidential Commissions of Inquiry were appointed, which recommended that secret files, including those of the CIA, be made public. President Clinton has acknowledged the facts, and certain practices, including experiments involving the use of radiation. He has publicly apologised to the victims and made funds available to compensate them. But only the tip of the iceberg has been found. Most specialists and survivors are convinced that these experiments are still going on, and that everything is being done to hush up the matter and discredit the victims or the most active researchers. The government often hides behind "defence secrecy" or the requirements of national security. Since none of the torturers involved in mind-programming have ever been prosecuted for illegal or immoral activities, this has, of course, encouraged the continuation of these practices.

- 7 / The study of the testimonies of survivors and therapists that we have published leads us to make the following remarks:

Even though the survivors' testimonies have been taken to competent therapists who have analysed and verified them, they remain personal testimonies. Given the complexity of the human psyche and mental programming techniques, one must always be cautious when dealing with personal testimony. If the survivors are born-again Christians, which some are, their testimony as survivors should be analysed in the light of their Christian testimony and the fruits of their lives.

What may lead us to believe that these testimonies are true as a whole is their large number, as well as the variety of geographical and social origins of the survivors, most of whom do not know each other. The mathematical probability that this is an invention or manipulation is practically zero. But this does not mean that we should automatically accept all the details of these accounts. It is well known that human memory can be very unreliable. Added to this is the problem of certain false memories, deliberately programmed by the torturers in their desire to cover their tracks.

Since the Illuminati will not fail to discredit, often without reason, the testimony of survivors and even therapists or those who assist survivors, the latter must always ensure that their conduct and research methodology are as above board as possible, so as not to be open to criticism, even though slander can never be avoided.

We recently learned, for example, that Fritz Springmeier's home in Oregon was raided by the FBI and police, who allegedly discovered "marijuana production equipment" and weapons. It is perfectly possible that these things were intentionally placed in his house by the investigators, when one knows how unscrupulous the CIA is. In any case, the judge placed Fritz Springmeier on electronic probation (with an electronic bracelet), pending trial. Springmeier himself claims total innocence in this case, and claims to be the victim of a frame-up, which is highly probable. (editor's note: Fritz Springmeier was finally sentenced to 8 years in prison, he was released in 2011 and placed under probation for 5 years).

Similarly, it is certain that most survivors were drugged and hypnotized. This does not make it easy for them to gain credibility, and it is relatively easy to dismiss their testimony wholesale on these grounds. A serious researcher will be aware of these dangers, and will be careful not to have his or her judgement distorted, to stick to the facts.

It is important that those who help the survivors are therefore well aware of all these dangers, and take all necessary precautions not to be caught out. In this respect, we could criticise Fritz Springmeier for being, to say the least, very imprudent in personally looking after Cisco Wheeler, as she herself says, "24 hours a day, 365 days a year". We believe that a committed Christian should never be involved with a person of the opposite sex in this way on a long-term basis (unless he or she is part of a large team, and is never alone with the victim), lest he or she be open to temptation or criticism. He could easily be accused of adultery or fornication by an outside slanderer who would judge on the basis of appearance, even if nothing wrong had been done.

Christians (such as Fritz Springmeier and Cisco Wheeler) put too much emphasis on the psychic or psychological aspects of mental programming, and not enough on the demonic aspects. It is true that they were interviewed on radio programmes aimed at the general, mostly non-Christian public. But they could have talked more about the intervention of demons in these personality disorders. Certain 'fractions' of the personality may well be demons that take control of the victims' bodies, which should have been cast out in the name of Jesus Christ, instead of engaging in ineffective psychotherapy in this area. Yet Cisco Wheeler admits in his interview that all Illuminati are completely possessed. It is very likely that their victims are too, and only their conversion to Jesus Christ can enable them to deal with this spiritual problem once and for all.

This allows us to talk about therapy and care for victims. This is probably the weakest point of these testimonies. It is clear that these therapies, which use the skills of psychiatry, psychology and the human sciences, are totally insufficient to completely heal the victims of mental programming. Indeed, these therapies are limited to action at the level of the psyche, i.e. the soul (thoughts, feelings and will), or the body (action on brain waves to control various states of consciousness). The mind of the victims is not affected by these therapies. Thus, even if these therapies can produce beneficial effects at the level of the psyche and the restructuring of the personality of the victims, they are powerless to solve their deep spiritual problems. The real therapy would be to lead them to Jesus

Christ, to go through a spiritual rebirth, as they are taught all aspects of the cross, to learn to walk by the spirit. Only the power of the preaching of the cross can enable the survivors to break permanently with such a burdened past and heredity, and make them understand that in Christ all things old have passed away and all things have become new![505]

We can add to this synthesis the importance of the notion of soul fragments during the traumatic process of Monarch programming. As we saw in the previous chapter, the splitting of the personality corresponds to a fragmentation of the soul whose different parts remain blocked, as if "frozen" in another space-time. This is a different dimension from ours, used by programmers to manage and control alter. It is in this dimension that they set up the partitioning structures to lock up, dominate and condition the soul fragments.

In this process of dissociation of the personality during traumas, there are therefore on the one hand the purely biological and physical consequences of neurological and chemical changes, which are now well understood by psychotraumatologists; and on the other hand the metaphysical consequences of the separation of the physical and energetic bodies, the "tearing out of the soul", creating a breach towards other dimensions of the being. Monarch programming is therefore both a scientific process and, above all, a spiritual and occult process in which external entities can interact.

Everything has a material side and a spiritual side... The spiritual aspect affects the material aspect and vice versa, they are two worlds that interact continuously. The mirror metaphor from Alice in Wonderland explains this notion of the spiritual world versus the material world very well. What do occultists do to see into the future or the past, or to communicate with demons? They use (among other things) a mirror to transcend our space-time (catoptromancy)...

Demonology is a key to Monarch programming, where demonic entities cooperate and have a gatekeeper role for each programming and memory. It is therefore imperative to take into account this spiritual and energetic domain to understand the subject as a whole.

---

[505] "Survivors of the Illuminati" (8), A209 - Word of Life.

CHAPTER 8

DEPROGRAMMING PROTOCOLS

"There is only one way to kill monsters: accept them" Julio Cortázar

1 - INTRODUCTION

This chapter is not intended to be a medical or therapeutic guide. It is intended to provide additional information to help understand as best as possible how the memory, mental programming and internal system of an I.D.T. works. This chapter is an expansion of the section entitled *"I.D.T. and Therapy"* in Chapter 5.

The term "deprogramming" may seem exaggerated or inappropriate in the sense that a human mind is not computer hardware and will never be programmable or deprogrammable at will in the same way as a computer can be; although transhumanism, which advocates the use of science and technology to improve the physical and mental characteristics of human beings, raises fears of such things. In fact, it is the victim who "deprograms" himself, the therapist merely guiding him in the process of becoming aware of the conditioning based on traumatic memories. Deprogramming consists of discovering the type of structure present in the inner world, determining the trigger codes and releasing the alter (soul fragments) trapped in the space-time where they experienced the abuse and programming. The deprogramming will also be done by reconstructing the memory puzzle so that a rational and chronological understanding can be made. Victims usually have programming to combat possible therapy, either through self-destruction or sabotage of therapeutic work, the aim of which is to silence the victim if they start to remember things and talk about them outside the cult.

The issue of deprogramming is obviously very delicate in the sense that there is no established protocol or official therapy to defuse and cancel MK programming. As we have seen in Chapter 5, modern psychiatry has totally abandoned the study and treatment of dissociative disorders and I.D.D., and more globally of psychotraumatology. Today, therefore, it does not provide any answers for establishing effective diagnoses and therapeutic protocols. The few therapists who work with survivors are looking for the best methods to stabilise the patient, defuse the programming, unload the traumatic memories and finally merge the alter personalities. Sometimes prayers of deliverance and even exorcism can be of great help in "cleansing" the parasitic entities. The intervention of a competent shaman for the recovery of the soul fragments can also help the survivor. Survivor Lynn Moss-Sharman reported how Native Americans in Canada performed intensive healing sessions to help victims of ritual abuse and mind control in their community. She herself has attended healing ceremonies in *sweat lodges* where elders work with victims. She says that they have the most impact on healing and she says that she would certainly not be alive if it were not for their intervention. The spiritual aspect is therefore just as important, if not more so, than the purely psychiatric aspect and prayer for the help of these victims is essential. Many testimonies report a recovery brought about by the grace of God and by conversion to Jesus Christ. Christ is certainly best placed to restore order to a soul that has been fractured by extreme trauma, programmed and bound to demonic entities.

2 - RESTORING A HEALTHY SPIRITUALITY

The programmers are well aware of the power of prayer for both physical and psychic healing, which is why they will install conditioning very early on so that the victim is resistant and even totally allergic to the idea of a loving and saving God. Conditioned since childhood, they cannot turn to something they do not believe in, or even violently reject. Cutting the victim off from God is an essential point for keeping her under spiritual control, so turning her back to the good God can also be a crucial point for her healing. Especially as there is usually some form of spirituality already present in these victims due to the pervasiveness of the occult in the environment they come from, they need to be steered in the right direction. Survivors coming out of a satanic/luciferian network will have strongly held beliefs from early childhood, some of which need to be defused and broken:

- Satan is stronger than God, he has the power, God is not able to do anything to protect me.

- God does not love me, he despises and rejects me. I am guilty of crimes that God can never forgive me, I have no hope of redemption.

- God wants to punish me, I am deeply afraid.

- My life is controlled by Satan, I irrevocably belong to Satan, he has taken my life and I am possessed by a spirit or demon that controls my life. Many survivors will find it difficult to accept that they have an I.D.T. because they may believe that their alter personalities are demons controlling them. This keeps the victim isolated and separate from their original personality. It is therefore essential to help the person understand that they have been used and held in these states of consciousness for the purpose of control and that they are not responsible for anything.

- *I am consecrated to Satan, I have vowed to serve him throughout my life in exchange for his protection and gifts.* These bonds or pacts require powerful spiritual work, deliverance must come through renunciation of Satan, exorcism prayer and if possible conversion to Jesus Christ, the only true Saviour and Healer. It must also be realised and kept in mind that the religious beliefs in which the alter personalities were involved are based on something real. Trying to change them overnight would be like telling a Christian or a Muslim that the foundations of their religion are meaningless. The whole "magical" aspect also plays an important part in the beliefs of a survivor of a satanist cult. The religious and spiritual side is an important part of the child's conditioning, but it is the physical and psychological (splitting) trauma that remains the focus for MK programming.

Survivor Svali reports that in some groups, a specific programme will orient the child against Christianity. Christianity is the antithesis of Luciferian occult practices, so they want their members to be unable to come into contact with the hope that Jesus Christ could bring. During torture, the child will often cry out for help or appeal to God. At this point, the programmer will say to the child: "God has abandoned you, He couldn't love you, that's why you hurt so much. If He was so powerful, He could stop this. They will even ask the child to pray and ask God to intervene. The child will then pray to God and then the abuser will further abuse the child. This situation will create a deep sense of despair in the little victim, the child will truly believe that he has been abandoned by God, that He has remained deaf to his call. The child will also be systematically abused and tortured when the name of Jesus Christ is mentioned, in order to create a psychological barrier to the mere mention of His name.[506]

Many readers may ask a legitimate question here: *'But why doesn't God intervene?'* Why doesn't he intervene in wars either? Why is there so much misery on this planet, including all the suffering of children, if God existed? These are questions that come up very often. We live in a fallen world under the yoke of Lucifer. Is not the fallen angel called *the prince of this world* in the Bible: *Now is the judgment of this world; now shall the prince of this world be cast out* (John 12:31), *My kingdom is not of this world* (John 18:36). This is the reason why these satanic/luciferian sects all connected to the fallen angels/demons are currently ruling this planet without being bothered at all. The issue of the suffering of these children in the networks is obviously unacceptable and even inconceivable to many of us. But it is up to us, human creatures, to become aware of the situation, to react and to work to stop these things at our level.

This extreme conditioning combined with occultism and demonology creates a powerful spiritual programming (a reverse sanctification) which it is therefore essential to break in order to establish new healthy and constructive spiritual notions. This spiritual programming can be the most damaging part of an MK-Monarch slave's system as it is designed to cut him or her off from the true Source of healing. It is an intentional distortion of Truth that teaches and reinforces false and inverted concepts of God. Some alter personalities may be very violent towards anything that refers to the Christian world, so it takes a lot of patience and understanding to reconcile the survivor to a positive spirituality based on love, gentleness, hope, grace and mercy. A new source of spirituality will greatly help the patient to dissolve the powerful occult attachments to the cult, to stop identifying with the abusers and to reclaim the parts of himself that have been "captured". Any intentional act to control and spiritually enslave a

---

[506] *How the Cult Programs People* - Svali, 2000.

child through terror, who is therefore not capable of making a contrary choice, can be reversed during therapy by a simple application of free will, as we all have control over our spirituality. Awareness of trauma and MK programming, and the application of free will, will enable this detachment and autonomy to be achieved. It is a question of setting up a physical, psychological and spiritual separation with the group of torturers. This separation will take place progressively as:

- The authority figure(s) of the group will be discredited
- Contradictions will be highlighted (ideology versus reality), e.g. "how can they preach love when they rape and exploit the victims."
- The patient starts to listen to the therapist, i.e. when reality starts to take over from the sectarian ideology.
- The patient begins to realise and express some reproaches towards the sectarian group.
- The patient begins to see himself as an opponent of the cult rather than a member of it.[507]

3 - SAFETY AND STABILITY

A key point is that the survivor must be safe before deprogramming can begin. This is to ensure that the survivor is both physically and psychologically safe for effective therapeutic work to begin, as it would be pointless to begin anything if there was a risk that the survivor would be severely abused for speaking out. If the abuse is still ongoing, the dissociative protective function will continue to operate and destabilise the person. Trying to dismantle and stop this dissociative process would then be like trying to stop the victim's only means of survival and protection. This is why the first step is to cut off all contact with the perpetrators in order to start a safe therapy allowing deprogramming. If the issue of safety arises, it will slow down the therapy because energy will be diverted to this fear rather than to the work of unloading the traumatic memories. Many survivors are still in contact with the cult when they start therapy, but it will progress much more quickly once this contact has been permanently broken.[508]

Stabilisation is about reducing risky behaviour and personality shifts. In Cathy O'Brien's autobiography, Mark Phillips gives a step-by-step account of the guidelines he put in place to stabilise O'Brien when they fled to Alaska to keep her safe from the Network[509]:

1. I maintained constant vigilance to ensure that Cathy would be physically and psychologically protected from any outside influence.

---

[507] "All Gods Children: The Cult Experience - Salvation Or Slavery?" - Carroll Stoner, Jo Anne Parke, 1977, p.231.

[508] *Breaking the Chain: breaking free of cult programming* - Svali, 2000. Omnia Veritas Ltd.

[509] *TRANCE Formation of America: True life story of a mind control slave* - Cathy O'Brien & Mark Phillips, 2013, p.47-48.

2. No memory could be verbalised by Cathy until she had written it down. The only questions I could ask had to be related to her story and addressed to the personality being consulted who was reliving her memories. These questions were only to be about the who, what, when, how and where of the memory. Even if I had been given the answers in advance, I was not to intervene. Our perceptions could have been radically different, which could create additional memory barriers between his personality fragments.

3. I basically explained to Cathy what mind control was and she understood that what had happened to her was not her fault. However, she also understood that she was becoming responsible for her actions here and now. It was through therapy that she asserted control over her own mind.

4. We spent many hours in 'intellectual discussions' about the religious beliefs Cathy had learned, in which they were 'logically' dismantled - just as if I were explaining how the illusion induced by a magician's tricks helped to blur reality.

5. Cathy would not be allowed to express any emotion when the memories were brought up and entered in her diary. I never asked her: 'How does it feel?' This is as important as the issue of safety for a quick recovery of the memory.

6. I provided Cathy with the necessary food, vitamins, water and sleep to improve her failing physical health.

7. I taught Cathy to visualise her memories on a 'mental cinema screen' rather than reliving them through the 'virtual reality' mechanism of the mind.

8. I taught Cathy how to put herself into a trance and control the depth of her trance through a certain self-hypnosis technique (some consider it to be meditation). This was put in place to avoid any possibility of contamination of her memories or confusion between them that might have occurred if I had used this hypnotic suggestion technique known as 'induced imagery'.

9. Cathy was not allowed to read books, newspapers or magazines, nor could she discuss any of the recovered memories with Kelly (her daughter). Cathy had lived with information control all her life and therefore had little opportunity to grapple with the contamination of memories. This rule was also understood and respected by Kelly whose memories were beginning to surface.

10. All the ways of behaving and other social conventions adopted by Cathy were re-examined in logical discussions between us. All pre-established ways of behaving, including daily routines, were either reworked or completely removed.

11. I demanded that she wear a watch on her wrist day and night to alert me whenever she felt she was experiencing the slightest 'black hole'. In the absence of trauma, missing time is a major sign of the transition from

one personality to another. On the other hand, regaining a sense of time indicates that one is recovering.

"Write it down, Mark orders me. I don't want to hear it, I want to be able to read it, so that I can understand it properly (...) Writing it down will revive the logical part of your brain. When you write down your memories, it transforms an incomprehensible emotion into something logical and thus makes it understandable. Once it's understandable, you can deal with the reality of your past in a logical way (...) Just transfer that view to a screen in your mind, like a movie screen. This will allow you to access your memories without abreaction (...) That is to say, he explains, without reliving it. As I said, you have already survived it once. There's no point in reliving it. It's just memories now, and you already know that. Look at the screen of your mind through the eyes of the one who endured those events. Smell the smells. And then write it all down. That's why I said the pen is mightier than the sword. This technique will give you back control of your memory, and ultimately your mind."[510]

Before beginning the work of becoming aware of and overcoming the programming, therapist Ellen P. Lacter has developed a list of tools that can stabilise and secure the patient. Lacter has developed a list of tools that can stabilise and secure the patient[511]:

1 - Obtaining a family tree, educational, professional and residential history for future reference.

2 - Create a special formula or prayer to "protect the space" at the beginning of each session.

3 - Maintain a deep respect for the patient's free will.

4 - To explore the patient's deepest spiritual values and beliefs, in order to determine the role that this 'spiritual source' can play in the therapeutic work.

5 - Create an internal "box" (or container) to store pain, fear, toxic states (drugs, alcohol...), all that may be undesirable and harmful to the progress of the therapy. There may be several "storage boxes" in the inner world.

6 - Create an inner place of healing and recuperation. A peaceful and serene "resting place" where alter personalities can be "released" from the places where the abuse occurred and receive help from other alters to heal emotionally and physically.

7 - Create an inner space to work on programming awareness and resolution. This "workroom" or "meeting room" will have the function of working with an overview of the system, but also on trauma and information retrieval. The patient will decide which alter will work in this area and will design the room in his or her own way.

8 - Establish a procedure for obtaining information in this "workroom".

---

[510] *"For the sake of National Security"* - Cathy O'Brien & Mark Phillips, 2015, p.21.

[511] "Ritual Abuse and Mind-Control: The manipulation of attachment", chap: Torture-based mind control: psychological mechanisms and psychotherapeutic approaches to overcoming mind control, Ellen P. Lacter, 2011, p.116.

4 - RECLAIMING THE 'INNER WORLD'

The virtual creation of a "storage box" or of different "rooms" may seem something strange or fanciful in therapy. But as mentioned in the previous chapter, the inner world of a split personality is very large, it is a dimension that forms a real universe that can be arranged. Just as the programmer arranges and structures the inner world for enslavement, the therapist as well as the patient can also use their creativity to bring elements into this dimension. Elements that will help to secure the inner system with the alter, as well as to structure the therapy. Dr. Ellen Lacter reported, for example, the case of a patient who put his questions in a bucket which he then plunged into the bottom of a well (symbolising his subconscious) to bring it up in order to obtain information or images.

In a 2003 *S.M.A.R.T.* conference, ritual abuse and mind control survivor Carol Rutz explains the usefulness of these therapeutic elements injected into this inner world. It can be a storage area for memories or a soothing and safe place for alter: *"When I left the therapist's office, I had to put away the things I had just worked on so that I could live well during the week without being bombarded by new information that had come up. So I created a safe inner place to put the memories we were working on in each session, the aim being that I wouldn't be drowned out by all the stuff between sessions. It was a toy box and I put a teddy bear on it at the end of each session before leaving the office. During the week, we could also keep a diary and then let the memories come out of the box during the next week's therapy. This box was different from the safe place my alters had been able to build for shelter and healing (...) The same visualisation that had been used by the executioners for programming allowed us to undo that same programming. We created an inner healing place where any alter who wanted to, could enter and stay to receive help from other alters. I have found that there are alters who cannot speak because of programming or because they are pre-verbal alters, and another alter personality has volunteered to be used to work on memory retrieval."* [512]

For Svali, the good news is that this 'inner landscape' is very malleable. Once the different parts have been 'found', the structures holding them captive are discovered and they are finally released, they can be encouraged and helped to settle permanently in the safe places of the inner world. Structures installed in the mind to harm and control the victim can then be removed. The survivor's healing and deprogramming work thus uses to its advantage what programmers use to enslave: that is, the unlimited malleability of the "inner landscape."

Patients can create many other new, soothing places in their inner worlds because there are no limits in this dimension of being. Survivor Jen Callow writes: *"The environment of our inner world has also evolved. At the end of each session, our therapist makes sure that any new alter personality that has been*

---

[512] "Healing from ritual abuse and mind control" - Ritual Abuse Secretive Organizations and Mind Control Conference, SMART 2003, www.ritualabuse.us.

discovered will find a comfortable place that provides its basic needs. We build a mansion full of rooms with a large common area, bathrooms with large tubs for bubble baths, a large kitchen with large tubs and a large table, play areas, etc. Each room can be furnished and decorated to suit the individual. Each room can be furnished and decorated according to the wishes of its resident, it can have a lockable door and a window (...) We can also create many more buildings if we wish. We now have a healing area filled with medicinal plants, various remedies, with a very nice view: gardens and meadows, an ocean with beaches, forests (...) We are creating spaces for sports, dance, arts... Each thing created encourages us to work together, to cooperate, to interact and to have more moments of relaxation and fun."[513]

This inner world has been set up by the programmers with different internal structures; knowing their nature will help the therapist to discover how many alter personalities are present in the system and with whom it is most important to work. The approach is to explore each part of the structure to find out what its functions are and how many alters "live" in it or are indirectly connected to it. When the programming is made aware by the patient and the alter personalities trapped in the structures understand that it is an illusion, the structure usually dissolves itself. When large structures disappear in this way, some patients may feel a "void" and they may be replaced by something else. The programmers usually secure these structures with traps and guardians (demons), or even with an alter programmed to be a *good and loyal soldier.*

5 - THE ALLIANCE WITH ALTER PERSONALITIES

As MK programming is based on I.D.T., the stabilisation protocols and the fusion of the alter are therefore applied in deprogramming (see *"I.D.T. and Therapy"* in Chapter 5). *The alliance* with the alters will consist in associating and cooperating with them in order to make them participate in the therapeutic work. Each alter personality in a system that has been programmed takes great care to perform its assigned function and they are usually terrified of failing in their mission. It is important to map this system of alter personalities both horizontally (their numbers and functions) and vertically (their hierarchical organisation). As we have already noted, alter personalities are organised hierarchically, and those in the lowest levels of the hierarchy will be punished by those in the higher levels. Alters at higher levels of the hierarchy are afraid of being punished or killed by the external perpetrators. No alter should be neglected, all have a role to play in therapy. According to therapist Alison Miller, it is important to work with the most 'charismatic' Alters in the system, those at the top of the hierarchy, especially those who have believed the lies, false promises and threats of their tormentors and have finally become aware of the deception. These are the alter "tormentors", the persecutors we have already

---

[513] "Healing the Unimaginable: Treating Ritual Abuse and Mind Control" - Alison Miller, 2012, p.273.

mentioned. It is very important to recognise that these alters are no different from any others in that their job is also to maintain the survival of the victim. It is important not to banish or attempt to mask or dismiss certain alters by labelling some as "good" and others as "bad". By working with these "leaders", the therapist will be able to gain the cooperation of other alters lower in the internal hierarchy. In the documentary *"When the Devil Knocks"*, therapist Cheryl Malmo says of these alters: *"I knew immediately that I had to befriend 'Tim' because you want to have these angry, hostile alters as your helpers. When the devil knocks on the door, invite him in for tea. "*

The therapist will thus gradually establish trust with this hierarchy of alter. The aim is to gradually show them in a calming manner what really happened to them, but also their false beliefs. The alter observers and reporters can also help the therapist a lot by participating in the reconstitution of the puzzle because they will help to determine which memories need to be worked on the most. Memories are broken up into a thousand pieces like puzzle pieces and each alter contains certain pieces. So the alters need to work together to put the memory puzzle together. Some therapists therefore invite all the alter personalities affected by a particular experience to meet in an inner meeting room, in order to work on reconstructing this memory chronologically. As we have seen, many survivors have testified to having parts of themselves come out of their physical bodies during abuse. They therefore saw the scene with the keen eye of a bird, in a detached and objective way, while other alters seemed to hide deep inside the body when the abuse occurred. These different external and internal points of view will mean that these scenes will be recorded in much greater detail than the alter who was directly raped and tortured. Survivor Trish Fotheringham explains that *experiences are often fragmented at the time they occur. This means that one alter could be "out" during an event, while one or more other alters would turn away from the feelings, emotional state and pain associated with what was being experienced, without actually being out of the body. It is for this reason that each piece of memory of each alter must be accessed and consulted so that the experiences can be considered recovered and healed. "*[514]

In the book Ritual Abuse and Mind Control, therapist Ellen P. Lecter quotes a conversation she had with survivor Carol Rutz: "If it was ritual abuse, there might be four or five alters involved: one might be a child, the other might be an adult. Lecter quotes from a conversation she had with survivor Carol Rutz: "If it was ritual abuse, there might be four or five alters involved: one for pain, one for ritual, one for transportation, etc. I think that's why people with D.I.D. have trouble remembering what happened. It's because you usually have different alter personalities that emerge successively during the same event. So it's not possible to remember the whole experience unless you access the memories of each alter that was involved. If you can get the presenting alter to go beyond its fear and pain, then you will be able to reach the rest. Many times

---

[514] "Ritual Abuse in the Twenty-first Century: Psychological, Forensic, Social and Political Considerations" - James Randall Noblitt & Pamela Perskin Noblitt, 2008, p.497.

I remembered events from long before, which helped me to finally put it all together and understand the ramifications of it all."[515]

What Carol Rutz describes here can be illustrated in one of the minutes of the Dutroux case that we have already described in chapter 4 on ritual abuse in relation to a witness X: *"When she woke up* (from the hypnotic trance), *she had the impression that there were several people who were present at what she described* (sacrificial ritual and orgy) *and that these people (these Nathalie's) faded away in front of one another. She thinks she disappeared about ten times. "*

In *"Breaking the Chain"*, Svali writes that the very first programming on the child, of "breaking the heart", is difficult to undo because it touches on the issue of abandonment and rejection of the original, infant personality. This concerns the child's early life experiences and involves its relationship with its parents and close family members. Working on these memories requires an effort by the whole internal alter system to come together to help the personality fragments that suffered this extreme initial parental rejection to recognise the importance of the present moment and the fact that these adults were truly unhealthy. Making them aware of the present moment is essential as they usually live stuck in the time-space where these traumas occurred. These alter child and even baby personalities will often feel depressed and angry. Some alters may then take on the role of "nurturer" to comfort them and make them understand that they are lovely children, no matter what these adults may have done to them. External therapeutic help and a good internal system of alter "nurturers" can greatly assist in the healing process by providing a new perspective and relief for these young, wounded and abandoned alters.

The first abuses aimed at splitting the personality occur very early in the child's life (0 to 24 months). Some alter who have never forgotten them will be able to share the memories with other alter who are totally amnesic. This must be done very gradually because these abuses occurred very early in life. For this, the creation of an internal "nursery" (set up as required) can help the process. The older, compassionate 'nanny' will be able to help and care for the children in this nursery. It is important to trust and validate what these alter children will say as they begin to move through the therapy and share their experiences. Often these will be pre-verbal alter children as they are still very young, so they need a way to express themselves. The presence of older alter children, who are close to the alter babies, can help them to verbalise their needs and fears. Generally, alter children have no trust in adults, even in the alter adult personalities of the system to which they belong. External therapeutic help is also important for healing, in order to train and structure the internal system so that it can provide help and good care for the injured children. It is about balancing the needs of the alter child between external care and the need for internal care from the alter system. The alter child can be helped by anchoring sessions, focusing on the

---

[515] "Ritual Abuse and Mind-Control: The manipulation of attachment", chap: Torture-based mind control: psychological mechanisms and psychotherapeutic approaches to overcoming mind control, Ellen P. Lacter, p.113.

present moment and realising that the physical body is now older and living a safe life.[516]

It must be borne in mind that many of the alter who suffered such horrors were deliberately kept at the age when the abuse took place. As we have seen, they are soul fragments stuck in a certain space-time. They are stuck in an age where they still believe everything they were told by their abusers, no matter how fantastical and unreal it may be. When the patient tries to remember what happened to him, the terror that is still present in his young alter will flood him, regardless of his age. Many alters are therefore stuck in the past, in an *eternal present* where they are still physically that child in contact with the aggressor(s). They need to be informed as much as possible of their current situation so that they realise that they are no longer in danger. This will enable them to stop punishing the other alter and learn to work as a group to regain their composure. It is necessary to explain to these fragments that they had to deal with unhealthy and violent people but that today all that is finished, that they are not in contact with them any more and that they do not have to follow the directives and the rules of these torturers any more. They can now come back to the present moment to make their own rules. It is also possible to change the programmed function of an alter to a new role in which he or she will use his or her skills and qualities in the service of therapy. It may be helpful to explain to alters, in simple words for younger ones, what post-traumatic stress, dissociation, amnesia, alter and flashbacks are.

Some alters may also have been programmed not to communicate directly with the outside world (never emerging to speak "out loud"), so it may take a considerable time before these alters are detected and begin to make contact with the therapist. Many of them will not have emerged from childhood, so they know nothing of the present world. They are alters who are not supposed to communicate with the outside world until they are triggered by a controller or programmer. They are fragments that will be very frightened and hostile when they "come out". It is also possible to use an intermediary alter, a mediator, to dialogue with these reluctant fragments. Even if they have already observed the outer world, the *real* world (our dimension) from the inside, they have rarely "come out" to interact with it directly, i.e. by taking control of the physical body. They therefore had a very limited life experience, limited to cult activities and "training" (programming); their rewards were sex, drugs and power. The patient may be very frightened of disclosing certain information, in relation to their abusers, but also because some alter will be terrified and humiliated by their own memories. They will therefore be afraid of the other's rejection if they talk about what they have done. The therapist must accept them, no matter what they may have been forced to do.

In therapy, it is also advisable to develop a holistic view of the victim's traumatic history and alter system. One way to access this global vision is to get in touch with the patient's *true self* (the original personality) or the *"inner guide"*, which are sometimes considered the same thing but not systematically.

---

[516] *Breaking the Chain: Breaking free of cult programming* - Svali, 2000.

According to some therapists, there is a part in each internal system that has the function of helping the patient at a higher level, a part called *ISH: Internal Self Helper*. This alter (if it is one) can be considered superior to the others, connected to God. It is a source of wisdom and an inner guide knowing all the other alter personalities, it accesses all the memories and life experiences of the person. *"The Inner Self Helper (ISH) should be identified as soon as possible. The therapist should not be afraid to work closely with the ISH, who will always be a protector of the alter personalities and will ensure that the treatment is respected. He will get the best possible agreements with the alter."*[517]

In her book Reaching for the Light, survivor Emilie Rose writes about this Inner Helper, this special source of wisdom: "Every survivor of ritual abuse has an inner part that has somehow remained connected to life, even in the midst of torture and death... It can have many names: the strong one, the spirit keeper, the healer, the mystic, the grandparent, the sage. Whatever we call it, we can affect our healing by seeking out this part of ourselves, inviting it to emerge, befriending it, nurturing it and assisting it to become more involved in our lives... This strong part of ourselves has a natural and innate desire for life and healing. It has knowledge of pain, healing and spirit. It may be the place where our connection to a higher power resides and it guides us on a true healing journey if we give it the opportunity."[518]

Dr. Sarah Krakauer calls this part the *inner wisdom*. In her book *Treating Dissociative Identity Disorder: The Power of the Collective* Heart, she reports on a patient who connected with this inner guide: *"Seven months after Lynn began therapy with me, she showed curiosity about the workings of the inner wisdom. While in a meditative state, she spontaneously asked her inner wisdom, "Why do you know all this and I don't? The inner wisdom then replied: You can think of me as the father you never had, someone you can count on and who will always be there, no matter what happens... I know all the different parts and how they fit together, because I can see the totality...' Lynn reported that she saw a beautiful yellow inner light after hearing this wisdom. She described: "This is the first time I've seen yellow like this. It's so pretty. It's a really reassuring experience, that I'm not alone anymore. A father is supposed to be the one who takes care of you... I feel a real calm, a sense of peace. Before discovering this yellow light, Lynn had already found that after seeking guidance in the theatre, she was able to go to a place where she saw a violet light that was both soothing and energising. It was something she had discovered for herself and she frequently went there during her meditations."*[519]

Perhaps the *ISH*, appearing to be a higher part of the being, corresponds to the *'spirit of superconsciousness'* described in the Kahuna tradition (in

---

[517] "Treatment philosophies in the management of multiple personality" - D. Caul, American Psychiatric Association, Atlanta, Georgia, 1978.

[518] "Healing the Unimaginable: Treating Ritual Abuse and Mind Control" - Alison Miller , 2012, p.246.

[519] Treating Dissociative Identity Disorder: The Power of the Collective Heart " - Sarah Y. Krakauer, 2001, p.130-131.

Chapter 6), which can override all other categories of soul fragments. In her article entitled *"The inner self helper concepts of inner guidance"*, therapist Christine Comstock concludes by writing: *"As with all psychological hypotheses, the existence of the ISH can neither be proven nor disproven. However, there is sufficient historical and clinical evidence to make it reasonable to believe that such a structure could exist and be beneficial. In the past, the concept of the dissociation of the "I" into an alter who observes and experiences has been found to be beneficial to the patient. The extension of the notion of "inner guidance" in the form of ISH to patients with IDD seems to be something that is logical and consistent with the experience described by these patients. According to many experienced clinicians, this phenomenon of inner guidance in the form of a separate psychic structure may be a useful clinical conceptualisation in the treatment of I.D.D."[520]*

It is obvious that the phenomenon of I.D.T. deserves a very thorough scientific research, because it leads to other dimensions of the being... but let's remind ourselves once again that this is the Pandora's box of the "nameless religion": all the discoveries concerning the arcane of the human psyche (and well beyond) allowing individual and global control must not be divulged in the profane world, an essential rule that allows to keep the power.

The words that were used by the perpetrators and programmers during the abuse, torture and programming sessions have a profoundly devastating effect on the victims. Memory work aims to ensure that the survivor can remember exactly what the programmer was saying to them along with the mental imagery that accompanied these phrases during the sessions. This is an essential point that will greatly help to deactivate the MK programming. It is therefore important to list and work on these words so that they lose their power to influence the victim. These words or phrases will lose their power even more when the traumatic memories are gradually emptied of their negative charge. The negative charge is that subconscious inner pain which, when triggered by stimuli, will activate programming. These words or phrases may have been used to define the role or nature of an alter and to name the alter, they may also be threats, insults, agreements (obtained under duress), commands and directives, specific trigger words aimed at bringing out an alter, access codes which may also include numbers, etc. Some of these commands can be replaced, for example by renaming alter personalities with new names and assigning them new roles. Prayers and blessings can also be used to counteract verbal attacks (programming commands) that remain in the subconscious.

During the therapeutic process, one of the greatest dangers is the programming of self-destruction and suicide. According to Svali, among the Luciferian elites, this programming is systematic. From early childhood, the victim is conditioned to believe that he or she will die if he or she leaves "the Family", the Network. This is the basis of suicide programming, which is closely

---

[520] "The inner self helper concepts of inner guidance: historical antecedents, its role within dissociation, and clinical utilization" - Christine M. Comstock, Journal Dissociation, Vol.4, N°3, 09/1991.

linked with the programming of loyalty and fidelity to the biological family and the Hierarchical Order. If the victim begins to access certain memories and decides to leave the network, or begins therapy, this sabotage or self-destructive programming should be triggered. This will then manifest as a feeling of being suddenly overwhelmed with overwhelming guilt and a deeply depressed state. Only the programmer and a few people have the code to deactivate this programming, which ensures that the victim will contact the group again. If the victim breaks this programming, they will need assistance and help, perhaps hospitalisation as breathing or heart rate may be severely impacted. Alter personalities may be programmed to commit self-harm or even suicide if there is an attempt at external disclosure or deprogramming. These alters are programmed to believe that the only way to escape suicide and self-destruction is to contact the programmer who knows the codes to stop the process.

One alter may punish another alter by scarifying it, for example, which is why it is important to make the whole alter system aware that they share the same physical body and that they are one individual.

The programming of an alter personality that can lead the victim to suicide is done by imprinting the belief that it is honourable to die for the cause of the "Family"; that traitors must kill themselves quickly before the group finds them to kill them in a slow and painful way; that their life will be so unbearable that it is better to kill themselves, etc.

According to Ellen Lacter, when the implanted commands *"don't remember"* and *"don't talk"* begin to break down, the rest of the programming becomes easier to recognize and overcome. Access to the different traumatic memories, which leads to the reconstruction of the chronological puzzle, will gradually release all the unconscious emotional charge that cements and allows the triggering of the programming. The more the scattered and repressed traumatic memories are made aware and reassembled, the more the emotional charge they contain will diminish, and the more the programming will lose its effectiveness. This is how the MK programming is gradually defused.

6 - PROCESSING TRAUMATIC MEMORIES

a/ General

Working with traumatic (dissociative) memories is a therapeutic process in which fragments of both psychological and physical memories (cellular memory) are reassociated. The treatment of a dissociative memory therefore consists of reassembling and making aware all the parts that make it up so that it can be definitively integrated, because as we have seen, the memory of an experience can be broken down into several pieces. Following this integration, the emotions and physical sensations associated with this memory will disappear and be replaced by a memory of what happened similar to any other conscious memory. This means that the repressed traumatic memory becomes a chronological and autobiographical memory with no negative charge. Once this process is complete, the different alter personalities associated with these memories can then be merged together. In some cases, this seems to happen automatically as soon as the memories are processed and made aware.

At the biological level, memories are linked to the different senses (sight, hearing, smell, touch, taste, but also physical pain or sexual pleasure), they are also linked to the different types of emotions. These memories are managed by the hippocampus, which transmits them to the cerebral cortex so that they are well integrated into the consciousness. This is how they move from the unconscious to the conscious level. Dissociative memories remain disconnected from consciousness, this is called traumatic amnesia, a 'forgotten' memory that has not been made conscious. These memories can arise suddenly and unexpectedly, usually in the form of flashbacks, which are eruptions of memories that suddenly come back to consciousness, they can be visual, auditory, emotional and even physical. Indeed, these flashbacks can trigger cellular memories linked to certain areas of the body, which can manifest as pain, paralysis and even physical marks. When these subconscious memories arise, they are relived as if they were actually happening in the present moment. When a person experiences an upwelling of traumatic memories resulting in a heavy emotional state, they will absolutely need to anchor themselves in the present moment. They need to open their eyes (usually closed during a flashback) and focus on their direct environment: sounds (the therapist's voice, for example), name and touch the objects around them in the room, they can also touch their clothes, naming them one by one, etc. Anchoring techniques are important in working with traumatic memories, as they prevent the patient from being overwhelmed by emotion and pain.

Generally, a patient will not be ready to do this work on traumatic memories until the alter personality system is cooperative. As we saw earlier, a relationship with the alters must be established so that all those who have been involved in the same experience, the same memory, can take part in the process. According to therapist Alison Miller, a memory cannot be fully integrated (and the programming dissolved) until all the fragments of the person involved in the traumatic memory align to put together their own piece of the memory, their piece of the puzzle, to establish the complete and chronological picture of the experience. Furthermore, if all the fragments of the patient are not cooperative, some alter may punish those who would disclose things prematurely.

Mind control groups deliberately create alter personalities who record everything and know the entire system and its history. Stella Katz calls this alter the *"Gatekeeper"*, whose function is to observe from the inside and record everything without ever intervening. Once accessed, these alter personalities can be of great help in determining both the content of a memory and the chronological list of the patient's alters who have successively experienced the traumatic experience.

There is also the issue of traumatic memories from the pre-verbal age, when the victim was still a baby. This type of memory cannot be verbalised to express the experience and feelings. Between the ages of 0 and 3, the declarative or explicit memory system that requires the maturation of the hippocampus is not yet operational. These will be implicit memories (emotional, behavioural, somato-sensory, perceptual, non-verbal). These implicit memories are linked to the amygdala of the right hemisphere, which matures earlier than the hippocampus

b/ The revival process

The term *"revivification"* and its restoration process was described by the survivor Brice Taylor. Unlike Fabian therapy, which we will also discuss, which only deals with non-traumatic conscious memories, this is the treatment of unconscious traumatic memories with the aim of fully integrating them into consciousness. The most difficult part of this work is certainly the emotional and sometimes physical pain that is associated with these dissociated memories. Revivification is a tool that can be useful when it is not possible to do a therapy session every time a traumatic memory comes to the surface of consciousness.

Brice Taylor introduces this technique: "As a survivor of extreme birth trauma, I spent years in therapy. I had abreactions and flashbacks about my incestuous past, ritual abuse and government mind control, until I was able to practice this revival process. To learn how to use this tool, I was helped by a member of the intelligence community who had some knowledge of MK programming and deprogramming. Revivification is an extremely valuable tool that helped me to deal with and archive the huge amount of painful memories. In this way I was able to recover the memory of my past and finally use my mind in a healthy and constructive way in the present moment. I think it is important to share this technique so that survivors can be helped in a simple way in their memory recovery process."

Reliving can begin when the patient is no longer in denial about past trauma and after they have learned to feel and express their emotions. According to Brice Taylor, it is not necessary to continually re-experience the abreactions or flashbacks physically and emotionally to unravel the memories. According to her, survivors need to re-experience cellular memories only when they are still in denial about the reality of their past. Re-experiencing will also allow the patient, who is overwhelmed by intrusive memories, which usually prevent him/her from functioning in daily life, to learn to contain, channel and manage these "flashes" of memories until he/she can finally process them properly.

When a patient has flashbacks at home, or when a memory is "triggered" by something in his environment, in public or in private, he can take a notepad and write down one or two words that will later serve to refresh his memory about what triggered the dissociated memory and its content. Following these notes, he can resume his activities without having to be constantly "harassed" by this memory. In the 48 hours following the flashback(s), the patient is advised to take notes on the trigger(s) and to examine the content of this memory. The examination of the memory is done in a calm environment, with deep introspection, in order to write down in detail the visual and auditory content, but also the odour and taste aspects that are linked to this traumatic memory. One criterion for determining whether these are genuine dissociated memories is that they are visually three-dimensional and contain strong sensory elements, such as sounds and smells.

To practice this type of amnesic memory exercise, the patient can first practice projecting conscious, non-traumatic memories onto a "mental screen". This consists of focusing on the details of this memory with the "mind's eye", i.e. closing the eyes to imagine the scene as real as possible. In this scene, the person can look, touch, smell and taste what was present, but also listen to sounds, words, sentences, etc. The work can therefore begin with non-dissociated memories that have not caused emotional shocks or physical pain. Once the patient is comfortable with this "mental screen", he or she can tackle memories that were previously amnesiac and that are beginning to emerge.

Here is how Brice Taylor describes the different phases of the process:

- 1/ Take a notebook.
- 2/ The patient must have previously listed elements that may trigger traumatic memories.
- 3/ The patient should be in a quiet, safe place to process these memories (preferably within 48 hours of their emergence). He will start by referring to his list of triggers.
- 4/ It is useful for the patient to have a diary or computer in which to store the dissociated memories that are brought back.
- 5/ Then the patient visualises this memory on an imaginary screen in his mind. He must concentrate on this memory with his mental eye, focusing on the sensory system, i.e. taste, smell, hearing, touch and sight. He must be interested in everything that was present at the time of the traumatic experience. They should also focus on the words and phrases that were spoken at the time. In people who have experienced ritual abuse and mind control, the words spoken during the dissociative states are very important because they contain the conditioning and programming. Alters who have heard what has been said may not repeat it in such a therapy session, they may, for example, recount the scene without the "soundtrack". They should be asked to give the full content of the memory, including the auditory content. The patient should try to see the scene through the eyes of the alter personality(ies) who experienced the event. He does not need to relive the scene or re-experience the painful emotions or sensations in the body. They just need to look at the memory in the same way as you would look at a film on a screen, but take care to retrieve as much information as possible. If the patient has survived the traumatic event once, he/she is now able to watch it with a certain distance in order to retrieve the bare essentials: i.e. all the details that will help him/her to become aware of what happened and which alter personality(ies) was/are involved in it. During this exercise, the patient should not judge what he/she sees on the mental screen, nor should he/she try to change the content. When the patient has dissociated the emotional content from the memory, it is then possible for him/her to describe precisely what he/she sees while the therapist takes note of the information. The therapist can therefore ask the patient to slow down or

repeat something without fear of re-traumatising the patient. It is as if the patient has a remote control with which he can zoom in, slow down or speed up the scene, pause, rewind or stop the story.

For this work of mental projection of a traumatic memory, the therapist Alison Miller advises starting the story in "normal life", i.e. in the situation that preceded the traumatic event (for example the car journey), and then ending it in the situation that followed the trauma. This is to broaden the chronology of the memory because the alter personalities at the beginning and end of a traumatic experience are usually not the same as those who suffered the traumas at the heart of the story. Thus, it will help the patient to better understand how his or her traumatic experiences are related to his or her daily life, to his or her conscious autobiographical memory and in what context they occurred.

- 6/ If the patient starts to experience an abreaction with bodily sensations during the visualisation, he can quickly write on a piece of paper: "*My body is trying to react to this memory*", and then thanks to the dissociative process already highly developed in him, he will move away from this memory which provokes a physical reaction. By dissociating from the physical or emotional pain, he can, for example, put it in a box in his inner world. He can also replace the images that trigger the abreaction with a maths problem. This will allow him to detach himself from the painful sensations, as he will then activate another area of his brain. If the body continues to react despite these measures, the patient should stop the mental projection session and anchor himself in the present moment with the methods listed above. The patient can then resume the mental projection session if he/she is able to maintain the dissociative barrier between the physical and emotional bodies and the traumatic memory. The same techniques can be applied when the emotional pain becomes too great. During this process, the patient can also choose to go voluntarily and fully into the emotional feeling of the memory in order to express it and make it burst as much as possible.

- 7/ If the patient feels sad, cries or is angry as a result of the traumatic memories, he or she can undertake another activity. A healthy young child who falls down and gets hurt will cry for a while, but very soon he will focus his attention on something that will bring him out of his negative state. Children are thus able to change their emotional states quickly. The patient can do the same thing by quickly choosing to do an activity that will put him in a positive mental and emotional state. He can play sports, garden, call a friend, walk the dog, paint, sing, take a bath, watch a comedy, all things that can bring him relaxation and joy. However, it is not about suppressing negative emotions such as sadness or anger. The patient should be able to feel and express them for as long as they need and want to. The patient's healing process is largely based on having control over himself and his own experiences. This part of the revival process may be appropriate for patients who are constantly stuck in old painful emotions.

When survivors are able to take charge and love themselves instead of destroying themselves, their abusers (or controllers) have lost. Survivors need to realise that only they can choose self-love instead of scarification for example. When they stop behaving as the programming has conditioned them, they become autonomous and free, with only their own minds as limits: they recover their own identity.

Brice Taylor points out that in this process it is easier to write down the traumatic memories first rather than verbalise them directly. This is also what Mark Phillips advocates, and is one of the rules he established in Cathy O'Brien's recovery and deprogramming protocol. The act of writing down the memories provokes, thanks to the coordination of the eyes and the hand, certain neuronal connections in the brain which will give the patient better access to his own cerebral capacities. In addition, writing down the memories means that they will be much richer in detail. Over time, the different "capsules" of traumatic memories will begin to come together to form a picture of what really happened in the patient's life. This more or less well put together jigsaw puzzle will explain many things that were previously misunderstood, such as undesirable behaviour or unexplained phobias. Brice Taylor explains that it is not necessary to dwell on every detail of memory to know whether it is valid or not, because with time and with enough recovery of traumatic memories, the pieces of memories will begin to validate each other by fitting together to form the puzzle of life. It is this overview of one's own life, hitherto shattered into pieces, that will help to provide the patient with the self-compassion, self-love and self-esteem that are so valuable to his or her healing and new life.

Here is an excerpt from Cathy O'Brien's book *"For National Security Purposes"* which illustrates the process of recovery from traumatic memories:

The answers come only slowly to the surface, but they bring up years of memories, all linked together. The whole thing seems to me to be one endless nightmare. When Mark comes home that night, there are sheets of paper scattered everywhere, covered with fragments of memories written in so many different scripts.

- I remembered a lot of things, but it doesn't make sense. I can't put the events in order.

I show him the pieces of paper and start crying:

- How can I remember when these things happened when I had no sense of time?

- It's simple," says Mark, "you have to ask yourself the right questions. Look beyond the moment. What season is it? Is there snow? Can you feel the warmth of the summer sun? Can you smell the spring flowers? Are you at school? Who is your teacher? What are you wearing? When did you have these clothes on? Are your brothers or sisters born yet? How old is Kelly? Look around you through the eyes of the person you used to be and to whom all this happened. Do people seem really tall to you, like when you were a little girl? What do you see at eye level? Their knees? Their eyes? Just time it as accurately as you can and leave the rest to the investigators (...)

You can look through old magazines and newspapers (...) You should start cutting out pictures, sentences, headlines - anything that catches your eye. When you have a box full of these cuttings, you can make a collage. It will be like putting the pieces of your mind back together (...)

- Dr. Patrick used the term "polyfragmented" to describe those little pieces that you glue back together. She also thinks that my idea of gluing could be beneficial to you.

Suddenly, my scribblings of memories seem to have a purpose after all. From then on I write down all the flashes that come up, whether they seem significant or not. I keep a pen and paper with me at all times. Memories often flash across the screen of my mind, sometimes to the point of breaking my concentration at the least opportune moments. A quick note of a word or phrase is enough to stop these intrusions, and allows me to get back to what I was doing before. It's as if my brain knows I'm going to write everything down later, and the flashes stop momentarily. Then, when I find myself in a position to concentrate properly, I let myself go into a deeper state, ask myself the questions Mark taught me, find the smells again and start writing down what is waiting to be retrieved photographically.

- Keep in mind, Mark advised me, that if a memory seems like it couldn't have happened, then you need to examine it closely to see if it's something you've been told or glimpsed in a film. Start by deprogramming the programme. Find the beginning and the end, what happened before and what happened after. Leave the written record of that memory out for three weeks. The truth does not disappear. Filling in the gaps with what might have happened, however, will disappear (...)

Writing down my memories as Mark taught me allows me to reconstruct them as they happened, but without the drama. I can deepen my trance with relaxation, watch events unfold photographically on my mind's screen, smell smells and recognise physical sensations without having to experience them again. Emotions had no existence of their own in the dissociative state I was in, and they still don't in this process of recovering my memory. Mark taught me to avoid the question often asked by therapists: "How does it feel?"[521]

c/ The inner theatre

In a 2006 *S.M.A.R.T.* lecture, survivor Lynn Schirmer described a tool that helps focus on particular memories and can be combined with the mind screen described above. It is a psychology tool that was developed by Dr. Lowell Routley and his colleagues, a model of theatre, a metaphor for consciousness and mind devised by neurobiologist Bernard J. Baars.

In '*In the Theater of Consciousness The Workspace of the Mind*', Bernard J. Baars describes how this 'theatre' works, which can be used to work on memories. In a theatre there is the stage, the actors, the lights, the set, the director

---

[521] *For the sake of National Security* - Cathy O'Brien & Mark Phillips, 2015, p.29-30.

and the audience. When you enter a theatre before the show, you see the stage, the audience and some doors at the side leading to the dressing rooms. As the lights start to go down and the audience falls silent, a single spotlight pierces the darkness to illuminate the stage. You know then that the writers, actors, sound and lighting engineers are all there, unseen but working together in the same direction and guided by a script that is about to be revealed to the audience. As the auditorium fades away, only the focus of consciousness remains, i.e. the spotlight illuminating the stage, everything else being in darkness. This theatre metaphor allows us to work on memories: the actors and the sets represent the content of the memory, traumatic or not, the spotlights represent the focus of attention on this memory, the conscious content emerges when the spotlights are directed towards the actors on the stage of the memory. These spotlights have an essential role because as soon as they direct the light towards a particular character, that character emerges into consciousness. Only those characters illuminated by the spotlights can convey information to the audience. In return, the audience, the public, can applaud or whistle, ask to hear more or, on the contrary, have an actor removed from the stage by throwing tomatoes at him. The audience of this theatre can also interact with the actors by exchanging information with them. But there is only one way to reach the audience as a whole, and that is through a character lit by the spotlight on stage. The audience is the raison d'être of all this experimental theatre.

The theatre stage represents the patient's interior, where he or she experiences the different perceptions, this place is called the fusion space. A simple exercise is used to access this place: the person has to visualise an object of their choice and try to determine the place where they feel something is happening inside them. This exercise may seem very simple, but for MK survivors, conditioned to avoid any kind of introspection, it can be something quite new and an important discovery. The ability to see into the fusion space can be a powerful tool. With practice, it is here that the person will be able to observe the elements of programming, in this "stage play", and even intervene directly by themselves.

The main actor in the scenario is usually the core, the true "I", the original personality, which can sometimes control the body. The various actors (alters) who are not in the spotlight, who are off stage, represent subsets, routines, skills, memories, feelings intended to act out particular behaviours or experiences. These different actors can enter the stage at any time to share the spotlight with the main actor causing a blending process in this fusion space. A trauma survivor may suddenly experience intense physical pain that is in fact another part of him/herself stuck in a traumatic memory, with the alters being able to blend with each other. According to Lynn Schirmer, this technique of introspection in the inner theatre allows us to examine this space of fusion. The patient can see objects and settings that have been set up and used by the programmers. It is a tool to get in touch with the inner world and to interact with it.

7 - FABIAN THERAPY

While therapies aimed at bringing up dissociative memories using hypnosis or other techniques such as EMDR (eye movement desensitisation and reprogramming) will bring the survivor face to face with his or her traumatic past, there is a non-frontal therapeutic method that avoids direct 'contact' with painful memories. Memories that can trigger certain implanted commands such as self-destruction and suicide programming.

This memory processing technique was disclosed by Kerth Barker, an *insider who was* himself a survivor of satanic ritual abuse and had been connected to the Network at some level. This therapeutic process was passed on to him by insiders who used their knowledge of MK programming to develop and establish a safe and effective protocol for discharging traumatic memories in a gradual manner, without having to relive them directly (it would appear that within the "Family" there are differing views on the MK issue).

Barker named this technique the *"Fabian"* therapy, in reference to the Fabian military strategy of avoiding a frontal and direct attack by setting up an indirect and progressive struggle. The aim of this therapeutic protocol is to unload and progressively cancel the impact of traumatic memories, which has the consequence of deactivating the programming that relies on these painful memories repressed at a subconscious level. These dissociative memories are toxic "capsules" that remain blocked in the subconscious, their presence will sabotage the individual's ability to think rationally and to act according to his or her own will. Therapeutic work that aims to discharge these unconscious toxic memories is therefore essential to deprogram the MK conditioning. This method will act on the repressed traumatic memories in an indirect way through work on the conscious memories: i.e. the sustained stimulation of semantic and episodic memories, two distinct forms of explicit memory.

Semantic memory is the memory that contains all the information that has been consciously memorised: telephone numbers, history lessons, etc. This semantic memory is made up of words or symbols. Episodic memory is made up of your life experiences. These are real events that you have consciously experienced, such as a walk in the woods or a football match. This episodic memory is composed of images, sounds, smells, tastes and emotions. Episodic memories are therefore like films that contain sensory perceptions and emotions. There is also the memory of subjective events, such as dreams (depending on one's ability to recall them) and imagination, i.e. the ability to imagine a fictitious event with the possibility of recalling it later.

Fabian therapy is designed to avoid the inappropriate triggering of implanted programming. This type of therapy only deals with conscious memories, i.e. episodic, semantic and subjective memories (dreams and imagination). There will never be a direct confrontation with dissociated and repressed traumatic memories. Sustained work on the conscious memories will be able to act indirectly on the repressed memories. In fact, all the layers of memory, down to the deepest, are interconnected in what can be called an "energetic mental field" that interacts with the brain and nervous system.

According to the Fabian therapy, memories are not made up of neurons but of stable subatomic energy, neurons being only a physical interface for these mnemonic energies (all the processes that facilitate the operations of memory). In this "energy field", each memory, whether conscious or unconscious, is connected to all the others by a kind of web. This means that if you work intensively on a certain area of the memory, it will automatically influence all other areas of the web: called the *"memory field"*. By working intensely on the episodic memory, you will subtly and indirectly work on the pain, on the trauma and on the amnesia of other repressed memories. These dissociated traumatic memories contain strong emotions that represent a powerful negative emotional charge. Working on conscious memories in a structured and intense way will slowly release the negative charge of these repressed memories. When enough of the negative charge is released, the implanted programming associated with these memories will cease to have power, thus gradually freeing the MK slave.

The commands implanted during programming are made up of words and images, mainly words, and the words are semantic. It will therefore be necessary to work on the conscious semantic memory in order to gradually release the negative charge of the commands implanted in the repressed and unconscious memory. The scientists who developed this therapy conducted experiments with people who had been subjected to mental control. They were hooked up to a *biofeedback* device that measured their heart rate and breathing. The researchers then slowly read aloud a vocabulary list mixing neutral words and command words commonly used in MK programming. While reading, the subject paid no attention to the command words, but each time one of these words was spoken, the *biofeedback* device showed a reaction. The MK victims connected to this device were not aware that these words were triggers, yet they stimulate the slave unconsciously because of the pain contained in the suppressed traumatic memory. The power of these words can be deactivated by working on the vocabulary in a structured way.

The Fabian Therapy is divided into four areas:

- Keeping journals.

- E.M.A. (Episodic Memory Analysis) is the systematic analysis of certain non-traumatic conscious memories.

- The extraversion technique.

- Vocabulary exercises to influence semantic memory, aimed at releasing the negative charge contained in the words related to the implanted commands.

a/ The newspaper

In Fabian therapy, the patient will keep three diaries:
- The daily diary of episodic memory.
- The daily diary of dream memory.
- The cathartic and memory journal of the imagination.

The episodic diary: Every evening, the patient will write down in this diary his/her full name (the host personality), the date and an episodic memory of the day (meeting an old friend, a trip to the park...). The memory should preferably be a significant and positive episode, without any negative emotions. This episodic memory must be something that was experienced in the real world and not something that was seen on television or the internet. In the diary, the patient will simply describe this memory so that he or she can easily recall it afterwards. At the end of each week, the patient should review all the episodic memories of the week. Similarly, at the end of the month, he will review everything he wrote in his diary during those few weeks. These reviews of episodic memories should be done by imagining the scene as precisely as possible in the mind, in order to record it as well as possible. This exercise can also be done at the end of the year.

In a subtle way, this work on episodic memory helps to unload negative memories weighing on the subconscious. This work requires a medium-term (a few months) or even long-term (several years) commitment in order to expect tangible results. By detecting gaps in memory on certain days, the patient will know that a change of alter has occurred on that day.

The dream diary: This diary should also be filled in daily if the dream memory is present. A number of people have found that once they start writing their episodic diary daily, they also start having vivid nightmares. In addition, once the patient has undertaken an E.M.A. (Episodic Memory Analysis) on a regular basis, this will also indirectly stimulate nightmares during sleep. Nightmares are unpleasant, but this is actually a good sign, because it is through them that the subconscious mind discharges the negative charge contained in traumatic memories.

The patient does not have to analyse his dreams in his diary, he should simply write down the content as objectively as possible, regardless of whether the dream was joyful or terrorising. Focusing on the dreams by recalling them and writing them down will also release the negative charge contained in the memory field. This is a natural healing process of the mind.

Imagination and cathartic diary: This diary does not have to be kept daily but only when the patient feels the need to do so. Its purpose is to use the imagination to release negative emotions. With this diary, the patient will try to purge the negativity, it is not a question of intellectualising what is written in it as it is a purely cathartic process. The content of the diary can be words, drawings, photos, etc. It is a very personal diary. The idea is to express the bad feelings that sometimes come up for no apparent reason, by putting them into images and words. It is a purely emotional process and not an intellectual one, an additional way of releasing the negative emotional charge from the memory field.

b/ E.M.A. - Episodic Memory Analysis

M.E.A. is the systematic analysis of unrepressed episodic memories. This analysis requires a therapist. These unrepressed episodic memories are conscious memories that should be free of pain and negative emotions. They are memories of ordinary, happy experiences of everyday life. The therapist acts as a guide, asking a series of questions to help the patient delve deeply into his or her memories. In this therapeutic process, the negative unconscious memories are indirectly influenced by this intense focus on the positive conscious memories.

The memory field is like a spider's web in which all the memories are linked together by threads. If you stimulate one area of the web, it will stir up everything else. So if you stimulate one area of the patient's conscious memory intensely, it will more or less influence all the other areas of the memory, also the dissociated memories. The aim of this type of analysis is to make the patient consciously immerse himself in a memory in order to recall it as deeply as possible in his "mental screen". The therapist's role is to use his or her intuition to guide the process by questioning the patient about the memory in order to encourage him or her to dive deeper and deeper into it, without intellectualising anything. This protocol does not require a hypnotic state or any kind of altered state of consciousness, the patient just needs to close his eyes when he recalls the memories. All memories worked on in M.A.E. must be of a happy nature, they must not contain any negative emotions. Furthermore, they must be recent memories that have not yet been processed, i.e. raw memories that the patient has not yet spoken about. To help you understand this process, here is an example:

- Therapist: Can you think of an appropriate memory that we could work on today?

- Patient: I went to a football match the other day.

- T: Very good. For a better recollection of this memory, what was the date and time that this episode started?

- P: It happened two days ago. I think it was at 4pm.

- T: Okay, let's start with your olfactory memory, do you remember the smells?

- P (eyes closed): I remember the smell of popcorn in the queue where I was waiting to buy a hot dog. There were smells of cooking, of hot dogs.... Let's see... There was also that smell of stale beer on the floor near the refreshment stand. When I went to the toilets, I remember it smelled very strongly of urine. In the stands I was sitting next to a man wearing disgusting aftershave. I also remember someone smoking a cigar. It was a hot day, I remember the body odour.

- T: Was it your own body odour or was it someone else's?

- P: There were the smells of several people. There was something else, I'm not sure what it was.... Oh yes, my friend had put sun cream on his arms, he gave me some...

- T: What was that smell?

- P: There was a slight smell of coconut, but mostly a smell of chemicals.

- T: Well... Is there another memory of a smell?
- P: *No.*
- T: Okay, so now let's go through your memories of the tastes in this episode.

etc...

In a methodical and systematic way, each of the sensory perceptions contained in this episodic memory, this life scene, will be reviewed. The therapist's questions are designed to maintain the patient's attention and to focus on the experience and its recollection. A session of this type should last between half an hour and forty-five minutes. The mind of an MK victim has been altered, so even ordinary episodic memory recall may contain distortions. If the therapist hears something that seems totally irrational, he or she does not have to question or analyse it, but simply continue the process without dwelling on it. The therapist should not make any judgements or evaluations, but simply help the patient to maintain a focus on the experience and its memory.

There are a number of perceptions contained in an episodic memory, the Fabian therapy works with a list of eight perceptions as follows:

N°1: Olfactory (smell)
No. 2: Gustative (taste)
No. 3: Auditory (sound)
No. 4: Tactile (touch)
No. 5: Vision (sight)
No. 6: Kinetics (movements)
No. 7: Emotional (emotions)
No. 8: Linguistics (language)

The therapist will work with each of these perceptions in the exact order listed. These eight categories are used sequentially, so the therapist must direct the patient to follow this sequence in the correct order. The session ends when the last category has been reviewed. The review of smell, taste and sound at the beginning of the session will allow the patient to re-experience the memory directly without personal alteration, he will not evaluate it but re-experience it. The review of emotions and language will take place at the end of the session as these perceptions are likely to be evaluated and modified by the ego. As far as possible, the therapist should avoid mixing the different categories of memory perceptions. For example, when analysing category 3, which is the memory of sounds, it would not be good to encourage the patient to focus on the content of a conversation he or she has heard, because this is what is analysed later in category 8 (language). In category 3, the therapist leads the patient into the pure perception of auditory memory. For example, the therapist will ask if the conversation was loud, soft, and compare it to other auditory perceptions. Focusing on tactile perceptions (category 4) of an episodic memory, the therapist may ask such questions as: *"Is this hot or cold?* These perceptions include: temperature, pressure/weight, discomfort/comfort, wetness and dryness on the skin, satiety/hunger...

Category 5 reviews visual memory, involving colours, shapes, patterns, brightness and darkness. It also refers to the visual perception of movements, such as a ball flying through the air or movements of a crowd. But this type of visual perception of movement must be distinguished from the movements experienced by one's own body which are the movements that concern category 6 involving the perception of physical (kinetic) movement retained in the memory, both the individual's own movements and the movements of objects that directly affect the individual. For example, in a car, there will be the sensation of the body following the movements of the car around bends as well as accelerating and braking. If it is a memory of walking down the street, it is only the movement of the body, unless it comes into contact with something. At a football match, where there is a lot of physical contact, there are the individual's own movements as well as those of others that will interfere and influence him. Thus there may be some confusion of perceptions between categories 5 and 6. Personal movements fall under category 6, but a movement such as a bird flying will fall under category 5. One way of dealing with this confusion is to deal with perceptions of movement in category 5 (visual) last, and then follow this logic with category 6. Category 7, emotions, is both the perception of the emotions of others and the subjective perception of one's own emotions. The patient can know his or her own subjective emotional reactions, but cannot really know the subjective experiences of others. To avoid the patient speculating about what people were really feeling, the memory and perception of other people's emotions should be limited to describing their outward expressions such as facial expression, tone of voice and body language. With such physical indicators, the patient may be able to detect basic emotional responses such as anger, disgust, fear, joy, sadness, boredom, indifference and surprise. The patient should not focus on what was going on inside the others, but only on their emotions displayed by the face, body and tone of voice. In this category 7, the patient's perception of the emotions of others must therefore be objective, while the perception of his or her own emotions is subjective. The patient's own subjective emotional reactions may indeed be more complex. The patient must be allowed to describe his or her own emotional reactions to whatever memory he or she has chosen. The patient's subjective emotions can be described with e.g. melancholy, optimism, bewilderment, conflict, euphoria, anger, etc., whereas the description of other people's emotions is much simpler and more objective: e.g. *"He looked angry because his face was red"*, or *"His face expressed a feeling of disgust"*. Category 8, the last one, will deal with perceptions related to language and the meaning it takes. This phase is therefore more intellectual, here the patient is guided to focus on all the conversations that took place in this episodic memory. The patient will also focus on all the written things he or she has read in this episode as well as the meaning of visual symbols such as a road sign or a cross on a church steeple.

Generally speaking, an episodic memory chosen for this type of work must be a positive memory. The patient can therefore choose to voluntarily program a "happy" experience into his or her schedule so that it can be used later in an M.E.A. session. For example, they may plan to go to a football match so that they can review this episodic memory a few days later in therapy. Recent memories, which are easy to recall, are a good choice, but old memories that are also easy to recall will work in the same way. It is best to start with sessions dealing with recent memories, once the patient becomes comfortable with the process, older memories can then be exploited.

In one session you can review a memory from the previous week and in the next session review an episodic memory from two years ago. The M.E.A. process can be applied to any memory that the patient can reasonably recall. The more this process is applied, the more the patient's ability to recall episodic memories will increase. With practice, the patient may even end up accessing memories from early childhood.

A few imperative rules to follow: it is essential that the patient has not consumed drugs or alcohol in the weeks or months prior to the M.E.A. sessions. It is also important that he/she avoids consuming drinks containing caffeine before a session. He/she must have had a good night's sleep in order to be at full capacity. All memories processed must be positive, containing no loss of consciousness, no pain and no negative emotions.

Thus, the Fabian process will allow the negative charge of repressed or hidden memories to be evacuated indirectly. The M.E.A. acts as a catalyst, the feelings contained in the repressed traumatic memories will come to the surface in different ways, through dreams, drawings, flashbacks of traumatic memories, etc. This type of therapy does not dwell on the negative memories that arise, it simply allows them to emerge. It is the focus on the present life that allows one to avoid dwelling on them.

c/ Extraversion exercises

The extroversion exercises will help the patient to get out of the painful memories of the past that may arise. As traumatic memories can cause the patient to totally collapse, these exercises consist of bringing the patient back into the present moment to stabilise them. When practising M.E.A., the therapist should always lead the patient to focus on positive memories, but if a negative memory comes up or the patient becomes angry for no apparent reason, the therapist should use extroversion techniques to bring the patient back into the present moment. The basic principle being that any inappropriate negative emotion comes from a dislocation of time, i.e. an event in the patient's past has made him/her angry, and now this anger may come up inappropriately in front of the therapist. In such a case, both the patient and the therapist need to focus on the present moment and the present environment. The therapist can ask the patient to tell him/her the current date, to write on a piece of paper where he/she is at the moment and to describe the room by going through it completely. Then the patient can move around the room touching things, naming them, feeling the textures, etc. This can also be done outside during a walk. As already described, these techniques of anchoring in the present moment use the different perceptions such as sight, hearing, touch, etc. Walking, sports, gardening, etc., are activities that help the patient to focus his or her attention "here and now". It is an attitude and a lifestyle to be adopted, meaning that the patient should aim to be socially extroverted: he/she should develop a sense of security in his/her social relationships, which will help him/her not to remain focused "alone in his/her corner" on his/her past in a negative way. Extroversion is more than a therapeutic technique, it is a global attitude that will facilitate access to a balanced life.

During the M.E.A. sessions, through a review of episodic memories, the therapist leads the patient into a deep state of introversion (diving into the past), but when this process is complete, it is important that the therapist brings the patient back into a state of extraversion: back to the present moment.

The patient in Fabian therapy should not get stuck on the traumatic memories that may emerge in the process. Although this is a sign that dissociated memories are coming up, when this happens, the patient should understand that throughout the therapy it is best to stay away from these memories. If there is a need for emotional release, they can use their cathartic journal to release these negative emotions. After this cathartic release, the patient should return to the present moment.

According to Kerth Barker, the Fabian Therapy will heal the whole memory field through all those therapeutic exercises aimed at intensely working and stimulating conscious memories. There are two aspects to this 'memory field': the conscious or unconscious memories and the mental mechanisms that access them. The Fabian therapy restores, through an indirect process, the mind's ability to access these traumatic memories while at the same time unloading the negative "capsules".

d/ Semantic destimulation technique

Here the term "semantics" refers to the meaning of words and symbols used in MK programming. Words and symbols (graphic or gestural) that unconsciously push the victim towards an action or the repression of an action. Therefore the victim is enslaved by the stimulation of command words or symbols. To deprogram the victim semantically, the power of these triggers must be reduced. All these implanted commands systematically contain a negative emotional charge.

Take a woman with MK-Monarch programming who has received an implanted command stating, for example, *"You are sexually serviced by anyone when your owner tells you to"*. The words of this command contain a negative emotional charge that was induced during the trauma and it is the inability to cope with this negative charge that forces the victim to unconsciously obey this programming. The key words in this command phrase are *'sexually', 'owner'* and *'command'*. The technique of semantic destimulation aims to gradually unload this negative implant.

The therapist will create three lists of words, each list containing one of the key command words, such as: *angel, boat, coat, landlord, porch, tree, waterfall*. The therapist will then ask the patient to go through the list and define each word with the help of a dictionary. Then the patient is asked to make up sentences with each of the words on the list. The therapist will not pay any special attention to the key command words, they will be treated in the same way as neutral words that do not stimulate any reaction. By doing this, the process will be able to influence the memory and subtly discharge the negative emotions of the traumatic memory containing one of these control words. Semantic memory recall is the ability to understand and use words to communicate. In a sense, the MK programming process hijacks the recall function of semantic memory so that it can be used to control the victim. However, by asking the patient to work on vocabulary, the patient will gradually regain full control of their semantic memory recall ability. The idea here is to strengthen this function in the patient. This will change the way he deals with the language contained in the memory field. A principle of Fabian therapy is that by increasing the mnemonic abilities of the mind, you decrease the power of dissociated memories. By simply working with vocabulary and asking the patient to make sentences with words defined with a dictionary, you decrease the power of the implanted commands.

e/ Typical therapy session

In a typical Fabian therapy session, the patient sits opposite the therapist, each with a pencil and notebook in front of them to take notes. No hypnosis or altered states of consciousness are required. The therapist begins by asking the patient if anything is bothering him or her that might interfere with concentration during the session. The patient may, if they wish, bring their diary to share content with the therapist. The first exercise will be the semantic destimulation exercise described above. When the patient creates sentences with the word lists, the therapist does not intervene, but listens. Once this protocol has been completed, a ten minute break can be taken before starting the episodic memory analysis, the E.M.A., which is the core of the session and will last for thirty to forty-five minutes. At the end of the session, the therapist must bring the patient back down to earth in the present moment, his or her attention must be focused in *the here and now*. The session can be followed by a walk outside to plan the next session. The frequency of the sessions will depend on the emotional state of the patient. Generally, sessions can be once a week. This can be spaced out to once a month, but they can also be daily if the patient feels it is necessary. These sessions, while discharging traumatic memories, will help to stabilise the patient emotionally and anchor him or her in the present moment.

f/ Advanced E.M.A. technique

The M.E.A. technique described above is the classic protocol, relatively easy to understand and practice. But there are more advanced techniques, including a scheme for doing much deeper M.E. work.

This method uses a circle divided into eight equal sections forming a pie chart, with rays intersected by eight concentric circles that divide this pie chart into equal sections. The eight spokes represent the eight categories mentioned above: olfactory, gustatory, auditory, tactile, visual, kinetic, emotional and linguistic. While each concentric circle represents a period of the patient's life: the central circle represents the unconscious memories of the pre-natal period and birth, the other concentric circles symbolise the evolution from early childhood, adolescence, young adulthood, etc., to the last outer circle which represents the most recent life experiences.

This pattern will be used to help the therapist shift the patient's focus to different areas of his or her vast memory field. The patient should be calm, deeply relaxed and free of inner conflict during such a session. The aim is to guide the patient to different areas of the circular pattern in a random way. For example, the therapist may ask the patient to recall a recent happy memory by asking him/her to immerse him/herself in a single perception of the memory in one of the eight categories, such as the recall of a smell for example. The therapist will then guide the patient to a memory in a different time zone by choosing a different category of perception, such as sight or language.

A classic M.E.A. session intensively studies the memory of a single episodic memory with the eight perceptions associated with it. Whereas this advanced M.E.A. technique, instead of intensively analysing all the perceptions of an episode, will juggle from episode to episode, choosing each time only one category of perception of the memory. For example, the patient might remember the smell of a flower when he was gardening a week ago, then the taste of corn on the cob from a picnic 10 years ago, the feeling of cold rain following a hot day out hiking six months ago, and so on. This protocol should take about 20 minutes. It is necessary to have already practised a lot of classical E.M.A. to be able to do this exercise which can sometimes allow access to completely forgotten memories from early childhood (non-traumatic), or even to pre-natal memories.

8 - THE INTERIOR CASTLE (TERESA OF AVILA)

To conclude this chapter, here are some excerpts from Teresa of Avila's masterpiece, *"The Interior Castle"* or *"The Book of Abodes"*. It is a castle that metaphorically represents the human soul that has to pass through different levels in order to reach perfection. Just as the programmer executioner incorporates dark castles and dungeons into the inner world of the MK slaves to keep the alters imprisoned, here is an inner castle that gradually leads the human to divine union with his Creator. Perhaps the survivors can incorporate this castle into their inner world?

Today I was offered what will be the basis of this writing: to consider our soul as a castle made entirely of a single diamond or crystal very clear. Let us consider that the castle has many dwellings, some at the top, some at the bottom, some on the sides; and in the centre, in the middle of all of them, is the main one, where the most secret things take place between God and the soul. You will find, I believe, consolation in revelling in this inner castle. You may enter it and walk about it at any hour. The gateway to this castle is prayer. You must not picture these dwellings one after the other, like a string of them, but fix your gaze on the centre. Let the soul, therefore, abandon itself into the hands of God, with the least possible concern for its progress.

Before going any further, I would like to ask you to consider what it is like to see this shining and beautiful castle. This oriental pearl, this tree of life planted in the living waters of life. This water flows into every home and every power. It is true that you cannot enter all the mansions by your own strength, however great it may seem to you, unless the Lord of the castle himself installs you there. He is very fond of humility. And humility is walking in the truth. For self-knowledge is so necessary, that you can never do better (than to know yourself).

Although I speak of only seven mansions, there are many in each one, below, above, on the sides with beautiful gardens, fountains, labyrinths... You will wish to be drawn into the praise of the great God who created this castle in his image and likeness. I see nothing that can be compared to the great beauty of a soul and its vast capacity. And He Himself says that He created us in His image and likeness (Gen 1:26). Now, if this is so, and it is a fact, we have no reason to tire of trying to understand the beauty of this castle. Fix your eyes on the Crucified One and everything will seem easy. He will not fail, one day or another, to call us to come closer to Him. (Excerpts) "The Interior Castle" - St Teresa of Avila

- There are many mansions in my Father's house - John 14:2

CHAPTER 9

MIND CONTROL IN THE ENTERTAINMENT INDUSTRY

"I learned that just below the surface, there is another world, and then different worlds again when you dig deeper. I knew this when I was a kid, but I couldn't find the proof. It was just like a feeling. There's goodness in the blue sky and the flowers, but there's another force, a wild, decadent pain, that goes with it too." - David Lynch

1 - INTRODUCTION

The ancient druids used the sacred branches of the *holly* tree to make their magic wands, with which they channelled and amplified powers... The holly tree was a symbol of death and resurrection, eternal life and fertility, all the way back to the time of Nimrod and the Great Babylon. Nimrod's Babylon is associated with slavery and the cult of World Government (Nimrod being recognised by Freemasons as the first *'Grand Master'*).

Every year the Academy Awards (the ultimate symbol of Hollywood culture) are held at the Dolby Theatre (formerly the Kodak Theatre before the group went bankrupt in 2012) located on Hollywood Boulevard in Los Angeles. Adjacent to the theatre is *the Hollywood & Highland Center,* also called *the Babylon Courtyard.* It is a huge shopping mall with a setting that is an exact replica of the ancient Babylon from the 1916 film *"Intolerance"*. While visiting the place, we can discover four monumental columns surmounted by elephants standing on their hind legs, surrounding a gigantic arch with the representations of two curious mythical characters: Enki, a Sumerian god, and the Assyrian god Nisroch... The decor is set for a temple of consumption dedicated to Hollywood...

If you want to see the Ancient Babylonian system at work today, look no further than Hollywood: *The Sacred Wood*; a reference to the holly wood used by the druids to fashion their tools of magic. Today, Hollywood is the nerve centre of the world's film and television propaganda, the magic wand immersing people in illusion, even bewitching them with its charms...

The spectator who watches a film will unconsciously encode behaviours that he will reproduce or at least integrate as a possibility of behaviour to adopt. Hollywood scripts inject thoughts, behaviours and attitudes into the spectator's mind which thus become things that can potentially be reproduced in such and such a situation, just as the actor did... but it so happens that an actor is paid to reproduce emotions and behaviours which thus become human... even if they are totally deviant and inhuman... Scripts (from Hollywood to reality TV) thus encode potentials into the matrix, it is a form of global programming.

This analysis may seem to be an aberration, as people think that their critical mind is systematically on guard and that all these productions do not influence them in any way, as they say: *'It's only cinema'*. But as we saw in the first chapter, social engineering is a key to mental control over the masses, and cinema plays a major role in conditioning them through 'cultural psychiatry': the art of propaganda aimed at systematically targeting the subconscious of the masses. Television series and reality TV, like the cinema, literally imprint in the minds of young people behaviours to be integrated and reproduced. These are real doctrines that are imposed indirectly via scenarios in the form of 'simple entertainment', whether humorous or totally horrific, and these two things are mixed together today in a very unhealthy way (ever more attractive and addictive productions). Lifestyles are thus programmed in the scripts of the entertainment industry before they are actually embodied in everyday life, with people unfortunately mimicking what they consume all the time on their screens, big or small. The sorcerer-controllers have mastered this, they program the youth and encode their doctrines in previously *cooked* brains to prepare the world of tomorrow...

The entertainment industry seems to be particularly affected by occultism and mind control, probably because of the fact that of all industries, it is the one that exposes itself the most publicly, so inevitably cracks appear in the spotlight and sometimes reveal symptoms of trauma and programming. Moreover, as we shall see, the music and fashion industry takes great pleasure in exposing ever more explicit MK symbolism to the public. This entertainment industry plays an essential role in the mind control of the masses, so it must itself be perfectly controlled and connected to the spirit world in order to channel and spread the "Luciferian light" here on earth. Artists destined for world fame must therefore be perfect mediums and puppets to infuse this "light" into the masses. Trauma-based mental programming is the perfect tool for this. We are all victims of mind control to varying degrees, but show business celebrities are probably the most. Their opulence and degenerate behaviour is promoted in the media so that we envy their lifestyle and consume their productions, not knowing that to achieve such a situation they are under absolute physical, psychic and spiritual bondage. The traumas they endure are often expressed through their globally distributed art, so that everyone can be indirectly traumatised... and they call it *entertainment...*

2 - PAEDO-CRIME IN SHOW BUSINESS

Little stars who are introduced into the "Hollywood system" often go through all kinds of trauma and abuse. It is becoming very clear today that child sexual abuse is not something anecdotal in Hollywood and that the whole of show business is seriously affected. It is a widespread phenomenon, a kind of "epidemic" that is transmitted like a vampire bite.

In August 2011, during an interview on *ABCNews' Nightline*, former child actor Corey Feldman, the hero of The *Goonies*, denounced: *"I can tell you that the number one problem in Hollywood has been, is and always will be pedophilia. It's the biggest problem for children in this industry... It's all done quietly, it's the big secret (...) There are so many people who have grown up in this industry and have been in it for so long that they feel they are above the law. This has to change, it has to stop."*

Feldman also reveals this in his autobiography entitled *"Coreyography"* released in 2014. He said that when he was 14 years old he was literally surrounded by paedophiles. He didn't realise what these *'vultures'* really were and what they wanted until he was older... but the damage was done...

In 2008, he and his friend Corey Haim revealed in the reality series *Two Corey* that they had been gang raped. In 2011, Alison Arngrim, the actress who played the "blonde pest" Nellie Oleson in the series *"Little House on the Prairie"*, also confirmed that the two Coreys were abused in the 1980s. She told *FoxNews*: *"What was said at the time was that they were drugged to be sexually abused. It's horrible, they were kids who were underage. There are all sorts of stories about them, for example that they were sexually abused and totally corrupted by every possible means imaginable, by people who were normally supposed to be looking after them (...) There's not just one person to blame, I'm sure there wasn't just one person raping Corey Haim, and they certainly weren't the only ones to go through this. I'm sure there were dozens of people who knew about the situation who chose to keep quiet."*[522]

Alison Arngrim, a member and spokesperson for *protect.org*, an organisation that protects children from physical and sexual abuse, also confides that all this Hollywood lust allows sexual predators to flourish: *"No one wants to stop this horror,"* she explains, *"It's almost a voluntary sacrifice of their children that many parents are unwittingly making (...) I've heard from victims all over the country. They all tell the same kind of stories and they are all threatened... Corey Feldman may have opened a can of worms by finally speaking out, but it doesn't have to end there."*[523]

In 2010, Allison Arngrim herself revealed in her autobiography *'Confessions of a Prairie Bitch'* the sexual abuse she herself suffered as a child.

Another child star from another era confirms that Hollywood has a long-standing problem with child abuse and molestation. Paul Peterson, star of the Donna Reed show, a popular sitcom from the 1950s and 1960s, told *FoxNews*: *"When I saw this interview* (with Corey Feldman), *a whole series of names and faces from my own history came to mind (...) Some of these people, who I know very well, are still around (...) From my point of view, Corey has been very brave. It would be really wonderful if these allegations could get through the various*

---

[522] "Recent Charges of Sexual Abuse of Children in Hollywood Just Tip of Iceberg, Experts Say" - Meagan Murphy, FoxNews.com, 05/12/2011.

[523] Ibid.

layers of protection to actually identify these people. Those who are part of the child pornography network of this world, it's huge and has no boundaries, just as it has no age limits for children. "[524]

Martin Weiss, a Hollywood casting agent, was charged in 2011 with sexually abusing a child under the age of 12. The victim reportedly told authorities that Weiss confided in him that what he was doing *"was common practice in the entertainment industry."* [525]

Another Hollywood predator is Jason James Murphy, also a casting agent, arrested for the kidnapping and rape of a child. Murphy had, among other things, recruited young actors for the productions of *"Bad News Bears"*, *"The School of Rock"*, *"Cheaper by the Dozen II"* and *"Three Stooges"*.

Fernando Rivas, the award-winning director of the popular series *"Sesame Street"*, has been charged with possession and distribution of child pornography and *sexual coercion of a child...*

In 2004, actor Brian Peck, who starred in the *X-Men* and *Living Dead* films, was sentenced to 16 months in prison for sexual abuse of a child actor. He was a coach for the children's channel *Nickelodeon*. The documentary *"An Open Secret"* (Amy Berg, 2015) tells the story of five victims who claim to have been raped while attending major Hollywood film studios as children. In the documentary, we learn that Brian Peck was initially charged with the following: *lewd act on a child, sodomy of a person under 16, attempted sodomy of a person under 16, sexual penetration with an object, oral copulation on a person under 16, oral copulation with anaesthesia or control by substance.*

The hard-hitting documentary *"An Open Secret"* also contains the testimony of Todd Bridges, the Willy from the famous *"Arnold and Willy"* series, *who* was sexually abused from the age of 11. It also includes interviews with Michael Egan, who accuses the director of the *X-Men* films, Bryan Singer, of raping him.

Bill Cosby of 'The *Cosby Show*' fame has also been accused of sexual abuse of minors by dozens of women. The scandal broke in 2014 when former supermodel Janice Dickinson publicly revealed that Bill Cosby had drugged and raped her in 1982. Actress Barbara Bowman also accused him of sexual assault when she was a teenager, as did actress Andrea Constand. A bust of the actor was even removed from *Disney's Hollywood Studios* in Florida following all these disturbing accusations...

Actress Mia Farrow and her adopted daughter Dylan have publicly stated that Woody Allen raped Dylan when she was 7 years old. Woody Allen, who married his adopted daughter Soon-Yi in 1997, has been accused of raping Dylan... Actress Susan Sarandon said on *The Daily Best*: *"I think he completely destroyed his family in a terrible way, and then washed his hands of it. He's always had a reputation for liking young girls, I mean really young girls. And then this woman Soon-Yi was very vulnerable. I think it was hard on the kids, especially Mia. You can't do that kind of thing. You just can't."*

---

[524] Ibid.

[525] Ibid.

We can also cite the case of director Roman Polanski accused (but never convicted) of raping a 13-year-old girl, Samantha Geimer. One day in March 1977, she was at Jack Nicholson's house in Los Angeles for a photo shoot with Polanski. He made her drink champagne, gave her a sedative and then abused her. That night, on her way home, Samatha wrote in her diary: *'Roman Polanski took my picture today. He raped me, damn it!'*[526]

In 2003 in Thierry Ardisson's show "*Tout le monde en parle*", the obscure singer Marilyn Manson tells how as a child, he discovered sexuality in his grandfather's cellar... He describes that in this cellar were female lingerie, dildos "*coated with Vaseline*" according to his own words, and zoophilic photos... Marilyn Manson concludes on his grandfather by declaring: *You see, when I was a kid, my grandfather seemed monstrous to me... but when I grew up, I realised that my grandfather was... well, I'm like him, so he's not so bad.* Why did his grandfather seem so *monstrous* to him? Why did he become *like him afterwards*? Marilyn Manson most probably suffered ritual abuse in his childhood. In his song '*Disassociative*', he describes his disassociated states: "*I can never get out of this, I don't want to just float in fear like a dead astronaut in space...*" The sad reality of Monarch slaves.

The situation of the entertainment industry in England is also very worrying. Indeed, the testimony of former child star Ben Fellows is damning. He was involved in many TV shows and series as a child, and now as an adult, he denounces how drugs and sex, including with minors, are the norm in show business: "*In fact, in all the productions I was involved in, whether it was on the BBC or other TV channels, and even in the theatre, I was a target in one way or another. Looking back, it would not be an exaggeration to say that the problem is both institutional and systemic in the entertainment industry (...) After an audition for a Coca Cola commercial, the police came to my parents' house. They warned my mother that I had unknowingly become a potential target for a known (never dismantled) paedophile ring. Indeed, it turned out that this well-known casting director had taken shirtless photos of me, and that these photos had then found their way into what was described as a catalogue that was passed on to other paedophiles in the company, but also to outside paedophiles.*"[527]

Ben Fellows has worked extensively for the *BBC*, the British television station that found itself at the centre of a huge celebrity paedophile scandal following the Jimmy Savile case. In 2013, during a protest against the *Bilderberg* Group, Ben Fellows publicly stated at a press conference: "*When they said Jimmy Savile was the only paedophile on the BBC... I was a BBC child myself... and I can tell you there are plenty of paedophiles on the BBC! The BBC children are run by paedophiles! When I went to auditions they would ask me to take my top off and pretend to lick an ice cream (...) I was drugged, I was drunk, and don't think it was a line of coke in the toilet... It was in milkshake... They would put this drug in to give you a buzz on the shows... I was taken to Esther Rantzen's*

---

[526] "*Polanski affair: He raped me, damn it!* " - Doan Bui, Le Nouvel Observateur, 10/2013.

[527] "Jimmy Savile wasn't the only one at the BBC', says investigative journalist and former child actor Ben Fellows" - 21stcenturywire.com, 10/2011.

house and we were given alcohol and drugs as children!! And she also has children! Was she interviewed by the police ? Was she questioned ?! No... Jimmy Savile must have died before we opened the file... "

Jimmy Savile, the popular British TV star, knighted by the *Queen Mother,* close friend of Margaret Thatcher and friend of Prince Charles, was revealed to be a "devil on legs" following the avalanche of revelations that followed his death in 2011. Savile raped hundreds of children and teenagers, both in his dressing room and in the *BBC* offices (there are over 340 charges against him). The *BBC* has been accused of clearly turning a blind eye to the crimes of its star presenter. Actress Julie Fernandez, for example, says she was raped at the age of 14 by Savile in *"a room full of people",* she says... [528]

In 2007, a complaint was already filed against Savile. A private investigator, Mark Williams-Thomas, conducted a 12-year investigation and spoke to several of the victims of the 42-year star of *Top of the Pops.* His investigation was used as the basis for a short documentary exposing Savile's perverse and criminal actions (*'The Other Side of Jimmy Savile',* 2012). The documentary was bought by the *BBC,* which obviously decided not to broadcast it because it implicated BBC executives, and also because the *BBC* was preparing a Christmas show to celebrate its favourite presenter: Jimmy Savile.

Savile even had free access to schools, orphanages and hospitals as part of his 'charity work'. *Duncroft Boarding school,* Leeds Hospital, *Stoke Mandeville* Hospital, among others, were among his *hunting grounds.* In 1988, he even obtained a position as team leader in the *Broadmoor* psychiatric hospital, to which he held the keys! He also had his friend Alan Franey appointed as director.

Savile's nephew, Guy Marsden, also gave evidence. He explained that he was 13 in 1967 when Savile took him to the London villa of a celebrity of the day *'for the first of a series of sordid social gatherings'.* Over 18 months, Marsden and other children were taken to numerous parties where the boys, the youngest of whom were in their teens, were raped by men. [529]

The Savile case also contains evidence of ritual abuse involving torture and murder. Dr. Valerie Sinason, president of the Institute of *Psychotherapy and Disability* in London, told the *Sunday Express* that she had a patient who was ritually abused by Savile and others at *Stoke Mandeville* Hospital in 1975, while she was a patient there. She says she was taken to a very secluded area of the hospital, ending up in the basement in a room filled with candles. Several adults were present, including Jimmy Savile who, like the others, was wearing a gown and a mask. She recognised him by his distinctive voice and the fact that his blond hair was sticking out of the mask. According to her, he was not the leader of the group. She was assaulted, raped and beaten. Therapist Sinason had a first contact with this victim in 1992. In 1993, a second victim contacted her saying she had been "loaned" sexual favours at a party in a London villa in 1980. She

---

[528] "I was sexually assaulted by Savile on Jim'll Fix It when I was just 14', says TV actress" - Daily Mail, October 2012.

[529] "England: BBC paedophile star Jimmy Savile plagued even orphanages" - DondeVamos 10/2012.

said that the first part of the evening began with an orgy, but that she was then led into another room to find Savile acting as a sort of master of ceremonies amidst a group of people wearing robes and masks and singing, she said, in Latin. The young victim was an adult by then but obviously suffered greatly from the sexual abuse.[530]

Following the initial revelations of satanic ritual abuse at *Stoke Mandeville* Hospital, another victim aged 50, who was only 13 at the time, contacted the *Sunday Express* to testify: *"I was taken to a dark cellar and put in front of three men in a circle, with one man sitting in the middle on a throne wearing a shiny robe with a cigar in his mouth. Two other men stood on either side of him, wearing blue robes and masks (...) I was forced to stand, wearing a white robe with nothing underneath, in front of this throne while this man watched me, blowing smoke from his cigar in my face to make me sick, I was terrified (...).I was then taken by the man with the cigar, whom I recognised as Jimmy Savile, to an altar where my white dress was removed and I was tied to it... Savile then climbed onto the altar to rape me. The other participants shouted Satan's name and laughed hysterically, frantically."[531]*

Another young woman testified about the criminal acts of Jimmy Savile and his clique: "I don't have to prove anything to anyone, but I would like to participate in exposing the violence and corruption that can flourish at the highest level in Western democracies. (...) I have made an official statement which has been corroborated by two other witnesses, saying that Savile was involved in rape and ritual murder in the 1980s and 1990s. I know this because I was a 'favourite'. I went through a lot of the rapes, filmed or not. I had disassociated states, personalities and talents that attracted everyone. This witness speaks of ceremonies that took place all over England, involving child rape, orgies, torture and ritual murder of children. At the age of 4, she would have come across Savile, who had already experienced the same rituals many times. She then saw him many, many times... [532]

3 - SOME QUOTES...

a/ Personality disorders

When I was a child, I didn't have my own "I". Growing up, I lived through characters I played as I lost myself in different parts of my personality. " - Angelina Jolie - "The Story of the World's Most Seductive Star", Rhona Mercer, 2009, chap.1

---

[530] "Jimmy Savile was part of satanic ring" - express.co.uk, 01/2013.

[531] "I was raped at 13 by Jimmy Savile in satanist ritual" - express.co.uk, 01/2013.

[532] "England: on the satanic rituals of Jimmy Savile" - Donde Vamos, 06/2013.

"You can never spend enough money to cure that feeling of being broken, of being in confusion. " Winona Ryder

- Roseanne Barr:

In 2013, on Abby Martin's show on the *Russia Today* channel, actress Roseanne Barr (from the famous American series *"Roseanne"*) did not beat about the bush to expose the situation regarding the Hollywood system...

I think that fear is cultivated, there are no people more afraid than these Hollywood people. They fear for their careers, they fear that they're not at the top of the pyramid any more, even though they might be in the middle... You know Hollywood is a system that retains its power structures with all its culture of racism and sexism... They feed that continuously and make a lot of money from it. They are at the behest of their masters who run everything. I'm lucky to be able to talk about it, but I feel like I'm doing it on behalf of everyone... Sometimes I go to parties in Hollywood, and I meet people there, and some of them, big celebrities, take me by the arm and lead me into a corner and say, "I just want to thank you for everything you're saying..." It means a lot to me, but clearly we're dealing with a culture of fear. You know, there's also a big culture of mind control, MK-Ultra mind control rules in Hollywood. Mental programming rules in Hollywood. "

It couldn't be clearer! She said on the same Russia Today programme shortly afterwards: Some time ago we talked here about mind control, MK-Ultra. I already talked about it here, but what I didn't say is that this kind of mind control works so that people never report the real culprits. Rather than pointing out what could help us... They will never denounce the culprits..."

Roseanne Barr is one of the few people in Hollywood brave enough to speak out about the most sensitive issue of all, that of Monarch-like mental programming. In this TV interview with Abby Martin, she makes it clear that many stars don't speak out because they simply can't, their personalities being split up and under the control of people who run their lives from top to bottom.

Roseanne claims to have been a victim herself and publicly declared in 1994 that she had dissociative identity disorder. She revealed the difficulties she had in making transitions between *"someone"* and *"nobody"*, which are the names of two of her alter personalities. Her other alter names are *Baby, Cindy, Susan, Joey and Heather*. The former *sitcom* queen finds it hard to keep to herself what has been inflicted on her since childhood. In an interview with *Esquire* magazine, she said it took her ten years of hard therapeutic work to merge her different personalities. *I didn't have blackouts for a long time because I used to have them all the time* (a connection - co-consciousness - between all the alters) (...) There was *always a conflict with the conflicting parts in me, but I learned to get them to listen to each other. I learned to make them know that they are on the same team and that we inhabit the same body, something we didn't know before* (...) *It's like living in a labyrinth... but the alters don't get along and some of them have really strange ways of defending themselves... "* [533]

---

[533] Roseanne Says Having 7 Personalities Is Tough " - ABC News, 16/07/2001.

This is not the first time Roseanne Barr has publicly denounced MK programming in a mainstream media appearance. On August 16, 2001, in an interview on *CNN* [534]with journalist Larry King, she said:

- Larry King: Well, some people believe that what you had, or still have, is a serious psychological disorder.

- Roseanne Barr: I love how you guys are going at it...

- LK: Others believe that this is just a psychological trend...

- RB: A trend?

- LK: They wonder whether this disorder was intentionally induced or whether it occurred naturally.

- RB: Well I have a psychologist who says he was induced intentionally. The CIA started working on this after they brought some Nazis back to the US to take over the American Psychiatric Association.

- LK: What do you mean?

- RB: I am telling you the truth. It's manipulation on their part, it's research to create people with multiple personalities.

- LK: So you were captured by the Nazis?

- RB: By the government, in a way. I think the government has implanted some kind of electronic chip in my head...

(...)

- LK: Let me read you a passage from Esquire magazine that quotes a page from your diary. Do you write notes about yourself?

- RB: Of course, I have thousands and thousands.

- LK: Thousands of notebooks?

- RB: Yes.

- LK: Well, here's this excerpt: "This is my life, my real story in Hollywood. It's the story of a woman with many, many facets: a woman, a young poet, a dancer, an actress, a singer, a freedom fighter, a warrior, a messenger, a performer, a mother, a lover, a wife, an actress, a producer, a pioneer director, an autistic child, a survivor of post-traumatic shock, a borderline bipolar, an overweight woman, a woman with Tourette's syndrome and multiple personality disorder, a victim of psychiatry, an obsessive-compulsive, an implanter of false memories, a heretic witch, an old crone... take your pick. There are 300 diagnoses showing that doctors are my only friends. "

- RB: It is true that doctors are my dearest friends.

(...)

- LK: Do you ever get angry at God for doing this to you, when your multiple personalities take over?

- RB: No because I believe that God... Honestly I believe that God gives you a multiple personality when there's too much stress in your life that you can't handle. It's a gift for a child.

- LK: So something else can take over during extreme stress?

- RB: Indeed.

- LK: Are there other people who experience this?

---

[534] Larry King Live " - Roseanne Tells Her Story, CNN, 08/2001.

- RB: Yes.... but I mean it's not us that are screwed up. It's the place we are in that is out of whack, so we have to adapt to it...

- Joan Baez:

In 1992, the famous singer Joan Baez wrote a song, *"Play Me Backwards"*, in reference to satanic messages allegedly encoded in some records. She herself states that the theme of the song is satanic ritual abuse. Is it an autobiographical song? Here are some explicit verses:

You don't have to go to hell to feel the curse of the devil...
I saw them light the candles, I heard them beat the drum...
A man in a mask takes off my clothes...
Mum, I'm freezing and I have nowhere to run...
I pay for protection, I filter the truth from the lies...
Pursuing memories, Recovering evidence...
I would stand at your altar and tell all I know...
I came to claim my childhood at the chapel of the (sacrificial) baby Rose...

In 2004 at a concert in Charlottesville, Joan Baez told her audience that she had multiple personalities and that one of her alter egos was a 15-year-old black teenager named *Alice*. Journalist Ronald Bailey reports how he was stunned to see the rich, famous white folk singer transform into a poor black teenager from Arkansas giving her opinion on the current presidential elections. The journalist reports that her accent, patois and attitude were just right, the only thing missing was the skin colour of *Alice*'s face. [535]

- Britney Spears:

In January 2008, TMZ.com reported on Britney Spears: "Some sources paint a very disturbing picture of Britney Spears... We're told she sometimes has a British accent... but it's more than just a British accent, Britney is said to have multiple personalities, and some people around her call her 'the English girl'. It has been reported that when Britney Spears loses her British personality, she has no idea what she did during the time she had that personality. Another source tells us that Brit' has a number of other identities such as "the crying girl", "the diva", "the inconsistent one", etc..."

Britney Spears explains: "This alter takes over when I'm on stage, she's really wild and daring. She's a much more impulsive performer than me. Her name is 'Britannia'. When she's around, I feel like I own the world, whereas I'm usually pretty shy."

In 2008, Britney Spears suddenly snapped. She shaved her head with scissors and when asked why she did it, she said *she was tired of people touching her and didn't want to have things put inside her anymore...*

Was it a deterioration of the programming? Indeed, at a certain age, the amnesic walls tend to dissolve, which can totally unbalance the person.

---

[535] *Joan Baez and me"* - Ronald Bailey, reason.com, 04/11/2004.

After this episode, she was committed to the *Promises* Clinic in Malibu where she inscribed a 666 on her bald head and shouted that she was the Anti-Christ, before attempting to hang herself with a sheet...

She was then placed under guardianship, which means that her father (and his *'fiancé'*) now have full control over her life, diet, clothing, bank account and medical *care*. Since her psychiatric internment, Britney and all her possessions have been under the complete control of her masters. She is now described by those around her as *"a doll who is told everything she has to do"*. A 2011 *Sun* article describes Britney as a zombie with robotic behaviour who has totally lost control of her career (she probably never had control). To be clearer, Britney is a mind-controlled, completely manipulated person by her masters/managers. She is not alone in this but it just became more obvious and transparent when she reached her thirties, the age when Monarch slaves usually experience violent *outbursts*. In the same year, 2011, stars Nickeloedon and Amanda Bynes experienced the same kind of behaviour, which landed them in psychiatric hospitals.

- Amanda Bynes:

Actress Amanda Bynes, like Britney Spears, has been diagnosed with bipolar disorder. Official diagnoses of Dissociative Identity Disorder are rare, especially among V.I.P.'s. This is because the D.I.D. on which MK programming is based is not supposed to be detected or even supposed to exist. If a personality disorder begins to emerge and cause damage, it will be diagnosed as *borderline* personality disorder, narcissistic disorder, *with* bipolar disorder being the most common celebrity diagnosis: Catherine Zeta-Jones, Jim Carrey, Tim Burton, Chris Brown, Axl Rose, DMX, Francis Ford Coppola, Linda Hamilton, Mel Gibson, Sinead O'Connor, George Michael, Brooke Shields, Carrie Fisher, Hugh Laurie, Maurice Benard, Jean Claude Van Damme, Ben Stiller, Owen Wilson, Winona Ryder, Rosie O'Donnell, Patty Duke... and many more...

Amanda Bynes was hospitalised in 2013 (not for the first time) for severe mental health problems and according to doctors *'schizophrenic tendencies'*, i.e. a severe personality disorder. The psychiatric hospital stated that she was aware that there was a *'good Amanda and a bad Amanda'*. When she spoke of the bad Amanda, she was simultaneously making exorcism gestures, pulling at her body and hitting herself as if to draw out the demon within her. The staff tried to reassure her that he was safe with his parents, but Amanda became hysterical, screaming for over an hour: *"They're going to kill him! Just like they tried to kill me!* She was so out of control that she had to be physically restrained. [536]

Foxnews reported during the hospitalization that "drugs had nothing to do with it (editor's note: the tests were negative) and that it was only a mental

---

[536] "Ammanda Bynes: 10 hours of sanity, 1 hour of crazy" - TMZ.com, 2013.

disorder (...) It was deep anger and severe post-traumatic stress that triggered this psychotic episode."[537]

The stressful life of Hollywood will be the official explanation for his post-traumatic stress... and his *deep anger...*

In October 2014, Amanda Bynes was again hospitalised in a psychiatric ward following a series of *tweets* she had posted. Her shocking statements on the social network *Tweeter* clearly described the symptoms of an MK slave: sexual abuse from a young age by her father and *'brainwashing'*. Her *tweets* were quickly removed, but screenshots from the internet[538] revealed:

- I need to tell the truth about my father
- My father physically and verbally abused me as a child.
- So let me live my own life free from sadness and misery.
- I won't be manipulated, I won't be brainwashed by anyone, ever again.
- I can't hear the sound of his incestuous voice ever again and I just want to be honest.
- So today I'm going to see a lawyer to file a complaint against my father.
- My mother knows that my father raped his own daughter and she never called the police, whereas I could have had him arrested and put in jail for the rest of his perverted life.

Within hours, the *tweets were* removed and Bynes was once again hospitalised in a psychiatric ward... This case reminds us of the attempted whistleblowing by a French model we saw in the introduction to Chapter 7, a woman who also ended up in a psychiatric hospital... Like Britney Spears, Amanda Bynes was interned under Californian law *5150-ed* which means that an individual can be forcibly hospitalised, usually with heavy anti-psychotic medication. Is Bynes following the same path as Britney Spears? One thing is for sure, this trend of *"psychotic episodes"* and psychiatric confinements is alive and well and is repeated again and again in the entertainment industry.

- Nicki Minaj:

In 2011, Nicki Minaj told V magazine: "I just always want to act like 'Me', but 'Me' changes every day. I would wither and die if I had to wake up and be the same person every day. I wouldn't let those voices be silent anymore, I just let them speak."

Nicki Minaj had a very troubled childhood, including constant conflict between her mother and father. She told *New York* magazine: *"To get out of that violence, I imagined being a different person. Cookie' was my first identity that stayed with me for a while. Then it was "Harajuku Barbie," then "Nicki Minaj."*

She also cites the alter-egos: "Roman Zolanski", "Martha" and "Nicki Teresa".

---

[537] "Amanda Bynes suffering PTSD problems, wants to get better" - Fox411, 2013.

[538] "Amanda Bynes Tweets About Father's Abuse and Microchip in Her Brain; Now Under Involuntary Psychiatric Hold" - TheVigilantCitizen.com, 10/2014.

In 2010, in an MTV documentary entitled *"My Time Now"*, the singer talks about the birth of her alter *Roman*:

- Nicki Minaj: Roman is a crazy boy who lives inside me, he says some things I would never want to say. He was born just a few months ago. I think it was rage that made him... He was conceived in rage, so he's badmouthing everyone and even threatening to hit people. He is violent.

- Journalist: It must be nice to have an oblivious loudmouth that you can blame for everything!

- Nicki Minaj: He wants to be blamed but I don't want to blame him. I ask him to leave, but he can't, he's here for a reason. People have brought him out, people have made an incantation for him and so he's not leaving.

At the 2012 *Grammy Awards*, the closing performance was a Nicki Minaj *show featuring* the exorcism of her alter *Roman*. At the beginning of the show, Nicki is in a confessional where she appears to be possessed. Her entire performance is a representation of a Catholic exorcism aimed at delivering her from her inner demon: *Roman*... A performance *art that* becomes a sort of black mass for the general public, glorifying the demonic entity inside her. She would later say on Ryan Seacrest's radio show: *"People around Roman say he's not good enough, because he can't blend in. His mother and people around him are afraid of him because they've never seen anything like him. He wants to prove that he is an incredible person but also that he is confident, that he is sure of himself. But he's never going to change, he's never going to be exorcised, even when he's sprinkled with holy water, he always gets up again. "*

It is possible that Nicki Minaj invented her different personalities and her inner demon *Roman* only for artistic purposes, but it is interesting to observe how this culture of *'multiple personalities'* is transmitted to the public, to the secular world, during a stage performance reaching millions of people... Her alter *Roman*, whether fictional, a truly disassociated personality fragment or a demonic entity, is thus represented to the audience as an independent and autonomous identity that takes possession of the singer's body and can be cast out by an exorcism... This is a way of glamorising and fashioning demonic possession and personalities split by trauma, in other words, infusing a culture of death into popular culture in the form of an entertainment.

- Eminem:
The rapper Eminem also says he has another personality living inside him, he calls it *Slim Shaddy*, on his website he says: *"Slim Shaddy is just the demon in my head, I think I shouldn't think about it... "*

In his song 'Low Down Dirty' he writes: "Because my split personality has an identity crisis. I'm Dr. Hyde and Mr. Jekyll, disrespectful. Hearing voices in my head with those echoing whispers. Or "All these fucking voices in my head, I can't take it anymore" in his song "Elevator".

There is no doubt that a certain milieu in the music industry is promoting *'multiple personalities'* as a *trend*... Is having a bunch of alter-egos, each one crazier than the last, becoming a fashion? ... This is how the witchdoctors infuse their culture of MK and occultism into the secular world: by its vulgarisation and trivialisation. The mass that applauds and asks for more is thus corrupted with something highly occult that serves beyond the spectacle and the glitter to a real enslavement of the human. We will come back to this later...

It is also possible that an alter of a really split and programmed subject can himself amuse himself by presenting several *personalities* to his audience, by playing on different names and characters, whereas his real alternation of personalities does not depend on him, but on the goodwill of his programmer or his masters.

- Christina Aguilera:

In 2002, Christina Aguilera released her album *"Stripped"* under the name of her hyper-sexualised alter personality: *Xtina*. As did Janet Jackson who revealed her sultry alter *Damita Jo* in 2004. In 2006, mtv.com published an article entitled: *"Christina's New* Split-Personality *Album Is Mature And* 'Dirty'". For Christina Aguilera, there is also talk of post-traumatic stress disorder and *borderline* personality disorder.

- Rihanna:

The more naked I am, the more self-confident I am", the famous star said on an American TV set. Psychologist Jo Hemmings said: *"Rihanna's unpredictable behaviour could indicate that she suffers from narcissistic personality disorder. The symptoms are an exaggerated sense of self-importance and a constant need for admiration, which Rihanna demonstrates by posting half-naked photos of herself on Twitter. If she does indeed suffer from this condition, with psychological help she could identify the disorder that is destroying her and get better. "* [539]

- Miley Cyrus:

Perhaps the most hyper-sexualised and slutty star of the moment is Miley Cyrus, who started her career as a child on the *Disney Channel* series *Hannah Montana*. Cyrus explains in *Marie Claire* magazine: *"You're a pop star! That means you have to be blonde, have long hair and wear tight, glittery things. During that time, I was a fragile little girl who played a 16-year-old with a wig and tons of make-up (...) For a long time, every day I was made to look beautiful, and when I wasn't on the set I thought: 'Who the fuck am I? " I was formatted to look like someone I'm not. "* [540]

According to Nicole Knepper, a psychologist specialising in teenage behaviour and an influential blogger in the US, Miley Cyrus may have a personality disorder, which would explain her highly questionable behaviour (hypersexuality, lack of impulse control, sudden mood swings and drug use). Nicole Knepper told *RadarOnline*: *"This is not normal behaviour. Even for the rich and famous! (...) I'm not saying that Miley Cyrus necessarily has a mood*

---

[539] "Rihanna: elle souffrait de troubles psychologiques" - aufeminin.com, 2012.

[540] "Miley Cyrus: How Disney destroyed her" - gala.co.uk, 2015.

disorder, I'm just saying that someone who has these behaviours and these symptoms is cause for concern and it makes you wonder about the causes (...).Someone who has a rapid change in mood, has insomnia, drinks alcohol regularly, talks unabashedly about sex, drugs and alcohol, that's alarming and those are warning signs of something much more serious. " [541]

In 2014, Miley Cyrus was admitted to a psychiatric hospital. The media explained that it was the death of her dog some time before that had deeply destabilized her... At the same time as she was hospitalised, a particularly crazy psychedelic video clip was released featuring her as a brainwashed junkie: "Blonde SuperFreak Steals the Magic Brain" (an official production), in which she screams from the very first minute: "Where the fuck is my brain!!! ".

- Mary J. Blige:

Singer Mary J. Blige will say of her alter "Brook": "I had to separate the two because Mary is kind and smart, while Brook is crazy, ignorant, she doesn't care about anything... Mary is quiet, the wild one is Brook. " [542]

Mary J. Blige has publicly stated on The Oprah Winfrey Show that she was sexually abused as a child and suffers from severe mental illness: "I was abused and I abused myself... I was tired of life... I was suicidal, ready to kill myself. I hated my image, I hated the sound of my voice, I hated myself completely. "

- Beyoncé:

Beyonce has publicly displayed another personality whom she calls "Sacha Fierce". Here is what she said about it in several media:

When I see a video of myself on stage or on TV, I think, 'Who is that girl? That's not me, I would never do that. " - Beyonce, 2003.

"I wouldn't want Sacha if I met her backstage" - Beyonce, Parade Magazine 2006.

I have someone else who takes over when it's time for me to work and when I'm on stage. This alter ego protects me and who I really am. " [543]

"Sasha Fierce's account is settled, I killed her. " Beyonce, Allure Magazine 2010

- Laurieann Gibson:

Choreographer Laurieann Gibson, known for her work with Lady Gaga, started a singing career in 2014. The introduction to the public of her alter named "Harlee" was done in a very peculiar way... She introduced this alter personality to the media scene with a one-minute mini video clip showing Harlee injured and sequestered in creepy, morbid basements, her tormentors being two men

---

[541] "Miley Cyrus: is her questionable behaviour due to mental illness? " - closermag.co.uk, 2013.

[542] "Mary J. Blige Unveils Alter Ego 'Brook' In Busta Video" - MTV News, 2006.

[543] "Beyonce adopts 'Fierce' alter-ego" - news.bbc.co.uk, 2008.

who rape her and spray her with a high-pressure water jet... This video in which she does not sing (strange for a singing career promotion) is entitled *"Harlee coming soon!* Perhaps this is how the alter *Harlee* was born... in basements and traumas...

- Lady Gaga:

Stefani Joanne Angelina Germanotta, better known as Lady Gaga, names her alter personalities: *"Jo Calderone"*, *"Mother Monster"* and *"Gypsy Queen"*. When Jo Calderone appears, Gaga is dressed as a man and behaves exactly like a macho man. In 2011, at the *MTV Video Music Awards*, Jo Calderone appeared publicly on stage stating:

I'm Jo, Joe Calderone, and I've been told I'm a bastard... Gaga? That one... She dared to leave me! She says it's always the same with guys, including me. Of course, I'm a guy, a real guy. They say we're all crazy. I admit I've gone mad, but in the madness department, she's pretty much the Gaga, isn't she? She's a fucking queen of crazy! Take the morning for example... She gets up, she puts on heels, she goes to the bathroom, I can hear the water running, and when she comes out of the bathroom wet, she still has her heels on... And what's with those heels? At first I thought it was sexy, but now I'm confused... She told me I was no better than the last one. That's not true! ... Honestly I think it's great, I think it's great that she's a fucking super-star... A star of the song as they say... But how do I shine?! I wouldn't mind being in the shadows if I had the impression that she was sincere with me... Maybe she is, mind you... Sometimes I think she's like that, that's her true nature. After all, when she gets on stage, she doesn't put any limits on herself... And the spotlights? All those big lights follow her everywhere she goes, they even follow her home, I assure you... I want my share too... When we fuck, she covers her face because she doesn't want me to see her. The girl is just incapable of being sincere even when no one is looking at her. I'd like to see the real Gaga... But Jo, she tells me... I'm not real, I'm playing a character. But you and I are real..."

Obviously there is a serious inner conflict between the alter *Gaga* and the alter *Calderone*... In case it's all just an acting game, again it's just propagating a certain fashion of split personality. It's all about promoting split personality in the secular world by making it *cool* and fun. The transmission of the Luciferian culture to the general public is done through a whole occult symbolism but also through the trivialisation of the multiple split personality. The aim is to contaminate popular culture with Luciferian subculture so that the people will finally acclaim and demand anti-Christian and enslaving productions... We will come back to Lady Gaga later...

- Tila Tequila:

Tila Tequila is an American singer, model and reality TV star. This unstable personality not only has a *multi-layered* character, she also seems not to be alone in her body... In 2010, she publicly declared that she had a dissociative identity disorder. One of her personalities calls herself *"Jane"* and allegedly tried to kill her. She said on the social network *Twitter: "Jane was there! She tried to kill me! She slashed my body with a knife! I'm terrified, there's blood everywhere! Everything in my room is broken! I woke up with blood everywhere! Jane tried to kill me! I took some pictures, it's really disgusting... I told you guys I have a multiple personality... I fell asleep and woke up with knives everywhere, and everything is broken around me! For people who have multiple personality or bipolar disorder, it's fucking stuff like that that happens! Jane left, I locked the doors.* " Later, Tila Tequila dismissed speculation by some fans that she had hurt herself or attempted suicide: *"I never hurt myself! I never did! I'm telling you, it was Jane!!..."* [544]

- Mel Gibson:
Much more discreetly than a Tila Tequila, a Beyonce or a Lady Gaga, Mel Gibson has confessed to having another personality named *"Bjorn"*... The famous actor spoke about it in 2007 in front of journalist Michael Parkinson on the *BBC's "Parkinson"* programme:

"I have an alter-ego called Bjorn (...) Bjorn is a Viking kind of guy (...) It goes back to a dark age, somewhere where the father would come and visit me, I know it's something bad (...) Bjorn is a former murderer (...) he's a wild guy. He has so much energy (...) I don't want to be Bjorn ever again."

Mel Gibson, who has also been diagnosed with bipolar disorder, says that he has to push this alter *into the sand* inside his mind, but that sometimes a hand still resurfaces and he has to push it back out... He also says that sometimes he lets *Bjorn* participate and play roles, which makes sense with the Viking film *Braveheart*. According to psychiatrist Colin Ross, Mel Gibson also revealed his alter *Bjorn* to the German investigative newspaper *Der Spiegel*.

It should be noted here that Mel Gibson was the lead actor in the MK-Ultra themed film *'Conspiracy'*.

- Joaquin Phoenix:
Joaquin Phoenix grew up in a family of actors and his parents were members of the *Children of God* sect. He made his debut on television and landed his first film role at the age of 10... He continued his career through numerous films including *8 millimetres, Firebomb, Hotel Rwanda, Two Lovers, Gladiator*...

In 2000, he said in an interview with the Australian magazine *Juice:*
- Journalist: Who will you take to the premiere of "Gladiator"?
- Joaquin Phoenix: I'll be honest and I know this is going to sound strange, but my partner right now is myself. That's what happens when you have multiple personality disorder and you're overly egocentric.

- Lindsay Lohan:
Lindsay Lohan, a famous American actress and singer who has been in and out of rehab, said in a reality TV documentary about her: *"Everything is*

---

[544] "Tila Tequila Shocks Fans With 'Multiple Personality' Rant" - starpulse.com, 2010.

going great and then I hear a voice in my head saying, oh oh, it's time to sabotage everything! ("Lindsay" OWN). The actress has serious self-destructive tendencies, be it through scarification, drugs and alcohol. Her life is rather chaotic, like many celebrities... Doctors have diagnosed her with *Narcissistic Personality Disorder* characterised by a disproportionate egocentricity, lack of empathy and an exaggerated sense of self-importance. In a 2010 article by Bill Zwecker for the *Chicago Sun-Times*, it was noted about Lindsay Lohan that *"multiple personalities plague the actress, who at times transforms into 'Diane' or 'Margot'.*

A long-time associate of Lindsay Lohan told the press that she believes the actress has multiple personality disorder and that this may be one of the reasons she suffers from these recurring addictions: *"Some of us have wondered if Lindsay is bipolar because of her recurring mood swings. But I think it goes much deeper than that because Lindsay sometimes called herself Diane or Margot. "*

- Iggy Pop:

In the book *'Iggy Pop: Open Up and Bleed: The Biography'*, Paul Trynka tells us that in 1975, the singer James Newell Osterberg ('Iggy Pop' being an alter-ego) was hospitalised due to his drug addiction. He underwent psychotherapy with Dr. Murray Zucker, who said: *"I always feel that Iggy enjoys playing with his brain so much that he himself doesn't know what's coming out or what's going in. Sometimes he seems to have total control over it, playing with different characters (...) But at other times you get the feeling that he's not in control, he's just going through it. It's not just a lack of discipline, it's not necessarily bipolar, it's God knows what! "*

- Anne Heche:

Actress Anne Heche, star of the American series *Ally Mac Beal*, has written an autobiography entitled *"Call Me Crazy"* in which she recounts her father's incest and the unfortunate psychological consequences she endured as a result of this trauma.

In September 2001, she gave an interview to Barbara Walters on *ABC News*[545]:

I'm not crazy... but I have a crazy life, I was raised in a crazy family and it took me 31 years to get that craziness out of me (...) I had another personality, I had a fantasy world. I called this other personality "Celestia". My other world was called the 'Fourth Dimension' and I thought I was from another planet. "

Anne Heche played the role of two twins in the *Another World* series from 1988 to 1992, and it was then, at the age of 25, that she says her personality disorders began to manifest themselves and lead to moments of madness. Celestia, her other personality, believed she was the reincarnation of God, spoke a different language and had special powers...

---

[545] "Exclusive: Anne Heche Interview" - 20/20 ABC News - 09/2001.

- Anne Heche: I told my mother after seven years of therapy that I had been sexually abused by my father... and she hung up on me (...) In New York, I heard the voice of God and I thought I was totally crazy. I had no idea what to do. I existed in two different people.

- Barbara Walters: So even though you thought you were Jesus or Celestia, you were also aware that this was an aberration?

- AH: Absolutely, that's what makes you crazy, you're absolutely aware of it. On the one hand I was Anne Heche, an actress with lots of friends and I thought people would think I was totally crazy if I told them about it... And at the same time I heard God saying to me "You're from heaven".

- BW: How did that manifest itself? How much control did you have over the situation?

- AH: Oh in so many different ways! What could I do? When I was Celestia, I spoke a different language. I spoke a language that God and I had. I could also see into the future, I could heal people...

- BW: Do you remember what language it was?

- AH: Of course!

- BW: Can you say anything in that language right now?

- AH: Well the word god for example. There are many prayers. The word for god in my language is "kiness". A'kiness, a'ta fortatuna donna...

- BW: And it's a language you never had...

- AH: ... I don't know where it came from, but I knew what it meant. I was in my mind, and God was teaching me.

- BW: You say you were under the influence of voices and visions almost constantly for almost seven years. You struggled with the demons and managed, unimaginably, to juggle this with your professional activity.

- AH: Yes, it's amazing to combine those two things. I would go to work and then come back to my dressing room because I had to write down the messages I was hearing from God about love.

- BW: You would go into your lodge and you were another person. You would close the door and then you were another person, you were Jesus?

- AH: I was Celestia.

- BW: Celestia is also Jesus?

- AH: No, Celestia, as I said before, is the reincarnation of god, here on earth.

- BW: You know Anne, there are doctors and therapists who might diagnose this as a form of mental illness, like split personality, schizophrenia or bipolar disorder. Does that apply to you?

- AH: I don't think so. The most interesting thing is that I went to a therapist for years... It's amazing what you can hide.

- Megan Fox:

Megan Fox who, as we saw in Chapter 7, had a real obsession with the Wizard of Oz as a child, told *Wonderland* magazine in 2009: *"I could end up like that* (referring to Marilyn Monroe) *because I'm constantly struggling with the idea that I have a borderline personality, that I have symptoms of mild schizophrenia. I really think I have mental problems but I haven't been able to find out exactly what they are. "*

She also told Rolling Stone magazine in 2009: "I have a lot to be happy about but that doesn't mean I don't struggle, I'm very vulnerable. I can be aggressive, hurtful, bossy and selfish, too much so. I am emotionally unpredictable, anywhere. I am a control freak. My temper is ridiculously bad. I destroyed the house. As a child she had "panic attacks that manifested themselves in violence, raging tantrums. Like I didn't know how to control myself or what to do. The interview also tells us that she can't fall asleep with someone who is in contact with her (hypersensitivity); she needs "cocoons" and pillows to feel safe; she can't sleep in the dark; she doesn't like to look at herself in the mirror; she admits (like Angelina Jolie) to drawing blood during sex without going into details... She admits to self-mutilation and also alludes to an eating disorder as well as her bisexuality.

- Sia Furler:

The Australian-born international star (whose videos *"Chandelier"* and *"Elastic Heart"* have caused controversy for their paedophile content) has declared that she suffers from bipolar disorder as a result of smoking too much cannabis as a teenager... In 2014, on a famous American radio show, *"The Howard Stern Show"*, she declared: *"What I think is that I smoked too many joints when I was a kid, my brain wasn't formed yet, I fucked up my brain"*... But on the same show, she also confided that her father, Phil B. Colson (also a professional musician), had a dual personality: *Phil* and *Stan*...

- Sia Furler: He had two very different personalities, one was called Phil and the other Stan...

- Journalist: He named his personalities Phil and Stan himself?

- SF: Yes... Phil was the best dad, he was fun but he was also articulate, present and very caring. When Stan would come in, then there would be some terrifying stuff going on (...) It was scary, like a certain energy that would come into the room. An intimidating energy... it intimidated everyone.

- J: How often have you experienced this?

- SF: I don't know, I don't remember.

Sia always assumed that her father suffered from dissociative identity disorder but that it was never diagnosed or treated. She claimed that he never physically abused her. However, when you grow up with a split parent (she does not describe what *"terrifying things"* the alter Stan did), unfortunately the risk of severe trauma is high... Her bipolar disorder may not be caused by THC (the active ingredient in cannabis). It is possible that her family is mired in this *'transgenerational dissociation'* passing from one generation to the next via traumatic experiences, possibly with programming on the split individuals. Sia did not get to the top of the music industry by chance...

- Tyler Perry:

The famous Hollywood producer Tyler Perry had a particularly difficult childhood. In 2010 on *The Oprah Winfrey Show*, he tearfully described the dissociative process that allowed him to escape the pain and terror of trauma: *"I could go to this park (in my mind) where my mum and aunt used to take me. So I'm there in that park running and playing, they were such beautiful days. So whenever someone would do something horrible and unbearable to me, I could go to that park, inside my mind, until it was over (...) All I remember is that he* (editor's note: his father) *grabbed me hard, I was slammed against a fence so hard that my hands were bleeding, and he was hitting me... I was just trying to preserve my life... and I felt myself trying to get to that place, that park, in my mind, where I could stand it... I was trying to get to that park and I couldn't... It made me so angry... I kept trying and trying... When I finally got there and saw the grass in my mind... I saw myself running out of myself... And I couldn't catch that little boy... I couldn't catch that little boy to bring him back to me... I could not bring myself back to my person... I thought I was dying and I didn't understand... It took me so long to understand what had happened. "*

- Barbara Streisand:

The famous singer and actress told Ladies Home Journal in 1994: "I live with a lot of anxiety (...) I'm always changing. So I tell the man I'm interested in that if he likes to have affairs with lots of women, then I'm perfect for him!"[546]

- Anna Nicole Smith:

Anna Nicole Smith, who died in 2007 at the age of 39, was an American former *playmate*, actress and singer. In August 2006 Nicole Smith was filmed in her home, a private recording that was later publicly revealed as the *'clown video'*. The recording showed Anna Nicole Smith in a pathetic state of neglect and clown make-up.

This video was filmed on her property in a sadistic manner by her partner or alleged "master" Howard K. Stern. The video was released to the public shortly after Anna's death. In the video, we can see the star completely disassociated, behaving and sounding like a 4 or 5 year old child. The mass media claimed that she was under the influence of drugs during this video recording, which is probably the case, but drugs alone cannot explain such a state. There were clear symptoms of deep psychological trauma.

When Howard K. Stern asks her, camera in hand, if she has eaten hallucinogenic mushrooms, you can see that she has no idea what a *"mushroom trip"* is... because at that moment she is a little girl of 4 years old, totally ignorant of such things. When Stern tells her that this recording is going to be worth a lot of money, she replies: *"Why? What recording?"* This woman has been in front of cameras and lenses all her life, she knows what a videotape is... but not at the age of 4... We see in this video that she is completely dissociated. A personality disorder that Howard K. Stern took great pleasure in exposing in a video recording designed to ridicule the poor woman...

---

[546] "Thanks for the Memories: the truth has set me free" - Brice Taylor, 1999, p.200.

Anna Nicole Smith was pregnant with a daughter at the time of this *"clown video"*, little Dannielynn Birkhead, who six years later would embody the Spring-Summer 2013 collection of the prestigious brand *Guess Kids*... A child born in the Network and injected into the fashion world at the age of 6, following in the footsteps of her mother...

It is obvious that celebrities play with the personalities that they expose publicly, they usually make a distinction between *private* and *public* persona, it is a way to preserve themselves but also to play with their image. Sometimes they also create a new identity when working on an unusual project, as in the case of musician Garth Brooks who created an alter-ego called Chris Gaines to release an album in a totally different style. Another example is Ashlee Simpson who became Vicky Valentine to switch from guitar to electronic music. We could also mention David Bowie and his alter-egos *Ziggy Stardust* and *Thin White Duke*, but also Prince and his female alter *Camille*, Laurie Anderson and her alter *Fenway Bergamot*...

Clearly the world's performers have very complex personalities... and we find that in some cases this seems to go far beyond simply playing a role or a character, and a line is crossed into what appears to be dissociative identity disorder resulting from severe trauma.

Sometimes celebrities even seem to be possessed and act as mediums...

b/ The demons of cinema and music

> - *I know I have demons, I don't know if I want to get rid of them but I would like to experience them in a different way. Maybe come face to face with them. I've never really had time to go to therapy, just a little bit here and there... but not enough to help me.*
> - *Of course I have demons... Sometimes I'm thirty different people...* Johnny Depp
> - *Vanity Fair*, 1997 and *US Magazine*, 1999

> - *Keanu is a very complex guy with a lot of demons in him, and I'm going to try to use and exploit that.* Taylor Hackford on actor Keanu Reeves - *Movieline*, 2000

> - *I am a tormented person, I have many demons inside me. My pain is as great as my joy.* Madonna - Los Angeles Times, 1991

Whitney Houston's vocal coach, Gary Catona, told the *Daily Mail* that "she had demons inside her ... that she was many people in one, and the question was which of them would appear ... and when."[547]

In 2002, when American journalist Diane Sawyer asked Whitney Houston what the 'worst demon' in her life was, she didn't say 'cocaine', 'drugs' or 'alcohol'... no, Witney's answer was: '*The worst demon is me. I am my best friend or my worst enemy.* " An unsurprising statement for someone with a profound personality disorder. Whitney Houston has revealed some particularly

---

[547] "How Whitney lost her dazzling voice because of her 'extra-curricular activities" - dailymail.co.uk, February 2012.

disturbing things about her relationship with Bobby Brown, another celebrity... Here's a clip from a 2009 interview Houston did with Oprah Winfrey:

- Whitney Houston: There were times when he would turn everything upside down, he would break glass things in the house. We had a giant picture of us with my kid and he cut my head out of the picture... He did stuff like that. Then I thought it was really strange... Cutting my head out of a picture was a bit much for me, it was a sign. And then there were other things... like when he started painting eyes all over the bedroom. Just eyes... evil eyes looking all over the room.

- Oprah Winfrey: He painted on the walls?

- WH: Yes, on the walls, on the carpets, on the cupboard doors. When I opened a door, there was a drawing, and when I closed it, there was another drawing. Eyes and faces... It was really strange...

- OW: What did you do then?

- WH: I was looking at things and thinking: "Lord, what's really going on here? I was getting scared because I felt that something was going to explode, that something was going to happen..."

In 2004, her partner Bobby Brown, himself a singer and actor and visibly disturbed, said in an interview with Jamie Foster for *Sister 2 Sister* magazine:

When I was younger I was diagnosed with attention deficit disorder, I know that's the same as bipolar disorder (...) When I first came to Betty Ford I was wondering what was wrong with me. I was trying in vain to understand why I had these extreme mood swings. That is, one minute I could be happy and the next I was in a rage, full of fire and anger, but I didn't know why. I went to the doctors, they talked to me, they did brain tests and they diagnosed me as bipolar."

Actress Angelina Jolie said she was "very sexualised from the age of four in nursery school (...) I made up a game where I would kiss the boys... Then we would go further and take our clothes off. I was in a lot of trouble then!"

For many early childhood professionals, a hypersexualised attitude in a young child is seen as a sign of suspected sexual abuse. Angelina Jolie, who also appears to be psychologically very disturbed, has admitted to having tried all kinds of drugs, but she seems to have a particular taste for... blood. When she was first married to Johnny Lee Miller, she wrote her husband's name on a white T-shirt in his blood. When she was married to Billy Bob Thornton, they both wore a vial of each other's blood around their necks. Her biography also reveals that as a child she had a fascination with knives, that she collected them, and that as a teenager her unhappiness manifested itself in scarification, among other things. A biography reveals: '*Some people go shopping, I scarify myself. When I started having sex, sex was not enough for me, my emotions were not strong enough, something wanted to come out... One day, wanting to feel an even more intense fusion, I grabbed a knife and slashed my boyfriend... then he slashed me too. He was a really good guy, a nice guy who wasn't the threatening or violent type. We had this particular exchange... We were covered in blood and I could feel my heart racing.*"

Jolie's biography also tells us that during a sado-masochistic session, Jolie asked her partner to slash her chin, a small scar that remains to this day.

She says: "I wanted him to help me out and it frustrated me because he couldn't help me. Scarification obviously couldn't help her, in fact it nearly killed her. In particular, there was an accident where Jolie slashed her neck and stomach and then carved a cross on her arm. She ended up in the emergency room and later said, "I almost cut my jugular."[548]

Angelina Jolie was thus sexualised from the age of 4, then later "adept" of bloody scarifications... Some therapists will clearly recognise here signs strongly suggesting that Angelina Jolie was a victim of sexual abuse in her early childhood. Abuses which could have split her personality and the following statement seems to confirm that she was undergoing dissociative states from her childhood: *"When I was a child, I didn't have my own "Self". As I grew up, I lived through characters that I played by losing myself in different parts of my personality."*

Another example is actor David Carradine who was found dead in a Bangkok hotel room at the age of 72. Lieutenant-General Worapong Siewpreecha said the actor was found with *one rope tied around his neck and another to his sexual organ, both of which were tied together and hung from the wardrobe.* A sadomasochistic practice of depriving the brain of oxygen in order to increase the effect of the orgasm, a "game" that proved fatal...

In the entertainment industry, there is no shortage of examples of totally unhinged and self-destructive behaviour, a world where the boundaries between fiction, reality, madness and sanity seem to no longer exist. A world where drama and horror are written not only in fictional scenarios but also in the lives of its actors... But is it possible that some of the greatest stars of cinema and song are possessed or influenced by demonic entities? Do they serve as mediums for certain spiritual forces that influence their creativity or their stage performances, consciously or unconsciously? Is the "deal with the devil" just a legend?

Man's status in this material universe is temporary and, as we have seen, can be influenced by entities linked to other dimensions. The Old and New Testaments are full of examples where angels intervened in human affairs under the direction of God. But the Bible also speaks of the unwanted and constant presence of *demons* or the *devil*, i.e. fallen spiritual entities influencing humans negatively. The Bible describes the different dimensions in which such beings reside: *"The angels who have not kept the dignity of their rank, but have left their own dwelling place, he has kept in perpetual chains in the depths of darkness, waiting for the great day of judgment."* Jude 1:6

Apart from the biblical aspect, objectively and rationally, we cannot deny today that the entertainment industry as a whole propagates an image of decadence and immorality based on violence, sex, drugs and exaggerated materialism... Like a mirror, our western society today reflects the content of these entertainment *programmes* infused permanently in the media.

Where does this spirit of decadence come from? Is it being infused into our world via entities using certain humans as mediums to embody a subculture

---

[548] "Angelina Jolie - The Biography: The Story of the World's Most Seductive Star" - Rhona Mercer, chap.1, 2009.

and thus influence humanity as a whole? Are these mediums "agents" of counter-initiation working to defile Creation (consciously or not)? Chapter 6 has already given us the beginnings of an answer to these questions...

In 2011, singer Ke$ha drank the blood of a (presumed) beef heart on stage during the *Future Music Festival* in Sydney. Her bloody "performance" in which she raised the heart above her head to let the blood flow into her mouth was an example of her song *Cannibal*... Kesha Rose Seber stood on stage covered in blood for over 45 minutes in front of thousands of cheering people. [549]Note here that the cover of her album *Cannibal* depicts her face with a tear splitting it vertically in two, a classic symbolism in the entertainment industry representing the splitting of the personality.

In 2014, at the *SXSW* Festival in Austin, Texas, Lady Gaga literally and willingly threw up on herself. During this "shock performance", the artist Millie Brown swallowed a greenish liquid and then put her fingers down her throat to vomit the contents of her stomach on the half-naked Gaga. All in a sexually explicit position on a mechanical horse....

Singer Miley Cyrus is increasingly provocative and sexually perverse. In November 2015, during a concert in Chicago for the launch of her new tour, Miley Cyrus arrived on stage almost naked, sporting a gigantic dildo in her crotch! It was in this outfit that she appeared in front of fans, many of whom were minors and even pre-teens.

The aim is to ensure that all these deviant, perverse and recurrent practices do not become shocking and that they gradually become part of our culture... Let's remember that Lady Gaga is the most popular pop star in the world and that her "performances" and behaviours permeate millions of young people. For example, Gaga has done photo shoots dressed with real raw red meat, or with horns implanted on her forehead, shots that are widely distributed around the world and unfortunately acclaimed.

An employee of the Chicos Intercontinental Hotel in London told The Sun newspaper: "Lady Gaga left a large amount of blood in the suite during her stay this summer. The incident was reported to the concierge, who was asked to turn a blind eye". Another source said: "Everyone in the hotel is convinced that Lady Gaga took a bloodbath, or at the very least, used all the blood for a costume or her stage appearance".

For some, this is simply a laughing matter... and many will see in these extreme acts only a provocation for publicity purposes: to create a *buzz* in the *celebrity* press and on the Internet. But this kind of completely deranged "artistic performance" is multiplying and becoming more and more extreme, just like a race to reverse moral values and the collapse of a civilisation. *L'ordo ab chao*... Order through chaos or from chaos to order... Everything is clear for those who still have eyes to see. The inversion of values is underway...

---

[549] "Ke$ha turns in a bloody shocker at Future Music Festival, drinks blood from a heart"- *The Daily Telegraph*, 2011.

- But the spirit expressly says that in the last days some will depart from the faith and hold to seducing spirits and doctrines of demons. 1 Timothy 4:1

- Woe to those who call evil good and good evil; who turn darkness into light and light into darkness; who turn bitter into sweet and sweet into bitter! Isaiah 5:20

- Know that in the last days difficult times will come. For men will be selfish, lovers of money, boastful, proud, blasphemers, rebellious to their parents, ungrateful, sacrilegious, unfeeling, unforgiving, slanderers, unrestrained, cruel, enemies of the good, traitors, impulsive, puffed up with pride, loving their own pleasure more than God. They will keep the outward form of piety, but they will deny its power. Stay away from such men. 2 Timothy 3:1-5.

Are some of the great stars of show business the mediums of a higher force? The question deserves to be asked and some artists' declarations seem to enlighten us on this subject, as we will see below...

What is mediumship? Psychologist and medium Jon Klimo defines mediumistic trance as: "The communication of information to a human being from a source that exists on another level than the physical dimension we know, and that does not come from the mind of the medium."

There are two forms of mediumship or channeling: intentional channeling and spontaneous channeling. Intentional channeling occurs when a person voluntarily seeks to make contact and be possessed by entities, in such cases the spirits usually wait for permission before entering the body. In spontaneous channeling, the spirits take control of the body when they wish, and the individual is then at their mercy.

Both types of channeling can take many forms. It can be a complete or partial loss of consciousness during the trance. It can also be done through sleep where the spirits will influence the individual in their dreams and nightmares. Another form of mediumship is automatism, where the entity takes control of a part of the body, usually the hand, to make it write or paint, this is called automatic writing or painting. A mediumistic trance may involve writing, painting, singing, dancing, composing music, and even giving speeches and teachings in the form of lectures. The medium can also hear words dictated in his or her mind, this is called "clairaudience", a paranormal hearing faculty. One thing to remember is that whatever the manner of channelling and the result obtained, it is recognised that without these demonic entities, the medium has strictly no power.[550]

Medium Jon Klimo confirms that mediumistic states are influenced by external entities: "If your mind can act on your own brain, then something similar of a non-physical nature may also be able to act on your brain, causing you to

---

[550] Cult Watch: What You Need to Know about Spiritual Deception " - John Ankerberg, John Weldon, 1991.

hear voices or have visions. An entity can speak or write by controlling your body in the same way that you usually control it with your mind."[551]

"The gods do not communicate directly to mortals, but through intermediate spirits. The mortal needs figures to communicate with the gods, and so the demon becomes the necessary figure... a source leading to sacrifices, initiations, incantations, prophecies, divinations, magic spells and sacred poems." Plato[552]

"In the same way, the muse inspires men because they are inspired and possessed... It is not through art or knowledge that you say what you say, but through possession." Socrates[553]

Keep yourselves constantly open to the demons that whisper in your ear. The term 'demon' has an old meaning which is close to the 'guiding spirit', the 'inspiring muse'. Anton Lavey[554]

"There are three main methods of invoking an entity (...) The third is the Theatrical method, perhaps the most attractive of all; it is at any rate certain to appeal to the artist's temperament, for it addresses his imagination through his sense of the aesthetic." Aleister Crowley[555]

The Bible teaches us that the channelling of spirits is nothing more than demonic possession, although *new-age* mediums prefer to speak of 'mutual cooperation' between the entity and the *channel*. It would seem that many artists intentionally or unintentionally channel entities in their creative process, whether it be in screenwriting, songwriting, acting or stage performance.

Let us specify that the interest of the Prince of this world and his army is not to spiritually elevate the human mass, but rather to make it fall with him... In our time, this entertainment industry putting forward its numerous mediums is used against the spiritual health of the human being although it can also infuse and divulge a part of the truth about our current situation... The ambiguity is there, on the one hand this industry plummets consciences to divert and debase them but on the other hand it can just as easily awaken people through its materialistic, decadent and sickening extremism, thus pushing the individual to question himself and to detach himself from it in order to return to the divine. Moreover, this industry permanently distils a symbolic occult knowledge in its productions, indeed everything is displayed for those who still have eyes to see: *"Don't talk about it, show it."*

A Law of this great theatre is to let the Truth shine through despite the semblance of darkness and confusion, to allow free will to be fulfilled. God does not permit the suppression of access to Truth in spite of this ambient *hubbub* and

---

[551] Channeling: Investigations on Receiving Information from Paranormal Sources " - Jon Klimo, 1987.

[552] "The Demon and the Angel: Searching for the Source of Artistic Inspiration" Edward Hirsch, 2003.

[553] "Actors and Acting" - Toby Cole, Helen Krich Chinoy (Eds.), Three Rivers Press, 1995.

[554] *Church of Satan"* - Anton Lavey, p.110.

[555] *Book 4"* - Aleister Crowley, 1980.

chaos attempting to divert and control human consciousness. The war is spiritual, it consists in diverting consciousness from the knowledge of God. Mind control of the masses is the *modus operandi of* the controlling sorcerers... but they must allow access to the Truth, they have no choice.

Here is an impressive series of quotes showing how demonic possession is more present than ever in our world, and particularly among the world's influential stars, both in the film and music industries.

"(In the studies of John Livingstone Nevius:) Wang Yung-ngen of Peking noted that people who had no ability for song became talented singers when possessed, and others without any natural ability for poetry could easily compose rhymes when under the possession of an entity."[556]

➤ Cinema:

- Rudolph Valentino:

In the 1920s, the actor Rudolph Valentino and his wife Natasha were both adepts of the occult and practised spiritualism: *'Every night Natasha would hold a séance to call on the spirit world for help with her creativity. Then, with pen and paper in hand, she would go into a trance and start writing. Once typed, the work would be given to the director the next day.* "[557]

- Mae West:

In the 1930s, the actress Mae West, known as the Queen of Sex and even the Statue of Libido, once said: 'When I'm good, I'm very good, but when I'm bad, I'm even better.'

His work has helped to overturn the biblical values of North America. West's contact with the spirit world led to a successful production of scripts. Screenplays that catapulted her onto the film scene. She allowed herself to be possessed by entities and spent entire evenings in psychic readings. One of her relatives, Kenny Kingston, said: *"When she was angry that no one could come up with an idea for a screenplay, she would pace around her room saying, 'Forces! forces! come to me and help me write a script. She would begin to hear voices and see images of a story unfolding before her. Mae would then call a stenographer, and for hours, while lying on her bed in a trance-like state, she would dictate things as the spirits passed them to her.* "[558]

---

[556] "Demonic Possession: a medical, historical, anthropological, and theological symposium" - John Warwick Montgomery, 1976.

[557] *Madam Valentino'* ' - Michael Morris, Abbeville Press, 1991.

[558] Psychic Kenny Kingston's Guide to Health and Happiness " - Kenny Kingston, (Windy Hill), 1984.

- Marilyn Monroe:

The famous 20th century sex symbol was known to go into deep trances. Kenny Kingston said she *"draws the spirit world to her for guidance."*[559]

Marilyn Monroe herself said: "Jekyll & Hyde... More than two, I am so many people. They shock me sometimes, I wish it was just me!"[560]

Lloyd Shearer wrote: "Before each take, Marilyn would close her eyes and go into a deep trance."[561]

Marilyn Monroe famously said: "Hollywood is a place where they pay you $50,000 for a kiss and 50 cents for your soul."

- James Dean:

James Dean was another known practitioner of the occult. He publicly admitted: *'I have a pretty good knowledge of satanic forces.'*[562]

His close friend Dennis Hopper said of him: "He was totally transformed when the camera started rolling. He would suddenly become the character... Strange things would come out of him."

James Dean's advice to Dennis Hooper about working with the spirit world was simple: *"Leave yourself open."*

Indeed, James Dean believed that another entity inhabited him when he was acting, he described it as follows: "as if there were two people in the same skin... one telescoping the other from behind... the one inside seemed to drift across the surface of the skin."

- Peter Sellers

British actor Peter Sellers, known for his role in the Pink Panther series, said: "It's a bit like being a medium and opening yourself up and saying, I want a character to inhabit my body or take over so I can produce what I want to produce."[563]

When Sellers was asked, "Do you hear his voice the same way you hear mine now? He said, "Yes, absolutely, as clear as this. A very clear voice, as if someone was talking but here (pointing to his head). Sometimes I call to get a hand and sometimes it happens like this. It can happen any time, really any time. (...) I play like a medium if you like, I let the character come through me..."

Peter Evans, Peter Sellers' biographer, will describe how 'the demon began to inhabit his body. Everything started to change in him. It wasn't just his walk and the way he stood, it wasn't just his voice, but his expressions, his eyes, his gestures... everything was different."

---

[559] *I still talk to...* " - Kenny Kingston, Valerie Porter, Seven Locks Press, 2000.

[560] Goddess: The Secret Life of Marilyn Monroe" - Anthony Summers, 1996.

[561] Ibid.

[562] James Dean, The Mutant King: a Biography " - David Dalton, 2001.

[563] Peter Sellers: The Mask Behind the Mask " - Peter Evans, 1980.

- Robin Williams:

In 1999, actor Robin Williams himself told *US Weekly* reporter James Kaplan that he opened himself up to possession when he was on stage: '*Yeah! Literally, it's like a possession. All of a sudden you're in it, and as you're playing in front of an audience, you get this energy that starts to flow into you... But there's also something else, it's possession, at one time you would have been burnt for it. But something gives you power in there. I mean, you're all in it... It's Dr Jekyll & Mr Hyde, you can actually become this other force. Maybe that's why I don't have to play evil characters (in the movies), on stage you can cross that line and then come back.*"

In the same article, James Kaplan added: "With a gift for imitation and improvisation that borders on demonic possession, Williams could even approach the art of his idol Jonathan Winters, a man whose genius once or twice led him to cross a line into madness."

Robin Williams was found to have committed suicide in 2014.

- Leonardo DiCaprio:

Total Eclipse director Agnieszka Holland said of actor Leonardo DiCaprio:

Leo is like a medium. He opens his body and mind to receive messages about another person's life."[564]

Leonardo DiCaprio's father said of his son: "I think Rimbaud was perhaps a medium, perhaps he was visited by aliens, and I think Leo has that ability too!"

In her book *Leonardo DI Caprio: The Modern Day Romeo*, Grace Catalano says: "With Leo, you can see thirty people emerge from him in one day."

- Marion Cotillard:

In 2014, actress Marion Cotillard said she felt possessed by *the ghost of Édith Piaf*. In an interview with the British newspaper *The Guardian*, the French actress said she had become so involved in her role as Édith Piaf that she could hear the singer's voice and felt pursued by her ghost for eight months. She said she tried everything to get rid of it. "*I tried exorcism with salt and fire. I also travelled to Bora Bora to escape it. I went to Machu Picchu in Peru, participated in shamanic ceremonies to cleanse myself. Finally, I realised why I couldn't let her go. She was abandoned by her mother. Her biggest fear was being alone.*"[565]

---

[564] *Leonardo DiCaprio"* - Nancy Krulik, 1998.

[565] "Marion Cotillard felt possessed by the ghost of Edith Piaf" - ici radio-canada.ca, 2014.

➤ Music:

To introduce this section, let us take the example of the composer Giuseppe Tartini, an Italian violinist of the Baroque period who wrote more than 400 works. His most famous piece is entitled *"Devil's Trill Sonata"*. The story behind this musical creation begins in a dream... Tartini is said to have told the French astronomer Jérôme Lalande that the devil appeared to him in a dream and asked him to be his servant. In his dream, at the end of the lesson, Tartini is said to have given the devil his violin to test his skill, the devil then began to play with such virtuosity that Tartini was left breathless. When the composer awoke, he immediately took out pencil and paper to write down the devil's sonata, desperately trying to recover what he had heard in his dream. Although his composition was ultimately very successful and loved by the public, Tartini lamented that it was still far from what he had heard in his dream. What he had written was, in his own words, *'so inferior to what I heard, that if I could subsist by any other means, I would have broken my violin and given up music forever."*[566]

Cyril Scott, the *'father of modern British music'*, was an eminent composer, poet and writer during his lifetime. He also studied theosophy and was interested in the use of music in the occult. Two of his books, *The Influence of* Music *on History* and *Morals and* Music: *Its Secret Influence Throughout the Ages, were* received through the channeling of one of his theosophical spirit guides. In the second book, Scott says that as a result of his contact with this spirit, he took *a particular interest in the evolution of Western music.* Scott was convinced that *the great initiates* (of the spirit world) *have vast and important plans for the musical future.* What is that plan? It is to use music as an occult medium through which altered states of consciousness, certain psychic abilities and close contact with the spirit world can be developed. Scott explains that *"The music of the future is to be used to bring people into close contact with the Devas (spirits), so that they will be able to receive the beneficial influence of these beings by attending concerts in which an appropriate type of sound has been used as an invocation (...) Scientifically calculated music can achieve two objectives: that of invoking the Devas and that of stimulating the psychic faculties of the listener, who will then be open to the influence of these spirits."*

Cyril Scott concludes his book by quoting the words of his spiritual guide: "Today, as we enter this new era, we seek, primarily through inspired music, to initiate the spirit of unification and brotherhood, and thus accelerate the vibration of this planet.[567] We are in the midst of a new age here...

---

[566] "Le Violon: les violonistes et la musique de violon du XVIe au XVIIIe siècle" - Arthur Pougin, 1924, p.106-107.

[567] "Music and Its Secret Influence Throughout the Ages" - Cyril Scott, 2013.

- Elvis Presley:

In one of the biographies of Elvis entitled *"If I Can Dream: Elvis' Own Story"*, Larry Geller writes that the famous singer himself acknowledged that he received help from the spirit world. According to Geller, who was Elvis' spiritual adviser, Presley always carried books with him when he travelled. Among his favourite books were *"Isis Unveiled"* by theosophist Helena Blavatsky, *"Autobiography of a Yogi"* by Paramahansa Yogananda, *"The Secret Teaching of All Ages"* by Freemason Manly P. Hall, Alice Bailey's *"Esoteric Healing"*, Levi H. Dowling's *"Aquarian Gospel of Jesus the Christ"* and the six volumes of Baird T. Spalding's *"Life and Teachings of the Masters of the Far East"*. Spalding. Elvis Presley was therefore an early *New-Ageer*, a great fan of the Theosophist Blavatsky who at one time published the magazine *Lucifer*. He was so fond of Blavatsky's book *"The Way of Silence"* that he sometimes even read parts of it on stage, and he also used it as inspiration for his own gospel group *"Voice"*.[568]

Journalist Steve Dunleavy reported some statements made by Elvis' bodyguard, Red West: "Elvis Presley was straddling his microphone in a very suggestive position... he was shaking in compulsive movements as if he was possessed by the spirit of an alien. For Red West, Elvis was possessed: "He had some kind of special power, he had psychic powers, Elvis proved that to me many times.[569]

His biographer Larry Geller also said: "Elvis believes that he is working under the aegis of the masters... and that they are helping him... In Elvis's mind, his life is divinely directed by the masters and enlightened beings, ascended entities who lived eons ago. He truly believed that he had been chosen to be a modern Christ."

Elvis himself admitted: "I've always felt an invisible hand behind me. I hear that same voice and I think it's my brother's (deceased) voice. That's what I think. I hear this guidance that directs my whole life. That's why I'm here and why I'm doing this. It's not by chance. (...) Elvis said that "his mission" was to use his "name and influence" to introduce people to the "spiritual world" through which he was used. He said that this 'Voice' used him as a 'channel' to reach millions of people through the 'universal language of music' (...) One day in the future, we will see how God's ministry will react when it sees the 'old age' beginning to crumble... I look forward to seeing this New Age..."[570]

According to Gary Herman, the author of "Rock and Roll Babylon" (2002), Elvis himself "acknowledged that there was a diabolical element in his success."

---

[568] *Elvis"* - Albert Goldman, 1981, p.436.

[569] "Elvis: What Happened? - Steve Dunleavy, 1977.

[570] If I Can Dream: Elvis' Own Story " - Larry Geller, 1990.

- Little Richard:

The famous American singer and rock'n'roll pioneer said: 'Rock'n'roll does not glorify God. You can't drink from the spring of God and the spring of the devil at the same time. I am one of the pioneers of this music, one of its builders. I know what it's made of because I built it."[571]

Richard also testified: "I was directed and commanded by another power. The power of darkness... A power that many believe does not exist. The power of the devil, Satan (...) My real opinion about Rock n' Roll, and I've talked about it a lot in the last few years, is this: I think this kind of music is demonic... A lot of the rhythms in today's music come from voodoo, from voodoo drums. If you study the music and its rhythms, as I did, you will see that this is a reality. I think that this style of music takes people away from Christ. It is contagious."[572]

- Jimi Hendrix:

"I can explain things much more easily through music. You hypnotize people that way... and when you have people at their weakest point, you can preach into their subconscious what you want. LIFE, October 1969
"The lord knows, I'm a voodoo child." Jimi Hendrix - Voodoo Chile, 1968

Jimi Hendrix's interest in spiritualism produced the song *'Voodoo Chile'*. Kwasi Dzidzornu aka Rocky Dijon, a Ghanaian-born conga player whose father was a voodoo priest and who often played alongside Hendrix, said: *"One of the first things I asked Jimi was where he got the voodoo rhythm from... A lot of the rhythms Jimi played on the guitar were very often the same rhythms my father played at voodoo ceremonies. The way Jimi danced to the rhythm of what he played also reminded me of the ceremonial dances to the rhythms my father played for Oxun, the god of thunder and lightning. This ceremony is called "Voodooshi".*[573]

For Hendrix, "Things like witchcraft and imagination, which are a form of exploration, have been banned by society and labelled as evil. This is because people are afraid to discover the full powers of their minds."[574]

Hendrix's producer Alan Douglas said: "One of the biggest things about Jimi was what he believed... He believed he was possessed by a spirit, and I believe that too. We had to deal with that all the time (...) he really believed it and he struggled all the time."

His lover Fayne Pridgeon said of Hendrix: "He used to say that a devil or something was inside him, you know he didn't know what made him act the way he did and what made him say what he said, the songs and so on, it just came out of him (...) He kept saying, 'I don't know what's going on with me. I really don't understand him. You know he used to grab his hair or stand in front of the mirror

---

[571] *The Dallas Morning News*, Little Richard, 10/1978, p.14A.

[572] The Life and Times of Little Richard" - Charles White, 2003.

[573] Scuse Me While I Kiss The Sky" - David Henderson, p. 251.

[574] *Jimi"* - Curtis Knight, Prayer Publishers Inc. New York, 1974.

and scream. Oh my God! It was so sad when he was screaming... He was maybe the first man or maybe the only man I saw crying, it broke my heart when he cried like that... It seemed to me that he was very tormented, totally torn and he was really obsessed by something very bad. He would sometimes ask me: "As you are from Georgia, you must surely know someone who exorcises demons."[575]

- The Beatles:

John Lennon said: "When real music comes to me, there's nothing to do because I'm like a channel. I feel like an empty temple filled with many spirits, each one passing through me, each one inhabiting me for a little while and then leaving and being replaced by another."[576]

Lennon's wife, Yoko Ono, also said: "They were psychics, they were not aware of everything they said, but it was coming through them."[577]

This is how Paul McCartney describes how he received one of his most famous songs: "The music for 'Yesterday' came to me in a dream. The melody was complete. You have to believe in magic. I myself can't even read or write music."[578]

John Lennon will say something very similar: "It's amazing, that melody (editor's note: the song 'In My Life') came into my head in a dream. That's why I don't pretend to know anything. I think the music is very mystical."[579]

The band's drummer, Ringo Starr, said of the song "Rain": "I felt like it was someone else playing."

The Beatles' publicist, Derek Taylor, said in an interview with the Saturday Evening Post: "It's incredible, absolutely incredible. Here are these four boys from Liverpool, they're tough, they're blasphemous, they're vulgar, but they've taken over the world. It's like they've founded a new religion. They are completely anti-Christ. I mean I am too, but they are so anti-Christ that they even shock me, which is not an easy thing."[580]

The San Francisco Chronicle of April 13, 1966, published this statement by John Lennon: "Christianity is going to disappear, it's going to diminish until it fades away. I don't want to argue about it. I am right and the future will prove it. We are more popular than Jesus Christ now. I don't know which will disappear first, Rock'N'Roll or Christianity."

---

[575] From the film "*Jimi Hendrix*", interview with Fayne Pridgeon, quoted in *Heartbeat of the Dragon*, p. 50.

[576] *People* magazine, 22 August 1988, p.70.

[577] The Playboy Interviews with John Lennon and Yoko Ono ", Berkeley, 1982.

[578] Paul McCartney, interview with Larry King Live, CNN June 2001.

[579] *The Beatles As Together*" - John Lennon, Reader's Digest, 2001.

[580] Saturday Evening Post, 08/1964, p. 25.

- David Bowie:

Bowie, who was a great admirer of the Satanist Aleister Crowley, told Rolling Stone magazine in 1976: "Rock has always been the devil's music (...) I think rock'n'roll is dangerous (...) I feel that we are just proclaiming something darker than ourselves."

In his song "Quicksand" he sings: "I'm close to the Golden Dawn, dressed in Crowley's outfit (...) I'm not a prophet or a stone age man, just a mortal with superhuman potential."

In the biography of Angie Bowie (his ex-wife) it is reported that in 1976 he said: "My major interest is Kabbalah and Crowley. That dark and rather scary world on the naughty side of the brain."

In 1983, in an interview with Musician magazine, David Bowie said: "I had this more than passing interest in Egyptology, mysticism and the Kabbalah. At the time it seemed perfectly obvious that it was an answer to life. My whole life was turning into this weird nihilistic fantasy world of impending doom, mythological characters and future totalitarianism."

- Michael Jackson:

Global pop culture icon Michael Jackson said: "I have a secret room, hidden by a wall and filled with mirrors. That's where I talk to Lee... that's where I hear his voice and feel his presence beside me. He is like my guardian angel. He even gave me permission to record his favourite song "I'll be seeing you".[581]

Michael Jackson was nicknamed *"Bambi"* or *"Peter Pan"* because he did not want to grow up, locking himself away in a "fairyland". An imaginary country illustrated in particular in the development of his *Neverland* ranch into a real amusement park. This man suffered enormously, probably because of a very traumatic childhood.

Here is another of his very explicit statements about the phenomenon of possession: "When I go on stage, there is a sudden magic coming from nowhere that takes hold of me, and when the spirit takes hold of you, you lose control of yourself."[582]

In a television interview, Oprah Winfrey asked him about his habit of putting his hand on his crotch when he danced, and Jackson replied: *"It's a subliminal phenomenon. It's the music that makes me do it, it's not premeditated, it happens spontaneously. I become a slave to the rhythm."*[583]

Jackson also said: "Many times when I'm dancing, I've felt touched by something sacred. In those moments, I feel my spirit soar and I become one with the whole."[584]

As with the Beatles, Michael Jackson's mediumship was also through dreams: "I wake up from sleep and think: Wow! I'll come out of sleep and I'll

---

[581] *"Michael Jackson"* - Psychic News, 14/02/1987.

[582] "Teen Beat: A tribute to Michael Jackson", 1984.

[583] *The Evening Star* - Oprah Winfrey interviews Michael Jackson, 1993.

[584] *Dancing The Dream"* - Michael Jackson, 1992.

say, 'Wow, put that down on paper. It's all strange, you hear words and it's all there in front of your eyes. I feel that somewhere, in some place, it's all been done and I'm just a messenger to the world. Rolling Stone, February 1983.

- Jim Morrison:

The co-founder and keyboardist of the famous band The Doors, Ray Manzarek, said: "Jim was authentic... He was not a showman. He wasn't an entertainer, he was a shaman. He was a man possessed."

In Siberia, when the shaman is ready to go into a trance, all the villagers are with him and play whatever instrument they can to help him go into a trance... It's the same with the Doors when we play live... I think it's our state with the drug that makes us go into a trance faster... It's like Jim is an electric shaman and we're the band that accompanies this electric shaman, hammering out the tempo behind him. Sometimes we don't want to get into these states, but the music hammers on and on, and little by little it takes over..."[585]

In a poem, Jim Morrison writes that he met the spirit of music after an intense energy discharge to see an apparition of the devil on a canal in Venice... I saw Satan or Satyr... A carnal shadow of my secret mind.[586]

Morrison admitted that he drank to silence the constant voices of demons.

The Doors' friend and photographer, Franck Lisciandro, said: "Jim drinks to calm the incessant voices of demons, ghosts and other spirits that demand their release... He drinks because there are demons and voices screaming in his head and he has found a way to quell them with alcohol."[587]

- Carlos Santana:

Santana has stated that he channels a spirit to create his music, in an article in *Rolling Stone* magazine in March 2000, we read: *"Metatron is an angel. Santana has been in regular contact with him since 1994. Carlos sits there facing the wall, candles lit, a yellow pad next to him, ready for the communications that are coming (...) It's a bit like receiving faxes (...) You meditate with candles and incense and sing... and all of a sudden you hear this voice saying, 'Write this...' (...) Metatron wants something from me, and I know exactly what it is. People who listen to music are connected to a higher level of themselves. That's why I'm having so much fun with this album, because it's a personal invitation from me to people: remember your divinity (...) The energy of angels and demons is the same energy, it depends on how you use it. It's a fuel (...) There's an invisible radio station that Jimi Hendrix and Coltrane picked up, and when you've picked it up, you channel that music."*

---

[585] *"No One Here Gets Out Alive"* - Jerry Hopkins and Daniel Sugerman, 1995, pp. 157-60.

[586] "Jim Morrison Search for God" - Michael J. Bollinger, 2012.

[587] "Break On Trought: The Life and Death of Jim Morrison" - Riordan & Prochnicky, 2006.

Santana also said: "Sometimes I do things on the guitar that I didn't even know how to do. I don't actually know how to do it, it just goes through me. It's one of the highest states someone can reach."

- John Mc Laughlin:

John Mc Laughlin of the Mahavishnu Orchestra testified: "One night we were playing, and suddenly the spirit came into me, and I played... but it wasn't me playing anymore." - *Circus*, April 1972

"When I let the spirit possess me, it is an intense pleasure. My role as a musician is to make everyone aware of their own divinity." - *Newsweek*, March 1972

- The Rolling Stones:

Keith Richards of the Rolling Stones not only said: "*We get our songs from inspiration like a* séance", but he told the *Los Angeles Times* that his song "*Demon*" was auto-biographical and that he himself was possessed by four demons. In the song "*Demon*" Richards sings: "*It's like a mass. Demon in me, demon in me. It lives in me, the demon in me.*"

- Led Zeppelin:

The famous Jimmy Page, who was a devout follower of the Satanist Aleister Crowley, believed he was being used as a vehicle by demonic spirits. Other members of Led Zeppelin admitted to experiencing "automatic writing": "*He* (editor's note: Robert Plant) *often said that he could feel his pen being pushed by a higher authority.*"[588]

Robert Plant and Jimmy Page both claim that they don't know who wrote their cult/occult song 'Stairway to Heaven'. Robert Plant said: "*Pagey wrote the chords and he played them for me. So I was holding this piece of paper with a pencil, and for some reason I was in a very bad mood... Then all of a sudden my hand started writing words... I then sat down looking at those words and almost fell out of my seat.*"[589]

- Brian Wilson:

The composer of the Beach Boys' biggest hits once said: "We're doing witchcraft, we're trying to do witch-music."[590]

Wilson openly acknowledged that he too was tormented by voices in his head. Nick Kent wrote of him: "Those voices in his head, they don't say anything distinct, they're a dark, ghostly whisper in the deep recesses of his brain."[591]

---

[588] *Hammer of the Gods' '*, Stephen Davis, 2001, p. 262.

[589] Ibid.

[590] The Dark Stuff: Selected Writings on Rock Music " - Nick Kent, 2002.

[591] Ibid.

Brian Wilson was a friend of the Satanist criminal Charles Manson, he even said about him: "The witch doctor is Charley Manson, who is a friend of mine. He thinks he's God and the Devil. He sings, plays and writes poetry and maybe one day he'll be an artist for Brother Records."[592]

Warner Brothers Records president Larry Waronker said he had met at least five different personalities inhabiting Brian Wilson's body: *"There are a lot of people here, I met five different personalities."* - *Rolling Stone,* August 1988

- Fleetwood Mac:

Fleetwood Mac singer Stevie Nicks, who was dubbed "the blonde priestess of the occult" by Rolling Stone magazine, once said: "It's amazing, sometimes when we're on stage I feel like there's a presence coming in to move the pieces... We don't have any control over it and it's a magical thing. " - Circus, April 1971

- Kurt Cobain:

In his book *Kurt Cobain,* Christopher Sandford wrote: "Kurt had many inner demons, many weaknesses and physical problems (...) He was a shy and at the same time aggressive personality, he struggled with the demons that plagued and tormented him." In April 1994, Kurt Cobain, a heroin addict, committed suicide by shooting himself in the head, leaving a farewell letter addressed to Boddah, his imaginary childhood friend... Kurt Cobain is referred to as a member of the infamous Forever 27 Club, a group of famous musicians who died at the age of 27, including Brian Jones, Jimi Hendrix, Janis Joplin and Jim Morrison.

- Tori Amos:

Singer Tori Amos said: "I think music comes from other dimensions, it would be arrogant to think that you can create music just by yourself, there's a co-creation going on. I don't know with whom, but it's a fact that we all have access to that tap (...) I feel it's a very nice thing that they come and use my body to transmit what they want. It's an energy, a force that comes and visits me."[593]

Tori Amos told SPIN magazine in 1996: "I want to marry Lucifer (...) I don't see Lucifer as an evil force (...) I feel his presence and his music. I feel like he comes and sits on my piano. She even wrote a song called "Father Lucifer" which begins with the words: "Father Lucifer, you never seemed so sane..."

- D'Angelo

In June 2012, singer D'Angelo told GQ magazine: "You know what they say about Lucifer, before he was cast out? Every angel has his specialty that is praised. They say he can play all instruments with just one finger and then the music is just great. He was exceptionally beautiful, Lucifer, the angel that he

---

[592] Ibid.

[593] *Axcess* magazine Volume 2, Issue 2; p.49.

was. But then he went down to hell. Lucifer was fearsome. There are forces at work and I don't think a lot of these fuckers who are making music today know about these things. It's deep, I felt it, I felt outside forces influencing me. It's a very powerful psychic tool that we are involved in. I learned at a very young age that what we sang in choirs was just as important as the work of the preacher. Singing is a ministry in itself. The stage is our pulpit, we can use all that energy as well as music, lights, colours and sound. But you have to be careful..."

In 2014, at the *Red Bull Music Academy Festival* in New York, D'Angelo gave an interview to Nelson Georges in which he said that it is *'spirit'* that infuses him in the artistic process. The singer says that he *surrenders to a higher power and becomes a medium through which this 'spirit' works.* The question is what kind of spirit it is...

- Nicki Minaj:

"When I write rap, my brain doesn't think, it doesn't think at all. You just have to let it go without thinking and it just happens" ... This statement may indeed be smiling coming from the bimbo Nicki Minaj...

In 2010, in the *MTV* documentary *"My Time Now,"* Nicki Minaj said after leaving the stage following a concert, when asked how she was doing: *"I don't even know! I was like in a trance the whole time!"*

- Beyoncé:

In 2004, *Rolling Stone* magazine published an article entitled: *"Beyonce: a woman possessed - Beyonce is held by a spirit so powerful it even has a name: Sasha!".* As we saw earlier in this chapter, it is her alter personality named *Sasha Fierce* living *inside her.*

Beyoncé also talks about her trance-like states when she is on stage, in an interview with *Marie Claire* magazine in 2008, she described what appears to be a dissociative trance during concerts: *"I have out-of-body experiences. If I hurt my leg or fall, I don't feel anything. I'm in a special state, I don't even pay attention to my body or my face anymore."*

In 2013, Beyoncé told Amy Wallace of GQ magazine: "It's like a blackout. When I'm on stage, I don't know what's going on: I'm somewhere else. The article concludes with a quote from the star: "I am far more powerful than my mind can process or even understand."

In a 2010 interview on BET TV, Beyoncé said: 'Sasha is my alter-ego. When people meet me and talk to me, they usually expect to see Sasha, but I'm actually a lot more reserved than she is, it's nothing like that. In the dressing rooms I'm not there any more because it's Sasha who emerges, she can do certain things that I would normally be embarrassed to do, even if I try to behave in that way, it doesn't work, by myself it doesn't work. I also remember just before I went on stage I raised my hands to the sky and it was like something went inside me and that's when I knew I was going to win a BET Award."

- Ke$ha:

Ke$ha has stated that she has had several supernatural experiences that influenced her album *Warrior*. In an interview with Ryan Seacrest, she revealed that she *"had sex with a ghost"* (incubus: a male demon who is supposed to take on a body to sexually abuse a sleeping woman) and said that this sexual relationship inspired her latest single *"Supernatural"*: *"It's a song about supernatural experiences... but erotic. I had some experiences with the supernatural... I don't know his name, it was a ghost! I'm very open about it."*

- Lady Gaga:

Lady Gaga learned from her mother that strange dreams and nightmares may be secret rituals... Gaga has revealed that her nightmares inspire her music, videos and performances. In 2010, she told *Rolling Stone* magazine about a frightening dream she has on a recurring basis: *"This ghost drags me into a room, and there's a young blonde girl whose arms and legs are being torn apart by ropes... I never see her get cut up, but I watch her moan. Then the ghost says to me, 'If you want me to stop hurting her and if you want your family to be safe, you have to cut your wrist. I think he must have a sick cutting tool. And there's this honey... He wants me to mix this honey into a cream and then spread it on the wound and the bandage. When I come out of this dream, I open my eyes and there is nothing like this around me... And my mother said to me: "Isn't this an illuminati ritual?"*

Gaga confided that she turned to her friend and spiritual advisor, the renowned Deepak Chopra, to help her interpret a dream in which she eats a human heart...

- This is terrifying! The devil is trying to take me... Deepak, I am a good girl!

- You are very creative, my Gaga. You should put this in a video clip...

- I suppose in his own way he is teaching me to respect and honour my madness. It's part of who I am (...) I have morbid dreams but I put them on show. A lot of my work is an exorcism for the fans, but for me too."[594]

The young singer Gaga told *Vanity Fair* magazine that she believes her late aunt's spirit is inside her... She believes her aunt Joanne's spirit was "transferred" to her mother's womb, she said: *"When I was born, it was almost like I was carrying on her unfinished business. She was a poet and pure of heart, a beautiful person. She died a virgin (...) And one of my guides told me that he could feel that I had two hearts in my chest, and that's what I think too."[595]*

In 2011, Gaga also told *Bazaar* magazine that she did not write her song *'Born This Way'*, but that the late British fashion designer Alexander McQueen passed on the lyrics from the dead. Indeed, Lady Gaga and McQueen, who committed suicide in 2010, were close friends: *"It's all planned, just after he*

---

[594] The Broken Heart and Violent Fantasies of Lady Gaga " - Neil Strauss, Rolling Stone, 2010.

[595] Lady GaGa: My aunt lives inside me " - digitalspy.co.uk, 2010.

died I wrote 'Born This Way'. I think he's in heaven pulling the fashion strings, being the puppeteer and planning it all. "... Says Gaga...

A 2010 *Herald Sun* article reported that Lady Gaga believes she is haunted by a ghost named "Ryan" and that he follows her around the world on tour. She said the constant presence terrifies her. A member of her team told the *Daily Star* newspaper: *"She's been telling us for months that there's a ghost called 'Ryan' who travels the world with her (...) He hasn't done anything particularly violent or scary, but she's freaked out by his presence. She's very spiritual and she's a person in tune with the spiritual world, but this is all going a bit too far, even for her."*

Gaga even contacted a psychic and held a séance to communicate with the entity and tell it to go away. Lady Gaga seems to be obsessed with the spirit world, at 24 she had already spent tens of thousands of dollars on "ghost hunters", including a device that measures electromagnetic fields to detect spirits...[596]

- To conclude:

It is overwhelmingly clear that many of the world's celebrities are emotional, psychological and spiritual wrecks, leading or having led chaotic, morbid and destructive lives of debauchery. Many of the world's biggest stars end up dying before their time and in similar circumstances (the official nature of the death is sometimes to be taken conditionally in such cases), here are some examples:

- Whitney Houston: "overdose
- Heath Ledger: "overdose
- Phillip Seymour Hoffman: "overdose
- Jim Morrison: "overdose
- David Carradine: "asphyxiation
- Michael Jackson: "overdose
- Robin Williams: "asphyxiation
- Cory Monteith: "overdose
- Kurt Cobain: "bullet in the head
- Jimi Hendrix: "overdose".
- Janis Joplin: "overdose
- Marilyn Monroe: "overdose
- Anna Nicole Smtih: "overdose
- Amy Winehouse: "overdose".
- Brittany Murphy: "overdose
- etc...

Eating disorders, obsessive-compulsive disorders (OCD), bipolar and *borderline* disorders, histrionic (narcissistic) personality disorders, depression and dissociative identity disorders make up the sad array of psychological conditions of entertainment industry celebrities. What do they all have in common to suffer so much? What is the source of this malaise?

---

[596] "Lady Gaga holds a seance to get rid of ghost" - Herald Sun, 11/2010.

The French psychotherapist and sexologist Patrick Dupuis perhaps sheds light on this question with what he calls the *"Initial Violence"*, i.e. the source that generates perversity, violence and self-destruction: *"Without wind, there is no storm, without childhood traumas, there is no depression, no phobias, no perversions. No natural drive system is capable of generating violence on its own without being subjected to a violent constraint (abuse, forcing, control, pressure) from the environment... Homo sapiens does not have a destructive instinct or a death drive, any more than any other animal on earth. He only has a construction instinct which is reversible into its opposite under the effect of a traumatic shock. The psychic device that I call the construction instinct (of the self and of the world) is reversible into its opposite (into a destruction instinct) under the effect of serious environmental disturbances that we call infantile traumas. The term perversion describes this process of inversion, which is a dynamic process (and not a natural property of perversity), but most of the time we do not link the violent or perverse behaviour to the violence that generated it, and this is due to the lack of a valid theorization of the process, and also because of the law of silence that still weighs on this type of hidden violence. "*[597]

This chaos and unease that is omnipresent in the entertainment industry is necessarily rooted in a traumatic past but also in a close relationship with the occult and the spirit world.

Are childhood traumas the price to pay for access to creative genius, to certain psychic powers, to the ability to open up easily to the spirit world through dissociation and possession, and ultimately to glory? A child who has been consecrated to Satan since birth, who has undergone repeated traumatic ritual abuse, becomes in spite of himself closely linked to demons... He will navigate between the world of humans and the world of spirits in dissociative states, altered states of consciousness caused by drugs, alcohol, music, but also violence on himself or others...

His split personality and MK programming will only enhance his ability to channel inspiration from an *"Beyond"* to serve as a bridge medium here on earth, thus furthering the agenda for the establishment of Luciferian rule. A human who is dedicated to Lucifer/Satan from birth, who is disassociated and split by trauma, is wide open to demonic possession (which does not necessarily involve *walking on the ceiling and spitting nails*), will serve as a human slave to transmit Luciferian culture to this earth via the best tool: the entertainment industry... This without escaping the inner chaos, self-destruction and final sacrifice of the slave. The Prince of this world needs agents/slaves on the ground to effectively influence humanity as a whole, to transmit the doctrine - Luciferian subculture - and for this the entertainment industry is the propaganda platform par excellence.

---

[597] *"La violence initiale"* - Patrick Dupuis, mondesfrancophones.com, 2010.

c/ The pact with the devil?

Several celebrities have publicly declared that they have literally *sold their soul to the devil* for fame and fortune... All this may of course lead to a smile, as the secular world is nowadays totally closed to such ideas.

Joseph Niezgoda's book *'The Lennon Prophecy, A New Examination of the Death Clues of the Beatles'* has pieced together a puzzle to prove that John Lennon made a deal with Satan in exchange for fame and fortune. Joseph Niezgoda, a first-generation Beatles fan who has read every book ever written about the famous rock band, has found a love of music, but also a love of Satan...

Niezgoda introduces his book with Lennon's famous quote to his friend Tony Sheridan in the mid-1960s: *'I sold my soul to the devil'*. He then describes how this group of musicians, made up of young Englishmen, ended up achieving worldwide fame...

Niezgoda cites the date of 27 December 1960 as the beginning of the pact. On that night, the Beatles were playing the *Town Hall Ball Room* in Litherland, England. At the time, Lennon was just a twenty-year-old rock singer in a mediocre band comparable to many other bands. But that night, the Beatles provoked an incredible reaction from the audience, one that was completely different from other times: while they were playing, the crowd unexpectedly jumped on stage and all the girls started to get hysterical. This had never happened before, but it was to become a systematic behaviour later on. And so, overnight, *Beatlemania* was born. The four young musicians and singers remembered that night as the turning point in their careers. Had the pact been made on the winter solstice a few days earlier? Had the pact been made on the winter solstice a few days earlier, thus preparing the crowd for the totally over-the-top reaction on 27 December? A date remembered as the 'anniversary of *Beatlemania'*.

Niezgoda also notes that this concert marks the beginning of John Lennon's openly anti-Christian behaviour. Several of Lennon's biographies report numerous public desecrations with no apparent purpose other than to blaspheme Jesus Christ.

Twenty years later, on December 9, 1980, Mark David Chapman shot John Lennon five times with a revolver in front of the famous Dakota Building in New York, where he and his wife Yoko Ono had a flat (on the same floor where Roman Polanski's occult film *Rosemary's Baby* was shot). Lennon died shortly after the attack. Mark Chapman later claimed that he had been instructed to kill Lennon by a *'voice in his head'* that insisted: *'Do it, do it, do it...'*. Five years later, while in prison, Chapman asked to be exorcised by a priest, and later claimed that he had been delivered from five or six demons.

A large part of Niezgoda's book investigates the 'clues' left by the Beatles themselves on the album covers and in their music. Clues that lead to the occult. To support his thesis, Niezgoda researched witchcraft, mysticism, numerology, anagrams, etc. He claims that clues to Lennon's death are revealed in the album covers of *Rubber Soul, Yesterday and Today, A Collection of Beatles Oldies, Sgt.*

Pepper's Lonely Hearts Club Band, Yellow Submarine, Magical Mystery Tour, but also in Lennon's solo albums like *Imagine* and *Walls and Bridges.*

The cover of the Beatles' 1966 album *'Yesterday and Today'* does not reveal anything about John Lennon's death, but it does explicitly show that the band was involved in Satanism. The cover, dubbed *'The Butcher's Cover'*, shows the Beatles posing in white butcher's coats with large chunks of raw meat on their laps, as well as a decapitated baby dummy... This very creepy photo is a clear reference to child sacrifices in Satanic rituals. This is not an avant-garde piece of art or a bad joke, as some Beatles fans claim.

Niezgoda also reports some song lyrics that reveal the mysterious prediction of John Lennon's death, as well as his connection with Satan. His songs were often passed on to him in his dreams, especially the most successful ones. In one of his last songs, *'Help me to help myself'*, it seems that he realised that his time had come. The song begins with the words: *"Well, I've been trying so hard to stay alive, but the angel of destruction keeps harassing me from everywhere. But I know in my heart that we never really left..."*. At the end of the song, Lennon can be heard whispering: *'I see, I see.'* As Niezgoda points out, there is nothing in his book that is not already in the public domain. All he has done is tie the pieces together to reveal the issue of the occult and the strong likelihood that the Beatles received supernatural help in their rise to fame.[598]

In December 2004, the famous Bob Dylan gave an interview to Ed Bradley for the television show *60 Minutes* (*CBS*), here are some excerpts:

- Bradley: Why do you go on? Why are you still here?
- Dylan: It's a matter of destiny, I made a good deal with her... a long time ago and... I'm coming to the end.
- Bradley: What case is this?
- Dylan: To get to where I am now.
- Bradley: Can I ask you who you made this 'good deal' with?
- Dylan: (laughs) With... You know, the Commander-in-Chief.
- Bradley: ... of this land?
- Dylan: Of this earth, and the world we cannot see.

Here, when Bob Dylan speaks of the *Commander-in-Chief*, he is referring to Lucifer, Commander-in-Chief of the fallen angels (demons), the Prince of this world. An uplifting interview in which he also states:

- Bradley: Do you ever look back on your productions and say, "Wow, that surprises me! "
- Dylan: I used to do it but I don't do it anymore. I don't know how I came to write these songs.
- Bradley: What do you mean by that?
- Dylan: All those early songs were written like magic... Darkness at the break of noon, shadows even the silver spoon, a handmade blade, the child's balloon" Well, try sitting down and writing something like that, there's a magic

---

[598] "John Lennon's Pact with Satan" - Margaret C. Galitzin / The Lennon Prophecy - Joseph Niezgoda.

in it... and it's not the Siegfried and Roy type of magic, you know? It's a different kind of penetrating magic. And you know, I did it, I did it for a while.

Famous rapper Kanye West said on stage: "I sold my soul to the devil, I know it's a rotten deal, but it comes with a few surprises like a happy meal."

Katy Perry quipped in an interview: *"I wanted to be the Amy Grant of music. But it didn't work out, so... I sold my soul to the devil."*... She is now a world-renowned star, with one clip in particular that refers directly to MK programming, more on that later.

Roger Morneau, the author of *A Trip Into the Supernatural*, spent several years in a Canadian cult involved in spiritualism and demon worship. In 1995, in a video interview with Dan & Karen Houghton of the *Hart Research Center*, Morneau reported the words of a famous jazz musician with whom he was dining at a party:

If I want power, I go straight to its source. How do you think I became so famous? I said, "You must be lucky. He said, "There is no such thing as luck. Either there is some power working for you somewhere, or you are not advancing in this world..." Then we talked about spirit worship (...) He told me that the so-called spirits of the dead are demons. "They are fallen angels, beautiful beings (...) We worship spirits. We worship Lucifer and all his angels. They are all as beautiful as when they were cast out of Heaven (...) So we are in a war, good against evil. We are the bad guys, but we are not so bad. I see this case as the forces of good and evil, one person believes in God, the other believes in Lucifer, it's like politics."

Former porn star Shelley Lubben testified on the 700 Club (Out of Pornography and Into the Light - CBN): "As soon as the camera started rolling, it was like Satan came to me... I could almost see the devil saying to me: 'You see Shelley, everyone is going to love you now, I'm going to make you famous'. The producer was astonished: "Where did you find this girl? I immediately went from being an amateur to a professional making adult films with porn stars. It was destroying me, I had lost my femininity, I lost my whole personality in porn.

This is what she says about her first day on set in 1992: "As soon as I walked in, I felt like a dark satanic presence was invading me. It was terrifying, dark, it had nothing to do with prostitution. I knew I was in Satan's territory. It was like Satan's final frontier. I thought, Oh, my God, I can't believe I'm doing this." Shelley went through with it and her career took off, fame and money soon became an obsession...

4 - MARILYN MONROE: HOLLYWOOD'S FIRST MIND-CONTROLLED SLAVE

Marilyn Monroe is perhaps the most iconic figure in American culture and the most recognisable sex symbol of all time. However, behind Marilyn's photogenic smile was a fragile person who was exploited and subjected to mind control by powerful 'masters'.

Marilyn Monroe is the ultimate sex symbol, embodying everything that Hollywood stands for: glamour and glitz. Her iconic sultry blonde persona forever revolutionised the film industry, and even today, this icon greatly influences popular culture.

While Marilyn represents all that is glamorous in Hollywood, the disturbing story of her private life also represents the dark side of Hollywood... Marilyn was effectively manipulated by high-level 'mind doctors' who controlled every aspect of her life and effectively stole her soul. Her death at the early age of 36 is one of the first *'celebrity death mysteries'* in popular culture. While there are many facts pointing to murder, his death is still classified as a *"probable suicide"*.

While many biographers explain that Marilyn's misfortunes originated solely from 'psychological problems', the assembly of the facts of her life combined with the knowledge of the dark side of Hollywood reveal something even darker: Marilyn Monroe was one of the first celebrities subjected to Monarch mind control. Through traumas and a psychological programme, Marilyn gradually became a high-level puppet for the American elite, she even became JFK's presidential model.

When Monroe's programming deteriorated and she began to sink, some say she was *"thrown off the freedom train"*, the term for slaves who are disposed of when they are no longer useful to their masters (and potentially dangerous because of the revelations they might make).

Marilyn, whose real name was Norma Jeane, was declared a ward of the state at the age of 11. She never knew her father and her mother was psychologically very unstable. The little girl was therefore placed in numerous foster homes, orphanages and other homes. She was placed in a number of foster homes, orphanages and other homes, where she was mistreated and sexually abused. This unstable and traumatic youth made her an ideal candidate for mind control, including Beta programming (sexual slavery). These children who no longer have a family are easy prey, they are at the mercy of unidentifiable adults and are therefore targets for the Network.

Norma Jeane started her career as a stripper in Los Angeles, where she was introduced to a certain Anton LaVey (who later founded the Church of Satan). According to Fritz Springmeier, LaVey himself was an MK programmer and the young Norma Jeane became one of his sex slaves, as did Jayne Mansfield (actress and singer). Mansfield and Monroe had a lot in common: they were both 'luscious blondes', the model of women who are credited with the sexualisation of Hollywood; they both worked (*playmates*) for *Playboy* magazine; they both had an 'affair' with the Satanist Anton LaVey; they both had an 'affair' with Robert F. Kennedy and JFK (the affair was actually playing the role of "presidential models"); both died in their thirties.

Norma Jeane's physical transformation into the iconic Marilyn Monroe began when she joined the *Blue Book Modeling* Agency. She underwent plastic surgery, a change of hair colour and finally a change of name... A radical transformation that allowed her to take on many film roles. It was in 1956 that she officially and legally changed her name from Norma Jeane to the future world icon: Marilyn Monroe. A strong symbolic act which in terms of mind control represents the suppression of her original personality, in order to allow her alter personality to fully exist. From that moment on, *Marilyn* was only what her controllers wanted her to be.

As her biographers reveal, Marilyn had little or no personal freedom. Her masters isolated her in order to control her better and avoid that outsiders help her to become aware that she was being manipulated. The only people she had contact with were her psychiatrists and her masters. The proof that these individuals were the only people in Marilyn's life is that they inherited almost all of her fortune. Monroe consulted psychiatrists on an almost daily basis, were they conditioning and programming sessions? One thing is for sure, she was getting worse as these sessions increased in frequency.

In 1955, while staying at the *Waldford Astoria Hotel* in New York, she wrote a poem entitled *"The Surgeon Story"*. In it, she describes being drugged and *"cut open"* (magic surgery?) by Lee Strasberg (her "mentor") and Margaret Hohenberg (her psychiatrist). This account is usually described as a simple recollection of a nightmare reported by Marilyn, but some researchers argue that it is in fact a description of a mind control session. She describes that the operation did not bother her, because she was prepared for it, was she in a state of dissociation and trance? She also mentions the fact that she could *only* see *"white"*, *which* could refer to sensory isolation (a method used in MK-Ultra). Once *"opened"*, the doctors found in her only a *"fine sawdust, like that coming out of a rag doll"*. Marilyn sees herself as an empty doll, typical of an MK slave who has lost contact with her original personality. This is the text entitled *'The Surgeon's Story'*:

Strasberg - he is the best and most competent surgeon to open me up, which I don't object to since Dr. H. prepared me for it - she gave me an anaesthetic and she is also the one who diagnosed my case and agrees with what needs to be done - an operation - to bring me back to life and cure me of this terrible disease or whatever it is (...). has given me an anaesthetic to try to relieve me medically, Strasberg opens me up - and after everything in the room turns WHITE, in fact I can't see anyone, just white objects - they open me up - Strasberg and the Hohenberg chick - and there is absolutely nothing in there - Strasberg is deeply disappointed but even more intellectually amazed that he could have made such a mistake. He thought he was going to find much more than he had ever hoped to find... and instead there was absolutely nothing - devoid of any sentient living human creature - the only thing that came out was very fine sawdust - such as is found inside Raggedy Ann (rag doll) dolls - and the sawdust spills out onto the floor and the table, Dr. H. She is baffled because she suddenly realises that she is faced with a new situation where the patient... exists from the extreme void. Strasberg sees her dreams and hopes for the operating room fall by the wayside. Dr. H. has to give up his dreams and hopes of lasting psychiatric treatment - Arthur is disappointed - Abandoned.[599]

---

[599] Translation by *Eyael* from pensinemutine.eklablog.com.

Marilyn Monroe is said to have had two pregnancies that ended in miscarriages. While her biographers claim that these were miscarriages, other sources say that they were actually induced. Lena Pepitone, who was Marilyn Monroe's maid, seamstress and confidante, wrote a book in which she reported that the star said: "Don't take my baby. They took him from me... and I'll never see him again". The book reveals that Marilyn had not miscarried but that *they* took her baby, a common practice in MK-Ultra and Satanism.

At the height of her career, Monroe found herself linked with US President John F. Kennedy. Some historians have described this relationship as a mere 'fling', but she was probably being used as a 'presidential dummy' - a slave for the 'good pleasure' of presidents and other notables.

Adam Gorightly, in his book An Interpretation of Kubrick's Eyes Wide Shut writes: "These presidential dummies would have been used by artists and politicians as sex toys: mind-controlled puppets programmed to perform various perverse acts at the behest of their manipulative master. It is assumed that Marilyn Monroe was the first Monarch sex slave to achieve "celebrity" status.

The last months of Marilyn Monroe's life were characterised by inconsistent behaviour and several 'intimate' relationships with individuals in power. As a Beta slave, she was also used sexually by people in the industry. In June Dimaggio's book *"Marilyn, Joe & Me"*, the author describes how she was forced to be in the service of old men and had to completely disassociate herself from reality (an important aspect of MK programming) in order to be able to perform repulsive acts: *"Marilyn couldn't afford emotions when she had to sleep with wrinkled old men in order to survive in the business. She had to protect herself by virtually "unplugging" from her emotions during those times - as if she were playing a role to get out of the horror of the situation. When these rich, high-profile tycoons owned her body and soul, she could not live on her own. At that time, she told me, she would come home exhausted from photo shoots and powerful old geezers phoning her, which gave her goose bumps. After some of the horrors of these sex sessions, she would stay in the shower for over an hour. She wanted to wash away the terrible experience she had just endured."*

In 1962, Marilyn began shooting Something's Got to Give but was so psychologically unstable that she was eventually fired and sued by *20th Century Fox* for half a million dollars in compensation. In his book *Goddess: The Secret Lives of Marilyn Monroe*, Anthony Summers reports that the film's producer, Henry Weinstein, said that Marilyn's behaviour during filming was horrifying: *"Very few people live in terror. We all experience anxiety, sadness and heartache, but this was pure animal terror".*

It was her psychiatrist Ralph Greenson who found her dead in her room on 5 August 1962. While her death was classified as a *"probable suicide"* by barbiturate poisoning, it still remains one of the most debated theories of all time, as there is indeed a great deal of evidence to support the murder theory. So much evidence has been destroyed that it is difficult not to believe in a cover-up. Jack Clemmons, the first LAPD officer to investigate the scene of her death, wrote a report stating that he clearly suspected murder. Three people were present in Marilyn Monroe's home at the time of her death: her housekeeper Eunice

Murray, her psychiatrist Dr. Ralph Greenson, and her general practitioner Dr. Hyman Engelberg. The investigation into Monroe's death revealed that Dr. Greenson called the police more than an hour after Dr. Engelberg pronounced him dead. The behaviour of the three people present at the scene was described as "incoherent". This is very reminiscent of the circumstances of the death of Michael Jackson, whose life can be compared in many ways with that of Marilyn Monroe, especially in the fact that it was their entourage that managed their lives from A to Z... like precious dolls of the entertainment industry (the same goes for Britney Spears and many others...).

Marilyn Monroe quickly became an outstanding global icon representing the sexy and glamorous side of Hollywood, but she also became, in the infamous world of MK-Ultra, the symbol of Beta Programming. Today, more than ever, young stars raised in the entertainment industry have followed in her footsteps (as if everything was planned for them). These young women, manipulated by "coaches", are led to fame and fortune. Women who have generally been subjected to mental control from an early age, leading later to psychotic breaks and sometimes even a mysterious early death. Systematically, these celebrities are staged at some point in their careers to embody the image of Marilyn Monroe, as if it were a sick need of those pulling the strings to make a point of symbolically revealing MK slavery. There is a plethora of videos or photos featuring big stars who embody the mythical image of Marilyn Monroe. There are too many of them for it to be a coincidence, and in some cases, the resemblance is not only aesthetic, so similar are the tragic destinies...[600]

5 - CANDY JONES: MANCHURIAN CANDIDATE

The Candy Jones case is one of the most documented cases of mind control in the fashion industry. How did a famous American model come to be subjected to the CIA's mind control experiments? In 2001, journalist Colin Bennett wrote an article for the *Fortean Times* magazine[601] exposing the whole affair:

To everyone she was known as the most famous American model of the 1940s. But she led a secret life as a Manchurian Candidate working for the secret service during the Cold War. Colin Bennett analysed this case of multiple personality and hypnotic mind control.

On December 31, 1972, in a luxurious New York flat owned by lawyer friends, the famous 61-year-old radio presenter Long John Nebel was married to Candy Jones, 47, an internationally renowned model. The guests at this happy event would certainly have a lot to talk about.

---

[600] "The Hidden Life of Marilyn Monroe, The Original Hollywood Mind Control Slave" - Vigilantcitizen.com - "The Hidden Life of Marilyn Monroe, Hollywood's First Mind Control Slave" - BistroBarBlog.

[601] Manchurian Candy" - Colin Bennet, *Fortean Times* 148, 07/2001.

John Nebel was the Arthur William "Art" Bell of the day, and his nightly radio show had an audience of millions, but that night his head was not at Watergate or in Vietnam... He had just married a woman whose face had been on the cover of eleven of the country's biggest magazines in the space of a month in 1943. During the Pacific offensive in World War II, pictures of Candy Jones in a polka-dot swimming costume adorned the interiors of ships, tanks and trenches.

It was a very quick marriage arranged on the basis of love at first sight, so Nebel did not know his wife well. During the reception, he noticed for a brief moment that she had lost all her exuberance and natural charm. Her voice became that of another woman and her usually fluid posture became rigid. The evening continued at a Chinese restaurant called "Ho Ho", where Nebel noticed the transformation again; it was as if she was uncomfortable with the décor, the mirrors and the Chinese candles. When it was time to go to bed, Candy spoke again in that strange voice Nebel had heard earlier in the evening. What was even more alarming was the fact that this strange Candy personality had a completely different attitude towards him. She" seemed cruel, mocking and cold. When Nebel asked her to explain this, Candy was surprised; indeed, she had not noticed the emergence of another voice or personality. However, a few weeks after their marriage, she finally confided in Nebel that she had once worked for the FBI for a while, mysteriously adding that she might have to leave town again without giving any explanation. Nebel then wondered if there was a connection between Candy's other personality and these strange trips she said she had taken for the FBI.

Candy Jones, whose real name is Jessica Wilcox, was born in 1925 in Atlantic City, New Jersey. She grew up to be a beautiful young blonde woman of 1.93 metres. Her typical American ice-queen face, like that of Grace Kelly, Jayne Mansfield and Marilyn Monroe, was very fashionable at that time. Although she grew up in a rather affluent environment, her manic-depressive (bipolar) father and mother abused her. Her father, who was separated from her mother, once crushed her fingers on a nutmeg grater. Her mother beat her legs so badly that Candy had to wear thick stockings to hide the marks. She was not allowed to be around other children and was often locked in a dark room by her mother. It was in this dark room that little Candy, in panic, developed a series of imaginary characters to keep her company. In the darkness of her prison, she visualised these characters appearing in the few reflections of a large wall mirror. The name of one of her magical friends was Arlene, who would later play a crucial role in Candy's life. Unlike the other characters in this fantasy world, Arlene did not disappear when Candy became an adult. She grew and matured with her, just like a secondary personality. Arlene's personality was a kind of mirror image of Candy's. She had traits of Candy's. She was a very good person, but she was not a good person. She had traits of Candy's mother: she was harsh, ruthless, sarcastic and cruel, with a small, squeaky voice very different from Candy's.

It was this voice that Nebel first heard on her wedding day. When she was herself, Candy was the most loving, charming and sociable of women. But when she was Arlene, she could become dangerously vicious, even attempting one night to strangle her new husband in a military and professional manner. Nebel soon realised and concluded, not without reason, that his new wife's mind was very disturbed. Candy seemed to be terrified of all things Chinese, she also had a great fear of doctors, psychiatrists and dentists, as well as drugs in general. Drugs were what Candy was most afraid of, whenever she heard about them, Candy's "protector" Arlene would vehemently declare that such things should never enter "her" body.

Nebel discovered that Candy's personality changes had a long history, and his research led him directly to the heart of an organisation that many of his listeners had been telling him about for years: The Central Intelligence Agency (CIA) of the United States of America. Nebel then took a big risk, as he had been practising hypnosis for many years as an amateur and decided to put Candy into a light trance to ask her some questions and record the answers. This was the beginning of one of the most amazing stories of our time, as told in Donald Bain's book "The Control of Candy Jones".

In 1945, while touring US military bases in the Philippines, Candy fell ill and was admitted to the Gulf Hospital in Leyte. It was there that she met a Dr. Gilbert Jensen (This is a pseudonym chosen by Donald Bain for legal reasons. Bain said that Nebel confided in him that he knew very well who this doctor was and that he had thought many times of killing him). This young doctor then prescribed vitamin injections, which probably saved his life, or at least his physical appearance. Jensen then left her his card and told her that he hoped to keep in touch with her. Several years after this event, she would meet Dr. Jensen again, with disastrous consequences...

In 1946, she married fashion king Harry Conover, who was later imprisoned for fraud, without much feeling. The marriage ended in divorce in 1959, leaving her with custody of her three sons and a modelling agency in New York. In 1960, an old acquaintance of Candy's, a retired army general, visited her at the agency to ask a small favour. He wanted her to allow the FBI to use her agency as a post office box. She agreed and even offered to deliver the mail to them when he was away on business. At the time, she viewed this arrangement as nothing more or less than a patriotic activity. She had no idea what was in store for her.

One of the first assignments given by this general (name unknown) was to deliver a letter to a man in San Francisco on one of his trips. This man was Dr. Gilbert Jensen, whom she only vaguely remembered. She had dinner with this man on November 16, 1960, a day that would forever shape her life. Jensen revealed to her that he was now working for the CIA and that he had an office in Oakland. He told Candy that if she wished, she could become more involved in secret intelligence matters, adding that it could be lucrative for her. With her three sons in public schools, Candy was running out of money and accepted the offer.

The first thing Jensen did was to hypnotize Candy. In doing so, he discovered the alter personality of "Arlene". He then strengthened this personality through the use of hypnotic techniques and intravenous injections of experimental drugs. He succeeded in making Arlene a leading personality in Candy's mind so that he was able to send her (with Arlene's voice and behaviour) on various missions, both nationally and internationally. The change from Candy to Arlene was radical, in addition to the change in personality, voice and behaviour, she wore a wig and specific make-up. Jensen wanted to create the "perfect messenger", the one who could not reveal anything about the message to be transmitted, neither where it came from, nor who sent it, even under torture.

This operation was extensive and very well organised. Candy, as Arlene, the virtual zombie, travelled to training camps, military bases and secret medical facilities throughout the United States. She was trained in all areas of covert action, including explosives handling, hand-to-hand combat, improvised weapons, camouflage and communication. Arlene learned to kill with her bare hands, was conditioned to resist pain and trained to resist interrogation techniques. Jensen, who took great pride in her work, promoted her within the army on several occasions as a "narco-hypnotic" success, the perfect warrior. An important point for Jensen was to demonstrate that the conditioning was so deep that Arlene could even kill herself on command. To give you an idea of the moral values of the people involved in this kind of program, Jensen once put a lighted candle in Candy's vagina without any reaction of fear or pain from her. He did this in front of 24 doctors in an auditorium at CIA headquarters in Langley, Virginia.

Candy, as Arlene, was sent to Taiwan at least twice on a test mission to deliver envelopes. There she was tortured with electric batons to see if she would break, which she did not. Perverse sexuality seems to have been an important part of this mental programming plan. She was often put naked on a stretcher, hypnotised and tortured on different parts of her body. She was subjected to coercive "Gestapo-like" interrogations and sexually abused by women against her will. The sexual abuse was done under hypnosis by Jensen himself.

Of course, none of this was part of the so-called fight against communism. It was more an example of what Churchill called "perverted science" operating in an intelligence service. The hypnosis and mental programming techniques used on Candy Jones came from American tactical and strategic research done in Vietnam, as did the saturation of unnecessary bombing, the use of defoliants, etc. The Americans would have been better off giving away more of their knowledge and expertise than they did in the past. The Americans would have been better off giving the Vietnamese free Japanese TV sets to put them to sleep, that would have been the easy way out. But perhaps we are talking about something more sinister than a failed cold war weapon. Weaponry that failed against the communists, but did it fail when it turned against the American state itself? Mark Chapman, Shiran-Shiran, John Hinckley, James Earl Ray and Lee Harvey Oswald are proof that there were other "Dr. Jensensens" at work in America.

Jensen knew that he was taking huge risks. He could not be sure that Arlene would not emerge unexpectedly at any time in Candy's daily life. In spite of his precautions, this of course happened, without which none of this would have been known to the public. Candy had no idea that she had made any trips or done anything outside of her visits to Jensen and her mail deliveries. That was all she knew, everything else was complete amnesia. Once her trip and mission were over, Jensen would snap her out of her trance and she would once again return to her daily life.

We know this story from the audio tapes of the hypnosis sessions where Nebel interviewed Candy. When Candy was played these tapes, she could not believe that she had been subjected to the things that Arlene described. From these many tapes recorded over a number of years, Donald Bain (the author of "The Control of Candy Jones") has skilfully articulated the four complex characters of Arlene, Nebel, Jensen and Candy. Arlene is an abstraction in Candy's head, Nebel a real character and Jensen a character who remains in the shadows. This drama was reinforced by the accumulation of evidence that Jensen had indeed existed and was probably engaged in the type of activities Candy/Arlene had described. In the mid-1970s, Nebel got cancer and, upset by Candy's story and the suspicion that she had seen Jensen several more times secretly during their marriage, he thought hard about getting revenge. He told Bain that he was going to kill Jensen, but Bain managed to talk him out of it.

Like Cathy O'Brien's one-off "America in Trance-Formation" and Annie McKenna's "Paperclip Dolls", Bain's book is a brilliant production. Disregarding the usual commercial framework, he has spent an enormous amount of time extracting the entire Candy Jones story from hundreds of audio tapes. The work was done over several years, but Jensen's own voice was missing, so information about him had to be reconstructed from the recorded dialogue. Although he was only a shadowy figure, Nebel was convinced that there was enough external evidence to show that he was much more real than Arlene.

The most difficult problem was to remove the many barriers placed like layers of cement by Jensen in Candy's mind. Nebel often tried to impersonate Jensen during the hypnosis sessions; however, Arlene always noticed this tactic and let her know. Arlene liked Jensen, while Candy did not like him at all. Nebel was also pretending to be Arlene's alter. Candy was much more comfortable talking about herself in this way, and she revealed a lot of information about the activities of this Dr. Jensen.

Donald Bain suggests that Candy, as Arlene, carried out many more experimental assignments for Jensen that were never discovered. He also went to Candy's agency to check, with the help of the business manager, the attendance schedules during the 1960s. Over a period of 10 years, it was found that Candy was often absent under the guise of 'business trips' for which no company was listed. Fragments of these trips emerged under hypnosis, on one occasion she said she had to deliver a rifle for Jensen.

(...) But what worried Nebel most before his death were the attempts by the CIA and Jensen to contact Candy. His adventures apparently took place between 1960 and 1971, but Bain said he couldn't be entirely sure it didn't go on. The courageous Nebel died of cancer shortly after Bain's book was published. He died without having found all the answers he was looking for about his wife's secret life. He had some consolation for a brief time as he had begun to tear the mask off America's hidden controllers. In a way similar to other glamorous personalities, Candy Jones unknowingly entered the mystery of elitist power, which is constantly denied. If Jayne Mansfield fell prey to the forces of consumerism and Marilyn Monroe fell victim to high state intrigue, Candy Jones was certainly one of the victims of both American intelligence and medical and psychiatric institutions. Both of which gave rise to the reinvigorated American military-industrial complex in the 1950s and 1960s.[602]

Even in adulthood, these women of high stature like Candy Jones remain fairy-tale children, just like the young models Jon Benet Ramsey and Sylvia Plath. Candy was probably chosen not only because she was deemed easily hypnotised, but also because she was one of the first media dolls, a kind of prototype. America has always been the world leader in mind control and illusory dreams, from television to dollhouse furniture. Like dolls, people become automatons, and all sorts of experiments and deep societal changes make this semi-transit of the mind a natural state.

Jensen may well have been involved in the early experiments as part of the MK-Ultra programme. Candy Jones' first husband had already made her a "super-doll", a perfect subject for Jensen. Bain's conclusion is that Jensen was working for the intelligence sector, but that he may also have had a much more complex project. If Candy represents the innocent imagination, situated between the world of Jules Verne and George Adamski, Jensen represents the dark side of science. This is the dark world of Auschwitz which, as we know, was run by a community of scientists, doctors and industrialists.

Like Marilyn Monroe, Candy Jones may have been a victim of the US military's early research into what are now called 'non-lethal weapons'. Perhaps the notion of 'Big Brother', like the coal miners, has finally become something archaic and obsolete, and perhaps Orwell was wrong and Huxley was right. Unlimited pleasure on the cheap, without pain or suffering, is the ultimate weapon used to break the will of the people without a drop of blood being shed.

(...) John Nebel must have wondered when his life took a certain turn with Candy Jones. For many years, this New York radio host had heard many listeners calling in to tell him about those things Candy was now describing when she was in a trance... As soon as Nebel heard Arlene's voice, he entered the world of American trance. A world in which entry wounds become exit wounds and in which Jack Ruby's last hours as a free man remain as enigmatic as Marilyn Monroe's last phone calls... or Candy Jones' mysterious travels.

---

[602] The Mind Manipulators - Alan Scheflin and Edward Opton, 1978 / Operation Mind-Control - Walter Bowart, 1978.

6 - THE MK-MONARCH SYMBOLISM
IN THE MUSIC INDUSTRY

"Signs and symbols rule the world, not laws and words" - Confucius

The music industry plays an important role, it is a powerful tool for indoctrination of the masses and there is much more than money at stake... The music offered/imposed to the people is as powerful a tool of control as the school system or the daily TV news. This type of social engineering shapes and forms the attitudes and values of a whole youth. Hence the interest in spending millions of dollars to constantly promote new global stars idolised by millions of young people. Just as the children of Satanic/Luciferian cults are programmed from an early age, the world's youth are also subject to systematic mental control. Although much less direct and coercive than ritual abuse, it is no less effective in conditioning minds.

Many of the clips that are viewed millions of times on the *YouTube* video platform are in fact only symbolic representations of the trauma-based Monarch mental programming process. These productions symbolically refer to a psychological process that is the splitting of the personality, the ultimate goal of MK-Monarch. The same symbols are systematically used by the Luciferian elite to promote their decadent and fallen *culture* among the laity. They do this by infusing the symbolism of mind control into high-profile productions, whether in the luxury industry, fashion and music productions with clips containing multiple lenses. The notion of multiple personalities and "crazy alter-egos" is becoming a *cool* thing and is spreading among glittering idols. The aim is to create a hegemonic and inescapable *MK culture* with an aesthetic and symbols that are now ubiquitous in the media, all wrapped up in attractive and addictive entertainment. Unconsciously, the younger generation therefore associates this vulgarised and simplified occultism with something positive, with a fashion, with a model to follow. Luciferian symbols such as the triangle and the one-eye are appearing more and more in the secular world. We acclaim, reclaim and consume these demonic suggestions, and so we unconsciously validate a whole Luciferian culture as something good for us. We like our music, we like our television programmes, our cartoons and our video games, we like content that very often clearly displays a Luciferian nature. As a result, our free will deliberately chooses to consume the devil's soup, because it is so sweet...

In March 2014, a *BBC* advert promoting *"Match of The Day"* (a football match) contained several flashes depicting triangles with an eye in the centre. The flashes lasted for a fraction of a second, during which time they could become imprinted on the minds of viewers. What was the point of such randomly appearing Masonic symbols in an advertisement for football matches? But what else can we expect from a TV station that for years protected an individual like Jimmy Savile? A monster who raped hundreds of children...

MTV also likes to systematically insert occult Masonic symbolism into its advertisements. The *MTV* group has set up its Toronto studios in a former Masonic lodge.

The *iHeartRadio Ultimate Pool Party* in Miami Beach is one of those large gatherings that serve to imbue the subconscious of youth with a particular symbolism. In June 2013, during Ke$ha's concert, the giant screen broadcast flashes and series of hypnotic images based on triangles, eyes, pentagrams and other typical Masonic and Luciferian symbolism for an hour.

Fashion photos and magazine covers are full of the symbolism of the one-eyed Lucifer, just as it is increasingly seen on the clothing of our major retailers.

Another example is Justin Bieber's *"Where Are U Now"* video clip, which is constructed with a multitude of drawings that mirror the image of the young singer, each drawing appearing for a fraction of a second on the screen. It turns out that in these hundreds of illustrations flashed on Bieber, we find many inverted crosses in the middle of his forehead, or masonic pyramids with the single eye, 666s, images that recur throughout the clip. It may be an unhealthy irony, but whatever one says, this is a clip that subliminally flashes Luciferian symbolism, a clip that is viewed millions of times, directly imprinting these images in the minds of young people. In short, as many people have already realised, all these *"winks"* are nothing more than the impregnation of the worldwide Luciferian cult into popular and secular culture. Let us specify here that it is not a question of demonising geometry and the equilateral triangle for example, these people have not invented anything, they only take up codes and symbols by appropriating them.

Our spirit is the citadel in which the Spirit of God desires to work with us for eternity, but Satan is trying to make this citadel his own to make it his throne... A choice must be made in the face of this corrupting and corrupting industry, the perfect platform by which Satan can reach the masses to stir them up, manipulate them and pervert them; let us quote Alexandre Dumas here: *"God fishes for souls with a line, Satan fishes for them with a net"*.

The music industry is well aware of the pattern of feeding an impressionable youth in demand of ever more extreme content. As the public becomes more and more insensitive to the things that are going on, the clips become more and more explicit in openly exposing the subject of trauma-based mind control, and this without any censorship even though it is probably the most despicable practice in the world. The world of Monarch slaves is clearly exposed in some of the clips, which feature violence, torture, sexual abuse and humiliation, not to mention drugs, all presented as something *cool* and trendy... It's all about social engineering, global mind control.

What could be more appropriate than the "music video" format and the great artistic freedom it allows to give free rein to the massive diffusion of occult knowledge barely concealed by symbolism and broadcast in a loop on TV channels and the web, 24 hours a day? The same codes are tirelessly injected into these productions... This is not a coincidence, a story is told to us in a veiled way if we still have eyes to see... One of the most hidden things in this world is therefore a knowledge that is paradoxically the most diffused daily under the noses of millions of people who are totally unaware of what is transmitted to them in a more or less direct way. This is probably a form of arrogance or black humour, or also a way of having humanity unconsciously validate these ignoble practices as something positive. The fact that the Monarch mind control process is symbolically encoded in some of the world's biggest media productions (music, film, fashion), is a serious indication that this is a non-marginal practice, systematically applied in the highest spheres of our society. But it is also a way of massively divulging an occult knowledge in this great theatre, where finally everything is displayed in broad daylight... There are Laws above the laws of this world that the "nameless religion" must imperatively respect.

Music videos and even some films are therefore an ideal means of visually and symbolically revealing something much deeper than a simple three or four minute song. According to the occult belief of the Luciferian Order, the *higher self* can only be communicated through myth, symbolism or music, in order to effectively penetrate the unconscious. In other words, don't talk about it, show it... This hermeticism systematically permeates major film and music productions: *"talk without talking, show without showing and hide without hiding"*, a very subtle art that the entertainment industry zealously pursues. All this MK symbolism is massively disseminated in the secular world so that people *see without seeing and hear without understanding*. The sorcerer-controllers think they are gods, and so they transmit their "light" in a more or less coded way with entertainment productions containing double meanings and explicit symbols conveying an occult doctrine that is finally exposed to the eyes of millions of lay people. This indirect disclosure allows them to compromise the masses so that we cannot say *"My God, we didn't know"*. Thus they somehow respect the Law of Free Will and the ability to make one's own choice when they clearly expose the most despicable things.

In the case of institutional paedocriminality, accepting systematic lies and thus abandoning the little victims to their fate, while the evidence is now becoming more and more blatant, makes people morally complicit in these crimes by not reacting and allowing them to happen... Permanent social engineering and people's denial of the corruption and atrocities committed by the ruling elite, which are now more obvious than ever, are two key points on which this precarious balance is based. A balance that ensures that public opinion does not tip over completely, while at the same time compromising it... because it is clear that today everything is revealed and exposed for those who choose to search for themselves by emancipating themselves from the social engineering programmes.

But let's go back to the music industry and its links to the MK-Monarch. In the introduction to the video *"Mary The Night"*, Lady Gaga gives a monologue that defines quite clearly the situation of a victim under mental control. She explains 'artistically' the traumas she went through to become a *super star*. The clip shows Lady Gaga lying on a gurney pushed by two nurses, describing how she perceives her sad reality: *"When I look back on my life, it's not that I don't want to see things exactly as they happened, it's just that I prefer to remember them in a poetic way. And to be honest, the lie of it all is much more honest, because I made it up. Psychiatry teaches us that trauma is probably the ultimate killer. Memories are not recycled like atoms and particles in quantum physics. They can be lost forever. My past is an unfinished painting and like the painter I have to fill in all the ugly holes to beautify the canvas. It's not that I'm dishonest, it's just that I hate reality..."*

A number of the big budget clips consistently feature the same symbolism, such as the artist being represented as a broken doll, mannequin, automaton or string puppet and the setting representing the 'inner world' of the slave. The process of dissociation and splitting is often represented by the passage through a mirror or the shattering of the mirror signifying that there is no way back or that the programming is broken; the rainbow has the same symbolism as the passage through the mirror. The Luciferian single eye or "all-seeing eye" is very common, as well as graphics representing duality such as the black and white checkerboard... and of course we find the Monarch butterfly recurring in these productions, as a signature. Pentagrams and goat heads, masks, pyramids, are also classic symbols impregnating this luciferian subculture... Don't talk about it, show it... and thus impregnate the profane popular culture to indirectly corrupt it.

Here are some examples of particularly explicit productions and I invite the reader to discover these clips for themselves on the internet, there are also much more detailed analyses of their symbolic content. It is obvious that a symbolic interpretation can appear very subjective, but a certain knowledge of MK processes allows us to identify clear indicators, all the more so when we find the same codes, the same symbolic imagery systematically used in many big budget productions.

- Let's start with the video for Laura Branigan's 1984 song *"Self Control"*, which is the forerunner of the mind control symbolism videos. On the face of it, the song, which was an international *hit,* tells the story of a girl who loves the nightclub scene. But it is the video that reveals the important aspect of the song. It shows the singer being stalked by a masked man, all combined with symbolism to make this production a tribute to the occult elite, a celebration of their most sadistic practice: Monarch mind control. In 1984, when this clip was released, the music industry was just beginning to embrace the video format as a promotional tool and the *Self Control* clip was a revolution in the entertainment industry. This video does not represent the nightlife of the average partygoer, it clearly shows us a woman losing her will and free will at the hands of a faceless master. The chorus sums it up perfectly:

You take my "Me".
You take control over me
You make me live only for the night
Before the morning arrives, mass is said
You take my "Me".
You take control over me

In this clip, the night world is a metaphor for dissociation. The first images show us a doll with brown hair symbolising Laura Branigan. We then see her getting ready for her night out, with strange characters around her that seem to emerge from nowhere: when she runs her hand through her hair, the next image shows a person next to her running his hand through her hair. The clip here represents what is going on in Laura's head, showing her alternate personalities. The next scene shows the young woman starting her evening, she is in the street standing in front of a shop window containing two mannequins floating horizontally in the air, an excellent way to represent a dissociated MK slave. Then a masked man appears in the back of a luxury car, her master, the occult elite. The next scene shows Laura dancing in a disco as the masked man appears again, with several masks clumped together in the background, symbolising that the programmers and slave masters themselves have a dissociated personality. Strangely, Laura decides to follow the strange and disturbing figure. She follows him because she no longer has control over herself, the lyrics of the second verse perfectly describing the state of an MK slave at the mercy of his master when in a state of dissociation, here symbolised by the 'world at night':

During the night, no control
Through the wall, something pierces
dressed in white as you walk down the street of my soul
A night without danger, I live in the forest of my soul
I know the night is not as it seems
I have to believe in something
So I persuade myself to believe that this night will never end

Laura cannot fight the will of the masked man who eventually takes her to an orgy, a part of the clip that is reminiscent of the famous scene in the film *Eye Wide Shut* in which masked characters have sex in a castle. In this scene, Laura is symbolically taken into the underground, occult world of the elite where she is used as a sex slave. Indeed, we see the masked man undressing the young woman, who appears to be in an altered state of consciousness, to be released into the *'party'*. This scene clearly depicts a woman being used as a sex slave in an elitist orgy.

Back home, Laura realises that she is not safe anywhere, not even in her bedroom, where there are masked people abusing her. In this final scene, the 'faceless' man is also present in the bedroom and abuses Laura. The clip ends with a very symbolic image: a close-up of the doll that introduced the clip. But here her dress is torn, her hair is a mess and one of her eyes is closed, a nod to Lucifer.

This production, released at the very beginning of the music video age, already contained all the characteristics and codes of a clip representing the MK. Thirty years later, the same scenarios, codes and symbolism are still present. Today more than ever, we see young starlets singing about their mind control in music videos celebrating the MK system of the "nameless religion".[603]

---

[603] "Self Control" by Laura Branigan: A Creepy 80's Video About Mind Control" - vigilantcitizen.com, 2015.

- The clip *"Wide Awake"* by Katy Perry begins by showing us Katy sitting in her dressing room, staring into a mirror, while removing her wig: a representation of the change of alter. This first introductory scene symbolises the dissociation that leads her into a fantasy world, which is none other than her inner world... Indeed, it is from this moment that the clip switches to another reality showing the star wandering in her inner world represented by a dark labyrinth full of dead ends and traps. She doesn't seem to know which way to go in her own mind and she gets caught in the various traps set by the programmer. Katy realises that she will not get out of the maze without the main element, the one that was taken away from her when she was programmed, that is, her true nature, what she really is. Then a little girl appears and comes to meet her, which represents the opportunity to reconnect with her original personality, she will then become her guide to find the path to freedom. The next scene shows Katy and the little girl hand in hand in a hallway filled with mirrors, with the little girl not appearing in the mirrors, meaning that she is not real, but just a part of Katy's psyche. In this scene, we see that Katy's dress is completely covered in butterflies... which will fly away in a cloud when Katy finally breaks one of the mirrors to escape from this inner world, from this programming.

The next scene is a complete contrast to the fantasy world of the labyrinth, we are out of Katy's head and back to a sad reality: Katy appears totally destroyed on a wheelchair in what seems to be a psychiatric hospital, still with the little girl by her side and a last butterfly fluttering above her. Two men with goat heads stand guard outside the hospital exit doors, and it is the little girl who makes them disappear by stamping her foot on the floor to free Katy from this psychiatric universe.

At the end of the clip we see this same little girl handing Katy a Monarch butterfly, we then discover that the little girl's name is Katheryn (Katy Perry's real name, her original personality). Back in her dressing room, Katy then realises as she opens her hand that she has been given a butterfly which she lets escape, this butterfly leading us from the dressing room to the stage for a new concert... in other words, the video comes full circle and brings us back to the starting point. Katy, who seems to have gone on a quest to conquer her "demons", is back in her "sexy pop star" persona, a pure product of the music industry. The 'Monarch' clips often represent this notion of an endless loop.

- Kerli's *'Walking On Air'* clip is also very explicit, showing the programming process through the symbolism of the little girl turning into a doll held by strings, like a puppet. The beginning of the clip shows us a strange character bringing a gift to Kerli, a doll in her likeness. A doll that Kerli takes inside a house that symbolically represents her inner world. We can see that in this house, Kerli and this doll (an alter) are constantly watched by a large eye that scrutinises them through a television screen. The fact that they are being watched by a television screen, rather than being watched by themselves, is representative of the systematic inversions practiced in mind control. The programmers do everything to make the child feel constantly watched and controlled. In this clip, inversions are everywhere: snow comes out of an umbrella, the oven freezes the chicken, while the fridge is used to cook it. In another scene, the inversion of the values of pleasure and pain is symbolically represented when Kerli lies on a bed with a mattress made of large stones. The confusion between pain and pleasure is part of the MK programming. It is on this bed of pebbles that Kerli lets out tears (symbolising her pain) which turn into... butterflies. We then see that the strange character from the beginning of the clip, probably the programmer, appears on the "other side" of a mirror placed next to the bed of stones, ordering him by signs to pass through the mirror to join him... The passage through the mirror will be the finality of the transformation. The next scene shows us the Kerli doll, which has come of age and become a puppet manipulated by a giant doll wearing the Monarch butterfly on its shoulder strap. The final scene shows this giant doll cutting the strings of the Kerli puppet with a chisel and locking it in a box. We then see the young Kerli waking up at home wondering about the strings hanging from her wrists... We then discover that Kerli is in fact locked in this box held in the hands of the giant doll, always with this notion of an endless loop, a sort of mise en abyme or fractal.

- Sigur Ros' 'Fjogur Piano' clip is difficult to understand because it is impossible to extract a coherent narrative from it, like most of those 'Monarch' clips that seem at first sight hermetic and mysterious. It is the symbolic content that gives them real meaning. This clip describes in a pictorial and symbolic way the endless loop of a Monarch slave's life, with the amnesia, violence and drugs that accompany it. The beginning of this production shows us a man and a woman on a bed, waking up in the middle of a strange room, they are very confused and don't seem to know what happened to them the day before. Furthermore they are surrounded by Monarch butterflies meticulously arranged on their bed. The room they are in shows frame marks on the walls, we will later see that these marks are those of frames containing butterfly collections. The couple wake up with all sorts of marks and bruises on their bodies, they are puzzled, not seeming to know the cause. It is then that two obscure characters enter the scene and come to get the "couple", starting by blindfolding them and giving them lollipops containing scorpions, symbolising psychotropic drugs, the man and the woman sucking greedily on these sweets showing that they are addicted to them. Then the two controllers lead the couple out of the room by simply blowing on them, without any physical contact, symbolising the self-sufficient mind control to direct the slaves without having to use force. The next scene shows the couple in the back of a fictitious car, "driven" by the controllers and placed in front of a cinema screen which shows images that make it look as if they are actually moving. This fictional car scene relates to dissociation, the process of pushing the subject's mind to disconnect from reality, i.e. to transport them somewhere but never actually physically. Following this strange escapade, it's back to the room... now filled with frames with collections of butterflies, the woman angrily brandishes one of these frames containing a butterfly under the man's nose, as if trying to make him understand something: *"Look, we're Monarch slaves"*. Then suddenly the woman disappears from the room and the man is left alone. This is another clue that this is probably a split personality and that the woman and the man are in fact one and the same split person. The man then goes into a rage and smashes a mirror with his fist, symbolising the attempt to break the programming, and then trashes the room until the woman reappears. He then begins to punch and scarify her, in effect a self-inflicted scarification. Eventually the couple go to sleep... and that's when we see the two dark controllers enter the room again to clean up and put everything back in order. The clip ends with the same image it started with: the couple wakes up again in confusion, unaware of the cause of all the scarring. Another day in the endless loop that is the life of a Monarch slave.

- Tool's '*Prison Sex*' video, whose theme song is the repetition of sexual violence by victims, has a symbolism related to traumatic amnesic walls and memory retrieval. The video features a small mannequin being dismembered and tortured by a disturbing being, a sort of black rubber humanoid. The clip shows this little one-eyed mannequin locked in a large cube made up of a multitude of drawers representing his memories, which he digs through in order to understand his dilapidated state. Little by little, he reconnects with the memories that allow him to access the little boy he once was. In this animation clip, it is not the Monarch butterfly but its caterpillar that signs the production, coming out of one of the drawers... Here again, the clip ends with the notion of endless loop and fractal: the cube composed of a multitude of drawers in which the little mannequin is locked, is in fact only the inside of the drawer of another much larger cube composed, like the first one, of a multitude of drawers, etc...

- The clip "*Shatter Me*" by violinist Lindsay Stirling is also 100% MK-Monarch. It represents the process of dissociation and splitting of personality through the symbolism of a *human-mechanical* ballerina enclosed in a glass globe and seeking to escape. Here again the image of the broken mirror and the splitting of the mechanical woman who literally explodes into a thousand pieces is symbolically very explicit. Even more so when Monarch butterflies flutter around throughout the clip. In these "Monarch" clips, duplicity is systematic, the song *"Shatter Me"* is about liberation from fear... But its symbolism communicates exactly the opposite: it clearly exposes the process of subjugation of a slave of MK programming.

- Candy Brooke's '*A Study in Duality*' clip is also pure implicit MK-Monarch propaganda. A clip that sums up what this whole industry really is: a combination of occultism and MK aimed at debasing and dehumanising. The clip is built on the concept of duality featuring the "good girl" versus the "bad girl", a theme particularly appropriate for MK-Monarch. The production shows a woman with a Monarch butterfly on her mouth, a strong symbolic image interspersed with quasi-subliminal flashes of torture such as a face being pulled apart at the mouth and eyelids; clearly reminiscent of the imagery of the film *Clockwork Orange*. Shocking images that hint at the torture inflicted to induce the dissociative states necessary for mind control. Why do these torture images appear for only a fraction of a second in this clip? Why are such subliminal horrors paralleled by imagery of a woman with a Monarch butterfly on her mouth? Why is this particular species of butterfly chosen so often? Another scene in this clip shows a masked executioner dressed in a black robe putting a woman, obviously robotic, into a bathtub with intravenous transfusion equipment next to her, suggesting that something terrifying is about to happen. This is the kind of totally creepy and dehumanising occult symbolism that is increasingly permeating popular culture via the entertainment industry.

- The clips *'Zombie'*, *'Mirrors'* or *'Wonderland'* by Natalia Kills also propagate a decadence linked to the MK-Monarch. They show the *artist* as an abused, humiliated and controlled woman by invisible forces. In the clip *'Mirrors'*, she is seen being forced through a mirror. In the clip *"Zombie"* we see her tied to a table in what appears to be a laboratory where she is being tortured by an invisible torturer, accompanied by explicit imagery showing mannequin heads covering her face as well as replacing it, dismembered mannequins also contribute to the dark atmosphere of this production. The clip *"Wonderland"* highlights the drug that allows to *follow the white rabbit down the rabbit hole...*

- Paramore's *'Brick by Boring Brick'* video tells the story of a little girl searching for her true 'Self' behind a wall she has built in her consciousness. The theme of the song tells us that this wall is the belief in 'fairy tales' that must be broken. The little girl wanders around with Monarch butterfly wings hanging from her back in a castle representing her inner world. In this castle we see her reflected in multiple deceptive mirrors. Again, there are systematic references to *'Alice in Wonderland'*.

- The clips *'Love Me'* by Lil' Wayne, *'Work B*tch'* by Britney Spears and *'Change Your Life'* by Iggy Azalea explicitly glorify Beta programming, i.e. sexual slavery.

- Jessie J's *'Price Tag'* video depicts the singer as a ridiculous puppet held together by strings or an automaton on a music box.

- Willow Smith's *'21st Century Girl'* video is pure Babylonian propaganda where the Monarch butterfly accompanies the girl like a relay passed on from generation to generation.

- Taylor Swift's *"Style"* video subtly represents dissociative identity disorder by playing with two characters mirroring each other, always with this notion of splitting and breaking.

This morbid MK subculture is not only confined to the Western world. In Asia, the very popular K-pop (South Korean pop) scene uses exactly the same codes:

- The clip *"Insane"* by A-JAX shows us a young man hospitalized in a psychiatric ward and undergoing hypnosis, the symbolism of dissociation and splitting is very significant and repetitive, notably once again by the passage through the mirror.

- The clip *'Hate You'* from Ladie's Code is also very explicit. It shows two young girls totally dehumanised and robotised, portrayed as dolls or puppets held by strings and manipulated by a 'trainer'.

- Andamiro's (Korea's *Lady Gaga*) *'Waiting'* video, which, under the guise of a song about a girl-boy heartbreak, actually represents the relationship between master and slave Monarch, as is often the case, it is the symbolism of the video that reveals something much heavier than the song's simple lyrics. Here again, the butterfly signs the production.

- Muse's 2015 track *"The Handler"* is one of the most explicit productions about Monarch mind control that has been produced, both in terms of the lyrics and the symbolism of the video, with its obvious Monarch butterflies. *Handler is* a term often used to describe the one who manipulates and manages the MK slave, a term that is difficult to translate into French and that would mean: trainer, manipulator or master, the one who *"holds the leash"*. Here are the lyrics of the song, which at first sight seems to be a love song, but whose background refers directly to the relationship between an MK slave and his master, the whole ambiguity is there, a representation of the Stockholm syndrome:

> You were my oppressor And I was programmed to obey Now you are my manipulator And I will carry out all your demands
> Leave me alone I must disassociate myself from you
> Admire my trance-formation And you have the power to do as you please
> My mind was totally lost And my heart a cold, unfeeling machine
> I will no longer let you control my feelings And I will no longer do what I'm told I'm no longer afraid to walk alone Let me go, let me be
> I must free myself from your grip You will never possess me again

It is interesting to report here also the lyrics of the song *"I Get Out!"* by Lauryn Hill:

> I'm getting out, I'm getting out of all your boxes,
> You can't hold me in these chains, I'm going out,
> Father has freed me from this bondage,
> Knowing my condition, this is why I have to change,
> Your stinking resolutions have nothing to do with a solution,
> but keep me away from freedom and maintain your pollutions,
> I can't stand your lies any longer,
> I don't want to try anymore,
> If I should die, oh Lord,
> That's why I chose to live,
> I don't want to be compromised anymore, I can't be bullied anymore,
> I will not sympathise any more,
> Because I now understand that you just want to use me
> You speak of love and you deceive me
> You never thought of releasing me
> But just as quickly we forget that nothing is certain
> You thought I was going to stand there and suffer
> Your plan to make me feel guilty is not working, it is suppressing me to death

For now I choose Life, I make sacrifices
If everything has to go, then let's go
This is how I choose to live
No more compromise
I see you before you are disguised
Blinding through this mind control
Stealing my eternal soul, tenderizing me with the material
To keep me as a slave, but I get by
What you see is what you will become
Oh you haven't seen anything yet
I don't care if you're upset
Look and do not distort the truth
And your hurt feelings are not excused
To keep me in this box, psychological lock
Repressing true expression, cementing repression
Organising this massive deception
While no one can be cured
I don't respect your system
I don't want to protect your system
When you talk I don't listen
Let my Father do it
Let me out of these chains,
All these traditions kill freedom
I just accepted what you said
Keeping me among the dead
The only way to know is to walk to learn, to learn and to grow
But faith does not grow quickly, and everyone believed you
While you had the sole authority
Just followed by the majority
Who is afraid of reality
This system is a farce
You better be smart to save your soul
And escape from this mental control
You spend your life sacrificing for this system of death
Where is the passion in this way of life?
Are you sure it is God you are serving?
Engaged in a system
Less and less good, although you deserve it
Who makes these schools? Who makes these rules?
An animal condition, oh keep us like slaves
Oh come out of this social purgatory...

7 - THE MK-MONARCH SYMBOLISM
IN THE FILM INDUSTRY

Some film productions also display the symbolism of Monarch mind control. As with the music videos, it is a question of identifying the different reading grids contained in all these productions.

Let's first look at the film *"Trouble jeu"* (*Hide & Seek* in V.O.) released in 2005. This film has been much criticized negatively because of its strangeness, it has been described as illogical with an ending considered absurd. It turns out that this film cannot be fully understood without knowing the key element on which it is based, i.e. trauma-based mind control: MK-Monarch. In a symbolic and theatrical way, this film describes this despicable process. The Monarch butterfly again appears regularly in this production to confirm its sad theme.

The film is about a little girl named Emily who has witnessed her mother's suicide and is suffering from severe traumatic symptoms. Her father, David (played by Robert De Niro) decides to help his daughter by leaving his psychiatrist's office and moving to the country with her to care for her full-time. Emily's behaviour becomes increasingly worrying as she claims to have a new friend called Charlie who she is having a lot of fun with. David believes that this is an imaginary friend created by Emily to cope with her trauma. However, some of the horrific things that are happening in the house, such as the cat found drowned in the bathtub, start to look very worrying, especially as Emily claims that Charlie is responsible. Charlie will also kill the father's girlfriend. In a scene where we see David patrolling the house for a possible murderer, he realises in a brief flash of insight that he himself is the 'famous' Charlie. The film reveals that this Charlie is in fact another personality of David's father, who is completely unaware of his existence. It is this alter personality, Charlie, who traumatizes and manipulates little Emily and commits horrible crimes.

This production depicts the relationship between a programmer executioner and his slave, in this case a totally dissociated psychiatrist who programs his own daughter. The programmers themselves usually have deep dissociative disorders. The final scene of the film shows us a drawing of little Emily representing herself with two heads on one body... a symbolic image revealing that she is dissociated and multiple.

The animated film *"Coraline"* (2009) is also a production that refers symbolically to MK-Monarch programming. Note that the little girl who does the voice of Coraline is Dakota Fanning who played the role of the girl in the film *"Trouble Jeu"* that we have just described above.

From the very beginning, the credits clearly sum up the whole process: we see ominous metal hands restoring an old doll to a new one. Her old outfit is completely cut away, she is literally turned inside out like a sock, the inner stuffing is removed and replaced with sand. She gets new hair, new eyes and new clothes are sewn on her. The creation of this new doll symbolises the creation of an alter personality.

Coraline is a little girl who has just moved into a new house with her parents. She is unhappy and constantly bored because her parents do not give her the attention she would like. As she explores her new home, she discovers a small door that leads to an alternative version of her reality, a place where her parents are fun and give her lots of attention. We find here the same theme as in 'The *Wizard of Oz*' or '*Alice in Wonderland*', i.e. a main character as a child who is bored in her everyday life and enters a strange, wonderful and magical world. In *Coraline*, the little girl goes through a door that propels her into a kind of vortex that gives access to the "wonderful" alternative reality, just as Alice goes through the mirror: the symbolism of the dissociative process, the disconnection from a certain reality. In this alternative reality, her "other parents" call Coraline *"our little doll"* and they tell her that if she accepts that they sew buttons on her eyes, soon *"she will see things their way"* and she will be able to stay with them forever... Sewing buttons on her eyes means that she will permanently become the puppet of the programmer executioner, who then, as the film says, *"devours her soul"*. But Coraline refuses this proposal and the illusion of the other world is shattered... We see the 'other mother' go into a rage showing her in her true light. Coraline finally sees the true aspect of her "other mother", a kind of skeletal monster with metallic hands, precisely the ones that made the doll in the opening credits. The whole film is based on this threatening hand, which represents the programmer manipulating the little girl and deceiving her psyche with a world created from scratch thanks to the passage through the small door: the dissociative process.

In 1985, Disney produced the film *"Return to Oz"*. While most viewers expected a logical sequel to the famous 1930 *Wizard of Oz*, this film surprised many by showing little Dorothy locked up in a squalid psychiatric hospital, strapped to a gurney for electroshock therapy... This Disney production explicitly depicts the plight of a little girl subjected to trauma-based mind control

The beginning of the film shows Dorothy finding a key with the Oz symbol, a key that represents the key to her original personality. The next scene shows this same key in the hands of a psychiatrist to whom she has been taken for electroshock treatment (for sleeping problems)... this psychiatrist who now holds the key will be able to become her programmer.

As Dorothy watches the machine that is to be used for the electroshock, she sees in a glass window not her reflection but that of another little girl, indeed, this machine is the *door to* her alter personality named "Ozma". The next scene shows Dorothy strapped to a stretcher about to receive electric shocks, but a power cut occurs just then... However, the rest of the film clearly suggests that Dorothy has suffered a deep trauma that has made her dissociate from reality, as it is from this point that the film shifts into an imaginary world. Indeed, Dorothy then returns to the magical world of Oz, a world that represents her dissociated psyche and entirely manipulated by the programmer (the psychiatrist). It is her alter personality Ozma who welcomes her on her stretcher and takes her to the land of Oz...

She then goes on a kind of quest through this alternative world. A particularly disturbing scene is the meeting between Dorothy and the witch

Mombi, who is none other than the head nurse of the psychiatric hospital. In this scene, we see the witch taking Dorothy into a room full of women's heads, lined up behind glass cases and watching the little girl from the corner of her eye... It is then that the witch Mombi removes her own head, just like unscrewing a toy, and replaces it with one of the many other heads present behind the glass cases. This scene is pure MK-Monarch symbolism, the collection of heads representing the different alter personalities that can emerge.

The ultimate goal of MK programming is the splitting of the basic personality into multiple alterations, and this is exactly what the last scenes of this film show us. We see little Dorothy, still in the world of Oz, in her inner world, staring at herself in a large mirror which does not reflect her own image but that of Ozma, the other little girl who represents her alter personality. The scene shows Dorothy approaching the mirror, taking the hand of the 'Ozma reflection' and pulling it through the mirror so that she is 'flesh and blood' before her. The mirror reflecting another identity is a strong symbol of the MK-Monarch. Dorothy's alter personality, Ozma, passes through the mirror and thus becomes real. Thus Dorothy's programming is completed, her programmed alter is present in her split mind, Ozma is now part of Dorothy...

The last scene shows Dorothy back home in the real world. She discovers Ozma again by looking at herself in the mirror in her room. This confirms that her personality has been split and that she is now multiple and programmed.

In this production, Disney has introduced a large number of elements that make it a real MK *anthem*, even more explicit than *'The Wizard of Oz'*.

In his film *"Death Proof"* (2007), Quentin Tarantino makes a clear reference to the MK-Monarch, a sad wink... Don't talk about it, but show it...

At first glance, this production seems to be nothing more or less than an homage to old B-movies, but it incorporates something very explicit that is not trivial.

But first of all, we have to go back to a 1977 film entitled *"Un espion de trop"* (*"Telefon"* in V.O.) featuring characters under MK-Ultra mind control who are triggered by a poem recited during a phone call. Following this call to bring out a pre-programmed alter personality, these people enter a trance-like state to carry out kamikaze missions on different targets.

Here is the poem that is used to trigger the programmed slaves:

The woods are charming, dark and deep,

But I have promises to keep and miles to go before I sleep,

Remember... (name of alter personality), the miles to go before you sleep.

In his film *"Death Proof"*, Quentin Tarantino took care to use the exact same poem. In one scene, we see a man approach a young woman and offer her a beer while saying *"Cheers butterfly"*, and then he starts to recite the same MK poem word for word...

Tarantino takes the exact poem that triggers the MK slaves in the 1977 film *'Telefon'* and adapts it in his own way in 2007. Whereas in *"Telefon"* the poem is used to trigger mind-controlled suicide bombers, in *"Death Proof"* the poem is used to trigger Beta programming, the sexual enslavement of a young woman. And to confirm that this is a reference to the MK-Monarch, Tarantino has chosen the word *"butterfly"* as the access code to the alter personality, this poem having the originality of varying according to the alter it is addressed to... *"Remember 'butterfly', miles before you sleep"*...

The next scene shows the young woman targeted starting an erotic dance in front of this man sitting on a chair in the middle of a bar. This woman, who did not know him before, ends up abandoning herself in his arms...

Here is an excerpt of dialogue from the 1977 film *"Telefon"*, where Charles Bronson refers directly to the MK-Ultra project to create Manchurian Candidates:

- Tell me, Borzov, who is the most secret agent in the world?

- The one who manages to remain eternally secret?

- Of course, but the one who surpasses them all is the ideal agent, the one who does not know he is an agent.

8 - SUPER-ATHLETES UNDER MENTAL CONTROL

The entertainment industry also includes high-level sport and mind control methods are also applied to train *super-athletes*... The champion is like an elite soldier whose physical and psychic strength must be optimal in a world where *"the show must go on"*, where performances must be ever more spectacular. High-level sport is a real show business and results must excel year after year to satisfy the public and sponsors. In this context, it is easy to understand why MK is also used in the field of sport.

In her autobiography, Cathy O'Brien reports on how an individual with a multiple personality can have extraordinary physical abilities, particularly with regard to sleep and hunger. The switch from one alter personality to another will somehow "reset the clock", i.e. the biological clock will be different from one alter to another and the feelings of hunger and fatigue will therefore vary according to which alter is in control of the body. This is a phenomenon that is difficult to understand because of the basic biological needs of the physical body, just as it is difficult to understand how an alter can be the only one to feel the effects of a drug.

MK-slaves can function on very little sleep or very limited food, which means that their minds, their brains, remain in an easily controlled, easily hypnotised state. Cathy O'Brien, who has been on the MK-Monarch protocol since early childhood, also describes that when she was training to run, her trainer would induce a trance in her so that she had no sense of time and distance. The mind control methods made it easier for her to get rid of pain and fatigue instantly. This phenomenon causes exceptional endurance in MK subjects, whether in sports or in the military.

Cathy O'Brien claims that some American baseball players are controlled by key codes and other triggers. According to her, members of the *Dodgers* team were under mental control and conditioned to win or lose according to the bets and wishes of their owners. Brice Taylor claims that the same *Dodgers* team (coached at the time by Tommy Lasorda) was rewarded with sex slaves (women as well as children) according to their sports results...

A little known fact is that the famous tennis player Serena Williams has several alter, one of which is called "Psycho-Serena", the alter present on the tennis court, the *super-athlete*. It seems that the world's number one female tennis player has developed a dissociative identity disorder. In the biographical documentary *"Venus and Serena"* (2012), she reveals and lists her different alterations in front of the camera: *"Yes, I really do have different personalities and different attitudes. There's Psycho-Serena, she's always on the court, she's training, she's in the game, she's incredible, she's a super-athlete. There's "Summer", she helps me a lot, for example when I have a long letter to write or for other things, it's "Summer" who does it. And there's this other girl, Megan, she's a horny girl, you can't keep up with her. There's also "Taquanda", she's a tough one, she's not Christian (laughs), she's from the ghetto. She was at the US Open in 2009* (editor's note: the report then shows a clip of a match where "Taquanda" is seen vulgarly insulting and violently threatening a ball boy). *At that particular match, I wasn't there, but I got the feedback."[604]*

This last statement - *"I wasn't there"* - means that she has no memory of that angry scene because it wasn't "she" who was playing that US Open match, which shows that there really are amnesic walls between her different alter. Serena clearly states in this biographical documentary that she has several independent personalities, so she would have a dissociative identity disorder, something common to MK slaves.

During a match at Wimbledon in July 2014, Serena, considered by many to be the best tennis player of all time, appeared on the court completely disoriented, literally not knowing how to play tennis or even how to hold a ball, a scene that was totally unbelievable. *The* headlines in the newspapers read: *"incredible discomfort"*, *"disoriented and unable to hold a ball"*, *"bordering on the ridiculous"*... The US Tennis Federation claimed that the player was *"suffering from a virus"* without giving any further details... but then why did she come on court to make a fool of herself like that? Or was it the *Psycho-Serena* alter that wasn't there that day?

Did you know that Tiger Woods, the best golfer of all time, has amnesia during competitions and is unable to remember his best shots?

Eldrick Woods is the son of Earl Woods, a former colonel and Green Beret of the Special Forces in Vietnam. Eldrick was nicknamed "Tiger" after a Vietnamese soldier who fought alongside his father. Tiger started playing golf at the age of two. He appeared in 1978 on *The Mike Douglas* Show, where the little guy demonstrated his clean swing. Tiger Woods was a child star from a very young age, adored by the media and destined to become the best, in the same way as the singer Michael Jackson. A former golfer and commentator for the *Professional Golfers' Association of America* (PGA) said Woods was *programmed by his father.*

Indeed, his incredible golfing ability defies logic, norms and statistics. But is this only due to the hypnosis used on him? Tiger's father was involved in

---

[604] "Venus and Serena - Discover the truth behind the legends" - Maiken Baird, Michelle Major, 2012.

psychological and memory control operations on soldiers when he was in the army, notably in Vietnam. Earl Woods decided to use the same techniques on his son and commissioned a military psychiatrist, Jay Bunza, to reprogram Tiger like a computer. Bunza worked on a strange project to hypnotise Tiger before his golf games. In interviews, Tiger has stated that he completely forgets entire sections of certain competitions. In the documentary *Tiger's Prowl: His Life*, he reveals: *"I have these blackout moments, I don't remember. I know I was there, but I don't remember how I played (...) It's like a trance, I let my subconscious play and I don't know what the result will be. There are many shots where I don't remember anything. I just remember getting ready, taking the club out of the bag and so on, but once I hit the ball I don't remember seeing it go... It's a very strange thing."*

Jay Bunza's techniques produced extraordinary results, but how is it possible that Tiger doesn't remember his most wonderful shots?

In 2008, former 'multi-functional' athlete Herschel Walker revealed that he had dissociative identity disorder. He explains this in detail in his book *'Breaking Free*: *My Life with* Dissociative *Identity Disorder'.*

In the same year, the American channel *ABC News* devoted a report to him.[605] It was reported that Walker is a true sports legend: he played for the Georgia *Bulldogs* football team in the 1980s, set several world records in athletics and won the famous Heisman Trophy in 1982. But Walker now claims that it was not *he* who won the famous trophy at the time. A champion who played 15 seasons of American football, who was even a dancer in the *Fort Worth Ballet*, a businessman, a public figure, a husband, he is none of those things, he says: *"These are personalities who can do different things for you. In competition, I'm a totally different person."*

Herschel Walker says that his alter named *'Warrior'* took on the football games by taking all the pain that could come from the violent physical contact. The *"Hero"* alter is the public and media figure, while the *"Sentinel"* alter's role was to protect his friends and family. In 1983 the athlete married Cindy Grossman, today the couple is separated and Cindy says: *"At first it was just very strange behaviour (...) he had the ability to hide that because I think all the alters inside were focused on football.* When his career and competitions ended, Cindy says her husband's inner subconscious system began to go haywire: *"I started to discover the alters (...) I noticed the changes in his voice, he would sometimes get hoarse and say strange things, like he didn't know who I was. He would call me "Miss Lady". It's hard to explain, even his face would change. The first thing I thought was that he had the devil inside him. I wasn't necessarily asking for an exorcism, I was just trying to get answers (...) I think he has a lot of alter, but I don't know how many, I can't tell, but I've met a number of them."*

When his sporting career ended, Walker recounts how his alter personalities began to take control in an anarchic way. It was from this point that he began to develop a morbid fascination with weapons and death. He writes in his book: *"The visceral enjoyment I get from seeing the impact and then the*

---

[605] Herschel Walker: Tell the World My Truth - Bob Woodruff, ABC News, 2008.

spraying of the brain with blood is like fireworks. He has been on the verge of murder with a gun several times, including against his wife: *"He put the gun to my head and said, 'I'll blow your brains out. I must have had the strength of God in me then because I looked him in the eye and said, 'Go ahead and pull the trigger, I know where I'm going, but do you know where you're going? There was someone fundamentally wrong in front of me."*

Walker has never denied threatening his wife in this way, but he says he does not remember it. During a therapy session with his wife, Dr. Jerry Mungadze, his therapist, said he saw a totally enraged alter personality emerge that literally wanted to kill everyone in the room. Dr. Mungadze reports: *"His eyes changed. The eyes that emerged didn't give a damn about me, and when he said he was going to kill me, I readily believed him... It wasn't Herschel, it was an enraged alter.* Finally that day, Walker deflected his anger by punching a hole in the cabinet door, and then another alter emerged, this time a young boy: *"He was in terrible pain because he had just broken his hand.* Herschel doesn't remember this violent scene either, but he makes it clear that he has to deal with all these things and that his illness is not an excuse for violence. After 8 years of therapy, without any medication, he has much more control over his alter personalities.

CHAPTER 10

PROPAGANDA AND OFFENSIVE AND DEFENSIVE NETWORK TECHNIQUES

Crimes against children thrive on a conspiracy of silence, and intimidation. We hope that one day paedophiles will be arrested and prosecuted. But what can be done when these same criminals are in charge of the justice system? "Dutch Injustice: When Child traffickers rule a nation", 2012)

What a misfortune for those people who act in secret to hide their plans from the Lord. They prepare their affairs in the shadows. They say, "Who can see us? Who knows what we are doing? - Isaiah 29:15

Blessed are those who hunger and thirst for righteousness, for they will be filled. - Matthew 5:6

1 - POWER NETWORKS

L et us first define the word "network". It is a term derived from the Latin word *"retis"*, plural *"retes"*, *"rets"*, meaning *"net"*. The term *"rets"*, most often used in the plural, meant a net for catching birds, fish or game. In a figurative sense, it meant an artifice by which one takes hold of someone or their mind. In scientific terms, it is a set of points that communicate with each other.

The word 'network' is currently defined as, among other things:
- An organised whole whose elements, dependent on a centre, are distributed at various points.
- A clandestine organisation whose members work in liaison with each other.

Networks are a grouping of entities (individuals, associations, various organisations, etc.) that are connected to each other. Networks are deployed in many fields: politics, the judiciary, the media, religion, the scientific and medical fields, associations, sports, etc. The aim of these networks is to bring together a maximum number of people and to create bridges from one network to another. These networks can be more or less apparent and even totally hidden. This system of operation is not in itself a negative thing, and is generally very effective. However, we live in an age where elitist networks are simply used to enslave a mass of humans at the bottom of a large pyramid hierarchy. The connections between these different networks such as Freemasonry (the various Luciferian lodges), mafia organisations and certain sectarian and religious communities are at the head of what can be called a 'meta-network' which seems to structure our society today. A meta-network organised to control and manipulate society at all levels, in a global manner, in order to establish a *New World Order*, the reign of the "civilising and liberating god": Lucifer.

Freemasonry is one of the organisations that has built the most powerful and extensive network. Indeed, its members are present on all continents and in all fields, including the most influential circles: politics, justice, humanitarian aid, intelligence, media, education, health, police, etc. Freemasonry currently forms a sort of structure of our society, a mesh that passes through banks, public administration (taxes, social security, etc.) to national education and the courts (two essential points). It functions as a transmission belt that takes care of transmitting information from one section to another when necessary. It is therefore a network that criss-crosses the whole of society, with multiple ramifications and pawns that can be moved according to the issues at stake.

One of the characteristics of these secret societies, but also of the intelligence services and classified government projects, is to maintain a compartmentalisation of information within the network. Indeed, each individual in the network only receives what is *"good to know"*, i.e. he will only have access to what he needs to know to do his *job*. They remain totally unaware of the globality of the project(s), receiving only what is strictly necessary in terms of information for the work they are doing at their level. Here is how this notion of systematic information compartmentalisation is described by Mark Phillips:

In fact, "need to know" is a phrase officially used by the CIA and other "alphabet" agencies like the FBI, NSA and DIA. Basically, it means that you are only told what you "need to know" to carry out your part of an operation without you being fully aware of what you are working for. In my case, I believed that the government was developing mind control in order to rid society of crime and mental illness. No one felt it necessary to tell me that the purpose was actually to control the population, to create the superhuman war machines of 'Special Forces' or to use them to torture and brutalise innocent people (...) I had no idea about any of this. I was just focused on 'my part' and excited about the prospects, and it never occurred to me for a moment that I might be contributing to the greatest threat humanity has ever faced."[606]

Faced with these networks, particularly the Masonic ones, it is difficult to establish a notion of counter-power, as the members (the *brothers*) are systematically present in each organisation and in each so-called opposing political party... All the while knowing that they have all taken an oath to serve the same occult interests (those of GADLU, the *Great Architect Of The Universe*) and to systematically cover each other in case of trouble. No matter the political party or the seriousness of the offences of which they would be incriminated, the oath of loyalty to a "brother" always comes first... One cannot therefore speak of independence and neutrality concerning the French justice system, which is today totally infiltrated by the Masonic network. Freemasons systematically do each other favours, a lodge "brother" will always come before

---

[606] *"On the grounds of national security"* - Cathy O'Brien & Mark Phillips, 2015, p.186.

a layman, so we are dealing with a kind of generalized masonic conflict of interest, extremely harmful to our society and to the proper functioning of a real justice system supposed to be rendered in the name of the people. When they take up their duties, each magistrate and each lawyer takes an oath to render justice fairly to all citizens. The question that arises today is this: does the Masonic oath, this systematic solidarity between "brothers", not hinder the manifestation of the truth in many legal proceedings? It should be noted that Italy and England oblige legal professionals to declare their membership of any Masonic obedience, which is unfortunately not the case in France.

Members of occult networks can also manipulate each other for various interests. The 'return of the lift' technique makes it possible to make people accountable to whom one has 'done a favour' at an opportune moment. The compromising information contained in heavy files also makes it possible to maintain constant pressure and blackmail on the members of the network. The files can even include real traps (such as photos or videos taken during a sexual situation where children are introduced) to maintain constant blackmail and control over the person. As the saying goes: *"they are all holding each other by the short hairs", not to* say by the c..... The members of the network are conditioned to obey and keep quiet, as they are usually all involved in dirty business. Many suffer from dissociative disorders linked to their early childhood, causing them to perpetuate despicable acts, which reinforces the records that serve to control them and keep them silent. It is a vicious circle in which the law of silence reigns.

The influence peddling of these networks is particularly virulent in the judiciary, and for good reason... Hubert Delompré, the administrator of the site deni-justice.net, denounces, for example, the Masonic signs inserted in certain letters circulating between magistrates. These signs (called triponctuation) indicate to the recipient who reads the letter that he or she should pay particular attention to the paragraph between two of these signs. This means that the content is binding on all the 'brothers' and that they must do everything possible to ensure that the message is successful, whether or not the judgment is justified. This is what is known as influence peddling and when the letters contain this kind of sign, the judgement always ends up in a conviction against the layman. Chantal Arnaud (ardechejustice.fr) speaks in these cases of *"masonic judgements"*, i.e. false information and allegations are made by the judges themselves, who take the liberty of writing anything and everything. According to her, these practices, concerning certain magistrates, can be attacked for forgery, as the manipulations are so flagrant. These malpractices even go so far as to make certain documents disappear from the file as evidence. There really are aberrations in the judgements given in the name of the people without anyone being able to react, since all this takes place in the courts, often behind closed doors... and by the magistrates themselves. The difficulty with these shameful judgements is that they are imposed de facto, as the magistracy embodies "the law". It is therefore very difficult for an ordinary citizen to counter such actions by a judicial system that imposes an almost unassailable, intimidating and threatening steamroller. The term generally used by the media to soften these aberrations is: *"judicial dysfunction"*... It is not a question of dysfunctions but rather of an organisation that leaves no room for the slightest error...

This world of justice is a corporatist world where clerks, bailiffs, lawyers, judges, prosecutors, eat together, go out together and marry each other... We find this same functioning in the political and journalistic world. So everyone protects themselves, it's a kind of caste above the people. The pyramid structure of society is not something new, but the problem is the influence peddling and the conflicts of interest that plague society, whether it be at the legal, media, political or pharmaceutical level... When the judicial system clearly abuses its power, it is time to sound the alarm. All court decisions are rendered in the name of the French people, so the *"dysfunctions"* and other judicial *"errors"* should be judged in turn by the French people to condemn and dismiss these magistrates who abuse their power. Some people call this system of corruption: *'The Republic of Friends'*; but should we say *'The Republic of Brothers'*?

What is perverse in these networks is the secret with a capital "S", it is a parallel hierarchy, an invisible power. In the France 5 documentary *"Grand-Orient: les frères invisibles de la république"*, the Freemason Alain Bauer declares without any restraint in front of a camera that *"what is studied in a lodge on Monday becomes a law proposal on Friday and a law the following week, the process, even if I accelerate it for the sake of the subject, is extremely fast because everything is linear"*.

Fred Zeller, who was head of the Grand Orient de France from 1971 to 1973, declared: "The influence of Masonry is perhaps even more important than under the third or fourth republics, it is placed at another level. There is no association, grouping or union in which Freemasons are not to be found and in the most eminent positions of responsibility. (INA.fr video archive)

2 - OPERATION OF THE NETWORK WHEN A PROTECTIVE PARENT SOUNDS THE ALARM

The numerous cases related to paedo-crime have helped to determine how the Network works to systematically cover up the case and eventually recover the child or children at the heart of the case.

It all starts with a complaint filed by the protective parent (usually the mother who still has full confidence in her country's justice system) who discovers that her child or children are being sexually abused by the father (or other family members). From then on, this family is identified and the first complaint is usually filed without any further action, but in France this usually leads to the placement of the child in the ASE (Aide Sociale à l'Enfance). The judge, totally ignoring the evidence of abuse that the protective parent brings in his file, will place the child in a home. According to the report of the CEDIF committee on child protection: *"The removal of children from their families has become a real social phenomenon in France. On the other hand, the little-publicised scandals surrounding involuntary placements also show that social services can become the instrument of children's misfortune, through clumsy and sometimes ill-intentioned interventions. Moreover, as Mr Pierre Naves, Inspector General of Social Affairs, acknowledges, half of the placements decided upon are not justified."*

Some sources claim that the general councils receive several thousand euros per month from our taxes for each child taken into care by the ASE. In France, abusive placements are increasing all the time... for what reason?

As we saw in Chapter 7, children in care are ideal targets for the network, especially those with dissociative disorders as a result of sexual abuse. They are the second-class victims, not destined for elite positions. The protective parent is ignored, or even deprived of his or her rights towards the child, because *"psychological expertises"*, carried out by members of the network, will serve to devalue his or her word. If the parent insists by becoming too virulent (especially if he or she is socially isolated), he or she may be subjected to abusive psychiatric internment, thus allowing his or her mental health to be ruined by shock chemical treatment (see the Patricia Poupard case). All these arbitrary decisions are made through the courts, which as we have seen are gangrenous. If the abuser is not already part of the "family", an agreement will be made with him: in exchange for immunity, he will have to "lend" his child to the network. This whole process is covered by the successive interventions of various "lightning rods" (social services, pseudo-child protection associations, crooked lawyers, etc.) whose function is to channel the case so that it is suppressed and does not become a threat to the network (the notion of "lightning rod" will be defined later).

It can be seen that these methods of isolating the child from the protective parent and generally ending up with the child in the hands of the abusive parent are perfectly run thanks to a network system, a well-oiled machine, whose members are all connected and know perfectly well the measures to be taken in cases of paedophile crime. Indeed, the process is always the same, the aim being first to get the protective parent:

- Is ruined by the cost of endless proceedings, to the great joy of the lawyers involved.

- Isolated, he is seen as a madman and a bad parent... and when the Masonic network gets involved, he finds himself in situations where even the administration seems to harm him at all levels. A more or less subtle form of societal harassment is put in place.

The following is a general overview of what has been found in child abuse cases (through the systematic repetition of protocols):

- No serious investigation is made to verify the child's accusations (complaint usually dismissed).

- No protection for victims and parents who report abuse.

- No appropriate medical examination of the child (including lower tract MRI or anoscopy).

- The word of the child systematically denied. The Outreau affair is now systematically used to claim that the word of children cannot be trusted: see the book by journalist Jacques Thomet *"Retour à Outreau: contre-enquête sur une manipulation pédocriminelle"*.

- No statistics on the rape (and disappearance) of minors. Indeed, this subject seems so taboo that no figures are available on the number of children raped, the number of convictions and the number of cases that have been dismissed.

- Total media silence on the highly sensitive issue of child abuse cases.

3 - THE LIGHTNING ROD STRATEGY

In his book *"L'affaire Vincent: au cœur du terrorisme d'état"* (2010), French activist Christian 'Stan' Maillaud, an ex-gendarme, describes a technique he calls the *"lightning rod strategy"*. It is an infiltration method to retrieve and channel sensitive files in order to cover them up. Here is how Stan Maillaud defines these methods:

The 'lightning rod strategy' is simple, practically unstoppable, and systematically employed in cases of paedophile crime, or any case that might disturb the order of organised crime (ed. note: the Network).

It consists of the establishment of a clever sham whose purpose is to interfere with any advocacy, whether legal, communications or otherwise, undertaken or likely to be undertaken by victims or victims' families. The actions in question must then be channelled and directed, as must public attention and debate, in a direction that does not profoundly threaten the interests of organised crime. The preferred terrain on which organised crime wants to confine victims and victims' families is obviously its judicial sham spread throughout our perverted societies.

Thus, the 'lightning rod' is most often in the form of judicial auxiliaries, but also of associations, the combination of the two being the most effective for organised crime. Concerning these associations, or other civic organisations, there are on the one hand those that are set up from scratch by organised crime - such as the famous "Child Focus", a so-called association against paedophile crime sponsored by the Belgian King "him self" - and on the other hand those whose origin is sincere but which are quickly infiltrated by real agents of organised crime.

The aim of the operations is then to excel in illusion, in order to deceive all the victims and families of victims as well as the general public and to attract into its web as many victims as possible in search of the help that is denied to them by the judicial and political sham.

And when it comes to illusionism, impostors have only one choice of procedures, mastering the rules of the rigged playing field, and having no more states of mind or moral sense than the criminals they serve and protect. This is how it is common to see the impostures of associations committed in ceremonies or charity galas where champagne - from Rothschild! - cakes and petits fours generously regale entire assemblies of well-heeled notables, rather like the demonstrations purporting to combat poverty and hunger in the world. With subsidies flowing like water for these associations, such pompous festivities are de rigueur in the thickest obscenity and cynicism (...)

As far as court officers are concerned, in the context that we are in today, their profession is in essence a perfect sham, just like the judiciary in general. For in order not to risk being disbarred, no lawyer ventures to confront in depth the criminal excesses of an institution to which he is otherwise subject, but in fact limits himself to treating only the symptoms. Every lawyer is only a piece of the rigged chessboard and knows it, a "master" piece, without which he would no longer be a lawyer. For a good lawyer, in our real context of judicial and societal imposture, is a "dead" lawyer, i.e. one who has fallen out of favour with the institution and will not survive for long for lack of clients; or a lawyer who has been disbarred or is about to be disbarred, or a lawyer who courageously gives up his hat.

Of course, the same is true for any magistrate, but I am only dealing here with the strategy of lightning rods, it is the servile auxiliary of justice that is in the limelight, because apart from the fact that I have just raised, regarding the profound dishonesty of such a profession in the current state of our judicial institution and our society, one must fear the propensity that lawyers willingly have to serve as lightning rods for your defence. Many are used to this kind of manoeuvre, where an obscure negotiation with the opposing party, with a prosecutor or a court president, intervenes behind your back to define the outcome of your case. The gullible client, most of the time, does not see that he is being fooled, and is the victim of the illusions of a real play in which his legal assistant overflows with melodramatic effects to make him believe that he is fiercely defending his cause...

4 - THE 'FALSE MEMORY SYNDROME' AND 'PARENTAL ALIENATION' SYNDROME

False memory syndrome is a theory that memory can be fabricated or 'contaminated' by illusory memories. This theory, invented by the former Lutheran pastor Ralph Underwager, is usually used to defend parents accused of incest. Many therapists have been sued for implanting false memories in their patients, thus becoming the perpetrators instead of the abusers. In most cases, this is an attack on the adult victim's word when she recalls sexual abuse during childhood. This *"false memory syndrome"* is not a recognised diagnosis, neither by the American Psychiatric Association nor by the WHO (World Health Organisation). The term "syndrome" is completely inappropriate because this theory does not describe any set of symptoms that can be used to establish a real diagnosis. However, even today, "false memory experts" come to court to discredit the word of the victims. Richard J. Lowenstein (President of the *International Society for the Study of Dissociation*) stated in 1992: *"I know of no research or clinical description that would empirically validate the existence of such a symptom. False memory syndrome is a syndrome without signs and symptoms (the defining characteristics of a syndrome)".*

In an interview with the Dutch paedophile magazine *'Paidika: The Journal of Paedophilia'* on the subject of 'loving children', Dr. Ralph

Underwager clearly invited paedophiles to proudly affirm their sexual choices: *'Paedophiles waste a lot of time and energy defending their choice. I don't think a paedophile has to do that. Paedophiles can proudly and courageously stand up for their choice. They can say that what they want is to find the best way to love. I am also a theologian and as such I believe that it is God's will that there should be closeness, intimacy and unity of the flesh, between people. A paedophile can say: 'This closeness is also possible for me according to the choice I have made. (...) What I think is that paedophiles can say that the search for intimacy and love is their choice. Boldly they can declare: "I believe that this is in fact part of God's will."*[607]

Ralph Underwager, former director of the *Institute for Psychological Therapies* in Minesota (USA), was regularly called to testify in court where he systematically attacked the credibility of people making accusations of sexual abuse. In 1993, he came to testify in France, in Aix en Provence, to defend the members of the sect *"La Famille"* (ex *Children of God*) who were under investigation for *"aggravated pimping, voluntary violence against minors, sequestration and corruption of minors"*. The 22 members of the sect were all acquitted in part thanks to Underwager.

Ralph Underwager is the official founder of the *False Memory Syndrome Foundation*. This foundation, which is not a competent scientific organisation in the field of psychiatry, is regularly called upon to assist in cases of paedophilia involving traumatic memories, especially those linked to satanic ritual abuse. When Underwager and other founding members of the *FMSF came under* accusations of paedophilia themselves, Underwager was quickly forced to resign and was replaced by Pamela Freyd, who claims to be a victim of the false accusations of sexual abuse that her daughter, Jennifer J. Frey, is making against her and her husband. Her daughter, a psychology professor at the University of Oregon, publicly accused her parents at a conference entitled *'Controversies around Recovered Memories of Incest and Ritualistic Abuse'*. A conference given in August 1993 in Ann Arbor, Michigan (USA). The mother then turned to psychiatrist Harold Lief (a member of the *FMSF* board of directors) to diagnose her daughter's "disorder": according to this psychiatrist, heterosexual couples do not rape their children and the repressed memories of sexual abuse do not exist, so the case is closed...

In 1995, at a conference of therapists grouped in the *Society for the Investigation, Treatment and Prevention of Ritual and Cult Abuse*, Walter Bowart (author of *the* book *Operation Mind Control*) stated that the *FMSF*, all those people working to pass off traumatic, dissociative memories as *"false memories"*, was a CIA creation designed to discredit and misinform the mental health community, and that it served primarily to silence victims of government mind control experiments.

In the French-speaking world, this theory of false memory syndrome is promulgated mainly by Hubert Van Gijseghem and Paul Bensoussan. These

---

[607] Joseph Geraci: Hollida Wakefield and Ralph Underwager - Padaika: Journal of Paedophilia, Vol.3, N°1, 1993.

"experts" intervene in numerous legal cases in order to put forward this theory to magistrates, police officers or social workers. Van Gijseghem regularly uses the *"parental alienation syndrome"* (PAS) to defend fathers accused of sexual abuse... Another *"syndrome"* with no scientific basis, invented by the paedophile Richard Gardner. Indeed, for Gardner, sexual activities between adults and children are part of the natural repertoire of human sexual activity. He even believes that paedophilia can enhance the survival of the human species by serving *'procreative purposes'*. According to him: *"Pedophilia has been considered the norm by a vast majority of people throughout the history of the world (...) it is a widespread and accepted practice by literally billions of people"*. Gardner believes that children spontaneously engage in sexual behaviour and can initiate sexual encounters by *'seducing'* the adult.[608]

Richard Gardner defines Parental Alienation Syndrome: PAS is a disorder specific to children, occurring almost exclusively in custody disputes, where one parent (usually the mother) conditions the child to hate the other parent (usually the father). Children usually side with the parent who does this conditioning, creating their own cabal against the father.

This means blaming the mother for any problems in the father's relationship with the child, the aim being to remedy this by increasing the child's contact with the father while reducing contact with the mother. All this is obviously imposed by court decisions. This is one of the reasons why in child abuse cases, the protective parent who reports the abuse is overwhelmed by the courts and has custody of his or her child taken away from him or her, and the child is automatically given to the alleged abuser.

Sherry Quick, a lawyer and president of the *American Coalition for Abuse Awareness (ACAA)*, reports that judges "tend to consistently believe" court-appointed experts when they say that the mother fabricated allegations of child abuse and then "brainwashed" the child into believing in the abuse in order to get back at the ex-husband... If the mother persists in her claims, she is perceived as obsessive and unstable and may even be committed to a psychiatric hospital while custody of the children will be given to the father...

In summary, Gardner's PAS theory and its various scales for distinguishing between true and false reports of child sexual abuse are not informed by science and have not been recognised by most child abuse experts. Rather than subjecting his theories to scientific evaluation, Gardner publishes most of his work through his own publishing house or in non-scientific journals. Because Gardner's theories are based on his own clinical observations - not on scientific data - they must be interpreted in the context of his atypical views on paedophilia and what he calls the climate of hysteria surrounding child sexual abuse cases. Gardner's theories are based on his presumption that there is nothing inherently wrong with sex between a child and an adult, and his belief that there is an epidemic of false allegations of sexual abuse made by vindictive wives in custody disputes. Gardner persists in these beliefs despite a wealth of clinical and experimental evidence to the contrary. This is not to suggest that

---

[608] True and false accusations of child sex abuse - Richard Gardner, 1992.

such allegations are always accurate or that parents never attempt to manipulate their children in custody disputes. However, all psychological expertise on which a child's safety will depend must be subjected to empirical testing. When a theory is unable to evolve and improve in response to research findings, it leaves the realm of science for that of ideology and dogma. Given the harms to children and their families in this area, legal and mental health professionals must constantly challenge their understandings to ensure that custody decisions are based on the best available science, rather than unfounded opinion, prejudice or ideology.[609]

Let's go back to Hubert Van Gijseghem... He was called as an 'expert' at the third Outreau trial which took place in Rennes in May 2015. The hearings were public, so many people were able to attend his intervention and report the facts. This adept of the theory of "false memories" and SAP ("parental alienation") then explained to the bar the best means, according to him, of gathering the child's word so that it is as reliable as possible. He emphasised the fact that the more the child is questioned *"outside the framework"*, the more his or her testimony will be *"polluted"*... According to him, a testimony collected by parents, by nursery assistants, by a teacher, but also by child assistance associations or by a psychologist is worthless and must be avoided at all costs... He also forbids places such as the house, the bedroom or the school to listen to the child so as not to establish a bond of familiarity... He recommends that the child should only be listened to in a police station, in a single hearing during which the child should feel pressure to tell the truth, *"here you have to tell the truth, the child has to be impressed"*, said Van Gijseghem, while recommending that the parents should not be present during this hearing.

He also recommends that the protective parent or any other person who could take a disturbing testimony (for the network) should be excluded, as this would automatically be *'contaminated'* by the child's interaction with others. According to Van Gijseghem's statements, who is careful to exclude any actor outside the institutions who could listen to the child's testimony, the child has to go to the police station himself to be interviewed once by a stranger... Furthermore, he warns against using drawings, toys, dolls or plans to make the child express his or her traumatic experiences, claiming that *'scientific research'* invalidates all this.

During his testimony in court, Van Gijseghem will repeatedly use the term *'scientific research versus the man in the street'*, as the flamboyant standard of the 'expert' that he is. But what scientific research is he talking about exactly? We won't know in this court of law. Van Gijseghem did not know how to answer Mr. Forster (lawyer for the civil party) when the latter asked him the title of his doctoral thesis of which he had found no trace... Forster also confronted him with a whole series of contradictory studies and research concerning his frivolous theories on the collection of the child's word and false memories. Faced with

---

[609] Does the Parental Alienation Syndrome have an empirical basis? A critical review of R. Gardner's theories and opinions - Stephanie J. Dallam, RN, MScN, family care practitioner and legal worker.

these contradictions, Van Gijseghem had nothing to say and remained silent, as this man's work is indeed very controversial in child psychology circles.

Van Gijseghem explained that parents, teachers and therapists have to be totally excluded in order to validate the child's word correctly. He said: *"There is a risk that the child will end up talking nonsense... The child will start telling fairy tales, satanic rituals, sacrifices, cannibalism, etc... myths from which we don't know where they come from..."* Van Gijseghem thus discredits everything related to traumatic ritual abuse, invalidating these testimonies by the fact that the child is *slipping* because his memory has been *contaminated* by adults: it is therefore a question of false memories, the case is closed, no need to investigate...

Van Gijseghem also states that a true story will tend to decrease in detail, while a false story will become more and more detailed over time, but again he does not elaborate on the research and sources behind these claims. However, traumatic memories can resurface over time in greater and greater sensory detail, thus making the testimony more and more complete. But according to him: *"the repressed memories are the result of an unrealized reconstruction, the person fills in the gaps with false memories."*

But if there are *'holes'*, it is because there is traumatic amnesia, and traumatic amnesia means hidden memories that can go back further in time. These are fractions of memories that must be reconstituted like a jigsaw puzzle in order to integrate them and verbalise them within a chronological framework: this is the challenge of survivors' testimonies, which are attacked precisely because they cannot give a precise and chronological account of the events. This is how survivors suffering from severe dissociative disorders find themselves totally discredited, unfortunately...

It is classic in this type of case to put forward the psychological state of the dissociated victim in order to discredit her testimony. The diagnosis of dissociative disorders should, on the contrary, be one more piece of evidence in the file to support the fact that the victim has indeed experienced severe trauma, or even mental control in the case of a dissociative identity disorder. Logically, in the face of severe dissociative disorders (as a consequence of severe trauma), the investigation should be more thorough rather than dismissed...

During the trial, Van Gijseghem clearly admitted to the president of the court that he was not competent in neuro-biological sciences or psychotraumatology, although it is precisely these areas of research that allow us to understand the functioning of traumatic memories linked to dissociative states.

Today we are in a situation where the judiciary seems at first sight to be totally unaware of psychotraumatology, and the magistracy does not seem to want to update itself on this knowledge which is nevertheless indispensable in order to understand and deal correctly with child abuse cases. It would seem that anything remotely related to dissociative disorders and traumatic memories should not be given any credit in child sexual abuse cases. Everything is done to stifle and discredit this field of research, especially when these questions are raised in a criminal court... The last thing we need is to open a Pandora's box in the middle of a courtroom!

There is therefore a communication war, or rather a *"memory war"*, *with regard to* the scientific research that allows us to understand how the brain works in the face of trauma. As a result, misinformation and withholding of information is taking place to prevent these studies from being widely disseminated and taught in medical schools, which could end up weighing heavily in the courts (see the conclusion of Chapter 5).

The treatment of victims with a view to their recovery is therefore affected by all this institutional 'negligence'. Here is what psychotraumatologist Muriel Salmona said on this subject: *"The problem with the public authorities is that on the one hand they are fighting against violence, they have passed recent laws, such as the law on incest in February 2010; but normally these laws should have included the provision of information and training for doctors, because doctors are not trained in all the new research and all the new knowledge we have. There should also be the creation of care centres, i.e. we should be able to receive the victims, but nothing is being done! And here, we absolutely need a huge political will to be able to take care of the victims. Taking care of victims really means avoiding suffering, avoiding the worsening of inequalities, avoiding situations of marginalisation, exclusion, distress... And an important point: it means avoiding the repetition of violence. When you have been a victim of violence, you can be a victim of violence again (...) But one of the ways of self-treatment is also violence against others (...) Violence against others is a drug, and in an unequal society there can be people who are designated as ready-made victims, available to use them and to "drug" themselves with them."* [610]

During the Outreau 3 trial in Rennes, psychotherapist Hélène Romano declared on Europe1: This is a great pity because there are recommendations on the hearing of children and teenagers which are not at all or hardly applied at the moment due to a lack of means and will, because it is said that listening to children is no longer of much use[611]... The sham of the first Outreau trial in 2004 played a large part in anchoring in public opinion that children "lie and talk nonsense" with regard to sexual abuse.

5 - FOCUSING ON THE INTERNET TOOL (CYBER-POLICE)

There are thousands of paedophile websites and millions of child pornography files circulating on the internet. This is why governments, media and associations focus on the web, thinking that this is where all child pornography is concentrated. Interpol and almost all national police forces are setting up internet monitoring units. Public campaigns are systematically aimed at raising awareness of paedophilia on the web, thus maintaining the idea that the whole problem is known and that governments are therefore providing the

---

[610] Muriel Salmona - UPP Femmes debout, round table on violence against women, 2011.

[611] Hélène Morano, Europe-Midi, Europe 1, 19/05/2015.

necessary responses to this scourge. There is no doubt that paedo-pornographic content on the web must be detected, removed and punished, but the issue of combating paedo-crime cannot be limited to the internet alone...

Belgian activist Marcel Vervloesem on the government's focus on the internet, while the real and not the virtual networks continue their activities without any judicial concern: *"The photos that end up on the internet have first been produced. The child was raped at the time the photo was taken and it is not the internet that rapes children. The perpetrators who rape children and produce this material, they are the rapists and they are the ones who put their pictures on the internet. This is what I have always said to the International Congress, I have always told them that we should not deal with the problem of the internet. No, it is not the internet that rapes, it is not the internet that tortures, no, the children who appear on the internet have been victims of these practices. Who are the perpetrators of these practices? That is what is important, the internet is not important. That's what I said at the Congress in Holland, in front of international lawyers, I clarified this position and I told them: "No! Internet is the end of the chain, before that the child is raped, tortured or whatever, and after that the photo is published by broadcasting it on the Internet, that's another step (...) When you see reports on television, you always hear: "We have uncovered a paedophile network on the Internet... That's rubbish!"*[612]

Indeed, the core of the problem is the producers of these child pornography materials who rape, torture and kill children. When cyber-police attack virtual networks on the Internet, they are attacking consumers of images and videos, not the core of the paedophile network, which is not virtual but real. The most dangerous paedophiles, such as Marc Dutroux, are usually not connected to the internet at all.

Moreover, the Internet is a global network without any regulation, an iceberg whose submerged part (the *dark web*, where Internet users circulate under total anonymity) contains the most ignoble practices of human beings. Therefore, from a technical point of view, the few sites closed by the authorities are only a drop in the ocean, ten others will bloom the next day. The fight against paedophile crime is not virtual, paedophile networks are not virtual. This governmental strategy of focusing on the internet is also a kind of lightning rod for the police forces to focus on the virtual, leaving the field open to the real producers of child pornography organised in networks. As we saw in the chapter on ritual abuse, the testimonies of the victims of these satanist networks very often report that the rapes, tortures and murders are photographed and filmed. However, the police obviously do not trace the source of all these atrocities, their function is not to dismantle the paedophile network, as the digital content disseminated on the Internet is only the end of the chain.

---

[612] *"The Networks of Horror"* - Stan Maillaud & Janet Seemann, 2010.

6 - "NATIONAL SECURITY

In the United States, the *National Security Act* was signed in 1947 to reorganise the armed forces and the intelligence services. Its main purpose was to protect military secrets and to push the CIA into a "secret war" against the Soviets: the Cold War. This legislation was the beginning of the lead cover-up that today, more than ever, allows for the cover-up of all 'sensitive' government projects, such as mind control programmes. It is under the protection of this 'national security' that projects such as Bluebird, Paperclip, Artichoke, MK-Ultra, etc. were developed. All psychotronic research is also covered by the *National Security Act*, making it impossible to publicly (officially) disclose anything about these programmes. With the various amendments that have been added to it over the years, including Reagan's in 1984, the US government is now able to hide and censor anything it wants... Simply by hiding behind the two words: "national security", it's that simple. It is a real smokescreen behind which some members of the government hide the crimes committed against innocent civilians. Mind control is certainly the most shocking practice that must be concealed from citizens at all costs thanks to what the *National Security Act* has become: an aberrant abuse of power. The secrecy of information, or withholding of information, is an excellent way to exercise power. Thus, this government has carte blanche to violate the laws of the land and the rights of its citizens.

The most telling example of what the *National Security* Act can be used for is the case of Cathy O'Brien, victim of the MK-Monarch. This case clearly demonstrates how the system works, literally blocking any legal recourse despite the amount of evidence accumulated - some of which was provided by FBI officials in the O'Brien case - that should logically lead to investigations, judgments and convictions, and finally to a public disclosure by the media of all these occult mind control activities. Cathy O'Brien's partner, Mark Phillips, said that his country had not been able to solve the problem in terms of justice, he was repeatedly told *that he could never get justice because of "National Security."*

This 'national security' also poses a problem in therapeutic terms, as all knowledge about dissociative disorders, MK programming and deprogramming is censored, blocked. Certain knowledge and technologies are therefore inaccessible to therapists and victims. This abuse of power also makes it possible to interpret the law in a certain way and to stifle the testimonies of survivors, always for reasons of 'national security'. Access to the courts for the unfortunate victims is also hampered by the cunning of the many judicial 'experts' who do everything to discredit them.

Thus, deprived of the benefit of the many discoveries brought about by DoD research and the technologies it has developed, psychiatric medicine is still at the learning curve in terms of establishing state-of-the-art patient care protocols. In other words, psychiatric actors themselves are becoming the second group of victims of mind/information control.

The profession of psychiatry is now in crisis and is at the classic crossroads between failure and success. It would appear that the path to success through the application of currently available technologies is blocked FOR NATIONAL SECURITY REASONS.

As a direct result of both the DoD's handling of psychiatric research secrecy and the resulting federal information withholding practices, psychiatric practitioners are on the defensive against their patients, the courts and, more recently, special interest advocacy groups. These groups launch attacks on psychiatric professionals that aim to destroy them. Well-funded organisations with highly dubious agendas, such as the False Memory Foundation (FMF) and the Church of Scientology, have publicly denounced the psychiatric profession. *TRANCE Formation of America: True life story of a mind control slave* - Cathy O'Brien & Mark Phillips, 2012, p.61.

Cathy O'Brien also describes how the juvenile court judge ruling on her daughter's case - also a victim of ritual abuse and MK programming - closed the door to the media and the public on the grounds of 'national security' while shocking violations of various laws ensued. Cathy O'Brien writes about her daughter's situation under *National Act Security* as follows *"Despite a public outcry that has grown to include a wide range of international rights organisations, as well as numerous documents/letters to the Governor(s) of Tennessee, most of which I have received copies of, Kelly is still having to be granted her right to a specialised re-education process for the proven mind control abuses she has suffered since birth, via the US government-funded 'MK-Ultra' operation. The handful of criminals at the helm of our country, our information and, subsequently, our "criminal" justice system, refuse to provide the known - yet classified - technological antidotes to a problem they do not want to admit exists. Over 70,000 (declassified) documents, various pieces of evidence, videos, medical records, affidavits, and other government insider testimony - which is only part of what Mark and I have accumulated over the years - establish the reality of the mind control abuse that Kelly and I suffered in "MK-Ultra". It is therefore absolutely inexcusable that these cover-ups continue or, as Andy Shookhoff, the only 'judge' involved in this case, stated during a Nashville, Tennessee juvenile court hearing, that 'the law does not apply in this case because of National Security'. After a decade of various suffocations, Kelly was released by the State of Tennessee without treatment. Placed in a secure environment, she is now awaiting the rehabilitation she so desperately needs."*[613]

Mark Phillips says that when they handed their file containing all the evidence to Judge Andy Shookhoff, he stood up and said: *'I don't know of any law for your case'*. The judge then said in open court: *"The laws do not apply in this case for reasons of national security.* This was a rather startling statement that was made in front of the entire courtroom audience, including dozens of lawyers and many citizens and journalists... So people knew what the case was about. For Mark Phillips, it meant that this judge had somehow validated their case and perhaps even saved their lives. This judge publicly stated that the US

---

[613] *TRANCE Formation of America: True life story of a mind control slave* - Cathy O'Brien & Mark Phillips, 2012, p.369.

government has a responsibility to cover up this case and not have to justify it... It was at this point that Mark Phillips and Cathy O'Brien realised that they would never be able to get justice in any state or criminal court in the US. However, this official and public statement by the judge was a big step forward. (For more on this case, see Appendix 2)

The truth is that the National Security Act has clearly been interpreted not to preserve the integrity of military secrets, but rather to protect criminal activity of the utmost gravity. We would be acting constitutionally by repealing this law and replacing it with the already existing rules for the conduct of the military in terms of National Security, rules that do not infringe on the constitutional rights of American citizens or those of their allies.[614]

According to Mark Phillips, all countries with a peace treaty with the US are subject to the terms of the *National Security Act* of 1947. This means that the issue of MK programming remains under a thick blanket of secrecy in many countries...

7 - SEXUAL SUBVERSION

This subject would deserve a book of its own, as the issue is so important and there is so much to say. What follows is an attempt to expose this recent phenomenon (which began in the middle of the 20th century), which both reverses moral values and attempts to corrupt children by impregnating society with all the "whims" of the Luciferian subculture: where incest and paedophilia are a heritage that is perpetuated from generation to generation...

This *culture of paedophilia and hyper-sexualisation is gradually* being imbued in popular culture to make sexual relations between adults and children acceptable and commonplace, and finally to legalise them. We also note that convictions against paedocriminals are becoming lighter and lighter year after year, a laxity on the part of the judicial institutions which indicates that these crimes are becoming less and less serious? ... When it comes to taking into account the dignity of the child (his word and his suffering), this is something that is nowadays totally put on the back burner and for good reason, the child is gradually becoming a *consumable good* in our consumer society that has gone adrift... This heavy subject is indeed a very hard pill to swallow, however there is still time to open our eyes!

a/ Alfred Kinsey

Alfred Charles Kinsey was a professor of entomology and zoology. He became famous after publishing two important studies on the sexual behaviour of men and women. In 1948 he published *'Sexual Behavior in the Human Male'* and in 1953 *'Sexual Behavior in the Human Female'*. In 1947, he founded the

---

[614] Ibid p.24.

Institute for Sex Research at Indiana University in Bloomington, which was later renamed the *Kinsey Institute for Research in Sex, Gender and Reproduction* (still active today). It was within this institute that Alfred Kinsey undertook the compilation of thousands of data to write his infamous report on the sexuality of adults... but also of children. According to the Kinsey Institute data, hundreds of children and even babies were used in research on sexuality.

The purpose of Kinsey's studies and the people who funded his 'scientific research' was to normalise a range of behaviours that had always been considered socially unacceptable, such as adultery, sodomy, incest and paedophilia. These studies also aimed to show that these behaviours were much more widespread than the public perceived, thus making them much more acceptable...

The Kinsey Institute is nothing more or less than a social engineering operation. All its 'studies' on sexuality were intended to infuse American society with propaganda financed by the Rockefeller Foundation, among others. Indeed, the reports produced by the Kinsey Institute (in the 1950s) were the starting point of the *sexual revolution* (or sexual liberation), which affected both adults and young people, as they had a definite influence on sex education programmes in schools. Alfred Kinsey is one of the precursors of early sexualisation.

After publishing his two reports on human sexuality, Kinsey began to travel around the United States lecturing at universities and to politicians. He quickly became the leading authority on sexuality and was hailed as *'the world's leading expert on human sexuality'*. He aimed in particular to bring about change in the laws concerning sex offenders and the sex education of children. The model of criminal law that was adopted after 1955 was based on Kinsey's research, among other things. Not only did his work influence sex education programmes for children, but it also influenced American laws, particularly with regard to the protection of women and children, as well as a reconsideration of the imprisonment of paedocriminals.

Kinsey stated, for example, that children are 100% orgasmic from birth and that they can benefit from having sex with adults, including incest. He advocated lowering the age of consent, but in fact aimed to completely legalise 'paedophilia'. For example, he states in his studies that *"Children need to be taught sex education as early as possible since they are sexualised from birth (...) They need to be taught about heterosexual and homosexual masturbation"*. According to Dr. Judith Reisman, the leading whistleblower on the sham Kinsey reports, he also claimed that sex offenders rarely repeat abuse, and therefore should not be imprisoned but paroled.

Here are the kinds of extreme results noted in Kinsey's studies in tabular form: a 4-year-old child is said to have had 26 orgasms in 24 hours. Dr. Reisman legitimately wonders where and under what circumstances Kinsey could have obtained such information? Under Table 31, Kinsey states that the data is based on observations of 317 male subjects. Then on page 177 of the report on male sexual behaviour, Kinsey writes: *"Orgasm in a 4-month-old girl is included in our report..."* How could anyone recognize such a thing in a 4-month-old baby?

Kinsey also writes: *"Among prepubescent boys and among little girls, orgasm is not readily recognised, partly because of the lack of ejaculation."*[615]

The question is what this man called an orgasm. On page 161 of his report on the man's sexual behaviour, he specifically describes what he considers to be an orgasm in these children: *"A gradual and sometimes prolonged process, leading to orgasm, which involves violent convulsions of all the bodies, rapid breathing, grunting or violent screaming, with sometimes an abundance of tears (especially in young children).* He also states that there are six categories of what he considers to be a child's orgasm: screaming, hysterical pain (especially in younger children), convulsions, the child hitting the *"partner"* (he uses the word partner to refer to the rapist), etc. For Kinsey, all this was part of orgasms and was used to build up his smoky reports.

Kinsey was very clear that all this data about children was provided by *'adult observers'*, defined as paedophiles by his own team members. Dr. Bankroft of the Kinsey Institute said that following the example of his mentor, Dr. Dickinson, Kinsey trained his own predators, men who were collecting data on what is purely and simply sexual abuse of children, even babies.

In 1990, on the *Phil Donahue* Show, Dr. Judith Reisman was confronted by Dr. Clarence Tripp, a close associate of Kinsey. He said on the show: *"I think we should talk about the children's case now, because a lot of things are mixed up. You know, we shouldn't rush into it... We want to savour it, because it's wonderful! It's a delight.* Judith Reisman said on the show: *"Do you know what Dr. Gebhard told me? He wrote me a letter, which I have available for anyone who wants it, in which he explains that "oral and manual techniques were used on the children"! If what I say is wrong, sue me!"*

This letter was written in March 1981. In it Dr. Gebhard explains where the sexual data on children came from. In this letter he admits that many paedophiles were employed to collect information for the Kinsey reports. He writes: *"Since sexual experimentation on infants and children is illegal, we therefore had to find other sources, some were parents, others were school nurses or teachers, or homosexual men (...) one of them was a man who had had many sexual encounters with men, women, children and infants, and being scientifically oriented, kept detailed records of each encounter (...).Some of these sources were accompanied by written evidence, photographs and sometimes films (...) The techniques employed were self-masturbation by the child, sex scenes between children and manual or oral adult-child sexual contact."*

Gebhard's letter completely refutes Dr. Bankroft's pedophile theories, but is in perfect agreement with what Kinsey had written in his report on male sexual behaviour. Geibhard mentions in his letter that photos and films were sent directly to Alfred Kinsey, which explains the sad discovery made by the director of his institute, June Reinisch... In 1984, in *Newsweek*, Reinsich stated that she had discovered a collection of paedo-pornography within the institute itself that was so disgusting that she could not continue to look at it.

---

[615] Sexual Behavior in the Human Male " - Alfred Kinsey, p.159.

In 1998, in the report "Secret History: Kinsey's Paedophiles" (Yorkshire TV), Gebhard said: "There is also a paedophile organisation in this country, they cooperated with us, and for some of them who were obviously not incarcerated, they gave us information. Dr. Reisman believes that the paedophile organisation Geibhard refers to was what later became NAMBLA (an American association advocating love between men and boys). To this day, pro-paedophile organisations such as NAMBLA systematically refer to the Kinsey impostor studies to make their claims and to trivialise paedomania.

In the same report, Dr. Clarence Tripp states: "Pedophilia is kind of non-existent, and the thing he (Kinsey) hated most was that people used words like 'child abuse'. What is that? Nobody knows (laughs) Child abuse? Are we talking about pulling his ears or hitting him with a pipe? Or are we talking about tickling him a bit? Do you put 'petting' and 'attacking' in the same basket? As Kinsey said: "With this kind of paranoia, you do more harm to the child than all the paedophiles in the world put together."

According to the research that has been done on this sad individual, he was himself a sick pervert. Alfred Kinsey's sadomasochistic tendencies have been documented by many biographers, including James Jones who reports that Kinsey once circumcised himself with a pocket knife in a bathtub without any anaesthetic. James Jones also reports that after the Rockefeller Foundation granted him funding, *"Kinsey went into the basement, tied a rope to a pipe and the other end around his scrotum, then climbed onto a chair and jumped."* His self-inflicted sexual abuse was clearly identified at the time of his death. Officially, Kinsey died of a heart attack, it would indeed be embarrassing to say that the father of the world's sexual revolution died as a result of self-mutilation.

To conclude with regard to this impostor, we note that he was a great admirer of the Satanist Aleister Crowley. After publishing his "famous" reports on male and female sexuality, Kinsey travelled abroad to study sexuality in various countries. According to Wardell Pomeroy, Kinsey's co-author, Kinsey was also looking for the document *'A prized item, the diaries of Aleister Crowley'*. Pomeroy writes that two weeks after Kinsey went to England to find the document, he went to Sicily to visit the 'temple' Crowley had built there, the Abbey of Thelema, where he practised satanic rituals. Kinsey even tried to acquire Crowley's *Magical Diaries* for his institute.[616] It should be noted that Aleister Crowley was expelled from Italy because he was accused of paedocriminality, including sacrifices.

Alfred Kinsey legitimised the sexual revolution, he did it academically but in an unscientific way, the real motive being not science but a well-orchestrated social engineering plan to change the morals of an entire country... and by implication the entire western world, the US being the influential culture that spills over into the world. One of his biographers, Jonathan Gathorne-Hardy, said: *"It's really interesting when you get into it, it's a real sick social plan... He didn't just want a little more tolerance of sexuality, it's something much more*

---

[616] "Kinsey: Crimes and Consequences the Red Queen and the Grand Scheme" - Judith Reisman, 1998.

monstrous. It was a powerful social plan perfectly orchestrated by the people who worked alongside him."

b/ Early sexualisation

Alfred Kinsey is the forerunner of early sexualisation, which today takes the form of sex education that is imposed on children at ever younger ages, particularly in school curricula.

In a booklet entitled *"Document on the basis of sex education"* published by the Pedagogical University of Central Switzerland (PHZ), it is stated that Kinsey's work has been successful and is being implemented in school curricula: "In *contrast to the rather hostile views on sexuality that prevailed in the first half of the twentieth century, most views on sexual development in the course of life are now based on scientific knowledge and take a favourable view of sexuality. They recognise that children and adolescents are sexual beings (...) From childhood, human beings are sexual beings with age-specific needs and individual forms of expression. Thus, for example, infants experience pleasure for the first time through sucking and suckling. Sexual curiosity and experimentation do not appear at puberty but exist from childhood onwards, in boys and girls, in different forms depending on age (...).One of the important tasks of the school is to provide all children and young people with this opportunity to learn about sexuality, gender roles and gender relations by explaining the social changes or common sense in society, so that they can access the values and norms of our society (...) The school complements the educational tasks of parents or carers in the area of sex education. It has an important role in transmitting social norms and values.*"

Sex education is not a problem in itself, but it is the age at which it is compulsory in a school environment that is a real problem. The general craze for sex education for children is to start it at kindergarten level. This official Swiss booklet intended to establish the basis for sex education in schools contains a table with a list of the stages of psycho-sexual development of children. It is noted that four-year-olds have *"orgasm-like reactions"*, *"pleasure in exposure and genital play"* and *"erotic interest in parents"*. The document states that a 5-year-old child practices *"role-playing like playing at having sex."*

This is what the booklet says about the sex educators who are responsible for 'training' children in schools: *"In the context of the empowerment of pupils, the transmission of sexual and reproductive health and rights topics or knowledge of regional psychosocial offers is of primary importance. The relevant skills are passed on by these specialists in the context of sexuality education in a valuable and sustainable way. They have a sound scientific background, up-to-date technical knowledge, sex education materials and proven didactic concepts in age-appropriate work with young people and adolescents."*

These sex educators would therefore have a *"solid scientific training (valuable and lasting)"*, based on the work of figures like Alfred Kinsey. This is a whole programme that aims to make marginal and criminal behaviour accepted as a norm, thus continuing the sexual revolution underway, the continuation of which is the *gender* theory. Gender theory consists of inculcating in very young children (and older ones) that they are neither boys nor girls but that it is up to them to decide their sex... All this in the name of *equality* and *freedom*, concepts dear to the Masonic lodges which are very active in the field of national education... In fact, the "specialised educators" in the field of sex education (often coming from LGBT associations - Lesbian, Gay, Bi, Trans -) are only the final link in the chain. These programmes are organised in the rectorates and ministries, which apply decisions taken upstream in the Masonic lodges that completely control the republican state.

Daniel Keller, Grand Master of the Grand Orient de France, told a Senate committee in March 2015: "Thank you for your invitation and for reminding me that I preside over an obedience with over 50,000 members. As you probably know, the Grand Orient de France includes in its ranks a large number of actors in the world of education, whether it be teachers or all those involved in extracurricular activities, from primary school to university. We consider that public schools are the pillar and crucible of the Republic." Basic rule: conditioning towards a certain ideology must start in early childhood...

c/ Hyper-sexualisation

There is also a phenomenon that is increasingly developing, which is the hyper-sexualisation of children and adolescents. *Early sexualisation* aims to 'educate' them from a very young age about sexuality, while *hyper-sexualisation* aims to make them physically desirable, to '*adultify*' them in a way.

Sylvie Richard Bessette (professor of sexology at the University of Quebec in Montreal) defines hyper-sexualisation as: "*Excessive use of body-centred strategies in order to seduce*". The problem is that today in some environments children are subjected to these practices, especially in the "Mini-Miss" competitions where little girls are dressed and made up to look like "miniature women". They adopt seduction codes that are not in keeping with their age (wiggling, winking, etc.). The little girls thus become objects of desire in spite of themselves.

Psychoanalyst Monique de Kermadec writes about the Mini-Miss competitions: "Their image is overly eroticized with young women's outfits. This can lead to self-image problems during adolescence and sometimes to eating disorders such as anorexia. And this damage is even greater when the child puts herself in a situation of seduction in front of the public. Naughty smiles and other teasing winks sexualise the behaviour in an abnormal way."[617]

Globally, hyper-sexualisation permeates the whole of society, notably through the entertainment industry which puts on stage starlets who are ever more naked, doing ever more sexually explicit dances, even pornographic (Miley Cyrus, Beyoncé, etc., MK dolls intended precisely to transmit this hyper-

---

[617] "*A pressure too heavy to bear*" - actu-match / www.parismatch.com, 14/01/2009.

sexualisation to young people). The clips and stage performances are viewed by millions of little girls whose subconscious is impregnated with all these things. One of the great trends of our decadent society is hyper-sexualisation.

In the Canadian documentary "Sexy inc, nos enfants sous influence" (2007), the sexologist Francine Duquet states: "We have really seen a break in the last five or six years where we are bombarded with more sexual messages. Children receive this as if it were normal. Also, when it comes to children or teenagers in particular, they are at an age where they want to fit the norm. They want to be like their idols, they want to be popular and the idea of popularity is a major concept in adolescence. Nowadays, being popular means being hot. You have to have some kind of sexual energy, you have to give off something sexual. But at the age of 11 or even 14, it's far from obvious... So we see mimicry: I dress the same, I do the same... There's also this whole fashion phenomenon, except for fashion at the moment for children, which is worrying on certain levels because clothes are eroticized, especially for little girls."

Social engineering programmes are particularly focused on the society of tomorrow: that is, the control of the consciousness (and especially the subconscious) of today's children and adolescents. We clearly see this propaganda for hyper-sexualisation when the media constantly encourage children to become little women or men, especially in advertisements of the fashion or cosmetics industry. A typical example is little Thylane Lena-Rose Blondeau (daughter of TV host Véronika Loubry and footballer Patrick Blondeau) who posed in 2011, at the age of 10, for *Vogue* magazine. Shocking pictures that have become a typical example of the hyper-sexualisation of a child.

There are now sexy thong-like clothes in girl's sizes, which have no breasts, but which are also offered bras. There are even *heeled slippers* for babies... A new market has opened up, and the pedophiles are enjoying it...

d/ Pro-pedophilia propaganda

In parallel with early sex education and the hyper-sexualisation of our children, there is a pro-pedophile propaganda whose aim is to progressively infuse a certain trivialisation and tolerance of these criminal activities in our society. Today paedocriminals have their international days: *International Love Boy Day* for "boy lovers" and *Alice Day* for "girl lovers".

Created in 1998, these international days have their own logos and slogans, distinctive signs and a particular vocabulary that form a real 'paedophile culture', putting forward 'scientific' works such as those of Alfred Kinsey to justify their serious deviances. They also have their own forums for exchange on the Internet, which can be very moderate in what they say, while some are much more virulent, particularly on the *dark web*.

Paedophile propaganda also appears in magazines (e.g. *Lolita*) and certain newspapers, in particular the daily newspaper *Libération*, which on 10 April 1979 published a plea by Gabriel Matzneff and Tony Duvert in favour of '*minority love affairs*'. This same newspaper published a petition in the 1970s asking Parliament to repeal articles of the law relating to sexual majority and the decriminalisation of sexual relations between an adult and a minor under 15 years of age. This petition was signed by many well-known personalities of the time such as Jack Lang, Simone de Beauvoir, Louis Aragon, Bernard Kouchner, André Glucksmann, etc.

In 1979, *Libération* even offered a full column to the paedocriminal Jacques Dugé to defend sodomy on children. The column entitled *"Jacques Dugé s'explique"* was an open letter to the examining magistrate in charge of studying this serious case, Dugé was indeed prosecuted for prostitution and sexual abuse of minors. This is what the paedocriminal wrote at the time in a famous national daily newspaper: '*A child who loves an adult knows very well that he cannot yet give, so he understands and accepts very well to receive. It is an act of love. It is one of his ways of loving and proving it. This was the behaviour with me of the few boys I sodomised. And then let's tell it like it is. He likes to feel in his body the virile member of the one he loves, to be united to him, by the flesh. This gives great satisfaction. He also has the satisfaction of being pleasured by the one who sodomises him, who comes inside him. This also gives him great joy, because to love is to give as well as to receive. This may be hard to admit for lay people, but it is the reality.* " - Libération, 25,26/01/1979.

It was during the 1970s that this paedophile propaganda was most virulent, taking advantage of the sexual revolution then underway (initiated by Alfred Kinsey). In May 1977, one could still read in *Libération:*

Birth of the "Pedophile Liberation Front".

A new group has just been created: FLIP, whose constitutive platform you can read below. Who are they? For the most part, readers of Libération who, following an open letter to paedophiles in our edition of 9/2/77, sent us an abundance of mail - we reported some of it in a double-page spread on 24 March 77 entitled: Adult-Child Relations. On April 2, 1977, a first meeting was held at Jussieu with about thirty people. It was a simple contact meeting. It is regrettable that the main concerns were of a judicial nature. Indeed, it was only a question of repression, defence and prosecution of paedophiles. Without ignoring these harsh realities, such a group has everything to gain if it broadens its field of reflection. The FLIP (Front de libération des Pédophiles) was born. Some essential objectives have already been launched:

- Fighting criminal injustice and critically reflecting on the family and school, based on a political analysis of sexuality between minors and adults.

- To join the struggle of children who want to change their way of life and of any political group that aims at the establishment of a radically new society where pederasty will exist freely.

- Develop a pederastic culture that expresses itself in a new way of life, and the emergence of a new art.

- To speak out in media outlets that give it the means and through the channels that are appropriate.

- Show solidarity with imprisoned paedophiles or victims of official psychiatry.

The "bourgeois tyranny" turns the child lover into a legendary monster who crushes thatched cottages. Together we will break monsters and thatched cottages.

There are many associations that campaign by bringing the word of paedocriminals into the public arena. Their strategy is to minimise the impact of paedophile acts on children, to relativise the notion of minors and sexual minority in order to lower the legal age and finally to trivialise paedophile statements. Two of the largest associations of this type are *NAMBLA* (*North American Man/Boy Love Association*) and *Martijn*, a Dutch association for the acceptance of sexual relations between adults and children founded in Hoogeveen in 1982. An attempt was made to dissolve the latter in 2012, as the court found that the association, which has a website, offered a *"digital and social network for sexual offenders.* The appeal court then declared that the texts and images published on the association's website were legal because they never directly called for sex with children. The association was nevertheless contrary to certain principles of Dutch law because it *'trivialised the dangers of sexual contact with young children, spoke positively of such contact, and even glorified it'*. In 2014, the Netherlands finally decided to ban the activities of the *Martijn* association for good. *"The Supreme Court (Hoge Raad), the highest judicial body in the kingdom, found that the integrity of the child was more important than the principle of freedom of expression.*"[618]

The main aim of paedophile propaganda is to minimise the consequences of these acts on children. The associations therefore use 'scientific' works such as the report by Robert Bauserman on the effects of child sexual abuse. Indeed, this report considers that "sexual relations" with children are not systematically harmful to them. Bauserman has been singled out as an activist who uses science inappropriately in an attempt to legitimise his views and tendencies.

Little by little, paedophiles are gaining ground, while children's rights are being steadily eroded. The ultimate goal is to whitewash the perpetrators and deny the children's status as victims, eventually classifying incest and paedocriminality as a simple *"sexual orientation"* just like heterosexuality or homosexuality. This is what is programmed for tomorrow's society...

To conclude this chapter, let's go back to the programme *"Ce soir ou jamais"* on France 3, broadcast on 31 May 2011, with a press review which revisited the accusations made by the politician Luc Ferry concerning a former paedophile minister who had been *"poached in Marrakech"*, according to his terms... During this programme, the famous lawyer Thierry Lévy revealed himself live during a stormy and shameful exchange with the Italian filmmaker Cristina Comencini:

- Thierry Lévy: I am talking about tolerance in general. Tolerance is something that at the moment is totally disappearing. And you speak of recent events as if they had liberated a situation that was blocked until then. But sex tourism has been repressed for over twenty years, very severely, very harshly,

---

[618] "Children's rights or freedom of expression, the Netherlands has chosen" - Jean-Pierre Stroobants, lemonde.fr, 19/04/2014.

ruthlessly. (...) You talk to us about the beauty of the world and the beauty of sex, but in concrete terms, in action, what are you doing, what are you doing if not constantly brandishing the stick, the stick of morality. But yes, what do you do?

- Cristina Comencini: On children?! Children... the beauty of sex on children?! I thought that the debate was very backward in Italy but I realise that in France it is much more ...

- TL: (interrupting her interlocutor)... Please! Sex with children... This is a subject that can no longer be discussed today. No one dares to talk about children's sexuality anymore (...) There is a kind of leaden blanket that falls from the blonde curls (editor's note: referring to her interlocutor) over the whole of society, which prohibits all behaviour that is a little different, a little abnormal....

- CC: A bit different !!?

- TL: But of course, and then we come back to paedophilia every time. Paedophilia is now a totally forbidden subject, you can't say a word about it without being demonised.

- CC: Why not talk about it? On the contrary, I think we should talk about it...

- TL: Really?!...

- CC: Yes I think so...

- TL: And how do you talk about it then?

- CC: Without saying that it is.......

- TL: (cutting him off again) Saying what, saying what? That all those who are attracted to children are criminals? That they should be put in prison for ever?

- CC: You have a system of speaking that is very authoritarian and does not allow the other person the freedom to express themselves......

CONCLUSION

Acquire truth, wisdom, instruction and discernment, and do not forsake them - Proverbs 23:23

Only small secrets need to be protected. The greatest secrets remain protected by public disbelief - Marshall McLuhan

Man is fire to lies but ice to truth - Jean de La Fontaine

Silence becomes a sin when it takes the place of protest and makes a man a coward - Abraham Lincoln

T
he subject of trauma-based mind control has at its core the physical and psychological abuse of children. The Child is at the heart of the eye of the storm that feeds on it, it is the Pandora's box that is currently ravaging our society... Purity and innocence incarnate in the crosshairs of the sorcerer-controllers.

From time to time a paedophile case is thrown into the public eye, usually the dismantling of a cyber network, but all this is the tree that hides the forest...

Why is it that in France, the judicial system seems to systematically protect child rapists to the detriment of child protectors who denounce them? Why is it that as soon as there is a case of paedocriminality, the judicial steamroller is set in motion to crush not only the case but also the people? Why was France called to order in a 2003 UN report? An investigation that was carried out in France by the rapporteur Juan Miguel Petit and that was presented to the 59th session of the UN Commission on Human Rights. This official report called for *an urgent investigation by an independent body into the shortcomings of the justice system with regard to child victims of sexual abuse and those who try to protect them (...) Given the number of cases that indicate a serious denial of justice for child victims of sexual abuse and those who try to protect them, it would be appropriate for an independent body, preferably the National Consultative Commission on Human Rights, to urgently investigate the current situation.*

For example, on page 14 of the report, it is noted that: "The Special Rapporteur has referred to the enormous difficulties faced by individuals, particularly mothers, who file complaints against those they suspect of abusing their children in the knowledge that they may face action for false accusations, which in some cases may lead to the loss of custody of their child(ren). Some of these mothers use legal remedies until they can no longer afford the costs of legal assistance, at which point they are left with the choice of continuing to hand over the child to the person they believe is abusing them, or seeking refuge with the child abroad. It would even appear that some judges and lawyers, aware of the weaknesses of the judicial system, have informally advised some parents to do so. These parents expose themselves to criminal prosecution for such actions in France and, often, in the country to which they travel."

Indeed, like the two examples given in the French testimonies in Chapter 4, many mothers have literally had to flee France for lack of real protection from the institutional paedocriminal network. Why are so many mothers harassed and persecuted, even locked up in psychiatric hospitals, for having naturally denounced the rape of their children? Why does a file as serious as that of the Zandvoort files[619] remain in the files of the Ministry of *Justice*, without any investigation having been launched? Why were some thirty key witnesses found dead in the Dutroux case?[620] This famous Belgian case is a textbook case for understanding how a case is suppressed when it starts to go back to the *'big fish'* of the Network... Why is everything orchestrated to methodically make children look like liars? Why is everything done to systematically discredit the word of adult survivors, for example by using the *"false memory syndrome"* or by relying on their psychological disorders to nullify their word? Why is the field of psychotraumatology so neglected by so-called public health institutions? Why are the consequences of deep trauma, i.e. dissociation and traumatic amnesia, generally hidden and avoided in the public debate?

The *consumption* and *modelling* of children would seem to be the preserve of a certain unsuspecting elite, but it is also a well-oiled institutional machine that allows them to practice their vice in complete peace of mind; until when?

The UN report cited above, which called for urgent action on the French situation, also tells us that *in several cases communicated to the Special Rapporteur, it was reported that the individuals accused of committing abuses were closely linked to members of the judiciary or to individuals holding high positions in the public administration, who were in a position to influence the outcome of the proceedings to their detriment, an argument that was also made by the National Division for the Repression of Offences against Persons and Property* .... But according to the political, journalistic, police and judicial authorities, there is no paedophile network in France, move along! ... Shouldn't we rather say that it is in *"good hands"*? ...

In Karl Zéro's documentary "Le fichier de la honte" (13ème Rue - 2010), we see the UN rapporteur Juan Miguel Petit declare: "There have been complaints and specific denunciations from mothers who say they are being pursued by groups, which can be likened to mafias or lodges, organising child pornography."

---

[619] See *"Les réseaux de l'horreur"* - Stan Maillaud, Janet Seeman, Marcel Vervloesem and *"Le livre de la honte"* - Laurence Beneux and Serge Garde, 2001.

[620] *30 dead witnesses..."* - Douglas De Coninck, 2004.

The silence of the French *mainstream* media on all these issues is disturbing! Many journalists - often paid by taxpayers - who are supposed to inform us about the reality of our society, now seem to be fully participating in a social engineering programme aimed at keeping people in a certain reality comparable to a matrix.

In April 2005, François Léotard (former Minister of Defence) told journalists opposite him on a major French radio station: *"I think that you and your colleagues, if I may say so, underestimate a part of the news that is completely under the radar, completely unknown to the media. You currently have 35 to 40,000 people in France who disappear every year... who disappear! It's quite fascinating and nobody looks into these thousands of disappearances. There are suicides that are fake suicides, car accidents that are assassinations, there are people who leave and are not found because they wanted to change their identity... What I mean is that there is an occult, hidden, underground, submarine world, that basically nobody tries to discover."*[621]

When François Léotard speaks of *"people who leave and are not found because they wanted to change their identity"*, we can probably include in this category all the mothers who fled France to protect their children from institutional paedocriminal persecution. As Juan Miguel Petit well noted in his report for the UN.

On 2 March 2009, Rachida Dati (then Minister of Justice) gave a press conference on the occasion of *'Children's Day'*. When Aude Chaney, the representative of the *Estelle Mouzin* association, *asked the* minister: *"How many unexplained disappearances, such as the case of Estelle Mouzin, are there in France?* Rachida Dati seemed unable to give a clear answer to this simple and precise question. She then turned to her advisers, but no one was able to give an exact figure to this obviously very embarrassing question. A palpable embarrassment settled over the room full of journalists and victims' families. It is astonishing that in a country like France the number of children who disappear every year is ignored... or not made public because it is too high?

On this disturbing issue, journalist Serge Garde says: "France is a country full of statistics, where we know, for example, how many salmon swim up the Loire every year, but we don't know how many children disappear."[622]

In 2001, Serge Garde had already asked a parliamentarian to ask the same question to the then Minister of Justice, Marylise Lebranchu, and she had replied in an embarrassed manner: *"I can't give you figures, because... it's impossible."*[623]

On 20 November 2001, Marylise Lebranchu declared before the National Assembly that 800 children had disappeared in France in 2000, while confirming that there are no figures for the disappearance of minors.

---

[621] "Les Grandes Gueules" - RMC, 7/04/2005.

[622] *"Les faits Karl Zéro"* - 13ème Rue, 22/05/2009.

[623] "Disappeared: what happened to them? " - Karl Zéro, 2014.

The number of disappearances must be much higher if we take into account foreign children who disappear or those who are undeclared at birth (particularly in networks). Out of 1000 foreign children (in 2001) who arrive without papers in France, only 200 remain under social control. The other 800 disappear into thin air.[624]

In the France 3 documentary *"Viols d'enfants: la fin du silence? "*, a girl stated that she had witnessed sacrifices of *"little children who were a bit Arab or things like that"*. In her testimony on TF1 in 2001, the survivor Véronique Liaigre stated: *"The children who are sacrificed are not declared, or are foreign children. In particular, when I was in Agen, they were little Africans, they were black. In Jallais I also saw some, in Nanterre too, but they were white children, French children, but they were children born of rape. Children born of rape? Yes, which had not been declared. They were given birth in the parents' home in abominable conditions. So, insofar as they were not declared, they were sacrificed? That's it..."*

Trauma-based programming is like a train wreck that loops around, like a virus or a vampire bite that transmits abomination from generation to generation. Slaves are programmed to become abusers themselves, but also programmers. Not everyone who is sexually and psychologically abused will automatically reproduce the abuse, but this human function of self-treatment through anaesthetic and dissociative behaviours such as violence against others is exploited to the extreme by some groups to perpetuate the abomination from generation to generation. Violence is a drug, literally, it creates an extreme stress that makes the person switch off by a sudden production of hormones like endogenous morphine, in order to anaesthetise the negative charge of his own traumatic memory. But these dissociative behaviours also recharge this traumatic memory, making it ever more explosive. These dissociative behaviours therefore become more and more necessary to the perpetrators and this creates a real vicious circle, an addiction to violence, destruction and even self-destruction. These people, who can be qualified as psychopaths whose empathy has been reduced to nothing since early childhood, do not consider the pain of others except when it gives them pleasure...

Does this make all perpetrators sick and irresponsible victims who repeat destructive patterns without any possibility of making another choice? A choice is always possible despite the enormous difficulties (psychological, family, network pressure). This is a delicate issue, but the day we really have to deal with it, we will have taken a huge step. It will mean that the criminals will be identified and put out of action. It will also mean that the Network is dismantled and that this infernal train of violence is finally stopped. So yes, we may wonder

---

[624] "Marylise Lebranchu reveals a frightening figure 800 children disappeared in 2000" - Serge Garde, l'Humanité, 14/12/2001

about the fate of all these people, but the final judgment will certainly not come from the justice of men.

It would be interesting to brain scan some of our 'elites' to see the state of their amygdala complex and hippocampus, brain structures that can actually prove with our scientific tools that there has been deep trauma in the person. Studies have found that these brain structures have a significantly smaller volume in people who have experienced severe trauma, including those with dissociative identity disorder. This neurological knowledge about the variation in hippocampal and amygdala volumes in relation to severe trauma could, for example, be used to validate testimonies of victims who claim to have suffered the worst atrocities but are unable to provide a coherent narrative.

As we have seen, the judicial system systematically discredits any disturbing testimony relating to ritual abuse, by putting forward the "disturbed" mental state of the witness, therefore "unreliable" and consequently carrying no weight in the scales of our *justice*... However, a cerebral MRI could prove and certify that there has indeed been a serious traumatic impact on this person, hence the fact that she is in a state that prevents her from explaining her experience clearly and chronologically. Following such a medical examination validating the fact that there was indeed deep trauma leading to severe dissociative disorders, the person's statements should therefore be studied more closely in order to conduct a serious investigation. Instead, the *justice* system relies on pseudo-experts of "false memories" who are not trained in psychotraumatology: the case is thus quickly closed...

It's a complicated question, but the fact is that the Network is trying to withhold information about scientific advances in psychotraumatology and all the recent neurological studies related to the impact that trauma can have on the human brain. This is so that this information cannot be put forward in an official way in criminal courts to defend victims effectively. Indeed, if medical universities do not train (or train very little) students on all the recent discoveries in psychotraumatology and dissociative processes, it becomes very difficult for a lawyer to put someone on the stand who can explain these things clearly and scientifically... When it comes to asking the *courts* to order brain scans to prove that there has been serious trauma, it is all the locked institutions that are standing in the way. Indeed, it is clear that MRIs of the lower voices and anuscopy, which would be essential examinations in paedocriminal cases, are very rarely carried out... so a brain MRI is unthinkable...

The whole issue of recognising victims would above all make it possible to take care of them in an effective way by providing them with appropriate therapies.

The phenomenon of dissociation in children, deliberately exploited by certain groups, is an occult knowledge, the cornerstone of secrecy and power, whether in the political, military, religious or mafia spheres. Initiates are well aware of the importance that these altered states of consciousness can have for the mental control of an individual. MK programming is therefore not simply about creating a sex slave, a *super starlet* or an assassin, it is above all an essential tool for global political control.

Fritz Springmeier describes the extent of this scourge in our modern world, a statement which at first sight seems alarming but which in the end turns out to be rather enlightening for understanding some of the workings (and blockages) of our modern society: *"Mind control is about infiltrating and controlling society from behind the scenes. You have to integrate that if you want to control an institution like the medical lobby for example. You have to put safe people in key positions because a weak link in the chain will always break. You can't afford to have weak links. If you want to control a very powerful lobby like the medical system, then you have to control a very wide spectrum of things like the hospital system, the medical schools, the medical association, etc. All this requires MK slaves at all levels of the system, at all strategic points. You can't have weak links. For example, a network of independent doctors practising alternative medicine; then you need to control the judicial system to be able to convict these "out of the box" doctors. You have to set up a vast hidden apparatus. If you don't understand the ins and outs of mental programming, you can't understand how you can have this kind of overall control over society."*[625]

As already quoted in the foreword, the famous hacker Kevin Mitnick said: *"The weak link in any security system is the human factor.* In order to secure a system of global domination, it is therefore imperative to *hack* the minds of the human pawns in strategic positions behind the democratic facades.

We can recall here the statements of Dr. Catherine Gould in 1994 in the documentary "In Satan's Name". We can recall here the statements of Dr. Catherine Gould in 1994 in the documentary "In Satan's Name": "There are certainly bankers, psychologists, media people, we have also heard from child protection services but also from police officers... because they have an interest in being present in all these socio-professional circles... When I started this work, I thought that the motivations behind paedophilia were limited to sex and money, but I started to realise in the course of my ten years of research that the motivations are much more sinister... Children are abused for indoctrination purposes. Ritual abuse of children is a protocol for formatting humans for a cult. It's about formatting children who have been so abused, so mind-controlled that they become very useful to the cult, at all levels... I think the purpose of this is to get maximum control, whether it's in this country or in another."

Dr. Lawrence Pazder also speaks of systematic infiltration: "They look normal and live a normal life at first glance. They are present in all strata of society, which they have carefully infiltrated. Any position of power or influence on society must be considered for them as a target for infiltration. The executioners have money available, many have impeccable positions: doctors, ministers, professions of all kinds."

In order to establish such an infiltration of institutions and various organisations, Freemasonry - most of whose members are unaware of the activity of the high degree back lodges - plays an essential role which is no longer in question today. The Masonic network practices a systematic subversion of traditional Christian values in favour of *illuminist* and *humanist* values replacing

---

[625] Interview with Fritz Springmeier by Wayne Morris - *"Survivors of the Illuminati"*, 1998.

God by Man; in other words, it is the Luciferian doctrine, counter-revelation, or counter-initiation, applied by High Masonry, but also by other initiatory secret societies of the pyramid type forming the whole of the Great Babylon: "the religion without a name".

This Luciferian doctrine corresponds to the four lies that led to original sin, aiming to apply them and anchor them in modern society. In the Garden of Eden, the serpent made four promises to Adam and Eve if they tasted the forbidden fruit:

- _Your eyes will be opened"_: you have been kept in a kind of intellectual blindness so that you cannot see the mysteries of God. Satan says he can open their eyes to all these occult things. The Gnostics seek this: to _open their eyes_ to discover what secrets God has hidden from men.

- _You shall not die"_: This is the transition from creature to creator. If the creature becomes eternal, then it becomes God.

- _You will become like gods"_: The creature and the Creator are also put on the same level. All these ideas are linked to Gnosis and to the Masonic doctrine. Gnosis is reflected today in the _new age_ movement, the new age, which advocates the deification of the human being who becomes a so-called creator, a divine being: _"we are gods"_.

- _You shall decide what is good and what is evil'_: Here again the creature puts himself in the place of God and we see the sad consequences in our modern society.

The 'famous' forbidden fruit thus seems to be linked to occult knowledge that promises man access to certain dimensions, to certain powers, while developing certain powers. This is partly what is contained in this book. We see that these four promises of Satan correspond to what the Luciferian secret societies have been working hard to apply in this world for several centuries, in order to sweep away the Creator and put his human creature at the centre of all things with the promise of deifying him. The global Luciferian network is thus working to establish its dominance to infuse its philosophy and spiritual belief throughout humanity.

Today, we see this doctrine coming to the fore, going hand in hand with the programmed degeneration of our civilisation, following a kind of apocalyptic messianism. Luciferism is symbolically represented by two mythical figures: Prometheus or Lucifer, who is considered by some circles as the benefactor of humanity, the "civilising" god who brings light (divine knowledge) to ignorant humans. Lucifer, the bearer of light, would thus give humans the possibility of becoming a god themselves, by their own means. This malignant and deceptive doctrine is gradually permeating the modern world so that the profane adopt these concepts of fallen life and thought against their will. The rebellion that was waged in Heaven by the rebellious angels continues on earth, and everything is done to ensure that it drags as many humans as possible down with it. Lucifer wanted to be his own god and so he drags human creatures into his rebellious dynamic by promising man to attain the status of a god himself.

Luciferians, Satanists, Neo-Gnostics, Kabbalists, Martinists, Theosophists of all stripes, all have this belief that they must evolve spiritually in order to gain power and eventually immortality to become gods themselves. But this requires certain sources of 'power', a rallying to the Fallen Angel to receive 'light'. Blood rituals (red magic), black magic, demonology, ritual child abuse and sex magic are tools to access this power and these openings to other dimensions to receive *enlightenment...* The most hardened occultists, thirsty for power, will fall into these totally perverse and demonic practices, all the more so if they are promised to become a creator god in the process. Satanic ritual abuse protocols are directly linked to sex magic and dissociative trances, two powerful catalysts for gaining power and access to other dimensions in the quest for immortality. Children subjected to torture and rape, totally dissociated and open to other dimensions, are exploited as bridges between two worlds and as a reservoir of demonic power. They serve as mediums, intermediaries that the sorcerer-abductor will use with sexual magic to exploit to the maximum this spiritual breach represented by the child in a state of dissociation. It is a real spiritual robbery, a physical, energetic and spiritual rape.

MK programming based on the *splitting of the soul* perfectly symbolises the culmination of Luciferian man's quest to become a creative god himself. By practising these horrors, he creates human dolls, empty shells, golem that he can fill and program according to his own desires. He manipulates the inner world of the slave as he wishes, just like a little god manipulating a robotic human, by playing in this other dimension that is the space-time of the inner universe of his victim. A universe that he arranges as he sees fit. The creation of a golem is the ultimate goal of Luciferian occultists, Kabbalists and Satanists of all kinds. Lucifer is not a true creator, he is not the creator of Heaven or Earth, which is why he takes pleasure in creating in his victims an inner world with a heaven, an earth and a hell of his own creation. He will arrange this world in his own way with an army of demonic entities that will cooperate with the programmer to control the victim. Thus a sort of satanic trinity is set up: *the Father* (the programmer), *the Son* (the child "Monarch") and *the Holy Spirit* (the demons). A dark trinity that will form the ultimate offence to God: the sabotage, misappropriation and exploitation of his beloved creature, the human being. The sabotage of man's consciousness to turn him away from God is applied today as much on MK slaves in the harshest way as on humanity as a whole in a more diffuse but equally abject way.

Without the tools of mind control based on dissociative identity disorder, drugs, hypnosis, psychotronics, etc., these occult organisations would fail in their plan of domination because they would not be able to keep their dastardly deeds secret on such a large scale. The witch-doctors have understood that this method of mind control using trauma and dissociation is also applicable on a societal scale and that it is something that is necessary to be able to rule 'easily and quietly'. This is what William Sargant tells us when he writes that *the methods of religious initiations are often so similar to modern political techniques of brainwashing and thought control that one sheds light on the mechanisms of the other.*

Ordo ab Chao", order is born out of chaos, is the motto of Freemasonry but it is also the heart of alchemical secrets. This formula can be used to achieve perfection on both the good and the evil side. For most Freemasons, it is above all a notion of personal development, a work consisting of defeating the *inner monster that* sows chaos, the dark forces of the mind and the ego, which must be fought and transcended in order to regain the Divine Order. In alchemy, the two most important operations are *"Dissolve"* (chaos) and *"Coagulate"* (ordo). *Dissolution* means the decomposition of the elements, then comes *Coagulation*, which consists in solidifying the dissolved element in a new state, a new order. We see today that this Masonic formula *Ordo ab Chao*, this alchemical work of decomposition and recomposition, is conscientiously applied in mind control programmes, whether on an individual or collective scale. Currently, *Ordo ab Chao* is not applied in a dynamic of spiritual upliftment, but in a dynamic of total control (although this situation paradoxically serves to create spiritual upliftment of the few).

The mental control of the masses is achieved by triggering a "dissociation" (social chaos) where the individual no longer identifies with himself, but becomes society itself (e.g. the *"Je suis Charlie"* or *"Je suis Paris"* movements following acts of terrorism). This social dissociation is caused by a whole series of destabilisations of society creating the ideal conditions to establish a new order, a new societal structure. This is the *"tabula rasa"* theory of Kurt Lewin, Eric Trist and many others...

The brainwashing of an individual goes through the erasure, the dissolution of his original personality in order to install a new internal system, it is the same for the people: destroy their roots, their values, their traditions, their beliefs, their family, even their notion of man or woman (*gender* theory), all this in order to obtain a totally dissociated/disconnected mass, without reference points, infantilised and malleable at will. The aim is to easily build a *New World Order*. The motto of creating *chaos* in order to establish a new *order* is applied, as we saw in Chapter 7, to MK-Monarch subjects who will inevitably need the programmer to be able to function again following the psychic chaos voluntarily created in them by the traumas. This formula, like a fractal, we find on a large scale in the current societal chaos: in order to be able to function again following the chaos that is inevitably taking shape, society (in a generalised post-traumatic stress) will need the sorcerer-controllers (the large-scale programmers) in order to re-establish itself and to function again in a *New World Order*, with a luciferian world religion. This is the project underway, and as we have seen the codes of this Luciferian subculture are gradually permeating the secular popular masses psychologically channelled into this *New World Order*. A new order in which traditional peoples and cultures (*the old world*) will be totally dissolved... This is the "Babylonian work", a worldwide mental programming with transhumanism at its core. Transhumanism advocates the use of science and technology to improve the physical and mental characteristics of human beings, even going so far as to consider old age as a disease... This is a continuation of the project aimed at the *"Luciferic deification of man"*... But *science without conscience is the ruin of the soul* (François Rabelais).

In 1736, Andrew Michael Ramsey gave a famous speech, known as *"Ramsey's Speech"*, to the St Thomas Lodge in Paris. This address clearly revealed the Babylonian spirit of the Masonic Order, which is working to *unite the subjects of all nations into a single brotherhood so as to create a new people whose cohesion will be cemented by the bonds of Virtue and Science.* This is taking place before our very eyes, and it is something that is more visible and comprehensible today than ever before, despite the chaos that masks the real spiritual issues. We are born and bathed in this matrix to such an extent that we do not even discern the ins and outs of it. So there is a real battle between two standards, *"the battle of the earthly city against the heavenly city"*, between Babylon, the city of Satan, and Jerusalem, the city of Jesus Christ, the world of sin against the world of grace. It goes without saying that a choice has to be made in this situation.

Professor Jean-Claude Lozac'hmeur writes about this *New World Order*:

The writings of the most representative theoreticians of these occultist traditions (Thomas More, Francis Bacon, Comenius, Guillaume Postel, Campanella) as well as contemporary history, allow us to specify the contours of this future totalitarian state.

From this data we know:

- that this civilisation (originally intended to be purely collectivist) will in all likelihood be a synthesis of capitalism and socialism,
- that it will spread to the whole world,
- Although seemingly democratic, it will be headed by a despot who is both 'king' and 'priest', surrounded by a privileged nomenklatura,
- that in this rationalised universe the family and marriage will have disappeared,
- that eugenics and euthanasia will be practiced,
- that the political and economic unification will be complemented by the unification of religions, replaced by a single cult, that of the "natural religion" known as "Noah's".[626]

The creation of strategically placed programmed MK pawns in our society is the prerequisite for the application of global mind control strategies to manipulate and dominate the mass. Today, more and more people are realising that our society is *walking on its head*, that our leaders are displaying ever more gross and blatant illogic (or inhuman and destructive logic) despite the media embellishment. The word *"psychopath"* to describe our rulers is becoming more and more common in the mouths of the people. There are certainly severe mental pathologies among our elites and their childhood is probably a factor. These severe psychiatric disorders are camouflaged behind a personality that has been worked on in the dark backstage and sanitised under the spotlight of the great political-media theatre. In his book *'Dialogues with Forgotten Voices: Relational Perspectives on Child Abuse Trauma and the Treatment of Severe Dissociative Disorders'*, Harvey Schwartz explains that addiction to power is the result of these occult subcultures: *'Those who have not been personally exposed to these extremes will be unable to fully understand the degenerative spiral of this power obsession. History has shown that when a person or group gains*

---

[626] "Les origines occultistes de la Franc-maçonnerie" - Jean Claude Lozac'hmeur, 2015, p.184.

power (Hitler, Idi Amin Dada, Pol Pot, Stalin, to name but a few), a pattern of extravagant sadism, irrational gratuitous cruelty and ultimately destructive exhibitionist violence leads to its explosion and collapse. History has yet to reveal that these same diabolical dynamics are at work outside the context of war and politics in the criminal groups that impose their power over children around the world in the form of unimaginable abuse."

During the ritual abuse, the children receive the transmission of *the "initiation"*, the "Initial Violence" which prepares them to become adults working for the "dark side". Since the Luciferian project is spread over several centuries, and therefore over several generations, the conditioning and even more so the mental programming of the children of the elite form an indispensable protocol. The programming of loyalty, fidelity and the law of silence is the foundation for controlling these children, who are destined to perpetuate the Luciferian globalist project. The aim is to achieve a society whose institutions and various layers of control are locked and held with an iron fist by individuals in the service of their inner demons... These children, dissociated and split up from an early age, have a "rewired" brain giving them certain intellectual and creative faculties, but also an energetic body that is totally open to the world of spirits, to conscious and unconscious mediumship. In luciferism, the dissociative process is seen as a state of spiritual enlightenment, allowing access to other dimensions.

These children are given *power, power* and *light*, they become channels used by fallen angels to embody and establish the Luciferian doctrine on this earth. Thus, little by little, a world has been set up that is indirectly governed by entities existing on another plane. Entities that need human beings well incarnated in flesh and blood to act here below in matter. In the same way that the Holy Spirit infuses itself into certain humans in a state of grace to inspire them with wisdom, intelligence, strength, charity, faith, hope... An anti-christian, counter-initiatic force can also infuse itself into humans, more particularly into those who have had their *doors wide open* since early childhood during their 'initiation' by extreme traumas. Some fragments of their souls are totally bound and enslaved to the fallen realm, to the "Prince of this world". This process is nothing less than a reversal of sanctification. These Luciferian bloodlines, *bound hand and foot to* demons for generations, represent the sub-human, resulting from this counter-initiation. Traumatic ritual abuse, sacrifice, magic, demonology, dissociation/possession/*'enlightenment'*, control of soul fragments, but also ceremonial sites with a particular telluric energy, all this occult knowledge is the tool that will enable connection with these fallen entities that offer this Luciferian human hierarchy the power to establish temporary dominion here on earth.

These lineages, holders of a particular blood inherited from an ancient "pact" with the fallen angels, recreate or deliberately awaken secret societies, schools, sects, through the intermediary of certain specially prepared individualities, who could be considered as a particular kind of "possessed" and charged with necessary powers, always of a psychic nature, of course, which allow them to provoke, for a certain period of time, more or less long but always limited, phenomena which constitute the "catalyst" element around which these groupings will be created. "Blood memory: counter-initiation, ancestor worship." - Alexandre de Dànann.

Freemasonry refers to mysterious *'Masters'*, foreign to humanity, who would inspire, through mediumship, certain high initiates connected to another dimension... This with the aim of receiving 'oracles', i.e. information allowing to act 'better' in the material world. As we have already seen, the Freemason Oswald Wirth was quite clear on this subject: *"The Masters - for this is how the initiates refer to them - wrap themselves in an impenetrable mystery; they remain invisible behind the thick curtain that separates us from the beyond... They work only on the drawing board, that is to say intellectually, by conceiving what must be built. These are the constructive intelligences of the World, effective powers for the Initiates who enter into relationship with the Unknown Superiors of the tradition."*[627] "The constructive intelligences of the world"... guiding the high Masonic lodges to set up the Luciferian New World Order. Today, this is very clear...

As we have seen, in a developing brain, repetitive extreme traumas that cause dissociation will shape the neural pathways and lead (under *"good guidance"*) to certain physical and intellectual abilities, but also to extraordinary psychic faculties. This violent *'spiritual unlocking'* opens the door to the spirit world. It is probable that in certain elitist circles, the fact of being *multiple*, of having a personality split into different alter, is seen as a spiritual mark of quality, an initiatory mark, *the* mark of *enlightenment* giving the access key to other dimensions. It is also the "trademark" of the Luciferian hierarchy known as the *"illuminati"*. It is probable that some initiates (or should we say *"traumatised"*) with multiple personalities can master their I.D.T. by changing alter personalities at will and according to their needs (see the case of Louise who totally mastered her switching from one personality to another - chapter 5). The deepest Alters, linked to occult sect activities, are perfectly aware of the internal system and can emerge when they want to, unlike the surface Alters who are totally unaware of the *"background"*.

But to what extent can one speak of superiority to the *ordinary* human, given that the 'initiatory' methods are nothing but pain, trauma and, finally, enslavement to demons and the Prince of this world? In the end, these infra-humans remain bound hand and foot to the entities on which their powers and might depend. This Luciferian slavery is perpetuated systematically on a chosen offspring to set up a *New World Order*. All this is accomplished in a state of mind of extreme superiority over the profane, *unenlightened* people, who are considered as cattle feeding "the beast"... to be corrupted and brought down at all costs...

One thing that is important to understand is that the children trapped and exploited by these cults fall into several categories. Firstly, there are the offspring of influential Luciferian families who systematically programme their offspring; secondly, there are children who are brought into these circles at a very young

---

[627] "Freemasonry made intelligible to its followers" Volume III - Oswald Wirth, 1986, p.219-130.

age and who are also destined to form the elite of tomorrow without having a blood link with the "Family". Finally, there are children who are literally used as fresh meat: children born of rape and not declared, kidnapped children or foreign children, all destined to be abused, tortured and finally sacrificed during the rituals. These children are used to 'initiate' the other children in the network, who are considered the 'chosen ones', into the ignoble practices of these groups.

Since the splitting of a human, i.e. the deliberate creation of a dissociative identity disorder, can only be done on very young children, it is clear that they automatically become priority targets for the perpetuation of counter-initiation and *enlightenment*. This is a large part of the explanation for the existence of *paedo-satanist* networks. Networks in which members involve their own children in the 'initiation' process, while also involving 'second-class' children, who can serve as both fresh meat and future MK slaves for the dirty work. As stated at the beginning of the conclusion: the Child is at the heart of this devastating cyclone...

It is high time to unmask this infernal chain so that the people know what is going on behind the scenes in this world. These files are systematically suppressed so as not to open the slightest breach in the greatest secrecy of domination. Potentially everything can come to a halt, so it goes without saying that in this great theatre, each and every one must do his or her part, with Providence perhaps only waiting for the right moment to intervene.

Despite the chaos and the constant smoke screens that try by all means to blind us, it is much easier today to get a global view of the world we live in than it was 50 years ago or even 20 years ago. Globalism, despite all its negative consequences, has the merit of giving us the opportunity to fully understand the world we live in.

As the Luciferian agenda of the *New World Order* advances, it is inevitably and inevitably revealed in an exponential manner. The hijacking, corruption and indoctrination of consciences is thus strengthened in proportion to the ever more flagrant unveiling. It is a snowball effect that paradoxically combines total revelation with ever greater obscurantism, the whole forming a kind of *chaos* of which the human mind is fortunately still capable of discerning the ins and outs... if it makes the effort.

The *light of* this 'nameless religion' is now so radiant in our world that it is finally being fully exposed for what it really is. The word *Revelation*, describing the times we live in, comes from the Greek word *Apokalupsis* meaning revelation and instruction. Indeed, today "all is clear" for those who no longer hide their faces in denial because they are detaching themselves from the virulent media propaganda to begin to re-inform themselves. This notion of unveiling, of revelation, as the Luciferian agenda progresses, is a law from which they cannot escape: it is the great "exposure" proper to the Apocalypse. This inescapable exposure/revelation is therefore at their peril, but they have no choice but to carry out the establishment of this *Luciferian New Order*. They are therefore currently relying to the maximum on social engineering (mind control of the masses) to corrupt and hijack consciousness (and the subconscious) by all means in an attempt to keep society in a certain matrix, a "comfortable cocoon" (although obviously increasingly unstable) that allows anything and everything to be infused smoothly, without people reacting. But we also see a tightening of *rights* and *freedoms under the* guise of the fight against terrorism; an ideal way to suppress all opinions that go against the ambient doxa maintained all the time by the controlled *mainstream* media. The media sow this automatically accepted 'public opinion' and thus create the phenomenon of *peer pressure*, a phenomenon described in the first chapter that can be summarised as follows: The sheep guard the sheep, the one who strays from the herd by being too critical of what is called the single thought, becomes a black sheep in the eyes of the other sheep. Thus, this constant social pressure makes one fear exclusion from the group.

The observation is that the masses are weighed down by work, debt and the daily routine to which they are committed, indulging in the evening in front of a television, using it mainly - and unconsciously - as a tool for relaxation. *Panem et circenses* (bread and circus/games), this expression from ancient Rome is more applicable than ever to our consumer society. A situation in which it is difficult to get things moving, as people are so enslaved and visibly lack the will to emancipate themselves from the 'journalistic' soup and the infantilizing and debilitating entertainment that is served up to them all the time during *prime time*. The youth is obviously targeted above all.

The subject matter of this book is particularly difficult to integrate and accept as it can upset a whole paradigm. The issue of a global *paedo-satanist* network drinking from the innocence of children is becoming known, and people can now understand this harsh reality more easily than even 10 years ago, because the unveiling is exponential. Thank you to all the researchers and independent investigators who have participated or are still participating in clearing up and exposing this difficult subject in order to disseminate information at all costs, many of whom have lost their feathers and even their lives...

The statement made by the former deputy prosecutor of Bobigny, Martine Bouillon, to the journalist Élise Lucet during a televised debate illustrates this point very well: "*We have just understood that paedophilia exists, we cannot yet understand that there are even worse things than paedophilia, I would say 'simple', and people resist with all their strength, with all their inner strength.* "

It is quite natural that people show a strong resistance, even a total denial, in front of the absolute horror that are paedocriminality, satanism and the massive corruption of their governments... But it is time to see clearly and if we don't accept everything, we must at least do our own research to validate or not these horrors. Especially since today everything is revealed, it is only thanks to the widespread corruption of institutions and the media and to the voluntary or involuntary blindness of the people subjected to social engineering that this infamous system is maintained in place.

The more a subject is studied and understood by a growing number of people, the more accessible and comprehensible it will become for the masses because it will be *"cleared"* in a certain way. Indeed, the more a path of understanding is cleared and deepened, the more it widens to give access to this knowledge to a growing number of people who will thus be able to understand it much more easily than the initial researchers...

The more information circulates, the more people it reaches, and the more mentally accessible it becomes to the majority who can then integrate it more easily into their paradigm. This information is obviously not available to everyone out of the blue, but subjects such as paedocriminality, satanism, MK programming, etc., will become more and more accessible to human minds because some people will have already done the work of *clearing the path*, i.e. the work of understanding and integration.

We can perhaps compare this process to the *100th monkey* theory: when enough individuals have discovered something and fully integrated it, it automatically becomes more accessible and understandable to other individuals of the same species. However, this requires a minimum amount of opening and research, as free will is always there to let us choose to open or close a door, but the path of understanding will already be cleared and more navigable than it was before... Hence the determination of our sorcerer-controllers to compartmentalise human consciousness into deep ruts so that it does not direct its attention towards subjects revealing their true tools of control, which in spite of themselves are becoming ineluctably more obvious day by day...

At the same time, we need providential help from God to be able to advance in this struggle, as the opposing party is itself supported by powerful forces of a supernatural order. The Network is organised as much militarily (a strict hierarchical organisation) as spiritually (a cult to the Prince of this world), unlike the profane peoples whose every effort has been made to distract them and especially to cut them off from their relationship with God... Alone, without God's help, we are no match for this dominant Luciferian Network, which works with fallen spiritual entities from which it receives its directives and power, hence the fact of its current domination.

This divine help, this providence, may depend on the number of humans who have become or will become aware of these things and act at their level to reverse the sabotage and corruption of the human being that is taking place.

The theory of a conscious critical mass being able to tip over and unblock a situation that was previously totally cemented and inextricable applies to very heavy subjects, things that are so shocking that they are generally unthinkable and unimaginable for most people... But the more these matters are understood and accepted by a growing number of people, the more there will be a chance to move the pieces on the Chessboard; the Real Chessboard, not the one of the justice of men, Freemasons and institutions, that one is today totally rigged.

If an entire people is not ready to *accept* a harsh reality, i.e. to face a heavy truth that could harm them with a shock or even worse, make them fall into chaotic madness, it is logical, from the point of view of the divine law that is supposed to preserve individuals, that they will access this information only with great difficulty, if at all... When consciousnesses begin to awaken and emancipate themselves from the matrix (the mental control of the masses), then they can begin to access information that is more or less upsetting.. but ultimately life-saving.

In other words, Heaven is waiting for the fruit to ripen before revealing certain things, while respecting the evolution of consciousness; despite the opposite forces which are trying to prevent the masses from accessing information that could bring them to another level of understanding of the matrix in which they have been immersed since birth. So the more consciences emancipate themselves from what they are fed daily in terms of information and turn to other sources for information, the more they will be ready to receive these heavy truths which can indeed be very shocking. Despite the horror, these are things that need to be revealed so that as many people as possible will look into these issues. Especially when it comes to children...

At present, in terms of information, everything is available for those who still have the time and courage to undertake a process of emancipation from this system based on global mental control: God does not allow us to be left without resources to understand the world in which we live: this is an essential Law.

Elitist Satanism/Luciferism scrupulously respects this Law (they have no choice) which eternally gives human souls the opportunity to access the Truth. They only have the power that God has allowed them for a limited period of time, and the war they wage in this great theatre that is our world is mainly against the consciousness/subconscious. They cannot censor everything, so the aim is to channel consciousness through systematic media propaganda: information control and social engineering being the main tools to condition people. The question of psychotronic technology also arises as to its ability to control our brains via scalar waves or pulsed microwaves, applied in a massive manner by literally showering the population with electromagnetic waves that can potentially influence the brain depending on the type of frequency broadcast. As for the strong addiction of the population to the *GSM* network (*Global System for Mobile communications*), it is no longer necessary to demonstrate this, it is enough to walk in the street and in public transport to realise it...

The Truth is there for those who seek a minimum and especially who ask for help from Heaven. It is a real spiritual war and we have, in spite of appearances, enough resources to learn and to be able to get out of the muddy ruts set up by the Great Babylon with its main tool: the Mental Control. But God will not allow us to be left without the resources to guide us to the Truth and to our salvation. The *New World Order* is in spite of itself subject to this Law, so it cannot censor the totality of things that allow human souls to access the Truth. In this great earthly theatre, both good and evil play a role in the evolution of human souls, as Bishop Delassus describes it very well in these words: *"They do not know, or they want to ignore, that above their master Satan, infinitely above, there is God, Almighty God. He created the world for His glory, the inexpressible glory which will be eternally rendered to Him by all His creatures, without exception, though in different ways, some manifesting His goodness, others manifesting His justice. Until the day of the supreme retributions, He leaves them to their own free will, so that both the evil and the good, the evil and the good, serve to accomplish the purposes of His infinite wisdom (...) God allows, we are, alas, witnesses to it, the errors of man and even rebellion against Him, but to a degree that will not be exceeded; He waits. Everything will serve His purposes, and when the trial has ceased, everything will be in its place; there will then be evil only for the obstinate guilty.* "[628]

This book aims first of all to *liberate children from the cellars*, i.e. to fight at one's level against paedo-satanism by informing the citizens about this reality. It is then intended particularly for therapists, psychiatrists, lawyers, magistrates, police officers, journalists, politicians and members of child welfare associations... In short, for all those who are still honest and have integrity and can possibly make things happen at their level.

At the same time, and this is essential, this book aims to make the reader aware who has not yet done so, that there really is a spiritual war here on earth. If there is a spiritual war, your soul needs to find the right path, that of the Lord Jesus Christ, who became flesh and blood for our salvation and to reform all the atrocities partially described in this book. His blood sacrifice on the cross was to be the last, the ultimate sacrifice... The great final reformation of the Son of God in the face of all these abominations.

In order to face these generations that perpetuate at all costs the adoration of the fallen angel, representing the infra-human sanctified by Lucifer, and therefore possessing a supernatural force of order; let us sanctify ourselves in Jesus Christ in order to also hand over our life to a supernatural force of opposition indispensable in such a fight.

Even in these seemingly darkest of times, God is always giving us knowledge and wisdom to oppose and counterbalance the Babylonian abomination.

- Ask, and it will be given to you; seek, and you will find; knock, and it will be opened to you. Matthew 7:7

- All that is hidden must be brought to light, all that is secret must be revealed. Mark 4:22

---

[628] "La Conjuration Antichrétienne - Le Temple Maçonnique voulant s'élever sur les ruines de l'Église Catholique" - Mgr Henri Delassus, Éd. Saint-Rémi 2008, p.310, 311.

APPENDIX

1

TRAUMA AND DISSOCIATION IN MASONIC MYTHOLOGY

Excerpts from the book *"Terror, Trauma and The Eye In The Triangle"*
Lynn Brunet - 2007, p. 64 to 83

The Temple of Solomon has often been interpreted as a metaphor for the human body. Freemason author Albert Mackey confirms this when he writes: "Third degree ceremonies in which a dilapidated building metaphorically represents the deterioration and infirmities associated with the age of the human body. The two columns, Jakin and Boaz, represent the entrance to the Temple. In Kabbalistic literature, these two pillars correspond to the right and left sides of the body with their mirroring effect (...) It is here that the link is made with the left and right functions of the human brain which each control the opposite side of the body, it is called controlaterality. These two pillars can also represent qualities such as severity and clemency, the concept of black and white (editor's note: some O.T.O. altars are surrounded by a black and a white column), *Adam and Eve, male and female, etc.* (editor's note: as we saw in chapter 7, these notions of controlaterality and the division of the two cerebral hemispheres seem to be an important point in the MK)

The Temple of Solomon was intended to provide a permanent home for the Ark of the Covenant, which since the time of Moses had been housed in a tent (...) In a plan of the Temple of Solomon, depicted in a Masonic document entitled "The Two Pillars", the Ark of the Covenant is located in the Holy of Holies with the incense altar next to it. (Editor's note: Lynn Brunet draws a parallel between the Ark of the Covenant and the thalamus, a structure in the heart of the brain)

The word thalamus is derived from the Greek word for an 'inner chamber', commonly used as a bridal chamber. The thalamus is located in the centre of the brain, is completely covered by the cortical hemisphere and is the main gateway that relays sensory information to the cerebral cortex, the main input streams to the cortex must pass through the thalamus. As Francis Cricks notes, "the idea that the thalamus is a key to consciousness is not new. Its role is to keep the somatosensory system, as well as the mental and emotional activity of an individual in harmony. He also observes that a large part of the thalamus is called the "pulvinar", a word that originally meant a "cushion" or "pillow"

(...) another variation means "sacred couch" or "seat of honour". Could this choice of terminology refer to the throne of grace of the Ark of the Covenant housed in the Holy of Holies? If so, the positioning of the altar of incense right next to the Holy of Holies could be a symbolic reference to the fact that the sense of smell is the only sense that does not involve a crossing of nerve pathways between the brain and the body: the right side of the nose is connected to the right side of the brain. The close relationship of the sense of smell to memory is well known (...) When Solomon recreated a "house" for the Ark, he placed the cherubim in such a way that their wings touched the side of each wall. In physiological terms, the wings of the cherubim may symbolically represent the two sides of the cerebral cortex that touch the inside of the skull walls and meet face to face in the inner chamber where consciousness resides. Seen in this way, the 'Throne of Grace' could then symbolically represent the brain's ability to organise chaos, i.e. the continuous mass of incoming sensory information processed instantaneously by the thalamus (...) The Middle Chamber (which marks the end of the initiation of the first three Masonic degrees: Apprentice, Fellow and Master) and its spiral staircase are two important Masonic symbols (...) Mackey writes that the Companions, the workers in the Temple, climb the spiral staircase to reach the Middle Chamber. He interprets this Middle Chamber as the place where Truth is received and the spiral staircase as a symbol of spiritual progression.

Research on the thalamus has shown that it contains a number of activity centres, called 'nuclei'. The main one is called the 'ventral caudal (or posterior) nucleus'. Neurologist Chihiro Ohye writes that "in the ventral caudal nucleus is an area called the ventral intermediate nucleus which contains scattered clusters of cells. Electrical stimulation of this part of the nucleus induces a sensation of spinning or elevation, a kind of ascension. (...) Psychologist Susan Blackmore states that some hallucinogenic experiences can impact on brain cells by producing a vision composed of spiral stripes that can appear as a tunnel on the visual cortex. In physiological terms, the symbol of the spiral staircase may therefore be a way of illustrating this physical sense of spinning and ascending with this hallucinatory vision. As for this place where "Truth" is received, it is possible that this Middle Chamber could be a familiar place for those who study meditation, an area of the brain that is neither right nor left, a state of totally centred calm where the individual can feel a sense of connection with the divine...) Located somewhere in the thalamus, the inner room or "bridal chamber" may be another way of representing the mystical concept of alchemical marriage (or chemical nuptials), represented as the concept of the hermaphrodite, or in Jungian terms, a condition in which the male and female aspects of the psyche are in total harmony (...)

In trauma terms, the Hiram legend can be seen as a metaphorical text that represents what happens physiologically when terror is used to produce the experience of 'inner light'. This 'inner light' is that sense of cosmic consciousness or immortality which is attained through the slow spiritual ascent represented in the second degree (...) Freemasonry belongs to the Gnostic tradition. The figure of Lucifer, the 'Light Bearer', the light of mystical experience, is at the heart of this tradition. The relationship between Lucifer and the psychology of trauma is highlighted in a play entitled 'The Tragedy of Man', written by the Hungarian Imre Madach and analysed by the anthropologist Geza Roheim. Lucifer, who is the central character of the play, is called "the Spirit of Denial". In the play, Lucifer invites Adam to fly into space (i.e. to disassociate himself from reality) in order to escape the scum of earthly life: 'the pain will cease when we give in and the last link that binds us to Mother Earth disappears'. This human ability to escape terror and intense emotional or physical pain through denial and disassociation may have been exploited by Freemasonry in order to achieve mystical experiences. By interfering with the brain process through physical or psychic trauma (shock, terror, hypnosis), the mind can experience a disruption of the sense of time and a sense of timelessness (...)

The myth of Isis and Osiris, used in the Scottish Rite may also be a metaphorical illustration of the traumatic process. Mackey writes that "Osiris was killed by a typhoon and his body cut into pieces, his mutilated remains thrown into the Nile and scattered to the four winds. His wife Isis, mourning the death and mutilation of her husband, searched for several days for the body parts, and after finding them, she reassembled the pieces to give him a decent burial. Osiris, thus restored, became one of the principal Egyptian deities and his cult was united with that of Isis, to form a fertile deity for the fertilisation of nature" (...) If we interpret the characters Isis and Osiris in terms of brain structures, Isis represents the right brain, the intuitive attributes, and Osiris represents the left brain, the logical and linguistic attributes. Damage caused by trauma can lead to problems with memory storage in the left hemisphere and can therefore affect the individual's ability to talk about the events they have experienced because the transfer of information from the right brain is "mutilated" or fragmented. It is then difficult for the individual to reconstruct the fragments of memory that are like pieces of a puzzle. These Egyptian gods could be interpreted as embodying this phenomenon of memory disorders of the fragmented mind following a traumatic experience (...) References to mutilation or self-mutilation in mythological gods are abundant in the magical and religious literature of ancient Egypt. Self-inflicted mutilation by the gods is usually due to emotional stress of various kinds. Budge notes that in other scenarios relating to the theme of death and resurrection in the Osirian myth of Horus, son of Isis and Osiris, Horus has the role of restoring life in an embrace, a gesture reminiscent of the Masonic 'Five Points of Companionship'. Horus came to Osiris, who was in the state of a dead man, and embraced him. By this embrace he transferred to him his own KA (double), or part of the power that dwelt in it. The embrace is in fact an act by which the life energy is transferred from the embracer to the embraced. Budge observes that the embrace can also be metaphorically seen as a restoration of information in the left brain language centre for the purpose of psychic healing after a major trauma. Alan Watt, in studying the theme of splitting in the myth of Osiris and other ancient myths, argues that the sacrificial dismemberment of a divine being is a voluntary process, that of self-sacrifice. He writes: "It follows logically that where there is dismemberment (deconstruction) at the beginning, there is reconstruction at the end (editor's note: Ordo ab Chao or Dissolve and then Coagulate) *It is the cosmic game of discovering what is hidden and remembering what has been dispersed. Watt's conclusion is related to a notion about memory in spiritual processes and the role of concentration in reducing scattered thoughts. I would argue that this myth is even more appropriate when applied to the nature of traumatic memory, its repression and recollection* (...) (editor's note: the Freemason) *Leadbeater suggests that initiation in its purest form involves some kind of connection with the divine and this is what the various Masonic degrees represent. The 'tearing into fragments' suggests that initiation requires an understanding of the use of shocks to produce a certain state of consciousness, which if produced correctly, can create the sensation of being 'one with the universe'. Such a state of consciousness is now considered by the medical field to be an example of a dissociative state. Casavis, in an analysis of the Greek origin of Freemasonry, notes the role that fragmentation plays in the Osirian Mysteries. He observes that the sacred plant of this Mystery cult was Erica, from the Greek word "eriko" which means "to break into pieces."*

Mackey reports that the most relevant Egyptian symbol for Freemasonry is that of the 'all-seeing eye', interpreted mystically as the eye of God, but also as 'the symbol of divine vigilance and care of the universe'. The adoption of the equilateral triangle is a symbol of divinity, which is found across different cultures. Mackey writes: "Among the Egyptians, the hare was the hieroglyph for open eyes, so it is because this fragile animal is supposed never to close its organs of vision, it is always on the lookout for its enemies. The hare was then adopted by the priests as a symbol of the mental illumination or mystical light which is revealed to the neophytes during the contemplation of the divine truth, during the course of their initiation. And so, according to Champollion, the hare was also the symbol of Osiris, a chief god, thus showing the close connection between the process of initiation in their sacred rites and the contemplation of the divine nature."

One of the consequences of severe trauma is a state known as 'hypervigilance'. This is a state of constant attention and exhausting fear, where the victim, like the rabbit or the hare, is constantly on the lookout for danger. When Osiris was resurrected, he possessed the 'all-seeing eye'. If the reconstruction of Osiris represents the recovery of traumatic memories, then this ability to 'see all' can be translated as the ability to face death or evil. These notions of facing death, the idea of the journey and rebirth in Masonic texts thus take on a certain significance with contemporary theories of memory and trauma.

From a physiological point of view, it is interesting to note that the neurons that seem to be most associated with consciousness are described as pyramidal cells. We can draw parallels with the symbolism of Isaac Newton's discovery of the breakdown of white light into the different colours of the rainbow through a triangular glass prism. The eye in the Masonic triangle embodies Newton's physics in that it can be a visual representation of splitting referring to dissociation, the illumination of consciousness (...)

Here, the Enlightenment philosophy of the link between Terror and Sublime described by Edmund Burke becomes relevant. All things that convey terror, he says, "are a source of the Sublime, they produce the strongest emotion that the mind is capable of feeling. Perhaps this echoes neurological research. The place where all these functions seem to coordinate is called the limbic system, comprising the thalamus, amygdala, hippocampus and other structures. As Pierre-Marie Lledo says: "Like the limbo in Christian mythology, the limbic system is the intermediary between the neo-mammalian brain of heaven and the reptilian brain of hell." (…)

On the 21st degree Masonic apron, the Noachite or Prussian Grade, is a winged human holding the index finger of his right hand to his lips and a key in his left hand. This representation is known as the Egyptian figure of Silence (...) In the Masonic system, the Tower of Babel is an image linked to memories and forgetting, linked to confusion and loss of language. According to the Freemasons: "Passing in front of the Tower makes you forget everything you know" (...) The winged figure of Silence on the 21st degree Masonic apron may also represent this process of dissociation. The inability to talk about the traumatic experience is represented by the right index finger held in front of the mouth, the right hand being controlled by the left brain, the side of the brain that affects language. The left hand (symbolising access to the right side of the brain where the dissociated traumatic memories are stored) holds the 'key' to access these memories (...)

The stories of the Flood and the Tower of Babel can be interpreted as another metaphor for how the brain functions during trauma. In much of the trauma literature, the experience is described as "leaving the body", a phenomenon related to the process of dissociation. A sense of peace is experienced as the person psychically disconnects from the terror, finding a natural way to escape. The flight of the 'soul' from the body in traumatic situations is represented by the release of the dove from Noah's Ark and symbolises, in physiological terms, the opioid effect released in the brain when terror 'floods' the physical body (...)After the Flood (of terror), the rainbow (dissociated identity) then becomes a symbol of hope because the flood of terror is forgotten and the individual can survive (...) The lives of individuals become psychologically 'divided' after experiencing something that could have killed them. In cabalistic texts, the rainbow is also linked with the Way of the Chameleon, the animal that changes colour according to its environment. This is related to the phenomenon of multiple personality, where the individual is able to adapt to different situations with different personalities (alter or fragments of personality). All this symbolism gives rise to the possibility that the story of Noah's Ark and the Ark of the Covenant may also correspond to metaphors for processes related to the human brain (...)

2

TRANSCRIPT OF A LECTURE BY CATHY O'BRIEN AND MARK PHILLIPS: MIND-CONTROL OUT OF CONTROL 31 OCTOBER 1996

Part 1: Mark Phillips

Thanks to John and thanks to the whole *Granada* forum. You all represent what I hope will one day happen in this country, but also in the whole world. You have heard from many people in the past who have enlightened you on many subjects. Tonight's - which is very appropriate for Halloween - is probably the worst story you will ever hear. I spent a lot of time trying to convince myself that it couldn't possibly be true. But sadly, the evidence is that this is not just about the Cathy O'Brien story. It's worth noting that Senator John DeCamp of the Franklin case in Nebraska has validated and supports everything you're going to hear tonight... In addition to that, there's a great deal of information that has emerged over the last three years. Information that has come from people who have been directly confronted with the subject. Not only therapists, but also generals, colonels from different branches of the military, as well as members of the intelligence community who have provided us with tons of documentation. This is not only in support of Cathy, but also for the hundreds of others in the same case... Cathy O'Brien's case is not unique, I wish it was, because if it were, I wouldn't be standing here tonight. Indeed, that would mean then that this problem is not widespread, unfortunately, that is not the case. What happened to Cathy O'Brien is something that happens all over the world. It's happening in daycares, it's happening in families... and not especially in totally uneducated, uncultured Appalachian savages who have been practicing incest for ages (laughs)... It's happening in a coordinated effort of the intelligence community, again on a global level.

My role in all this is relatively simple, but nevertheless complex. I'm going to give you a little bit of a presentation tonight... I'm also going to take a few minutes to give you some information about the MK-Ultra (...) I can't, like Cathy, talk about other cases of victims, except the obvious ones like Timothy Mc Veight. But we have not studied this testimony, we have no evidence, we only have Mr McVeight's confession and some other information supporting this case.

We spent 5 1/2 years lecturing to police authorities and therapists. This is what protects us today. We also dug up as much information as we could from other survivors, but also information from the law enforcement system, or should

I say from cooperative people: free thinkers, just like you. They knew there was something wrong with the system, but they didn't understand what it was.

I will give you some information about myself so that you understand my journey with Cathy. But our main concern, the thing we are focusing on, is of course to get this information out to the people in this country and all the other countries that are affected, the question is which ones are not? This also concerns Cathy O'Brien's daughter Kelly, who has been in various psychiatric institutions since she was 8 years old, just after I rescued them. She's still "committed" to this day. I don't know how many of you can imagine what it's like to be a child who has been raised in mental institutions... But I can assure you that it's not a pretty sight, even if Kelly is not abused like she was before she went there...

Mind control is not something new, it is thousands of years old. It's written in the *Egyptian Book of the Dead* under the words: *"The exact formula for trauma-based mind control"*. Adolf Hitler was particularly interested in mind control, he had entrusted it to his right-hand man: Henrich Himmler. The research focused in particular on Northern European families who systematically abuse their children sexually, physically and psychologically from generation to generation. Those of us who read the Bible and understand its interpretation of the *"sins of the father"* will understand what transgenerationals mean. In the case of these families, transgenerational abuse, which begins at birth, involves terrible sexual, physical and psychological abuse by parents of their children, or by other caregivers. Adolf Hitler knew that people who are victims of such abuse become very "receptive" to mind control. They also develop incredible skills, such as over-developed visual acuity. Now, I know it doesn't take a genius - pardon the pun - to figure out how we can use a person with such abilities... This is called *Special Forces*. The individuals who make up these "Special Forces" are monitored very carefully.

Now let's go back to the time when I was working for the Ministry of Defence on a project known as MK-Ultra. It was exactly the project that Hitler and Himmler had started with these abused children in transgenerational families. At that time I saw nothing of what Cathy O'Brien reported to me later, I saw no abuse. What I saw in the prison system and in psychiatric hospitals were people who had a chance to get their lives and their minds back. To me these were positive and caring things and I truly believed that this MK-Ultra programme could eventually reduce our prison and psychiatric populations. This was because I was seeing real rehabilitation without any use of trauma. I was sworn to secrecy about the things that I witnessed, the equipment that was developed, and I can assure you that from 1967 to 1973, when I was involved in this research as a subcontractor for the Department of Defense, I saw then that there was a 25 or 30 year technological advance, things that were totally unknown on this planet (...).I was hired for this job after months and months of psychological tests to check my ability to keep the secret; then I was given a pass from the Department of Defense. I knew of Himmler's studies under Adolf Hitler, I knew that he had wanted to train "very serious" people to strategically place them to control different regions in what he called, and George Bush also calls: the New World Order. You see, Bush was not the first to fantasise about this terrifying idea of a totalitarian government, enslaving the whole world through mind control...

Mind control takes many forms. All of you here in this room do not fall into this huge trap of information control and manipulation, and I thank the *Granada* forum again for allowing us to speak here, because we need your support. This book (*Transe-Formation of America*) is hardly distributed in bookstores and the few booksellers who distribute it deal directly with us, in order to preserve the completeness of the content and avoid any censorship. Initially, this book was published by our own means.

Today we have an opportunity in front of us because of the fact that many of the people Cathy mentioned in the book have been indicted for various reasons; facing charges, some have even fled their countries or resigned from their high positions. The corruption that we are going to talk about here goes far beyond what you know (...)

Cathy O'Brien is certainly a remarkable person, but I can assure you that the prognosis for recovery of someone who has been extremely abused before the age of 5, before the brain is fully formed, is very good. These people can lead a normal, balanced life, even though they have lived a period of life with horrible abuse. This is the thing that surprised me the most. Today there are many survivors in different stages of recovery and Cathy is the only one who has testified by writing a book. All this has been validated and we have not been locked in. I would like everyone in this room to understand that neither Cathy nor I are suicidal. We just came back from Arkansas, Cathy and I were invited to spend four days with investigators because they had identified a chapter in the book that they were able to validate. I told them, *"Pass this on to the press!* But these are people I consider friends of yours and mine... Now, if there are CIA agents in this conference room, you don't have to raise your hand (laughs) but I would like you to come and see me directly face to face. Especially if you are trying to undermine what we are doing. Because this project that Adolf Hitler developed, we in turn developed through Operation Paperclip, which was the exfiltration of Nazi and fascist scientists from Europe to America after the Second World War. They infiltrated our universities, our biggest companies, NASA, I would even say they developed NASA... This infiltration was done at all levels of our society with all this m****: pedo-pornography, blood rituals as well as vile beliefs involving human sacrifice... everything that can traumatize the human mind.

I have approached some researchers who say that Satan is behind this... I want to tell you that there are also real people behind this! I worked for an airline that was involved in this. I had no idea why I was recruited by *Capital International Airways*. It was because I was able to keep quiet. Most agents don't know who they are really working for. There are more than 86,000 in this country, now divide that number by 50 and you'll see what we're dealing with (an average of 1,720 agents per state). This country is crawling with *Big Brother*... The KGB (Russia) never had as many high-level operatives as we have now in this country. George Orwell's book *"1984"* was indeed a dark prophecy come true.

A lot of people say: *"We have to stop this New World Order by taking charge of ourselves"*, but it's already here, we are in the middle of it. Now let's try to understand who the actors are and what their tools are!

Mind control based on repetitive trauma to actually create a totally robotic human being is one such tool. *Fortunately*, it takes a lot of horrible trauma to get to that level of slavery. It requires other means than just pressing a button or a console (editor's note: nothing is less certain at the moment). Today, there is material available that we cannot protect ourselves from. The amazing thing is that these devices are available to everyone. I don't quite understand the philosophy behind the construction of such generators. There is a device called MDD1 which uses a double coil system pulsing electro-magnetic waves which act on our cerebral cortex by stopping logical thinking. You couldn't even control your chequebooks if these things were on, or even think about turning them off... any more than Cathy O'Brien would have thought about running away from her ordeal. This is not *battered woman syndrome*, it has nothing to do with economic dependence, it has to do with robotic mind control and there is tons of documentation on this. *America in Transformation* is Cathy's autobiography, I wrote the first part to introduce the subject. What's in the book is what she experienced and we can prove it. When it was printed, we had more than 27,000 documents in 5 binders. Today we have three tons of paperwork on the subject! (...)

I know now why the intelligence services did not want me as an officer. I know now why I was not aware of certain things... which unfortunately I am aware of now... Because I think I blew the whistle on certain things. There are a lot of whistleblowers nowadays (...) I can assure you that it would be against God and against who I am, if I didn't stand up here and speak and introduce Cathy O'Brien to you so that she could tell her story. (applause)

Cathy and I are very moved by the number of people who would have done the same thing as us. People say to us spontaneously: *"We really appreciate what you are doing"*, or: *"It's hard to believe, but I'm going to read this and all the accompanying documents."* Please do! Read the references at the end of the book, you will have some books written by doctors, intelligence officers, and many other professionals that present things related to what Cathy experienced.

In 1977, the US Congress officially admitted the existence of the MK-Ultra programme, and that's a good thing because I wouldn't have a shred of credibility if it hadn't been revealed publicly. If it hadn't been declassified, I couldn't even say its code name here in front of you.

In 1977, Congress also took up the case of Dr. Ewen Cameron, the founder of the American Psychiatric Association, a Washington lobby, controlling what psychiatrists do to *our heads* when we have disorders... Psychiatry is the youngest of the sciences of medicine and it is the most primitive of all (applause). There may be psychiatrists in this room, these therapists will know exactly what I'm talking about because the information they get from their lobby is carefully vetted / filtered... Information on the rehabilitation of victims of mind control is scarce. It took incredible efforts by a few therapists with integrity who were sued because they did not want to violate their patients' civil rights (medical confidentiality).

Cathy's and my situation was very different because I'm not a doctor or a psychiatrist, so I had no authorisation to practice and no licence for protection. When I rescued her on the eighth of February 1988, she didn't know her name, her age, or even where she was... I'd seen this sort of thing before with people involved in espionage, so I immediately thought Cathy was a mole. She was dressed like a prostitute, she walked like a prostitute, but she talked like a person who would lead a Christian choir... An extreme contrast that I couldn't understand. That was until I got enough information from some people connected with intelligence in this country, but also from abroad.

I was desperate to finally find an appropriate treatment that could result in Cathy O'Brien being freed for the second time in her life... the first time being at the time of her birth and that was it. Cathy O'Brien was a victim of the most horrific system of abuse known to man. It is the kind of mind control that Adolf Hitler thought he could use on certain people to place them in great positions of power, by having invisible strings to puppeteer their minds, actions and words. I don't know if we have politicians like that now, because it seems you don't have to put them under mind control. Indeed, they do whatever the corrupt members of Congress tell them to do. I've known several congressmen, they don't have to be sexually blackmailed, they don't have to be seduced by money or drugs... They're just corrupt... You see, a psychopath is a very social person, they're leaders, they're leaders... Unfortunately these psychopaths have no conscience, that is, no expression of the soul. They do not consider the pain of others, except when it gives them pleasure.

MK-Ultra was built with many sub-projects, including developing the perfect soldier, or the perfect spy. What I was told was that it covered our national security more than any soldier or diplomat could ever do. No one told me that they were being used (editor's note: MK slaves) for drug trafficking and prostitution. No one told me that we were using them for breeding, that is, providing children to sheikhs, to world leaders... No one told me that we were using them for money laundering.

When I rescued Cathy and her daughter, it took me a year to recover Cathy mentally, with a lot of help and a lot of love. Therapists don't provide all that, they can't love their patients, they can't keep them away from the phone, newspapers, TV, etc. They can't keep them away from the world. The patients then often end up relapsing because they are very suggestible. They see an advertisement for fried chicken and they can even smell it... As a former advertising executive, I dreamed of being able to produce such advertisements. I worked very hard to get someone to say: *"This is a good ad"*, but no one ever drooled when they saw my productions. But I used subliminal, I used a form of neuro-linguistics. Those who don't know about it should look into it. Tony Robbins is an advocate of neuro-linguistics, he taught it to George Bush and Bill Clinton. He's not a bad guy, Tony Robbins is a smart businessman and any smart businessman knows the value of neuro-linguistics. It's the language of the unconscious, well for me it's the subconscious.

The language of the subconscious contains codes, keys and triggers. Keys that were used to unlock all the doors in Cathy's mind that were specifically related to the abuse she had suffered. I then accessed information such as bank account numbers. People who work on MK-Ultra know very well that deprogramming is nothing but hacking... Just as I can hack a computer, I can hack the hard drive of a human brain. It was this *hacking* job that gave me incredible information like bank account numbers. Rather than go and loot those bank accounts and then have to go and hide in luxury for the rest of my life, I gave them to the FBI. Not because I knew it was dirty money or not, but because I didn't want to lose my skin. I provided everything in this book to the authorities over a period of three or four years: to all the federal states and to the law enforcement agencies that are directly involved in this case. I also provided the names of over a thousand agencies and individuals. I wanted this to be presented to Congress as it was in 1977 when the wife of a Canadian cabinet member was committed to a psychiatric hospital in Montreal where Dr. Ewen Cameron was practicing (editor's note: Velma Orlikow, wife of Canadian politician David Orlikow)... She came out a vegetable... This cabinet member, whose name I don't remember, did everything he could to try to find out what had happened to his wife. They had put her through electroshock and other horrible tortures along with drugs and hypnosis. Unfortunately, many other people have been subjected to Dr. Ewen Cameron's experiments... Some have recovered well and I am in contact with two of them. These people are very functional and one of them is going to do the same thing as us in the very near future. I don't know how many have been able to fully recover as well as Cathy in this country, because no therapist can devote sixteen or eighteen hours a day, seven days a week to a patient, while violating their civil rights to get them out legally... Can they legally get their patient out of the clutches of their master(s), legally get them out of that slavery and access the directories? In one of these directories (Cathy's) was Bill Clinton's personal phone number. It was a $20,000 cocaine *deal* with Dick Thornburgh... and the list goes on!

This is a small group, a gang... If you take the entire population of the United States, it's a very small fraction, it's these bandits that control all of us... They're such a minority that you wonder how they can do all of this (editor's note: in direct connection with a supernatural force). One also wonders how Clinton survives all the attacks against him. How did George Bush survive the attacks on him? Well, he didn't, he left office, but that didn't change anything. Whoever replaced him did exactly what Bush wanted, like implementing NAFTA (North American Free Trade Agreement) and the General Agreement on Tariffs and Trade (GATT).

But that's their job, my job and Cathy's job is to stand in front of citizens' assemblies like this one in front of you. We want to make sure that the information you receive will challenge you enough to go and spread it around, but also that you will study the subject and talk about it again and again: that's all we want. I am absolutely convinced that the information in this book will reach the eyes of those who can see. Just as this video filmed here at this conference will reach those who can still hear and see the truth. So that people will stand up and start asking why Shiran-Shiran had the same psychiatrist as Lee Harvey Oswald or Timothy McVeight. This psychiatrist (editor's note: Louis Jolyon West, who died in 1999) is very popular, he practised at *UCLA* (University of California at Los Angeles). He was also the first person to call me on my home phone number, an unlisted number and under a false name! Right into the bush, up there in Alaska after I rescued Cathy and her daughter.

I didn't have enough connections at that time for people to inform me about what I shouldn't do on my own; and at that time it was out of the question for me to hear that kind of stuff... I suffered from post-traumatic stress disorder because I was totally overwhelmed by what Cathy and her daughter Kelly were telling me... Then I showed this information to members of the intelligence community and other federal agents who validated it, thank you to them.

Now I would like to introduce Cathy O'Brien, the person who restored my spirituality. I wasn't a bad guy, but I needed a boost. I am proud to have been with her for over eight years now.

Part 2: Cathy O'Brien

I would like to thank each and every one of you for welcoming us here tonight to learn about a tool that is being used in secret to herald what Adolf Hitler and George Bush call the New World Order. I am talking about mind control...

I have enjoyed talking to some of you earlier this evening, people who say they have been personally subjected to mind control or have been subjected to it by people close to them. Mind control is widespread in this country and throughout the world.

These criminals who run our country operate on the philosophy of *"secret knowledge = power"*. Many government secrets and personal reputations were based on the belief that I could not be deprogrammed to remember things I was supposed to forget. They were wrong... For as intelligent as these officials are, their reasoning is hampered by their own immorality. They have no wisdom, they do not think deeply and they never consider the strength of the human spirit. They have never considered what would happen if a benevolent man like Mark Phillips learned their secrets and used them to restore the spirit rather than to control it.

I know I was very lucky to have survived after being a victim of the MK-Ultra mind control used by the CIA, the White House and the Pentagon: trauma-informed programming.

Now that I have regained my means and finally my free will: I testify. I speak of all that I have witnessed, all that I have seen and heard. All that I have recorded photographically behind the scenes of this attempted *New World Order*.

By exposing their secrets, their power is eroded (applause).

I also speak on behalf of the many victims of mind control and survivors who cannot think for themselves to say what they know and what they have endured.

I am speaking on behalf of my daughter Kelly who is now sixteen years old, a true political prisoner. She is currently in the state of Tennessee where she has been denied a pardon due to the political influence of her torturers. She is counting on Mark and me to get the message out for her. For Kelly's sake and yours, Mark and I have spared no effort in the facts and truths recorded in our book, which was self-published and therefore not censored. So you will find facts that you have a right and a need to know.

These realities have long been concealed from us under the guise of so-called *"national security"*. It is this same pretext of national security that has prevented us from seeing justice done despite all the evidence and documents in our possession. We have more than 27,000 documents and evidence: testimonies from government officials, medical records, far more than necessary for any legal process in this country, including Congress. But this national security pretext has blocked our access to justice. It is time for the truth to triumph. It is time for these truths to be brought to light in the name of humanity.

I would like to start by defining mind control through my experience. I realise that what I experienced was extreme, but also that this absolute robotic control that I endured is more limited than the type of global mind control that proliferates in society.

There are many levels of mind control, like a ladder... At one level there is total robotic control and at another level there is mind control such as occultism which is also proliferating in this country, or the *Global Education 2000* programme where children are losing their freedom of thought and critical thinking skills. There are so many different levels of society that are affected by mind control that it becomes imperative that all of this information be disseminated.

My experience as a victim can certainly be applied to all facets of mind control and mind manipulation (...) It's a subject that concerns us all, and suddenly the whole *New World Order makes* sense. The erosion of constitutional values, the erosion of the morality of this country, suddenly becomes clearer when we become aware of this issue of global mind control.

I was born in 1957 in Muskegon, Michigan, into a family that has practiced incest for generations. Which means that my father was sexually abused as a child, my mother was sexually abused as a child, and they in turn abused me... My father has sexually abused me for as long as I can remember. I have often heard him say that he started to replace my mother's nipple with his penis when I was just an infant.

I'm telling you this so that you can understand that my sexuality has been messed up since early childhood. It was put into an area of my brain that is very much like survival, like eating and drinking... I am telling you this so that you are better equipped to understand what is going on in society and to call things by their name.

Mark and I name names in our book, not so I can say I was in the White House with so-and-so, I don't bring up the whole glamour part. But it's so you know who the problem is and where it is.

The sexual abuse I endured was so horrific that I developed dissociative identity disorder, it was usually called multiple personality disorder. I'm glad they changed the term to dissociative identity disorder because it describes much better the compartmentalisation that occurs when a person endures a trauma that is too horrific to comprehend.

Even though I could not understand that what my father was doing to me was wrong, the pain and suffocation of his abuse was so unbearable that I developed a dissociative identity disorder. It was impossible to understand, there was no place in my mind to deal with such horror. So I automatically compartmentalised my brain, small areas separated by amnesic barriers to block out memories of the abuse so that the rest of my mind could continue to function normally, as if nothing had happened... When I saw my father at the dinner table, I didn't remember the sexual abuse. But as soon as he unbuttoned his trousers, a part of me, the part of my brain that knew how to deal with this horrible abuse would wake up, it was as if a neural junction opened up so that this part of my mind could suffer my father over and over again as needed... I certainly had a lot of experience in this "brain compartment" that dealt with my father's abuse, but I didn't have the full range of perceptions, I had a very limited perception, a very limited vision of things. That's why I'm glad that we don't talk in terms of *personalities* anymore about this disorder.

I built another compartment in my head to cope with my mother's abuse. Her abuse was primarily psychological. She herself suffered from a dissociative identity disorder and I do not hold her responsible for her actions as I do for my father, who was fully aware of what he was doing. My mother, despite her inability to control herself, was destroying any vestiges of self-esteem I might still have had. Her abuse was so horrible that I created another compartment in my mind just to deal with the unhealthy interactions I had with her. I also developed another compartment to deal with the paedo-pornography that my father subjected me to. He made his living digging up earthworms for fishing, as he had only been to primary school, so he supplemented the family income by producing paedo-pornography. Productions that he then distributed through the local Michigan mafia network.

At the time, there was a criminal faction in our government that targeted children like me for mind control. This is because of this compartmentalisation of memory which is something they felt was ideal for keeping government secrets. After all, if I couldn't remember, how could I talk about it? Furthermore, people with dissociative identity disorder develop a photographic memory behind these amnesic barriers. Indeed, the brain has a defence mechanism that makes it record the events related to the trauma in an extremely precise and detailed way. To give you an example, the many of you old enough to remember the assassination of John F. Kennedy will remember exactly where you were and what you were doing at the time. It was an event that traumatised the whole nation and it illustrates how the mind photographically records the events surrounding the trauma. So behind these amnesia barriers, I had a photographic memory that the government felt was perfect for programming. I could deliver and receive messages from leaders, or in my case also from the drug lords involved in funding the *New World Order* slush funds. They were interested in programming me so that I could deliver messages verbally. When I delivered these messages, I transmitted exactly word for word what I had been told, using the voice inflections of my torturers, without any conscious understanding of what I was saying. I was just a tape recorder, repeating like a parrot what had been recorded in my memory.

Another aspect that interested the government was that my dissociative disorder took away all sense of time. This was because I was moving from compartment to compartment in my brain without remembering what had happened before. I was therefore unable to keep track of time and its notion was absolutely foreign to me. Not knowing what I was doing before, I strangely had no concept of fatigue, yet I was doing way too much... A person with a dissociative identity disorder has great physical stamina, it's like a superhuman strength with the ability to go on indefinitely. People with this disorder also develop a much sharper than average visual acuity. That's why they are often seen with wide eyes, they take in more elements of their environment than a normal person. This makes them perfect snipers for commando operations or for the intelligence services. So the government was very interested in developing mind control.

So I was a *chosen one*, a prime candidate for mind control because of repeated sexual abuse. My sexuality had been exalted, so I was used as a sex slave and also received messages from government officials. This criminal faction of our government, so interested in people with dissociative identity disorder, knew full well that every child subjected to child pornography must have endured such horrific traumas that they were bound to suffer from this disorder. This government criminal group was therefore dedicated to this child pornography network in order to identify and target children like me for their projects. At that time, the politician connected to this local Michigan mafia, the politician who was protecting this pornography ring, was Gerald Ford. This is the same Gerald Ford who was elected President of the United States... I never saw him as a politician, I saw him as just another rapist, the same type as my father. Because Gerald Ford also raped me as a child and throughout the time I was under mind control, until Mark came to the rescue of me and my daughter in 1988.

Gerald Ford is not a paedophile per se, he is what I call a *"sexual experimenter"*. He will try anything, any age, any time, any place... until he has taken control. This is because he had a perversion of power in addition to having this interest in mind control.

It was Gerald Ford who came to the house to explain to my father how to educate me according to the government guidelines. My father had been caught sending child pornography through the mail, so he was contacted to let him know that if he sold me for this project, he would gain legal immunity... Since that day, my father has had no trouble with the law, thanks to the famous "National Security".

My father obviously thought this was a "wonderful" idea and immediately sold me on the project. He thought the government was turning a blind eye to child abuse... as I do too. My father continued to raise his five other children for the project, seven in all. The others are still waiting for their freedom as we speak...

Once my father agreed to sell me to the project, I was regularly taken to *Mackimac Island*, Michigan. It's a political haven where the governor of Michigan lives. It is a sort of *Bohemian Grove* (occult club) where politicians met and discussed the *New World Order* and mind control: mind control of the masses, mind control in the school system, how to use the occult as a basic trauma, etc.

One of my sexual abusers at the time was the Prime Minister of Canada: Pierre Trudeau. Pierre Trudeau is of the Jesuit faith, today they are the armed wing of the Vatican. There is a criminal faction within these Jesuits. I'm certainly not saying that all Catholics are bad, any more than all CIA agents are bad, or all our politicians. There is good and bad in everything. But nevertheless, Pierre Trudeau represented that criminal faction of Catholic Jesuits who wanted mind control of the masses to become the World Church in this *New World Order*. The money that this church brought in financed the controllers of the *New World Order*.

Another of my sexual abusers was the then Senator from Michigan and later Congressman Guy Vander Jagt. It was the same Guy Vander Jagt who remained head of the Republican National Committee and installed George Bush in the presidential office.

It was on *Mackimac Island*, when I was 13 years old, that I was handed over to a senator who became my landlord in this mind control project. This US Senator was Robert C. Byrd.

Senator Byrd is a Democrat from West Virginia, and again you'll notice that I'm revealing all the names regardless of political party. It's both Democrats and Republicans who are involved in these things. It's not about the parties, it's about who's for a *New World Order* and who's not...

Senator Byrd was in office then and he is in office now. He headed our Senate Appropriations Committee. That means that he held the purse strings of our country and he decided where the money would be spent. I know from behind the scenes that Senator Byrd was sending the money where it would benefit the *New World Order* controllers.

My father, who sold me on this project, for example, had a lucrative contract with the army to manufacture camshafts for military vehicles. This is how my father became extremely rich... for someone who never went beyond primary school...

It was Senator Byrd, who became my landlord, who would then decide where I would go and when I would go; what operations I would perform during the Reagan and Bush administrations; and where I would be taken for specific MK programming. Senator Byrd ran my whole life.

It was at this time that I made my First Communion at *St. Francis of Assisi* Church in Muskegon. After this first Communion, I also underwent a ritual called the *'rite of silence'*. This ritual was conducted by deputy Vander Jagt and the rector of our church, father Don... an occult blood ritual. It was so horrible, it was this inversion of the Catholic mass that confused my mind because when a person is functioning on a subconscious level, they are so traumatized that the conscience finds no place to deal with what they are going through. The subconscious has no way of discerning, questioning and reasoning as the usual conscious mind does. And this inversion of the Catholic mass into the occult totally messed with my mind. It was absolutely vile... This blood ritual was so horrible that my mind immediately accepted the mental manipulation they put me through: hypnotic language, neuro-linguistic programming, mind control... It then changed the way my brain worked until now. Remember, that part of my brain I told you about, an area that was triggered to deal with my father's perpetual abuse... In this ritual they changed that, so that they could now decide when, where and how that particular compartment of my brain would be opened and accessed. They replaced the trigger mechanism with hypnotic codes: keys and triggers, hand signals. There are also certain tones that can open up these neural junctions and allow access to compartmentalized memories. They then reworked all this.

As a result of this rite of *"keeping silent"*, it also became silent in my head... Because until then I would hear my own voice arguing back and forth with all these different perceptions coming from the multiple compartments before I could formulate a decision on anything. I remember before this ritual I still had my own ideas, I had hope that there was a place in the world where people didn't abuse each other. I had hope that I would have ten children who would be at least ten children on this earth who were not abused... I had hope for these things, but with this ritual I lost my ability to think freely. I had even lost my ability to hope. I had lost my free will entirely. This ritual silenced this debate that was constantly popping up in my head and all I could hear instead, at that point, were the voices of my tormentors directing me, telling me exactly what I was supposed to do. I could only robotically follow these instructions to carry them out.

When I was ready for high school, Senator Byrd ordered that I be sent to Central Catholic College in Muskegon. At that time there was a lot of information that the Catholics had been studying the effects of trauma on the human mind for a long time. They had been studying and keeping records of these things for a very long time, especially since the Spanish Inquisition. This information ties in with the research on Hitler and Himmler that the CIA had undertaken and was making progress on. The cross-referencing of the information that was emerging was very significant.

Muskegon College was a place where this information was gathered. It was in Muskegon that the very foundations and structure of *Global Education 2000* were implemented. There are many different names for this programme which is implemented in our school system and which the government strictly enforces on children and young people. *Global Education 2000 is* designed to increase the learning capacity of our young people while decreasing their capacity for critical analysis. They immediately accept everything they are told without question and simply swallow all the information they receive.

At school I got straight A's, I was very good at it because I used to record the lessons photographically. I also underwent occult rituals in the chapel of this college, like many other students, I was far from being the only one. In fact, at the time I really thought that everyone was involved in this kind of abuse. My whole environment was saturated with it... This occultism, these traumas, created a photographic record of everything I studied at school. I had no ability to analyse it critically or to use it creatively, but all the data was perfectly stored in my head.

It was while I was in college that Gerald Ford took over as president. I had been conditioned during that time to think that I *"had no place to escape, no place to hide.* This is a specific phrase that serves to put into the heads of mind control victims that there is absolutely nowhere to run and nowhere to hide: *"we are always keeping an eye on you"*. Of course that's what I thought, who could I turn to? Not my parents, not my church, not my school, not the local politicians... I couldn't even turn to the President of the United States! I felt really trapped, which is exactly what they want for total mind control. Since then, of course, I've discovered something else entirely and Mark wisely taught me during my deprogramming that I did have somewhere to run: straight to them! ... and that I didn't need to hide. Obviously they are the ones who are hiding, they are hiding all their abuses using *National Security* as a cover.

After I graduated from college, Senator Byrd ordered that I be sent to Nashville, Tennessee. At the time, Nashville was heavily involved in mind control through the country music industry, but especially through the proliferation of CIA cocaine within the country music community. This was already in full swing and political corruption in Tennessee was reaching fever pitch. The country music industry was providing a cover for mind-controlled slaves like me to be walked around the country to distribute and deliver large shipments of CIA cocaine.

In my experience, what the CIA calls the so-called *"war on drugs"* is nothing more than the elimination of their rivals in order to take over the world drug industry (applause). They are waging their *"anti-drug war"* on every street corner and today our streets have become a bloodbath.

The country music industry provided a cover for cocaine trafficking, so Senator Byrd wanted me to get into the business. At the same time, Byrd fancied himself some kind of artist and occasionally played the fiddle at the *Grand Ole Opry*. The first time I was sent to Nashville, he was playing that very night in that great concert hall. At his side (or rather behind him) was a musician named Wayne Cox... who later told me that playing music alongside Byrd was not only musical accompaniment, but also political. That night after the *show* I was again subjected to an occult ritual. The occult is frequently used as a basis for trauma for mind control. Who can understand this kind of trauma? Absolutely horrible blood rituals are a perfect basis for the trauma necessary for mind control aimed at the compartmentalisation of memory. I witnessed a scene where Wayne Cox murdered a homeless man at the Nashville train station, a place that was derelict at the time and squatted with homeless people. He shot him right between the eyes and cut off both his hands. This was Cox's *modus operandi* for murder.

After this blood ritual, this horrible trauma, it was decided that Cox would become my first "master", "supervisor", in MK-Ultra mind control. As my "master" and "supervisor", Wayne Cox would follow Senator Byrd's guidelines and instructions. Mostly he would put me through more traumas, enough to satisfy the many compartments that Senator Byrd wanted to create in my brain for MK programming. This was so that I could then perform various operations during the Reagan/Bush administration.

So thereafter I endured many occult rituals. At that time, Wayne Cox was working directly under Louisiana Senator J. Bennett Johnston. Cox took me to his home in Chatham, Louisiana. Bennett Johnston was running mind control operations in conjunction with a band of mercenaries. These mercenaries were going back and forth to South America, the arms trade was very active. But more importantly, when the planes dropped these guys in South America, they would come back loaded with cocaine, which was then distributed on our streets. Wayne Cox would trigger the MK functioning of these mercenaries by showing them the severed hand of one of his victims, which would take them back into the trauma of a ritual they had already undergone, making them access a specific compartment of their brain. He would also tell them that Bennett Johnston wanted them to *"reach out"*, he would then give them instructions which the guys followed to the letter. So Bennett Johnston was also involved in this...

In 1978, it was agreed that I had been through enough trauma to do a first test, this was to be my first operation. A large quantity of cocaine had arrived by plane and I was to deliver it to the neighbouring state of Arkansas. At that time, the drug trade around Bill Clinton was in full swing. He was governor of Arkansas at the time. So I delivered that cocaine to an airport in *Ouachita Forest* that I've since identified as Mena Airport. I also passed information and a small amount of cocaine from Bennett Johnston's personal stockpile to Bill Clinton. I handed him the package and he immediately snorted two lines of coke... it was not the first time I had seen Bill Clinton use cocaine. My sexual experiences with Bill Clinton were very limited, even though I was a sex slave. In my experience, Bill Clinton is bisexual, rather strongly homosexually oriented. I saw him mostly involved in homosexual activities. I had much more experience with Hilary Clinton. Hilary is also bisexual, with a strong homosexual bent. She was the one accessing my sexual programming to satisfy her perversions.

Also at that time, Bennett Johnston subjected me to other mind manipulations that involved not the occult but the theme of aliens. These guys who were manipulating my mind and programming me for MK, real criminals in charge of our country, pretending to be gods, demons, aliens... This was to make me feel totally helpless, to make me integrate the fact that they were always there behind me to harm me. And it worked very well at that time...

Bennett Johnston told me that he was an alien. He told me that he had participated in *the "Philadelphia Experiment"* and that when the ship disappeared, he came back as a spaceship... This is in line with the "air/water mirror" theme frequently used by NASA, it's a reversal/inversion. Because, again, the subconscious has no capacity for reasoning. Bennett Johnston then showed me, on the *General Dynamics* website, a 'top secret' stealth craft. It was a triangular thing that wasn't in any textbook, that nobody talked about, that you didn't see in the newspapers, but there it was, hanging in the air in front of my eyes... It was another one of those top secret military systems. To me at that time, it looked like a spaceship! I had never seen anything like it. So everything Bennett Johnston did was alien-related to me at the time. So it was easy to get me to accept the idea that everything that was happening was in fact perpetrated by aliens. I'm not saying that aliens don't exist, that would be stupid of me, but what I am saying is that these are people who actually claim to be ETs. If there is a reality of extra-planetary influence, we need to clear up the misinformation and mind control that our government is practicing.

I have it on good authority that their plan is to make us all feel powerless... under so-called alien domination and that our *"Independence Day" is coming...* So beware of that! Understand that these criminals are taking information and technology from us under the guise of "National Security". They are at least 25 years ahead of us in technology! Can you imagine what they have today? What has happened in the last 25 years? The microwave oven, computers, but they are still making progress and they are way ahead. So when they say, *"It's from the aliens!* by showing us incredible technology, don't fall into the trap of feeling totally helpless. Superstition begins where knowledge ends, and we have been isolated from that knowledge for a long time. People have always had different beliefs and I am sure that each of you has different belief systems. Whatever your belief system, it is imperative that you know that these criminals are humans, they are among us to harm us. They must be held accountable for their actions and their crimes against humanity. (applause)

In 1980, when my daughter Kelly was born. She came into this MK-Ultra program at a much more sophisticated technological stage than I was subjected to. In addition to the trauma, she was subjected to "harmonics" (MK programming system) at NASA sites from birth, before her brain even had a chance to build.

As soon as Kelly was born, Senator Byrd, knowing that I had been sufficiently traumatized, ordered that we both be transferred to Nashville to operate under the Reagan administration. In this country music industry, we were then handed over to our second "master", "supervisor", his name is Alex Houston. Alex Houston was a ventriloquist, hypnotist and country music performer. He mainly carried out criminal operations for the CIA to finance classified programmes. This involved the distribution of large quantities of cocaine throughout the United States and Canada. At that time, he was working to provide me with a cover to travel out of the country, to Canada, Mexico and the Caribbean, for criminal operations. My 'supervisor' (Houston) took me to various military and NASA facilities for MK programming, for specific operations that I was forced to participate in (...) They involved leaders such as the then president of Mexico, De la Madrid, as well as former president Salinas.

In 1984, a CIA base was established in Lampe, Missouri, a trauma centre working specifically on near death experiences (NDEs). This site is called *"Swiss Villa Amphiteater"*. They use the country music industry to handle large quantities of cocaine and then redistribute it. Lampe, Missouri is just across the river from Arkansas, and is closely linked to Bill Clinton's coke-dealing operations... which were booming at the time. It's also interesting to note that the Lampe operation was the place where the country industry was cleverly relocated, right there in Branson, so as to be close to Clinton's operation.

Lampe was also the place where I heard George Bush and Bill Clinton talking... From my point of view, they clearly seemed to be friends, there was no political conflict between them then. It's all a smokescreen to fool the public. Indeed, they don't adhere to these "political conflicts" because they have exactly the same agenda, which is the construction of this *New World Order*.

At the time, I heard George Bush tell Bill Clinton that when Americans become disillusioned with the Republicans leading them to the *New World Order*, it will be Bill Clinton, the Democrat, who will be put in the presidential office. This was all decided in 1984! And even long before that! In 1984 they were already discussing these things as an absolute fact. In this discussion, the preparations for NAFTA (North American Free Trade Agreement) were also discussed. At the time George Bush became president, Salinas became president of Mexico, and together they were going to set up NAFTA. This was the beginning of the control for a *New World Order*.

I was forced to participate in the creation of this criminal NAFTA. The opening of the Mexican border in Juarez to free trade. The free trade of drugs, the free trade of our children... The criminal roots of NAFTA are absolutely appalling... It's interesting that these political moves are already decided in advance.

Once I was deprogrammed, I was completely baffled when I realised that people had no awareness of this... It was so obvious to me... I couldn't realise that people were not aware of the situation and that they had been fooled by a smoke screen, without ever having tried to find out what was really going on behind the scenes, behind the veil.

But I can understand that honest and sincere people don't think that way, they don't have a criminal mind and their conscience is not directed towards that kind of thing. Just as these guys (elitist criminals) are themselves limited in their thinking by their immorality, honest people are somehow blinded to this kind of extreme criminal activity... Until their eyes are opened to the truth.

The people who were involved in these criminal activities were under the orders of George Bush. I don't pretend to know everything and I don't pretend that George Bush was at the top of it all, but he was the highest ranking person I knew at that time (...) Bush Sr. was respected for his great knowledge of building the *New World Order*. Look at his past: George Bush first started with the UN, then he became the head of our CIA. Then he indirectly led our country during three administrations: the Reagan presidency, his own presidency and then the Clinton presidency. Indeed, both Reagan and Clinton answer to Bush Sr. Mexican President De la Madrid also answers to Bush Sr. (...) King Fadh of Saudi Arabia also followed George Bush's orders, as did Canadian Prime Minister Brian Mulroney.

In 1983, I overheard Ronald Reagan and Brian Mulroney discussing the *New World Order*. Indeed, Senator Byrd acted as a pimp by pimping me out to Reagan when I attended a White House cocktail party.

Ronald Reagan certainly smoked us all out wonderfully. For those of you who don't want to believe he's involved in these things, he did tell you he was an actor! (laughs) And he did a very good job, over a long period of time. That was his role, that's what he was supposed to do.

I heard Reagan tell Mulroney that he believed the only way to achieve world peace was through mass mind control... I know from experience that there is no peace in the mind under mind control. How could there be world peace without people having peace in their minds?

The ramifications of mind control go very far. Under mind control, there is no freedom of thought. Without freedom of thought, there is no free will. Without God-given free will, there is no soul expression. What kind of *"world peace"* can we achieve without free will, without soul expression and without spirituality?

Mind control in all its forms must be exposed so that people retain their freedom of thought. So that they retain their free will and the expression of their soul, their spirituality. When people have a soul and a spirituality, they are able to Love. That is world peace! Not mind control! (applause)

In 1988 I was forced to participate in many operations against my will. Things that I certainly would never have done in my conscious mind. I suppose if I had had a part of me that was willing to do these things, mind control would not have been necessary. I'm appalled at what I was forced to participate in, but I'm relieved that this information is getting out, that people are passing the book from hand to hand. So, hand in hand, we can take our country back. You have the right and the need to know this information, and their control over the media will not suppress the Truth. The Truth is needed! ... (applause)

In 1988 Mark rescued me and my daughter Kelly. We couldn't think of escaping, I couldn't think of saving my daughter at all, any more than I could think of saving myself. And all my hopes and dreams as a child had certainly come to nothing... When Mark rescued us, we had no capacity to hope to meet a good person, we didn't even know it existed. We didn't have the capacity to trust anyone outside our environment (network). So I couldn't say to myself that Mark was a good guy, but I saw his attitude with his animals, and even though I had no capacity for reasoning, for awareness, something happened on an extra sensory level. We felt very strong things then. After all, considering that we only use 10% of our brain, we had been split up in certain parts of our brain, areas that were very receptive to various psychic levels, a bit like animal instinct. My daughter and I had noticed that animals loved Mark. He had three raccoons that he had rescued and they loved him very much, they would wrap their paws around his neck and he would give them kisses... For us it was something very important to witness this, because we had only known abuse of our animals until then. We had lived on a ranch, we had dogs, cats, horses, cows, chickens, etc., and everything that Alex Houston did to our animals was very important. If we didn't participate in the abominations, this would have happened to our pets, and we loved them more than anything.

Please keep in mind that those who abuse children often abuse animals. If you see someone abusing an animal, be vigilant. Make sure you know that their children are safe. I have never seen an exception to this rule.

So it was very revealing for us to see that these animals loved Mark. Also, at the time he rescued us, we were threatened by the CIA. I was 30 years old at the time, I was supposed to be killed as most MK slaves are killed around the age of 30. I was considered "too old" for sex, so I was to be suppressed. Mark saved me from certain death and he saved my daughter from a fate far worse than death... He even took the time to save our animals. He took horses, cows and chickens to safety. This had a profoundly positive impact on Kelly and I, and we began to trust him from that point on. Mark took us all the way to Alaska in safety and serenity. As we found ourselves safe for the first time in our lives and truly loved for the first time, memories of the past began to come back in flashes. Through these flashes of memory, I began to realise what had happened to me and my daughter, especially during the Reagan and Bush administrations.

As I became aware of all this, I became furious, I had rage for what my daughter had gone through, for all the torture inflicted, and for humanity as a whole. I would have been totally blinded and immobilised by this rage had it not been for Mark's wisdom to tell me that the best revenge was complete healing. This is because through this healing, through the photographic recording of all these events, I could expose these people for what they really are! To expose their plan, to expose this *New World Order,* and also to be able to get help for my daughter who is in desperate need right now...

So from then on I started to write down my traumatic memories. By putting them on paper, I was using a part of my brain other than verbalisation, thus bypassing the emotional. Bypassing the emotional is something necessary to bring logic, to make the incomprehensible finally understandable. It allowed me to understand and grasp what had happened to us and what we could do with all this information.

Kelly was not as lucky as I was because of the programming she endured, harmonic-based programming. The trauma memories and deprogramming did not allow her to access all parts of her brain as I did. This type of programming requires special equipment to help her recover and heal. She currently needs to receive treatment on her neural pathways with harmonic equipment. Without this, she ended up at *Humana* Hospital in Anchorage, Alaska, in an intensive care unit. By this time she was in horrible pain and only responded to psychological interventions and not to conventional medications. Kelly is now suffering from respiratory failure... Mind control has evolved to the point where they know the ins and outs of the human brain and mind so well that they can not only program the subconscious mind, but also go into the primitive mind, which is the area of our mind where basic biological reflexes such as blinking, breathing and heart rate are regulated. They can work on it and put deadly programs in place. In my daughter's case, it's respiratory failure which means she can't speak if she ever remembers anything, she's never been forced to, but in the spy business it can happen. By brainwashing, they can access the memories of the trapped spy. So today spies no longer have to carry the old cyanide pill with them, instead they suffer respiratory or heart failure. So no information will be passed on to the enemy, no chance...

My daughter, genetically selected, was raised and trained with mind control to be later introduced into the spy business. So she had this program in place, which then unfortunately got triggered. Because of the medical assistance she needed, she soon fell into the illegal and immoral detention of the state of Tennessee. Where she remains to this day... The violations of laws and rights that proliferated in her case are numerous.

We had an upstanding district attorney step in and tell the judge that he was violating constitutional and human rights in my daughter Kelly's case. As he was quoting a whole list of laws, the judge interrupted him to say, *"But the laws don't apply to this case for National Security reasons.* This raises some questions: What does "National Security" have to do with the rape and torture of a child's body and mind? Especially when validated by evidence and supporting documents!

For Kelly's sake and the sake of so many other mind control survivors, we must lift this veil of "National Security. We must get this *National Security Act* of 1947 repealed. (applause)

It is no longer "national security", but a threat to the nation when it is used to cover up such a crime against humanity as mind control. When it covers up the CIA's so-called "war on drugs", or covers up the sale of our country to the *New World Order*. This "National Security" that has nothing to do with the security of our nation.

This "National Security" has kept the mind control information from each of you for too long. We must get this information out. We must arm everyone with knowledge about MK, because knowledge is our only defense against mind control. We need to get detailed information so that we can all be more effective in our respective fields, so that we can take back the country and ultimately our world; for Kelly's sake; for the sake of all the other victims and survivors of mind control and I know there are many. For the love of humanity as we know it. It is the truth that sets us free. Help us spread the word, thank you. (applause)

3

DISSOCIATIVE EXPERIENCES SCALE (DES)
THE DISSOCIATIVE EXPERIENCES SCALE

The Dissociative Experiences Scale (DES) is a self-administered questionnaire for adults. It was developed by Eve Bernstein Carlson and Frank W. Putnam in 1986. The DES consists of 28 items that assess the frequency of various dissociative symptoms in the patient's daily life. This scale was developed to measure experiences of mental dissociation in adults and is the most widely used tool for the study of dissociative disorders in psychiatry. Altered states of consciousness under the influence of drugs or alcohol are not to be considered for this test.

The final result is an average of the scores of the 28 items, which is then divided by 28. This gives a score between 0 and 100. The average DES score for the general population ranges from 3.7 to 7.8. The results for psychiatric inpatients range from 14.6 to 17.0. In the Netherlands, 71 patients with dissociative identity disorder had a score of 49.4. Patients with a DES score of 25 or higher have a high probability of having a dissociative disorder.

In addition to the DES, there is also the *Multidimensional Inventory of Dissociation* (MID), which is based on the same principle but contains more than 200 items (available on the internet). Both the DES and the MID do not provide a definitive diagnosis; only with the help of a structured and thorough examination can a dissociative identity disorder be identified or excluded.

———————————

Circle a number to indicate the percentage of time this happens to you.

1. Some people experience while driving or staying in a car (or in the metro or bus) that they suddenly realise that they do not remember what happened during all or part of the journey.

0% Never	10%	20%	30%	40%	50%	60%	70%	80%	90%	100% Always

2. Sometimes people who are listening to someone speak suddenly realise that they have not heard what has just been said (in full or in part).

0% Never	10%	20%	30%	40%	50%	60%	70%	80%	90%	100% Always

3. Some people experience being in a place and having no idea how they got there.

0% Never	10%	20%	30%	40%	50%	60%	70%	80%	90%	100% Always

4. Some people have the experience of finding themselves wearing clothes they do not remember putting on.

0% Never	10%	20%	30%	40%	50%	60%	70%	80%	90%	100% Always

5. Some people experience finding new items in their belongings without remembering having bought them.

0% Never	10%	20%	30%	40%	50%	60%	70%	80%	90%	100% Always

6. Some people are approached by people they do not recognise. These strangers call them by a different name but claim to know them.

0% Never	10%	20%	30%	40%	50%	60%	70%	80%	90%	100% Always

7. Some people sometimes have the feeling that they are standing next to themselves or see themselves doing something, and in fact they see themselves as if they were looking at another person.

0% Never	10%	20%	30%	40%	50%	60%	70%	80%	90%	100% Always

8. Some people do not recognise friends or family members.

0% Never	10%	20%	30%	40%	50%	60%	70%	80%	90%	100% Always

9. Some people find that they have no memories of important events in their lives (e.g. wedding or graduation ceremonies).

0% Never	10%	20%	30%	40%	50%	60%	70%	80%	90%	100% Always

10. Some people experience being accused of lying when they sincerely believe they have not lied.

0% Never	10%	20%	30%	40%	50%	60%	70%	80%	90%	100% Always

11. Some people have the experience of looking in the mirror and not recognising themselves.

0% Never	10%	20%	30%	40%	50%	60%	70%	80%	90%	100% Always

12. Some people sometimes experience other people, objects, and the world around them as unreal.

0% Never	10%	20%	30%	40%	50%	60%	70%	80%	90%	100% Always

13. Some people sometimes feel that their body does not belong to them.

0% Never	10%	20%	30%	40%	50%	60%	70%	80%	90%	100% Always

14. Some people experience that they sometimes remember a past event in such an intense way that they feel as if they are reliving the event.

0% Never	10%	20%	30%	40%	50%	60%	70%	80%	90%	100% Always

15. Some people experience not being sure whether the things they remember really happened or whether they just dreamt them.

0% Never	10%	20%	30%	40%	50%	60%	70%	80%	90%	100% Always

16. Some people experience being in a familiar place but yet find it strange and unusual.

0% Never	10%	20%	30%	40%	50%	60%	70%	80%	90%	100% Always

17. Some people find that when they are watching television or a film they are so absorbed in the story that they are unaware of other events happening around them.

0% Never	10%	20%	30%	40%	50%	60%	70%	80%	90%	100% Always

18. Some people find that they sometimes become so involved in an imaginary thought or daydream that they feel it is actually happening to them.

0% Never	10%	20%	30%	40%	50%	60%	70%	80%	90%	100% Always

19. Some people find that they are sometimes able to ignore the pain.

0% Never	10%	20%	30%	40%	50%	60%	70%	80%	90%	100% Always

20. Some people just stare blankly into space, thinking of nothing and unaware of the passage of time.

0% Never	10%	20%	30%	40%	50%	60%	70%	80%	90%	100% Always

21. Sometimes people realise that when they are alone they talk out loud to each other.

0% Never	10%	20%	30%	40%	50%	60%	70%	80%	90%	100% Always

22. Some people react so differently in comparable situations that they almost feel as if they are two different people.

0% Never	10%	20%	30%	40%	50%	60%	70%	80%	90%	100% Always

23. Some people sometimes find that in certain situations they are able to do things they are not normally able to do, with surprising spontaneity and ease (e.g. sports, work, social situations, art...).

0% Never	10%	20%	30%	40%	50%	60%	70%	80%	90%	100% Always

24. Some people find that sometimes they cannot determine whether a memory is something concrete that they did or whether it is just the thought that they were going to do that thing (e.g. confusion about whether they actually mailed a letter or whether they just thought about mailing it).

0% Never	10%	20%	30%	40%	50%	60%	70%	80%	90%	100% Always

25. Some people do not remember doing something when they find evidence that they have done it.

0% Never	10%	20%	30%	40%	50%	60%	70%	80%	90%	100% Always

26. Some people sometimes find writings, drawings or notes in their belongings that they must have done but have no memory of.

0% Never	10%	20%	30%	40%	50%	60%	70%	80%	90%	100% Always

27. Some people find that they hear voices in their head telling them to do things or commenting on the things they do.

0% Never	10%	20%	30%	40%	50%	60%	70%	80%	90%	100% Always

28. Some people sometimes feel that they are looking at the world through a fog so that people and objects appear distant or indistinct.

0% Never	10%	20%	30%	40%	50%	60%	70%	80%	90%	100% Always

4

The *"Seven Level"* painting produced by the alter *Key* (Kim Noble)

OTHER TITLES

OMNIA VERITAS. OMNIA VERITAS LTD PRESENTS:
CURRENCY WARS SERIES by SONG HONGBING

THE SECRET HISTORY OF HIGH FINANCE

OMNIA VERITAS

Omnia Veritas Ltd presents:

Vladimir Putin & Eurasia

The providential advent of the "predestined man", the "absolute concept" Vladimir Putin, embodying the ''New Russia''.

by JEAN PARVULESCO

A singularly dangerous book, not to be placed in all hands...

OMNIA VERITAS. Omnia Veritas Ltd presents:

ARCHIBALD RAMSAY

THE NAMELESS WAR
THE JEWISH POWER AGAINST THE NATIONS

The author describes the anatomy of the machine of the Revolutionary International which today pursues the project of supranational world power, the age-old messianic dream of international Jewry...

Evidence of a centuries-old conspiracy against Europe and the whole of Christendom...

OMNIA VERITAS®   Omnia Veritas Ltd presents:

FREDERICK SODDY

THE ROLE OF MONEY
WHAT IT SHOULD BE CONTRASTED
WITH WHAT IT HAS BECOME

This book attempts to
clear up the mystery of
money in its social
aspect

This, surely, is what the public really wants to know about money

OMNIA VERITAS   Omnia Veritas Ltd presents:

Fatima
and the
GREAT CONSPIRACY

This meant creating, or making, money
out of nothing, being allowed to call it
money, and to lend it to the public at a
high interest rate.

This private syndicate acquiring a cast-iron monopoly over the supply
and circulation of the money not just of England, but of the whole world...

OMNIA VERITAS®
www.omnia-veritas.com